D1089171

THE
NEW
TESTAMENT

of Our Lord and Savior Jesus Christ

Translated from the Latin Vulgate

A Revision of the Challoner-Rheims Version
Edited by Catholic Scholars
Under the Patronage of
THE EPISCOPAL COMMITTEE
of the
CONFRATERNITY OF
CHRISTIAN DOCTRINE

2016 Reprint
SCEPTER PUBLISHERS

2016 reprint by Sinag-tala Publishers
with the special permission of the
CONFRATERNITY OF THE PRECIOUS BLOOD
5300 Fort Hamilton Parkway,
Brooklyn, N.Y. 11219, U.S.A. May 1986.
COPYRIGHT 1941, by
CONFRATERNITY OF CHRISTIAN DOCTRINE
International Copyright
under International Copyright Union

Nihil obstat
RT. REV. MSGR. HENRY J. GRIMMELSMAN, S.T.D.
REV. JOHN F. McCONNELL, M.M., S.T.L., S.S.L.
REV. JOSEPH J. TENNANT, S.T.D., S.S.L.

Imprimatur
† MOST REV. THOMAS H. McLAUGHLIN, S.T.D.,
Bishop of Paterson

Prayer to the Holy Spirit

COME, Holy Spirit, fill the hearts of Thy faithful
and enkindle in them the fire of Thy love.
V. Send forth Thy spirit and they shall be created.
P. And Thou shalt renew the face of the earth.

Let us Pray

O GOD, Who didst instruct the hearts of the faithful by the
light of the Holy Spirit, grant us in the same Spirit to be truly
wise, and ever to rejoice in His consolation. Through Christ
our Lord. Amen. *Indulgence of five years. Plenary indulgence,
under the usual conditions, if the prayer has been recited daily
for a month*

—*Preces et Pia Opera*, 265.

NOTES: My Daily Reading from the New Testament
Nihil obstat: James H. Griffiths, S.T.D., Censor Librorum, July 25th, 1941
Imprimatur: Thomas E. Molloy, S.T.D., Bishop of Brooklyn

ISBN: 978-971-554-062-9

SCEPTER PUBLISHERS
P.O. Box 1391, New Rochelle, NY 10802

FOREWORD TO
THE CONFRATERNITY REVISION
OF THE NEW TESTAMENT

BY MOST REV. AMLETO GIOVANNI CICOGNANI
APOSTOLIC DELEGATE TO THE UNITED STATES

"The excellent revision of the Rheims-Douay Version of the Scriptures made in 1750 by Bishop Challoner, Vicar Apostolic of the London District, is an admirable accomplishment. This work had become in many respects obsolete and unintelligible in its archaic expressions. A new revision meant an analytical, critical and literary work of such magnitude that to attempt it seemed not only a risk but almost a dream. The revision of the New Testament is now a happy reality, and has won the applause of the most competent scholars. Study for the revision continued over more than five years, under the direction of about thirty Biblical scholars from among the clergy, generously assisted by the active members of the Catholic Biblical Association of America. The names of these scholars have very appropriately been listed on the last page of the new volume of the New Testament as a tribute of undying gratitude. . . .

"The New Testament is the code of love and salvation. It carries the word of God, the revelation of our Lord through His teachings. It is of utmost importance, for every age, not least for our own, to hear it with the same clarity, vividness and comprehension with which it was first pronounced by our Lord.

"Search the Scriptures (cf. John 5, 39). They have been given 'for our instruction, that through . . . the consolation afforded by the Scriptures we may have hope' (Rom. 15, 4)."

Excerpts from the address to the Seventh National Congress of the Confraternity of Christian Doctrine, Philadelphia, November 16, 1941, reproduced here with the approval of His Excellency the Apostolic Delegate.

ON THE READING OF HOLY SCRIPTURE

FROM THE ENCYCLICAL LETTER, "SPIRITUS PARACLITUS," OF POPE BENEDICT XV (SEPTEMBER 15, 1920)

"Since the Holy Spirit, the Comforter, had bestowed the Scriptures on the human race for their instruction in Divine things, He also raised up in successive ages saintly and learned men whose task it should be to develop that treasure and so provide for the faithful plenteous 'consolation afforded by the Scriptures' (Rom. 15, 4). Foremost among these teachers stands St. Jerome.... The responsibility of our Apostolic office impels us to set before you his wonderful example and so promote the study of Holy Scripture in accordance with the teachings of our predecessors, Leo XIII and Pius X."

"And none can fail to see what profit and sweet tranquillity must result in well-disposed souls from such devout reading of the Bible. Whoever comes to it in piety, faith, and humility, and with a determination to make progress in it, will assuredly find therein and will eat the 'bread that comes down from heaven' (John 6, 50)."

"Hence, as far as in us lies, we, Venerable Brethren, shall, with St. Jerome as our guide, never desist from urging the faithful to read daily the Gospels, the Acts and the Epistles, so as to gather thence food for their souls.... But what, in his view, is the goal of such study? First, that from the Bible's pages we learn spiritual perfection.... Secondly, it is from the Bible that we gather confirmations and illustrations of any particular doctrine we wish to defend.... We confidently hope that his example will fire both clergy and laity with enthusiasm for the study of the Bible.... So convinced indeed was Jerome that familiarity with the Bible was the royal road to the knowledge and love of Christ that he did not hesitate to say: 'Ignorance of the Bible means ignorance of Christ' ('Prol. in Comment. in Isa.'; cf. 'Tract. de Ps. 77')."

"Jerome still calls to us. His voice rings out, telling us of the super-excellence of Holy Scripture, of its integral character and historical trustworthiness, telling us, too, of the pleasant fruits resulting from reading and meditating upon it."

"Our one desire for all the Church's children is that, being saturated with the Bible, they may arrive at the all-surpassing knowledge of Jesus Christ."

Pope Leo XIII granted to the faithful who shall read for at least a quarter of an hour the books of the Sacred Scripture with the veneration due to the Divine Word and as spiritual reading, an indulgence of 300 days.—Preces et Pia Opera, 645.

PREFACE

"The word of the Lord endures forever," is the saying of a great prophet (Isa. 40, 8) and of the Prince of the Apostles (1 Pet. 1, 25).

In her belief in the divine authority and the perfect truth of the Bible, as being the inspired Word of God, the Catholic Church has never hesitated. Nor has the Church forgotten that this sacred Book was destined by its Author to convey His message to all His faithful servants of every place and time. Neither has she overlooked the fact that this message must lie sealed and silent to many of her children unless given them in their own language, at least by the voice of their pastors, if not by means of the written page.

Further, the Church has always realized that Holy Scripture was committed to her charge by virtue of its very origin and object. Like the Apostolic Tradition of Christ's teaching, the Bible, too, is a treasury of divine revelation. As such, it can have no rightful guardian and dispenser except that Church which Christ formed and commissioned to teach to all the world the truths revealed for man's salvation. There can be no graver crime than the least corruption of that eternal truth which Christ has brought us. The Church is, therefore, watchful over Holy Scripture; and not only over its message, but likewise over its written transmission.

In exercising this guardianship, the Church has given special sanction to that Latin version which, because of its common use for centuries, won the name of "Vulgate." Her intention in this is primarily to declare which of many Latin versions is to be regarded as substantially accurate and safe in all matters of faith and morals. It was from this Latin text that most of the vernacular versions of Europe were made. It was also from this text that our first printed Catholic Bible in English was taken.

In 1560 the Catholic Church had been outlawed in England. The Catholics who remained in the country faced a particular danger to their faith from English versions of the Bible which altered the true meaning of the Scriptures. To meet this danger there was urgent need of a more faithful, a Catholic, version. This

[V]

PREFACE

need was met by the "Rheims and Douay Version."
It was so called because the New Testament was
printed at Rheims in 1582, and the Old Testament at
Douay in 1609-10. It was the work of exiled English
priests and educators, the chief of whom was Dr.
Gregory Martin.

The Rheims-Douay remained the standard English
version for Catholic use until near the time of the
American Revolution. By this time the language had
passed through many of those changes which are
natural to all living tongues. It was Bishop Challoner,
Vicar Apostolic of the London District, who saw the
pressing need of an English version of the Bible more
in keeping with the time. In spite of his heavy pastoral labors, he produced a new version of the entire
Bible in English in 1750. Challoner regarded his work
as merely a revision of the Rheims-Douay, as its title
page shows. The Catholic version in English which is
best known to us all, both in England and in America,
is still practically that of Challoner. Other Catholic
scholars sought to improve on his work, and some
of our current editions are indebted to them as well;
but Challoner's Bible has been the framework and
the substance of our own down to the present time.

But, in its turn, Challoner's version has suffered
loss of value because of progressive changes in our
language. The consequent need of revision in which
it stands has been recognized for a long time. Challoner's text was made the approved English version
for Catholics in America by the Archbishop of Baltimore and the Bishops of the United States in 1810.
The approbation was confirmed by the Hierarchy at
the First Provincial Council of Baltimore (1829), but
at the same time the emendation of the "Douay"
text, as Challoner's was still described, was earnestly
recommended. This matter of the improvement of
Challoner's version came up again at the Ninth
Provincial Council of Baltimore (1858). The Sacred
Congregation *de Propaganda Fide* sanctioned in a
particular way this desire for a better vernacular
version, suggesting that it be entrusted to a group of
theologians experienced in biblical studies.

PREFACE

Notwithstanding this encouragement to undertake a revision of the approved version, the closing decades of the last century, and the first of the present century, found the Church in America too much occupied with other concerns and not sufficiently equipped to attempt this work. Archbishop Kenrick undertook the great task of revising the entire Bible, but his work never met with general acceptance. The result was that we have continued to use editions of the English Bible which are, in language and substance, the text that Bishop Challoner gave us a hundred and ninety years ago.

The passage of time has neither lessened the weaknesses of this version nor done away with the demand for its improvement. In the meantime, however, the number of priests in America trained in the theological sciences, and notably in the specialized discipline of biblical studies, has greatly increased. Parallel to this growth there has been a marked increase of popular interest in the study of Holy Scripture. This progress has brought to light again the unsatisfactory condition of our vernacular version, it has reawakened the desire for a version accommodated to the needs of our time, and it has called attention to the fact that we now possess the adequate means to produce a worthy English text.

The English version which is presented in this volume is the answer of the Church in America to this need. Its preparation was requested and supervised by the Episcopal Committee of the Confraternity of Christian Doctrine. The principles upon which it rests were submitted to the Secretary and to other members of the Biblical Commission at Rome, and received complete approval. It is the accomplishment of some twenty-seven Catholic biblical scholars, all men of training and experience in their particular field, who have devoted more than five years to the work. Many other scholars have had part in it, whether as special editors or as critics. It enjoys, therefore, in the first place the authority necessary in any serious attempt to meet the requirements of an improved Catholic version in English. And it claims a scholarship commensurate with that authority.

PREFACE

While new in many of its aspects, this text is not a new version, but a revision of the work done by Bishop Challoner. While that venerable text has lost a great deal of its value with the lapse of time, it retains much that is commendable. To produce the type of version required in our day, it was necessary to eliminate many of the characteristics of the older version, and even to change many of its familiar passages; but there was no reason for setting it aside entirely. In fact, this revised text can claim the advantage of preserving in an improved form the version to which English-speaking Catholics have become accustomed.

The English text now being presented retains as much as possible of the version it seeks to replace. And yet, in striving for expression that is modern, much of the general style of Challoner's work has been improved upon. Many terms found in this version are no longer current in the sense in which he used them. The close adherence to Latin sentence structure, so evident in his text, is not the usage of our time. Such modifications are inevitable. It may be stated, however, that only such alterations in the Challoner text have been made in the revised edition as were necessary to give a simple and clear modern version.

However, this present text is much more than an effort to bring the language of Challoner's version into conformity with modern English idiom. It is a revision in the sense that it goes back to the source upon which Challoner drew, and reconsiders in a thorough way the accurate rendering of the divine message in the language of our day.

Like both the Rheims and the Challoner versions, the revised text rests upon the Latin Vulgate. This has been made necessary by a desire to have the version available for liturgical use. The excellence of the Vulgate as an ancient interpretation of the New Testament is an added advantage. The Clementine edition of the Vulgate is the main source of this revision. The readings of the Clementine, however, have been improved in not a few instances by recourse to the witnesses for a more ancient text of the

PREFACE

Vulgate. This tends to bring the text basic to the present version very close to the modern critical editions of the original Greek.

One immediate influence of the Vulgate will be observed in the spelling of proper names. The Latin form has been retained as more familiar to Catholics, and in some instances closer to the original pronunciation.

In addition to improving on Challoner's use of the Latin text, the revised version will show the results of a more thorough method of interpretation. The Latin text often reflects the peculiarities and idiom of its Semitic and Greek origin. In accordance with the rules of sound biblical interpretation, the present version takes this into account; and when the Latin text clearly supposes such elements, it renders them in the sense that is native to them. In no case, however, has the Latin text been set aside in favor of the Greek. It can, therefore, be said that the present version is in every sense a translation of the Vulgate.

As a further aid to the reading and understanding of the divine message, this new text abandons the old verse form of Challoner for the still older paragraphing of the Rheims-Douay Bible. Another improvement is offered in the addition of headings that show the main divisions of the books, and titles describing the contents of their subdivisions.

This revised version is presented with the confidence that it will advance the reading and appreciation of the New Testament. It is offered with the hope that it may awaken new interest in the Word of God, and that it may bring to God's children the manifold blessings of His Letter to them. At the same time, it is presented with the humble prayer that, as it has been prepared with all diligence and care, it may not interpret the divine message in any way except in the full sense intended by the Holy Spirit. It is He who has given it to us for our instruction, and that we may have hope. (Rom. 15, 4.)

THE BOOKS OF THE NEW TESTAMENT

St. Matthew	3
St. Mark	88
St. Luke	143
St. John	236
Acts of the Apostles	305
Romans	394
1 Corinthians	432
2 Corinthians	468
Galatians	491
Ephesians	504
Philippians	518
Colossians	527
1 Thessalonians	536
2 Thessalonians	544
1 Timothy	549
2 Timothy	560
Titus	567
Philemon	572
Hebrews	574
St. James	601
1 St. Peter	611
2 St. Peter	622
1 St. John	629
2 St. John	640
3 St. John	642
St. Jude	644
Apocalypse	648

THE FOUR GOSPELS

The Latin word commonly used for Gospel is *evangelium*, a term derived from the Greek. In the New Testament it means the glad news of salvation, first brought to earth by the Son of God, and afterwards delivered by word of mouth to the world by the Apostles. About the end of the first century or the beginning of the second, this word was applied to the books containing this glad news, and their authors were called "evangelists." The English word to express this Latin *evangelium* is "Gospel," from the Anglo-Saxon *godspel*, an abbreviated form of *good-spell*, i.e., "good tidings."

Though many non-inspired, or apocryphal, gospels eventually made their appearance, from the earliest period of ecclesiastical history only four Gospels were recognized as inspired and canonical. They contain the Gospel in four forms, or as the oldest titles express it, the Gospel according to Matthew, Mark, Luke and John. St. Irenæus, writing during the latter half of the second century, points out that our four Gospels were the only recognized ones: "It is not possible that the Gospels can be either more or fewer in number than they are." Origen tersely sums up the teaching of the Church for the first half of the third century when he says, "The Church has four Gospels, heretics have many more."

The four evangelists and their Gospels were believed to have been prefigured by the four living creatures mentioned in the vision of Ezechiel (1, 10). Explanations varied, but the opinion of St. Jerome is now the prevailing one. St. Matthew is symbolized by the "man," because he commences his Gospel with Christ's earthly ancestry and stresses His human and kingly character. St. Mark is represented by the "lion," because he starts his Gospel with St. John the Baptist, "the voice of one crying in the desert," and emphasizes the miraculous powers of the Savior. St. Luke is typified by the "ox," the animal of sacrifice, because he begins with the history of Zachary the priest offering sacrifice to God, and accentuates the universal priesthood of Christ. St. John is expressed by the "eagle," because from the very beginning of his Gospel he soars above the things of the earth and time and dwells upon the divine origin and nature of Jesus.

The titles prefixed to the four Gospels, though not original, are of early date. They are mentioned in the latter part of the second century in the churches of Lyons, Rome and Alexandria. Thus one can reasonably conclude that they were added to the Gospels during the first half of the second century. These titles indicate the human or secondary authors and not that the Gospels were written merely according to the preaching, mind or authority of St. Matthew, St. Mark, St. Luke and St. John.

Our present order of St. Matthew, St. Mark, St. Luke and St. John is chronological and sanctioned by tradition. The first three, though distinct in many ways, show a striking resemblance in content and form. They adopt a simple and convenient plan for the life of Jesus, the arrangement of which appears summarily in the preaching of St. Peter (Acts 10, 37-41): 1. His preparation for His ministry; 2. His preaching in Galilee; 3. His journey from Galilee to Jerusalem; 4. The last week in Jerusalem, together with His Passion, Death and Resurrection. Hence they are called the "Synoptists" and their writings the "Synoptic Gospels," because, whenever they are placed in parallel columns or are otherwise compared, they give us at a glance the same general view of our Lord's life. The fourth Gospel, on the contrary, written at the close of the first century, contains much new material, but in certain parts, either common or related to the Synoptic Gospels, St. John supplements them and thus prevents a false interpretation of their writings.

THE GOSPEL ACCORDING TO
ST. MATTHEW

Introduction

St. Matthew, one of the twelve Apostles, is the author of the first Gospel. This has been the constant tradition of the Church and is confirmed by the Gospel itself. He was the son of Alpheus and was called to be an Apostle while sitting in the tax-collector's place at Capharnaum. Before his conversion he was a publican, i. e., a tax-collector by profession. He is to be identified with the "Levi" of Mark and Luke. His apostolic activity was at first restricted to the communities of Palestine. Nothing definite is known about his later life. There is a tradition that points to Ethiopia as his field of labor; other traditions make mention of Parthia and Persia. It is likewise uncertain whether he died a natural death or received the crown of martyrdom. His feast is celebrated on September 21.

His Gospel was written to fill a sorely felt want for his fellow-countrymen, both believers and unbelievers. For the former it served as a token of his regard and as an encouragement in the trial to come, especially the danger of falling back to Judaism; for the latter it was designed to convince them that the Messias had come in the Person of Jesus, our Lord, in whom all the promises of the messianic kingdom embracing all people had been fulfilled in a spiritual rather than in a carnal way: "My kingdom is not of this world." His Gospel, then, answered the question put by the disciples of St. John the Baptist, "Art thou he who is to come, or shall we look for another?"

Writing for his countrymen of Palestine, St. Matthew composed his Gospel in his native Aramaic, the "Hebrew tongue" mentioned in the Gospel and the Acts of the Apostles. Soon afterwards, about the time of the persecution of Herod Agrippa I in 42 A. D., he took his departure for other lands. Another tradition places the composition of his Gospel either between the time of this departure and the Council of Jerusalem, i.e., between 42 A. D. and 50 A. D., or

[3]

THE HOLY GOSPEL OF JESUS CHRIST ACCORDING TO ST. MATTHEW

Prelude: The Coming of the Savior

Genealogy of Jesus

1 1 THE BOOK OF THE ORIGIN of Jesus Christ, the Son of David, the son of

> DEC. 1
> June 1

2 Abraham. Abraham begot Isaac, Isaac begot Jacob, Jacob begot Judas and his brethren. 3 Judas begot Phares and Zara of Thamar, Phares 4 begot Esron, Esron begot Aram. And Aram begot Aminadab, Aminadab begot Naasson, Naasson 5 begot Salmon. Salmon begot Booz of Rahab. Booz begot Obed of Ruth, Obed begot Jesse, 6 Jesse begot David the king.

And David the king begot Solomon of the 7 former wife of Urias. Solomon begot Roboam, 8 Roboam begot Abia, Abia begot Asa. And Asa begot Josaphat, Josaphat begot Joram, Joram 9 begot Ozias. And Ozias begot Joatham, Joatham 10 begot Achaz, Achaz begot Ezechias. And Ezechias begot Manasses, Manasses begot Amon, Amon

---

even later. Definitely, however, the Gospel itself, depicting the Holy City with its altar and temple as still existing, and without any reference to the fulfillment of our Lord's prophecy, shows that it was written before the destruction of the city by the Romans (70 A. D.), and this internal evidence confirms the early traditions.

The Gospel was soon translated into Greek—possibly during the lifetime of St. Matthew or a little later; certainly before the close of the first century. The original has been lost in the course of time. The Greek text, however, is in substantial conformity with the original. St. Matthew's Gospel, then, was the only book of the New Testament written in a language other than the Greek common to the people of the Empire.

begot Josias. And Josias begot Jechonias and 11 his brethren at the time of the carrying away to Babylon.

And after the carrying away to Babylon Jecho- 12 nias begot Salathiel, Salathiel begot Zorobabel. And Zorobabel begot Abiud, Abiud begot Elia- 13 chim, Eliachim begot Azor. And Azor begot 14 Sadoc, Sadoc begot Achim, Achim begot Eliud. And Eliud begot Eleazar, Eleazar begot Matthan, 15 Matthan begot Jacob. And Jacob begot Joseph, 16 the husband of Mary, and of her was born Jesus who is called Christ.

So all the generations from Abraham to David 17 are fourteen generations; and from David to the carrying away to Babylon fourteen generations; and from the carrying away to Babylon to Christ fourteen generations.

The Virgin Birth

Now the origin of Christ was in this wise. 18 When Mary his mother had been betrothed to Joseph, before they came together, she was found to be with child by the Holy Spirit. But Joseph 19 her husband, being a just man, and not wishing to expose her to reproach, was minded to put her away privately. But while he thought on these 20 things, behold, an angel of the Lord appeared to him in a dream, saying, "Do not be afraid, Joseph, son of David, to take to thee Mary thy wife, for that which is begotten in her is of the Holy Spirit. And she shall bring forth a son, and 21 thou shalt call his name Jesus; for he shall save his people from their sins." Now all this came to 22 pass that what was spoken by the Lord through the prophet might be fulfilled, "Behold, the virgin 23 shall be with child, and shall bring forth a son; and they shall call his name Emmanuel"; which

24 is, interpreted, "God with us." So Joseph, arising from sleep, did as the angel of the Lord had commanded him, and took unto him his wife.
25 And he did not know her till she brought forth her firstborn son. And he called his name Jesus.

The Magi

2 1 Now when Jesus was born in Bethlehem of Judea, in the days of King Herod, behold, Magi came from the East to

| DEC 2 |
| June 2 |

2 Jerusalem, ' saying, "Where is he that is born king of the Jews? For we have seen his star in
3 the East and have come to worship him." But when King Herod heard this, he was troubled,
4 and so was all Jerusalem with him. And gathering together all the chief priests and Scribes of the people, he inquired of them where the Christ
5 was to be born. And they said to him, "In Bethlehem of Judea; for thus it is written by the
6 prophet, 'And thou, Bethlehem, of the land of Juda, art by no means least among the princes of Juda; for from thee shall come forth a leader who shall rule my people Israel.' "
7 Then Herod summoned the Magi secretly, and carefully ascertained from them the time
8 when the star had appeared to them. And sending them to Bethlehem, he said, "Go and make careful inquiry concerning the child, and when you have found him, bring me word, that I too may go and worship him."
9 Now they, having heard the king, went their way. And behold, the star that they had seen in the East went before them, until it came and

---

1, 25: *Firstborn:* does not imply that Mary ever bore another child. Among the Jews this title belonged to an only child (if a son) to mark his rights and duties under the Law. Thus the apostolic doctrine of Mary's perpetual virginity is in no way denied by these words.

stood over the place where the child was. And 10
when they saw the star they rejoiced exceedingly. And entering the house, they found the 11
child with Mary his mother, and falling down
they worshipped him. And opening their treasures
they offered him gifts of gold, frankincense and
myrrh. And being warned in a dream not to 12
return to Herod, they went back to their own
country by another way.

The Flight into Egypt

But when they had departed, behold, an angel 13
of the Lord appeared in a dream to Joseph, saying, "Arise, and take the child and his mother,
and flee into Egypt, and remain there until I tell
thee. For Herod will seek the child to destroy
him." So he arose, and took the child and his 14
mother by night, and withdrew into Egypt, and
remained there until the death of Herod; that 15
what was spoken by the Lord through the prophet
might be fulfilled, "Out of Egypt I called my son."

The Innocents

Then Herod, seeing that he had been tricked 16
by the Magi, was exceedingly angry; and he sent
and slew all the boys in Bethlehem and all its
neighborhood who were two years old or under,
according to the time that he had carefully ascertained from the Magi. Then was fulfilled what 17
was spoken through Jeremias the prophet, "A 18
voice was heard in Rama, weeping and loud
lamentation; Rachel weeping for her children,
and she would not be comforted, because they
are no more."

The Return to Nazareth

But when Herod was dead, behold, an angel 19
of the Lord appeared in a dream to Joseph in

[7]

20 Egypt, ' saying, "Arise, and take the child and
his mother, and go into the land of Israel, for
21 those who sought the child's life are dead." So
he arose and took the child and his mother, and
22 went into the land of Israel. But hearing that
Archelaus was reigning in Judea in place of his
father Herod, he was afraid to go there; and
being warned in a dream, he withdrew into the
23 region of Galilee. And he went and settled in a
town called Nazareth; that there might be fulfilled what was spoken through the prophets,
"He shall be called a Nazarene."

I: THE PUBLIC MINISTRY OF JESUS

I

John the Baptist

3 1 NOW IN THOSE DAYS John the Baptist came, preaching in the desert of
2 Judea, ' and saying, "Repent, for the kingdom of
3 heaven is at hand." For this is he who was spoken
of through Isaias the prophet, when he said, "The
voice of one crying in the desert, 'Make ready
the way of the Lord, make straight his paths.'"
4 But John himself had a garment of camel's hair
and a leathern girdle about his loins, and
5 his food was locusts and wild honey. Then there
went out to him Jerusalem, and all Judea, and
6 all the region about the Jordan; and they were
baptized by him in the Jordan, confessing their
sins.

7 But when he saw many of the Pharisees and
Sadducees coming to his baptism, he said to
them, "Brood of vipers! who has shown you how
8 to flee from the wrath to come? Bring forth there-
9 fore fruit befitting repentance, and do not think
to say within yourselves, 'We have Abraham for

DEC. 3
June 3

[8]

our father'; for I say to you that God is able
out of these stones to raise up children to Abraham. For even now the axe is laid at the root of 10
the trees; every tree therefore that is not bringing forth good fruit is to be cut down and thrown
into the fire. I indeed baptize you with water, 11
for repentance. But he who is coming after me
is mightier than I, whose sandals I am not worthy
to bear. He will baptize you with the Holy Spirit
and with fire. His winnowing fan is in his hand, 12
and he will thoroughly clean out his threshing
floor, and will gather his wheat into the barn;
but the chaff he will burn up with unquenchable
fire."

The Baptism of Jesus

Then Jesus came from Galilee to John, at the 13
Jordan, to be baptized by him. And John was 14
for hindering him, and said, "It is I who ought
to be baptized by thee, and dost thou come to
me?" But Jesus answered and said to him, "Let 15
it be so now, for so it becomes us to fulfill all
justice." Then he permitted him. ' And when 16
Jesus had been baptized, he immediately came
up from the water. And behold, the heavens
were opened to him, and he saw the Spirit of
God descending as a dove and coming upon him.
And behold, a voice from the heavens said, "This 17
is my beloved Son, in whom I am well pleased."

The Temptation

Then Jesus was led into the desert by the 4 1
Spirit, to be tempted by the devil. And after fast- 2
ing forty days and forty nights, he was hungry.
And the tempter came and said to him, "If thou 3
art the Son of God, command that these stones
become loaves of bread." But he answered and 4
said, "It is written, 'Not by bread alone does

man live, but by every word that comes forth
from the mouth of God.' "

5   Then the devil took him into the holy city, and
6 set him on the pinnacle of the temple, and said
to him, "If thou art the Son of God, throw thyself
down; for it is written, 'He will give his angels
charge concerning thee; and upon their hands
they shall bear thee up, lest thou dash thy foot
7 against a stone.' " ' Jesus said to him, "It is
written further, 'Thou shalt not tempt the Lord
thy God.' "

8   Again, the devil took him to a very high mountain, and showed him all the kingdoms of the
9 world and the glory of them. And he said to him,
"All these things will I give thee, if thou wilt fall
10 down and worship me." Then Jesus said to him,
"Begone, Satan! for it is written, 'The Lord thy
God shalt thou worship and him only shalt thou
11 serve.' " Then the devil left him; and behold,
angels came and ministered to him.

II

Jesus in Capharnaum

12   NOW WHEN HE HEARD that John | DEC. 4
had been delivered up, he withdrew | June 4
13 into Galilee. And leaving the town of Nazareth,
he came and dwelt in Capharnaum, which is by
the sea, in the territory of Zabulon and Nephtha-
14 lim; that what was spoken through Isaias the
15 prophet might be fulfilled: "Land of Zabulon
and land of Nephthalim, by the way to the sea,
16 beyond the Jordan, Galilee of the Gentiles: the
people who sat in darkness have seen a great
light; and upon those who sat in the region and
17 shadow of death, a light has arisen." From that
time Jesus began to preach, and to say, "Repent,
for the kingdom of heaven is at hand."

The First Disciples Called

As he was walking by the sea of Galilee, he 18
saw two brothers, Simon, who is called Peter,
and his brother Andrew, casting a net into the
sea (for they were fishermen). And he said to 19
them, "Come, follow me, and I will make you
fishers of men." And at once they left the nets, 20
and followed him. And going farther on, he saw 21
two other brothers, James the son of Zebedee,
and his brother John, in a boat with Zebedee
their father, mending their nets; and he called
them. And immediately they left their nets and 22
their father, and followed him.

Mission of Preaching and Miracles

And Jesus went about all Galilee, teaching 23
in their synagogues, and preaching the gospel
of the kingdom, and healing every disease and
every sickness among the people. And his fame 24
spread into all Syria; and they brought to him
all the sick suffering from various diseases and
torments, those possessed, and lunatics, and
paralytics; and he cured them. And large 25
crowds followed him from Galilee and Decapolis and Jerusalem and Judea, and from beyond
the Jordan.

III

The Beatitudes

AND SEEING THE CROWDS, he went up the **5** 1
mountain. And when he was seated, his disciples
came to him. And opening his mouth he taught 2
them, saying, "Blessed are the poor in spirit, 3
for theirs is the kingdom of heaven. Blessed 4
are the meek, for they shall possess the earth.
Blessed are they who mourn, for they shall be 5
comforted. Blessed are they who hunger and 6
thirst for justice, for they shall be satisfied.

7 Blessed are the merciful, for they shall obtain
8 mercy. Blessed are the clean of heart, for they
9 shall see God. Blessed are the peacemakers,
10 for they shall be called children of God. Blessed
are they who suffer persecution for justice' sake,
11 for theirs is the kingdom of heaven. Blessed
are you when men reproach you, and persecute
you, and, speaking falsely, say all manner of evil
12 against you, for my sake. Rejoice and exult,
because your reward is great in heaven; for
so did they persecute the prophets who were
before you.

The Disciples Compared to Salt and Light

13   "You are the salt of the earth; | DEC. 5 |
but if the salt loses its strength, what | June 5 |
shall it be salted with? It is no longer of any use
but to be thrown out and trodden underfoot by
men.

14   "You are the light of the world. A city set
15 on a mountain cannot be hidden. Neither do men
light a lamp and put it under the measure, but
upon the lamp-stand, so as to give light to all
16 in the house. Even so let your light shine before men, in order that they may see your good
works and give glory to your Father in heaven.

The Old Law and the New

17   "Do not think that I have come to destroy
the Law or the Prophets. I have not come
18 to destroy, but to fulfill. For amen I say to you,
till heaven and earth pass away, not one jot
or one tittle shall be lost from the Law till all
19 things have been accomplished. Therefore whoever does away with one of these least commandments, and so teaches men, shall be called least
in the kingdom of heaven; but whoever carries
them out and teaches them, he shall be called
20 great in the kingdom of heaven. For I say to

you that unless your justice exceeds that of the Scribes and Pharisees, you shall not enter the kingdom of heaven.

Against Anger

"You have heard that it was said to the ancients, 'Thou shalt not kill'; and that whoever shall kill shall be liable to judgment. But I say to you that everyone who is angry with his brother shall be liable to judgment; and whoever says to his brother, 'Raca,' shall be liable to the Sanhedrin; and whoever says, 'Thou fool!', shall be liable to the fire of Gehenna. Therefore, if thou art offering thy gift at the altar, and there rememberest that thy brother has anything against thee, leave thy gift before the altar and go first to be reconciled to thy brother, and then come and offer thy gift. Come to terms with thy opponent quickly while thou art with him on the way, lest thy opponent deliver thee to the judge, and the judge to the officer, and thou be cast into prison. Amen I say to thee, thou wilt not come out from it until thou hast paid the last penny.

Chastity of Mind and Body

"You have heard that it was said to the ancients, 'Thou shalt not commit adultery.' But I say to you that anyone who so much as looks with lust at a woman has already committed adultery with her in his heart.

"So if thy right eye is an occasion of sin to thee, pluck it out and cast it from thee; for it is better for thee that one of thy members should perish than that thy whole body should be thrown into hell. And if thy right hand is an occasion of sin to thee, cut it off and cast it from thee; for it is better for thee that one of

thy members should be lost than that thy
whole body should go into hell.

Divorce

31 "It was said, moreover, 'Whoever puts away
his wife, let him give her a written notice of
32 dismissal.' But I say to you that everyone who
puts away his wife, save on account of immorality, causes her to commit adultery; and
he who marries a woman who has been put
away commits adultery.

Concerning Oaths

33 "Again, you have heard that it
was said to the ancients, 'Thou shalt

| DEC. 6 |
| June 6 |

not swear falsely, but fulfill thy oaths to the
34 Lord.' But I say to you not to swear at all:
neither by heaven, for it is the throne of God;
35 nor by the earth, for it is his footstool; nor by
Jerusalem, for it is the city of the great King.
36 Neither do thou swear by thy head, for thou
37 canst not make one hair white or black. But
let your speech be, 'Yes, yes'; 'No, no'; and
whatever is beyond these comes from the
evil one.

The New Law of Talion

38 "You have heard that it was said, 'An eye
39 for an eye,' and, 'A tooth for a tooth.' But I say
to you not to resist the evildoer; on the contrary, if someone strike thee on the right cheek,
40 turn to him the other also; and if anyone would
go to law with thee and take thy tunic,

5, 32: Unfaithfulness justifies separation from bed and
board, but the bond of marriage remains unbroken.
This truth is clear enough from the conclusion of this
verse, and still clearer in Mark 10, 11; Luke 16, 18;
Rom. 7, 2; 1 Cor. 7, 10f. 39.

let him take thy cloak as well; and whoever 41
forces thee to go for one mile, go with him two.
To him who asks of thee, give; and from him 42
who would borrow of thee, do not turn away.

The Love of Enemies

"You have heard that it was said, 'Thou 43
shalt love thy neighbor, and shalt hate thy
enemy.' But I say to you, love your enemies, 44
do good to those who hate you, and pray for
those who persecute and calumniate you, so 45
that you may be children of your Father in
heaven, who makes his sun to rise on the good
and the evil, and sends rain on the just and the
unjust. For if you love those that love you, 46
what reward shall you have? Do not even the
publicans do that? And if you salute your brethren 47
only, what are you doing more than others? Do
not even the Gentiles do that?

"You therefore are to be perfect, even as 48
your heavenly Father is perfect.

Purity of Intention

"Take heed not to do your good before men, **6** 1
in order to be seen by them; otherwise you
shall have no reward with your Father in heaven.

Almsgiving

"Therefore when thou givest alms, do not 2
sound a trumpet before thee, as the hypocrites do in the synagogues and streets, in
order that they may be honored by men.
Amen I say to you, they have received their
reward. But when thou givest alms, do not let 3
thy left hand know what thy right hand is doing,
so that thy alms may be given in secret; and 4
thy Father, who sees in secret, will reward thee.

Prayer

5   "Again, when you pray, you shall not be like the hypocrites, who love

| DEC. 7 |
| June 7 |

to pray standing in the synagogues and at the street corners, in order that they may be seen by men. Amen I say to you, they have received their
6 reward. But when thou prayest, go into thy room, and closing thy door, pray to thy Father in secret; and thy Father, who sees in secret, will reward thee.

7   "But in praying, do not multiply words, as the Gentiles do; for they think that by saying
8 a great deal, they will be heard. So do not be like them; for your Father knows what you
9 need before you ask him. In this manner therefore shall you pray: 'Our Father who art in
10 heaven, hallowed be thy name. Thy kingdom come, thy will be done on earth, as it is in
11 heaven. Give us this day our daily bread.
12 And forgive us our debts, as we also forgive
13 our debtors. And lead us not into temptation,
14 but deliver us from evil.' For if you forgive men their offenses, your heavenly Father will also
15 forgive you your offenses. But if you do not forgive men, neither will your Father forgive you your offenses.

Fasting

16   "And when you fast, do not look gloomy like the hypocrites, who disfigure their faces in order to appear to men as fasting. Amen I say to you, they have received their reward.
17 But thou, when thou dost fast, anoint thy
18 head and wash thy face, so that thou mayest not be seen fasting by men, but by thy Father, who is in secret; and thy Father, who sees in secret, will reward thee.

True Riches

"Do not lay up for yourselves treasures on 19 earth, where rust and moth consume, and where thieves break in and steal; but lay up for 20 yourselves treasures in heaven, where neither rust nor moth consumes, nor thieves break in and steal. 'For where thy treasure is, there also 21 will thy heart be.

"The lamp of the body is the eye. If thy eye 22 be sound, thy whole body will be full of light. But if thy eye be evil, thy whole body will be 23 full of darkness. Therefore if the light that is in thee is darkness, how great is the darkness itself!

"No man can serve two masters; for either he 24 will hate the one and love the other, or else he will stand by the one and despise the other. You cannot serve God and mammon.

Trust in God

"Therefore I say to you, do not | DEC. 8 | 25 be anxious for your life, what you | June 8 | shall eat; nor yet for your body, what you shall put on. Is not the life a greater thing than the food, and the body than the clothing? Look 26 at the birds of the air: they do not sow, or reap, or gather into barns; yet your heavenly Father feeds them. Are you not of much more value than they? But which of you by being 27 anxious about it can add to his stature a single cubit?

"And as for clothing, why are you anxious? 28 Consider how the lilies of the field grow; they neither toil nor spin, yet I say to you that not 29 even Solomon in all his glory was arrayed like one of these. But if God so clothes the grass of 30 the field, which flourishes today but tomorrow is thrown into the oven, how much more you, O you of little faith!

31 "Therefore do not be anxious, saying, 'What shall we eat?' or, 'What shall we drink?' or,
32 'What are we to put on?' (for after all these things the Gentiles seek); for your Father
33 knows that you need all these things. But seek first the kingdom of God and his justice, and all
34 these things shall be given you besides. Therefore do not be anxious about tomorrow; for tomorrow will have anxieties of its own. Sufficient for the day is its own trouble.

Avoiding Judgments

7 1 "Do not judge, that you may not be judged.
2 For with what judgment you judge, you shall be judged; and with what measure you mea-
3 sure, it shall be measured to you. But why dost thou see the speck in thy brother's eye, and yet dost not consider the beam in thy own eye?
4 Or how canst thou say to thy brother, 'Let me cast out the speck from thy eye'; and behold,
5 there is a beam in thy own eye? Thou hypocrite, first cast out the beam from thy own eye, and then thou wilt see clearly to cast out the speck from thy brother's eye.

6 "Do not give to dogs what is holy, neither cast your pearls before swine, or they will trample them under their feet and turn and tear you.

Power of Prayer

7 "Ask, and it shall be given you; seek, and you shall find; knock, and it shall be opened to
8 you. For everyone who asks, receives; and he who seeks, finds; and to him who knocks, it shall
9 be opened. Or what man is there among you, who, if his son asks him for a loaf, will hand him

a stone; or if he asks for a fish, will hand him a 10
serpent? Therefore, if you, evil as you are, know 11
how to give good gifts to your children, how much
more will your Father in heaven give good things
to those who ask him!

The Golden Rule

"Therefore all that you wish men to do to you, even so do you also to them; for this is the Law and the Prophets. 12

DEC. 9
June 9

Obstacles to Virtue

"Enter by the narrow gate. For wide is the 13
gate and broad is the way that leads to destruction, and many there are who enter that way.
How narrow there and close the way that 14
leads to life! And few there are who find it.

"Beware of false prophets, who come to you 15
in sheep's clothing, but inwardly are ravenous
wolves. By their fruits you will know them. Do 16
men gather grapes from thorns, or figs from
thistles? Even so, every good tree bears good 17
fruit, but the bad tree bears bad fruit. A good 18
tree cannot bear bad fruit, nor can a bad tree
bear good fruit. Every tree that does not bear 19
good fruit is cut down and thrown into the fire.
Therefore, by their fruits you will know them. 20

"Not everyone who says to me, 'Lord, Lord,' 21
shall enter the kingdom of heaven; but he who
does the will of my Father in heaven shall enter
the kingdom of heaven. Many will say to me in 22
that day, 'Lord, Lord, did we not prophesy in thy
name, and cast out devils in thy name, and work
many miracles in thy name?' And then I will de- 23
clare to them, 'I never knew you. Depart from
me, you workers of iniquity!'

Conclusion of the Sermon

24 "Everyone therefore who hears these my
25 words and acts upon them, shall be likened to a wise man who built his house on rock. And the rain fell, and the floods came, and the winds blew and beat against that house, but it did not
26 fall, because it was founded on rock. And everyone who hears these my words and does not act upon them, shall be likened to a foolish man who
27 built his house on sand. And the rain fell, and the floods came, and the winds blew and beat against that house, and it fell, and was utterly ruined."

Epilogue

28 And it came to pass when Jesus had finished these words, that the crowds were astonished
29 at his teaching; for he was teaching them as one having authority, and not as their Scribes and Pharisees.

A Leper

8 1 Now when he had come down from the mountain, great crowds | DEC. 10
 June 10 |
2 followed him. And behold, a leper came up and worshipped him, saying, "Lord, if thou wilt, thou
3 canst make me clean." And stretching forth his hand Jesus touched him, saying, "I will; be thou made clean." And immediately his leprosy was
4 cleansed. And Jesus said to him, "See thou tell no one; but go, show thyself to the priest, and offer the gift that Moses commanded, for a witness to them."

The Centurion's Servant

5 Now when he had entered Capharnaum, there came to him a centurion who entreated him,
6 saying, "Lord, my servant is lying sick in the house, paralyzed, and is grievously afflicted."

Jesus said to him, "I will come and cure him." 7
But in answer the centurion said, "Lord, I am not 8
worthy that thou shouldst come under my roof;
but only say the word, and my servant will be
healed. For I too am a man subject to authority, 9
and have soldiers subject to me; and I say to one,
'Go,' and he goes; and to another, 'Come,' and
he comes; and to my servant, 'Do this,' and he
does it."

And when Jesus heard this, he marvelled, and 10
said to those who were following him, "Amen I
say to you, I have not found such great faith in
Israel. And I tell you that many will come from 11
the east and from the west, and will feast with
Abraham and Isaac and Jacob in the kingdom of
heaven, but the children of the kingdom will be 12
put forth into the darkness outside; there will be
the weeping and the gnashing of teeth." Then 13
Jesus said to the centurion, "Go thy way; as thou
hast believed, so be it done to thee." And the
servant was healed in that hour.

Peter's Mother-in-law

And when Jesus had come into Peter's house, 14
he saw Peter's mother-in-law lying in bed, sick
with a fever. And he touched her hand, and 15
the fever left her; and she rose and began to
wait on them.

Other Miracles

Now when it was evening, they brought to him 16
many who were possessed, and he cast out the
spirits with a word, and cured all who were sick;
that what was spoken through Isaias the prophet 17
might be fulfilled, who said, "He himself took up
our infirmities, and bore the burden of our ills."

Sacrifice to Follow Christ

18 But when Jesus saw great crowds

DEC. 11 | June 11

about him, he gave orders to go
19 across the sea. Then a Scribe came and said to
20 him, "Master, I will follow thee wherever thou
goest." But Jesus said to him, "The foxes have
dens, and the birds of the air have nests; but the
21 Son of Man has nowhere to lay his head." And
another, who was one of his disciples, said to
him, "Lord, let me first go and bury my father."
22 But Jesus said to him, "Follow me, and leave the
dead to bury their own dead."

The Storm on the Lake

23 Then he got into a boat, and his disciples fol-
24 lowed him. And behold, there arose a great
storm on the sea, so that the boat was covered
25 by the waves; but he was asleep. So they came
and woke him, saying, "Lord, save us! we are
26 perishing!" But he said to them, "Why are you
fearful, O you of little faith?" Then he arose and
rebuked the wind and the sea, and there came
27 a great calm. And the men marvelled, saying,
"What manner of man is this, that even the wind
and the sea obey him?"

Expulsion of the Devils in Gerasa

28 Now when he had come to the other side, to
the country of the Gerasenes, there met him
two men who were possessed, coming from the
tombs, so exceedingly fierce that no one could
29 pass by that way. And behold, they cried out,
saying, "What have we to do with thee, Son of
God? Hast thou come here to torment us before
the time?"

30 Now not far from them there was a herd of
31 many swine, feeding. And the devils kept en-

treating him, saying, "If thou cast us out, send us into the herd of swine." And he said to them, 32 "Go!" And they came out and entered into the swine; and behold, the whole herd rushed down the cliff into the sea, and perished in the water. But the swineherds fled, and going away into 33 the town, they reported everything, and what had befallen the men possessed by demons. And behold, all the town came out to meet Jesus; and on 34 seeing him they entreated him to depart from their district.

A Paralytic at Capharnaum

And getting into a boat, he crossed over and came to his own town. And behold, they brought to him a paralytic lying on a pallet. And Jesus, seeing their faith, said to the paralytic, "Take courage, son; thy sins are forgiven thee." And behold, some of the Scribes 3 said within themselves, "This man blasphemes." And Jesus, knowing their thoughts, said, "Why 4 do you harbor evil thoughts in your hearts? For 5 which is easier, to say, 'Thy sins are forgiven thee,' or to say, 'Arise, and walk'? But that you 6 may know that the Son of Man has power on earth to forgive sins"—then he said to the paralytic—"Arise, take up thy pallet and go to thy house." And he arose, and went away to his 7 house. But when the crowds saw it, they were 8 struck with fear, and glorified God who had given such power to men.

9 1

2

DEC. 12
June 12

The Call of Matthew

Now as Jesus passed on from there, he saw 9 a man named Matthew sitting in the tax-collector's place, and said to him, "Follow me." And he arose and followed him. And it came to 10

pass as he was at table in the house, that, behold, many publicans and sinners came to the
11 table with Jesus and his disciples. And the
Pharisees seeing it, said to his disciples, "Why
does your master eat with publicans and sin-
12 ners?" But Jesus heard it, and said, "It is not
the healthy who need a physician, but they who
13 are sick. But go, and learn what this means: 'I
desire mercy, and not sacrifice.' For I have come
to call sinners, not the just."

The Question of Fasting

14 At that time the disciples of John came to
him, saying, "Why do we and the Pharisees often
15 fast, whereas thy disciples do not fast?" And
Jesus said to them, "Can the wedding guests
mourn as long as the bridegroom is with them?
But the days will come when the bridegroom
shall be taken away from them, and then they
16 will fast. And no one puts a patch of raw cloth on
an old garment, for the patch tears away from the
17 garment, and a worse rent is made. Nor do
people pour new wine into old wine-skins, else
the skins burst, the wine is spilt, and the skins
are ruined. But they put new wine into fresh
skins, and both are saved."

The Ruler's Daughter; the Woman with a Hemorrhage

18 As he was saying this to them, be-
hold, a ruler came up and worshipped | DEC. 13
him, saying, "My daughter has just now died; June 13
but come and lay thy hand upon her, and she
19 will return to life." And Jesus arose and followed
him, and so did his disciples.
20 Now a woman who for twelve years had been
suffering from hemorrhage, came up behind
21 him and touched the tassel of his cloak, saying

[24]

to herself, "If I touch but his cloak I shall be saved." But Jesus, turning and seeing her, said, 22 "Take courage, daughter; thy faith has saved thee." And the woman was restored to health from that moment.

And when Jesus came to the ruler's house, 23 and saw the flute players and the crowd making a din, he said, "Begone, the girl is asleep, not 24 dead." And they laughed him to scorn. But 25 when the crowd had been put out, he went in and took her by the hand; and the girl arose. And 26 the report of this spread throughout all that district.

Two Blind Men

Now as Jesus was passing on from there, two 27 blind men followed him, crying out and saying, "Have pity on us, Son of David!" And when 28 he had reached the house, the blind men came to him. And Jesus said to them, "Do you believe that I can do this to you?" They answered him, "Yes, Lord." Then he touched their eyes, 29 saying, "Let it be done to you according to your faith." And their eyes were opened. And Jesus 30 strictly charged them, saying, "See that no one knows of this!" But they went out and spread his 31 fame abroad throughout all that district.

A Dumb Demoniac

Now as they were going out, behold, there 32 was brought to him a dumb man possessed by a devil. And when the devil had been cast out, 33 the dumb man spoke; and the crowds marvelled, saying, "Never has the like been seen in Israel." But the Pharisees said, "By the prince of devils 34 he casts out devils."

The Mission of the Apostles

35   And Jesus was going about all the towns and villages, teaching in their synagogues, and preaching the gospel of the kingdom, and curing every kind of disease and
36 infirmity. But seeing the crowds, he was moved with compassion for them, because they were bewildered and dejected, like sheep without a
37 shepherd. Then he said to his disciples, "The harvest indeed is great, but the laborers are few.
38 Pray therefore the Lord of the harvest to send
10 1 forth laborers into his harvest." Then having summoned his twelve disciples, he gave them power over unclean spirits, to cast them out, and to cure every kind of disease and infirmity.
2   Now these are the names of the twelve apostles: first Simon, who is called Peter, and his
3 brother Andrew; James the son of Zebedee, and his brother John; Philip and Bartholomew; Thomas and Matthew the publican; James the
4 son of Alpheus, and Thaddeus; Simon the Cananean, and Judas Iscariot, he who betrayed him.
5   These twelve Jesus sent forth, having instructed them thus: "Do not go in the direction of the Gentiles, nor enter the towns of Samari-
6 tans; but go rather to the lost sheep of the house
7 of Israel. And as you go, preach the message,
8 'The kingdom of heaven is at hand!' ' Cure the sick, raise the dead, cleanse the lepers, cast out
9 devils. Freely you have received, freely give. ' Do not keep gold, or silver, or money in your girdles,
10 no wallet for your journey, nor two tunics, nor sandals, nor staff; for the laborer deserves his living.

10, 2: *First Simon, who is called Peter:* primacy in the Church belongs to Peter.

"And whatever town or village you enter, inquire who in it is worthy; and stay there until you leave. As you enter the house, salute it. If then that house be worthy, your peace will come upon it; but if it be not worthy, let your peace return to you. And whoever does not receive you, or listen to your words—go forth outside that house or town, and shake off the dust from your feet. Amen I say to you, it will be more tolerable for the land of Sodom and Gomorrah in the day of judgment than for that town.

Opposition Foretold

"Behold, I am sending you forth like sheep in the midst of wolves.

| DEC. 15 |
| June 15 |

Be therefore wise as serpents, and guileless as doves. But beware of men; for they will deliver you up to councils, and scourge you in their synagogues, and you will be brought before governors and kings for my sake, for a witness to them and to the Gentiles. But when they deliver you up, do not be anxious how or what you are to speak; for what you are to speak will be given you in that hour. For it is not you who are speaking, but the Spirit of your Father who speaks through you. And brother will hand over brother to death, and the father his child; children will rise up against parents and put them to death. And you will be hated by all for my name's sake; but he who has persevered to the end will be saved. When they persecute you in one town, flee to another. Amen I say to you, you will not have gone through the towns of Israel before the Son of Man comes.

"No disciple is above his teacher, nor is the servant above his master. It is enough for the disciple to be like his teacher, and for the servant to be like his master. If they have called the master of the house Beelzebub, how much more those of his household!

26 "Therefore do not be afraid of them. For there is nothing concealed that will not be disclosed, and nothing hidden that will not be 27 made known. What I tell you in darkness, speak it in the light; and what you hear whis- 28 pered, preach it on the housetops. And do not be afraid of those who kill the body but cannot kill the soul. But rather be afraid of him who is 29 able to destroy both soul and body in hell. Are not two sparrows sold for a farthing? And yet not one of them will fall to the ground without 30 your Father's leave. But as for you, the very 31 hairs of your head are all numbered. Therefore do not be afraid; you are of more value than many sparrows.

32 "Therefore, everyone who acknowledges me before men, I also will acknowledge him before 33 my Father in heaven. But whoever disowns me before men, I in turn will disown him before my Father in heaven.

34 "Do not think that I have come to send peace upon the earth; I have come to bring a 35 sword, not peace. For I have come to set a man at variance with his father, and a daughter with her mother, and a daughter-in-law with 36 her mother-in-law; and a man's enemies will 37 be those of his own household. He who loves father or mother more than me is not worthy of me; and he who loves son or daughter more 38 than me is not worthy of me. And he who does not take up his cross and follow me, is not 39 worthy of me. He who finds his life will lose it, and he who loses his life for my sake, will find it.

"He who receives you, receives me; and he 40
who receives me, receives him who sent him. He 41
who receives a prophet because he is a prophet,
shall receive a prophet's reward; and he who
receives a just man because he is a just man,
shall receive a just man's reward. And whoever 42
gives to one of these little ones but a cup of cold
water to drink because he is a disciple, amen I
say to you, he shall not lose his reward."

The Baptist's Deputation

Now it came to pass when Jesus | DEC. 16 | **11** 1
had finished giving instructions to | June 16 |
his twelve disciples, that he passed on from there
to teach and preach in their towns. But when 2
John had heard in prison of the works of Christ,
he sent two of his disciples to say to him, "Art 3
thou he who is to come, or shall we look for
another?" And Jesus answering said to them, 4
"Go and report to John what you have heard
and seen: the blind see, the lame walk, the lepers 5
are cleansed, the deaf hear, the dead rise, the
poor have the gospel preached to them. And 6
blessed is he who is not scandalized in me."

Christ's Witness Concerning John

Then, as they went away, Jesus began to say 7
to the crowds concerning John, "What did you
go out to the desert to see? A reed shaken by
the wind? But what did you go out to see? A 8
man clothed in soft garments? Behold, those who
wear soft garments are in the houses of kings.
But what did you go out to see? A prophet? Yes, 9
I tell you, and more than a prophet. This is he of 10
whom it is written, 'Behold, I send my messenger
before thy face, who shall make ready thy way
before thee.' Amen I say to you, among those 11
born of women there has not risen a greater than

John the Baptist; yet the least in the kingdom of
12 heaven is greater than he. But from the days of
John the Baptist until now the kingdom of
heaven has been enduring violent assault, and
13 the violent have been seizing it by force. For all
the Prophets and the Law have prophesied until
14 John. And if you are willing to receive it, he is
15 Elias who was to come. He who has ears to hear,
let him hear.

16   "But to what shall I liken this generation? It is
like children sitting in the market place, who call
17 to their companions, and say, 'We have piped to
you, and you have not danced; we have sung
18 dirges, and you have not mourned.' For John
came neither eating nor drinking, and they say,
19 'He has a devil!' The Son of Man came eating
and drinking, and they say, 'Behold a glutton and
a wine-drinker, a friend of publicans and sinners!' And wisdom is justified by her children."

The Impenitent Towns

20   Then he began to reproach the DEC. 17 / June 17
towns in which most of his miracles
were worked, because they had not repented.
21 "Woe to thee, Corozain! woe to thee, Bethsaida!
For if in Tyre and Sidon had been worked the
miracles that have been worked in you, they
would have repented long ago in sackcloth and
22 ashes. But I tell you, it will be more tolerable for
Tyre and Sidon on the day of judgment than for
23 you. And thou, Capharnaum, shalt thou be exalted
to heaven? Thou shalt be thrust down to hell!
For if the miracles had been worked in Sodom
that have been worked in thee, it would have re-
24 mained to this day. But I tell you, it will be more
tolerable for the land of Sodom on the day of
judgment than for thee."

Jesus Draws Men Gently to Himself

At that time Jesus spoke and said, "I praise 25 thee, Father, Lord of heaven and earth, that thou didst hide these things from the wise and prudent, and didst reveal them to little ones. Yes, 26 Father, for such was thy good pleasure. All 27 things have been delivered to me by my Father; and no one knows the Son except the Father; nor does anyone know the Father except the Son, and him to whom the Son chooses to reveal him.

"Come to me, all you who labor and are bur- 28 dened, and I will give you rest. Take my yoke 29 upon you, and learn from me, for I am meek and humble of heart; and you will find rest for your souls. For my yoke is easy, and my burden light." 30

The Disciples Pluck Grain on the Sabbath

At that time Jesus went through the standing**12** 1 grain on the Sabbath; and his disciples being hungry began to pluck ears of grain and to eat. But the Pharisees, when they saw it, said to him, 2 "Thy disciples are doing what it is not lawful for them to do on the Sabbath." But he said to 3 them, "Have you not read what David did when he and those with him were hungry? how he en- 4 tered the house of God, and ate the loaves of proposition which neither he nor those with him could lawfully eat, but only the priests? Or have 5 you not read in the Law, that on the Sabbath days the priests in the temple break the Sabbath and are guiltless? But I tell you that one greater 6 than the temple is here. But if you knew what 7 this means, 'I desire mercy, and not sacrifice,' you would never have condemned the innocent; for the Son of Man is Lord even of the Sabbath." 8

A Man with a Withered Hand

9 And when he had passed on from | DEC. 18 | June 18 |
that place he entered their syna-
10 gogue. And behold, a man with a withered hand
was there. And they asked him, saying, "Is it
lawful to cure on the Sabbath?" that they might
11 accuse him. But he said to them, "What man is
there among you who, if he has a single sheep
and it falls into a pit on the Sabbath, will not take
12 hold of it and lift it out? How much better is a
man than a sheep! Therefore, it is lawful to do
13 good on the Sabbath." Then he said to the man,
"Stretch forth thy hand." And he stretched it
forth, and it was restored, as sound as the other.
14 But the Pharisees went out and took counsel
against him, how they might do away with him.

The Mercy of Jesus

15 Then, knowing this, Jesus withdrew from the
place; and many followed him and he cured
16 them all, and warned them not to make him
17 known; that what was spoken through Isaias the
18 prophet might be fulfilled, who said, "Behold,
my servant, whom I have chosen, my beloved in
whom my soul is well pleased: I will put my
Spirit upon him, and he will declare judgment to
19 the Gentiles. He will not wrangle, nor cry aloud,
neither will anyone hear his voice in the streets.
20 A bruised reed he will not break, and a smoking
wick he will not quench, till he send forth judg-
21 ment unto victory; and in his name will the Gentiles hope."

Blasphemy of the Pharisees

22 Then there was brought to him a | DEC. 19 | June 19 |
possessed man who was blind and
dumb; and he cured him so that he spoke and

saw. And all the crowds were amazed, and they 23
said, "Can this be the Son of David?" But the 24
Pharisees, hearing this, said, "This man does not
cast out devils except by Beelzebub, the prince of
devils."

And knowing their thoughts Jesus said to 25
them, "Every kingdom divided against itself is
brought to desolation, and every city or house
divided against itself will not stand. And if Satan 26
casts out Satan, he is divided against himself;
how then shall his kingdom stand? And if I cast 27
out devils by Beelzebub, by whom do your children cast them out? Therefore they shall be your
judges. But if I cast out devils by the Spirit of 28
God, then the kingdom of God has come upon
you. Or, how can anyone enter the strong man's 29
house, and plunder his goods, unless he first
binds the strong man? Then he will plunder his
house. He who is not with me is against me, 30
and he who does not gather with me scatters.

"Therefore I say to you, that every kind of sin 31
and blasphemy shall be forgiven to men; but the
blasphemy against the Spirit will not be forgiven.
And whoever speaks a word against the Son of 32
Man, it shall be forgiven him; but whoever
speaks against the Holy Spirit, it will not be forgiven him, either in this world or in the world to
come. Either make the tree good and its fruit 33
good, or make the tree bad and its fruit bad; for
by the fruit the tree is known. You brood of vi- 34
pers, how can you speak good things, when you
are evil? For out of the abundance of the heart

12, 32: The sin against the Holy Spirit is to ascribe to the
devil the works of the Holy Spirit. One who thus attacks
directly this source of all grace, rejects the source of
salvation. It is morally impossible that he should ever
meet the conditions for absolution.

35 the mouth speaks. The good man from his good treasure brings forth good things; and the evil man from his evil treasure brings forth evil 36 things. But I tell you, that of every idle word men speak, they shall give account on the day of judg- 37 ment. For by thy words thou wilt be justified, and by thy words thou wilt be condemned."

The Sign of Jonas

38 Then certain of the Scribes and Pharisees answered him, saying, "Master, we would see a 39 sign from thee." But he answered and said to them, "An evil and adulterous generation de- mands a sign, and no sign shall be given it but 40 the sign of Jonas the prophet. For even as Jonas was in the belly of the fish three days and three nights, so will the Son of Man be three days and 41 three nights in the heart of the earth. The men of Nineve will rise up in the judgment with this generation and will condemn it; for they re- pented at the preaching of Jonas, and behold, a 42 greater than Jonas is here. The queen of the South will rise up in the judgment with this generation and will condemn it; for she came from the ends of the earth to hear the wisdom of Solomon, and behold, a greater than Solomon is here.

43 "But when the unclean spirit has gone out of a man, he roams through dry places in search of 44 rest, and finds none. Then he says, 'I will return to my house which I left'; and when he has come to it, he finds the place unoccupied, swept and 45 decorated. Then he goes and takes with him seven other spirits more evil than himself, and

---

12, 36: An idle word is one which profits neither the speaker nor the hearer. If the word is merely useless, its utterance is not seriously wrong.

they enter in and dwell there; and the last state of that man becomes worse than the first. So shall it be with this evil generation also."

Jesus and His Brethren

While he was still speaking to the crowds, his mother and his brethren [DEC. 20 | June 20] 46 were standing outside, seeking to speak to him. And someone said to him, "Behold, thy mother 47 and thy brethren are standing outside, seeking thee." But he answered and said to him who told 48 him, "Who is my mother and who are my brethren?" And stretching forth his hand towards 49 his disciples, he said, "Behold my mother and my brethren! For whoever does the will of my 50 Father in heaven, he is my brother and sister and mother."

On that day Jesus left the house and was **13** 1 sitting by the water's edge. And as great crowds 2 gathered about him, he got into a boat and sat down. And all the crowd stood on the shore.

Parable of the Sower

And he spoke to them many things in para- 3 bles, saying, "Behold, the sower went out to sow. And as he sowed, some seeds fell by the wayside, 4 and the birds came and ate them up. And other 5 seeds fell upon rocky ground, where they had not much earth; and they sprang up at once, because they had no depth of earth; but when the sun 6 rose they were scorched, and because they had no root they withered away. And other seeds fell 7 among thorns; and the thorns grew up and choked them. And other seeds fell upon good 8 ground, and yielded fruit, some a hundredfold, some sixtyfold, and some thirtyfold. He who has 9 ears to hear, let him hear!"

10 And the disciples came up and said to him,
11 "Why dost thou speak to them in parables?" And
he answered and said, "To you it is given to
know the mysteries of the kingdom of heaven,
12 but to them it is not given. For to him who has
shall be given, and he shall have abundance; but
from him who does not have, even that which he
13 has shall be taken away. This is why I speak to
them in parables, because seeing they do not see,
and hearing they do not hear, neither do they
14 understand. In them is being fulfilled the prophecy of Isaias, who says, 'Hearing you will hear, but
not understand; and seeing you will see, but not
15 perceive. For the heart of this people has been
hardened, and with their ears they have been
hard of hearing, and their eyes they have closed;
lest at any time they see with their eyes, and
hear with their ears, and understand with their
mind, and be converted, and I heal them.'

16 "But blessed are your eyes, for they see; and
17 your ears, for they hear. For amen I say to you,
many prophets and just men have longed to
see what you see, and they have not seen it; and to
hear what you hear, and they have not heard it.

18 "Hear, therefore, the parable of the sower.
19 When anyone hears the word of the kingdom, but
does not understand it, the wicked one comes
and snatches away what has been sown in his
heart. This is he who was sown by the wayside.
20 And the one sown on rocky ground, that is he
who hears the word and receives it immediately
21 with joy; yet he has no root in himself, but continues only for a time, and when trouble and
persecution come because of the word, he at once
22 falls away. And the one sown among the thorns,

13, 12: One grace prepares for another; one who fails to
correspond with grace will lose what he has.

that is he who listens to the word; but the care of this world and the deceitfulness of riches choke the word, and it is made fruitless. And the one 23 sown upon good ground, that is he who hears the word and understands it; he bears fruit and yields in one case a hundredfold, in another sixtyfold, and in another thirtyfold.''

The Weeds

Another parable he set before them, saying, "The kingdom of heaven is like a man who sowed good seed in his 24

| DEC. 21 |
| June 21 |

field; but while men were asleep, his enemy 25 came and sowed weeds among the wheat, and went away. And when the blade sprang up and 26 brought forth fruit, then the weeds appeared as well. And the servants of the householder came 27 and said to him, 'Sir, didst thou not sow good seed in thy field? How then does it have weeds?' He said to them, 'An enemy has done this.' And 28 the servants said to him, 'Wilt thou have us go and gather them up?' 'No,' he said, 'lest in 29 gathering the weeds you root up the wheat along with them. Let both grow together until the har- 30 vest; and at harvest time I will say to the reapers, Gather up the weeds first and bind them in bundles to burn; but gather the wheat into my barn.' ''

The Mustard Seed and the Leaven

Another parable he set before them, saying, 31 "The kingdom of heaven is like a grain of mustard seed, which a man took and sowed in his field. This indeed is the smallest of all the seeds; 32 but when it grows up it is larger than any herb and becomes a tree, so that the birds of the air come and dwell in its branches.''

[37]

33 He told them another parable: "The kingdom of heaven is like leaven, which a woman took and buried in three measures of flour, until all of it was leavened."

34 All these things Jesus spoke to the crowds in parables, and without parables he did not speak
35 to them; that what was spoken through the prophet might be fulfilled, "I will open my mouth in parables, I will utter things hidden since the foundation of the world."

Explanation of the Parable of the Weeds

36 Then he left the crowds and went into the house. And his disciples came to him, saying, "Explain to us the parable of the weeds in the
37 field." So answering them he said, "He who
38 sows the good seed is the Son of Man. The field is the world; the good seed, the sons of the kingdom; the weeds, the sons of the wicked one;
39 ' and the enemy who sowed them is the devil. But the harvest is the end of the world, and the
40 reapers are the angels. Therefore, just as the weeds are gathered up and burnt with fire, so will
41 it be at the end of the world. The Son of Man will send forth his angels, and they will gather out of his kingdom all scandals and those who work
42 iniquity, and cast them into the furnace of fire, where there will be the weeping, and the gnash-
43 ing of teeth. Then the just will shine forth like the sun in the kingdom of their Father. He who has ears to hear, let him hear.

The Treasure and the Pearl

44 "The kingdom of heaven is like a treasure hidden in a field; he who ┌─────────┐ finds it hides it, and in his joy goes and sells all that he has and buys that field.

                                      DEC. 22 / June 22

45 "Again, the kingdom of heaven is like a mer-
46 chant in search of fine pearls. When he finds a

single pearl of great price, he goes and sells all
that he has and buys it.

Parable of the Net

"Again, the kingdom of heaven is like a net 47
cast into the sea that gathered in fish of every
kind. When it was filled, they hauled it out, and 48
sitting down on the beach, they gathered the
good fish into vessels, but threw away the bad.
' So will it be at the end of the world. The angels 49
will go out and separate the wicked from among
the just, and will cast them into the furnace of 50
fire, where there will be the weeping, and the
gnashing of teeth.

Conclusion

"Have you understood all these things?" They 51
said to him, "Yes." And he said to them, "So 52
then, every Scribe instructed in the kingdom of
heaven is like a householder who brings forth
from his storeroom things new and old."

Jesus at Nazareth

And it came to pass when Jesus had finished 53
these parables, that he set out from that place.
And when he had come to his own country, he 54
began to teach them in their synagogues, so that
they were astonished, and said, "How did this
man come by this wisdom and these miracles?
' Is not this the carpenter's son? Is not his mother 55
called Mary, and his brethren James and Joseph
and Simon and Jude? And his sisters, are they 56
not all with us? Then where did he get all this?"
' And they took offense at him. But Jesus said to 57
them, "A prophet is not without honor except in
his own country, and in his own house." And be- 58
cause of their unbelief, he did not work many
miracles there.

Death of the Baptist

14 1 At that time Herod the tetrarch
2 heard about the fame of Jesus, and
he said to his servants, "This is John the Baptist;
he has risen from the dead, and that is why miraculous powers are working through him."

| DEC. 23 |
| June 23 |

3 For Herod had taken John, and bound him,
and put him in prison, because of Herodias, his
4 brother's wife. For John had said to him, "It is
5 not lawful for thee to have her." And he would
have liked to put him to death, but he feared the
people, because they regarded him as a prophet.

6 But on Herod's birthday, the daughter of
Herodias danced before them, and pleased
7 Herod. Whereupon he promised with an oath to
8 give her whatever she might ask of him. Then
she, at her mother's prompting, said, "Give me
9 here on a dish the head of John the Baptist." And
grieved as he was, the king, because of his oath
10 and his guests, commanded it to be given. He
11 sent and had John beheaded in the prison. And
his head was brought on a dish and given to the
12 girl, who carried it to her mother. His disciples
came, took away his body, and buried it. And
they went and told Jesus.

Jesus Feeds Five Thousand

13 When Jesus heard this, he withdrew by boat
to a desert place apart; but the crowds heard of
14 it and followed him on foot from the towns. And
when he landed, he saw a large crowd, and out of
15 compassion for them he cured their sick. Now
when it was evening, his disciples came to him,
saying, "This is a desert place and the hour is
already late; send the crowds away, so that they
may go into the villages and buy themselves
food."

But Jesus said to them, "They do not need to 16
go away; you yourselves give them some food."
They answered him, "We have here only five 17
loaves and two fishes." He said to them, "Bring 18
them here to me."

And when he had ordered the crowd to recline 19
on the grass, he took the five loaves and the two
fishes, and looking up to heaven, blessed and
broke the loaves, and gave them to his disciples,
and the disciples gave them to the crowds. And 20
all ate and were satisfied; and they gathered up
what was left over, twelve baskets full of fragments. Now the number of those who had eaten 21
was five thousand men, without counting women
and children.

Jesus Walks on the Water

And immediately afterwards he 22
made his disciples get into the boat
and cross the sea ahead of him, while he dismissed the crowd. And when he had dismissed 23
the crowd, he went up the mountain by himself
to pray. And when it was late, he was there alone,
' but the boat was in the midst of the sea, buf- 24
feted by the waves, for the wind was against
them. But in the fourth watch of the night he 25
came to them, walking upon the sea. And they, 26
seeing him walking upon the sea, were greatly
alarmed, and exclaimed, "It is a ghost!" And
they cried out for fear. Then Jesus immediately 27
spoke to them, saying, "Take courage; it is I, do
not be afraid."

But Peter answered him and said, "Lord, if it 28
is thou, bid me come to thee over the water."
' And he said, "Come." Then Peter got out of the 29
boat and walked on the water to come to Jesus.
But seeing the wind was strong, he was afraid; 30
and as he began to sink he cried out, saying,

DEC. 24
June 24

31 "Lord, save me!" And Jesus at once stretched forth his hand and took hold of him, saying to him, "O thou of little faith, why didst thou
32 doubt?" And when they got into the boat, the
33 wind fell. But they who were in the boat came and worshipped him, saying, "Truly thou art the Son of God."

Other Miracles

34 And crossing over, they came to the land at
35 Genesar. The inhabitants of that place, as soon as they recognized him, sent into that whole
36 country, and brought to him all the sick,' and they entreated him to let them touch but the tassel of his cloak; and all who touched it were saved.

Jesus and the Pharisees

15 1 Then Scribes and Pharisees from Jerusalem came to him, saying, | DEC. 25 / June 25 |
2 "Why do thy disciples transgress the tradition of the ancients? For they do not wash their hands
3 when they take food." But he answered and said to them, "And why do you transgress the commandment of God because of your tradition? For
4 God said, 'Honor thy father and thy mother'; and, 'Let him who curses father or mother be put
5 to death.' But you say, 'Whoever shall say to his father or mother, "Any support thou mightest
6 have had from me is dedicated to God," does not have to honor his father or his mother.' So you have made void the commandment of God by
7 your tradition. Hypocrites, well did Isaias proph-
8 esy of you, saying, 'This people honors me with
9 their lips, but their heart is far from me; and in vain do they worship me, teaching as doctrine the precepts of men.' "

10 Then he called the crowd to him, and said to

them, "Hear, and understand. ' What goes into 11
the mouth does not defile a man; but it is what
comes out of the mouth that defiles a man." Then 12
his disciples came up and said to him, "Dost thou
know that the Pharisees have taken offense at
hearing this saying?" But he answered and said, 13
"Every plant that my heavenly Father has not
planted will be rooted up. Let them alone; they 14
are blind guides of blind men. But if a blind man
guide a blind man, both fall into a pit."

But Peter spoke to him, saying, "Explain to us 15
this parable." And he said, "Are you also even 16
yet without understanding? Do you not realize 17
that whatever enters the mouth passes into the
belly and is cast out into the drain? But the 18
things that proceed out of the mouth come from
the heart, and it is they that defile a man. For out 19
of the heart come evil thoughts, murders, adulteries, immorality, thefts, false witness, blasphemies. These are the things that defile a man; 20
but to eat with unwashed hands does not defile a
man."

IV

The Canaanite Woman

AND LEAVING THERE, Jesus re- | DEC. 26 | 21
tired to the district of Tyre and Si- | June 26 |
don. And behold, a Canaanite woman came out 22
of that territory and cried out to him, saying,
"Have pity on me, O Lord, Son of David! My
daughter is sorely beset by a devil." He an- 23
swered her not a word. And his disciples came up
and besought him, saying, "Send her away, for
she is crying after us." But he answered and 24
said, "I was not sent except to the lost sheep of
the house of Israel." But she came and wor- 25
shipped him, saying, "Lord, help me!" He said in 26
answer, "It is not fair to take the children's bread

27 and to cast it to the dogs." But she said, "Yes, Lord; for even the dogs eat of the crumbs that
28 fall from their masters' table." Then Jesus answered and said to her, "O woman, great is thy faith! Let it be done to thee as thou wilt." And her daughter was healed from that moment.

Jesus Heals the Suffering

29 And when Jesus had departed from there, he went along the sea of Galilee; and he went up
30 the mountain and sat there. And great crowds came to him, bringing with them the dumb, the blind, the lame, the maimed, and many others; and they set them down at his feet, and he cured
31 them; so that the crowds marvelled to see the dumb speak, the lame walk, and the blind see. And they glorified the God of Israel.

Jesus Feeds Four Thousand

32 Then Jesus called together his disciples and said, "I have compassion on the crowd, for they have now been with me three days, and have nothing to eat; and I am unwilling to send them
33 away fasting, lest they faint on the way." And the disciples said to him, "But in a desert, where are we to get enough loaves to satisfy so great a
34 crowd?" Jesus said to them, "How many loaves have you?" And they said, "Seven, and a few little fishes."
35 And he bade the crowd recline on the ground.
36 Then taking the seven loaves and the fishes, he gave thanks, broke them and gave them to his disciples, and the disciples gave them to the
37 crowd. And they all ate and were satisfied; and they took up what was left of the fragments,
38 seven full baskets. Now those who had eaten were four thousand men, apart from children and women.

[44]

The Pharisees and Sadducees Ask a Sign

When he had dismissed the DEC. 27 June 27 39 crowd, he got into the boat, and came into the district of Magedan. And the **16** 1 Pharisees and Sadducees came to him to test him, and they asked him to show them a sign from heaven. But answering them he said, "When 2 it is evening you say, 'The weather will be fair, for the sky is red.' And in the morning you say, 3 'It will be stormy today, for the sky is red and lowering.' You know then how to read the face of 4 the sky, but cannot read the signs of the times! An evil and adulterous generation demands a sign, and no sign shall be given it but the sign of Jonas." And he left them and went away.

The Leaven of the Pharisees and Sadducees

And when his disciples crossed the sea, they 5 found that they had forgotten to bring bread. And he said to them, "Take heed and beware of 6 the leaven of the Pharisees and Sadducees!" But they began to argue among themselves, say- 7 ing, "We have brought no bread." But Jesus 8 knowing this, said, "You of little faith, why do you argue among yourselves that you have no bread? Do you not yet understand, nor remember 9 the five loaves among five thousand men, and how many baskets you took up? Nor the seven 10 loaves among four thousand, and how many large baskets you took up? Why do you not 11 understand that it was not of bread I said to you, 'Beware of the leaven of the Pharisees and Sad- ducees'?" Then they understood that he bade 12 them beware not of the leaven of bread, but of the teaching of the Pharisees and Sadducees.

[45]

Peter's Confession

13   Now Jesus, having come into the district of Cæsarea Philippi, began to ask his disciples, saying, "Who do men say the Son of Man is?"

14 But they said, "Some say, John the Baptist; and others, Elias; and others, Jeremias, or one of the

15 prophets." He said to them, "But who do you say

16 that I am?" Simon Peter answered and said, "Thou art the Christ, the Son of the living God."

17 Then Jesus answered and said, "Blessed art thou, Simon Bar-Jona, for flesh and blood has not revealed this to thee, but my Father in

18 heaven. And I say to thee, thou art Peter, and upon this rock I will build my Church, and the

19 gates of hell shall not prevail against it. And I will give thee the keys of the kingdom of heaven; and whatever thou shalt bind on earth shall be bound in heaven, and whatever thou shalt loose

20 on earth shall be loosed in heaven." Then he strictly charged his disciples to tell no one that he was Jesus the Christ.

Passion and Resurrection Foretold

21   From that time Jesus began to show his disciples that he must go to Jerusalem and suffer many things from the

<table>
<tr><td>DEC. 28</td></tr>
<tr><td>June 28</td></tr>
</table>

16, 18: *The gates of hell:* hostile, evil powers. Their aggressive force will struggle in vain against the Church. She shall never be overcome; she is indefectible. And since she has the office of teacher, and since she would be overcome if error prevailed, she is infallible.

16, 19: *Keys:* a symbol of authority. Peter has the power to admit into the Church and to exclude therefrom. Nor is he merely the porter; he has complete power within the Church. "To bind and loose" seems to have been used by the Jews in the sense to forbid or to permit; but 18, 18 as well as the present context requires a more comprehensive meaning. In heaven God ratifies the decisions which Peter makes on earth, in the name of Christ.

elders and Scribes and chief priests, and be put to death, and on the third day rise again. And 22 Peter taking him aside, began to chide him, saying, "Far be it from thee, O Lord; this will never happen to thee." He turned and said to Peter, 23 "Get behind me, satan, thou art a scandal to me; for thou dost not mind the things of God, but those of men."

The Doctrine of the Cross

Then Jesus said to his disciples, "If anyone 24 wishes to come after me, let him deny himself, and take up his cross, and follow me. For he who 25 would save his life will lose it; but he who loses his life for my sake will find it. For what does it 26 profit a man, if he gain the whole world, but suffer the loss of his own soul? Or what will a man give in exchange for his soul? For the Son 27 of Man is to come with his angels in the glory of his Father, and then he will render to everyone according to his conduct. Amen I say to you, 28 there are some of those standing here who will not taste death, till they have seen the Son of Man coming in his kingdom."

Jesus Transfigured

Now after six days Jesus took Peter, James **17** 1 and his brother John, and led them up a high mountain by themselves, and was transfigured 2 before them. And his face shone as the sun, and his garments became white as snow. And behold, 3 there appeared to them Moses and Elias talking together with him. Then Peter addressed Jesus, 4 saying, "Lord, it is good for us to be here. If thou wilt, let us set up three tents here, one for thee, one for Moses, and one for Elias." As he was still 5 speaking, behold, a bright cloud overshadowed them, and behold, a voice out of the cloud said,

"This is my beloved Son, in whom I am well
6 pleased; hear him." And on hearing it the disciples fell on their faces and were exceedingly
7 afraid. And Jesus came near and touched them,
and said to them, "Arise, and do not be afraid."
8 But lifting up their eyes, they saw no one but
Jesus only.

On the Coming of Elias

9 And as they were coming down from the
mountain, Jesus cautioned them, saying, "Tell
the vision to no one, till the Son of Man has risen
10 from the dead." And the disciples asked him,
saying, "Why then do the Scribes say that Elias
11 must come first?" But he answered and said,
"Elias indeed is to come and will restore all
12 things. But I say to you that Elias has come already, and they did not know him, but did to him
whatever they wished. So also shall the Son of
13 Man suffer at their hands." Then the disciples
understood that he had spoken to them of John
the Baptist.

A Possessed Boy

14 And when he had come to the   DEC. 29
crowd, a man approached him and   June 29
threw himself on his knees before him, saying,
"Lord, have pity on my son, for he is a lunatic,
and suffers severely; for often he falls into the
15 fire, and often into the water. And I brought him
to thy disciples, but they could not cure him."

16 Jesus answered and said, "O unbelieving and
perverse generation, how long shall I be with
you? How long shall I put up with you? Bring him
17 here to me." And Jesus rebuked him; and the
devil went out of him; and from that moment the
boy was cured.

18 Then the disciples came to Jesus privately and

said, "Why could not we cast it out?" He said   19
to them, "Because of your little faith; for amen I
say to you, if you have faith like a mustard seed,
you will say to this mountain, 'Remove from
here'; and it will remove. And nothing will be
impossible to you. But this kind can be cast out   20
only by prayer and fasting."

The Second Prediction of the Passion

Now while they were together in Galilee,   21
Jesus said to them, "The Son of Man is to be
betrayed into the hands of men, and they will   22
kill him; and on the third day he will rise again."
And they were exceedingly sorry.

Paying the Temple Tax

And when they had come to Capharnaum,   23
those who were collecting the didrachma came
to Peter, and said, "Does your Master not pay
the didrachma?" ' He said, "Yes." But when he   24
had entered the house, Jesus spoke first, saying,
"What dost thou think, Simon? From whom do
the kings of the earth receive tribute or customs;
from their own sons, or from others?" And he   25
said, "From others." Jesus said to him, "The
sons then are exempt. But that we may not   26
give offense to them, go to the sea and cast
a hook, and take the first fish that comes up. And
opening its mouth thou wilt find a stater; take
that and give it to them for me and for thee."

Against Ambition

At that hour the disciples came to Jesus, say-   **18** '
ing, "Who then is greatest in the kingdom of
heaven?" And Jesus called a little child to him,   2
set him in their midst, ' and said, "Amen I say to   3
you, unless you turn and become like little children, you will not enter into the kingdom of

4 heaven. Whoever, therefore, humbles himself as this little child, he is the greatest in the kingdom of heaven.

Avoiding Scandal

5 "And whoever receives one such little child for
6 my sake, receives me. But whoever causes one of these little ones who believe in me to sin, it were better for him to have a great millstone hung around his neck, and to be drowned in the depths of the sea.

7 "Woe to the world because of scandals! For it must needs be that scandals come, but woe to the
8 man through whom scandal does come! And if thy hand or thy foot is an occasion of sin to thee, cut it off and cast it from thee! It is better for thee to enter life maimed or lame, than, having two hands or two feet, to be cast into the everlasting
9 fire. And if thy eye is an occasion of sin to thee, pluck it out and cast it from thee! It is better for thee to enter into life with one eye, than, having two eyes, to be cast into hell-fire.

The Lost Sheep

10 "See that you do not despise one of these little ones; for I tell you, their angels in heaven always behold the face of
11 my Father in heaven. For the Son of Man came
12 to save what was lost. ' What do you think? If a man have a hundred sheep, and one of them stray, will he not leave the ninety-nine in the mountains, and go in search of the one that has
13 strayed? And if he happen to find it, amen I say to you, he rejoices over it more than over the
14 ninety-nine that did not go astray. Even so, it is not the will of your Father in heaven that a single one of these little ones should perish.

DEC. 30
June 30

Fraternal Correction

"But if thy brother sin against thee, go and 15 show him his fault, between thee and him alone. If he listen to thee, thou hast won thy brother. But if he do not listen to thee, take with thee one 16 or two more so that on the word of two or three witnesses every word may be confirmed. And if 17 he refuse to hear them, appeal to the Church, but if he refuse to hear even the Church, let him be to thee as the heathen and the publican. Amen I 18 say to you, whatever you bind on earth shall be bound also in heaven, and whatever you loose on earth shall be loosed also in heaven.

The Power of United Prayer

"I say to you further, that if two of you shall 19 agree on earth about anything at all for which they ask, it shall be done for them by my Father in heaven. For where two or three are gathered 20 together for my sake, there am I in the midst of them."

The Unmerciful Servant

Then Peter came up to him and said, "Lord, 21 how often shall my brother sin against me, and I forgive him? Up to seven times?" Jesus said to 22 him, "I do not say to thee seven times, but seventy times seven.

18, 18: To the Apostles as a body is given a part of the power granted to Peter. There will be no conflict of authority, since Peter is the head of the Church, including the Apostles, he alone having received "the keys of the kingdom of heaven."

18, 22: A sinner must be forgiven as often as he repents. The expression "seventy times seven" is for an indefinite number.

23 "This is why the kingdom of heaven is likened
to a king who desired to settle accounts with his
24 servants. And when he had begun the settlement, one was brought to him who owed him ten
25 thousand talents. And as he had no means of
paying, his master ordered him to be sold, with
his wife and children and all that he had, and
26 payment to be made. But the servant fell down
and besought him, saying, 'Have patience with
27 me and I will pay thee all!' And moved with
compassion, the master of that servant released
him, and forgave him the debt.

28 "But as that servant went out, he met one
of his fellow-servants who owed him a hundred
denarii, and he laid hold of him and throttled
29 him, saying, 'Pay what thou owest.' His fellow-
servant therefore fell down and began to entreat him, saying, 'Have patience with me and
30 I will pay thee all.' But he would not; but went
away and cast him into prison until he should
pay what was due.

31 "His fellow-servants therefore, seeing what
had happened, were very much saddened, and
they went and informed their master of what
32 had taken place. Then his master called him,
and said to him, 'Wicked servant! I forgave thee
all the debt, because thou didst entreat me.
33 Shouldst not thou also have had pity on thy
34 fellow-servant, even as I had pity on thee'? And
his master, being angry, handed him over to
the torturers until he should pay all that was due
35 to him. So also my heavenly Father will do to
you, if you do not each forgive your brothers
from your hearts."

V

AND IT CAME TO PASS when Jesus had brought these words to a close, that he departed from Galilee and came to the district of Judea beyond the Jordan. And great crowds followed him, and he cured them there. 2

DEC. 31
July 1

19 1

The Question of Divorce

And there came to him some Pharisees, 3 testing him, and saying, "Is it lawful for a man to put away his wife for any cause?" But he 4 answered and said to them, "Have you not read that the Creator, from the beginning, made them male and female, and said, 'For this 5 cause a man shall leave his father and mother, and cleave to his wife, and the two shall become one flesh'? Therefore now they are no 6 longer two, but one flesh. What therefore God has joined together, let no man put asunder." They said to him, "Why then did Moses command to give a written notice of dismissal, and to put her away?" He said to them, "Because Moses, by reason of the hardness of your heart, permitted you to put away your wives; but it was not so from the beginning. And I 9 say to you, that whoever puts away his wife, except for immorality, and marries another, commits adultery; and he who marries a woman who has been put away commits adultery."

His disciples said to him, "If the case of a 10 man with his wife is so, it is not expedient to marry." And he said, "Not all can accept this 11 teaching; but those to whom it has been given. For there are eunuchs who were born so from 12 their mother's womb; and there are eunuchs who were made so by men; and there are eunuchs who have made themselves so for the sake of the kingdom of heaven. Let him accept it who can."

Jesus Blesses the Children

13 Little children were brought to him then that he might lay his hands on them and pray;
14 but the disciples rebuked them. But Jesus said to them, "Let the little children be, and do not hinder them from coming to me, for of such is
15 the kingdom of heaven." And when he had laid his hands on them, he departed from that place.

The Danger of Riches

16 And behold, a certain man came to him and said, "Good Master,

JAN. 1
July 2

what good work shall I do to have eternal
17 life?" He said to him, "Why dost thou ask me about what is good? One there is who is good, and he is God. But if thou wilt enter into life,
18 keep the commandments." He said to him, "Which?" And Jesus said, "Thou shalt not kill, Thou shalt not commit adultery, Thou shalt not steal, Thou shalt not bear false witness,
19 Honor thy father and mother, and, Thou shalt love thy neighbor as thyself."

20 The young man said to him, "All these I have
21 kept; what is yet wanting to me?" Jesus said to him, "If thou wilt be perfect, go, sell what thou hast, and give to the poor, and thou shalt have treasure in heaven; and come, follow
22 me." But when the young man heard the saying, he went away sad, for he had great possessions.

23 But Jesus said to his disciples, "Amen I say to you, with difficulty will a rich man enter the
24 kingdom of heaven. And further I say to you, it is easier for a camel to pass through the eye

of a needle, than for a rich man to enter the kingdom of heaven." The disciples, hearing 25 this, were exceedingly astonished and said, "Who then can be saved?" And looking upon 26 them, Jesus said to them, "With men this is impossible, but with God all things are possible."

Then Peter addressed him, saying, "Behold, 27 we have left all and followed thee; what then shall we have?" And Jesus said to them, 28 "Amen I say to you that you who have followed me, in the regeneration when the Son of Man shall sit on the throne of his glory, shall also sit on twelve thrones, judging the twelve tribes of Israel. And everyone who has left house, or 29 brothers, or sisters, or father, or mother, or wife, or children, or lands, for my name's sake, shall receive a hundredfold, and shall possess life everlasting. But many who are first now 30 will be last, and many who are last now will be first.

Parable of the Laborers in the Vineyard

"For the kingdom of heaven is like a householder who went out early in the morning to hire laborers for his vineyard. And having agreed with the laborers 2 for a denarius a day, he sent them into his vineyard. And about the third hour, he went out 3 and saw others standing in the market place

| JAN. 2 | **20** 1 |
| July 3 | |

19, 24: Our Lord expresses in a paradoxical way the idea that it is very difficult for a rich man to be saved; v. 26 shows that it is not impossible with the help of God.

20, 1-16: The laborers in the vineyard all receive the same reward, a denarius. God is master of His gifts and His grace may make one who has served Him only for a short time as worthy of supernatural rewards as one who has borne the burden of the day and the heat.

4 idle; and he said to them, 'Go you also into the vineyard, and I will give you whatever is just.'
5 ' So they went. And again he went out about the sixth, and about the ninth hour, and did as
6 before. But about the eleventh hour he went out and found others standing about, and he said to them, 'Why do you stand here all day
7 idle?' They said to him, 'Because no man has hired us.' He said to them, 'Go you also into
8 the vineyard.' But when evening had come, the owner of the vineyard said to his steward, 'Call the laborers, and pay them their wages, be-
9 ginning from the last even to the first.' Now when they of the eleventh hour came, they re-
10 ceived each a denarius. And when the first in their turn came, they thought that they would receive more; but they also received each his
11 denarius. And on receiving it, they began to mur-
12 mur against the householder, ' saying, 'These last have worked a single hour, and thou hast put them on a level with us, who have borne
13 the burden of the day's heat.' But answering one of them he said, 'Friend, I do thee no injustice; didst thou not agree with me for a denarius?
14 Take what is thine and go; I choose to give to
15 this last even as to thee. Have I not a right to do what I choose? or art thou envious because
16 I am generous?' Even so the last shall be first, and the first last; for many are called, but few are chosen."

The Third Prediction of the Passion

17 And as Jesus was going up to Jerusalem, he took the twelve disciples aside by themselves, and said to them,

JAN. 3
July 4

18 "Behold, we are going up to Jerusalem, and the Son of Man will be betrayed to the chief priests

and the Scribes; and they will condemn him to
death, and will deliver him to the Gentiles to be   19
mocked and scourged and crucified; and on the
third day he will rise again."

The Mother of James and John

Then the mother of the sons of Zebedee came   20
to him with her sons; and worshipping, she made
a request of him. He said to her, "What dost   21
thou want?" She said to him, "Command that
these my two sons may sit, one at thy right hand
and one at thy left hand, in thy kingdom." But   22
Jesus answered and said, "You do not know
what you are asking for. Can you drink of the cup
of which I am about to drink?" They said to him,
"We can." He said to them, "Of my cup you   23
shall indeed drink; but as for sitting at my right
hand and at my left, that is not mine to give you,
but it belongs to those for whom it has been prepared by my Father."

And when the ten heard this, they were indig-   24
nant at the two brothers. But Jesus called them   25
to him, and said, "You know that the rulers of
the Gentiles lord it over them, and their great
men exercise authority over them. Not so is it   26
among you. On the contrary, whoever wishes to
become great among you shall be your servant;
and whoever wishes to be first among you shall   27
be your slave; even as the Son of Man has not   28
come to be served but to serve, and to give his
life as a ransom for many."

The Blind Men at Jericho

And as they were leaving Jericho, a great   29
crowd followed him. And behold, two blind men   30
sitting by the wayside heard that Jesus was
passing by, and cried out, saying, "Lord, Son of
David, have mercy on us!" And the crowd an-   31

grily tried to silence them. But they cried out all
the louder, saying, "Lord, have mercy on us, Son
32 of David!" Then Jesus stopped, and called them,
and said, "What will you have me do for you?"
33 They said to him, "Lord, that our eyes be
34 opened." And Jesus, moved with compassion for
them, touched their eyes; and at once they received their sight, and followed him.

VI

Triumphal Entry into Jerusalem

21 1 AND WHEN THEY DREW NEAR to $\boxed{\begin{array}{l}\text{JAN. 4}\\ \text{July 5}\end{array}}$
Jerusalem, and came to Bethphage,
on the Mount of Olives, then Jesus sent two dis-
2 ciples, saying to them, "Go into the village opposite you, and immediately you will find an ass
tied, and a colt with her; loose them and bring
3 them to me. And if anyone say anything to you,
you shall say that the Lord has need of them, and
4 immediately he will send them." Now this was
done that what was spoken through the prophet
5 might be fulfilled, "Tell the daughter of Sion:
Behold, thy king comes to thee, meek and seated
upon an ass, and upon a colt, the foal of a beast of
burden."

6 So the disciples went and did as Jesus had
7 directed them. And they brought the ass and the
colt, laid their cloaks on them, and made him sit
8 thereon. And most of the crowd spread their
cloaks upon the road, while others were cutting
branches from the trees, and strewing them on
9 the road. And the crowds that went before him,
and those that followed, kept crying out, saying,
"Hosanna to the Son of David! Blessed is he who
comes in the name of the Lord! Hosanna in the
10 highest!" And when he entered Jerusalem, all
the city was thrown into commotion, saying,

"Who is this?" But the crowds kept on saying, 11 "This is Jesus the prophet from Nazareth of Galilee."

Cleansing of the Temple

And Jesus entered the temple of God, and cast 12 out all those who were selling and buying in the temple, and he overturned the tables of the money-changers and the seats of those who sold the doves. And he said to them, "It is written, 13 'My house shall be called a house of prayer'; but you have made it a den of thieves."

And the blind and the lame came to him in the 14 temple, and he healed them. But the chief priests 15 and the Scribes, seeing the wonderful deeds that he did, and the children crying out in the temple, and saying, "Hosanna to the Son of David," were indignant, and said to him, "Dost thou hear 16 what these are saying?" And Jesus said to them, "Yes; have you never read, 'Out of the mouth of infants and sucklings thou hast perfected praise'?" And leaving them, he went out of the 17 city to Bethany and he stayed there.

Jesus Curses a Fig Tree

Now in the morning, on his way | JAN. 5 | 18
back to the city, he felt hungry. And | July 6 | 19
seeing a fig tree by the wayside, he came up to it, and found nothing on it but leaves; and he said to it, "May no fruit ever come from thee henceforward forever!" And immediately the fig tree withered up.

And upon seeing this the disciples marvelled, 20 saying, "How did it come to wither up immediately?" But Jesus answered and said to them, 21 "Amen I say to you, if you have faith and do not waver, not only will you do what I have done to the fig tree, but even if you shall say to this

mountain. 'Arise, and hurl thyself into the sea,'
22 it shall be done. And all things whatever you ask
for in prayer, believing, you shall receive.''

The Authority of Jesus

23　And when he had come into the temple, the
chief priests and elders of the people came to
him as he was teaching, and said, "By what
authority dost thou do these things? And who
24 gave thee this authority?" Jesus answered and
said to them, "I also will ask you one question,
and if you answer me this, I in turn will tell you
25 by what authority I do these things. Whence was
the baptism of John? from heaven, or from
men?" But they began to argue among them-
26 selves, saying, "If we say, 'From heaven,' he
will say to us, 'Why then did you not believe
him?' But if we say, 'From men,' we fear the
27 people, for all regard John as a prophet." And
they answered Jesus and said, "We do not
know." Then he in turn said to them, "Neither
do I tell you by what authority I do these things.

Parable of the Two Sons

28　"But what do you think? A man had two sons;
and he came to the first and said, 'Son, go and
29 work today in my vineyard.' But he answered
and said, 'I will not'; but afterwards he regretted
30 it and went. And he came to the other and spoke
in the same manner. And this one answered, 'I
31 go, sir'; but he did not go. Which of the two did
the father's will?" They said, "The first." Jesus
said to them, "Amen I say to you, the publicans
and harlots are entering the kingdom of God
32 before you. For John came to you in the way of
justice, and you did not believe him. But the
publicans and the harlots believed him; whereas

you, seeing it, did not even repent afterwards,
that you might believe him.

Parable of the Vine-dressers

"Hear another parable. There
was a man, a householder, who

| JAN. 6 | 33 |
| July 7 | |

planted a vineyard, and put a hedge about it, and
dug a wine vat in it, and built a tower; then he
let it out to vine-dressers, and went abroad.
But when the fruit season drew near, he sent his   34
servants to the vine-dressers to receive his
fruits. And the vine-dressers seized his servants,   35
and beat one, killed another, and stoned another.
Again he sent another party of servants more   36
numerous than the first; and they did the same
to these. Finally he sent his son to them, saying,   37
'They will respect my son.'

"But the vine-dressers, on seeing the son, said   38
among themselves, 'This is the heir; come, let us
kill him, and we shall have his inheritance.'
So they seized him, cast him out of the vineyard,   39
and killed him. When, therefore, the owner of   40
the vineyard comes, what will he do to those
vine-dressers?" They said to him, "He will   41
utterly destroy those evil men, and will let out
the vineyard to other vine-dressers, who will
render to him the fruits in their seasons."

Jesus said to them, "Did you never read in the   42
Scriptures, 'The stone which the builders rejected, has become the corner stone; by the Lord
this has been done, and it is wonderful in our
eyes'? Therefore I say to you, that the kingdom   43
of God will be taken away from you and will be
given to a people yielding its fruits. And he who   44
falls on this stone will be broken to pieces; but
upon whomever it falls, it will grind him to
powder."

45   And when the chief priests and Pharisees had
heard his parables, they knew that he was speak-
46 ing about them. And though they sought to lay
hands on him, they feared the people, because
they regarded him as a prophet.

The Marriage Feast

221   And Jesus addressed them, and JAN. 7 July 8
spoke to them again in parables,
2 saying, "The kingdom of heaven is like a king
3 who made a marriage feast for his son. And he
sent his servants to call in those invited to the
4 marriage feast, but they would not come. Again
he sent out other servants, saying, 'Tell those
who are invited, Behold, I have prepared my
dinner; my oxen and fatlings are killed, and
everything is ready; come to the marriage feast.'
5 But they made light of it, and went off, o ne to
6 his farm, and another to his business; and the
rest laid hold of his servants, treated them
shamefully, and killed them.

7   "But when the king heard of it, he was angry;
and he sent his armies, destroyed those mur-
8 derers, and burnt their city. Then he said to his
servants, 'The marriage feast indeed is ready,
but those who were invited were not worthy;
9 go therefore to the crossroads, and invite to the
10 marriage feast whomever you shall find.' And his
servants went out into the roads, and gathered all
whom they found, both good and bad; and the
marriage feast was filled with guests.

11   "Now the king went in to see the guests, and
he saw there a man who had not on a wedding
12 garment. And he said to him, 'Friend, how didst
thou come in here without a wedding garment?'
13 But he was speechless. Then the king said to
the attendants, 'Bind his hands and feet and cast
him forth into the darkness outside, where there

will be the weeping, and the gnashing of teeth.'
For many are called, but few are chosen." 14

Tribute to Caesar

Then the Pharisees went and took counsel how 15
they might trap him in his talk. And they sent to 16
him their disciples with the Herodians, saying,
"Master, we know that thou art truthful, and
that thou teachest the way of God in truth and
that thou carest naught for any man; for thou
dost not regard the person of men. Tell us, there- 17
fore, what dost thou think: Is it lawful to give
tribute to Cæsar, or not?" But Jesus, knowing 18
their wickedness, said, "Why do you test me,
you hypocrites? Show me the coin of the tribute." 19
So they offered him a denarius. ' Then Jesus said 20
to them, "Whose are this image and the inscription?" ' They said to him, "Cæsar's." Then he 21
said to them, "Render, therefore, to Cæsar the
things that are Cæsar's, and to God the things
that are God's." And hearing this they mar- 22
velled, and leaving him went off.

The Sadducees and the Resurrection

On that same day some of the | JAN. 8 | 23
Sadducees, who say there is no res- | July 9 |
urrection, came to him, and questioned him,
' saying, "Master, Moses said, 'If a man die 24
without having a son, his brother shall marry the
widow and raise up issue to his brother.' Now 25
there were among us seven brothers. And the
first, after having married a wife, died, and having no issue, left his wife to his brother. In like 26
manner the second, and the third down to the
seventh. And last of all the woman also died. 27
At the resurrection, therefore, of which of the 28
seven will she be the wife? For they all had her."
But Jesus answered and said to them, "You 29

[63]

err because you know neither the Scriptures nor
30 the power of God. For at the resurrection they
will neither marry nor be given in marriage, but
31 will be as angels of God in heaven. But as to the
resurrection of the dead, have you not read what
32 was spoken to you by God, saying, 'I am the God
of Abraham, and the God of Isaac, and the God
of Jacob'? He is not the God of the dead, but of
33 the living." And when the crowds heard this,
they marvelled at his teaching.

The Great Commandment

34 But the Pharisees, hearing that he had si-
35 lenced the Sadducees, gathered together. And
one of them, a doctor of the Law, putting him
36 to the test, asked him, "Master, which is the
37 great commandment in the Law?" Jesus said to
him, " 'Thou shalt love the Lord thy God with
thy whole heart, and with thy whole soul, and
38 with thy whole mind.' This is the greatest and the
39 first commandment. And the second is like it,
40 'Thou shalt love thy neighbor as thyself.' On
these two commandments depend the whole Law
and the Prophets."

The Son of David

41 Now while the Pharisees were
gathered together, Jesus questioned
42 them, saying, "What do you think of the Christ?
Whose son is he?" They said to him, "David's."
43 He said to them, "How then does David in the
44 Spirit call him Lord, saying, 'The Lord said to
my Lord: Sit thou at my right hand, till I make
45 thy enemies thy footstool'? If David, therefore,

JAN. 9
July 10

22, 45: David's son is David's Lord: there is implied a
claim to divinity.

[64]

calls him 'Lord,' how is he his son?" And no one 46
could answer him a word; neither did anyone
dare from that day forth to ask him any more
questions.

Hypocrisy of the Scribes and Pharisees

Then Jesus spoke to the crowds and to his **23** 1
disciples, ' saying, "The Scribes and the Pharisees 2
have sat on the chair of Moses. All things, there- 3
fore, that they command you, observe and do.
But do not act according to their works; for they
talk but do nothing. And they bind together 4
heavy and oppressive burdens, and lay them on
men's shoulders; but not with one finger of their
own do they choose to move them. In fact, all 5
their works they do in order to be seen by men;
for they widen their phylacteries, and enlarge their
tassels, and love the first places at suppers and 6
the front seats in the synagogues, and greetings 7
in the market place, and to be called by men
'Rabbi.' But do not you be called 'Rabbi'; for 8
one is your Master, and all you are brothers.
And call no one on earth your father; for one is 9
your Father, who is in heaven. Neither be called 10
masters; for one only is your Master, the Christ.
He who is greatest among you shall be your 11
servant. And whoever exalts himself shall be 12
humbled, and whoever humbles himself shall
be exalted.

23, 5: *Phylacteries:* little boxes containing Scripture texts
which were bound to the forehead and left arm when the
Jews were saying their prayers. A misinterpretation of
the Law made them think they were obliged to wear
them. The fringes, tassels attached to the cloak, were
prescribed by Num. 15, 37-41; Deut. 22, 12.

23, 7: *Rabbi:* means "my master."

23, 8-11: It would be blameworthy for Christians to give
or receive such titles as "master," "father," "doctor,"
without recognizing that one is "father in Christ," that is,
in union with and subordination to our Lord and to the
Father.

Woe to the Scribes and Pharisees

13 "But woe to you, Scribes and Pharisees, hypocrites! because you JAN. 10 July 11 shut the kingdom of heaven against men. For you yourselves do not go in, nor do you allow those going in to enter.

14 ["Woe to you, Scribes and Pharisees, hypocrites! because you devour the houses of widows, praying long prayers. For this you shall receive a greater judgment.]

15 "Woe to you, Scribes and Pharisees, hypocrites! because you traverse sea and land to make one convert; and when he has become one, you make him twofold more a son of hell than yourselves.

16 "Woe to you, blind guides, who say, 'Whoever swears by the temple, it is nothing; but whoever swears by the gold of the temple, he
17 is bound.' You blind fools! for which is greater, the gold, or the temple which sanctifies the
18 gold? 'And whoever swears by the altar, it is nothing; but whoever swears by the gift that is
19 upon it, he is bound.' Blind ones! for which is greater, the gift, or the altar which sanctifies
20 the gift? Therefore he who swears by the altar
21 swears by it, and by all things that are on it; and he who swears by the temple swears by it and
22 by him who dwells in it. And he who swears by heaven swears by the throne of God, and by him who sits upon it.

23 "Woe to you, Scribes and Pharisees, hypocrites! because you pay tithes on mint and anise and cummin, and have left undone the weightier matters of the Law, right judgment and mercy and faith. These things you ought to have done, while not leaving the others
24 undone. Blind guides, who strain out the gnat but swallow the camel!

"Woe to you, Scribes and Pharisees, hypo- 25
crites! because you clean the outside of the cup
and the dish, but within they are full of robbery
and uncleanness. Thou blind Pharisee! clean 26
first the inside of the cup and of the dish, that
the outside too may be clean.

"Woe to you, Scribes and Pharisees, hypo- 27
crites! because you are like whited sepulchres,
which outwardly appear to men beautiful, but
within are full of dead men's bones and of all
uncleanness. So you also outwardly appear just 28
to men, but within you are full of hypocrisy and
iniquity.

"Woe to you, Scribes and Pharisees, hypo- 29
crites! you who build the sepulchres of the
prophets, and adorn the tombs of the just,' and 30
say, 'If we had lived in the days of our fathers,
we would not have been their accomplices in
the blood of the prophets.' Thus you are wit- 31
nesses against yourselves that you are the sons
of those who killed the prophets.

"You also fill up the measure of your fathers. 32
Serpents, brood of vipers, how are you to 33
escape the judgment of hell? Therefore, be- 34
hold, I send you prophets, and wise men, and
scribes; and some of them you will put to
death, and crucify, and some you will scourge
in your synagogues, and persecute from town
to town; that upon you may come all the just 35
blood that has been shed on the earth, from the
blood of Abel the just unto the blood of
Zacharias the son of Barachias, whom you killed
between the temple and the altar. Amen I say 36
to you, all these things will come upon this
generation.

"Jerusalem, Jerusalem! thou who killest the 37
prophets, and stonest those who are sent to thee!
How often would I have gathered thy children

together, as a hen gathers her young under her
38 wings, but thou wouldst not! Behold, your
39 house is left to you desolate. For I say to you,
you shall not see me henceforth until you shall
say, 'Blessed is he who comes in the name of
the Lord!'"

Destruction of Jerusalem and End of the World

24 1 And Jesus left the temple and was
going away, when his disciples came
forward to show him the buildings of the temple.
2 But he answered and said to them, "Do you see
all these things? Amen I say to you, there will
not be left here one stone upon another that will
not be thrown down."

3 And as he was sitting on the Mount of Olives,
the disciples came to him privately, saying, "Tell
us, when are these things to happen, and what
will be the sign of thy coming and of the end of
the world?"

4 And in answer Jesus said to them, "Take care
5 that no one leads you astray. For many will come
in my name, saying, 'I am the Christ,' and they
6 will lead many astray. For you shall hear of wars
and rumors of wars. Take care that you do not
be alarmed, for these things must come to pass,
7 but the end is not yet. For nation will rise against
nation, and kingdom against kingdom; and there
will be pestilences and famines and earthquakes
8 in various places. But all these things are the
beginnings of sorrows.

9 "Then they will deliver you up to tribulation,
and will put you to death; and you will be hated
10 by all nations for my name's sake. And then
many will fall away, and will betray one another,
11 and will hate one another. And many false
prophets will arise, and will lead many astray.

And because iniquity will abound, the charity of 12
the many will grow cold. But whoever perse- 13
veres to the end, he shall be saved. And this 14
gospel of the kingdom shall be preached in the
whole world, for a witness to all nations; and
then will come the end.

Destruction of Jerusalem

"Therefore when you see the abomination of 15
desolation, which was spoken of by Daniel the
prophet, standing in the holy place — let him
who reads understand — then let those who 16
are in Judea flee to the mountains; and let him 17
who is on the housetop not go down to take anything from his house; and let him who is in the 18
field not turn back to take his cloak. But woe to 19
those who are with child, or have infants at the
breast in those days! But pray that your flight 20
may not be in the winter, or on the Sabbath. For 21
then there will be great tribulation, such as has
not been from the beginning of the world until
now, nor will be. And unless those days had been 22
shortened, no living creature would be saved.
But for the sake of the elect those days will be
shortened.

The Signs of the Last Day

"Then if anyone say to you, 'Be- 23
hold, here is the Christ,' or, 'There
he is,' do not believe it. For false christs and 24
false prophets will arise, and will show great
signs and wonders, so as to lead astray, if possible, even the elect. Behold, I have told it to 25
you beforehand. If therefore they say to you, 26
'Behold, he is in the desert,' do not go forth;
'Behold, he is in the inner chambers,' do not
believe it. For as the lightning comes forth from 27
the east and shines even to the west, so also will

JAN. 12
July 13

28 the coming of the Son of Man be. Wherever the body is, there will the eagles be gathered together.

29 　"But immediately after the tribulation of those days, the sun will be darkened, and the moon will not give her light, and the stars will fall from heaven, and the powers of heaven will be shaken.

30 And then will appear the sign of the Son of Man in heaven; and then will all tribes of the earth mourn, and they will see the Son of Man coming upon the clouds of heaven with great power and

31 majesty. And he will send forth his angels with a trumpet and a great sound, and they will gather his elect from the four winds, from one end of the heavens to the other.

Jerusalem's Impending Destruction

32 　"Now from the fig tree learn this parable. When its branch is now tender, and the leaves

33 break forth, you know that summer is near. Even so, when you see all these things, know that it is

---

24, 32-36: This passage seems at first sight, on account of its immediately preceding context, to refer to the Second Coming as well as to the destruction of Jerusalem; and so the words of our Lord, *This generation will not pass away till all these things have been accomplished*, would promise the Second Coming before the death of many of those then living. But He does not actually make this promise, for He says explicitly that no one knows, not even Himself (with a knowledge He may communicate), when it will come. *That day:* in the Bible, this predicted day always refers to the day of judgment. *This generation:* may mean that the Jewish nation would survive to the end of the world. The expression does not always necessarily refer to contemporaries. And despite their position, the words may be referred to the destruction of Jerusalem. The signs announcing it would enable the Christians to flee, whereas the end of the world was to come suddenly and there would be no escape from the calamities which preceded it.

near, even at the door. Amen I say to you, this 34
generation will not pass away till all these things
have been accomplished. Heaven and earth will 35
pass away, but my words will not pass away.

The Need of Watchfulness

"But of that day and hour no one knows, not 36
even the angels of heaven, but the Father only.
And as it was in the days of Noe, even so will be 37
the coming of the Son of Man. For as in the days 38
before the flood they were eating and drinking,
marrying and giving in marriage until the day
when Noe entered the ark, and they did not 39
understand until the flood came and swept them
all away; even so will be the coming of the Son
of Man.

"Then two men will be in the field; one will 40
be taken, and one will be left. Two women will 41
be grinding at the millstone; one will be taken,
and one will be left.

Exhortation to Vigilance

"Watch therefore, for you do not | JAN. 13 | 42
know at what hour your Lord is to | July 14 |
come. But of this be assured, that if the house- 43
holder had known at what hour the thief was
coming, he would certainly have watched, and not
have let his house be broken into. Therefore you 44
also must be ready, because at an hour that you
do not expect, the Son of Man will come. Who, 45
dost thou think, is the faithful and prudent
servant whom his master has set over his household to give them their food in due time? Blessed 46
is that servant whom his master, when he comes,
shall find so doing. Amen I say to you, he will 47
set him over all his goods. But if that wicked 48
servant says to himself, 'My master delays his
coming,' and begins to beat his fellow-servants, 49

50 and to eat and drink with drunkards, the master of that servant will come on a day he does not
51 expect, and in an hour he does not know, and will cut him asunder and make him share the lot of the hypocrites. There will be the weeping, and the gnashing of teeth.

Parable of the Ten Virgins

25 1 "Then will the kingdom of heaven be like ten virgins who took their lamps and went forth to
2 meet the bridegroom and the bride. Five of them
3 were foolish and five wise. But the five foolish, when they took their lamps, take no oil with
4 them, while the wise did take oil in their vessels
5 with the lamps. Then as the bridegroom was long in coming, they all became drowsy and
6 slept. And at midnight a cry arose, 'Behold, the bridegroom is coming, go forth to meet him!'
7 Then all those virgins arose and trimmed their
8 lamps. And the foolish said to the wise, 'Give us some of your oil, for our lamps are going out.'
9 The wise answered, saying, 'Lest there may not be enough for us and for you, go rather to those who sell it, and buy some for yourselves.'

10 "Now while they were gone to buy it, the bridegroom came; and those who were ready went in with him to the marriage feast, and the
11 door was shut. Finally there came also the other virgins, who said, 'Sir, sir, open the door for us!'
12 But he answered and said, 'Amen I say to you, I
13 do not know you.' Watch therefore, for you know neither the day nor the hour.

Parable of the Talents

14 "For it is like a man going abroad, who called his servants and handed
15 over his goods to them. And to one he gave five

JAN. 14
July 15

talents, to another two, and to another one, to each according to his particular ability, and then he went on his journey. And he who had received 16 the five talents went and traded with them, and gained five more. In like manner, he who had 17 received the two gained two more. But he who 18 had received the one went away and dug in the earth and hid his master's money.

"Then after a long time the master of those 19 servants came and settled accounts with them. And he who had received the five talents came 20 and brought five other talents, saying, 'Master, thou didst hand over to me five talents; behold, I have gained five others in addition.' His master 21 said to him, 'Well done, good and faithful servant; because thou hast been faithful over a few things, I will set thee over many; enter into the joy of thy master.'

"And he also who had received the two talents 22 came and said, 'Master, thou didst hand over to me two talents; behold, I have gained two more.' His master said to him, 'Well done, good and 23 faithful servant; because thou hast been faithful over a few things, I will set thee over many; enter into the joy of thy master.'

"But he who had received the one talent came 24 and said, 'Master, I know that thou art a stern man; thou reapest where thou hast not sowed and gatherest where thou hast not winnowed; and as I was afraid, I went away and hid thy 25 talent in the earth; behold, thou hast what is thine.' But his master answered and said to him, 26 'Wicked and slothful servant! thou didst know that I reap where I do not sow, and gather where I have not winnowed? Thou shouldst therefore 27 have entrusted my money to the bankers, and on my return I should have got back my own with interest. Take away therefore the talent 28

from him, and give it to him who has the ten
29 talents. For to everyone who has shall be given,
and he shall have abundance; but from him who
does not have, even that which he seems to have
30 shall be taken away. But as for the unprofitable
servant, cast him forth into the darkness outside,
where there will be the weeping, and the gnashing of teeth.'

The Last Judgment

31 "But when the Son of Man shall
come in his majesty, and all the

JAN. 15
July 16

angels with him, then he will sit on the throne
32 of his glory; and before him will be gathered all
the nations, and he will separate them one from
another, as the shepherd separates the sheep
33 from the goats; and he will set the sheep on his
right hand, but the goats on the left.

34 "Then the king will say to those on his right
hand, 'Come, blessed of my Father, take possession of the kingdom prepared for you from the
35 foundation of the world; for I was hungry and
you gave me to eat; I was thirsty and you gave
me to drink; I was a stranger and you took me
36 in;' naked and you covered me; sick and you
visited me; I was in prison and you came to me.'
37 Then the just will answer him, saying, 'Lord,
when did we see thee hungry, and feed thee;
38 or thirsty, and give thee drink? And when did
we see thee a stranger, and take thee in; or
39 naked, and clothe thee? Or when did we see
40 thee sick, or in prison, and come to thee?' And
answering the king will say to them, 'Amen I
say to you, as long as you did it for one of these,
the least of my brethren, you did it for me.'

41 "Then he will say to those on his left hand,
'Depart from me, accursed ones, into the ever-

lasting fire which was prepared for the devil and his angels. For I was hungry, and you did not 42 give me to eat; I was thirsty and you gave me no drink; I was a stranger and you did not take me 43 in; naked, and you did not clothe me; sick, and in prison, and you did not visit me.' Then they 44 also will answer and say, 'Lord, when did we see thee hungry, or thirsty, or a stranger, or naked, or sick, or in prison, and did not minister to thee?' Then he will answer them, saying, 45 'Amen I say to you, as long as you did not do it for one of these least ones, you did not do it for me.' And these will go into everlasting punish- 46 me nt, but the just into everlasting life.''

II: THE PASSION, DEATH AND RESURRECTION

1. The Last Supper

AND IT CAME TO PASS when Jesus had finished all these words, that he | JAN. 16 / July 17 | **26** 1 said to his disciples, "You know that after two 2 days the Passover will be here; and the Son of Man will be delivered up to be crucified."

The Council

Then the chief priests and the elders of the 3 people gathered together in the court of the high priest, who was called Caiphas, ' and they took 4 counsel together how they might seize Jesus by stealth and put him to death. But they said, 5 "Not on the feast, or there might be a riot among the people."

The Anointing at Bethany

Now when Jesus was in Bethany, in the house 6 of Simon the leper, a woman came up to him 7 with an alabaster jar of precious ointment, and

she poured it on his head, as he reclined at
8 table. But when the disciples saw this, they were
indignant, and said, "To what purpose is this
9 waste? for this might have been sold for much
and given to the poor."

10 But Jesus, perceiving it, said to them, "Why
do you trouble the woman? She has done me a
11 good turn. For the poor you have always with
12 you, but you do not always have me. For in pouring this ointment on my body, she has done it for
13 my burial. Amen I say to you, wherever in the
whole world this gospel is preached, this also
that she has done shall be told in memory of
her."

The Betrayal

14 Then one of the Twelve, called Judas Iscariot,
15 went to the chief priests, ' and said to them,
"What are you willing to give me for delivering
him to you?" But they assigned him thirty pieces
16 of silver. And from then on he sought out an opportunity to betray him.

Preparation

17 Now on the first day of the Unleavened Bread,
the disciples came to Jesus and said, "Where
dost thou want us to prepare for thee to eat the
18 passover?" But Jesus said, "Go into the city to
a certain man, and say to him, 'The Master says,
My time is near at hand; at thy house I am keep-
19 ing the Passover with my disciples.'" And the
disciples did as Jesus bade them, and prepared
the passover.

The Betrayer

20 Now when the evening arrived, he reclined at
21 table with the twelve disciples. And while they
were eating, he said, "Amen I say to you, one of
22 you will betray me." And being very much sad-

dened they began each to say, "Is it I, Lord?"
But he answered and said, "He who dips his 23
hand into the dish with me, he will betray me.
The Son of Man indeed goes his way, as it is 24
written of him; but woe to that man by whom the
Son of Man is betrayed! It were better for that
man if he had not been born." And Judas who 25
betrayed him answered and said, "Is it I,
Rabbi?" He said to him, "Thou hast said it."

The Holy Eucharist

And while they were at supper, Jesus took 26
bread, and blessed and broke, and gave it to his
disciples, and said, "Take and eat; this is my
body." And taking a cup, he gave thanks and 27
gave it to them, saying, "All of you drink of this;
for this is my blood of the new covenant, which is 28
being shed for many unto the forgiveness of sins.
But I say to you, I will not drink henceforth of 29
this fruit of the vine, until that day when I shall
drink it new with you in the kingdom of my
Father."

Peter's Denials Predicted

And after reciting a hymn, they ┌─────────┐ 30
went out to Mount Olivet. Then │ JAN. 17 │ 31
                                │ July 18 │
                                └─────────┘
Jesus said to them, "You will all be scandalized
this night because of me; for it is written, 'I will
smite the shepherd, and the sheep of the flock
will be scattered.' But after I have risen, I will 32
go before you into Galilee." But Peter answered 33
and said to him, "Even though all shall be scandalized because of thee, I will never be scandalized." Jesus said to him, "Amen I say to thee, 34
this very night, before a cock crows, thou wilt
deny me three times." Peter said to him, "Even 35
if I should have to die with thee, I will not deny
thee!" And all the disciples said the same thing.

2. The Passion and Death of Jesus

The Agony in the Garden

36 THEN JESUS CAME WITH THEM to a country place called Gethsemani, and he said to his disciples, "Sit down here, while I go over yonder
37 and pray." And he took with him Peter and the two sons of Zebedee, and he began to be sad-
38 dened and exceedingly troubled. Then he said to them, "My soul is sad, even unto death. Wait
39 here and watch with me." And going forward a little, he fell prostrate and prayed, saying, "Father, if it is possible, let this cup pass away from me; yet not as I will, but as thou willest."
40 Then he came to the disciples and found them sleeping. And he said to Peter, "Could you not, then, watch one hour with me?
41 Watch and pray, that you may not enter into temptation. The spirit indeed is willing, but
42 the flesh is weak." Again a second time he went away and prayed, saying, "My Father, if this cup cannot pass away unless I drink
43 it, thy will be done." And he came again and found them sleeping, for their eyes were
44 heavy. And leaving them he went back again, and prayed a third time, saying the same
45 words over. Then he came to his disciples, and said to them, "Sleep on now, and take your rest! Behold, the hour is at hand when the Son of Man will be betrayed into the hands of
46 sinners. Rise, let us go. Behold, he who betrays me is at hand."

Jesus Arrested

47 And while he was yet speaking, behold Judas, one of the Twelve, came and with him a great crowd with swords and clubs, from the

chief priests and elders of the people. Now his 48
betrayer had given them a sign, saying, "Whomever I kiss, that is he; lay hold of him." And 49
he went straight up to Jesus and said, "Hail,
Rabbi!" and kissed him. And Jesus said to him, 50
"Friend, for what purpose hast thou come?"
Then they came forward and set hands on Jesus
and took him.

And behold, one of those who were with 51
Jesus reached out his hand, drew his sword,
and struck the servant of the high priest, cutting off his ear. Then Jesus said to him, "Put 52
back thy sword into its place; for all those who
take the sword will perish by the sword. Or 53
dost thou suppose that I cannot entreat my
Father, and he will even now furnish me with
more than twelve legions of angels? How then 54
are the Scriptures to be fulfilled, that thus it
must take place?"

In that hour Jesus said to the crowds, "As 55
against a robber you have come out, with swords
and clubs, to seize me. I sat daily with you in
the temple teaching, and you did not lay hands
on me." Now all this was done that the Scrip- 56
tures of the prophets might be fulfilled. Then
all the disciples left him and fled.

Jesus before the Sanhedrin

Now those who had taken Jesus | JAN. 18 | 57
led him away to Caiphas the high | July 19 |
priest, where the Scribes and the elders had
gathered together. But Peter was following him 58
at a distance, even to the courtyard of the high
priest, and he went in and sat with the attendants to see the end. Now the chief priests 59
and all the Sanhedrin were seeking false
witness against Jesus, that they might put
him to death, ' but they found none, though 60

many false witnesses came forward. But last

61 of all two false witnesses came forward, and said, "This man said, 'I am able to destroy the temple of God, and to rebuild it after three days.' "

62 Then the high priest, standing up, said to him, "Dost thou make no answer to the things

63 that these men prefer against thee?" But Jesus kept silence. And the high priest said to him, "I adjure thee by the living God that thou tell us whether thou art the Christ, the Son of

64 God." Jesus said to him, "Thou hast said it. Nevertheless, I say to you, hereafter you shall see the Son of Man sitting at the right hand of the Power and coming upon the clouds of heaven."

65 Then the high priest tore his garments, saying, "He has blasphemed; what further need have we of witnesses? Behold, now you

66 have heard the blasphemy. What do you think?" And they answered and said, "He is liable to

67 death." Then they spat in his face and buffeted him; while others struck his face with the

68 palms of their hands, saying, "Prophesy to us, O Christ! who is it that struck thee?"

Peter's Denial

69 Now Peter was sitting outside in the courtyard; and a maidservant came up to him and said, "Thou also wast with Jesus the Galilean."

70 But he denied it before them all, saying, "I

71 do not know what thou art saying." And when he had gone out to the gateway, another maid saw him, and said to those who were there, "This man also was with Jesus of Nazareth."

72 And again he denied it with an oath, "I do not

73 know the man!" And after a little while the bystanders came up and said to Peter, "Surely

thou also art one of them, for even thy speech betrays thee." Then he began to curse and to 74 swear that he did not know the man. And at that moment a cock crowed. And Peter remem- 75 bered the word that Jesus had said, "Before a cock crows, thou wilt deny me three times." And he went out and wept bitterly.

Now when morning came all the chief priests 27 1 and the elders of the people took counsel to-gether against Jesus in order to put him to death. And they bound him and led him away, 2 and delivered him to Pontius Pilate the proc-urator.

The End of Judas

Then Judas, who betrayed him, when he saw that he was con- | JAN. 19 | 3
July 20 | demned, repented and brought back the thirty pieces of silver to the chief priests and the elders, ' saying, "I have sinned in betraying 4 innocent blood." But they said, "What is that to us? See to it thyself." ' And he flung the 5 pieces of silver into the temple, and withdrew; and went away and hanged himself with a halter.

And the chief priests took the pieces of silver, 6 and said, "It is not lawful to put them into the treasury, seeing that it is the price of blood." And after they had consulted together, they 7 bought with them the potter's field, as a burial place for strangers. For this reason that field 8 has been called even to this day, Haceldama, that is, the Field of Blood. Then what was spoken 9 through Jeremias the prophet was fulfilled, "And they took the thirty pieces of silver, the price of him who was priced, upon whom the children of Israel set a price, and they gave 10 them for the potter's field, as the Lord directed me."

Jesus before Pilate

11 Now Jesus stood before the procurator, and the procurator asked him, saying, "Art thou the king of the Jews?" Jesus said to him,
12 "Thou sayest it." And when he was accused by the chief priests and the elders, he made
13 no answer. Then Pilate said to him, "Dost thou not hear how many things they prefer
14 against thee?" But he did not answer him a single word, so that the procurator wondered exceedingly.

15 Now at festival time the procurator used to release to the crowd a prisoner, whomever
16 they would. Now he had at that time a notorious
17 prisoner called Barabbas. Therefore, when they had gathered together, Pilate said, "Whom do you wish that I release to you? Barabbas, or
18 Jesus who is called Christ?" For he knew that
19 they had delivered him up out of envy. Now, as he was sitting on the judgment-seat, his wife sent to him, saying, "Have nothing to do with that just man, for I have suffered many
20 things in a dream today because of him." But the chief priests and the elders persuaded the crowds to ask for Barabbas and to destroy
21 Jesus. But the procurator addressed them, and said to them, "Which of the two do you wish that I release to you?" And they said, "Barab-
22 bas." ' Pilate said to them, "What then am I to do with Jesus who is called Christ?" They
23 all said, "Let him be crucified!" The procurator said to them, "Why, what evil has he done?" But they kept crying out the more, saying, "Let him be crucified!"

24 Now Pilate, seeing that he was doing no good, but rather that a riot was breaking out, took water and washed his hands in sight of the crowd, saying, "I am innocent of the blood

of this just man; see to it yourselves." And all 25 the people answered and said, "His blood be on us and on our children."

The Scourging and Crowning

Then he released to them Barab- | JAN. 20 | 26
bas; but Jesus he scourged and de- | July 21 |
livered to them to be crucified. Then the soldiers 27 of the procurator took Jesus into the prætorium, and gathered together about him the whole cohort. And they stripped him and put on him a 28 scarlet cloak; and plaiting a crown of thorns, 29 they put it upon his head, and a reed into his right hand, and bending the knee before him they mocked him, saying, "Hail, King of the Jews!" And they spat on him, and took the reed 30 and kept striking him on the head.

The Way of the Cross

And when they had mocked him, they took 31 the cloak off him and put his own garments on him, and led him away to crucify him. Now as 32 they went out, they found a man of Cyrene named Simon; him they forced to take up his cross. And they came to the place called Gol- 33 gotha, that is, the Place of the Skull.

The Crucifixion

And they gave him wine to drink mixed with 34 gall; but when he had tasted it, he would not drink. And after they had crucified him, they 35 divided his garments, casting lots, [to fulfill what was spoken through the prophet, "They divided my garments among them, and upon my vesture they cast lots."] And sitting down they kept 36 watch over him. And they put above his head the 37 charge against him, written, "This is Jesus, the King of the Jews."

38 Then two robbers were crucified with him, one
39 on his right hand and one on his left. Now the
passers-by were jeering at him, shaking their
40 heads, ' and saying, "Thou who destroyest the
temple, and in three days buildest it up again,
save thyself! If thou art the Son of God, come
41 down from the cross!" In like manner, the chief
priests with the Scribes and the elders, mock-
42 ing, said, "He saved others, himself he cannot
save! If he is the King of Israel, let him come
down now from the cross, and we will believe
43 him. He trusted in God; let him deliver him
now, if he wants him; for he said, 'I am the Son
44 of God.'" And the robbers also, who were
crucified with him, reproached him in the same
way.

The Death of Jesus

45 Now from the sixth hour there | JAN. 21
was darkness over the whole land | July 22
46 until the ninth hour. But about the ninth hour
Jesus cried out with a loud voice, saying, "Eli,
Eli, lema sabacthani," that is, "My God, my
47 God, why hast thou forsaken me?" And some of
the bystanders on hearing this said, "This man
48 is calling Elias." And immediately one of them
ran and, taking a sponge, soaked it in common
wine, put it on a reed and offered it to him to
49 drink. But the rest said, "Wait, let us see wheth-
50 er Elias is coming to save him." But Jesus
again cried out with a loud voice, and gave up
his spirit.

27, 46: The words of our Lord were a quotation of Ps.
21, 2. Taken in their context they do not express anything
like despair. They do, however, express a poignant sense
of dereliction.

And behold, the curtain of the temple was torn 51
in two from top to bottom; and the earth quaked,
and the rocks were rent, ' and the tombs were 52
opened, and many bodies of the saints who had
fallen asleep arose; and coming forth out of the 53
tombs after his resurrection, they came into the
holy city, and appeared to many. Now when the 54
centurion, and those who were with him keeping guard over Jesus, saw the earthquake and
the things that were happening, they were very
much afraid, and they said, "Truly he was the
Son of God." And many women were there, 55
looking on from a distance, who had followed
Jesus from Galilee, ministering to him. Among 56
them were Mary Magdalene, and Mary the
mother of James and Joseph, and the mother of
the sons of Zebedee.

The Burial

Now when it was evening, there came a certain 57
rich man of Arimathea, Joseph by name, who was
himself a disciple of Jesus. He went to Pilate and 58
asked for the body of Jesus. Then Pilate ordered
the body to be given up. And Joseph taking the 59
body, wrapped it in a clean linen cloth, ' and laid 60
it in his new tomb, which he had hewn out in the
rock. Then he rolled a large stone to the entrance
of the tomb, and departed. But Mary Magdalene 61
and the other Mary were there, sitting opposite
the sepulchre.

Precautions of the Chief Priests

And the next day, which was the one after the 62
Day of Preparation, the chief priests and the
Pharisees went in a body to Pilate, ' saying, "Sir, 63
we have remembered how that deceiver said,
while he was yet alive, 'After three days I will
rise again.' Give orders, therefore, that the 64

sepulchre be guarded until the third day, or else his disciples may come and steal him away, and say to the people, 'He has risen from the dead'; and the last imposture will be worse than the
65 first." Pilate said to them, "You have a guard;
66 go, guard it as well as you know how." So they went and made the sepulchre secure, sealing the stone, and setting the guard.

3. The Resurrection of Jesus

The Women at the Grave

28 1   NOW LATE IN THE NIGHT of the JAN. 22 / July 23 Sabbath, as the first day of the week began to dawn, Mary Magdalene and the other
2 Mary came to see the sepulchre. And behold, there was a great earthquake, for an angel of the Lord came down from heaven, and drawing near
3 rolled back the stone, and sat upon it. His countenance was like lightning, and his raiment like
4 snow. And for fear of him the guards were terri-
5 fied, and became like dead men. But the angel spoke and said to the women, "Do not be afraid; for I know that you seek Jesus, who was
6 crucified. He is not here, for he has risen even as he said. Come, see the place where the Lord
7 was laid. And go quickly, tell his disciples that he has risen; and behold, he goes before you into Galilee; there you shall see him. Behold, I
8 have foretold it to you." And they departed quickly from the tomb in fear and great joy, and
9 ran to tell his disciples. And behold, Jesus met them, saying, "Hail!" And they came up and
10 embraced his feet and worshipped him. Then Jesus said to them, "Do not be afraid; go, take word to my brethren that they are to set out for Galilee; there they shall see me."

[86]

The Guards and the Chief Priests

Now while they were going, behold, some 11
of the guards came into the city and reported to
the chief priests all that had happened. And when 12
they had assembled with the elders and had consulted together, they gave much money to the
soldiers, ' telling them, "Say, 'His disciples 13
came by night and stole him while we were sleeping.' And if the procurator hears of this, we will 14
persuade him and keep you out of trouble." And 15
they took the money, and did as they were instructed; and this story has been spread abroad
among the Jews even to the present day.

Commission of the Apostles

But the eleven disciples went into Galilee, to 16
the mountain where Jesus had directed them to
go. And when they saw him they worshipped 17
him; but some doubted. And Jesus drew near 18
and spoke to them saying, "All power in heaven
and on earth has been given to me. Go, there- 19
fore, and make disciples of all nations, baptizing
them in the name of the Father, and of the Son,
and of the Holy Spirit, ' teaching them to observe 20
all that I have commanded you; and behold, I
am with you all days, even unto the consummation of the world."

THE GOSPEL ACCORDING TO
ST. MARK
Introduction

The second Gospel was written by St. Mark who, in the New Testament, is sometimes called John Mark. Both he and his mother, Mary, were highly esteemed in the early Church, and his mother's house in Jerusalem served as a meeting place for Christians there. He was associated with St. Paul and St. Barnabas (who was Mark's cousin) on their missionary journey through the island of Cyprus. Later he accompanied St. Barnabas alone. We know also that he was in Rome with St. Peter and with St. Paul. Tradition ascribes to him the founding of the Church in Alexandria. His feast falls on April 25.

It is historically certain that St. Mark wrote the second Gospel, that he wrote it in Rome sometime before the year 60 A. D., that he wrote it in Greek for the Gentile converts to Christianity. Tradition tells us that St. Mark was requested by the Romans to set down the teachings of St. Peter. This seems to be confirmed by the position which St. Peter has in this Gospel. In this way the second Gospel is a record of the life of Jesus as seen through the eyes of the Prince of the Apostles.

St. Mark's purpose is to show to the Romans that Jesus is the Savior, and that He is divine. To this end he attends more to the miracles of our Lord than to His sermons, giving only a few of the parables at length. The author, however, gives in some detail the events he narrates, and leaves the impression of an eyewitness. His language is simple, and yet earnest and full of charm.

THE HOLY GOSPEL OF JESUS CHRIST ACCORDING TO ST. MARK

I: THE PUBLIC MINISTRY OF JESUS

I

John the Baptist

THE BEGINNING OF THE GOSPEL OF JESUS CHRIST, the Son of God. **1** 1
As it is written in Isaias the prophet, "Behold I 2
send my messenger before thee, who shall prepare
thy way, the voice of one crying in the desert: 3
'Make ready the way of the Lord, make straight
his paths,' " there came John in the desert, 4
baptizing and preaching a baptism of repentance
for the forgiveness of sins. And all the country 5
of Judea went out to him, and all the inhabitants
of Jerusalem; and they were baptized by him in
the river Jordan, confessing their sins. And 6
John was clothed in camel's hair, with a
leathern girdle about his loins, and he ate
locusts and wild honey. And he preached, 7
saying, "One mightier than I is coming after
me, the strap of whose sandals I am not worthy
to stoop down and loose. I have baptized you 8
with water, but he will baptize you with the
Holy Spirit."

The Baptism of Jesus

And it came to pass in those days, that Jesus 9
came from Nazareth in Galilee and was baptized by John in the Jordan. And immediately 10
on coming up from the water he saw the
heavens opened and the Spirit, as a dove, descending and remaining upon him. And there 11
came a voice from the heavens, "Thou art my
beloved Son, in thee I am well pleased."

12 And immediately the Spirit drove him forth
13 into the desert. And he was in the desert forty
days and forty nights, being tempted the while
by Satan, and was with the wild beasts, and the
angels ministered to him.

II

In Galilee

14 AND AFTER JOHN HAD BEEN DELIVERED
up, Jesus came into Galilee, preaching the
15 gospel of the kingdom of God, ¹ and saying, "The
time is fulfilled, and the kingdom of God is at
hand. Repent and believe in the gospel."

The First Disciples Called

16 And passing along by the sea of Galilee, he
saw Simon and his brother Andrew, casting
their nets into the sea (for they were fishermen).
17 And Jesus said to them, "Come, follow me, and
18 I will make you fishers of men." And at once
19 they left the nets, and followed him. And
going on a little farther, he saw James the son
of Zebedee, and his brother John; they also
20 were in their boat mending the nets. Immediately he called them. And they left their father
Zebedee in the boat with the hired men, and
followed him.

21 And they entered Capharnaum. And immediately on the Sabbath he went into the
22 synagogue and began to teach them. And they
were astonished at his teaching; for he was
teaching them as one having authority, and not
as the Scribes.

The Cure of a Demoniac

Now in their synagogue there was 23
a man with an unclean spirit, and he
cried out, saying, "What have we to do with 24
thee, Jesus of Nazareth? Hast thou come to
destroy us? I know who thou art, the Holy One
of God." And Jesus rebuked him, saying, "Hold 25
thy peace, and go out of the man." And the 26
unclean spirit, convulsing him and crying out
with a loud voice, went out of him. And they 27
were all amazed, so that they inquired among
themselves, saying, "What is this? What new
doctrine is this? For with authority he commands even the unclean spirits, and they obey
him." And rumor concerning him went forth 28
immediately into all the region round about
Galilee.

> JAN. 24
> July 25

Peter's Mother-in-law

And as soon as they came out of the syna- 29
gogue, they, with James and John, came to the
house of Simon and Andrew. Now Simon's 30
mother-in-law was keeping her bed sick with a
fever, and they immediately told him about
her. And drawing near, he took her by the hand 31
and raised her up; and the fever left her at
once, and she began to wait on them.

Other Miracles

Now when it was evening, and the sun had 32
set, they brought to him all who were ill and
who were possessed. And the whole town had 33
gathered together at the door. And he cured 34
many who were afflicted with various diseases,
and cast out many devils; and he did not permit them to speak, because they knew him.

And rising up long before daybreak, he went 35
out and departed into a desert place, and there

36 he prayed. And Simon, and those who were
37 with him, followed him. And they found him
and said to him, "They are all seeking thee."
38 And he said to them, "Let us go into the neighboring villages and towns, that there also I may
39 preach. For this is why I have come." ' And
he was preaching in their synagogues, and
throughout all Galilee, and casting out devils.

A Leper

40 And a leper came to him, entreating him,
and kneeling down he said, "If thou wilt,
41 thou canst make me clean." And Jesus, having
compassion on him, stretched forth his hand
and touched him, and said to him, "I will; be
42 thou made clean." And when he had spoken, immediately the leprosy left him, and he was made
43 clean. Then he strictly charged him, and im-
44 mediately drove him away. And he said to him,
"See thou tell no one; but go, show thyself to
the high priest, and offer for thy purification
the things that Moses commanded, for a wit-
45 ness to them." But he went out, and began to
publish and to spread abroad the fact, so that
Jesus could no longer openly enter a town, but
remained outside in desert places. And they kept
coming to him from every direction.

A Paralytic at Capharnaum

2 1   And after some days, he again | JAN. 25
2 entered Capharnaum and it was | July 26
reported that he was at home. And many
gathered together, so that there was no longer
room, not even around the door. And he spoke
3 the word to them. And they came, bringing to
4 him a paralytic, carried by four. And since they
could not bring him to Jesus because of the

crowd, they stripped off the roof where he was, and, having made an opening, they let down the pallet on which the paralytic was lying. And 5 Jesus, seeing their faith, said to the paralytic, "Son, thy sins are forgiven thee."

Now some of the Scribes were sitting there 6 and reasoning in their hearts, "Why does this 7 man speak thus? He blasphemes. Who can forgive sins, but only God?" And at once Jesus, 8 knowing in his spirit that they so reasoned within themselves, said to them, "Why are you arguing these things in your hearts? Which is 9 easier, to say to the paralytic, 'Thy sins are forgiven thee,' or to say, 'Arise, and take up thy pallet, and walk'? But that you may know that 10 the Son of Man has power on earth to forgive sins"—he said to the paralytic— ' "I say to thee, 11 arise, take up thy pallet, and go to thy house." And immediately he arose and, taking up his 12 pallet, went forth in the sight of all, so that they were all amazed, and glorified God, saying, "Never did we see the like."

The Call of Levi

And he went forth again by the water's edge, 13 and all the crowd kept coming to him, and he taught them. And as he was passing along, he 14 saw Levi, the son of Alpheus, sitting in the tax-collector's place, and he said to him, "Follow me." And he arose and followed him. ' And it 15 came to pass as he was at table in Levi's house, that many publicans and sinners were at table with Jesus and his disciples, for there were many and they also followed him. And the Scribes and 16 the Pharisees, seeing that he ate with sinners and publicans, said to his disciples, "Why does your master eat and drink with publicans and

17 sinners?" And Jesus heard this, and said to them, "It is not the healthy who need a physician, but they who are sick. For I have not come to call the just, but sinners."

The Question of Fasting

18 And the disciples of John and the Pharisees were fasting. And they came, and said to him, "Why do the disciples of John and of the Pharisees fast, whereas thy disciples do not fast?"
19 And Jesus said to them, "Can the wedding guests fast as long as the bridegroom is with them? As long as they have the bridegroom
20 with them they cannot fast. But the days will come when the bridegroom shall be taken away from them, and then they will fast on that day.
21 No one sews a patch of raw cloth on an old garment; else the new patch tears away from
22 the old, and a worse rent is made. And no one pours new wine into old wine-skins; else the wine will burst the skins, and the wine is spilt, and the skins will be ruined. But new wine must be put into fresh skins."

The Disciples Pluck Grain on the Sabbath

23 And it came to pass again as he
was going through the standing
grain on the Sabbath, that his disciples began, as they went along, to pluck the ears of grain.

JAN. 26
July 27

24 But the Pharisees said to him, "Behold, why are they doing what is not lawful on the Sabbath?"
25 And he said to them, "Have you never read what David did when he and those who were with him
26 were in need, and hungry? how he entered the house of God, when Abiathar was high priest, and ate the loaves of proposition, which he could not lawfully eat, but only the priests? and how he gave them to those who were with him?"

And he said to them, "The Sabbath was made 27 for man, and not man for the Sabbath. Therefore 28 the Son of Man is Lord even of the Sabbath."

A Man with a Withered Hand

And again he entered the synagogue. And a **3** 1 man with a withered hand was there. And they 2 were watching him, whether he cured on the Sabbath, that they might accuse him. And he 3 said to the man with the withered hand, "Stand forth in the midst." And he said to them, "Is it 4 lawful on the Sabbath to do good, or to do evil? to save a life, or to destroy it?" But they kept silence. And looking round upon them with 5 anger, and being grieved at the blindness of their hearts, he said to the man, "Stretch forth thy hand." And he stretched it forth, and his hand was restored. But the Pharisees went out and 6 immediately took counsel with the Herodians against him, how they might do away with him.

The Mercy of Jesus

And Jesus with his disciples withdrew to the 7 sea; and there followed him a large crowd from Galilee and Judea, ' and from Jerusalem, and 8 from Idumea, and from beyond the Jordan. And of those about Tyre and Sidon, a large crowd, hearing what he was doing, came to him. And 9 he told his disciples to have a small boat in readiness for him, because of the crowd, lest they should throng him. For he healed many, so 10 that as many as had ailments were pressing upon him to touch him. And the unclean spirits, when- 11 ever they beheld him, fell down before him and cried out, saying, "Thou art the Son of God." 12 And he charged them strictly not to make him known.

The Choice of the Twelve

13 And going up a mountain, he called to him men of his own choos- | JAN. 27 / July 28 |

14 ing, and they came to him. And he appointed twelve that they might be with him and that he

15 might send them forth to preach. To them he gave power to cure sicknesses and to cast out

16 devils. There were Simon, to whom he gave the

17 name Peter; ' and James the son of Zebedee, and John the brother of James (these he surnamed

18 Boanerges, that is, Sons of Thunder); and Andrew, and Philip, and Bartholomew, and Matthew, and Thomas, and James the son of Alpheus, and Thaddeus, and Simon the Canan-

19 ean, and Judas Iscariot, he who betrayed him.

III

Blasphemy of the Scribes

20 AND THEY CAME TO THE HOUSE, and again a crowd gathered so that they could not so

21 much as take their food. But when his own people had heard of it, they went out to lay hold of him, for they said, "He has gone mad."

22 And the Scribes who had come down from Jerusalem said, "He has Beelzebub" and, "By

23 the prince of devils he casts out devils." And he called them together, and said to them in para-

24 bles, "How can Satan cast out Satan? And if a kingdom is divided against itself, that kingdom

25 cannot stand. And if a house is divided against

26 itself, that house cannot stand. And if Satan has risen up against himself, he is divided, and

27 cannot stand, but is at an end. But no one can enter the strong man's house and plunder his goods, unless he first binds the strong man. Then he will plunder his house.

28 "Amen I say to you, that all sins shall be for-

given to the sons of men, and the blasphemies wherewith they may blaspheme; but whoever 29 blasphemes against the Holy Spirit never has forgiveness, but will be guilty of an everlasting sin." For they said, "He has an unclean spirit." 30

Jesus and His Brethren

And his mother and his brethren came, and 31 standing outside, they sent to him, calling him. Now a crowd was sitting about him, and they 32 said to him, "Behold, thy mother and thy brethren are outside, seeking thee." And he answered 33 and said to them, "Who are my mother and my brethren?" And looking round on those who 34 were sitting about him, he said, "Behold my mother and my brethren. For whoever does the 35 will of God, he is my brother and sister and mother."

Parable of the Sower

And again he began to teach by 4 1 the water's edge. And as a great crowd gathered about him, he got into a boat and sat on board. And all the crowd remained on land facing the sea.

| JAN. 28 |
| July 29 |

And he taught them many things in parables, 2 and he said to them in his instruction, "Hear! 3 Behold, the sower went out to sow. And as he 4 sowed, some seed fell by the wayside, and the birds came and ate it up. And other seed fell 5

3, 31: *Brethren*: relatives of Jesus, not blood brothers. This wider use of the term was common among the Jews. Jesus does not disclaim the bonds of physical relationship, but He seizes the opportunity to give a lesson on the greater dignity of spiritual relationship. St. Augustine says that Mary was more blessed in that she believed in Christ than in that she had given Him birth.

upon rocky ground, where it had not much earth, and it sprang up at once, because it had no depth

6 of earth, ' but when the sun rose it was scorched, and because it had no root it withered away.

7 And other seed fell among thorns, and the thorns grew up and choked it, and it yielded no fruit.

8 And other seed fell upon good ground, and yielded fruit that grew up, made increase and produced, one thirty, another sixty, and another

9 a hundredfold." Then he said, "He who has ears to hear, let him hear."

10 And when he was alone, those who were with him and the Twelve asked him about the para-

11 bles. And he said to them, "To you it is given to know the mystery of the kingdom of God; but to those outside, all things are treated in para-

12 bles, ' that 'Seeing they may see, but not perceive; and hearing they may hear, but not understand; lest perhaps at any time they should be converted, and their sins be forgiven them.' "

13 And he said to them, "Do you not know this parable? How then will you understand all

14 the parables? ' The sower sows the word.

15 And those by the wayside are they in whom the word is sown; as soon as they have heard, Satan at once comes and takes away the word

16 that has been sown in their hearts. And those likewise who are sown on the rocky ground are they who, when they have heard the word,

17 receive it immediately with joy; and they have no root in themselves, but continue only for a time; then, when trouble and persecution come

18 because of the word, they at once fall away. And those who are sown among the thorns are they

19 who listen to the word; but the cares of the world, and the deceitfulness of riches, and the desires about other things, entering in, choke

20 the word, and it is made fruitless. And those

who are sown upon good ground are they who hear the word, and welcome it, and yield fruit, one thirty, another sixty, and another a hundredfold."

Purpose of This Teaching

And he said to them, "Is a lamp brought to be put under the measure, or under the couch? Is it not rather to be put upon the lamp-stand? For there is nothing hidden that will not be manifest; nor is anything concealed that will not come to light. If anyone has ears to hear, let him hear." And he said to them, "Take heed what you hear. With what measure you measure, it shall be measured to you, and more shall be given to you. For to him who has shall be given; and from him who does not have, even that which he has shall be taken away."

JAN. 29
July 30

Seed Grows of Itself

And he said, "Thus is the kingdom of God, as though a man should cast seed into the earth, then sleep and rise, night and day, and the seed should sprout and grow without his knowing it. For of itself the earth bears the crop, first the blade, then the ear, then the full grain in the ear. But when the fruit is ripe, immediately he puts in the sickle because the harvest has come."

The Mustard Seed

And he said, "To what shall we liken the kingdom of God; or to what parable shall we compare it? It is like a grain of mustard seed, which, when sown upon the earth, is the smallest of all the seeds upon the earth; yet when it is sown, it grows up and becomes larger than any herb, and puts out great branches, so that the birds of the air can dwell beneath its shade."

33 And in many such parables he spoke the word to them, according as they were able to 34 understand it; but without a parable he did not speak to them. But privately he explained all things to his disciples.

The Storm on the Lake

35 And he said to them on that day, when evening had come, "Let us cross over to the 36 other side." And sending away the crowd, they took him just as he was, in the boat; and there 37 were other boats with him. And there arose a great squall, and the waves were beating into the boat, so that the boat was now filling. 38 And he himself was in the stern of the boat, on the cushion, asleep. And they woke him and said to him, "Master, does it not concern 39 thee that we are perishing?" Then rising up, he rebuked the wind, and said to the sea, "Peace, be still!" And the wind fell and there came a 40 great calm. And he said to them, "Why are you fearful? Are you still without faith?" And they feared exceedingly and said to one another, "Who, then, is this, that even the wind and the sea obey him?"

Expulsion of the Devils in Gerasa

5 1 And they came to the other side of the sea, to the country of the | JAN. 30 / July 31 |
2 Gerasenes; and as soon as he stepped out of the boat, there met him from the tombs a man 3 with an unclean spirit. This man lived in the tombs and no one could any longer bind him, 4 even with chains, for often had he been bound with fetters and chains, and he had rent the chains asunder and broken the fetters into pieces. And no one was able to control him.

And constantly, night and day, he was in the   5
tombs and on the mountains, howling and
gashing himself with stones.

And when he saw Jesus from afar, he ran   6
and worshipped him, ' and crying out with a   7
loud voice, he said, "What have I to do with
thee, Jesus, Son of the most high God? I adjure
thee by God, do not torment me!" ' For he was   8
saying to him, "Go out of the man, thou unclean spirit."

And he asked him, "What is thy name?"   9
And he said to him, "My name is Legion, for
we are many." And he entreated him earnestly   10
not to drive them out of the country.

Now a great herd of swine was there on the   11
mountainside, feeding. And the spirits kept en-   12
treating him, saying, "Send us into the swine,
that we may enter into them." And Jesus im-   13
mediately gave them leave. And the unclean
spirits came out and entered into the swine;
and the herd, in number about two thousand,
rushed down with great violence into the sea,
and were drowned in the sea.

But the swineherds fled and reported it in   14
the town and in the country; and people came
out to see what had happened. And they came   15
to Jesus, and saw the man who had been afflicted by the devil, sitting clothed and in his
right mind, and they were afraid. And those who   16
had seen it reported to them how it had happened to the possessed man, and about the
swine. And they began to entreat him to depart   17
from their district.

And as Jesus was getting into the boat, the   18
man who had been afflicted by the devil began
to entreat him that he might remain with him.
And he did not allow him, but said to him, "Go   19

home to thy relatives, and tell them all that
the Lord has done for thee, and how he has
20 had mercy on thee." And he departed, and
began to publish in the Decapolis all that Jesus
had done for him. And all marvelled.

*The Daughter of Jairus; the Woman with
a Hemorrhage*

21 And when Jesus had again crossed
over in the boat to the other side,
a great crowd gathered together to him, and he

> JAN. 31
> Aug. 1

22 was at the water's edge. And there came one
of the rulers of the synagogue named Jairus.
23 And seeing Jesus, he fell at his feet, ' and entreated him much saying, "My daughter is at
the point of death; come, lay thy hands upon
her, that she may be saved and live."

24 And he went away with him, and a great
crowd was following him and pressing upon him.
25 And there was a woman who for twelve years
26 had had a hemorrhage, and had suffered much
at the hands of many physicians, and had
spent all that she had, and found no benefit,
27 but rather grew worse. Hearing about Jesus,
she came up behind him in the crowd and
28 touched his cloak. For she said, "If I touch
29 but his cloak, I shall be saved." And at once
the flow of her blood was dried up, and she felt
in her body that she was healed of her affliction.

30 And Jesus, instantly perceiving in himself
that power had gone forth from him, turned to
the crowd, and said, "Who touched my cloak?"
31 And his disciples said to him, "Thou seest the
crowd pressing upon thee, and dost thou say,
32 'Who touched me?'" And he was looking round
33 to see her who had done this. But the woman,
fearing and trembling, knowing what had happened within her, came and fell down before

him, and told him all the truth. But he said to 34
her, "Daughter, thy faith has saved thee. Go in
peace, and be thou healed of thy affliction."

While he was yet speaking, there came some 35
from the house of the ruler of the synagogue,
saying, "Thy daughter is dead. Why dost thou
trouble the Master further?" But Jesus, having 36
heard what was being said, said to the ruler of
the synagogue, "Do not be afraid, only have
faith." And he allowed no one to follow him 37
except Peter and James, and John the brother
of James.

And they came to the house of the ruler of the 38
synagogue and he saw a tumult, people weeping
and wailing greatly. And going in he said to them, 39
"Why do you make this din, and weep? The girl
is asleep, not dead." And they laughed him to 40
scorn. But he, putting them all out, took the
father and mother of the girl and those who were
with him, and entered in where the girl was
lying. And taking the girl by the hand, he said to 41
her, "Talitha cumi," which is interpreted, "Girl,
I say to thee, arise." And the girl rose up imme- 42
diately and began to walk; she was twelve years
old. And they were utterly amazed. ¹ And he 43
charged them strictly that no one should know
of it, and directed that something be given her
to eat.

Jesus at Nazareth

And leaving that place, he went ┌─────────┐ **6** 1
into his own country, and his dis- │ FEB. 1 │
ciples followed him. And when the S │ Aug. 2 │ had
                                    └─────────┘
come, he began to teach in the synagogue. And 2
many, when they heard him, were astonished at
his doctrine, saying, "Where did he get all this?"
and, "What is this wisdom that is given to him?"
and, "What mean such miracles wrought by his

3 hands? Is not this the carpenter, the son of Mary, the brother of James, Joseph, Jude, and Simon? And are not also his sisters here with us?" And
4 they took offense at him. And Jesus said to them, "A prophet is not without honor except in his own country, and among his own kindred, and in his
5 own house." And he could not work any miracle there, beyond curing a few sick people by laying
6 his hands upon them. And he marvelled because of their unbelief.

The Mission of the Apostles

And he made a circuit of the villages, teaching.
7 And he summoned the Twelve and began to send them forth two by two; and he gave them
8 power over the unclean spirits. And he instructed them to take nothing for their journey, but a staff only — no wallet, no bread, no money in
9 their girdle; but to wear sandals, and not to
10 put on two tunics. And he said to them, "Wherever you enter into a house, stay there until you
11 leave the place. And whoever does not receive you, or listen to you — go forth from there, and shake off the dust from your feet for a witness
12 against them." And going forth, they preached
13 that men should repent, and they cast out many devils, and anointed with oil many sick people, and healed them.

Death of the Baptist

14 And King Herod heard of him, for his name had become well known;
and he kept saying, "John the Baptist has risen from the dead, and that is why miraculous powers
15 are working through him." But others were saying, "It is Elias." But others were saying, "It is
16 a prophet, like one of the prophets." **But when**

FEB. 2
Aug. 3

Herod heard of this, he said, "It is John whom I beheaded; he has risen from the dead."

For Herod himself had sent and taken John, 17 and bound him in prison, because of Herodias, his brother Philip's wife, whom he had married. For John had said to Herod, "It is not lawful for 18 thee to have thy brother's wife." But Herodias 19 laid snares for him, and would have liked to put him to death, but she could not. For Herod feared 20 John, knowing that he was a just and holy man, and protected him; and when he heard him talk, he did many things, and he liked to hear him.

And a favorable day came when Herod on his 21 birthday gave a banquet to the officials, tribunes and chief men of Galilee. And Herodias' own 22 daughter having come in and danced, she pleased Herod and his guests. And the king said to the girl, "Ask of me what thou willest, and I will give it to thee." And he swore to her, "Whatever thou 23 dost ask, I will give thee, even though it be the half of my kingdom." Then she went out and said 24 to her mother, "What am I to ask for?" And she said, "The head of John the Baptist." And she 25 came in at once with haste to the king, and asked, saying, "I want thee right away to give me on a dish the head of John the Baptist." And grieved 26 as he was, the king, because of his oath and his guests, was unwilling to displease her. But send- 27 ing an executioner, he commanded that his head be brought on a dish. Then he beheaded him in 28 the prison, and brought his head on a dish, and gave it to the girl, and the girl gave it to her mother. His disciples, hearing of it, came and 29 took away his body, and laid it in a tomb.

Return of the Disciples

And the apostles came together to meet Jesus 30 and reported to him all that they had done and

31 taught. And he said to them, "Come apart into a desert place and rest a while." For there were many coming and going, and they had no leisure

32 even to eat. And they got into the boat and went

33 off to a desert place apart. And many saw them leaving and recognized them; and from all the towns they hurried on foot to the place, and got there ahead of them.

Jesus Feeds Five Thousand

34 And when he landed, Jesus saw a large crowd, and had compassion on them, because they were like sheep without a shepherd. And he began to teach them many

| FEB. 3 |
| Aug. 4 |

35 things. Now when the day was far spent, his disciples came, saying, "This is a desert place and

36 the hour is already late; send them away, so that they may go to the hamlets and villages round about and buy themselves food to eat."

37 But he answered and said to them, "You yourselves give them some food." And they said to

38 him, "Are we to go and buy two hundred denarii worth of bread and give them to eat?" And he said to them, "How many loaves have you? Go and see." When they had found out, they said, "Five, and two fishes."

39 And he ordered them to make all the people

40 recline in groups on the green grass. And they

41 reclined in groups of hundreds and fifties. And he took the five loaves and the two fishes and, looking up to heaven, blessed and broke the loaves, and gave them to his disciples to set before the people; and the two fishes he divided

42 among them all. And all ate and were satisfied;

43 and they gathered up what was left over, twelve baskets full of fragments, besides what was left

44 over of the fishes. Now those who had eaten were five thousand men.

Jesus Walks on the Water

And immediately afterwards he made his disciples get into the boat and cross the sea ahead of him to Bethsaida, while he himself dismissed the crowd. And when he had dismissed them, he went away to the mountain to pray. And when it was late, the ship was in the midst of the sea, and he alone on the land. And seeing them straining at the oars, for the wind was against them, about the fourth watch of the night he came to them, walking upon the sea, and he would have passed by them. But they, seeing him walking upon the sea, thought it was a ghost, and cried out. For they all saw him, and were troubled. Then he immediately spoke to them, and said to them, "Take courage; it is I, do not be afraid." And he got into the boat with them, and the wind fell. And they were utterly beside themselves with astonishment, for they had not understood about the loaves, because their heart was blinded.

Other Miracles

And crossing over, they came to the land at Genesareth and moored the boat. And when they had gotten out of the boat, the people at once recognized him; and they hurried through that whole country, and began to bring the sick on their pallets, wherever they heard he was. And wherever he went, into village or hamlet or town, they laid the sick in the market places, and entreated him to let them touch but the tassel of his cloak; and as many as touched him were saved.

Jesus and the Pharisees

7 1 And the Pharisees and some of the Scribes who had come from

FEB. 4
Aug. 5

2 Jerusalem gathered about him. And when they saw that some of his disciples were eating bread with defiled (that is, unwashed) hands, they 3 found fault. For the Pharisees and all the Jews do not eat without frequent washing of hands, 4 holding the tradition of the ancients. And when they come from the market, they do not eat without washing first. And there have been handed down to them many other things to observe: washing of cups and pots, and brazen vessels 5 and beds. So the Pharisees and Scribes asked him, "Why do not thy disciples walk according to the tradition of the ancients, instead of eating 6 bread with defiled hands?" But answering he said to them, "Well did Isaias prophesy of you hypocrites, as it is written, 'This people honors me with their lips, but their heart is far from me; 7 and in vain do they worship me, teaching as 8 doctrine the precepts of men.' For, letting go the commandment of God, you hold fast the tradition of men, the washing of pots and of cups; and many other things you do like to these."

9 And he said to them, "Well do you nullify the commandment of God, that you may keep your 10 own tradition! For Moses said, 'Honor thy father and thy mother', and, 'Let him who curses 11 father or mother be put to death.' But you say, 'Let a man say to his father or his mother, "Any support thou mightest have had from me is Cor- 12 ban" ' (that is, given to God). And you do not

---

7, 11: *Corban:* a gift to God which could be put to no other use. A son could evade giving support to his parents by declaring Corban what might have been given them. Jesus here illustrates how the Pharisees' teaching frustrated the Law of Moses.

allow him to do anything further for his father or mother. You make void the commandment of God by your tradition, which you have handed down; and many suchlike things you do." 13

Then he called the crowd to him again, and said to them, "Hear me, all of you, and understand. There is nothing outside a man that, entering into him, can defile him; but the things that come out of a man, these are what defile a man. If anyone has ears to hear, let him hear." 14 15 16

And when he had entered the house away from the crowd, his disciples began to ask him about the parable. And he said to them, "Are you also, then, without understanding? Do you not realize that nothing from outside, by entering a man, can defile him? For it does not enter his heart, but his belly, and passes out into the drain." Thus he declared all foods clean. "And," he said, "the things that come out of a man are what defile a man. For from within, out of the heart of men, come evil thoughts, adulteries, immorality, murders, thefts, covetousness, wickedness, deceit, shamelessness, jealousy, blasphemy, pride, foolishness. All these evil things come from within, and defile a man." 17 18 19 20 21 22 23

IV

The Canaanite Woman

AND HE AROSE AND DEPARTED from there for the district of Tyre and Sidon. And he entered a house, and wanted no one to know it, but he could not keep it secret. For immediately a woman, whose little daughter had an unclean spirit, on hearing of him, came in and fell down at his feet. Now the woman was a Gentile, a Syrophœnician by birth. And she besought him to cast the devil out of her daughter. 24 25 26

FEB. 5 | Aug. 6

27 But he said to her, "Let the children first have
their fill, for it is not fair to take the children's
28 bread and to cast it to the dogs." But she answered and said to him, "Yes, Lord; for even
the dogs eat under the table of the children's
29 crumbs." And he said to her, "Because of this
answer, go thy way; the devil has gone out of thy
30 daughter." And when she went to her house, she
found the girl lying upon the bed, and the devil
gone.

Healing of a Deaf-Mute

31　And departing again from the district of Tyre,
he came by way of Sidon to the sea of Galilee,
through the midst of the district of Decapolis.
32 And they brought to him one deaf and dumb,
and entreated him to lay his hand upon him.
33 And taking him aside from the crowd, he put his
fingers into the man's ears, and spitting, he
34 touched his tongue. And looking up to heaven,
he sighed, and said to him, "Ephpheta," that is,
35 "Be thou opened." ' And his ears were at once
opened, and the bond of his tongue was loosed,
36 and he began to speak correctly. And he charged
them to tell no one. But the more he charged
them, so much the more did they continue to
37 publish it. And so much the more did they
wonder, saying, "He has done all things well.
He has made both the deaf to hear and the dumb
to speak."

Jesus Feeds Four Thousand

8 1　In those days when again there was a great
crowd, and they had nothing to eat, he called his
2 disciples together and said to them, "I have

7, 27: Jesus repeatedly pointed out that the Messias
had come to bring the kingdom of God first to the children
of Israel.

compassion on the crowd, for behold, they have now been with me three days, and have nothing to eat; ' and if I send them away to their homes fasting, they will faint on the way, for some of them have come from a distance." And his disciples answered him, "How will anyone be able to satisfy these with bread, here in a desert?" He asked them, "How many loaves have you?" And they said, "Seven."

And he bade the crowd recline on the ground. Then taking the seven loaves, he gave thanks, broke them and gave them to his disciples to distribute; and they set them before the crowd. And they had a few little fishes; and he blessed them, and ordered them to be distributed. And they ate and were satisfied; and they took up what was left of the fragments, seven baskets. Now those who had eaten were about four thousand. And he dismissed them.

The Pharisees Ask a Sign

And immediately getting into the boat with his disciples, he came into the district of Dalmanutha. And the Pharisees came forth, and began to dispute with him, demanding from him a sign from heaven, to test him. ' And sighing deeply in spirit, he said, "Why does this generation demand a sign? Amen I say to you, a sign shall not be given to this generation."

FEB. 6
Aug. 7

The Leaven of the Pharisees

And he left them, and getting back into the boat, crossed the sea. And they had forgotten to bring bread, and they had but one loaf with them in the boat. And he began to charge them, saying, "Take heed; beware of the leaven of the Pharisees, and of the leaven of Herod!" And they began to argue among themselves, saying,

17 "We have no bread." ' But Jesus knowing this, said to them, "Why do you argue because you have no bread? Do you not yet perceive, nor
18 understand? Is your heart still blinded? ' Though you have eyes do you not see, and though you have ears do you not hear? And do you not
19 remember? When I broke the five loaves among five thousand, how many baskets full of fragments did you take up?" They said to him,
20 "Twelve." ' "And when I broke the seven loaves among four thousand, how many large baskets of fragments did you take up?" They said,
21 "Seven." ' And he said to them, "How is it that you do not yet understand?"

A Blind Man at Bethsaida

22 And they came to Bethsaida and they brought him a blind man and entreated him to touch him.
23 And taking the blind man by the hand, he led him forth outside the village; and applying spittle to his eyes, he laid his hands upon him, and
24 asked him if he saw anything. And the man looked up, and said, "I see men as though they
25 were trees, but walking about." Then again he laid his hands upon the man's eyes, and he began to see, and was restored so that he saw
26 all things plainly. And he sent him to his house, saying, "Go to thy house, and if thou enter the village, tell nobody."

Peter's Confession

27 And Jesus and his disciples went out into the villages of Cæsarea Philippi; and on the way he asked his disciples, saying to them, "Who do men say that I am?"

FEB. 7
Aug. 8

28 They answered him, saying, "John the Baptist; others, Elias, and others, one of the prophets."

Then he said to them, "But who do you say that 29
I am?" Peter answered and said to him, "Thou
art the Christ." And he strictly charged them to 30
say nothing about him to anyone.

Passion and Resurrection Foretold

And he began to teach them that the Son of 31
Man must suffer many things, and be rejected
by the elders and chief priests and Scribes, and
be put to death, and after three days rise again.
And what he said he spoke openly. And Peter 32
taking him aside, began to chide him. But he, 33
turning and seeing his disciples, rebuked Peter,
saying, "Get behind me, satan, for thou dost not
mind the things of God, but those of men."

The Doctrine of the Cross

And calling the crowd together with his 34
disciples, he said to them, "If anyone wishes
to come after me, let him deny himself, and
take up his cross, and follow me. For he who 35
would save his life will lose it; but he who
loses his life for my sake and for the gospel's
sake will save it. For what does it profit a man, 36
if he gain the whole world, but suffer the loss
of his own soul? Or what will a man give in 37
exchange for his soul? For whoever is ashamed 38
of me and of my words in this adulterous and
sinful generation, of him will the Son of Man
also be ashamed when he comes with the holy
angels in the glory of his Father." And he said 39
to them, "Amen I say to you, there are some
of those standing here who will not taste death,
till they have seen the kingdom of God coming
in power."

8, 39: *Who will not taste death:* i.e., even in the lifetime
of some of His listeners He will manifest the power of
His kingdom.

Jesus Transfigured

9 1 Now after six days Jesus took Peter, James and John, and led them up a high mountain off by themselves, and was transfigured before 2 them. And his garments became shining, exceedingly white as snow, as no fuller on earth 3 can whiten. And there appeared to them Elias with Moses, and they were talking with Jesus. 4 And Peter addressed Jesus, saying, "Rabbi, it is good for us to be here. And let us set up three tents, one for thee, and one for Moses, 5 and one for Elias." For he did not know what to 6 say, for they were struck with fear. And there came a cloud overshadowing them, and there came a voice out of the cloud, saying, "This is 7 my beloved Son; hear him." And suddenly looking round, they no longer saw anyone with them but only Jesus.

On the Coming of Elias

8 And as they were coming down from the mountain, he cautioned them to tell no one what they had seen, except 9 when the Son of Man should have risen from the dead. And they kept what he said to themselves, discussing with one another what the words, "When he shall have risen from the 10 dead," might mean. And they asked him, saying, "Why then do the Pharisees and Scribes 11 say that Elias must come first?" But he answered and said to them, "Elias is to come first and will restore all things. But how then is it written of the Son of Man, that he should suffer

FEB. 8
Aug. 9

9, 11: Jesus refers to the Jewish tradition that Elias was to come as precursor of the messianic age, and explains that he has come in the person of the Baptist.

many things and be despised? But I say to you 12 that Elias has come, and they did to him whatever they wished, as it is written of him."

A Possessed Boy

And on coming to his disciples, he saw a 13 great crowd around them, and the Scribes arguing with them. And immediately all the 14 crowd, on seeing him, were amazed and struck with fear, and running up, began to greet him. And he asked them, "What are you arguing 15 about among yourselves?" And one of the crowd 16 answering, said, "Master, I have brought to thee my son, who has a dumb spirit; and 17 wherever it seizes him it throws him down, and he foams and grinds his teeth; and he is wasting away. And I told thy disciples to cast it out, but they could not."

And he answered and said to them, "O unbe- 18 lieving generation, how long shall I be with you? How long shall I put up with you? Bring him to me." And they brought him to him; and the 19 spirit, when it saw Jesus, immediately threw the boy into convulsions, and he fell down on the ground, and rolled about foaming at the mouth. So he asked his father, "How long 20 is it since this has come upon him?" And he said, "From his infancy. Oftentimes it has 21 thrown him into the fire and into the waters to destroy him. But if thou canst do anything, have compassion on us and help us." But Jesus said 22 to him, "If thou canst believe, all things are possible to him who believes." At once the 23 father of the boy cried out, and said with tears, "I do believe; help my unbelief."

Now when Jesus saw that a crowd was 24 rapidly gathering, he rebuked the unclean spirit, saying to it, "Thou deaf and dumb spirit, I command thee, go out of him and enter

25 him no more." And crying out and violently convulsing him, it went out of him, and he became like one dead, so that many said, "He
26 is dead." But Jesus took him by the hand, and raised him and he stood up.

27 And when he had come into the house, his disciples asked him privately, "Why could not
28 we cast it out?" ' And he said to them, "This kind can be cast out in no way except by prayer and fasting."

The Second Prediction of the Passion

29 And leaving that place, they were passing through Galilee, and he did

| FEB. 9 |
| Aug. 10 |

30 not wish anyone to know it. For he was teaching his disciples, and saying to them, "The Son of Man is to be betrayed into the hands of men, and they will kill him; and having been killed,
31 he will rise again on the third day." But they did not understand the saying, and were afraid to ask him.

Against Ambition and Envy

32 And they came to Capharnaum. When he was at home, he asked them, "What were you
33 arguing about on the way?" But they kept silence, for on the way they had discussed with one another which of them was the greatest.
34 And sitting down, he called the Twelve and said to them, "If any man wishes to be first, he shall be last of all, and servant of all."
35 And he took a little child, and set him in their midst, and taking him into his arms, he said
36 to them, "Whoever receives one such little child for my sake, receives me; and whoever receives me, receives not me but him who sent me."

John said to him, "Master, we saw a man 37 who was not one of our followers casting out devils in thy name, and we forbade him." But 38 Jesus said, "Do not forbid him, because there is no one who shall work a miracle in my name, and forthwith be able to speak ill of me. For he 39 who is not against you is for you. For whoever 40 gives you a cup of water to drink in my name, because you are Christ's, amen I say to you, he shall not lose his reward.

Avoiding Scandal

"And whoever causes one of these little ones 41 who believe in me to sin, it were better for him if a great millstone were hung about his neck, and he were thrown into the sea. If thy hand 42 is an occasion of sin to thee, cut it off! It is better for thee to enter into life maimed, than, having two hands, to go into hell, into the unquenchable fire, 'Where their worm dies not, 43 and the fire is not quenched.' And if thy foot 44 is an occasion of sin to thee, cut it off! It is better for thee to enter into life everlasting lame, than, having two feet, to be cast into the hell of unquenchable fire, 'Where their worm 45 dies not, and the fire is not quenched.' And if 46 thy eye is an occasion of sin to thee, pluck it out! It is better for thee to enter into the kingdom of God with one eye, than, having two eyes, to be cast into hell-fire, 'Where their 47 worm dies not, and the fire is not quenched.' For everyone shall be salted with fire, and every 48 victim shall be salted. Salt is good; but if the 49 salt becomes insipid, what shall you season it with? Have salt in yourselves, and be at peace with one another."

9, 42: . . . *cut it off:* no sacrifice, however painful it may be, is too great if one may save his soul thereby.

V

10 1 AND LEAVING THAT PLACE, he came to the district of Judea beyond the Jordan, and crowds again flocked to him. And as had been his custom, he again began to teach them.

FEB. 10
Aug. 11

The Question of Divorce

2 And some Pharisees coming up asked him, testing him, "Is it lawful for a man to put away 3 his wife?" But he answered and said to them, 4 "What did Moses command you?" ' They said, "Moses permitted us to write a notice of dis- 5 missal, and to put her away." But Jesus said to them, "By reason of the hardness of your heart 6 he wrote you that commandment. But from the beginning of creation God made them male 7 and female. 'For this cause a man shall leave his mother and father, and cleave to his wife, 8 and the two shall become one flesh.' Therefore now they are no longer two, but one flesh. 9 What therefore God has joined together, let no man put asunder."

10 And in the house, his disciples again asked 11 him concerning this. And he said to them, "Whoever puts away his wife and marries 12 another, commits adultery against her; 'and if the wife puts away her husband, and marries another, she commits adultery."

Jesus Blesses the Children

13 And they were bringing little children to him that he might touch them; but the disciples re-

---

10, 4: *Moses permitted us . . . to put her away:* the Mosaic Law permitted divorce for certain causes. In the verses immediately following here, Jesus abrogates divorce and declares the indissolubility of marriage.

buked those who brought them. But when Jesus 14
saw him, he was indignant, and said to them,
"Let the little children come to me, and do not
hinder them, for of such is the kingdom of God.
Amen I say to you, whoever does not accept the 15
kingdom of God as a little child will not enter
into it." And he put his arms about them, and 16
laying his hands upon them, he began to bless
them.

The Danger of Riches

And as he was going forth on his 17
journey, a certain man running up

FEB. 11
Aug. 12

fell upon his knees before him, and asked him,
"Good Master, what shall I do to gain eternal
life?" But Jesus said to him, "Why dost thou 18
call me good? No one is good but only God.
Thou knowest the commandments: Thou shalt 19
not commit adultery, Thou shalt not kill, Thou
shalt not steal, Thou shalt not bear false witness,
Thou shalt not defraud, Honor thy father and
mother." And he answered and said, "Master, 20
all these I have kept ever since I was a child."
And Jesus, looking upon him, loved him, and 21
said to him, "One thing is lacking to thee; go,
sell whatever thou hast, and give to the poor,
and thou shalt have treasure in heaven; and
come, follow me." But his face fell at the saying, 22
and he went away sad, for he had great possessions.

And Jesus looking round, said to his disciples, 23
"With what difficulty will they who have riches
enter the kingdom of God!" But the disciples 24
were amazed at his word. But Jesus again addressed them, saying, "Children, with what
difficulty will they who trust in riches enter the
kingdom of God! It is easier for a camel to pass 25
through the eye of a needle, than for a rich man

26 to enter the kingdom of God." But they were astonished the more, saying among themselves,
27 "Who then can be saved?" ' And looking upon them, Jesus said, "With men it is impossible, but not with God; for all things are possible with God."
28 Peter began to say to him, "Behold, we have
29 left all and followed thee." Answering, Jesus said, "Amen I say to you, there is no one who has left house, or brothers, or sisters, or mother, or father, or children, or lands, for my sake and
30 for the gospel's sake, ' who shall not receive now in the present time a hundredfold as much, houses, and brothers, and sisters, and mothers, and children, and lands—along with persecutions,
31 and in the age to come life everlasting. But many who are first now will be last, and many who are last now will be first."

The Third Prediction of the Passion

32 They were now on their way, going up to Jerusalem; and Jesus was walking on in front of them, and they were in dismay, and those who followed were afraid. And again taking the Twelve, he began to tell
33 them what would happen to him, ' saying, "Behold, we are going up to Jerusalem, and the Son of Man will be betrayed to the chief priests and the Scribes; and they will condemn him to death,
34 and will deliver him to the Gentiles; ' and they will mock him, and spit upon him, and scourge him, and put him to death; and on the third day he will rise again."

FEB. 12
Aug. 13

Ambition of James and John

35 And James and John, the sons of Zebedee, came to him, saying, "Master, we want thee to
36 do for us whatever we ask." But he said to them,

"What do you want me to do for you?" ' And 37 they said, "Grant to us that we may sit, one at thy right hand and the other at thy left hand, in thy glory." ' But Jesus said to them, "You do 38 not know what you are asking for. Can you drink of the cup of which I drink, or be baptized with the baptism with which I am to be baptized?" ' And they said to him, "We can." And Jesus 39 said to them, "Of the cup that I drink, you shall drink; and with the baptism with which I am to be baptized, you shall be baptized; ' but as for 40 sitting at my right hand or at my left, that is not mine to give, but it belongs to those for whom it has been prepared."

And when the ten heard this, they were at 41 first indignant at James and John. But Jesus 42 called them and said to them, "You know that those who are regarded as rulers among the Gentiles lord it over them, and their great men exercise authority over them. But it is not so 43 among you. On the contrary, whoever wishes to become great shall be your servant; ' and who- 44 ever wishes to be first among you shall be the slave of all; ' for the Son of Man also has not 45 come to be served but to serve, and to give his life as a ransom for many."

The Blind Bartimeus

And they came to Jericho. And as he was 46 leaving Jericho with his disciples and a very great crowd, Bartimeus, a blind man, the son of Timeus, was sitting by the wayside, begging. And hearing that it was Jesus of Nazareth, he 47 began to cry out and say, "Jesus, Son of David, have mercy on me!" And many angrily tried to 48 silence him. But he cried out all the louder, "Son of David, have mercy on me!" Then Jesus 49 stopped and commanded that he should be

called. And they called the blind man and said
to him, "Take courage. Get up, he is calling thee."
50 And throwing off his cloak, he sprang to his feet
51 and came to him. And Jesus addressed him,
saying, "What wouldst thou have me do for
thee?" And the blind man said to him, "Rabboni,
52 that I may see." And Jesus said to him, "Go thy
way, thy faith has saved thee." And at once he
received his sight, and followed him along the
road.

VI

Triumphal Entry into Jerusalem

11 1 AND WHEN THEY DREW NEAR to | FEB. 13 |
Jerusalem and to Bethany, at the | Aug. 14 |
Mount of Olives, he sent two of his disciples,
2 ' and said to them, "Go into the village opposite
you, and immediately on entering it you will
find a colt tied, upon which no man has yet sat;
3 loose it, and bring it. And if anyone say to you,
'What are you doing?' you shall say that the
Lord has need of it, and immediately he will
send it here."

4 And they went their way and found a colt
tied at a door outside in the street, and they
5 loosed it. And some of the bystanders said to
them, "What are you doing, loosing the colt?"
6 But they answered them as Jesus had told them
to do, and they let them go.

7 And they brought the colt to Jesus, and threw
8 their cloaks over it, and he sat upon it. And
many spread their cloaks upon the road, while
others were cutting branches from the trees,
9 and strewing them on the road. And those who
went before him, and those who followed, kept
crying out, saying, "Hosanna! Blessed is he
10 who comes in the name of the Lord! Blessed is
the kingdom of our father David that comes!

Hosanna in the highest!" And he went into 11
Jerusalem, into the temple. And when he had
looked round upon all things, then, as it was
already late, he went out to Bethany with the
Twelve.

Jesus Curses a Fig Tree

And the next day, after they had left Beth- 12
any, he felt hungry. And seeing in the distance 13
a fig tree in leaf, he went to see if he might
find anything on it. But when he came up to it,
he found nothing but leaves; for it was not the
season for figs. Then he spoke to it saying, 14
"May no one ever eat fruit of thee henceforward forever." And his disciples heard.

Cleansing of the Temple

And they came to Jerusalem. And he en- 15
tered the temple, and began to cast out those
who were selling and buying in the temple;
and he overturned the tables of the money-
changers and the seats of those who sold the
doves. He would not allow anyone to carry a 16
vessel through the temple, And he began to 17
teach, saying to them, "Is it not written, 'My
house shall be called a house of prayer for all
the nations'? But you have made it a den of
thieves."

And the chief priests and the Scribes heard 18
it, and they sought a way to destroy him; for
they were afraid of him, because all the crowd
were astonished at his teaching. And when it 19
was evening he went out of the city.

And as they passed by in the morning, they 20
saw the fig tree withered from the roots. And 21
Peter, remembering, said to him, "Rabbi, behold, the fig tree that thou didst curse is withered
up." But Jesus answered and said to them, 22

[123]

23 "Have faith in God. Amen I say to you, whoever says to this mountain, 'Arise, and hurl thyself into the sea,' and does not waver in his heart, but believes that whatever he says will
24 be done, it shall be done for him. Therefore I say to you, all things whatever you ask for in prayer, believe that you shall receive, and they
25 shall come to you. And when you stand up to pray, forgive whatever you have against anyone, that your Father in heaven may also for-
26 give you your offenses. But if you do not forgive, neither will your Father in heaven forgive you your offenses."

The Authority of Jesus

27   And they came back to Jerusalem.
And as he was walking in the temple, | FEB. 14 / Aug. 15 |
the chief priests and the Scribes and the elders
28 came to him, ' and said to him, "By what authority dost thou do these things?" and, "Who
29 gave thee this authority to do these things?" But Jesus answered and said to them, "I also will ask you one question, and answer me; then I will tell you by what authority I do these things.
30 Was the baptism of John from heaven, or from
31 men? Answer me." But they began to argue among themselves, saying, "If we say, 'From heaven,' he will say, 'Why then did you not
32 believe him?' ' But if we say, 'From men' "—they feared the people; for all regarded John
33 as really a prophet. And they answered Jesus and said, "We do not know." And Jesus answering, said to them, "Neither do I tell you by what authority I do these things."

Parable of the Vine-dressers

And he began to speak to them in parables. **12** 1 "A man planted a vineyard, and put a hedge about it, and dug a wine vat, and built a tower; then he let it out to vine-dressers, and went abroad. And at the proper time he sent a ser- 2 vant to the vine-dressers to receive from the vine-dressers some of the fruit of the vineyard; but they seized him, and beat him, and sent 3 him away empty-handed. And again he sent 4 another servant to them; but this one they wounded in the head and treated shamefully. And again he sent another, and him they killed, 5 and many others; beating some, and killing some. Now he still had one left, a beloved son; 6 and him he sent to them last of all, saying, 'They will respect my son.'

"But the vine-dressers said to one another, 7 'This is the heir; come, let us kill him, and the inheritance will be ours.' So they seized him 8 and killed him, and cast him out of the vine-yard. What therefore will the owner of the vine- 9 yard do? He will come and destroy the vine-dressers, and will give the vineyard to others. And have you not read this Scripture: 'The 10 stone which the builders rejected, has become the corner stone; by the Lord this has been 11 done, and it is wonderful in our eyes'?" And 12 they sought to lay hands on him, but they feared the crowd; for they knew that he had aimed this parable at them. And leaving him, they went their way.

12, 1-12: God is the landowner of the parable. He had sent His prophets, and lastly His Son, to the vine-dressers, the Jews.

Tribute to Caesar

13   And they sent to him certain of the Pharisees and Herodians, that

FEB. 15
Aug. 16

14 they might trap him in his talk. And they came and said to him, "Master, we know that thou art truthful, and that thou carest naught for any man; for thou dost not regard the person of men, but dost teach the way of God in truth. Is it lawful to give tribute to Cæsar; or shall we not give

15 it?" But knowing their craftiness, he said to them, "Why do you test me? Bring me a denarius

16 to look at." So they brought one. Then he said to them, "Whose are this image and the inscrip-

17 tion?" They said to him, "Cæsar's." And Jesus answered and said to them, "Render, therefore, to Cæsar the things that are Cæsar's, and to God the things that are God's." And they marvelled at him.

The Sadducees and the Resurrection

18   And there came to him Sadducees, who say there is no resurrection, and they began to ques-

19 tion him, saying, "Master, Moses has written for us that 'if a man's brother die, leaving a wife but no children, his brother shall take the widow

20 and raise up issue to his brother.' Now there were seven brothers. And the first took a wife,

21 and dying, left no issue. And the second took her, and died, without leaving issue either; and the

22 third likewise. And the seven took her in the same way, and left no issue. Last of all the wo-

23 man also died. At the resurrection, therefore, when they rise, of which of them will she be wife? For the seven had her as wife."

24   And Jesus answered and said to them, "Is not

this why you err—because you know neither the
Scriptures nor the power of God? For when they   25
rise from the dead, they will neither marry nor be
given in marriage, but are as angels in heaven.
But as to the dead rising, have you not read in   26
the book of Moses about the Bush, how God
spoke to him, saying, 'I am the God of Abraham,
and the God of Isaac, and the God of Jacob'?
He is not the God of the dead, but of the living.   27
You are therefore entirely wrong."

The Great Commandment

And one of the Scribes came forward who had   28
heard them disputing together; and seeing that
he had answered them well, he asked him which
was the first commandment of all. But Jesus   29
answered him, "The first commandment of all
is, 'Hear, O Israel! The Lord our God is one
God; and thou shalt love the Lord thy God with   30
thy whole heart, and with thy whole soul,
and with thy whole mind, and with thy whole
strength.' This is the first commandment.' And   31
the second is like it, 'Thou shalt love thy neighbor
as thyself.' There is no other commandment
greater than these." And the Scribe said to him,   32
"Well answered, Master, thou hast said truly
that he is one and that there is no other besides him; and that he should be loved with the   33
whole heart, and with the whole understanding,
and with the whole soul, and with one's whole
strength; and that to love one's neighbor as
oneself is a greater thing than all holocausts
and sacrifices." And Jesus, seeing that he had   34
answered wisely, said to him, "Thou art not
far from the kingdom of God." And no one
after that ventured to ask him questions.

The Son of David

35 　And while Jesus was teaching in
the temple, he addressed them, say-
ing, "How do the Scribes say that the Christ is
36 the Son of David? For David himself says, by the
Holy Spirit, 'The Lord said to my Lord: Sit thou
at my right hand, till I make thy enemies thy
37 footstool.' David himself, therefore, calls him
'Lord'; how, then, is he his son?" And the mass
of the common people liked to hear him.

FEB. 16
Aug. 17

Hypocrisy of the Scribes and Pharisees

38 　And in the course of his teaching he said to
them, "Beware of the Scribes, who like to walk
about in long robes, and to be greeted in the
39 market place, and to have the front seats in the
40 synagogues and the first places at suppers; who
devour the houses of the widows, making pretense of long prayers. These shall receive a
heavier sentence."

The Widow's Mite

41 　And Jesus sat down opposite the treasury, and
observed how the crowd were putting money
into the treasury; and many rich people were
42 putting in large sums. And there came one poor
widow, and she put in two mites, which make a
43 quadrans. And he called his disciples together,
and said to them, "Amen I say to you, this poor
widow has put in more than all those who have
44 been putting money into the treasury. For they
all have put in out of their abundance; but she
out of her want has put in all that she had—all
that she had to live on."

Destruction of Jerusalem and End of the World

And as he was going out of the temple, one of **13** 1 his disciples said to him, "Master, look, what wonderful stones and buildings!" And Jesus 2 answered and said to him, "Dost thou see all these great buildings? There will not be left one stone upon another that will not be thrown down."

And as he was sitting on the Mount of Olives, 3 opposite the temple, Peter and James and John and Andrew asked him privately, "Tell us, when 4 are these things to happen, and what will be the sign when all these things will begin to come to pass?"

And in answer Jesus began to say to them, 5 "Take care that no one leads you astray. For 6 many will come in my name, saying, 'I am he'; and they will lead many astray. But when you 7 hear of wars and rumors of wars, do not be alarmed; for they must come to pass, but the end is not yet. For nation will rise against nation, and 8 kingdom against kingdom; and there will be earthquakes in various places, and famines. These things are the beginning of sorrows.

"But be on your guard. For they will deliver 9 you up to councils, and you will be beaten in synagogues, and you will stand before governors and kings for my sake, for a witness to them. And the gospel must first be preached to all the 10 nations. And when they lead you away to deliver 11

13, 2-37: This long prophecy deals with both the destruction of Jerusalem and the end of the world. The elements of the prophecy are so intermingled that it is difficult at times to determine to which cataclysm Jesus refers.

you up, do not be anxious beforehand what you are to speak; but speak whatever is given you in that hour. For it is not you who are speaking, but
12 the Holy Spirit. And brother will hand over brother to death, and the father his child; children will rise up against parents and put them
13 to death. And you will be hated by all for my name's sake; but he who has persevered to the end will be saved.

Destruction of Jerusalem

14 "And when you see the abomination of desolation, standing where it ought not—let him who reads understand—then let those who are in Judea flee to the mountains;

| FEB. 17 |
| Aug. 18 |

15 and let him who is on the housetop not go down and enter to take anything from his house;
16 and let him who is in the field not turn back to
17 take his cloak. But woe to those who are with child, or have infants at the breast in those days!
18 But pray that these things may not happen in
19 winter. For in those days will be tribulations, such as have not been from the beginning of the creation which God created until now, nor will
20 be. And unless the Lord had shortened the days, no living creature would be saved. But for the sake of the elect whom he has chosen, he has shortened the days.

The Signs of the Last Day

21 "And then, if anyone say to you, 'Behold, here is the Christ; behold, there he is,' do not believe
22 it. For false christs and false prophets will arise, and will show signs and wonders, so as to lead
23 astray, if possible, even the elect. Be on your guard, therefore; behold, I have told you all things beforehand.

"But in those days, after that tribulation, the 24
sun will be darkened, and the moon will not give
her light, and the stars of heaven will be falling, 25
and the powers that are in heaven will be shaken.
And then they will see the Son of Man coming 26
upon clouds with great power and majesty. And 27
then he will send forth his angels, and will
gather his elect from the four winds, from the
uttermost parts of the earth to the uttermost
parts of heaven.

Jerusalem's Impending Destruction

"Now from the fig tree learn this parable. 28
When its branch is now tender, and the leaves
break forth, you know that summer is near.
Even so, when you see these things coming to 29
pass, know that it is near, even at the door. Amen 30
I say to you, this generation will not pass away
till all these things have been accomplished.
Heaven and earth will pass away, but my words 31
will not pass away.

The Need of Watchfulness

"But of that day or hour no one knows, neither 32
the angels in heaven, nor the Son, but the Father
only. Take heed, watch and pray, for you do not 33
know when the time is: just as a man, when he 34
leaves home to journey abroad, puts his servants
in charge, to each his work, and gives orders to
the porter to keep watch. Watch, therefore, for 35
you do not know when the master of the house
is coming, in the evening, or at midnight, or at
cockcrow, or early in the morning; lest coming 36
suddenly he find you sleeping. And what I say to 37
you, I say to all, 'Watch.' "

II: THE PASSION, DEATH AND RESURRECTION

1. The Last Supper

The Council

14 1   NOW IT WAS TWO DAYS before the Passover and the feast of the Unleavened Bread; the chief priests and the Scribes were seeking how they might seize him 2 by stealth and put him to death; for they said, "Not on the feast, or there might be a riot among the people."

FEB. 18
Aug. 19

The Anointing at Bethany

3   And when he was at Bethany, in the house of Simon the leper, and was reclining at table, there came a woman with an alabaster jar of ointment, genuine nard of great value; and breaking the 4 alabaster jar, she poured it on his head. But there were some who were indignant among themselves, and said, "To what purpose has this 5 waste of the ointment been made? for this ointment might have been sold for more than three hundred denarii, and given to the poor." And they grumbled at her.

6   But Jesus said, "Let her be. Why do you trou- 7 ble her? She has done me a good turn. For the poor you have always with you, and whenever you want you can do good to them; but you do not 8 always have me. She has done what she could; she has anointed my body in preparation for 9 burial. Amen I say to you, wherever in the whole world this gospel is preached, this also that she has done shall be told in memory of her."

The Betrayal

10   And Judas Iscariot, one of the Twelve, went 11 to the chief priests to betray him to them. And

they, when they heard it, were glad, and promised to give him money. And he sought out an opportunity to betray him.

Preparation

And on the first day of the Unleavened Bread, 12 when it was customary for them to sacrifice the passover, the disciples said to him, "Where dost thou want us to go and prepare for thee to eat the passover?" And he sent two of his disciples, 13 and said to them, "Go into the city, and there will meet you a man carrying a pitcher of water; follow him. And wherever he enters, say to the 14 master of the house, 'The Master says, "Where is my guest chamber, that I may eat the passover there with my disciples?" ' And he will show you 15 a large upper room furnished; there make ready for us." And his disciples went forth, and came 16 into the city, and found just as he had told them; and they prepared the passover.

The Betrayer

Now when evening arrived, he 17 came with the Twelve. And while | FEB. 19 / Aug. 20 | 18 they were at the table eating, Jesus said, "Amen I say to you, one of you will betray me—one who is eating with me." But they began to be sad, and 19 to say to him one by one, "Is it I?" But he said to 20 them, "It is one of the Twelve, who dips into the dish with me. The Son of Man indeed goes his 21 way, as it is written of him; but woe to that man by whom the Son of Man is betrayed! It were better for that man if he had not been born."

The Holy Eucharist

And while they were eating, Jesus took bread, 22 and blessing it, he broke and gave it to them, and said, "Take; this is my body." ' And taking a 23

cup and giving thanks, he gave it to them, and
24 they all drank of it; ' and he said to them, "This
is my blood of the new covenant, which is being
25 shed for many. Amen I say to you, that I will
drink no more of the fruit of the vine, until that
day when I shall drink it new in the kingdom of
God."

Peter's Denials Predicted

26 And after reciting a hymn, they went out to
27 the Mount of Olives. And Jesus said to them,
"You will all be scandalized this night; for it is
written, 'I will smite the shepherd, and the sheep
28 will be scattered.' But after I have risen, I will
29 go before you into Galilee." But Peter said to
him, "Even though all shall be scandalized, yet
30 not I." Jesus said to him, "Amen I say to thee,
today, this very night, before a cock crows twice,
31 thou wilt deny me three times." But he went on
speaking more vehemently, "Even if I should
have to die with thee, I will not deny thee!"
And they all said the same thing.

2. The Passion and Death of Jesus

The Agony in the Garden

32 AND THEY CAME to a country | FEB. 20
place called Gethsemani, and he | Aug. 21
said to his disciples, "Sit down here, while I
33 pray." And he took with him Peter and James
and John, and he began to feel dread and to be
34 exceedingly troubled. And he said to them, "My
soul is sad, even unto death. Wait here and
35 watch." And going forward a little, he fell on the
ground, and began to pray that, if it were possible,
36 the hour might pass from him; ' and he said,
"Abba, Father, all things are possible to thee.
Remove this cup from me; yet not what I will,
but what thou willest."

Then he came and found them sleeping. And 37
he said to Peter, "Simon, dost thou sleep?
Couldst thou not watch one hour? Watch and 38
pray, that you may not enter into temptation.
The spirit indeed is willing, but the flesh is weak."
And again he went away and prayed, saying the 39
same words over. And he came again and found 40
them sleeping, for their eyes were heavy. And
they did not know what answer to make to him.
And he came the third time, and said to them, 41
"Sleep on now, and take your rest! It is enough;
the hour has come. Behold, the Son of Man is
betrayed into the hands of sinners. Rise, let us 42
go. Behold, he who will betray me is at hand."

Jesus Arrested

And while he was yet speaking, Judas Iscariot, 43
one of the Twelve, came and with him a great
crowd with swords and clubs, from the chief
priests and the Scribes and the elders. Now his 44
betrayer had given them a sign, saying, "Whomever I kiss, that is he; lay hold of him, and lead
him safely away." And when he came, he went 45
straight up to him, and said, "Rabbi!" and kissed
him. And they seized him and held him. 46

But one of the bystanders drew his sword, and 47
struck the servant of the high priest, and cut off
his ear. And Jesus, addressing them, said, "As 48
against a robber you have come out, with swords
and clubs, to seize me. I was daily with you in 49
the temple teaching, and you did not lay hands
on me. But it is so that the Scriptures may be
fulfilled."

Then all his disciples left him and fled. And 50.51
a certain young man was following him, having
a linen cloth wrapped about his naked body, and
they seized him. But leaving the linen cloth 52
behind, he fled away from them naked.

Jesus before the Sanhedrin

53   And they led Jesus away to the | FEB. 21 |
high priest; and all the priests and | Aug. 22 |
the Scribes and the elders gathered together.

54 But Peter followed him at a distance, even to
the courtyard of the high priest, and was sitting
with the attendants at the fire and warming

55 himself. Now the chief priests and all the
Sanhedrin were seeking witness against Jesus,
that they might put him to death, but they found

56 none. For while many bore false witness against

57 him, their evidence did not agree. And some
stood up and bore false witness against him,

58 saying, "We ourselves have heard him say, 'I
will destroy this temple built by hands, and
after three days I will build another, not built by

59 hands.' " And even then their evidence did not
agree.

60   Then the high priest, standing up in their
midst, asked Jesus, saying, "Dost thou make no
answer to the things that these men prefer

61 against thee?" But he kept silence, and made no
answer. Again the high priest began to ask him,
and said to him, "Art thou the Christ, the Son of

62 the Blessed One?" ' And Jesus said to him, "I
am. And you shall see the Son of Man sitting at
the right hand of the Power and coming with the
clouds of heaven."

63 But the high priest tore his garments and said,

64 "What further need have we of witnesses? ' You
have heard the blasphemy. What do you
think?" And they all condemned him as liable to

65 death. And some began to spit on him, and to
blindfold him, and to buffet him, and to say to
him, "Prophesy." And the attendants struck him
with blows of their hands.

Peter's Denial

And while Peter was below in the courtyard, 66
there came one of the maidservants of the high
priest; ' and seeing Peter warming himself, she 67
looked closely at him and said, "Thou also wast
with Jesus of Nazareth." But he denied it, saying, 68
"I neither know nor understand what thou
art saying." And he went outside into the vestibule;
and the cock crowed. And the maidservant, 69
seeing him again, began to say to the bystanders,
"This is one of them." ' But again he denied it. 70
And after a little while the bystanders again said
to Peter, "Surely thou art one of them, for thou
art also a Galilean." But he began to curse and 71
to swear: "I do not know this man you are talking
about." And at that moment a cock crowed a 72
second time. And Peter remembered the word
that Jesus had said to him, "Before a cock crows
twice, thou wilt deny me three times." And he
began to weep.

Jesus before Pilate

And as soon as it was morning, | FEB. 22 | **15** 1
the chief priests held a consultation | Aug. 23 |
with the elders, the Scribes and the whole
Sanhedrin. And they bound Jesus and led him
away, and delivered him to Pilate. And Pilate 2
asked him, "Art thou the king of the Jews?" And
he answered him and said, "Thou sayest it."
And the chief priests accused him of many things. 3
And Pilate again asked him, saying, "Hast thou 4
no answer to make? Behold how many things
they accuse thee of." But Jesus made no further 5
answer, so that Pilate wondered.

Now at festival time he used to release to 6
them one of the prisoners, whomever they had

7 petitioned for. Now there was a man called Barabbas imprisoned with some rioters, one who
8 in the riot had committed murder. And the crowd came up, and began to ask that he do for them
9 as he was wont. But Pilate addressed them, saying, "Do you wish that I release to you the king of
10 the Jews?" For he knew that the chief priests had
11 delivered him up out of envy. But the chief priests stirred up the crowd to have him release Barab-
12 bas for them instead. But Pilate again spoke and said to them, "What then do you want me to do
13 to the king of the Jews?" But they cried out
14 again, "Crucify him!" But Pilate said to them, "Why, what evil has he done?" But they kept crying out the more, "Crucify him!"

The Scourging and Crowning

15 So Pilate, wishing to satisfy the crowd, released to them Barabbas; but Jesus he
16 scourged and delivered to be crucified. Now the soldiers led him away into the courtyard of the prætorium, and they called together the
17 whole cohort. And they clothed him in purple, and plaiting a crown of thorns, they put it upon
18 him, ' and began to greet him, "Hail, King of
19 the Jews!" And they kept striking him on the head with a reed, and spitting upon him; and bending their knees, they did homage to him.

The Way of the Cross

20 And when they had mocked him, they took the purple off him and put his own garments on
21 him, and led him out to crucify him. And they forced a certain passer-by, Simon of Cyrene, coming from the country, the father of Alexander
22 and Rufus, to take up his cross. And they brought him to the place called Golgotha, which translated, is the Place of the Skull.

The Crucifixion

And they gave him wine to drink 23
mixed with myrrh; but he did not | FEB. 23 / Aug. 24 |
take it. Then they crucified him, and divided 24
his garments, casting lots for them to see what
each should take. Now it was the third hour and 25
they crucified him. And the inscription bearing 26
the charge against him was, "The King of the
Jews."

And they crucified two robbers with him, 27
one on his right hand and one on his left. And 28
the Scripture was fulfilled, which says, "And he
was reckoned among the wicked." And the 29
passers-by were jeering at him, shaking their
heads, and saying, "Aha, thou who destroyest
the temple, and in three days buildest it up
again; come down from the cross, and save 30
thyself!" In like manner, the chief priests with 31
the Scribes said in mockery to one another, "He
saved others, himself he cannot save! Let the 32
Christ, the King of Israel, come down now from
the cross, that we may see and believe." And
they who were crucified with him reproached
him.

The Death of Jesus

And when the sixth hour came, there was 33
darkness over the whole land until the ninth
hour. And at the ninth hour Jesus cried out 34
with a loud voice, saying, "Eloi, Eloi, lama
sabacthani?" which, translated is, "My God,
my God, why hast thou forsaken me?" And 35
some of the bystanders on hearing this said,
"Behold, he is calling Elias." But someone ran, 36
soaked a sponge in common wine, put it on a

[139]

reed and offered it to him to drink, saying, "Wait, let us see whether Elias is coming to
37 take him down." But Jesus cried out with a loud voice, and expired.

38 And the curtain of the temple was torn in
39 two from top to bottom. Now when the centurion, who stood facing him, saw how he had thus cried out and expired, he said, "Truly
40 this man was the Son of God." And some women were also there, looking on from a distance. Among them were Mary Magdalene, Mary the mother of James the Less and of
41 Joseph, and Salome. These used to accompany him and minister to him when he was in Galilee —besides many other women who had come with him to Jerusalem.

The Burial

42 Now when it was evening, as it was the Day of Preparation, that is, the eve of the Sabbath,
43 there came Joseph of Arimathea, a councillor of high rank, who was himself looking for the kingdom of God. And he went in boldly to
44 Pilate and asked for the body of Jesus. But Pilate wondered whether he had already died. And sending for the centurion, he asked him
45 whether he was already dead. And when he learned from the centurion that he was, he
46 granted the body to Joseph. And Joseph bought a linen cloth, and took him down, and wrapped him in the linen cloth, and laid him in a tomb which had been hewn out of a rock. Then he
47 rolled a stone to the entrance of the tomb. But Mary Magdalene and Mary the mother of Joseph were looking on and saw where he was laid.

3. The Resurrection of Jesus

The Women at the Grave

AND WHEN THE SABBATH WAS | FEB. 24 | **16** 1
PAST, Mary Magdalene, Mary the | Aug. 25 |
mother of James, and Salome, bought spices,
that they might go and anoint him. And very 2
early on the first day of the week, they came to
the tomb, when the sun had just risen. And 3
they were saying to one another, "Who will
roll the stone back from the entrance of the
tomb for us?" And looking up they saw that the 4
stone had been rolled back, for it was very
large. But on entering the tomb, they saw a 5
young man sitting at the right side, clothed in a
white robe, and they were amazed. He said to 6
them, "Do not be terrified. You are looking for
Jesus of Nazareth, who was crucified. He has
risen, he is not here. Behold the place where
they laid him. But go, tell his disciples and Peter 7
that he goes before you into Galilee; there you
shall see him, as he told you." And they de- 8
parted and fled from the tomb, for trembling
and fear had seized them; and they said nothing
to anyone, for they were afraid.

Apparitions of Jesus

Now when he had risen from the dead early 9
on the first day of the week, he appeared first
to Mary Magdalene, out of whom he had cast
seven devils. She went and brought word to 10
those who had been with him, as they were
mourning and weeping. And they, hearing that 11
he was alive and had been seen by her, did
not believe it.

After this he was manifested in another form 12
to two of them, as they were walking on their

13 way into the country. And they went and brought word to the rest, and even then they did not believe.

Commission of the Apostles

14 At length he appeared to the Eleven as they were at table; and he upbraided them for their lack of faith and hardness of heart, in that they had not believed those who had seen him

15 after he had risen. And he said to them, "Go into the whole world and preach the gospel to

16 every creature. He who believes and is baptized shall be saved, but he who does not believe

17 shall be condemned. And these signs shall attend those who believe: in my name they shall cast out devils; they shall speak in new

18 tongues; ' they shall take up serpents; and if they drink any deadly thing, it shall not hurt them; they shall lay hands upon the sick and they shall get well."

4. The Ascension of Jesus

The Ascension

19 SO THEN THE LORD, after he had spoken to them, was taken up into heaven, and sits at

20 the right hand of God. But they went forth and preached everywhere, while the Lord worked with them and confirmed the preaching by the signs that followed. Amen.

THE GOSPEL ACCORDING TO
ST. LUKE
Introduction

St. Luke was born at Antioch, Syria, according to the Church historian Eusebius. He was a Gentile by birth (Col. 4, 10-14) and a physician by profession (Col. 4, 14). According to a legend of the sixth century he was also a painter.

He was one of the earliest converts to the faith and later became the missionary companion of St. Paul, whom he accompanied on part of the second and third missionary journeys (Acts 16, 10-17; 20, 5—21, 17), and attended during the Cæsarean (Acts 24, 23) and Roman captivity (Acts 27—28; Col. 4, 14). Little is known with certainty of his subsequent life.

The unanimous tradition of the Church ascribes the third Gospel to St. Luke. Allusions to and citations from the Gospel are most frequent in early Christian writings, and even heretics made diligent use of this inspired book. The Gospel itself shows that its author was a person of literary powers, a physician and a companion of St. Paul.

This Gospel was written before the destruction of Jerusalem, A. D. 70, for it does not refer to the fulfillment of Christ's prophecy. Since the Acts of the Apostles closes its narrative with the year A. D. 63 or 64, the Gospel of St. Luke, his first book, must have been written prior to A. D. 63.

Little is known with certainty about the place of composition. Some of the ancient authors suggest Achaia (Greece); some of the manuscripts mention Alexandria or Macedonia; while modern writers also defend Cæsarea, Ephesus or Rome.

The Gospel is addressed to a certain Theophilus, a man of conspicuous rank or office. Indirectly, however, this Sacred Writing was intended for the Gentile converts. The purpose of the Gospel is clearly indicated in the prologue (1, 1-4). These converts from paganism had received instruction before Baptism. St. Luke wishes now to give them a deeper and more accurate knowledge of the truths of their religion, and

THE HOLY GOSPEL OF JESUS CHRIST
ACCORDING TO ST. LUKE

Prologue

1 1 INASMUCH AS MANY have under- | FEB. 25
taken to draw up a narrative con- | Aug. 26
cerning the things that have been fulfilled among
2 us, even as they who from the beginning were
eyewitnesses and ministers of the word have
3 handed them down to us, I also have determined,
after following up all things carefully from the
very first, to write for thee, most excellent
4 Theophilus, an orderly account, ' that thou
mayest understand the certainty of the words in
which thou hast been instructed.

---

at the same time to show them on what a firm basis
their faith is founded. There are some characteristic
features that are accentuated more by St. Luke than
by the other evangelists. Many of these show the influence of St. Paul. The theme of the universality of
salvation can be considered as running through the
Gospel. Divine forgiveness and salvation are offered
to all. The Gospel also sharply contrasts the position
of pagan and Jewish womanhood, and presents many
types of womanhood to its readers. The subject of
prayer is also stressed. Not only does the evangelist
record more frequently than the others Christ as an
example of prayer, but also His instructions on
prayer. As an artist St. Luke shows his skill in por-
traying living characters and he has remained an inspiration to painters for centuries. As a historian he is
comparable with the great Greek and Latin writers.
In his Gospel there is a steady movement of events
from Nazareth to Jerusalem, whereas in the Acts it
is from Jerusalem to Rome.

Prelude: The Coming of the Savior

Annunciation of the Baptist

IN THE DAYS OF HEROD, king of Judea, there 5
was a certain priest named Zachary, of the course
of Abia; and his wife was of the daughters of
Aaron, and her name was Elizabeth. Both were 6
just before God, walking blamelessly in all the
commandments and ordinances of the Lord. But 7
they had no son, for Elizabeth was barren; and
they were both advanced in years.

Now it came to pass, while he was officiating 8
in the order of his course as priest before God,
according to the custom of the priest's office, 9
that he was chosen by lot to enter the temple of
the Lord to burn incense. And the whole multi- 10
tude of the people were praying outside at the
hour of incense. And there appeared to him an 11
angel of the Lord, standing at the right of the
altar of incense. And Zachary, seeing him, was 12
troubled, and fear fell upon him.

But the angel said to him, "Do not be afraid, 13
Zachary, for thy petition has been heard, and thy
wife Elizabeth shall bear thee a son and thou
shalt call his name John. And thou shalt have joy 14
and gladness, and many will rejoice at his birth.
For he shall be great before the Lord; he shall 15
drink no wine or strong drink, and shall be filled
with the Holy Spirit even from his mother's
womb. And he shall bring back to the Lord their 16
God many of the children of Israel, and he shall 17
himself go before him in the spirit and power
of Elias, to turn the hearts of fathers to their children and the incredulous to the wisdom of the
just; to prepare for the Lord a perfect people."

And Zachary said to the angel, "How shall I 18
know this? For I am an old man and my wife is
advanced in years."

19 And the angel answered and said to him, "I am Gabriel, who stand in the presence of God; and I have been sent to speak to thee and to 20 bring thee this good news. And behold, thou shalt be dumb and unable to speak until the day when these things come to pass, because thou hast not believed my words, which will be fulfilled in their proper time."

21 And the people were waiting for Zachary, and they wondered at his 22 tarrying so long in the temple. But when he did come out he could not speak to them, and they realized that he had seen a vision in the temple. And he kept making signs to them, but he remained dumb.

FEB. 26
Aug. 27

23 And it came to pass, when the days of his service were completed, that he departed to his 24 own house. Now after these days Elizabeth his wife conceived, and she secluded herself for 25 five months, saying, "Thus has the Lord dealt with me in the days when he deigned to take away my reproach among men."

Annunciation of the Savior

26 Now in the sixth month the angel Gabriel was sent from God to a town of Galilee called Naza- 27 reth, to a virgin betrothed to a man named Joseph, of the house of David, and the virgin's 28 name was Mary. And when the angel had come to her, he said, "Hail, full of grace, the Lord is with thee. Blessed art thou among women." 29 When she had heard him she was troubled at his word, and kept pondering what manner of greeting this might be.

30 And the angel said to her, "Do not be afraid, 31 Mary, for thou hast found grace with God. Behold, thou shalt conceive in thy womb and shalt bring forth a son; and thou shalt call his name Jesus.

He shall be great, and shall be called the Son 32 of the Most High; and the Lord God will give him the throne of David his father, and he shall be king over the house of Jacob forever; and of his 33 kingdom there shall be no end."

But Mary said to the angel, "How shall this 34 happen, since I do not know man?"

And the angel answered and said to her, "The 35 Holy Spirit shall come upon thee and the power of the Most High shall overshadow thee; and therefore the Holy One to be born shall be called the Son of God. And behold, Elizabeth thy kins- 36 woman also has conceived a son in her old age, and she who was called barren is now in her sixth month; for nothing shall be impossible with 37 God."

But Mary said, "Behold the handmaid of the 38 Lord; be it done to me according to thy word." And the angel departed from her.

The Visitation

Now in those days Mary arose and went with haste into the hill country, to a town of Juda. And she entered the 40 house of Zachary and saluted Elizabeth. And it 41 came to pass, when Elizabeth heard the greeting of Mary, that the babe in her womb leapt. And Elizabeth was filled with the Holy Spirit, and 42 cried out with a loud voice, saying, "Blessed art thou among women and blessed is the fruit of thy womb! And how have I deserved that the 43 mother of my Lord should come to me? For be- 44 hold, the moment that the sound of thy greeting came to my ears, the babe in my womb leapt for joy. And blessed is she who has believed, be- 45 cause the things promised her by the Lord shall be accomplished."

| FEB. 27 | 39 |
| Aug. 28 | |

46   And Mary said, "My soul magnifies the Lord,
47, 48 and my spirit rejoices in God my Savior; because he has regarded the lowliness of his handmaid; for, behold, henceforth all generations
49   shall call me blessed; because he who is mighty
has done great things for me, and holy is his
50   name; and his mercy is from generation to gener-
51   ation on those who fear him. He has shown might
with his arm, he has scattered the proud in the
52   conceit of their heart. He has put down the
mighty from their thrones, and has exalted the
53   lowly. He has filled the hungry with good things,
54   and the rich he has sent away empty. He has
given help to Israel, his servant, mindful of his
55   mercy — even as he spoke to our fathers — to
Abraham and to his posterity forever."

56   And Mary remained with her about three
months and returned to her own house.

Birth of the Baptist

57   Now Elizabeth's time was fulfilled
that she should be delivered, and

FEB. 28
Aug. 29

58   she brought forth a son. And her neighbors and
kinsfolk heard that the Lord had magnified his
mercy towards her, and they rejoiced with her.
59   And it came to pass on the eighth day, that they
came to circumcise the child, and they were going to call him by his father's name, Zachary.
60   And his mother answered and said, "Not so, but
he shall be called John."
61   And they said to her, "There is none of thy
62   kindred that is called by this name." And they
kept inquiring by signs of his father what he
63   would have him called. And asking for a writing-
tablet he wrote the words, "John is his name."
64   And they all marvelled. And immediately his
mouth was opened and his tongue loosed, and
65   he began to speak, blessing God. And fear came

on all their neighbors; and all these things
were spoken abroad in all the hill country of
Judea. And all who heard them laid them up 66
in their heart, saying, "What then will this
child be?" For the hand of the Lord was with
him. And Zachary his father was filled with the 67
Holy Spirit, and prophesied, saying, ' "Blessed 68
be the Lord, the God of Israel, because he has
visited and wrought redemption for his people,
and has raised up a horn of salvation for us, 69
in the house of David his servant, ' as he 70
promised through the mouth of his holy ones,
the prophets from of old; salvation from our ene- 71
mies, and from the hand of all who hate us, to 72
show mercy to our forefathers and to be mindful
of his holy covenant, of the oath that he swore to 73
Abraham our father, that he would grant us,
' that, delivered from the hand of our enemies, 74
we should serve him without fear, in holiness 75
and justice before him all our days. And thou, 76
child, shalt be called the prophet of the Most
High, for thou shalt go before the face of the
Lord to prepare his ways, ' to give to his people 77
knowledge of salvation through forgiveness of
their sins, because of the loving-kindness of 78
our God, wherewith the Orient from on high
has visited us, ' to shine on those who sit in 79
darkness and in the shadow of death, to guide
our feet into the way of peace."

And the child grew and became strong in 80
spirit; and was in the deserts until the day of
his manifestation to Israel.

The Birth of Jesus

Now it came to pass in those | FEB. 29 | **2** 1
days, that a decree went forth from | Aug. 30 |
Cæsar Augustus that a census of the whole
world should be taken. This first census took 2

3 place while Cyrinus was governor of Syria. And all were going, each to his own town, to register.

4 And Joseph also went from Galilee out of the town of Nazareth into Judea to the town of David, which is called Bethlehem—because he

5 was of the house and family of David— ' to register, together with Mary his espoused wife,

6 who was with child. And it came to pass while they were there, that the days for her to be

7 delivered were fulfilled. And she brought forth her firstborn son, and wrapped him in swaddling clothes, and laid him in a manger, because there was no room for them in the inn.

The Shepherds at the Crib

8 And there were shepherds in the same district living in the fields and keeping watch over

9 their flock by night. And behold, an angel of the Lord stood by them and the glory of God shone round about them, and they feared exceedingly.

10 And the angel said to them, "Do not be afraid, for behold, I bring you good news of

11 great joy which shall be to all the people; for today in the town of David a Savior has been

12 born to you, who is Christ the Lord. And this shall be a sign to you: you will find an infant wrapped in swaddling clothes and lying in a

13 manger." And suddenly there was with the angel a multitude of the heavenly host praising

14 God and saying, "Glory to God in the highest, and on earth peace among men of good will."

15 And it came to pass, when the angels had departed from them into heaven, that the shepherds were saying to one another, "Let us go over to Bethlehem and see this thing that has come to pass, which the Lord has made known to us."

So they went with haste, and they found 16 Mary and Joseph, and the babe lying in the manger. And when they had seen, they understood 17 what had been told them concerning this child. And all who heard marvelled at the things told 18 them by the shepherds. But Mary kept in mind 19 all these things, pondering them in her heart. And the shepherds returned, glorifying and 20 praising God for all that they had heard and seen, even as it was spoken to them.

Circumcision and Presentation

And when eight days were ful- | MAR. 1 | 21
filled for his circumcision, his name | Aug. 31 |
was called Jesus, the name given him by the angel before he was conceived in the womb.

And when the days of her purification were 22 fulfilled according to the Law of Moses, they took him up to Jerusalem to present him to the Lord—as it is written in the Law of the 23 Lord, "Every male that opens the womb shall be called holy to the Lord"—' and to offer a sacrifice 24 according to what is said in the Law of the Lord, "a pair of turtledoves or two young pigeons."

And behold, there was in Jerusalem a man 25 named Simeon, and this man was just and devout, looking for the consolation of Israel, and the Holy Spirit was upon him. And it had 26 been revealed to him by the Holy Spirit that he should not see death before he had seen the Christ of the Lord. And he came by in- 27 spiration of the Spirit into the temple. And when his parents brought in the child Jesus, to do for him according to the custom of the Law, ' he also received him into his arms and blessed 28 God, saying, ' "Now thou dost dismiss thy ser- 29 vant, O Lord, according to thy word, in peace;

30 because my eyes have seen thy salvation,
31 which thou hast prepared before the face of
32 all peoples: a light of revelation to the Gentiles,
and a glory for thy people Israel."

33 And his father and mother were marvelling
34 at the things spoken concerning him. And
Simeon blessed them, and said to Mary his
mother, "Behold, this child is destined for the
fall and for the rise of many in Israel, and for a
35 sign that shall be contradicted. And thy own
soul a sword shall pierce, that the thoughts of
many hearts may be revealed."

36 There was also Anna, a prophetess, daughter
of Phanuel, of the tribe of Aser. She was of a
great age, having lived with her husband seven
37 years from her maidenhood, and by herself as
a widow to eighty-four years. She never left
the temple, with fastings and prayers wor-
38 shipping night and day. And coming up at that
very hour, she began to give praise to the Lord,
and spoke of him to all who were awaiting
the redemption of Jerusalem.

39 And when they had fulfilled all things prescribed in the Law of the Lord, they returned
40 to Galilee, into their own town of Nazareth. And
the child grew and became strong. He was full
of wisdom and the grace of God was upon him.

The Child Jesus in the Temple

41 And his parents were wont to go
every year to Jerusalem at the Feast

MAR. 2
Sept. 1

42 of the Passover. And when he was twelve years
old, they went up to Jerusalem according to the
43 custom of the feast. And after they had fulfilled
the days, when they were returning, the boy
Jesus remained in Jerusalem, and his parents
44 did not know it. But thinking that he was in the

caravan, they had come a day's journey before it occurred to them to look for him among their relatives and acquaintances. And not finding him, 45 they returned to Jerusalem in search of him.

And it came to pass after three days, that they 46 found him in the temple, sitting in the midst of the teachers, listening to them and asking them questions. And all who were listening to him 47 were amazed at his understanding and his answers. And when they saw him, they were as- 48 tonished. And his mother said to him, "Son, why hast thou done so to us? Behold, in sorrow thy father and I have been seeking thee."

And he said to them, "How is it that you 49 sought me? Did you not know that I must be about my Father's business?" And they did not 50 understand the word that he spoke to them.

And he went down with them and came to 51 Nazareth, and was subject to them; and his mother kept all these things carefully in her heart. And Jesus advanced in wisdom and age 52 and grace before God and men.

I: THE PUBLIC MINISTRY OF JESUS

I

John the Baptist

NOW IN THE FIFTEENTH YEAR of | MAR. 3 | **3** 1
the reign of Tiberius Cæsar, when | Sept. 2 |
Pontius Pilate was procurator of Judea, and Herod tetrarch of Galilee, and Philip his brother tetrarch of the district of Iturea and Trachonitis,

---

2, 52: As God, our Lord has infinite knowledge; as man, He had from the beginning the greatest possible infused knowledge and also the beatific vision. His human mind, however, could advance in experimental knowledge, which is only acquired through the medium of mental faculties and bodily senses.

2 and Lysanias tetrarch of Abilene, during the high priesthood of Annas and Caiphas, the word of God came to John, the son of Zachary, in the
3 desert. And he went into all the region about the Jordan, preaching a baptism of repentance for
4 the forgiveness of sins, as it is written in the book of the words of Isaias the prophet, "The voice of one crying in the desert, 'Make ready the way of
5 the Lord, make straight his paths. Every valley shall be filled, and every mountain and hill shall be brought low, and the crooked ways shall be made straight, and the rough ways shall be smooth;
6 and all mankind shall see the salvation of God.' "

7 He said therefore to the crowds that went out to be baptized by him, "Brood of vipers! who has shown you how to flee from the wrath to come?
8 Bring forth therefore fruits befitting repentance, and do not begin to say, 'We have Abraham for our father'; for I say to you that God is able out of these stones to raise up children to Abraham.
9 For even now the axe is laid at the root of the trees; every tree, therefore, that is not bringing forth fruit is to be cut down and thrown into the fire."

10 And the crowds asked him, saying, "What
11 then are we to do?" And he answered and said to them, "Let him who has two tunics share with him who has none; and let him who has food do likewise."

12 And publicans also came to be baptized, and they said to him, "Master, what are we to do?"
13 But he said to them, "Exact no more than what has been appointed you."

14 And soldiers also asked him, saying, "And we—what are we to do?" And he said to them, "Plunder no one, accuse no one falsely, and be content with your pay."

Now as the people were in expectation, and all 15
were wondering in their hearts about John,
whether perhaps he might be the Christ, John 16
addressed them, saying to all, "I indeed baptize
you with water. But one mightier than I is coming, the strap of whose sandals I am not worthy
to loose. He will baptize you with the Holy
Spirit and with fire. His winnowing fan is in his 17
hand, and he will clean out his threshing floor,
and will gather the wheat into his barn; but the
chaff he will burn up with unquenchable fire."
So with many different exhortations he kept on 18
preaching the gospel to the people.

But Herod the tetrarch, being reproved by him 19
concerning Herodias, his brother's wife, and
concerning all the evil things that Herod had
done, crowned all this by shutting up John in 20
prison.

The Baptism of Jesus

Now it came to pass when all the | MAR. 4 | 21
people had been baptized, Jesus also | Sept. 3 |
having been baptized and being in prayer, then
heaven was opened, and the Holy Spirit de- 22
scended upon him in bodily form as a dove, and a
voice came from heaven, "Thou art my beloved
Son, in thee I am well pleased."

Genealogy of Jesus

And Jesus himself, when he began his work, 23
was about thirty years of age, being—as was

3, 16: The Messias will baptize with the Holy Spirit and
with fire; cf. Mal. 3, 2. His action, symbolized by puri-
fying fire, will be more penetrating and powerful than
that of John.

3, 17: Here Jesus is described in His capacity as judge.
In this verse fire does not symbolize an agent of purification, as in v. 16, but rather a destructive agency.

supposed—the son of Joseph, the son of Heli,
24 the son of Matthat, ' the son of Levi, the son of
25 Melchi, the son of Janne, the son of Joseph, the
son of Matthathias, the son of Amos, the
son of Naum, the son of Esli, the son of Nagge,
26 ' the son of Maath, the son of Matthathias, the
son of Semei, the son of Josech, the son of Joda,
27 ' the son of Joanna, the son of Resa, the son of
Zorobabel, the son of Salathiel, the son of Neri,
28 ' the son of Melchi, the son of Addi, the son of
Cosam, the son of Elmadam, the son of Her,
29 ' the son of Jesus, the son of Eliezer, the son of
30 Jorim, the son of Matthat, the son of Levi, ' the
son of Simeon, the son of Judas, the son of
Joseph, the son of Jona, the son of Eliachim,
31 ' the son of Melea, the son of Menna, the son of
Matthata, the son of Nathan, the son of David,
32 ' the son of Jesse, the son of Obed, the son of
Booz, the son of Salmon, the son of Naasson,
33 ' the son of Aminadab, the son of Aram, the son
of Esron, the son of Phares, the son of Judas,
34 ' the son of Jacob, the son of Isaac, the son of
Abraham, the son of Thare, the son of Nachor,
35 ' the son of Seruch, the son of Ragau, the son of
36 Phalec, the son of Eber, the son of Sale, ' the son
of Cainan, the son of Arphaxad, the son of Sem,
37 the son of Noe, the son of Lamech, ' the son of
Mathusale, the son of Enoch, the son of Jared,
38 the son of Malaleel, the son of Cainan, ' the son
of Enos, the son of Seth, the son of Adam, who
was of God.

The Temptation

4 1   Now Jesus, full of the Holy Spirit, returned
from the Jordan, and was led by the Spirit about
2 the desert ' for forty days, being tempted the
while by the devil. And he ate nothing those days;
and when they were completed he was hungry.

And the devil said to him, "If thou art the Son 3
of God, command that this stone become a loaf
of bread." And Jesus answered him, "It is writ- 4
ten, 'Not by bread alone shall man live, but by
every word of God.'"

And the devil led him up, and showed him all 5
the kingdoms of the world in a moment of time.
And he said to him, "To thee will I give all this 6
power and their glory; for to me they have been
delivered, and to whomever I will I give them.
Therefore if thou wilt worship before me, the 7
whole shall be thine." And Jesus answered and 8
said to him, "It is written, 'The Lord thy God
shalt thou worship, and him only shalt thou
serve.'"

Then he led him to Jerusalem and set him on 9
the pinnacle of the temple and said to him, "If
thou art the Son of God, throw thyself down
from here; for it is written, 'He will give his 10
angels charge concerning thee, to preserve thee';
and, 'Upon their hands they shall bear thee up, 11
lest thou dash thy foot against a stone.'"

And Jesus answered and said to him, "It is 12
said, 'Thou shalt not tempt the Lord thy God.'"
And when the devil had tried every tempta- 13
tion, he departed from him for a while.

II

Jesus at Nazareth

AND JESUS RETURNED in the | MAR. 5 | 14
power of the Spirit into Galilee; and | Sept. 4 |
the fame of him went out through the whole
country. And he taught in their synagogues, and 15
was honored by all.

And he came to Nazareth, where he had been 16
brought up; and according to his custom, he
entered the synagogue on the Sabbath and stood

17 up to read. And the volume of Isaias the prophet was handed to him. And after he opened the volume, he found the place where it was written,
18 "The Spirit of the Lord is upon me because he has anointed me; to bring good news to the poor
19 he has sent me, ' to proclaim to the captives release, and sight to the blind; to set at liberty the oppressed, to proclaim the acceptable year of the Lord, and the day of recompense."

20 And closing the volume, he gave it back to the attendant and sat down. And the eyes of all in the
21 synagogue were gazing on him. But he began to say to them, "Today this Scripture has been ful-
22 filled in your hearing." And all bore him witness, and marvelled at the words of grace that came from his mouth. And they said, "Is not this Joseph's son?"

23 And he said to them, "You will surely quote me this proverb, 'Physician, cure thyself! What-ever things we have heard of as done in Caphar-naum, do here also in thy own country!' "
24 But he said, "Amen I say to you, no prophet is
25 acceptable in his own country. In truth I say to you, there were many widows in Israel in the days of Elias, when heaven was shut up for three years and six months, and a great famine came
26 over all the land; and to none of them was Elias sent, but rather to a widowed woman in Sarepta
27 of Sidon. And there were many lepers in Israel in the time of Eliseus the prophet; and not one of them was cleansed, but only Naaman the Syrian."

28 And all in the synagogue, as they heard these
29 things, were filled with wrath. And they rose up and put him forth out of the town, and led him to the brow of the hill, on which their town was built, that they might throw him down headlong.

But he, passing through their midst, went his 30
way.

And he went down to Capharnaum, a town of 31
Galilee. And there he was teaching them on the
Sabbath. And they were astonished at his teach- 32
ing, for his word was with authority.

The Cure of a Demoniac

Now in the synagogue there was a ⎡ MAR. 6 ⎤ 33
man possessed by an unclean devil, ⎣ Sept. 5 ⎦
and he cried out with a loud voice, ¹ saying, "Let 34
us alone! What have we to do with thee, Jesus
of Nazareth? Hast thou come to destroy us? I
know thee, who thou art, the Holy One of God."
And Jesus rebuked him, saying, "Hold thy peace, 35
and go out of him." And when the devil had
thrown him down into the midst, he went out of
him, without harming him at all. And amaze- 36
ment came upon all, and they discussed it with
one another, saying, "What is this word? For
with authority and power he commands the
unclean spirits, and they come out." And rumor 37
concerning him went forth into every place of
the region roundabout.

Peter's Mother-in-law

But he rose from the synagogue and entered 38
Simon's house. Now Simon's mother-in-law was
suffering from a great fever, and they besought
him for her. And standing over her he rebuked 39
the fever, and it left her; and she rose at once
and began to wait on them.

Other Miracles

Now when the sun was setting, all who had 40
persons sick with various diseases brought them
to him. And he laid his hands upon each of them
and cured them. And devils also came forth 41

from many, crying out and saying, "Thou art the Son of God." And he rebuked them, and did not permit them to speak, because they knew that he was the Christ.

42 Now when it was day, he went out and departed into a desert place. And the crowds were seeking after him, and they came to him, and tried to detain him, that he might not depart
43 from them. But he said to them, "To the other towns also I must proclaim the kingdom of God,
44 for this is why I have been sent." And he was preaching in the synagogues of Galilee.

The First Disciples Called

5 1 Now it came to pass, while the crowds were pressing upon him to hear the word of God, that he was standing by Lake Genesareth.
2 And he saw two boats moored by the lake, but the fishermen had left them and were washing
3 their nets. And getting into one of the boats, the one that was Simon's, he asked him to put out a little from the land. And sitting down, he began
4 to teach the crowds from the boat. But when he had ceased speaking, he said to Simon, "Put out into the deep, and lower your nets for a catch."

5 And Simon answered and said to him, "Master, the whole night through we have toiled and have taken nothing; but at thy word I will
6 lower the net." And when they had done so, they enclosed a great number of fishes, but
7 their net was breaking. And they beckoned to their comrades in the other boat to come and help them. And they came and filled both the boats, so that they began to sink.

8 But when Simon Peter saw this, he fell down at Jesus' knees, saying, "Depart from me, for I

am a sinful man, O Lord." For he and all who 9
were with him were amazed at the catch of fish
they had made; ¹ and so were also James and 10
John, the sons of Zebedee, who were partners
with Simon. And Jesus said to Simon, "Do not
be afraid; henceforth thou shalt catch men."
And when they had brought their boats to land, 11
they left all and followed him.

A Leper

And it came to pass, while he was 12
in one of the towns, that, behold,
there was a man full of leprosy. And when he
saw Jesus he fell on his face and besought him,
saying, "Lord, if thou wilt, thou canst make me
clean." And stretching forth his hand he touched 13
him, saying, "I will; be thou made clean." And
immediately the leprosy left him. And he charged 14
him to tell no man, but, "Go, show thyself to the
priest, and offer the gift for thy purification, as
Moses commanded, for a witness to them."

But so much the more the tidings spread 15
concerning him, and great crowds gathered together to hear him and to be cured of their sicknesses. But he himself was in retirement in the 16
desert, and in prayer.

And it came to pass on one of the days, that 17
he sat teaching. And there were Pharisees and
teachers of the Law sitting by, who had come
out of every village of Galilee and Judea and out
of Jerusalem. And the power of the Lord was
present to heal them.

A Paralytic at Capharnaum

And behold, some men were carrying upon 18
a pallet a man who was paralyzed, and they
were trying to bring him in and to lay him before
him. And as they found no way of bringing him 19

MAR. 7
Sept. 6

in, because of the crowd, they went up onto the
roof and lowered him through the tiles, with his
20 pallet, into the midst before Jesus. And seeing
their faith, he said, "Man, thy sins are forgiven
thee."

21 And the Scribes and Pharisees began to argue,
saying, "Who is this man who speaks blasphemies? Who can forgive sins, but God only?"

22 But Jesus, knowing their thoughts, answered
and said to them, "Why are you arguing in your
23 hearts? 'Which is easier, to say, 'Thy sins are
24 forgiven thee,' or to say, 'Arise and walk'? ' But
that you may know that the Son of Man has
power on earth to forgive sins"—he said to the
paralytic—"I say to thee, arise, take up thy
pallet and go to thy house."

25 And immediately he arose before them, took
up what he had been lying on, and went away to
26 his house, glorifying God. And astonishment
seized upon them all, and they glorified God and
were filled with fear, saying, "We have seen
wonderful things today."

The Call of Levi

27 And after this he went forth; and
he saw a publican, named Levi, sit-

ting in the tax-collector's place, and he said to
28 him, "Follow me." And leaving all things, he
29 arose and followed him. And Levi gave a great
feast for him at his house; and there was a
great gathering of publicans and of others, who
30 were at the table with them. And the Pharisees
and their Scribes were grumbling, saying to his
disciples, "Why do you eat and drink with publi-
31 cans and sinners?" And Jesus answered and
said to them, "It is not the healthy who need a
32 physician, but they who are sick. I have not come
to call the just, but sinners, to repentance."

The Question of Fasting

Now they said to him, "Why do the disciples of 33 John fast often and make supplications, and likewise those of the Pharisees, whereas thy disciples eat and drink?" He said to them, "Can 34 you make the wedding guests fast as long as the bridegroom is with them? But the days will 35 come—and when the bridegroom shall be taken away from them, then they will fast in those days."

And he spoke a parable also to them, "No one 36 puts a patch from a new garment on an old garment; else not only does he tear the new one, but the patch from the new garment does not match the old. And no one pours new wine into 37 old wine-skins; else the new wine will burst the skins, and will be spilt itself, and the skins ruined. But new wine must be put into fresh 38 skins, and both are saved. And no man after 39 drinking old wine immediately desires new; for he says, 'The old is better.'"

The Disciples Pluck Grain on the Sabbath

Now it came to pass on the second first Sabbath, that he was going through standing grain, and his disciples were plucking and eating the ears of grain, rubbing them with their hands. But some of the Phari- 2

| MAR. 9 |
| Sept. 8 |

6 1

5, 34f: Jesus is the bridegroom, and His wedding guests (literally, children of the bridegroom) are His disciples. It is repugnant to Jewish custom to think of fasting and mourning during the period of the wedding festivities. But when He is taken away from them, then His disciples will fittingly fast and mourn.

5, 36-39: In these two similes Jesus refers to the differences between the old dispensation, which was coming to an end, and the new order, which was foretold by the prophets and which He began to establish. These two orders are incompatible and cannot be made to match.

sees said to them, "Why are you doing what is
3 not lawful on the Sabbath?" And Jesus answered and said to them, "Have you not, then,
read what David did when he and those with
4 him were hungry? how he entered the house of
God, and took, ate, and gave to those who were
with him, the loaves of proposition, which no
5 one may lawfully eat except the priests?" And
he said to them, "The Son of Man is Lord even
of the Sabbath."

A Man with a Withered Hand

6   And it came to pass on another Sabbath, that
he entered the synagogue and taught. And a man
7 was there and his right hand was withered. And
the Scribes and the Pharisees were watching
whether he cured on the Sabbath, that they
8 might find how to accuse him. But he knew their
thoughts, and he said to the man with the
withered hand, "Arise and stand forth in the
9 midst." And he arose and stood forth. But
Jesus said to them, "I ask you, is it lawful on the
Sabbath to do good, or to do evil? to save a life,
10 or to destroy it?" And having looked around
upon them all, he said to the man, "Stretch
forth thy hand." And he stretched it forth, and
11 his hand was restored. But they were filled with
fury, and began to discuss among themselves
what they should do to Jesus.

The Choice of the Twelve

12   Now it came to pass in those days, that he
went out to the mountain to pray, and continued
13 all night in prayer to God. And when day broke,
he summoned his disciples; and from these he
chose twelve (whom he also named apostles):

Simon, whom he named Peter, and his brother 14
Andrew; James and John; Philip and Bartholomew; Matthew and Thomas; James the son of 15
Alpheus, and Simon called the Zealot; Jude the
brother of James, and Judas Iscariot, who 16
turned traitor.

III

The Sermon on the Mount: The Scene

AND COMING DOWN with them, he took his 17
stand on a level stretch, with a crowd of his
disciples, and a great multitude of people from
all Judea and Jerusalem, and the sea coast of
Tyre and Sidon, who came to listen to him and 18
to be healed of their diseases. And those who
were troubled with unclean spirits were cured.
And all the crowd were trying to touch him, for 19
power went forth from him and healed all.

The Beatitudes and Woes

And he lifted up his eyes to his disciples, and 20
said, "Blessed are you poor, for yours is the
kingdom of God. Blessed are you who hunger 21
now, for you shall be satisfied. Blessed are you
who weep now, for you shall laugh. Blessed shall 22
you be when men hate you, and when they shut
you out, and reproach you, and reject your name
as evil, because of the Son of Man. Rejoice on 23
that day and exult, for behold your reward is
great in heaven. For in the selfsame manner their
fathers used to treat the prophets. But woe to 24
you rich! for you are now having your comfort.
Woe to you who are filled! for you shall hunger. 25
Woe to you who laugh now! for you shall mourn
and weep. Woe to you when all men speak well 26
of you! In the selfsame manner their fathers
used to treat the prophets.

The Rules of Charity

27   "But I say to you who are listen- | MAR. 10
ing: Love your enemies, do good to | Sept. 9
28 those who hate you. Bless those who curse you,
29 pray for those who calumniate you. And to him
who strikes thee on the one cheek, offer the
other also; and from him who takes away thy
30 cloak, do not withhold thy tunic either. Give to
everyone who asks of thee, and from him who
31 takes away thy goods, ask no return. And even
as you wish men to do to you, so also do you to
32 them. And if you love those who love you, what
merit have you? For even sinners love those who
33 love them. And if you do good to those who do
good to you, what merit have you? For even
34 sinners do that. And if you lend to those from
whom you hope to receive in return, what merit
have you? For even sinners lend to sinners that
35 they may get back as much in return. But
love your enemies, and do good, and lend, not
hoping for any return, and your reward shall be
great, and you shall be children of the Most
High, for he is kind towards the ungrateful and
36 evil. Be merciful, therefore, even as your Father
is merciful.

37   "Do not judge, and you shall not be judged;
do not condemn, and you shall not be condemned. Forgive, and you shall be forgiven;
38 'give, and it shall be given to you; good measure,
pressed down, shaken together, running over,
shall they pour into your lap. For with what
measure you measure, it shall be measured to
you."

Self-examination

39   And he spoke a parable also to them, "Can
a blind man guide a blind man? Will not both fall

into a pit? No disciple is above his teacher, but 40 when perfected, everyone will be like his teacher. But why dost thou see the speck in thy brother's 41 eye, and yet dost not consider the beam in thy own eye? And how canst thou say to thy brother, 42 'Brother, let me cast out the speck from thy eye,' while thou thyself dost not see the beam in thy own eye? Thou hypocrite, first cast out the beam from thy own eye, and then thou wilt see clearly to cast out the speck from thy brother's eye.

"For there is no good tree that bears bad fruit, 43 nor is there a bad tree that bears good fruit. For 44 every tree is known by its fruit. For from thorns men do not gather figs, neither from a bramble do they harvest grapes. The good man from the 45 good treasure of his heart brings forth that which is good; and the evil man from the evil treasure brings forth that which is evil. For out of the abundance of the heart the mouth speaks.

Conclusion of the Sermon

"But why do you call me, 'Lord, Lord,' and 46 not practise the things that I say? Everyone who 47 comes to me and hears my words and acts upon them, I will show you what he is like: ' he is like a 48 man building a house, who dug deep and laid a foundation upon rock. And when a flood came, the stream broke against that house and could not shake it; because it was founded on rock. But 49 he who has heard my words and has not acted upon them is like a man who built his house upon the ground without a foundation; against which the stream broke and straightway it fell in, and great was the wreck of that house."

The Centurion's Servant

7 1 When he had finished all his discourse in the hearing of the people, 2 he entered Capharnaum. Now a servant of a certain centurion, to whom he was dear, was 3 sick to the point of death. And the centurion, hearing of Jesus, sent to him elders of the Jews, beseeching him to come and save his servant. 4 And when they came to Jesus, they entreated him earnestly, saying to him, "He is worthy that 5 thou shouldst do this for him, ' for he loves our nation and himself has built us our synagogue."

6 So Jesus went with them. And when he was now not far from the house, the centurion sent friends to say to him, "Lord, do not trouble thyself, for I am not worthy that thou shouldst 7 come under my roof; ' this is why I did not think myself worthy to come to thee. But say the 8 word, and my servant will be healed. For I too am a man subject to authority, and have soldiers subject to me; and I say to one, 'Go,' and he goes; and to another, 'Come,' and he comes; and to my servant, 'Do this,' and he does it." 9 Now when Jesus heard this, he marvelled, and turning to the crowd that followed him, said, "Amen I say to you, not even in Israel have I 10 found such great faith." And when the messengers returned to the house, they found the servant in good health who had been ill.

MAR. 11
Sept. 10

The Widow's Son

11 And it came to pass soon afterwards, that he went to a town called Naim; and his disciples 12 and a large crowd went with him. And as he drew near the gate of the town, behold, a dead man was being carried out, the only son of his mother, and she was a widow; and a large

gathering from the town was with her. And the 13
Lord, seeing her, had compassion on her, and
said to her, "Do not weep." · And he went up 14
and touched the stretcher; and the bearers stood
still. And he said, "Young man, I say to thee,
arise." And he who was dead, sat up, and began 15
to speak. And he gave him to his mother.

But fear seized upon all, and they began to 16
glorify God, saying, "A great prophet has risen
among us," and "God has visited his people."
And this report concerning him went forth 17
throughout the whole of Judea, and all the
country roundabout.

The Baptist's Deputation

And John's disciples brought him word of all 18
these things. And John summoned two of his 19
disciples and sent them to the Lord, saying, "Art
thou he who is to come, or shall we look for
another?"

And when the men had come to him, they said, 20
"John the Baptist has sent us to thee, saying,
'Art thou he who is to come, or shall we look for
another?' " In that very hour he cured many of 21
diseases, afflictions and evil spirits, and to many
who were blind he granted sight. And he an- 22
swered and said to them, "Go and report to
John what you have heard and seen: the blind
see, the lame walk, the lepers are cleansed, the
deaf hear, the dead rise, the poor have the gospel
preached to them. And blessed is he who is not 23
scandalized in me."

7, 19: The Baptist asked this question for the benefit of
his disciples and the people. He wished to convince them
fully that Jesus was the Messias.

Christ's Witness Concerning John

24 Then, as the messengers of John left, he began to say to the crowds concerning John, "What did you go out to the desert to see? A reed shaken by the wind?

MAR. 12
Sept. 11

25 But what did you go out to see? A man clothed in soft garments? Behold, those who wear fine clothes and live in luxury are in the houses of
26 kings. But what did you go out to see? A prophet? Yes, I tell you, and more than a prophet.
27 This is he of whom it is written, 'Behold, I
28 send my messenger before thy face, who shall make ready thy way before thee.' I say to you, among those born of women there is not a greater prophet than John the Baptist; yet the least in the kingdom of God is greater than he."
29 And when they had heard him, all the people and the publicans justified God, having been
30 baptized with the baptism of John. But the Pharisees and the lawyers, not having been baptized by him, brought to naught God's purpose concerning themselves.

The Stubborn Children

31 "To what then shall I liken the men of this
32 generation? And what are they like? They are like children sitting in the market place, calling to one another and saying, 'We have piped to you, and you have not danced; we have sung
33 dirges, and you have not wept.' For John the Baptist came neither eating bread nor drinking
34 wine, and you say, 'He has a devil.' The Son of Man came eating and drinking, and you say, 'Behold a man who is a glutton, and a wine-

---

7, 29: *Justified God:* acknowledged in their baptism the mercy of God manifest in the Baptist's preaching.

drinker, a friend of publicans and sinners!'
And wisdom is justified by all her children." 35

The Penitent Woman

Now one of the Pharisees asked him to dine 36
with him; so he went into the house of the
Pharisee and reclined at table. And behold, a 37
woman in the town who was a sinner, upon
learning that he was at table in the Pharisee's
house, brought an alabaster jar of ointment;' and 38
standing behind him at his feet, she began to
bathe his feet with her tears, and wiped them
with the hair of her head, and kissed his feet,
and anointed them with ointment.

Now when the Pharisee, who had invited him, 39
saw it, he said to himself, "This man, were he a
prophet, would surely know who and what manner of woman this is who is touching him, for
she is a sinner."

And Jesus answered and said to him, "Simon, 40
I have something to say to thee." And he said,
"Master, speak."' "A certain money-lender had 41
two debtors; the one owed five hundred denarii,
the other fifty. As they had no means of paying, 42
he forgave them both. Which of them, therefore,
will love him more?"' Simon answered and said, 43
"He, I suppose, to whom he forgave more."
And he said to him, "Thou hast judged rightly."
And turning to the woman, he said to Simon, 44
"Dost thou see this woman? I came into thy
house; thou gavest me no water for my feet; but
she has bathed my feet with tears, and has wiped
them with her hair. Thou gavest me no kiss; but 45
she, from the moment she entered, has not
ceased to kiss my feet. Thou didst not anoint my 46
head with oil; but she has anointed my feet with
ointment. Wherefore I say to thee, her sins, 47

[171]

many as they are, shall be forgiven her, because she has loved much. But he to whom little is
48 forgiven, loves little." ' And he said to her, "Thy
49 sins are forgiven." And they who were at table with him began to say within themselves, "Who
50 is this man, who even forgives sins?" ' But he said to the woman, "Thy faith has saved thee; go in peace."

The Ministering Women

8 1   And it came to pass afterwards, that he was journeying through towns and villages, preaching and proclaiming the good news of the kingdom of God. And with

MAR. 13
Sept. 12

2 him were the Twelve, and certain women who had been cured of evil spirits and infirmities: Mary, who is called the Magdalene, from whom
3 seven devils had gone out, ' and Joanna, the wife of Chuza, Herod's steward, and Susanna, and many others, who used to provide for them out of their means.

Parable of the Sower

4   Now when a very great crowd was gathering together and men from every town were resort-
5 ing to him, he said in a parable: "The sower went out to sow his seed. And as he sowed, some seed fell by the wayside and was trodden under foot,
6 and the birds of the air ate it up. And other seed fell upon the rock, and as soon as it had sprung up it withered away, because it had no moisture.
7 And other seed fell among thorns, and the thorns
8 sprang up with it and choked it. And other seed fell upon good ground, and sprang up and yielded fruit a hundredfold." As he said these things he cried out, "He who has ears to hear, let him hear!"

But his disciples then began to ask him what 9
this parable meant. He said to them, "To you it 10
is given to know the mystery of the kingdom of
God, but to the rest in parables, that 'Seeing they
may not see, and hearing they may not understand.'

"Now the parable is this: the seed is the word 11
of God. And those by the wayside are they who 12
have heard; then the devil comes and takes away
the word from their heart, that they may not
believe and be saved. Now those upon the rock 13
are they who, when they have heard, receive the
word with joy; and these have no root, but
believe for a while, and in time of temptation
fall away. And that which fell among the thorns, 14
these are they who have heard, and as they go
their way are choked by the cares and riches
and pleasures of life, and their fruit does not
ripen. But that upon good ground, these are they 15
who, with a right and good heart, having heard
the word, hold it fast, and bear fruit in patience.

Purpose of This Teaching

"Now no one, when he has lighted a lamp, 16
covers it with a vessel, or puts it under a couch,
but he puts it upon a lamp-stand, that they who
enter may see the light. For there is nothing 17
hidden that will not be made manifest; nor
anything concealed that will not be known and
come to light. Take heed, therefore, how you 18
hear; for to him who has shall be given; and from
him who does not have, even what he thinks he
has shall be taken away."

Jesus and His Brethren

Now his mother and brethren came to him; 19
and they could not get to him because of the
crowd. And it was told him, "Thy mother and thy 20

brethren are standing outside, wishing to see
21 thee." But he answered and said to them,
"My mother and my brethren are they who hear
the word of God, and act upon it."

The Storm on the Lake

22 Now it came to pass on one of
those days, that he and his disciples
got into a boat, and he said to them, "Let us cross
over to the other side of the lake." And they put
23 out to sea. But as they were sailing, he fell
asleep. And a squall swept down upon the lake,
24 and they were filling and were in peril. So they
came and woke him, saying, "Master, we are
perishing." Then he arose and rebuked the wind
and the raging of the water; and they ceased,
25 and there came a calm. And he said to them,
"Where is your faith?" But they were afraid,
and marvelled, saying to one another, "Who,
then, is this, that he commands even the winds
and the sea, and they obey him?"

MAR. 14
Sept. 13

Expulsion of the Devils in Gerasa

26 And they sailed to the country of the Gera-
27 senes, which is opposite Galilee. Now when he
landed, there met him a certain man who for a
long time was possessed by a devil, and wore no
clothes, and lived in the tombs, not in a house.
28 And when he saw Jesus, he fell down before him,
and crying out with a loud voice said, "What
have I to do with thee, Jesus, Son of the most
high God? I pray thee, do not torment me."
29 For he was charging the unclean spirit to go
forth from the man. For many times it had laid
hold of him; and he was bound with chains and
fetters, and kept under guard, but he would
break the bonds asunder, and be driven by the
devil into the deserts.

And Jesus asked him, saying, "What is thy 30 name?" And he said, "Legion," because many devils had entered into him. And they entreated 31 him not to command them to depart into the abyss.

Now a herd of many swine was there, feeding 32 on the mountainside. And they kept entreating him to give them leave to enter into them. And he gave them leave. And the devils came out 33 from the man and entered into the swine; and the herd rushed down the cliff into the lake and were drowned.

And when the swineherds saw what had hap- 34 pened, they fled and reported it in the town and in the country; and people came out to see what 35 had happened. And they came to Jesus, and found the man from whom the devils had gone out sitting at his feet, clothed and in his right mind, and they were afraid. And those also who 36 had seen it reported to them how he had been saved from Legion. And all the people of the Gera- 37 sene district besought him to depart from them; for they were seized with great fear.

And he got into a boat and went back. ' But 38 the man from whom the devils had gone out prayed him that he might remain with him. But Jesus sent him away, saying, ' "Return to thy 39 house, and tell all that God has done for thee." And he departed, publishing throughout the whole town all that Jesus had done for him.

8, 32f: He granted the devils permission to enter the swine, thereby showing His Apostles the reality of de- moniac possession and expulsion, the power of Satan as well as the dependence of the devil upon the permissive will of God and upon His own superior power.

The Daughter of Jairus; the Woman with a Hemorrhage

40 Now it came to pass when Jesus had returned, that the crowd welcomed him, for they were all waiting for him.

MAR. 15
Sept. 14

41 And behold, there came a man named Jairus, and he was a ruler of the synagogue; and falling at the feet of Jesus, he entreated him to come to 42 his house, for he had an only daughter about twelve years of age, and she was dying.

And it happened as he went that he was 43 pressed upon by the crowds. And a certain woman who for twelve years had had a hemorrhage, and had spent all her means on physicians, but 44 could not be cured by anyone, came up behind him and touched the tassel of his cloak; and at once her hemorrhage ceased.

45 And Jesus said, "Who touched me?" But as all were denying it, Peter, and those who were with him, said, "Master, the crowds throng and press upon thee, and dost thou say, 'Who touched 46 me?'" But Jesus said, "Someone touched me; for I perceived that power had gone forth from 47 me." But the woman, seeing that she had not escaped notice, came up trembling, and falling down at his feet, declared in the presence of all the people why she had touched him, and how she 48 had been healed instantly. And he said to her, "Daughter, thy faith has saved thee; go in peace."

49 While he was yet speaking, there came one from the house of the ruler of the synagogue, saying to him, "Thy daughter is dead; do not 50 trouble him." But Jesus on hearing this answered the father of the girl, "Do not be afraid; only have faith and she shall be saved."

51 And when he came to the house, he allowed

no one to enter with him, except Peter and James and John, and the girl's father and mother. And all were weeping and mourning for 52 her. But he said, "Do not weep; she is asleep, not dead." And they laughed him to scorn, know- 53 ing that she was dead. But he, taking her by the 54 hand, cried out, saying, "Girl, arise!" And her 55 spirit returned, and she rose up immediately. And he directed that something be given her to eat. And her parents were amazed, but he 56 charged them to tell no one what had happened.

The Mission of the Apostles

Then having summoned the twelve apostles, he gave them power and authority over all the devils, and to cure diseases. And he sent them forth to preach 2 the kingdom of God, and to heal the sick. And 3 he said to them, "Take nothing for your journey, neither staff, nor wallet, nor bread, nor money; neither have two tunics. And whatever house 4 you enter, stay there, and do not leave the place. And whoever does not receive you—go 5 forth from that town, and shake off even the dust from your feet for a witness against them." And going forth, they went about from village 6 to village, preaching the gospel and working cures everywhere.

MAR. 16
Sept. 15

9 1

Now Herod the tetrarch heard of all that 7 was being done by him, and was much per- plexed, because it was said ' by some, "John 8 has risen from the dead"; and by some, "Elias has appeared"; and by others, "One of the prophets of old has risen again." But Herod 9 said, "John I beheaded; but who is this about whom I hear such things?" And he endeavored to see him.

10 And the apostles on their return reported to him all that they had done. And taking them with him, he withdrew apart to a desert place,
11 which belongs to Bethsaida. But the crowds on learning it followed him. And he welcomed them, and spoke to them of the kingdom of God, and those in need of cure he healed.

Jesus Feeds Five Thousand

12 Now the day began to decline; and the Twelve came up and said to him, "Send the crowds away, so that they may go into the villages and farms roundabout and find lodging and provisions, for we are in a desert place
13 here." But he said to them, "You yourselves give them some food." And they said, "We have not more than five loaves and two fishes, unless we are to go and buy food for all this
14 crowd." For there were about five thousand men present.

Then he said to his disciples, "Make them
15 recline in groups of fifties." And they did so,
16 and made them all recline. And he took the five loaves and the two fishes, and looking up to heaven, blessed them and broke the loaves, and gave them to his disciples to set before the
17 crowds. And all ate and were satisfied; and what was left over to them was gathered up, twelve baskets of fragments.

IV

Peter's Confession; Passion and Resurrection Foretold

18 AND IT CAME TO PASS as he was praying in private, that his disciples also were with him, and he asked them, saying, "Who do the
19 crowds say that I am?" And they answered and

said, "John the Baptist; and others, Elias; and others, that one of the ancient prophets has risen again."

And he said to them, "But who do you say 20 that I am?" Simon Peter answered and said, "The Christ of God." But he strictly charged 21 them, and commanded them not to tell this to anyone, ' saying, "The Son of Man must suffer 22 many things, and be rejected by the elders and chief priests and Scribes, and be put to death, and on the third day rise again."

The Doctrine of the Cross

And he said to all, "If anyone wishes to come after me, let him ┌─────────┐ 23
│ MAR. 17 │
│ Sept. 16 │
└─────────┘
deny himself, and take up his cross daily, and follow me. For he who would save his life will 24 lose it; but he who loses his life for my sake will save it. For what does it profit a man, if he 25 gain the whole world, but ruin or lose himself? For whoever is ashamed of me and my words, 26 of him will the Son of Man be ashamed when he comes in his glory and that of the Father and of the holy angels. But I say to you truly, there 27 are some of those standing here who will not taste death, till they have seen the kingdom of God."

Jesus Transfigured

Now it came to pass about eight days after 28 these words, that he took Peter, James and John and went up the mountain to pray. And 29 as he prayed, the appearance of his countenance was changed, and his raiment became a radiant white. And behold, two men were talking with 30 him. And these were Moses and Elias, ' who, 31 appearing in glory, spoke of his death, which he was about to fulfill in Jerusalem.

32 　　Now Peter and his companions were heavy with sleep. But when they were fully awake, they saw his glory and the two men who were
33 standing with him. And it came to pass as they were parting from him, that Peter said to Jesus, "Master, it is good for us to be here. And let us set up three tents, one for thee, and one for Moses, and one for Elias," not knowing
34 what he said. But as he was speaking thus, there came a cloud and overshadowed them; and they were afraid as they entered the
35 cloud. And there came a voice out of the cloud, saying, "This is my beloved Son; hear him."
36 And after the voice had passed, Jesus was found alone. And they kept silence and told no one at that time any of these things that they had seen.

A Possessed Boy

37 　　Now it came to pass on the following day, when they came down from the mountain,
38 that a large crowd met him. And behold, a man from the crowd cried out, saying, "Master, I pray thee to look at my son, for he is my only
39 child; and behold, a spirit seizes him and he suddenly cries out; and it throws him down and convulses him so that he foams, and bruis-
40 ing him sorely, it scarcely leaves him. And I prayed thy disciples to cast it out, but they could not."
41 　　But Jesus answered and said, "O unbelieving and perverse generation, how long shall I be with you and put up with you? Bring thy son
42 here to me." And as he was yet coming near, the devil cast him down and threw him into
43 convulsions. But Jesus rebuked the unclean spirit and healed the boy, and restored him to
44 his father. And all were astounded at the majesty of God.

[180]

The Second Prediction of the Passion

But while all marvelled at all the things that he was doing, he said to his disciples, "Store up these words in your minds: the Son of Man is to be betrayed into the hands of men." But they did not understand 45 this saying, and it was hidden from them, that they might not perceive it; and they were afraid to ask him about this saying.

MAR. 18
Sept. 17

Against Ambition and Envy

Now a discussion arose among them, which 46 of them was the greatest. But Jesus, knowing 47 the reasoning of their heart, took a little child and set him at his side, and said to them, 48 "Whoever receives this little child for my sake, receives me; and whoever receives me, receives him who sent me. For he who is the least among you, he is the greatest."

But John answered and said, "Master, we 49 saw a man casting out devils in thy name, and we forbade him, because he does not follow with us." And Jesus said to him, "Do 50 not forbid him; for he who is not against you is for you."

V

The Unfriendly Samaritans

NOW IT CAME TO PASS, when the days had 51 come for him to be taken up, that he steadfastly set his face to go to Jerusalem, and sent 52 messengers before him. And they went and entered a Samaritan town to make ready for him; and they did not receive him, because his 53 face was set for Jerusalem. But when his disciples James and John saw this, they said, 54

[181]

"Lord, wilt thou that we bid fire come down from heaven and consume them?"

55 But he turned and rebuked them, saying, "You do not know of what manner of spirit
56 you are; for the Son of Man did not come to destroy men's lives, but to save them." And they went to another village.

Sacrifice to Follow Christ

57 And it came to pass as they went on their journey, that a man said to him, "I will follow
58 thee wherever thou goest." And Jesus said to him, "The foxes have dens, and the birds of the air have nests, but the Son of Man has nowhere to lay his head."

59 And he said to another, "Follow me." But he said, "Lord, let me first go and bury my
60 father." But Jesus said to him, "Let the dead bury their dead, but do thou go and proclaim
61 the kingdom of God." And another said, "I will follow thee, Lord, but let me first bid fare-
62 well to those at home." Jesus said to him, "No one, having put his hand to the plow and looking back, is fit for the kingdom of God."

The Seventy-two Disciples

10 1 Now after this the Lord appointed seventy-two others, and

MAR. 19
Sept. 18

sent them forth two by two before him into every town and place where he himself was about to
2 come. And he said to them, "The harvest indeed is great, but the laborers are few. Pray therefore the Lord of the harvest to send forth laborers into his harvest.

9, 62: Undivided attention is required of the disciples of Jesus.

"Go. Behold, I send you forth as lambs in the ³ midst of wolves. Carry neither purse, nor wallet, ⁴ nor sandals, and greet no one on the way. Whatever house you enter, first say, 'Peace to ⁵ this house!' And if a son of peace be there, your ⁶ peace will rest upon him; but if not, it will return to you. And remain in the same house, eating ⁷ and drinking what they have; for the laborer deserves his wages. Do not go from house to house. And whatever town you enter, and they ⁸ receive you, eat what is set before you, ' and ⁹ cure the sick who are there, and say to them, 'The kingdom of God is at hand for you.' ' But ¹⁰ whatever town you enter, and they do not receive you—go out into its streets and say, ' 'Even the ¹¹ dust from your town that cleaves to us we shake off against you; yet know this, that the kingdom of God is at hand.' I say to you, that it will be ¹² more tolerable for Sodom in that day than for that town.

The Impenitent Towns

"Woe to thee, Corozain! woe to thee, Beth- ¹³ saida! For if in Tyre and Sidon had been worked the miracles that have been worked in you, they would have repented long ago, sitting in sackcloth and ashes. But it will be more tolerable for ¹⁴ Tyre and Sidon at the judgment than for you. And thou, Capharnaum, shalt thou be exalted to ¹⁵ heaven? Thou shalt be thrust down to hell.

"He who hears you, hears me; and he who ¹⁶ rejects you, rejects me; and he who rejects me, rejects him who sent me."

10, 4: The disciples are not to spend much unnecessary time in long oriental salutations, but are rather to devote themselves without delay and distraction to their higher calling.

Return of the Disciples

17 Now the seventy-two returned with joy, saying, "Lord, even the devils are subject to us in thy
18 name." ' But he said to them, "I was watching
19 Satan fall as lightning from heaven. Behold, I have given you power to tread upon serpents and scorpions, and over all the might of the enemy;
20 and nothing shall hurt you. But do not rejoice in this, that the spirits are subject to you; rejoice rather in this, that your names are written in heaven."

Jesus Draws Men Gently to Himself

21 In that very hour he rejoiced in the Holy Spirit and said, "I praise thee, Father, Lord of heaven and earth, that thou didst hide these things from the wise and prudent, and didst reveal them to little ones. Yes,

MAR. 20
Sept. 19

22 Father, for such was thy good pleasure. All things have been delivered to me by my Father; and no one knows who the Son is except the Father, and who the Father is except the Son, and him to whom the Son chooses to reveal him."
23 And turning to his disciples he said, "Blessed
24 are the eyes that see what you see! For I say to you, many prophets and kings have desired to see what you see, and they have not seen it; and to hear what you hear, and they have not heard it."

The Great Commandment:
The Good Samaritan

25 And behold, a certain lawyer got up to test him, saying, "Master, what must I do to gain
26 eternal life?" But he said to him, "What is
27 written in the Law? How dost thou read?" ' He answered and said, "Thou shalt love the Lord thy God with thy whole heart, and with thy

whole soul, and with thy whole strength, and with thy whole mind; and thy neighbor as thyself."

And he said to him, "Thou hast answered 28 rightly; do this and thou shalt live." But he, 29 wishing to justify himself, said to Jesus, "And who is my neighbor?"

Jesus answered, "A certain man was going 30 down from Jerusalem to Jericho, and he fell in with robbers, who after both stripping him and beating him went their way, leaving him half-dead. But, as it happened, a certain priest was 31 going down the same way, and when he saw him, he passed by. And likewise a Levite also, 32 when he was near the place and saw him, passed by. But a certain Samaritan as he journeyed 33 came upon him, and seeing him, was moved with compassion. And he went up to him and 34 bound up his wounds, pouring on oil and wine. And setting him on his own beast, he brought him to an inn and took care of him. And the next 35 day he took out two denarii and gave them to the innkeeper and said, 'Take care of him; and whatever more thou spendest, I, on my way back, will repay thee.'

"Which of these three, in thy opinion, proved 36 himself neighbor to him who fell among the robbers?" ' And he said, "He who took pity on 37 him." And Jesus said to him, "Go and do thou also in like manner."

Martha and Mary

Now it came to pass as they were on their journey, that he entered a certain village; and a woman named Martha 38 welcomed him to her house. And she had a sister 39 called Mary, who also seated herself at the Lord's feet, and listened to his word. But 40 Martha was busy about much serving. And she

MAR. 21
Sept. 20

came up and said, "Lord, is it no concern of thine that my sister has left me to serve alone? Tell her therefore to help me."

41 But the Lord answered and said to her, "Martha, Martha, thou art anxious and troubled about
42 many things; ' and yet only one thing is needful. Mary has chosen the best part, and it will not be taken away from her."

Lessons on Prayer

11 1 And it came to pass as he was praying in a certain place, that when he ceased, one of his disciples said to him, "Lord, teach us to pray,
2 even as John also taught his disciples." And he said to them, "When you pray, say: 'Father, hallowed be thy name. Thy kingdom come!
3, 4 Give us this day our daily bread, ' and forgive us our sins, for we also forgive everyone who is indebted to us. And lead us not into temptation.'"

5 And he said to them, "Which of you shall have a friend and shall go to him in the middle of the night and say to him, 'Friend, lend me three
6 loaves, ' for a friend of mine has just come to me from a journey, and I have nothing to set before
7 him'; ' and he from within should answer and say, 'Do not disturb me; the door is now shut, and my children and I are in bed; I cannot get up and give to thee'?

8 "I say to you, although he will not get up and give to him because he is his friend, yet because of his persistence he will get up and give him all
9 he needs. And I say to you, ask, and it shall be given to you; seek, and you shall find; knock,
10 and it shall be opened to you. For everyone who asks receives; and he who seeks finds;
11 and to him who knocks it shall be opened. But if one of you asks his father for a loaf, will he

hand him a stone? or for a fish, will he for a fish
hand him a serpent? ' or if he asks for an egg, 12
will he hand him a scorpion? Therefore, if you, 13
evil as you are, know how to give good gifts to
your children, how much more will your heavenly
Father give the Good Spirit to those who ask
him!"

Blasphemy of the Pharisees

And he was casting out a devil, | MAR. 22 | 14
and the same was dumb; and when | Sept. 21 |
he had cast out the devil, the dumb man spoke.
And the crowds marvelled. ' But some of them 15
said, "By Beelzebub, the prince of devils, he
casts out devils." And others, to test him, de- 16
manded from him a sign from heaven.

But he, seeing their thoughts, said to them: 17
"Every kingdom divided against itself is brought
to desolation, and house will fall upon house.
If, then, Satan also is divided against himself, 18
how shall his kingdom stand? Because you say
that I cast out devils by Beelzebub. Now, if I 19
cast out devils by Beelzebub, by whom do
your children cast them out? Therefore they
shall be your judges. But if I cast out devils by 20
the finger of God, then the kingdom of God
has come upon you. When the strong man, fully 21
armed, guards his courtyard, his property is
undisturbed. But if a stronger than he attacks 22
and overcomes him, he will take away all his
weapons that he relied upon, and will divide
his spoils. He who is not with me is against me; 23
and he who does not gather with me scatters.

11, 19: The "children" of the Pharisees are their disciples. They taught them formulas and practices to cast
out devils.

24 "When the unclean spirit has gone out of a man, he roams through waterless places in search of rest; and finding none, he says, 'I

25 will return to my house which I left.' And when he has come to it, he finds the place swept.

26 Then he goes and takes seven other spirits more evil than himself, and they enter in and dwell there; and the last state of that man becomes worse than the first."

The Praise of Mary

27 Now it came to pass as he was saying these things, that a certain woman from the crowd lifted up her voice and said to him, "Blessed is the womb that bore thee, and the breasts that

28 nursed thee." But he said, "Rather, blessed are they who hear the word of God and keep it."

The Sign of Jonas

29 And as the crowds were gathering together, he began to say, "This generation is an evil generation: it demands a sign, and no sign

30 shall be given it but the sign of Jonas. For even as Jonas was a sign to the Ninevites, so will

31 also the Son of Man be to this generation. The queen of the South will rise up in the judgment with the men of this generation and will condemn them; for she came from the ends of the earth to hear the wisdom of Solomon, and be-

32 hold, a greater than Solomon is here. The men of Nineve will rise up in the judgment with this generation and will condemn it; for they repented at the preaching of Jonas, and behold, a greater than Jonas is here.

11, 24-26: Jesus warns that a devil cast out may return with reinforcements, to an individual or to a society; here there is a warning to those who are rejecting Him. He uses a parable to present the idea: the impure spirit is like a robber who goes into the desert, etc.

A Lesson from a Lamp

"No one lights a lamp and puts
it in a cellar or even under the | MAR. 23
measure, but upon the lamp-stand, that they | Sept. 22
who enter in may see the light. The lamp of 34
thy body is thy eye. If thy eye be sound, thy
whole body will be full of light. But if it be evil,
thy body also will be full of darkness. Take 35
care, therefore, that the light that is in thee is
not darkness. If, then, thy whole body is full 36
of light, having no part in darkness, it will all be
illumined, as when a bright lamp illumines
thee."

Denunciation of the Pharisees

Now after he had spoken, a Pharisee asked 37
him to dine with him. And he went in and
reclined at table. But the Pharisee began to 38
ponder and ask himself why he had not washed
before dinner.

But the Lord said to him, "Now you Pharisees 39
clean the outside of the cup and the dish, but
within you are full of robbery and wickedness.
Foolish ones! did not he who made the outside 40
make the inside too? Nevertheless, give that 41
which remains as alms; and behold, all things
are clean to you.

"But woe to you Pharisees! because you pay 42
tithes on mint and rue and every herb, and disregard justice and the love of God. But these
things you ought to have done, while not leaving
the others undone. Woe to you Pharisees! be- 43
cause you love the front seats in the synagogues
and greetings in the market place. Woe to you! 44
because you are like hidden tombs, over which
men walk unaware."

11, 41: Worldly possessions should be used for good
purposes; the hearts of the Pharisees as well as their
vessels will be clean, if they use them so.

Denunciation of the Lawyers

45 But one of the lawyers, answering, said to him, "Master, in saying these things, thou in-
46 sultest us also." But he said, "Woe to you lawyers also! because you load men with oppressive burdens and you yourselves with one
47 of your fingers do not touch the burdens. Woe to you! for you build the tombs of the prophets,
48 whereas your fathers killed them. So then you are witnesses and approve the deeds of your fathers; for they indeed killed them, and you
49 build their tombs. For this reason also the wisdom of God has said, 'I will send them prophets and apostles; and some of them they
50 will put to death and persecute, that the blood of all the prophets that has been shed from the foundation of the world may be required of this
51 generation, from the blood of Abel unto the blood of Zacharias, who was slain between the altar and the temple.' Yes, I say to you, it shall
52 be required of this generation. Woe to you lawyers! because you have taken away the key of knowledge; you have not entered yourselves and those who were entering you have hindered."

53 After he had said these things to them, the Pharisees and the lawyers began to press him hard and to provoke him to speak on many
54 things, ' setting traps for him and plotting to seize upon something out of his mouth, that they might accuse him.

The Leaven of the Pharisees

12 1 Now when immense crowds had gathered together, so that they were treading on one another, he began to say to his disciples, "Beware of the leaven of the Phari-
2 sees, which is hypocrisy. But there is nothing

concealed that will not be disclosed, and nothing hidden that will not be made known. For what 3 you have said in darkness will be said in the light; and what you have whispered in the inner chambers will be preached on the housetops.

Encouragement in Persecution

"But I say to you, my friends: Do not be 4 afraid of those who kill the body, and after that have nothing more that they can do. But 5 I will show you whom you shall be afraid of; be afraid of him who, after he has killed, has power to cast into hell. Yes, I say to you, be afraid of him. Are not five sparrows sold for two 6 farthings? And yet not one of them is forgotten before God. Yes, the very hairs of your head 7 are all numbered. Therefore do not be afraid, you are of more value than many sparrows.

"And I say to you, everyone who acknowledges 8 me before men, him will the Son of Man also acknowledge before the angels of God. But 9 whoever disowns me before men will be disowned before the angels of God. And every- 10 one who speaks a word against the Son of Man, it shall be forgiven him; but to him who blasphemes against the Holy Spirit, it will not be forgiven.

"And when they bring you before the syna- 11 gogues and the magistrates and the authorities, do not be anxious how or wherewith you shall defend yourselves, or what you shall say, for 12 the Holy Spirit will teach you in that very hour what you ought to say."

A Warning against Avarice

Now one out of the crowd said to him, "Mas- 13 ter, tell my brother to divide the inheritance with me." But he said to him, "Man, who has 14

appointed me a judge or arbitrator over you?"
15 And he said to them, "Take heed and guard
yourselves from all covetousness, for a man's
life does not consist in the abundance of his
possessions."

16 But he spoke a parable to them, saying, "The
land of a certain rich man brought forth abun-
17 dant crops. And he began to take thought within
himself, saying, 'What shall I do, for I have
18 no room to store my crops?' And he said, 'I will
do this: I will pull down my barns and build
larger ones, and there I will store up all my
19 grain and my goods. And I will say to my soul,
Soul, thou hast many good things laid up for
many years; take thy ease, eat, drink, be
20 merry.' But God said to him, 'Thou fool, this
night do they demand thy soul of thee; and the
things that thou hast provided, whose will they
21 be?' So is he who lays up treasure for himself,
and is not rich as regards God."

Trust in God

22 But he said to his disciples,
"Therefore I say to you, do not be
anxious for your life, what you shall eat; nor yet

MAR. 25
Sept. 24

23 for your body, what you shall put on. The life is a
greater thing than the food, and the body than
24 the clothing. Consider the ravens: they neither
sow nor reap, they have neither storeroom nor
barn; yet God feeds them. Of how much more
25 value are you than they! But which of you by
being anxious about it can add to his stature a
26 single cubit? Therefore if you are not able to do
even a very little thing, why are you anxious
concerning the rest?

27 "Consider how the lilies grow; they neither
toil nor spin, yet I say to you that not even
Solomon in all his glory was arrayed like one

of these. But if God so clothes the grass which 28
flourishes in the field today but tomorrow is
thrown into the oven, how much more you, O
you of little faith!

"And as for you, do not seek what you shall 29
eat, or what you shall drink; and do not exalt
yourselves ' (for after all these things the nations 30
of the world seek); but your Father knows that
you need these things. But seek the kingdom of 31
God, and all these things shall be given you
besides.

"Do not be afraid, little flock, for it has pleased 32
your Father to give you the kingdom. Sell what 33
you have and give alms. Make for yourselves
purses that do not grow old, a treasure unfailing
in heaven, where neither thief draws near nor
moth destroys. For where your treasure is, there 34
also will your heart be.

The Watchful Servants

"Let your loins be girt about and your lamps 35
burning, ' and you yourselves like men waiting 36
for their master's return from the wedding; so
that when he comes and knocks, they may
straightway open to him. Blessed are those 37
servants whom the master, on his return, shall
find watching. Amen I say to you, he will gird
himself, and will make them recline at table, and
will come and serve them. And if he comes in 38
the second watch, and if in the third, and finds
them so, blessed are those servants!

"But of this be assured, that if the householder 39
had known at what hour the thief was coming,
he would certainly have watched, and not have
let his house be broken into. You also must be 40
ready, because at an hour that you do not expect,
the Son of Man is coming."

And Peter said to him, "Lord, dost thou speak 41
this parable for us or for all alike?"

Exhortation to Vigilance

42 And the Lord said, "Who, dost | MAR. 26
thou think, is the faithful and pru- | Sept. 25
dent steward whom the master will set over his
household to give them their ration of grain in
43 due time? Blessed is that servant whom his
44 master, when he comes, shall find so doing. Truly
I say to you, he will set him over all his goods.
45 But if that servant says to himself, 'My master
delays his coming,' and begins to beat the men-
servants and the maids, and to eat and drink, and to
46 get drunk,' the master of that servant will come on
a day he does not expect, and in an hour he does
not know, and will cut him asunder and make
47 him share the lot of the unfaithful. But that
servant who knew his master's will, and did not
make ready for him and did not act according to
his will, will be beaten with many stripes.
48 Whereas he who did not know it, but did things
deserving of stripes, will be beaten with few.
But of everyone to whom much has been given,
much will be required; and of him to whom they
have entrusted much, they will demand the more.

The Necessity of Struggle

49 "I have come to cast fire upon the earth, and
50 what will I but that it be kindled? But I have a
baptism to be baptized with; and how distressed
51 I am until it is accomplished! Do you think that
I came to give peace upon the earth? No, I tell
52 you, but division. For henceforth in one house
five will be divided, three against two, and two
53 against three. They will be divided, father against
son and son against his father; mother against
daughter and daughter against the mother;
mother-in-law against her daughter-in-law and
daughter-in-law against her mother-in-law."

Time for Reconciliation

And he said also to the crowds, "When you 54
see a cloud rising in the west, you say at once,
'A shower is coming,' and so it comes to pass.
And when you see the south wind blow, you say, 55
'There will be a scorching heat,' and so it comes
to pass. You hypocrites! you know how to judge 56
the face of the sky and of the earth; but how is it
that you do not judge this time? But why even of 57
yourselves do you not judge what is right?

"And when thou art going with thy opponent 58
to the ruler, take pains to be quit of him on the
way; lest he deliver thee to the judge, and the
judge to the officer, and the officer cast thee into
prison. I say to thee, thou wilt not come out from 59
it until thou hast paid the very last mite."

The Necessity of Repentance

Now there came at that very time some who 13 1
brought him word about the Galileans, whose
blood Pilate had mingled with their sacrifices.
And he answered and said to them, "Do you 2
think that these Galileans were worse sinners
than all the other Galileans, because they have
suffered such things? I tell you, no; but unless 3
you repent, you will all perish in the same manner. Or those eighteen upon whom the tower of 4
Siloe fell and killed them; do you think that they
were more guilty than all the other dwellers in
Jerusalem? I tell you, no; but unless you repent, 5
you will all perish in the same manner."

A Barren Fig Tree

And he spoke this parable: "A ⎡ MAR. 27 ⎤ 6
certain man had a fig tree planted in ⎣ Sept. 26 ⎦
his vineyard; and he came seeking fruit thereon,
and found none. And he said to the vine-dresser, 7

'Behold, for three years now I have come seeking fruit on this fig tree, and I find none. Cut it down, therefore; why does it still encumber the
8 ground?' But he answered him and said, 'Sir, let it alone this year too, till I dig around it and
9 manure it. Perhaps it may bear fruit; but if not, then afterwards thou shalt cut it down.' "

A Stooped Woman

10 Now he was teaching in one of their syna-
11 gogues on the Sabbath. And behold, there was a woman who for eighteen years had had a sickness caused by a spirit; and she was bent over
12 and utterly unable to look upwards. When Jesus saw her, he called her to him and said to her, "Woman, thou art delivered from thy infirmity."
13 And he laid his hands upon her, and instantly she was made straight, and glorified God.

14 But the ruler of the synagogue, indignant that Jesus had cured on the Sabbath, addressed the crowd, saying, "There are six days in which one ought to work; on these therefore come and be
15 cured, and not on the Sabbath." But the Lord answered him and said, "Hypocrites! does not each one of you on the Sabbath loose his ox or ass from the manger, and lead it forth to water?
16 And this woman, daughter of Abraham as she is, whom Satan has bound, lo, for eighteen years, ought not she to be loosed from this bond on the Sabbath?"

17 And as he said these things, all his adversaries were put to shame; and the entire crowd rejoiced at all the glorious things that were done by him.

The Mustard Seed

18 He said therefore, "What is the kingdom of
19 God like, and to what shall I liken it? It is like a grain of mustard seed, which a man took and

cast into his own garden; and it grew and became a large tree, and the birds of the air dwelt in its branches."

The Leaven

And again he said, "To what shall I liken the 20 kingdom of God? It is like leaven, which a 21 woman took and buried in three measures of flour, until all of it was leavened."

The Narrow Gate

And he passed on through towns and vil- 22 lages, teaching and making his way towards Jerusalem. But someone said to him, "Lord, are 23 only a few to be saved?"

But he said to them, ' "Strive to enter by the 24 narrow gate; for many, I tell you, will seek to enter and will not be able. But when the master 25 of the house has entered and shut the door, you will begin to stand outside and knock at the door, saying, 'Lord, open for us!' And he shall say to you in answer, 'I do not know where you are from.' Then you shall begin to 26 say, 'We ate and drank in thy presence, and thou didst teach in our streets.' And he shall 27 say to you, 'I do not know where you are from. Depart from me, all you workers of iniquity.' There will be the weeping, and the gnashing of 28 teeth, when you shall see Abraham and Isaac and Jacob and all the prophets in the kingdom of God, but you yourselves cast forth outside. And they will come from the east and from the 29 west, from the north and from the south, and will feast in the kingdom of God. And behold, 30 there are those last who will be first, and there are those first who will be last."

13, 30: Many Gentiles will be called to salvation and take the place destined for the chosen people of Israel.

Jesus and Herod

31 On that same day certain Phari- | MAR. 28
sees came up, saying to him, "De- | Sept. 27
part and be on thy way, for Herod wants to
32 kill thee." And he said to them, "Go and say
to that fox, 'Behold, I cast out devils and perform cures today and tomorrow, and the third
33 day I am to end my course. Nevertheless, I
must go my way today and tomorrow and the
next day, for it cannot be that a prophet perish
outside Jerusalem.'

34 "Jerusalem, Jerusalem, thou who killest the
prophets, and stonest those who are sent to
thee! How often would I have gathered thy
children together, as a hen gathers her young
35 under her wings, but thou wouldst not! Behold,
your house is left to you. And I say to you, you
shall not see me until the time comes when
you shall say, 'Blessed is he who comes in the
name of the Lord!'"

A Man with Dropsy

14 1 And it came to pass, when he entered the
house of one of the rulers of the Pharisees on
the Sabbath to take food, that they watched
2 him. And behold, there was a certain man
3 before him who had the dropsy. And Jesus
asked the lawyers and Pharisees, saying, "Is it
lawful to cure on the Sabbath?"

4   But they remained silent. And he took and
5 healed him and let him go. Then addressing
them, he said, "Which of you shall have an
ass or an ox fall into a pit, and will not im-
6 mediately draw him up on the Sabbath?" And
they could give him no answer to these things.

The Last Seat

But he also spoke a parable to those invited, **7**
observing how they were choosing the first
places at table, and he said to them, "When **8**
thou art invited to a wedding feast, do not
recline in the first place, lest perhaps one more
distinguished than thou have been invited by
him, and he who invited thee and him come **9**
and say to thee, 'Make room for this man';
and then thou begin with shame to take the last
place. But when thou art invited, go and re- **10**
cline in the last place; that when he who invited thee comes in, he may say to thee, 'Friend,
go up higher!' Then thou wilt be honored in
the presence of all who are at table with thee.
For everyone who exalts himself shall be **11**
humbled, and he who humbles himself shall
be exalted."

Poor Guests

But he also said to him who had invited **12**
him, "When thou givest a dinner or a supper,
do not invite thy friends, or thy brethren, or
thy relatives, or thy rich neighbors, lest perhaps they also invite thee in return, and a
recompense be made to thee. But when thou **13**
givest a feast, invite the poor, the crippled, the
lame, the blind; and blessed shalt thou be, **14**
because they have nothing to repay thee with;
for thou shalt be repaid at the resurrection of
the just."

Parable of a Great Supper

Now when one of those who were [MAR. 29] **15**
at table with him had heard this, he [Sept. 28]
said to him, "Blessed is he who shall feast in
the kingdom of God."

16 But he said to him, "A certain man gave a
17 great supper, and he invited many. And he
sent his servant at supper time to tell those
18 invited to come, for everything is now ready. And
they all with one accord began to excuse themselves. The first said to him, 'I have bought
a farm, and I must go out and see it; I pray
19 thee hold me excused.' And another said, 'I
have bought five yoke of oxen, and I am on my
way to try them; I pray thee hold me excused.'
20 And another said, 'I have married a wife, and
therefore I cannot come.'

21 "And the servant returned, and reported
these things to his master. Then the master of the
house was angry and said to his servant, 'Go
out quickly into the streets and lanes of the
city, and bring in here the poor, and the crip-
22 pled, and the blind, and the lame.' And the
servant said, 'Sir, thy order has been carried
23 out, and still there is room.' Then the master
said to the servant, 'Go out into the highways
and hedges, and make them come in, so that
24 my house may be filled. For I tell you that
none of those who were invited shall taste
of my supper.'"

Following of Christ

25 Now great crowds were going along with him.
26 And he turned and said to them, [1] "If anyone
comes to me and does not hate his father and
mother, and wife and children, and brothers
and sisters, yes, and even his own life, he
27 cannot be my disciple. And he who does not
carry his cross and follow me, cannot be my
disciple.

14, 26: *Hate:* i.e., love less. Jesus does not command us
to have a feeling of hatred towards our relatives, but
teaches that we should pay no attention to their requests
if these are detrimental to our spiritual welfare.

"For which of you, wishing to build a tower, 28
does not sit down first and calculate the outlays
that are necessary, whether he has the means
to complete it? Lest, after he has laid the 29
foundation and is not able to finish, all who
behold begin to mock him, ' saying, 'This man 30
began to build and was not able to finish!'

"Or what king setting out to engage in battle 31
with another king, does not sit down first and
consider whether he is able with ten thousand
men to meet him who with twenty thousand is
coming against him? Or else, whilst the other 32
is yet at a distance, he sends a delegation and
asks the terms of peace. So, therefore, every 33
one of you who does not renounce all that he
possesses, cannot be my disciple.

"Salt is good; but if even the salt loses its 34
strength, what shall it be seasoned with? It is 35
fit neither for the land nor for the manure heap,
but must be thrown out. He who has ears to
hear, let him hear."

The Lost Sheep

Now the publicans and sinners | MAR. 30 | **15** 1
were drawing near to him to listen | Sept. 29 |
to him. And the Pharisees and the Scribes mur- 2
mured, saying, "This man welcomes sinners
and eats with them."

But he spoke to them this parable, saying, 3
"What man of you having a hundred sheep, and 4
losing one of them, does not leave the ninety-
nine in the desert, and go after that which is lost,
until he finds it? And when he has found it, he 5
lays it upon his shoulders rejoicing. And on 6
coming home he calls together his friends and
neighbors, saying to them, 'Rejoice with me,
because I have found my sheep that was lost.'

7 I say to you that, even so, there will be joy in heaven over one sinner who repents, more than over ninety-nine just who have no need of repentance.

The Lost Coin

8 "Or what woman, having ten drachmas, if she loses one drachma, does not light a lamp and sweep the house and search carefully until 9 she finds it? And when she has found it, she calls together her friends and neighbors, saying, 'Rejoice with me, for I have found the drachma 10 that I had lost.' Even so, I say to you, there will be joy among the angels of God over one sinner who repents.''

The Prodigal Son

11 And he said, "A certain man had two sons. 12 And the younger of them said to his father, 'Father, give me the share of the property that falls to me.' And he divided his means between them.

13 "And not many days later, the younger son gathered up all his wealth, and took his journey into a far country; and there he squandered his 14 fortune in loose living. And after he had spent all, there came a grievous famine over that country, 15 and he began himself to suffer want. And he went and joined one of the citizens of that country, who sent him to his farm to feed swine. 16 And he longed to fill himself with the pods that the swine were eating, but no one offered to give them to him.

17 "But when he came to himself, he said, 'How many hired men in my father's house have bread in abundance, while I am perishing here 18 with hunger! I will get up and go to my father, and will say to him, Father, I have sinned against 19 heaven and before thee. I am no longer worthy

to be called thy son; make me as one of thy hired men.' And he arose and went to his father. 20

"But while he was yet a long way off, his father saw him and was moved with compassion, and ran and fell upon his neck and kissed him. And the son said to him, 'Father, I have sinned 21 against heaven and before thee. I am no longer worthy to be called thy son.' But the father 22 said to his servants, 'Fetch quickly the best robe and put it on him, and give him a ring for his finger and sandals for his feet; and bring out 23 the fattened calf and kill it, and let us eat and make merry; because this my son was dead, 24 and has come to life again; he was lost, and is found.' And they began to make merry.

"Now his elder son was in the field; and as 25 he came and drew near to the house, he heard music and dancing. And calling one of the ser- 26 vants he inquired what this meant. And he said 27 to him, 'Thy brother has come, and thy father has killed the fattened calf, because he has got him back safe.' But he was angered and would 28 not go in.

"His father, therefore, came out and began to entreat him. But he answered and said to his 29 father, 'Behold, these many years I have been serving thee, and have never transgressed one of thy commands; and yet thou hast never given me a kid that I might make merry with my friends. But when this thy son comes, who has 30 devoured his means with harlots, thou hast killed for him the fattened calf.'

"But he said to him, 'Son, thou art always 31 with me, and all that is mine is thine; but we 32 were bound to make merry and rejoice, for this thy brother was dead, and has come to life; he was lost, and is found.'"

The Unjust Steward

16 1 And he said also to his disciples, | MAR. 31 |
"There was a certain rich man who | Sept. 30 |
had a steward, who was reported to him as
2 squandering his possessions. And he called him
and said to him, 'What is this that I hear of thee?
Make an accounting of thy stewardship, for thou
canst be steward no longer.'

3 "And the steward said within himself, 'What
shall I do, seeing that my master is taking away
the stewardship from me? To dig I am not able;
4 to beg I am ashamed. I know what I shall do, that
when I am removed from my stewardship they
5 may receive me into their houses.' And he summoned each of his master's debtors and said to
the first, 'How much dost thou owe my master?'
6 And he said, 'A hundred jars of oil.' He said to
him, 'Take thy bond and sit down at once and
7 write fifty.' Then he said to another, 'How much
dost thou owe?' He said, 'A hundred kors of
wheat.' He said to him, 'Take thy bond and
write eighty.'

8 "And the master commended the unjust
steward, in that he had acted prudently; for
the children of this world, in relation to their
own generation, are more prudent than the
9 children of the light. And I say to you, make
friends for yourselves with the mammon of
wickedness, so that when you fail they may receive you into the everlasting dwellings.

16, 8: The unjust behavior of the steward is not commended, but the master admires his worldly wisdom in
providing for his future.

16, 9: The Greek reading is, "when it shall fail." *Mammon of wickedness:* riches, which often lead men to sin.
The disciples of Jesus during their short span of life are
to use their wealth to relieve the poor and needy.

"He who is faithful in a very little thing is 10
faithful also in much; and he who is unjust in
a very little thing is unjust also in much. There- 11
fore, if in the case of the wicked mammon you
have not proved faithful, who will entrust to you
what is true? And if in the case of what belongs 12
to another you have not proved faithful, who
will give you what is your own? No servant can 13
serve two masters; for either he will hate the
one and love the other, or else he will stand by
the one and despise the other. You cannot serve
God and mammon."

Pretenses of the Pharisees

Now the Pharisees, who were fond of money, 14
were listening to all these things, and they
began to sneer at him. And he said to them, 15
"You are they who declare yourselves just in
the sight of men, but God knows your heart;
for that which is exalted in the sight of men is
an abomination before God. Until John came, 16
there were the Law and the Prophets; since
then the kingdom of God is being preached,
and everyone is forcing his way into it. Yet it 17
is easier for heaven and earth to pass away
than for one tittle of the Law to fail.

"Everyone who puts away his wife and marries 18
another commits adultery; and he who marries
a woman who has been put away from her
husband commits adultery.

The Rich Man and Lazarus

"There was a certain rich man who used to 19
clothe himself in purple and fine linen, and who
feasted every day in splendid fashion. And there 20
was a certain poor man, named Lazarus, who
lay at his gate, covered with sores, ' and longing 21
to be filled with the crumbs that fell from the

[205]

rich man's table; even the dogs would come
22 and lick his sores. And it came to pass that the
poor man died and was borne away by the
angels into Abraham's bosom; but the rich man
23 also died and was buried in hell. And lifting
up his eyes, being in torments, he saw Abraham
24 afar off and Lazarus in his bosom. And he cried
out and said, 'Father Abraham, have pity on
me, and send Lazarus to dip the tip of his finger
in water and cool my tongue, for I am tormented
in this flame.'

25   "But Abraham said to him, 'Son, remember
that thou in thy lifetime hast received good
things, and Lazarus in like manner evil things;
but now here he is comforted whereas thou art
26 tormented. And besides all that, between us and
you a great gulf is fixed, so that they who wish
to pass over from this side to you cannot, and
they cannot cross from your side to us.'

27   "And he said, 'Then, father, I beseech thee
to send him to my father's house, for I have
28 five brothers, ' that he may testify to them, lest
29 they too come into this place of torments.' And
Abraham said to him, 'They have Moses and
30 the Prophets, let them hearken to them.' But he
answered, 'No, father Abraham, but if someone
from the dead goes to them, they will repent.'
31 But he said to him, 'If they do not hearken to
Moses and the Prophets, they will not believe
even if someone rises from the dead.'"

Avoiding Scandal

17 1 And he said to his disciples, "It ⎡ APR. 1 ⎤
is impossible that scandals should ⎣ Oct. 1 ⎦
not come; but woe to him through whom they
2 come! It were better for him if a millstone were
hung about his neck and he were thrown into

the sea, than that he should cause one of these little ones to sin.

Forgiveness of Injuries

"Take heed to yourselves. If thy brother sin, 3 rebuke him; and if he repent, forgive him. And if seven times in the day he sin against 4 thee, and seven times in the day turn back to thee, saying, 'I repent,' forgive him."

Efficacy of Faith

And the apostles said to the Lord, "Increase 5 our faith." And the Lord answered, "If you have 6 faith even like a mustard seed, you will say to this mulberry tree, 'Be uprooted and be planted in the sea,' and it will obey you.

The Unprofitable Servant

"But which of you is there, having a servant 7 plowing or tending sheep, who will say to him on his return from the field, 'Come at once and recline at table!' But will he not say to him, 8 'Prepare my supper, and gird thyself and serve me till I have eaten and drunk; and afterwards thou thyself shalt eat and drink'? Does he 9 thank that servant for doing what he commanded him?' I do not think so. Even so you 10 also, when you have done everything that was commanded you, say, 'We are unprofitable servants; we have done what it was our duty to do.'"

Ten Lepers

And it came to pass as he was going to Jeru- 11 salem, that he was passing between Samaria and Galilee. And as he was entering a certain 12 village, there met him ten lepers, who stood afar off 'and lifted up their voice, crying, "Jesus, 13 master, have pity on us." 'And when he saw 14

them he said, "Go, show yourselves to the priests." And it came to pass as they were on
15 their way, that they were made clean. But one of them, seeing that he was made clean, re-
16 turned, with a loud voice glorifying God, 'and he fell on his face at his feet, giving thanks; and he was a Samaritan.

17 But Jesus answered and said, "Were not the
18 ten made clean? But where are the nine? 'Has no one been found to return and give glory to
19 God except this foreigner?" And he said to him, "Arise, go thy way, for thy faith has saved thee."

Coming of the Kingdom of God

20 And on being asked by the Phar-
 isees, "When is the kingdom of God | APR. 2 |
                 | Oct. 2 |
 coming?" he answered and said to them, "The
21 kingdom of God comes unawares. Neither will they say, 'Behold, here it is,' or 'Behold, there it is.' For behold, the kingdom of God is within you."

22 But he said to the disciples, "The days will come when you will long to see one day of the
23 Son of Man, and will not see it. And they will say to you, 'Behold, here he is; behold, there
24 he is.' Do not go, nor follow after them. ' For as the lightning when it lightens flashes from one end of the sky to the other, so will the Son of
25 Man be in his day. But first he must suffer many things and be rejected by this generation.
26 "And as it came to pass in the days of Noe, even so will it be in the days of the Son of Man.

17, 21: *Within you:* i.e., in the midst of you and within your power to reach through faith, justice and love. It has already begun and the Pharisees might recognize it if they had eyes to see and ears to hear. The Messias is already reigning.

They were eating and drinking, they were marry- 27
ing and giving in marriage, until the day when
Noe entered the ark, and the flood came and
destroyed them all. Or as it came to pass in the 28
days of Lot. They were eating and drinking,
they were buying and selling, they were planting
and building; but on the day that Lot went out 29
from Sodom, it rained fire and brimstone from
heaven and destroyed them all. In the same wise 30
will it be on the day that the Son of Man is
revealed. In that hour let him who is on the 31
housetop and his goods in the house, not go down
to take them away; and likewise let him who is
in the field not turn back. Remember Lot's wife. 32
Whoever tries to save his life will lose it; and 33
whoever loses it will preserve it. I say to you, 34
on that night there will be two on one bed;
one will be taken, and the other will be left.
Two women will be grinding together; one will 35
be taken, and the other will be left. Two men
will be in the field; one will be taken, and the
other will be left."

And they answered and said to him, "Where, 36
Lord?" He said to them, "Wherever the body 37
is, there will the eagles be gathered together."

The Godless Judge

And he also told them a parable | APR. 3 | **18** 1
— that they must always pray and | Oct. 3 |
not lose heart — saying, "There was a judge 2
in a certain town who did not fear God and did
not respect man. Now there was a certain widow 3
in that town, and she kept coming to him, saying,
'Do me justice against my adversary.' And he 4
would not for a long time. But afterwards he
said within himself, 'Although I do not fear God,
nor even respect man, yet because this widow 5

bothers me, I will do her justice, lest by her continual coming she finally wear me out.'"

6 And the Lord said, "Hear what the unjust
7 judge says; and will not God avenge his elect, who cry to him day and night? And will he be
8 slow to act in their case? I tell you that he will avenge them quickly. Yet when the Son of Man comes, will he find, do you think, faith on the earth?"

The Pharisee and the Publican

9 But he spoke this parable also to some who trusted in themselves as being just and despised
10 others. "Two men went up to the temple to pray, the one a Pharisee and the other a publican.
11 The Pharisee stood and began to pray thus within himself: 'O God, I thank thee that I am not like the rest of men, robbers, dishonest,
12 adulterers, or even like this publican. I fast twice a week; I pay tithes of all that I possess.'
13 But the publican, standing afar off, would not so much as lift up his eyes to heaven, but kept striking his breast, saying, 'O God, be merciful to me the sinner!'

14 "I tell you, this man went back to his home justified rather than the other; for everyone who exalts himself shall be humbled, and he who humbles himself shall be exalted."

Jesus Blesses the Children

15 Now they were bringing the babes also to him that he might touch them; but when the
16 disciples saw it, they rebuked them. But Jesus called them together and said, "Let the little children come to me, and do not hinder them,
17 for of such is the kingdom of God. Amen I say to you, whoever does not accept the kingdom of God as a little child will not enter into it."

The Danger of Riches

18 And a certain ruler asked him, saying, "Good Master, what shall I do to gain eternal life?" But Jesus said to him, 19 "Why dost thou call me good? No one is good but only God. Thou knowest the command- 20 ments: Thou shalt not kill, Thou shalt not commit adultery, Thou shalt not steal, Thou shalt not bear false witness, Honor thy father and mother." And he said, "All these I have 21 kept ever since I was a child." But when Jesus 22 heard this, he said to him, "One thing is still lacking to thee; sell all that thou hast, and give to the poor, and thou shalt have treasure in heaven; and come, follow me." When he heard 23 these things, he was much grieved, for he was very rich.

But Jesus, seeing him become sad, said, 24 "With what difficulty will they who have riches enter the kingdom of God! For it is easier for 25 a camel to pass through the eye of a needle, than for a rich man to enter the kingdom of God." And they who heard it said, "Who then 26 can be saved?" He said to them, "Things that 27 are impossible with men are possible with God."

And Peter said, "Behold, we have left all 28 and followed thee." And he said to them, 29 "Amen I say to you, there is no one who has left house, or parents, or brothers, or wife, or children, for the sake of the kingdom of God, who shall not receive much more in the present 30 time, and in the age to come life everlasting."

The Third Prediction of the Passion

But Jesus taking to himself the Twelve said 31 to them, "Behold, we are going up to Jerusalem, and all things that have been written by the

APR. 4
Oct. 4

prophets concerning the Son of Man will be ac-
32 complished. For he will be delivered to the Gentiles, and will be mocked and scourged and spit
33 upon; and after they have scourged him, they
will put him to death; and on the third day he will
rise again."

34 And they understood none of these things and
this saying was hidden from them, neither did
they get to know the things that were being said.

VI

A Blind Man at Jericho

35 NOW IT CAME TO PASS as he drew near to
Jericho, that a certain blind man was sitting by
36 the wayside, begging; but hearing a crowd pass-
37 ing by, he inquired what this might be. And they
told him that Jesus of Nazareth was passing by.
38 And he cried out, saying, "Jesus, Son of David,
39 have mercy on me!" And they who went in
front angrily tried to silence him. But he cried
out all the louder, "Son of David, have mercy on
40 me!" Then Jesus stopped and commanded that
he should be brought to him. And when he drew
41 near, he asked him, ' saying, "What wouldst
thou have me do for thee?" And he said, "Lord,
42 that I may see." And Jesus said to him, "Re-
43 ceive thy sight, thy faith has saved thee." And
at once he received his sight, and followed him,
glorifying God. And all the people upon seeing
it gave praise to God.

Zacchaeus the Publican

19 1   And he entered and was passing ⎡ APR. 5
2 through Jericho. And behold there ⎣ Oct. 5
was a man named Zacchæus; and he was a lead-
3 ing publican, and he was rich. And he was trying
to see Jesus, who he was, but could not, on ac-

count of the crowd, because he was small of
stature. So he ran on ahead and climbed up into 4
a sycamore tree to see him, for he was going to
pass that way.

And when Jesus came to the place, he looked 5
up and saw him, and said to him, "Zacchæus,
make haste and come down; for I must stay in
thy house today."

And he made haste and came down, and wel- 6
comed him joyfully. And upon seeing it all began 7
to murmur, saying, "He has gone to be the guest
of a man who is a sinner." But Zacchæus stood 8
and said to the Lord, "Behold, Lord, I give one-
half of my possessions to the poor, and if I have
defrauded anyone of anything, I restore it four-
fold." Jesus said to him, "Today salvation has 9
come to this house, since he, too, is a son of
Abraham. For the Son of Man came to seek and 10
to save what was lost."

Parable of the Gold Pieces

Now as they were listening to these things, he 11
went on to speak a parable, because he was near
Jerusalem, and because they thought that the
kingdom of God was going to appear immediately.

He said therefore, "A certain nobleman went 12
into a far country to obtain for himself a kingdom and then return. And having summoned 13
ten of his servants, he gave them ten gold pieces
and said to them, 'Trade till I come.'

"But his citizens hated him; and they sent a 14
delegation after him to say, 'We do not wish this
man to be king over us.' And it came to pass 15
when he had returned, after receiving the kingdom, that he ordered the servants to whom he
had given the money to be called to him in order

that he might learn how much each one had made by trading.

16 "And the first came, saying, 'Lord, thy gold
17 piece has earned ten gold pieces.' And he said to him, 'Well done, good servant; because thou hast been faithful in a very little, thou shalt have authority over ten towns.'

18 "Then the second came, saying, 'Lord, thy
19 gold piece has made five gold pieces.' And he said to him, 'Be thou also over five towns.'

20 "And another came, saying, 'Lord, behold thy gold piece, which I have kept laid up in a napkin;
21 for I feared thee, because thou art a stern man. Thou takest up what thou didst not lay down,
22 and thou reapest what thou didst not sow.' He said to him, 'Out of thy own mouth I judge thee, thou wicked servant. Thou knewest that I am a stern man, taking up what I did not lay down and
23 reaping what I did not sow. Why, then, didst thou not put my money in a bank, so that I on my
24 return might have gotten it with interest?' And he said to the bystanders, 'Take away the gold piece from him, and give it to him who has the
25 ten gold pieces.' But they said to him, 'Lord, he has ten gold pieces.'

26 "I say to you that to everyone who has shall be given; but from him who does not have,
27 even that which he has shall be taken away. But as for these my enemies, who did not want me to be king over them, bring them here and slay them in my presence.'"

28 And when he had said these things, he went ahead, going up to Jerusalem.

Triumphal Entry into Jerusalem

29 And it came to pass, when he drew near to Bethphage and Bethany, at the mountain called Olivet, that he sent

APR. 6
Oct. 6

two of his disciples, ' saying, "Go into the village 30
opposite; on entering it you will find a colt of an
ass tied, upon which no man ever yet sat; loose it
and bring it. And if anyone ask you, 'Why are 31
you loosing it?' you shall answer him thus, 'Because the Lord has need of it.' "

And they who were sent away and found 32
the colt standing, even as he had told them. And 33
as they were loosing the colt, its owners said to
them, "Why are you loosing the colt?" And they 34
replied, "Because the Lord has need of it."

And they brought it to Jesus, and throwing 35
their cloaks over the colt they set Jesus on it. And 36
as he went, they kept spreading their cloaks
upon the road. And when he was drawing near, 37
being by now at the descent of the Mount of
Olives, the whole company of the disciples began
to rejoice and to praise God with a loud voice for
all the miracles that they had seen, saying, 38
"Blessed is he who comes as king, in the name
of the Lord! Peace in heaven, and glory in the
highest!"

And some of the Pharisees from the crowds 39
said to him, "Master, rebuke thy disciples." He 40
said to them, "I tell you that if these keep silence, the stones will cry out."

And when he drew near and saw the city, he 41
wept over it, saying, "If thou hadst known, in 42
this thy day, even thou, the things that are for
thy peace! But now they are hidden from thy
eyes. For days will come upon thee when thy 43
enemies will throw up a rampart about thee, and
surround thee and shut thee in on every side,
and will dash thee to the ground and thy children 44
within thee, and will not leave in thee one stone
upon another, because thou hast not known the
time of thy visitation."

Cleansing of the Temple

45 And he entered the temple, and began to cast out those who were selling and buying in it,
46 saying to them, "It is written, 'My house is a house of prayer,' but you have made it a den of thieves."

47 And he was teaching daily in the temple. But the chief priests and the Scribes and the leading men of the people sought to destroy
48 him; but they found nothing that they could do to him, for all the people hung upon his words.

The Authority of Jesus

20 1 And it came to pass on one of the days, as he was teaching the people

APR. 7
Oct. 7

in the temple and preaching the gospel, that the chief priests and Scribes together with the
2 elders came up and spoke to him, saying, "Tell us, by what authority dost thou do these things? Or who is it that gave thee this au-
3 thority?" But he answered and said to them, "I also will ask you one question. Answer me:
4 was the baptism of John from heaven, or from
5 men?" But they began to argue among themselves, saying, "If we say, 'From heaven,' he will say, 'Why then did you not believe him?'
6 But if we say, 'From men,' all the people will stone us; for they are convinced that John was
7 a prophet." And they answered that they did
8 not know whence it was. Then Jesus said to them, "Neither do I tell you by what authority I do these things."

Parable of the Vine-dressers

9 But he began to speak to tne people this parable: "A man planted a vineyard, and let it out to vine-dressers, and went abroad for a

long time. And at the proper time he sent a 10
servant to the vine-dressers, that they might
give him part of the fruit of the vineyard; but
they beat him and sent him away empty-
handed. And he sent yet a second servant; but 11
him also they beat, and treated shamefully and
sent away empty-handed. And he sent yet a 12
third; but him also they wounded and cast out.
But the owner of the vineyard said, 'What 13
shall I do? I will send my beloved son; perhaps
when they see him, they will respect him.'

"But the vine-dressers, on seeing him, argued 14
with one another, saying, 'This is the heir; let
us kill him, that the inheritance may become
ours.' So they cast him out of the vineyard 15
and killed him. What therefore will the owner
of the vineyard do to them? He will come and 16
destroy those vine-dressers, and will give the
vineyard to others."

Upon hearing this, they said to him, "By no
means." But he looked on them and said, "What 17
then is this that is written, 'The stone which
the builders rejected, has become the corner
stone'? Everyone who falls upon that stone will 18
be broken to pieces; but upon whomever it
falls, it will grind him to powder."

And the chief priests and the Scribes sought 19
to lay hands on him that very hour, but they
feared the people; for they knew that he had
aimed this parable at them.

Tribute to Caesar

So watching their opportunity, they sent forth 20
spies, who should pretend to be just men, that
they might trap him in his talk and deliver
him up to the ruling power and to the authority
of the procurator. And they asked him, saying, 21

"Master, we know that thou speakest and
teachest rightly, and showest no favor to any,
22 but teachest the way of God in truth. Is it law-
23 ful for us to give tribute to Cæsar, or not?" But
knowing their craftiness, he said to them, "Why
24 do you test me? ' Show me a denarius. Whose
image and inscription does it bear?" Answering
25 they said, "Cæsar's." And he said to them,
"Render, therefore, to Cæsar the things that
are Cæsar's, and to God the things that are
26 God's." And they could not take hold of what
he said before the people; and marvelling at
his answer, they kept silence.

The Sadducees and the Resurrection

27 Now there came to him certain
of the Sadducees, who say that APR. 8 Oct. 8
there is no resurrection, and they questioned
28 him, ' saying, "Master, Moses has written for
us: 'If a man's brother die, having a wife, and he
be childless, his brother shall take the widow
29 and raise up issue to his brother.' Now there
were seven brothers. And the first took a wife
30 and died childless. And the next took her; and
31 he also died childless. Then the third took her;
and in like manner all seven, and they died
32 without leaving children. Last of all the woman
33 also died. At the resurrection, therefore, of
which of them will she be wife? For the seven
had her as wife."

34 And Jesus said to them, "The children of this
35 world marry and are given in marriage. But
those who shall be accounted worthy of that
world and of the resurrection from the dead,
36 neither marry nor take wives. For neither shall
they be able to die any more, for they are equal
to the angels, and are sons of God, being sons

of the resurrection. But that the dead rise, even 37
Moses showed in the passage about the Bush,
when he calls the Lord the God of Abraham, and
the God of Isaac, and the God of Jacob. Now 38
he is not the God of the dead, but of the living,
for all live to him."

And certain of the Scribes answered and said, 39
"Master, thou hast said well." And they did 40
not dare to question him any further.

The Son of David

But he said to them, "How do they say that 41
the Christ is the Son of David? For David him- 42
self says in the Book of Psalms, 'The Lord said
to my Lord: Sit at my right hand,' till I make 43
thy enemies thy footstool.' David therefore calls 44
him 'Lord'; how, then, is he his son?"

Hypocrisy of the Scribes and Pharisees

And in the hearing of all the people he said 45
to his disciples, "Beware of the Scribes, who like 46
to walk about in long robes, and love greetings
in the market place, and front seats in the
synagogues and first places at suppers; who 47
devour the houses of the widows, making pretense of long prayers. These shall receive a
heavier sentence."

The Widow's Mite

But looking up he saw the rich
who were putting their gifts into the
treasury. And he saw also a certain poor widow 2
putting in two mites. And he said, "Truly I say 3
to you, this poor widow has put in more than
all. For all these out of their abundance have 4
put in as gifts to God; but she out of her want
has put in all that she had to live on."

| APR. 9 | **21** 1 |
| Oct. 9 | |

Destruction of Jerusalem and End of the World

5 And as some were saying of the temple that it was adorned with beautiful stones and of-
6 ferings, he said, "As for these things that you behold, the days will come in which there will not be left one stone upon another that will
7 not be thrown down." And they asked him, saying, "Master, when are these things to hap-pen, and what will be the sign when these things will begin to come to pass?"

8 And he said, "Take care not to be led astray. For many will come in my name, saying, 'I am he,' and, 'The time is at hand.' Do not, there-
9 fore, go after them. But when you hear of wars and insurrections, do not be terrified; these things must first come to pass, but the end will
10 not be at once." Then he said to them, "Nation will rise against nation, and kingdom against
11 kingdom; and there will be great earthquakes in various places, and pestilences and famines, and there will be terrors and great signs from heaven.

12 "But before all these things they will arrest you and persecute you, delivering you up to the synagogues and prisons, dragging you before
13 kings and governors for my name's sake. It shall
14 lead to your bearing witness. Resolve therefore in your hearts not to meditate beforehand how
15 you are to make your defense. For I myself will give you utterance and wisdom, which all your adversaries will not be able to resist or gainsay.
16 But you will be delivered up by your parents and brothers and relatives and friends; and some of
17 you they will put to death. And you will be hated
18 by all for my name's sake; yet not a hair of your
19 head shall perish. By your patience you will win your souls.

Destruction of Jerusalem

"And when you see Jerusalem | APR. 10 | 20
being surrounded by an army, then | Oct. 10 |
know that her desolation is at hand. Then let 21
those who are in Judea flee to the mountains;
and let those who are in her midst go out, and
let those who are in the country not enter her.
For these are days of vengeance, that all things 22
that are written may be fulfilled. But woe to 23
those who are with child, or have infants at the
breast in those days! For there will be great
distress over the land, and wrath upon this
people. And they will fall by the edge of the 24
sword, and will be led away as captives to all the
nations. And Jerusalem will be trodden down by
the Gentiles, until the times of the nations be
fulfilled.

The Signs of the Last Day

"And there will be signs in the sun and moon 25
and stars, and upon the earth distress of nations
bewildered by the roaring of sea and waves; men 26
fainting for fear and for expectation of the things
that are coming on the world; for the powers of
heaven will be shaken. And then they will see 27
the Son of Man coming upon a cloud with great
power and majesty. But when these things begin 28
to come to pass, look up, and lift up your heads,
because your redemption is at hand."

Jerusalem's Impending Destruction

And he spoke to them a parable. "Behold 29
the fig tree, and all the trees. When they now 30
put forth their buds, you know that summer is
near. Even so, when you see these things com- 31
ing to pass, know that the kingdom of God is
near. Amen I say to you, this generation will not 32

pass away till all things have been accomplished.
33 Heaven and earth will pass away, but my words
will not pass away.

The Need of Watchfulness

34   "But take heed to yourselves, lest your hearts
be overburdened with self-indulgence and
drunkenness and the cares of this life, and that
35 day come upon you suddenly ' as a snare. For
come it will upon all who dwell on the face of all
36 the earth. Watch, then, praying at all times,
that you may be accounted worthy to escape all
these things that are to be, and to stand before
the Son of Man."

37   Now in the daytime he was teaching in the
temple; but as for the nights, he would go out
and pass them on the mountain called Olivet.
38 And all the people came to him early in the morning in the temple, to hear him.

II: THE PASSION, DEATH AND RESURRECTION

1. The Last Supper

The Council and the Betrayal

22 1   NOW THE FEAST of the Unleavened Bread, which is called the
2 Passover, was drawing near; and the chief
priests and the Scribes were seeking how they
might put him to death, for they feared the
people.

| APR. 11 |
| Oct. 11 |

3   But Satan entered into Judas, surnamed
4 Iscariot, one of the Twelve. And he went away
and discussed with the chief priests and the
5 captains, how he might betray him to them. And
they were glad, and agreed to give him money.
6 He accordingly promised, and sought out an
opportunity to betray him without a disturbance.

Preparation

Now the day of the Unleavened Bread came, 7
on which the passover had to be sacrificed. And 8
he sent Peter and John, saying, "Go and prepare
for us the passover that we may eat it." But they 9
said, "Where dost thou want us to prepare it?"
And he said to them, "Behold, on your entering 10
the city, there will meet you a man carrying a
pitcher of water; follow him into the house into
which he goes. And you shall say to the master 11
of the house, 'The Master says to thee, "Where
is the guest chamber, that I may eat the passover
there with my disciples?"' And he will show you 12
a large upper room furnished; there make
ready." And they went, and found just as he had 13
told them; and they prepared the passover.

The Holy Eucharist

And when the hour had come, he reclined at 14
table, and the twelve apostles with him. And 15
he said to them, "I have greatly desired to eat
this passover with you before I suffer; for I say 16
to you that I will eat of it no more, until it has
been fulfilled in the kingdom of God." And hav- 17
ing taken a cup, he gave thanks and said, "Take
this and share it among you; for I say to you that 18
I will not drink of the fruit of the vine, until the
kingdom of God comes."

And having taken bread, he gave thanks and 19
broke, and gave it to them, saying, "This is my
body, which is being given for you; do this in
remembrance of me." In like manner he took 20
also the cup after the supper, saying, "This cup
is the new covenant in my blood, which shall be
shed for you.

The Betrayer

21   "But behold, the hand of him who betrays me is with me on the table. APR. 12 Oct. 12

22 For the Son of Man indeed goes his way, as it has been determined; yet woe to that man by

23 whom he will be betrayed." And they began to inquire among themselves which of them it might be that was about to do this.

Contention among the Apostles

24   Now there arose also a dispute among them, which of them was reputed to be the greatest.

25 But he said to them, "The kings of the Gentiles

26 lord it over them, and they who exercise authority over them are called Benefactors. But not so with you. On the contrary, let him who is greatest among you become as the youngest,

27 and him who is the chief as the servant. For which is the greater, he who reclines at table, or he who serves? Is it not he who reclines? But

28 I am in your midst as he who serves. But you are they who have continued with me in my trials.

29 And I appoint to you a kingdom, even as my

30 Father has appointed to me, that you may eat and drink at my table in my kingdom; and you shall sit upon thrones, judging the twelve tribes of Israel."

Peter's Denials Predicted

31   And the Lord said, "Simon, Simon, behold, Satan has desired to have you, that he may sift

32 you as wheat. But I have prayed for thee, that thy faith may not fail; and do thou, when once thou hast turned again, strengthen thy brethren."

33 But he said to him, "Lord, with thee I am ready

34 to go both to prison and to death!" But he said, "I tell thee, Peter, a cock will not crow this day,

until thou hast denied three times that thou knowest me."

And he said to them, ' "When I sent you 35 forth without purse or wallet or sandals, did you lack anything?" ' And they said, "Nothing." Then 36 he said to them, "But now, let him who has a purse take it, and likewise a wallet; and let him who has no sword sell his tunic and buy one. For I say to you that this which is written must 37 yet be fulfilled in me, 'And he was reckoned among the wicked.' For that which concerns me is at its end." And they said, "Lord, behold, 38 here are two swords." And he said to them, "Enough."

2. The Passion and Death of Jesus

The Agony in the Garden

AND HE CAME OUT and went, according to his custom, to the Mount of Olives, and the disciples also followed him. 39

APR. 13
Oct. 13

But when he was at the place, he said to them, 40 "Pray, that you may not enter into temptation." And he himself withdrew from them about a 41 stone's throw, and kneeling down, he began to pray, ' saying, "Father, if thou art willing, re- 42 move this cup from me; yet not my will but thine be done." And there appeared to him an angel 43 from heaven to strengthen him. And falling into an agony he prayed the more earnestly.

And his sweat became as drops of blood run- 44 ning down upon the ground. And rising from 45 prayer he came to the disciples, and found them sleeping for sorrow. And he said to them, "Why 46 do you sleep? Rise and pray, that you may not enter into temptation."

Jesus Arrested

47 And while he was yet speaking, behold, a crowd came; and he who was called Judas, one of the Twelve, was going before them, and 48 he drew near to Jesus to kiss him. But Jesus said to him, "Judas, dost thou betray the Son of Man with a kiss?"

49 But when they who were about him saw what would follow, they said to him, "Lord, shall we 50 strike with the sword?" And one of them struck the servant of the high priest and cut off his 51 right ear. But Jesus answered and said, "Bear with them thus far." And he touched his ear and 52 healed him. But Jesus said to the chief priests and captains of the temple and elders, who had come against him, "As against a robber have 53 you come out, with swords and clubs. When I was daily with you in the temple, you did not stretch forth your hands against me. But this is your hour, and the power of darkness."

Peter's Denial

54 Now having seized him, they led him away to the high priest's house; but Peter was follow-55 ing at a distance. And when they had kindled a fire in the middle of the courtyard, and were 56 seated together, Peter was in their midst. But a certain maidservant saw him sitting at the blaze, and after gazing upon him she said, "This man 57 too was with him." But he denied him, saying, 58 "Woman, I do not know him." ' And after a little while someone else saw him and said, "Thou, too, art one of them." But Peter said, "Man, I 59 am not." And about an hour later another in-sisted, saying, "Surely this man, too, was with 60 him, for he also is a Galilean." But Peter said, "Man, I do not know what thou sayest." And at

that moment, while he was yet speaking, a cock crowed. And the Lord turned and looked upon 61 Peter. And Peter remembered the word of the Lord, how he said, "Before a cock crows, thou wilt deny me three times." And Peter went out 62 and wept bitterly.

Jesus before the Sanhedrin

And the men who had him in custody began to mock him and beat 63

APR. 14
Oct. 14

him. And they blindfolded him, and kept striking 64 his face and asking him, saying, "Prophesy, who is it that struck thee?" And many other things 65 they kept saying against him, reviling him.

And as soon as day broke, the elders of the 66 people and the chief priests and Scribes gathered together; and they led him away into their Sanhedrin, saying, "If thou art the Christ, tell us." And he said to them, "If I tell you, you will not 67 believe me; and if I question you, you will not 68 answer me, or let me go. But henceforth, the Son 69 of Man will be seated at the right hand of the power of God."

And they all said, "Art thou, then, the Son of 70 God?" He answered, "You yourselves say that I am." And they said, "What further need have we 71 of witness? For we have heard it ourselves from his own mouth."

Jesus before Pilate

And the whole assemblage rose, and took him **23** 1 before Pilate. And they began to accuse him, 2 saying, "We have found this man perverting our nation, and forbidding the payment of taxes to Cæsar, and saying that he is Christ a king." So 3 Pilate asked him, saying, "Art thou the king of the Jews?" And he answered him and said, "Thou sayest it." ' And Pilate said to the chief 4 priests and to the crowds, "I find no guilt in this man."

5   But they persisted, saying, "He is stirring up the people, teaching throughout all Judea, and
6   beginning from Galilee even to this place." But Pilate, hearing Galilee, asked whether the man
7   was a Galilean. And learning that he belonged to Herod's jurisdiction, he sent him back to Herod, who likewise was in Jerusalem in those days.

Jesus before Herod

8   Now when Herod saw Jesus, he was exceedingly glad; for he had been a long time desirous to see him, because he had heard so much about him, and he was hoping to see some miracle done
9   by him. Now he put many questions to him, but he made him no answer.

10 Now the chief priests and Scribes were stand-
11 ing by, vehemently accusing him. But Herod, with his soldiery, treated him with contempt and mocked him, arraying him in a bright robe, and
12 sent him back to Pilate. And Herod and Pilate became friends that very day; whereas previously they had been at enmity with each other.

Jesus Again before Pilate

13 And Pilate called together the chief priests and the rulers and the
APR. 15
Oct. 15
14 people, and said to them, "You have brought before me this man, as one who perverts the people; and behold, I, upon examining him in your presence have found no guilt in this man as touching those things of which you accuse
15 him. Neither has Herod; for I sent you back to him, and behold, nothing deserving of death has
16 been committed by him. I will therefore chastise him and release him."

Now at festival time it was necessary for him 17
to release to them one prisoner. But the whole 18
mob cried out together, saying, "Away with this
man, and release to us Barabbas!"— one who 19
had been thrown into prison for a certain riot
that had occurred in the city, and for murder.
But Pilate spoke to them again, wishing to re- 20
lease Jesus. But they kept shouting, saying, 21
"Crucify him! Crucify him!" And he said to 22
them a third time, "Why, what evil has this man
done? I find no crime deserving of death in him.
I will therefore chastise him and release him."

But they persisted with loud cries, demanding 23
that he should be crucified; and their cries prevailed. And Pilate pronounced sentence 24
what they asked for should be done. So he re- 25
leased to them him who for murder and riot had
been put in prison, for whom they were asking;
but Jesus he delivered to their will.

The Way of the Cross

And as they led him away, they laid hold of a 26
certain Simon of Cyrene, coming from the country, and upon him they laid the cross to bear it
after Jesus. Now there was following him a great 27
crowd of the people, and of women, who were
bewailing and lamenting him. But Jesus turning 28
to them said, "Daughters of Jerusalem, do not
weep for me, but weep for yourselves and for
your children. For behold, days are coming in 29
which men will say, 'Blessed are the barren,
and the wombs that never bore, and breasts that
never nursed.' Then they will begin to say to the 30
mountains, 'Fall upon us,' and to the hills, 'Cover
us!' For if in the case of green wood they do 31
these things, what is to happen in the case of the
dry?" Now there were also two other male- 32
factors led to execution with him.

The Crucifixion

33 And when they came to the place called the Skull, they crucified him there, and the robbers, one on his right hand and
34 the other on his left. And Jesus said, "Father, forgive them, for they do not know what they are doing." Now in dividing his garments, they cast lots.

35 And the people stood looking on; and the rulers with them kept sneering at him, saying, "He saved others; let him save himself, if he is
36 the Christ, the chosen one of God." And the soldiers also mocked him, coming to him and
37 offering him common wine, and saying, "If thou art the King of the Jews, save thyself!"

38 And there was also an inscription written over him in Greek and Latin and Hebrew letters, "This is the King of the Jews."

39 Now one of those robbers who were hanged was abusing him, saying, "If thou art the Christ,
40 save thyself and us!" But the other in answer rebuked him and said, "Dost not even thou
41 fear God, seeing that thou art under the same sentence? And we indeed justly, for we are receiving what our deeds deserved; but this man
42 has done nothing wrong." And he said to Jesus, "Lord, remember me when thou comest into
43 thy kingdom." And Jesus said to him, "Amen I say to thee, this day thou shalt be with me in paradise."

The Death of Jesus

44 It was now about the sixth hour, and there was darkness over the whole land until the
45 ninth hour. And the sun was darkened, and the curtain of the temple was torn in the middle.
46 And Jesus cried out with a loud voice and said,

"Father, into thy hands I commend my spirit."
And having said this, he expired.

Now when the centurion saw what had hap- 47
pened, he glorified God, saying, "Truly this was
a just man." And all the crowd that collected 48
for the sight, when they beheld what things
had happened, began to return beating their
breasts. But all his acquaintances, and the 49
women who had followed him from Galilee,
were standing at a distance looking on.

The Burial

And behold, there was a man 50
named Joseph, a councillor, a good

APR. 17
Oct. 17

and just man—he had not been party to their 51
plan of action—of Arimathea, a town of Judea,
who was himself looking for the kingdom of
God. He went to Pilate and asked for the body 52
of Jesus. And he took him down, and wrapped 53
him in a linen cloth, and laid him in a rock-
hewn tomb where no one had ever yet been
laid. And it was Preparation Day, and the Sabbath 54
was drawing on. And the women who had come 55
with him from Galilee, followed after, and beheld the tomb, and how his body was laid.
And they went back and prepared spices and 56
ointments. And on the Sabbath they rested, in
accordance with the commandment.

3. The Resurrection of Jesus

The Women at the Grave

BUT ON THE FIRST DAY of the week at early **24** 1
dawn, they came to the tomb, taking the spices
that they had prepared, and they found the 2
stone rolled back from the tomb. But on enter- 3
ing, they did not find the body of the Lord
Jesus. And it came to pass, while they were 4

wondering what to make of this, that, behold,
two men stood by them in dazzling raiment.
5 And when the women were struck with fear
and bowed their faces to the ground, they said
6 to them, "Why do you seek the living one
among the dead? He is not here, but has
risen. Remember how he spoke to you while he
7 was yet in Galilee, saying that the Son of Man
must be betrayed into the hands of sinful men,
and be crucified, and on the third day rise."

8.9 And they remembered his words. And having
returned from the tomb, they reported all these
10 things to the Eleven, and to all the rest. Now, it
was Mary Magdalene and Joanna and Mary, the
mother of James, and the other women who were
with them, who were telling these things to the
11 apostles. But this tale seemed to them to be
nonsense, and they did not believe the women.

12 But Peter arose and ran to the tomb; and
stooping down, he saw the linen cloths laid
there; and he went away wondering to himself
at what had come to pass.

Emmaus

13 And behold, two of them were
going that very day to a village
named Emmaus, which is sixty stadia from
14 Jerusalem. And they were talking to each other
15 about all these things that had happened. And
it came to pass, while they were conversing
and arguing together, that Jesus himself also
16 drew near and went along with them; but their
eyes were held, that they should not recognize
17 him. And he said to them, "What words are
these that you are exchanging as you walk and
are sad?"

18 But one of them, named Cleophas, answered

APR. 18
Oct. 18

and said to him, "Art thou the only stranger in Jerusalem who does not know the things that have happened there in these days?" And 19 he said to them, "What things?"

And they said to him, "Concerning Jesus of Nazareth, who was a prophet, mighty in work and word before God and all the people; and 20 how our chief priests and rulers delivered him up to be sentenced to death, and crucified him. But we were hoping that it was he who should 21 redeem Israel. Yes, and besides all this, today is the third day since these things came to pass. And moreover, certain women of our company, 22 who were at the tomb before it was light, astounded us, ' and not finding his body, they 23 came, saying that they had also seen a vision of angels, who said that he is alive. So some of 24 our company went to the tomb, and found it even as the women had said, but him they did not see."

But he said to them, "O foolish ones and slow 25 of heart to believe in all that the prophets have spoken! Did not the Christ have to suffer 26 these things before entering into his glory?" And beginning then with Moses and with all the 27 Prophets, he interpreted to them in all the Scriptures the things referring to himself.

And they drew near to the village to which 28 they were going, and he acted as though he were going on. And they urged him, saying, 29 "Stay with us, for it is getting towards evening, and the day is now far spent." And he went in with them. And it came to pass when he re- 30 clined at table with them, that he took the bread and blessed and broke and began handing it to them. And their eyes were opened, and 31 they recognized him; and he vanished from

32 their sight. And they said to each other, "Was not our heart burning within us while he was speaking on the road and explaining to us the Scriptures?"

33 And rising up that very hour, they returned to Jerusalem, where they found the Eleven gathered together and those who were with
34 them, ' saying, "The Lord has risen indeed, and
35 has appeared to Simon." And they themselves began to relate what had happened on the journey, and how they recognized him in the breaking of the bread.

Jesus Appears to the Eleven

36 Now while they were talking of these things, Jesus stood in their midst, and said to them, "Peace to you! It is I,
37 do not be afraid." But they were startled and panic-stricken, and thought that they saw a spirit.

APR. 19
Oct. 19

38 And he said to them, "Why are you disturbed,
39 and why do doubts arise in your hearts? See my hands and feet, that it is I myself. Feel me and see; for a spirit does not have flesh and
40 bones, as you see I have." And having said
41 this, he showed them his hands and his feet. But as they still disbelieved and marvelled for joy, he
42 said, "Have you anything here to eat?" And they offered him a piece of broiled fish and a honey-
43 comb. And when he had eaten in their presence, he took what remained and gave it to them.

The Last Instructions of Jesus

44 And he said to them, "These are the words which I spoke to you while I was yet with you, that all things must be fulfilled that are written in the Law of Moses and the Prophets and the Psalms

concerning me." Then he opened their minds, 45
that they might understand the Scriptures. And 46
he said to them, "Thus it is written; and thus
the Christ should suffer, and should rise again
from the dead on the third day; and that re- 47
pentance and remission of sins should be
preached in his name to all the nations, beginning from Jerusalem. And you yourselves 48
are witnesses of these things. And I send forth 49
upon you the promise of my Father. But wait
here in the city, until you are clothed with
power from on high."

4. The Ascension of Jesus
The Ascension

NOW HE LED THEM OUT towards Bethany, and 50
he lifted up his hands and blessed them. And it 51
came to pass as he blessed them, that he parted
from them and was carried up into heaven. And 52
they worshipped him, and returned to Jerusalem
with great joy. And they were continually in the 53
temple, praising and blessing God. Amen.

THE GOSPEL ACCORDING TO
ST. JOHN
Introduction

St. John, "the disciple whom Jesus loved," was the last to write his Gospel. He was a young man when first called to the apostolate and lived to an advanced old age. At Ephesus, where he lived till about the year 100 A. D., he wrote the Gospel at the request of the Elders.

John and James were the sons of Zebedee, of the town of Bethsaida. They were fishermen by trade. They had attached themselves as disciples to John the Baptist, and from him learned that Jesus was the Messias. They were among the first whom Jesus invited to follow Him, and later were called to be with Him permanently. They were among the chosen Twelve. With Peter, they were permitted to share some of the more hidden experiences of their Master.

John was particularly intimate with Jesus, as his title of "beloved disciple" and his position at the Last Supper clearly show. To him our Lord entrusted the care of the Blessed Virgin. We do not wonder, therefore, that he was able to reach such spiritual heights in his Gospel, or that tradition has assigned to him the symbol of the eagle.

The purpose of the Gospel is stated in 20, 31: ". . . that you may believe that Jesus is the Christ, the Son of God, and that believing you may have life in his name." To establish this truth, the evangelist recounts certain of our Lord's miracles, and the teachings which were associated with them. He assumes that his readers know the Synoptic Gospels, and in some points completes their narrative. But all other possible motives of the Gospel are subordinate to his main theme, which he unfolds with convincing force.

THE HOLY GOSPEL OF JESUS CHRIST ACCORDING TO ST. JOHN

Prologue

The Word in Himself

IN THE BEGINNING was the Word, and the Word was with God; and the Word was God. He was in the beginning with God. All things were made through him, and without him was made nothing that has been made. In him was life, and the life was the light of men. And the light shines in the darkness; and the darkness grasped it not.

1 1

2

3

4

5

The Word's Mission

There was a man, one sent from God, whose name was John. This man came as a witness, to bear witness concerning the light, that all might believe through him. He was not himself the light, but was to bear witness to the light. It was the true light that enlightens every man who comes into the world. He was in the world, and the world was made through him, and the world knew him not. He came unto his own, and his own received him not. But to as many as received him he gave the power of becoming sons of God; to those who believe in his name:

6

7

8

9

10

11

12

1, 1: St. John employs the term "Word," in referring to the eternal co-existence of Jesus with the Father. This term "Word" designates the Son as a kind of intellectual emanation from the Father. He enjoys the divine nature and yet is distinct from the Father. It was this eternal divine Person who became man in order to reveal God to us, and to accomplish our redemption.

1, 5: *Light* is God's revelation and grace; *Darkness* is man's sinful nature. *Shines:* i.e., is always in the world, in both the past and the present. *Grasped:* this may refer to man's failure to appreciate the light.

13 who were born not of blood, nor of the will of the flesh, nor of the will of man, but of God.

The Word Incarnate

14 And the Word was made flesh, and dwelt among us. And we saw his glory — glory as of the only-begotten of the Father — full of grace
15 and of truth. John bore witness concerning him, and cried, "This was he of whom I said, 'He who is to come after me has been set above me,
16 because he was before me.' " And of his fullness
17 we have all received, grace for grace. For the Law was given through Moses; grace and truth
18 came through Jesus Christ. No one has at any time seen God. The only-begotten Son, who is in the bosom of the Father, he has revealed him.

I: THE PUBLIC MINISTRY OF JESUS

I

The Witness of John the Baptist

19 AND THIS IS THE WITNESS of John, when the Jews sent to him from Jerusalem priests and Levites to ask him,

APR. 21
Oct. 21

20 "Who art thou?" And he acknowledged and did not deny; and he acknowledged, "I am not the
21 Christ." And they asked him, "What then? Art thou Elias?" And he said, "I am not." "Art thou the Prophet?" And he answered, "No."
22 They therefore said to him, "Who art thou? that we may give an answer to those who sent us.
23 What hast thou to say of thyself?" He said, "I am the voice of one crying in the desert, 'Make straight the way of the Lord,' as said Isaias the prophet."
24 And they who had been sent were from among
25 the Pharisees. And they asked him, and said to him, "Why, then, dost thou baptize, if thou art

not the Christ, nor Elias, nor the Prophet?" John 26 said to them in answer, "I baptize with water; but in the midst of you there has stood one whom you do not know. He it is who is to come after 27 me, who has been set above me, the strap of whose sandal I am not worthy to loose."

These things took place at Bethany, beyond 28 the Jordan, where John was baptizing.

The next day John saw Jesus coming to him, 29 and he said, "Behold, the lamb of God, who takes away the sin of the world! This is he of whom I 30 said, 'After me there comes one who has been set above me, because he was before me.' And 31 I did not know him. But that he may be known to Israel, for this reason have I come baptizing with water."

And John bore witness, saying, "I beheld the 32 Spirit descending as a dove from heaven, and it abode upon him. And I did not know him. But 33 he who sent me to baptize with water said to me, 'He upon whom thou wilt see the Spirit descending, and abiding upon him, he it is who baptizes with the Holy Spirit.' And I have seen and have 34 borne witness that this is the Son of God."

The First Disciples

Again the next day John was standing there, and two of his dis-ciples. And looking upon Jesus as he walked by, 36 he said, "Behold the lamb of God!" And the two 37 disciples heard him speak, and they followed Jesus.

| APR. 22 | 35 |
| Oct. 22 |

But Jesus turned round, and seeing them fol- 38 lowing him, said to them, "What is it you seek?" They said to him, "Rabbi (which interpreted means Master), where dwellest thou?" He said 39

[239]

to them, "Come and see." They came and saw where he was staying; and they stayed with him that day. It was about the tenth hour.

40 Now Andrew, the brother of Simon Peter, was one of the two who had heard John and had

41 followed him. He found first his brother Simon and said to him, "We have found the Messias

42 (which interpreted is Christ)." And he led him to Jesus. But Jesus, looking upon him, said, "Thou art Simon, the son of John; thou shalt be called Cephas (which interpreted is Peter)."

43 The next day he was about to leave for Galilee, and he found Philip. And Jesus said to him,

44 "Follow me." Now Philip was from Bethsaida, the town of Andrew and Peter.

45 Philip found Nathanael, and said to him, "We have found him of whom Moses in the Law and the Prophets wrote, Jesus the son of Joseph of

46 Nazareth." And Nathanael said to him, "Can anything good come out of Nazareth?" Philip said to him, "Come and see."

47 Jesus saw Nathanael coming to him, and said of him, "Behold a true Israelite in whom there is

48 no guile!" Nathanael said to him, "Whence knowest thou me?" Jesus answered and said to him, "Before Philip called thee, when thou wast

49 under the fig tree, I saw thee." Nathanael answered him and said, "Rabbi, thou art the Son of God, thou art King of Israel."

50 Answering, Jesus said to him, "Because I said to thee that I saw thee under the fig tree, thou dost believe. Greater things than these shalt

51 thou see." And he said to him, "Amen, amen, I say to you, you shall see heaven opened, and the angels of God ascending and descending upon the Son of Man."

1, 42: *Cephas:* in Aramaic this means "rock."

The Marriage Feast at Cana

And on the third day a marriage | APR. 23 | **2** 1
took place at Cana of Galilee, and | Oct. 23 |
the mother of Jesus was there. Now Jesus too 2
was invited to the marriage, and also his disciples. And the wine having run short, the 3
mother of Jesus said to him, "They have no
wine." And Jesus said to her, "What wouldst 4
thou have me do, woman? My hour has not yet
come." His mother said to the attendants, "Do 5
whatever he tells you."

Now six stone water-jars were placed there, 6
after the Jewish manner of purification, each
holding two or three measures. Jesus said to 7
them, "Fill the jars with water." And they filled
them to the brim. And Jesus said to them, 8
"Draw out now, and take to the chief steward."
And they took it to him.

Now when the chief steward had tasted the 9
water after it had become wine, not knowing
whence it was (though the attendants who had
drawn the water knew), the chief steward called
the bridegroom, ' and said to him, "Every man 10
at first sets forth the good wine, and when they
have drunk freely, then that which is poorer.
But thou hast kept the good wine until now."

This first of his signs Jesus worked at Cana of 11
Galilee; and he manifested his glory, and his

2, 4: *What wouldst thou have me do:* literally, "What to
me and to thee," is an expression which can vary in
meaning with its context, and with the speaker's tone
of voice. The circumstances show that it was not a rebuke. *Woman:* an honorable address in the language
spoken by our Lord. *My hour:* is used of the opening of
Christ's public ministry, or of that ministry as a whole.

2, 11: *Signs:* St. John speaks always of Christ's miracles
as "signs" or "works." We retain the term "sign," but
it is to be understood in the same sense as "miracle"
in the Synoptic Gospels.

12 disciples believed in him. After this he went down to Capharnaum, he and his mother, and his brethren, and his disciples. And they stayed there but a few days.

Cleansing of the Temple

13 Now the Passover of the Jews was at hand,
14 and Jesus went up to Jerusalem. And he found in the temple men selling oxen, sheep and doves,
15 and money-changers at their tables. And making a kind of whip of cords, he drove them all out of the temple, also the sheep and oxen, and he poured out the money of the changers and
16 overturned the tables. And to them who were selling the doves he said, "Take these things away, and do not make the house of my Father a house
17 of business." And his disciples remembered that it is written, "The zeal for thy house has eaten me up."

18 The Jews therefore answered and said to him, "What sign dost thou show us, seeing that thou
19 dost these things?" In answer Jesus said to them, "Destroy this temple, and in three days I
20 will raise it up." The Jews therefore said, "Forty-six years has this temple been in build-
21 ing, and wilt thou raise it up in three days?" But
22 he was speaking of the temple of his body. When, accordingly, he had risen from the dead, his disciples remembered that he had said this, and they believed the Scripture and the word that Jesus had spoken.

23 Now when he was at Jerusalem for the feast of the Passover, many believed in his name,
24 seeing the signs that he was working. But Jesus did not trust himself to them, in that he knew all
25 men, and because he had no need that anyone should bear witness concerning man, for he himself knew what was in man.

Nicodemus

Now there was a certain man among the Pharisees, Nicodemus by name, a ruler of the Jews. This man came to Jesus at night, and said to him, "Rabbi, we know that thou hast come a teacher from God, for no one can work these signs that thou workest unless God be with him." Jesus answered and said to him, "Amen, amen, I say to thee, unless a man be born again, he cannot see the kingdom of God." Nicodemus said to him, "How can a man be born when he is old? Can he enter a second time into his mother's womb and be born again?"

Jesus answered, "Amen, amen, I say to thee, unless a man be born again of water and the Spirit, he cannot enter into the kingdom of God. That which is born of the flesh is flesh; and that which is born of the Spirit is spirit. Do not wonder that I said to thee, 'You must be born again.' The wind blows where it will, and thou hearest its sound but dost not know where it comes from or where it goes. So is everyone who is born of the Spirit."

Nicodemus answered and said to him, "How can these things be?"

Answering him, Jesus said, "Thou art a teacher in Israel and dost not know these things? Amen, amen, I say to thee, we speak of what we know, and we bear witness to what we have seen; and our witness you do not receive. If I have spoken of earthly things to you, and you do not believe, how will you believe if I speak to you

APR. 24
Oct. 24

3 1
2
3
4

5
6
7
8

9

10
11
12

2, 23-25: The faith of those attracted to Christ was imperfect, and He knew it. Hence He did not reveal Himself to them (Chrysostom), or admit them to a more intimate understanding of His teaching and Person.

13 of heavenly things? And no one has ascended into heaven except him who has descended from heaven: the Son of Man who is in heaven.

14 "And as Moses lifted up the serpent in the desert, even so must the Son of Man be lifted

15 up, that those who believe in him may not perish, but may have life everlasting."

16 For God so loved the world that he gave his only-begotten Son, that those who believe in him may not perish, but may have life everlast-

17 ing. For God did not send his Son into the world in order to judge the world, but that the world

18 might be saved through him. He who believes in him is not judged; but he who does not believe is already judged, because he does not believe in the name of the only-begotten Son of God.

19 Now this is the judgment: The light has come into the world, yet men have loved the darkness rather than the light, for their works were evil.

20 For everyone who does evil hates the light, and does not come to the light, that his deeds may

21 not be exposed. But he who does the truth comes to the light that his deeds may be made manifest, for they have been performed in God.

The Witness of John the Baptist

22 After these things Jesus and his disciples came into the land of Judea, and he stayed there with them and bap-
APR. 25 Oct. 25

23 tized. Now John was also baptizing in Aennon near Salim, for there was much water there.

24 And the people came and were baptized. For John had not yet been put into prison.

25 Now there arose a discussion about purification between some of John's disciples and the

---

3, 17: *To judge:* here in the sense of "to punish."

Jews. And they came to John and said to him, 26
"Rabbi, he who was with thee beyond the Jordan, to whom thou hast borne witness, behold
he baptizes and all are coming to him."

John answered and said, "No one can receive 27
anything unless it is given to him from heaven.
You yourselves bear me witness that I said, 'I am 28
not the Christ but have been sent before him.'
He who has the bride is the bridegroom; but the 29
friend of the bridegroom, who stands and hears
him, rejoices exceedingly at the voice of the
bridegroom. This my joy, therefore, is made full.
He must increase, but I must decrease." 30

He who comes from above is over all. He who is 31
from the earth belongs to earth, and of the
earth he speaks. He who comes from heaven
is over all. And he bears witness to that which 32
he has seen and heard, and his witness no one
receives. He who receives his witness has set 33
his seal on this, that God is true. For he whom 34
God has sent speaks the words of God, for not
by measure does God give the Spirit. The Father 35
loves the Son, and has given all things into his
hand. He who believes in the Son has ever- 36
lasting life; he who is unbelieving towards the
Son shall not see life, but the wrath of God
rests upon him.

The Samaritan Woman

When, therefore, Jesus knew that | APR. 26 | **4** 1
the Pharisees had heard that Jesus | Oct. 26 |
made and baptized more disciples than John—
¹ although Jesus himself did not baptize, but 2
his disciples—he left Judea and went again 3
into Galilee. Now he had to pass through 4
Samaria.

He came, accordingly, to a town of Samaria 5
called Sichar, near the field that Jacob gave to

6 his son Joseph. Now Jacob's well was there. Jesus therefore, wearied as he was from the journey, was sitting at the well. It was about 7 the sixth hour. There came a Samaritan woman to draw water.

8 Jesus said to her, "Give me to drink"; ' for his disciples had gone away into the town to 9 buy food. The Samaritan woman therefore said to him, "How is it that thou, although thou art a Jew, dost ask drink of me, who am a Samaritan woman?" For Jews do not associate with Samaritans.

10 Jesus answered and said to her, "If thou didst know the gift of God, and who it is who says to thee, 'Give me to drink,' thou, perhaps, wouldst have asked of him, and he would have given 11 thee living water." The woman said to him, "Sir, thou hast nothing to draw with, and the well is deep. Whence then hast thou living 12 water? Art thou greater than our father Jacob who gave us the well, and drank from it, him-13 self, and his sons, and his flocks?" In answer Jesus said to her, "Everyone who drinks of this water will thirst again. He, however, who drinks of the water that I will give him shall never 14 thirst; but the water that I will give him shall become in him a fountain of water, springing 15 up unto life everlasting." The woman said to him, "Sir, give me this water that I may not thirst, or come here to draw."

16 Jesus said to her, "Go, call thy husband 17 and come here." The woman answered and said, "I have no husband." Jesus said to her, "Thou 18 hast said well, 'I have no husband,' ' for thou hast had five husbands, and he whom thou now hast is not thy husband. In this thou hast spoken truly."

The woman said to him, "Sir, I **19** see that thou art a prophet. Our **20** fathers worshipped on this mountain, but you say that at Jerusalem is the place where one ought to worship." Jesus said to her, "Woman, **21** believe me, the hour is coming when neither on this mountain nor in Jerusalem will you worship the Father. You worship what you do not know; **22** we worship what we know, for salvation is from the Jews. But the hour is coming, and is now **23** here, when the true worshippers will worship the Father in spirit and in truth. For the Father also seeks such to worship him. God is spirit, **24** and they who worship him must worship in spirit and in truth."

The woman said to him, "I know that Messias **25** is coming (who is called Christ), and when he comes he will tell us all things." Jesus said to **26** her, "I who speak with thee am he."

And at this point his disciples came; and they **27** wondered that he was speaking with a woman. Yet no one said, "What dost thou seek?" or, "Why dost thou speak with her?" The woman **28** therefore left her water-jar and went away into the town, and said to the people, "Come and **29** see a man who has told me all that I have ever done. Can he be the Christ?" They went forth **30** from the town and came to meet him. Mean- **31** while, his disciples besought him, saying, "Rabbi, eat." But he said to them, "I have food to eat **32** of which you do not know." The disciples **33** therefore said to one another, "Has someone brought him something to eat?"

4, 23: *In spirit and in truth:* not merely with the external observances of Jews and Samaritans, but internally and according to God's will. *Such to worship him:* God desires as His worshippers those who have this internal disposition.

34 Jesus said to them, "My food is to do the will of him who sent me, to accomplish his work.
35 Do you not say, 'There are yet four months, and then comes the harvest'? Well, I say to you, lift up your eyes and behold that the fields
36 are already white for the harvest. And he who reaps receives a wage, and gathers fruit unto life everlasting, so that the sower and the reaper
37 may rejoice together. For herein is the proverb
38 true, 'One sows, another reaps.' I have sent you to reap that on which you have not labored. Others have labored, and you have entered into their labors."

39 Now many of the Samaritans of that town believed in him because of the word of the woman who bore witness,

APR. 28
Oct. 28

40 "He told me all that I have ever done." When therefore the Samaritans had come to him, they besought him to stay there; and he stayed two
41 days. And far more believed because of his
42 word. And they said to the woman, "We no longer believe because of what thou hast said, for we have heard for ourselves and we know that this is in truth the Savior of the world."

43 Now after two days he departed from that
44 place and went into Galilee, for Jesus himself bore witness that a prophet receives no honor
45 in his own country. When, therefore, he had come into Galilee, the Galileans received him, having seen all that he had done in Jerusalem during the feast, for they also had gone to the feast.

4, 36-38: Under this agricultural figure Christ illustrates the whole plan of His mission. The sowers were God's earlier messengers, as Moses and the prophets. The one who sows for this harvest is Christ. The reapers are the Apostles. In this spiritual harvest both sowers and reapers will rejoice together.

The Official's Son

He came again therefore to Cana of Galilee, 46
where he had made the water wine. And there
was a certain royal official whose son was lying
sick at Capharnaum. When he heard that Jesus 47
had come from Judea into Galilee, he went to
him and besought him to come down and heal
his son, for he was at the point of death.

Jesus therefore said to him, "Unless you see 48
signs and wonders, you do not believe." The 49
royal official said to him, "Sir, come down before my child dies." Jesus said to him, "Go thy 50
way, thy son lives."

The man believed the word that Jesus spoke
to him, and departed. But even as he was now 51
going down, his servants met him and brought
word saying that his son lived. He asked of 52
them therefore the hour in which he had got
better. And they told him, "Yesterday, at the
seventh hour, the fever left him." The father 53
knew then that it was at that very hour in which
Jesus had said to him, "Thy son lives." And
he himself believed, and his whole household.

This was a second sign that Jesus worked 54
when coming from Judea into Galilee.

II

The Cure at the Pool of Bethsaida

AFTER THIS THERE WAS A FEAST | APR. 29 | **5** 1
of the Jews, and Jesus went up to | Oct. 29 |
Jerusalem. Now there is at Jerusalem, by the 2
Sheepgate, a pool called in Hebrew Bethsaida,
having five porticoes. In these were lying a great 3
multitude of the sick, blind, lame, and those
with shrivelled limbs, waiting for the moving
of the water. For an angel of the Lord used to 4
come down at certain times into the pool, and

the water was troubled. And the first to go down into the pool after the troubling of the water was cured of whatever infirmity he had.

5 Now a certain man was there who had been
6 thirty-eight years under his infirmity. When Jesus saw him lying there, and knew that he had been in this state a long time, he said to
7 him, "Dost thou want to get well?" The sick man answered him, "Sir, I have no one to put me into the pool when the water is stirred; for while I am coming, another steps down before
8 me." Jesus said to him, "Rise, take up thy
9 pallet and walk." And at once the man was cured. And he took up his pallet and began to walk. Now that day was a Sabbath.

10 The Jews therefore said to him who had been healed, "It is the Sabbath; thou art not allowed
11 to take up thy pallet." He answered them, "He who made me well said to me, 'Take up thy
12 pallet and walk.'" They asked him then, "Who is the man who said to thee, 'Take up thy pallet
13 and walk'?" But the man who had been healed did not know who it was, for Jesus had quietly gone away, since there was a crowd in the place.
14 Afterwards Jesus found him in the temple, and said to him, "Behold, thou art cured. Sin no more, lest something worse befall thee."
15 The man went away and told the Jews that it was Jesus who had healed him.

16 And this is why the Jews kept persecuting Jesus, because he did such things on the Sab-
17 bath. Jesus, however, answered them, "My
18 Father works even until now, and I work." This, then, is why the Jews were the more anxious to put him to death; because he not only broke the Sabbath, but also called God his own Father, making himself equal to God.

Christ's Claim to Divinity

In answer therefore Jesus said to them, "Amen, amen, I say to you, | APR .30 / Oct. 30 | 19 the Son can do nothing of himself, but only what he sees the Father doing. For whatever he does, this the Son also does in like manner. For the 20 Father loves the Son, and shows him all that he himself does. And greater works than these he will show him, that you may wonder. For as the 21 Father raises the dead and gives them life, even so the Son also gives life to whom he will. For 22 neither does the Father judge any man, but all judgment he has given to the Son, that all men 23 may honor the Son even as they honor the Father. He who does not honor the Son, does not honor the Father who sent him.

"Amen, amen, I say to you, he who hears my 24 word, and believes him who sent me, has life everlasting, and does not come to judgment, but has passed from death to life.

"Amen, amen, I say to you, the hour is com- 25 ing, and now is here, when the dead shall hear the voice of the Son of God, and those who hear shall live. For as the Father has life in himself, 26 even so he has given to the Son also to have life in himself; and he has granted him power to 27 render judgment, because he is Son of Man. Do 28 not wonder at this, for the hour is coming in which all who are in the tombs shall hear the voice of the Son of God. And they who have done 29 good shall come forth unto resurrection of life; but they who have done evil unto resurrection of judgment. Of myself I can do nothing. As I hear, 30 I judge, and my judgment is just because I seek not my own will, but the will of him who sent me.

Justification of Christ's Claims

31 "If I bear witness concerning myself, my wit-
32 ness is not true. There is another who bears
witness concerning me, and I know that the
33 witness that he bears concerning me is true. You
have sent to John, and he has borne witness to
34 the truth. I however do not receive the witness of
man, but I say these things that you may be
35 saved. He was the lamp, burning and shining;
and you desired to rejoice for a while in his
light.

36 "The witness, however, that I have is greater
than that of John. For the works which the
Father has given me to accomplish, these very
works that I do, bear witness to me, that the
37 Father has sent me. And the Father himself,
who has sent me, has borne witness to me. But
38 you have never heard his voice, or seen his face.
And you have not his word abiding in you, since
39 you do not believe him whom he has sent. You
search the Scriptures, because in them you
think that you have life everlasting. And it is
40 they that bear witness to me, yet you are not
willing to come to me that you may have life.

41.42 "I do not receive glory from men. But I know
that you have not the love of God in you.
43 I have come in the name of my Father, and you
do not receive me. If another come in his own
44 name, him you will receive. How can you believe who receive glory from one another, and
do not seek the glory which is from the only
45 God? Do not think that I shall accuse you to the
Father. There is one who accuses you, Moses,
46 in whom you hope. For if you believed Moses
you would believe me also, for he wrote of me.
47 But if you do not believe his writings, how will
you believe my words?"

Jesus Feeds Five Thousand

After this Jesus went away to the other side of the sea of Galilee, **6** 1

MAY 1
Oct. 31

which is that of Tiberias. And there followed 2 him a great crowd, because they witnessed the signs he worked on those who were sick. Jesus 3 therefore went up the mountain, and sat there with his disciples.

Now the Passover, the feast of the Jews, was 4 near. When, therefore, Jesus had lifted up his 5 eyes and seen that a very great crowd had come to him, he said to Philip, "Whence shall we buy bread that these may eat?" But he said this to 6 try him, for he himself knew what he would do.

Philip answered him, "Two hundred denarii 7 worth of bread is not enough for them, that each one may receive a little." One of his disciples, 8 Andrew, the brother of Simon Peter, said to him, "There is a young boy here who has five 9 barley loaves and two fishes; but what are these among so many?" Jesus then said, "Make the 10 people recline."

Now there was much grass in the place. The men therefore reclined, in number about five thousand. Jesus then took the loaves, and when 11 he had given thanks, distributed them to those reclining; and likewise the fishes, as much as they wished. But when they were filled, he said 12 to his disciples, "Gather the fragments that are left over, lest they be wasted." They therefore 13 gathered them up; and they filled twelve baskets with the fragments of the five barley loaves left over by those who had eaten.

When the people, therefore, had seen the sign 14 which Jesus had worked, they said, "This is indeed the Prophet who is to come into the world." So when Jesus perceived that they 15 would come to take him by force and make him king, he fled again to the mountain, himself alone.

Jesus Walks on the Water

16 Now when evening had come, his
17 disciples went down to the sea. And
getting into a boat, they went across the sea
towards Capharnaum. And it was already dark,
18 but Jesus had not come to them. Now the sea
was rising, because a strong wind was blowing.
19 But after they had rowed some twenty-five or
thirty stadia, they beheld Jesus walking upon the
sea, and drawing near to the boat; and they were
20 frightened. But he said to them, "It is I, do not
21 be afraid." They desired therefore to take him
into the boat; and immediately the boat was at
the land towards which they were going.

| MAY 2 |
| Nov. 1 |

The Discourse on the Eucharist

22 The next day, the crowd which had remained
on the other side of the sea observed that there
had been but one boat at that place, and that
Jesus had not gone into the boat with his disciples, but that his disciples had departed alone.
23 But other boats from Tiberias came near the
place where they had eaten the bread, when the
24 Lord gave thanks. When therefore the crowd
perceived that Jesus was not there, nor his disciples, they themselves got into the boats and
25 came to Capharnaum, seeking Jesus. And when
they had found him on the other side of the sea,
they said to him, "Rabbi, when didst thou come
here?"

26 Jesus answered them and said, "Amen, amen,
I say to you, you seek me, not because you have
seen signs, but because you have eaten of the
27 loaves and have been filled. Do not labor for

the food that perishes, but for that which endures unto life everlasting, which the Son of Man will give you. For upon him the Father, God himself, has set his seal."

They said therefore to him, "What are we to do that we may perform the works of God?" 28 In answer Jesus said to them, "This is the work 29 of God, that you believe in him whom he has sent." They said therefore to him, "What sign, 30 then, dost thou, that we may see and believe thee? What work dost thou perform? Our fathers 31 ate the manna in the desert, even as it is written, 'Bread from heaven he gave them to eat.'"

Jesus then said to them, "Amen, amen, I say 32 to you, Moses did not give you the bread from heaven, but my Father gives you the true bread from heaven. For the bread of God is that which 33 comes down from heaven and gives life to the world."

They said therefore to him, "Lord, give us always this bread." 34

| MAY 3 |
| Nov. 2 |

But Jesus said to them, "I am the bread of 35 life. He who comes to me shall not hunger, and he who believes in me shall never thirst. But 36 I have told you that you have seen me and you do not believe. All that the Father gives to me 37 shall come to me, and him who comes to me I will not cast out. For I have come down from 38 heaven, not to do my own will, but the will of him who sent me. Now this is the will of him 39 who sent me, the Father, that I should lose nothing of what he has given me, but that I should raise it up on the last day. For this is 40 the will of my Father who sent me, that whoever beholds the Son, and believes in him, shall have everlasting life, and I will raise him up on the last day."

41 The Jews therefore murmured about him because he had said, "I am the bread that has
42 come down from heaven." And they kept saying, "Is this not Jesus the son of Joseph, whose father and mother we know? How, then, does he say, 'I have come down from heaven'?"

43 In answer therefore Jesus said to them, "Do
44 not murmur among yourselves. No one can come to me unless the Father who sent me draw him, and I will raise him up on the last day.
45 It is written in the Prophets, 'And they all shall be taught of God.' Everyone who has listened
46 to the Father, and has learned, comes to me; not that anyone has seen the Father except him
47 who is from God, he has seen the Father. Amen, amen, I say to you, he who believes in me has life everlasting.

48·49 "I am the bread of life. Your fathers ate the
50 manna in the desert, and have died. This is the bread that comes down from heaven, so that if
51 anyone eat of it he will not die. I am the living
52 bread that has come down from heaven. If anyone eat of this bread he shall live forever; and the bread that I will give is my flesh for the life of the world."

53 The Jews on that account argued with one another, saying, "How can this man give us his flesh to eat?"

54 Jesus therefore said to them, "Amen, amen, I say to you, unless | MAY 4 / Nov. 3 |
you eat the flesh of the Son of Man, and drink his
55 blood, you shall not have life in you. He who eats my flesh and drinks my blood has life everlasting and I will raise him up on the last day.
56 For my flesh is food indeed, and my blood is
57 drink indeed. He who eats my flesh, and drinks
58 my blood, abides in me and I in him. As the

living Father has sent me, and as I live because of the Father, so he who eats me, he also shall live because of me. This is the bread that has come down from heaven; not as your fathers ate the manna, and died. He who eats this bread shall live forever." 59

These things he said when teaching in the synagogue at Capharnaum. 60

Many of his disciples therefore, when they heard this, said, "This is a hard saying. Who can listen to it?" But Jesus, knowing in himself that his disciples were murmuring at this, said to them, "Does this scandalize you? What then if you should see the Son of Man ascending where he was before? It is the spirit that gives life; the flesh profits nothing. The words that I have spoken to you are spirit and life. But there are some among you who do not believe." For Jesus knew from the beginning who they were who did not believe, and who it was who should betray him. 61 62 63 64 65

And he said, "This is why I have said to you, 'No one can come to me unless he is enabled to do so by my Father.'" From this time many of his disciples turned back and no longer went about with him. 66 67

Jesus therefore said to the Twelve, "Do you also wish to go away?" Simon Peter therefore answered, "Lord, to whom shall we go? Thou hast words of everlasting life, and we have come to believe and to know that thou art the Christ, the Son of God." 68 69 70

Jesus answered them, "Have I not chosen you, the Twelve? Yet one of you is a devil." Now he was speaking of Judas Iscariot, the son of Simon; for he it was, though one of the Twelve, who would betray him. 71 72

III

Jesus Goes Secretly to the
Feast of Tabernacles

7 1 NOW AFTER THESE THINGS Jesus
went about in Galilee, for he did not

MAY 5
Nov. 4

wish to go about in Judea because the Jews were
2 seeking to put him to death. Now the Jewish
3 feast of Tabernacles was at hand. His brethren
therefore said to him, "Leave here and go into
Judea that thy disciples also may see the works
4 that thou dost; for no one does a thing in secret
if he wants to be publicly known. If thou dost
these things, manifest thyself to the world."
5 For not even his brethren believed in him.

6 Jesus therefore said to them, "My time has
not yet come, but your time is always at hand.
7 The world cannot hate you, but it hates me
because I bear witness concerning it, that its
8 works are evil. As for you, go up to the feast,
but I do not go up to this feast, for my time is
not yet fulfilled."

9 When he had said these things he stayed on
10 in Galilee. But as soon as his brethren had gone
up to the feast, then he also went up, not publicly, but as it were privately.

11 The Jews therefore were looking for him at
the feast, and were saying, "Where is he?"
12 And there was much whispered comment among
the crowd concerning him. For some were saying, "He is a good man." But others were saying,
13 "No, rather he seduces the crowd." Yet for fear
of the Jews no one spoke openly of him.

14 When, however, the feast was already half
over, Jesus went up into the temple and began
15 to teach. And the Jews marvelled, saying, "How
does this man come by learning, since he has
not studied?"

The Source of Christ's Teachings

Jesus answered them and said, "My teaching 16 is not my own, but his who sent me. If anyone 17 desires to do his will, he will know of the teaching whether it is from God, or whether I speak on my own authority. He who speaks on his own 18 authority seeks his own glory. But he who seeks the glory of the one who sent him is truthful, and there is no injustice in him. Did not Moses 19 give you the Law, and none of you observes the Law? Why do you seek to put me to death?" 20 The crowd answered and said, "Thou hast a devil. Who seeks to put thee to death?"

Jesus answered and said to them, "One work 21 I did and you all wonder. For this reason Moses 22 gave you the circumcision"—not that it is from Moses, but from the fathers—"and on a Sabbath you circumcise a man. If a man receives circum- 23 cision on a Sabbath, that the Law of Moses may not be broken, are you indignant with me because I made a whole man well on a Sabbath? Judge not by appearances but give just judg- 24 ment."

Christ's Origin

Some therefore of the people of | MAY 6 | 25
Jerusalem were saying, "Is not this | Nov. 5 |
the man they seek to kill? And behold, he speaks 26 openly and they say nothing to him. Can it be that the rulers have really come to know that this

---

7, 21: *One work:* the cure of the sick man at the pool of Bethsaida.

7, 22: Circumcision was established as a sign of the covenant made with Abraham. Moses, however, provided the laws which governed it. When the recipient was a Jew, the Jews interpreted these laws as permitting circumcision, and all things necessary thereto, on the Sabbath.

27 is the Christ? Yet we know where this man is from; but when the Christ comes, no one will know where he is from."

28 Jesus therefore, while teaching in the temple, cried out and said, "You both know me, and know where I am from. Yet I have not come of myself, but he is true who has sent me, whom
29 you do not know. I know him because I am from him, and he has sent me."

30 They wanted therefore to seize him, but no one laid hands on him because his hour had not
31 yet come. Many of the people, however, believed in him, and they kept saying, "When the Christ comes will he work more signs than this man
32 works?" The Pharisees heard the crowd whispering these things about him, and the rulers and Pharisees sent attendants to seize him.

33 Jesus then said, "Yet a little while I am with
34 you, and then I go to him who sent me. You will seek me and will not find me; and where I am
35 you cannot come." The Jews therefore said among themselves, "Where is he going that we shall not find him? Will he go to those dispersed among the Gentiles, and teach the Gentiles?
36 What is this statement that he has made, 'You will seek me and will not find me, and where I am you cannot come'?"

37 Now on the last, the great day of the feast, Jesus stood and cried out, saying, "If anyone
38 thirst, let him come to me and drink. He who believes in me, as the Scripture says, 'From within him there shall flow rivers of living water.'"
39 He said this, however, of the Spirit whom they who believed in him were to receive; for the Spirit had not yet been given, since Jesus had not yet been glorified.

40 Some of the crowd, therefore, when they had heard these words, said, "This is truly the

Prophet." Others said, "This is the Christ." 41
Some, however, said, "Can the Christ come
from Galilee? Does not the Scripture say that 42
it is of the offspring of David, and from Bethlehem, the village where David lived, that the
Christ is to come?" So there arose a division 43
among the crowd because of him. And some of 44
them wanted to seize him, but no one laid hands
on him.

The attendants therefore came to the chief 45
priests and Pharisees; and these said to them,
"Why have you not brought him?" ' The at- 46
tendants answered, "Never has man spoken as
this man." The Pharisees then answered them, 47
"Have you also been led astray? ' Has any one 48
of the rulers believed in him, or any of the
Pharisees? But this crowd, which does not 49
know the Law, is accursed."

Nicodemus, he who had come to him at 50
night, who was one of them, said to them, "Does 51
our Law judge a man unless it first give him a
hearing, and know what he does?" They an- 52
swered and said to him, "Art thou also a Galilean? Search the Scriptures and see that out of
Galilee arises no prophet."

The Adulteress

And they returned each one to his | MAY 7 | 53
own house. But Jesus went to the | Nov. 6 | 8 1
Mount of Olives. And at daybreak he came 2
again into the temple, and all the people came
to him; and sitting down he began to teach them.

Now the Scribes and Pharisees brought a 3
woman caught in adultery, and setting her in the
midst, ' said to him, "Master, this woman has 4
just now been caught in adultery. And in the 5
Law Moses commanded us to stone such per-

[261]

6 sons. What, therefore, dost thou say?" Now they were saying this to test him, in order that they might be able to accuse him. But Jesus, stooping down, began to write with his finger on the ground.

7 But when they continued asking him, he raised himself and said to them, "Let him who is without sin among you be the first to cast a stone

8 at her." And again stooping down, he began to

9 write on the ground. But hearing this, they went away, one by one, beginning with the eldest. And Jesus remained alone, with the woman standing in the midst.

10 And Jesus, raising himself, said to her, "Woman, where are they? Has no one condemned

11 thee?"¹ She said, "No one, Lord." Then Jesus said, "Neither will I condemn thee. Go thy way, and from now on sin no more."

The Light of the World

12 Again, therefore, Jesus spoke to them, saying, "I am the light of the world. He who follows me does not walk in the darkness, but will have the

13 light of life." The Pharisees therefore said to him, "Thou bearest witness to thyself. Thy witness is not true."

14 Jesus answered and said to them, "Even if I bear witness to myself, my witness is true, because I know where I came from and where I go. But you do not know where I came from or where

15 I go. You judge according to the flesh; I judge

16 no one. And even if I do judge, my judgment is true, because I am not alone, but with me is he

17 who sent me, the Father. And in your Law it is

18 written that the witness of two persons is true. It is I who bear witness to myself, and he who sent me, the Father, bears witness to me."

[262]

They therefore said to him, "Where is thy 19 father?" Jesus answered, "You know neither me nor my Father. If you knew me, you would then know my Father also."

Jesus spoke these words in the treasury, while 20 teaching in the temple. And no one seized him, because his hour had not yet come.

The Son of God

Again, therefore, Jesus said to 21 them, "I go, and you will seek me, and in your sin you will die. Where I go you cannot come." The Jews therefore kept saying, 22 "Will he kill himself, since he says, 'Where I go you cannot come'?"

MAY 8 Nov. 7

And he said to them, "You are from below, I 23 am from above. You are of this world, I am not of this world. Therefore I said to you that you will 24 die in your sins; for if you do not believe that I am he, you will die in your sin."

They therefore said to him, "Who art thou?" 25 Jesus said to them, "Why do I speak to you at all! I have many things to speak and to judge con- 26 cerning you; but he who sent me is true, and the things that I heard from him, these I speak in the world." And they did not understand that he 27 was speaking to them about the Father.

Jesus therefore said to them, "When you have 28 lifted up the Son of Man, then you will know that I am he, and that of myself I do nothing; but that I preach only what the Father has taught me. And he who sent me is with me; he 29 has not left me alone, because I do always the things that are pleasing to him." When he was 30 speaking these things, many believed in him.

8, 24: *I am he:* i.e., the Messias.

The Children of Abraham

31   Jesus therefore said to the Jews who had
come to believe in him, "If you abide in my
32 word, you shall be my disciples indeed, ' and
you shall know the truth, and the truth shall
33 make you free." They answered him, "We are
the children of Abraham, and we have never
yet been slaves to anyone. How sayest thou,
'You shall be free'?"

34   Jesus answered them, "Amen, amen, I say
to you, everyone who commits sin is a slave
35 of sin. But the slave does not abide in the house
36 forever; the son abides there forever. If therefore the Son makes you free, you will be free
37 indeed. I know that you are the children of
Abraham; but you seek to kill me because my
38 word takes no hold among you. I speak what I
have seen with the Father; and you do what you
have seen with your father."

39   They answered and said to him, "Abraham
is our father." Jesus said to them, "If you are
the children of Abraham, do the works of
40 Abraham. But as it is, you are seeking to kill
me, one who has spoken the truth to you
which I have heard from God. That is not what
41 Abraham did. You are doing the works of your
father." They therefore said to him, "We have
not been born of fornication; we have one
Father, God."

42   Jesus therefore said to them, "If   MAY 9
God were your Father, you would   Nov. 8
surely love me. For from God I came forth and
have come; for neither have I come of myself,
43 but he sent me. Why do you not understand
my speech? Because you cannot listen to my
44 word. The father from whom you are is the
devil, and the desires of your father it is your
will to do. He was a murderer from the begin-

ning, and has not stood in the truth because there is no truth in him. When he tells a lie he speaks from his very nature, for he is a liar and the father of lies. But because I speak the 45 truth you do not believe me. Which of you can 46 convict me of sin? If I speak the truth, why do you not believe me? He who is of God hears 47 the words of God. The reason why you do not hear is that you are not of God."

Christ and Abraham

The Jews therefore in answer said to him, 48 "Are we not right in saying that thou art a Samaritan, and hast a devil?" Jesus answered, 49 "I have not a devil, but I honor my Father, and you dishonor me. Yet I do not seek my own 50 glory; there is one who seeks and who judges. Amen, amen, I say to you, if anyone keep my 51 word, he will never see death."

The Jews therefore said, "Now we know that 52 thou hast a devil. Abraham is dead, and the prophets, and thou sayest, 'If anyone keep my word he will never taste death.' Art thou 53 greater than our father Abraham, who is dead? And the prophets are dead. Whom dost thou make thyself?"

Jesus answered, "If I glorify myself, my 54 glory is nothing. It is my Father who glorifies me, of whom you say that he is your God. And you do not know him, but I know him. 55 And if I say that I do not know him, I shall be like you, a liar. But I know him, and I keep his word. Abraham your father rejoiced that he 56 was to see my day. He saw it and was glad." The Jews therefore said to him, "Thou art not 57 yet fifty years old, and hast thou seen Abraham?"

8, 56: *He saw it:* Abraham can be said to have seen Christ's day either in faith and prophetic vision, or from his place in limbo when Christ was born.

58 Jesus said to them, "Amen, amen, I say to
59 you, before Abraham came to be, I am." They
therefore took up stones to cast at him; but
Jesus hid himself, and went out from the temple.

The Man Born Blind

9 1 And as he was passing by, he saw
2 a man blind from birth. And his
disciples asked him, "Rabbi, who has sinned,
this man or his parents, that he should be born
3 blind?" Jesus answered, "Neither has this man
sinned, nor his parents, but the works of God
4 were to be made manifest in him. I must do
the works of him who sent me while it is day;
5 night is coming, when no one can work. As
long as I am in the world I am the light of the
world."

MAY 10
Nov. 9

6 When he had said these things, he spat on
the ground and made clay with the spittle, and
7 spread the clay over his eyes, and said to him,
"Go, wash in the pool of Siloe (which is interpreted 'sent')." So he went away, and
8 washed, and returned seeing. The neighbors
therefore and they who were wont to see him
before as a beggar, began saying, "Is not this
he who used to sit and beg?" Some said, "It is
9 he." But others said, "By no means, he only
resembles him." Yet the man declared, "I
am he."

10 They therefore said to him, "How were thy
11 eyes opened?" He answered, "The man who
is called Jesus made clay and anointed my eyes,
and said to me, 'Go to the pool of Siloe and
wash.' And I went and washed, and I see."
12 And they said to him, "Where is he?" He said,
"I do not know."

8, 58: *I am:* the use of the present emphasizes His
eternal existence.

They took him who had been blind to the 13
Pharisees. Now it was a Sabbath on which 14
Jesus made the clay and opened his eyes. Again, 15
therefore, the Pharisees asked him how he
received his sight. But he said to them, "He
put clay upon my eyes, and I washed, and I see."

Therefore some of the Pharisees said, "This 16
man is not from God, for he does not keep the
Sabbath." But others said, "How can a man
who is a sinner work these signs?" And there
was a division among them. Again therefore 17
they said to the blind man, "What dost thou
say of him who opened thy eyes?" But he said,
"He is a prophet."

The Jews therefore did not believe of him 18
that he had been blind and had got his sight,
until they called the parents of the one who
had gained his sight, and questioned them, 19
saying, "Is this your son, of whom you say
that he was born blind? How then does he now
see?" His parents answered them and said, "We 20
know that this is our son, and that he was born
blind; but how he now sees we do not know, 21
or who opened his eyes we ourselves do not
know. Ask him; he is of age, let him speak for
himself." These things his parents said because 22
they feared the Jews. For already the Jews had
agreed that if anyone were to confess him to be
the Christ, he should be put out of the synagogue. This is why his parents said, "He is of 23
age; question him."

They therefore called a second | MAY 11 | 24
time the man who had been blind, | Nov. 10 |
and said to him, "Give glory to God! We ourselves know that this man is a sinner." He 25
therefore said, "Whether he is a sinner, I do
not know. One thing I do know, that whereas

[267]

26 I was blind, now I see." They therefore said
to him, "What did he do to thee? How did he
27 open thy eyes?" He answered them, "I have
told you already, and you have heard. Why
would you hear again? Would you also become
28 his disciples?" They heaped abuse on him
therefore, and said, "Thou art his disciple, but
29 we are disciples of Moses. We know that God
spoke to Moses; but as for this man, we do
30 not know where he is from." In answer the man
said to them, "Why, herein is the marvel, that
you do not know where he is from, and yet he
31 opened my eyes. Now we know that God does
not hear sinners; but if anyone is a worshipper
32 of God, and does his will, him he hears. Not
from the beginning of the world has it been
heard that anyone opened the eyes of a man
33 born blind. If this man were not from God, he
34 could do nothing." They answered and said to
him, "Thou wast altogether born in sins, and
dost thou teach us?" And they turned him out.

35 Jesus heard that they had turned him out,
and when he had found him, said to him, "Dost
36 thou believe in the Son of God?" He answered
and said, "Who is he, Lord, that I may believe
37 in him?" And Jesus said to him, "Thou hast
both seen him, and he it is who speaks with
38 thee." ' And he said, "I believe, Lord." And
falling down, he worshipped him.

39 And Jesus said, "For judgment have I come
into this world, that they who do not see may
40 see, and they who see may become blind." And
some of the Pharisees who were with him heard
this, and they said to him, "Are we also blind?"
41 Jesus said to them, "If you were blind, you would
not have sin. But now that you say, 'We see,'
your sin remains.

The Good Shepherd

"Amen, amen, I say to you, he | MAY 12 | **10** 1
who enters not by the door into the | Nov. 11 |
sheepfold, but climbs up another way, is a thief
and a robber. But he who enters by the door is 2
shepherd of the sheep. To this man the gate- 3
keeper opens, and the sheep hear his voice, and
he calls his own sheep by name and leads them
forth. And when he has let out his own sheep, he 4
goes before them; and the sheep follow him because they know his voice. But a stranger they 5
will not follow, but will flee from him, because
they do not know the voice of strangers."

This parable Jesus spoke to them, but they 6
did not understand what he was saying to them.

Again, therefore, Jesus said to them, "Amen, 7
amen, I say to you, I am the door of the sheep.
All whoever have come are thieves and robbers; 8
but the sheep have not heard them. I am the 9
door. If anyone enter by me he shall be safe,
and shall go in and out, and shall find pastures.
The thief comes only to steal, and slay, and 10
destroy. I came that they may have life, and have
it more abundantly.

" I am the good shepherd. The good shepherd 11
lays down his life for his sheep. But the hireling, 12
who is not a shepherd, whose own the sheep are
not, sees the wolf coming and leaves the sheep
and flees. And the wolf snatches and scatters
the sheep; but the hireling flees because he is a 13
hireling, and has no concern for the sheep.

"I am the good shepherd, and I know mine 14

10, 8: The Greek text reads, "all who have come before
me." This can refer to pretenders, e.g., Judas the Galilean,
or to the Scribes and Pharisees, who taught largely their
own doctrine.

15 and mine know me, ' even as the Father knows
me and I know the Father; and I lay down my
16 life for my sheep. And other sheep I have that
are not of this fold. Them also I must bring,
and they shall hear my voice, and there shall be
17 one fold and one shepherd. For this reason the
Father loves me, because I lay down my life that
18 I may take it up again. No one takes it from me,
but I lay it down of myself. I have the power to
lay it down, and I have the power to take it up
again. Such is the command I have received
from my Father."

19 Again there arose a division among the Jews
20 because of these words. Many of them were
saying, "He has a devil and is mad. Why do you
21 listen to him?" Others were saying, "These are
not the words of one who has a devil. Can a
devil open the eyes of the blind?"

At the Feast of the Dedication

22 Now there took place at Jerusalem | MAY 13
the feast of the Dedication; and it | Nov. 12
23 was winter. And Jesus was walking in the
24 temple, in Solomon's portico. The Jews therefore gathered round him, and said to him, "How
long dost thou keep us in suspense? If thou art
the Christ, tell us openly."

25 Jesus answered them, "I tell you and you do
not believe. The works that I do in the name of
my Father, these bear witness concerning me.
26 But you do not believe because you are not of
27 my sheep. My sheep hear my voice, and I know
28 them and they follow me. And I give them everlasting life; and they shall never perish, neither
29 shall anyone snatch them out of my hand. What
my Father has given me is greater than all; and
no one is able to snatch anything out of the hand
30 of my Father. I and the Father are one."

The Jews therefore took up stones to stone 31
him. Jesus answered them, "Many good works 32
have I shown you from my Father. For which of
these works do you stone me?" The Jews an- 33
swered him, "Not for a good work do we stone
thee, but for blasphemy, and because thou, being a man, makest thyself God."

Jesus answered them, "Is it not written in 34
your Law, 'I said you are gods'? If he called 35
them gods to whom the word of God was addressed (and the Scripture cannot be broken),
do you say of him whom the Father has made 36
holy and sent into the world, 'Thou blasphemest,'
because I said, 'I am the Son of God'? If I do not 37
perform the works of my Father, do not believe
me. But if I do perform them, and if you are 38
not willing to believe me, believe the works, that
you may know and believe that the Father is in
me and I in the Father."

They sought therefore to seize him; and he 39
went forth out of their hands.

Jesus in Perea

And again he went away beyond the Jordan, 40
to the place where John was at first baptizing;
and there he stayed. And many came to him; 41

10, 29: *What . . . is greater than all:* this gift may have
been Christ's power, the work of redemption, or the
flock itself. Generally, however, it is understood to be
Christ's divine nature. It is taken in this sense by the
Lateran Council.

10, 34 ff: The judges who administered the Law were
called gods, because they represented God. If they,
merely men, and so often unfaithful to their duties, as in
Ps. 81, could enjoy this title, how much more right to it
has He who was made holy, i.e., especially set aside for
God's work!

and they were saying, "John indeed worked no
42 sign. All things, however, that John said of this
man were true." And many believed in him.

The Raising of Lazarus

11 1   Now a certain man was sick, | MAY 14 |
Lazarus of Bethany, the village of | Nov. 13 |
2 Mary and her sister Martha. Now it was Mary
who anointed the Lord with ointment, and wiped
his feet dry with her hair, whose brother Lazarus
3 was sick. The sisters therefore sent to him, saying, "Lord, behold, he whom thou lovest is sick."
4 But when Jesus heard this, he said to them,
"This sickness is not unto death, but for the
glory of God, that through it the Son of God may
5 be glorified." Now Jesus loved Martha and her
6 sister Mary, and Lazarus. So when he heard
that he was sick, he remained two more days in
7 the same place. Then afterwards he said to his
disciples, "Let us go again into Judea."
8 The disciples said to him, "Rabbi, just now
the Jews were seeking to stone thee; and dost
9 thou go there again?" Jesus answered, "Are
there not twelve hours in the day? If a man walks
in the day, he does not stumble, because he sees
10 the light of this world. But if he walks in the
night, he stumbles, because the light is not in
him."
11 These things he spoke, and after this he said
to them, "Lazarus, our friend, sleeps. But I go
12 that I may wake him from sleep." His disciples
therefore said, "Lord, if he sleeps, he will be
13 safe." Now Jesus had spoken of his death, but
they thought he was speaking of the repose of
14 sleep. So then Jesus said to them plainly, "Laza-
15 rus is dead; and I rejoice on your account that
I was not there, that you may believe. But let us
16 go to him." Thomas, who is called the Twin,

said therefore to his fellow-disciples, "Let us also go, that we may die with him."

Jesus therefore came and found him already 17 four days in the tomb. Now Bethany was close to 18 Jerusalem, some fifteen stadia distant. And 19 many of the Jews had come to Martha and Mary, to comfort them on account of their brother. When, therefore, Martha heard that Jesus was 20 coming, she went to meet him. But Mary remained at home.

Martha therefore said to Jesus, | MAY 15 | 21 "Lord, if thou hadst been here my | Nov. 14 | brother would not have died. But even now I 22 know that whatever thou shalt ask of God, God will give it to thee."

Jesus said to her, "Thy brother shall rise." 23 Martha said to him, "I know that he will rise at 24 the resurrection, on the last day." Jesus said to 25 her, "I am the resurrection and the life; he who believes in me, even if he die, shall live; and 26 whoever lives and believes in me, shall never die. Dost thou believe this?" She said to him, 27 "Yes, Lord, I believe that thou art the Christ, the Son of God, who hast come into the world."

And when she had said this, she went away 28 and quietly called Mary her sister, saying, "The Master is here and calls thee." As soon as she 29 heard this, she rose quickly and came to him, ' for Jesus had not yet come into the village, but 30 was still at the place where Martha had met him.

When, therefore, the Jews who were with 31 her in the house and were comforting her, saw Mary rise up quickly and go out, they followed her, saying, "She is going to the tomb to weep there."

When, therefore, Mary came where Jesus 32 was, and saw him, she fell at his feet, and said to him, "Lord, if thou hadst been here, my

33 brother would not have died." When, therefore, Jesus saw her weeping, and the Jews who had come with her weeping, he groaned in

34 spirit and was troubled, ' and said, "Where have you laid him?" They said to him, "Lord, come

35. 36 and see." And Jesus wept. The Jews therefore

37 said, "See how he loved him." But some of them said, "Could not he who opened the eyes of the blind, have caused that this man should not die?"

38 Jesus therefore, again groaning in himself, came to the tomb. Now it

MAY 16
Nov. 15

was a cave, and a stone was laid against it.

39 ' Jesus said, "Take away the stone." Martha, the sister of him who was dead, said to him, "Lord, by this time he is already decayed, for

40 he is dead four days." Jesus said to her, "Have I not told thee that if thou believe thou shalt

41 behold the glory of God?" They therefore removed the stone. And Jesus, raising his eyes, said, "Father, I give thee thanks that thou

42 hast heard me. Yet I knew that thou always hearest me; but because of the people who stand round, I spoke, that they may believe

43 that thou hast sent me." When he had said this, he cried out with a loud voice, "Lazarus,

44 come forth!" And at once he who had been dead came forth, bound feet and hands with bandages, and his face was tied up with a cloth. Jesus said to them, "Unbind him, and let him go."

The Council

45 Many therefore of the Jews who had come to Mary, and had seen what he did, believed

46 in him. But some of them went away to the Pharisees, and told them the things that Jesus had done.

The chief priests and the Pharisees therefore 47 gathered together a council, and said, "What are we doing? for this man is working many signs. If we let him alone as he is, all will be- 48 lieve in him, and the Romans will come and take away both our place and our nation."

But one of them, Caiphas, being high priest 49 that year, said to them, "You know nothing at all; nor do you reflect that it is expedient for 50 us that one man die for the people, instead of the whole nation perishing." This, however, he 51 said not of himself; but being high priest that year, he prophesied that Jesus was to die for the nation; and not only for the nation, but 52 that he might gather into one the children of God who were scattered abroad. So from that 53 day forth their plan was to put him to death.

Jesus in Ephrem

Jesus therefore no longer went about openly 54 among the Jews, but withdrew to the district near the desert, to a town called Ephrem; and there he stayed with his disciples.

Now the Passover of the Jews was at hand; 55 and many from the country went up to Jeru- salem before the Passover, in order to purify themselves. And they were looking for Jesus. 56 And as they stood in the temple they were say- ing to one another, "What do you think, that he is not coming to the feast?" But the chief priests and Pharisees had given orders that, if anyone knew where he was, he should report it, so that they might seize him.

11, 51: Although Caiphas saw only the present, temporal significance of his words, he was led to make the state- ment by God who intended the higher sense. It was not necessary that Caiphas realize the prophetic character of his counsel.

The Anointing at Bethany

12 1 Jesus therefore, six days before the Passover, came to Bethany where Lazarus, whom Jesus had raised to life, 2 had died. And they made him a supper there; and Martha served, while Lazarus was one of those reclining at table with him.

| MAY 17 |
| Nov. 16 |

3 Mary therefore took a pound of ointment, genuine nard of great value, and anointed the feet of Jesus, and with her hair wiped his feet dry. And the house was filled with the odor of 4 the ointment. Then one of his disciples, Judas Iscariot, he who was about to betray him, said, 5 "Why was this ointment not sold for three 6 hundred denarii, and given to the poor?" Now he said this, not that he cared for the poor, but because he was a thief, and holding the purse, 7 used to take what was put in it. Jesus therefore said, "Let her be—that she may keep it for the 8 day of my burial. For the poor you have always with you, but you do not always have me."

9 Now the great crowd of the Jews learned that he was there; and they came, not only because of Jesus, but that they might see Lazarus, whom he had raised from the dead. 10 But the chief priests planned to put Lazarus to 11 death also. For on his account many of the Jews began to leave them and to believe in Jesus.

Triumphal Entry into Jerusalem

12 Now the next day, the great crowd which had come to the feast, when they heard that 13 Jesus was coming to Jerusalem, took the branches of palms and went forth to meet him. And they cried out, "Hosanna! Blessed is he who comes in the name of the Lord, the king of Israel!"

And Jesus found a young ass, and sat upon 14
it, as it is written, "Fear not, daughter of Sion; 15
behold, thy king comes, sitting upon the colt
of an ass." These things his disciples did not 16
at first understand. But when Jesus was glorified, then they remembered that these things
were written about him, and that they had done
these things to him.

The crowd therefore, which was with him 17
when he called Lazarus from the tomb and
raised him from the dead, bore witness to him.
And the reason why the crowd also went to 18
meet him was that they heard that he had
worked this sign. The Pharisees therefore said 19
among themselves, "Do you see that we avail
nothing? Behold, the entire world has gone
after him!"

Last Words of Jesus to the People

Now there were certain Gentiles among those 20
who had gone up to worship on the feast. These 21
therefore approached Philip, who was from Bethsaida of Galilee, and asked him, saying, "Sir,
we wish to see Jesus." Philip came and told 22
Andrew; again, Andrew and Philip spoke to
Jesus.

But Jesus answered them, "The hour has 23
come for the Son of Man to be glorified. Amen, 24
amen, I say to you, unless the grain of wheat
falls into the ground and dies, it remains alone. 25
But if it dies, it brings forth much fruit. He who
loves his life, loses it; and he who hates his life
in this world, keeps it unto life everlasting.
If anyone serves me, let him follow me; and 26
where I am there also shall my servant be. If
anyone serves me, my Father will honor him.

27 "Now my soul is troubled. And
what shall I say? Father, save me
from this hour! No, this is why I came to this
28 hour. Father, glorify thy name!" There came
therefore a voice from heaven, "I have both
29 glorified it, and I will glorify it again." Then
the crowd which was standing round and had
heard, said that it had thundered. Others said,
30 "An angel has spoken to him." Jesus answered
and said, "Not for me did this voice come,
but for you.

31 "Now is the judgment of the world; now will
32 the prince of the world be cast out. And I, if I
be lifted up from the earth, will draw all things
33 to myself." Now he said this signifying by what
34 death he was to die. The crowd answered him,
"We have heard from the Law that the Christ
abides forever. And how canst thou say, 'The
Son of Man must be lifted up'? Who is this
35 Son of Man?" Jesus therefore said to them,
"Yet a little while the light is among you. Walk
while you have the light, that darkness may not
overtake you. He who walks in the darkness
36 does not know where he goes. While you have
the light, believe in the light, that you may
become sons of light."

These things Jesus spoke, and he went away
and hid himself from them.

Incredulity

37 Now though he had worked so many signs in
38 their presence, they did not believe in him; that
the word which the prophet Isaias spoke might
be fulfilled, "Lord, who has believed our report,
and to whom has the arm of the Lord been re-

12, 27: *Troubled*: this emotion is human fear and sadness,
occasioned by the impending Passion. St. Thomas calls
this scene a brief anticipation of the Agony in the Garden.

vealed?" This is why they could not believe, 39
because Isaias said again, "He has blinded their 40
eyes, and hardened their hearts; lest they see
with their eyes, and understand with their
mind, and be converted, and I heal them." Isaias 41
said these things when he saw his glory and
spoke of him.

And yet, even among the rulers, many be- 42
lieved in him; but because of the Pharisees they
did not acknowledge it, lest they should be put
out of the synagogue. For they loved the glory of 43
men more than the glory of God.

But Jesus cried out, and said, "He who be- 44
lieves in me, believes not in me but in him who
sent me. And he who sees me, sees him who 45
sent me. I have come a light into the world, 46
that whoever believes in me may not remain in
the darkness. And if anyone hears my words, 47
and does not keep them, it is not I who judge
him; for I have not come to judge the world, but
to save the world. He who rejects me, and does 48
not accept my words, has one to condemn him.
The word that I have spoken will condemn him
on the last day. For I have not spoken on my own 49
authority, but he who sent me, the Father, has
commanded me what I should say, and what I
should declare. And I know that his command- 50
ment is everlasting life. The things, therefore,
that I speak, I speak as the Father has bidden
me."

12, 39: *They could not believe:* faith is a gift of God
which often cannot be received because of an obstacle
which man puts in its way. The obstacle here is their
obstinacy. Isaias had foretold this.

II: THE PASSION, DEATH AND RESURRECTION
1. The Last Supper
The Washing of the Feet

13 1 BEFORE THE FEAST OF THE PASS-
OVER, Jesus, knowing that the hour
had come for him to pass out of this world to the
Father, having loved his own who were in the
world, loved them to the end.

MAY 19	Nov. 18

2 And during the supper, the devil having already put it into the heart of Judas Iscariot, the
3 son of Simon, to betray him, Jesus, ' knowing
that the Father had given all things into his
hands, and that he had come forth from God and
4 was going to God, rose from the supper and laid
aside his garments, and taking a towel girded
5 himself. Then he poured water into the basin
and began to wash the feet of the disciples, and
to dry them with the towel with which he was
girded.

6 He came, then, to Simon Peter. And Peter
said to him, "Lord, dost thou wash my feet?"
7 ' Jesus answered and said to him, "What I do
thou knowest not now; but thou shalt know
8 hereafter." Peter said to him, "Thou shalt never
wash my feet!" Jesus answered him, "If I do
not wash thee, thou shalt have no part with me."
9 Simon Peter said to him, "Lord, not my feet only,
10 but also my hands and my head!" Jesus said to
him, "He who has bathed needs only to wash,
and he is clean all over. And you are clean, but

13, 10: *Needs only to wash:* the words "his feet" are
added here in some MSS. If we retain them, the sense is:
He who has bathed, on returning home needs only to
wash the dust from his feet. Or it might also mean that
the liturgical and social requirements are satisfied with
this partial bathing.

not all." For he knew who it was that would be- 11
tray him. This is why he said, "You are not all
clean."

Now after he had washed their feet and put 12
on his garments, when he had reclined again,
he said to them, "Do you know what I have done
to you? You call me Master and Lord, and you 13
say well, for so I am. If, therefore, I the Lord and 14
Master have washed your feet, you also ought to
wash the feet of one another. For I have given 15
you an example, that as I have done to you, so
you also should do. Amen, amen, I say to you, no 16
servant is greater than his master, nor is one who
is sent greater than he who sent him. If you 17
know these things, blessed shall you be if you do
them. ' I do not speak of you all. I know whom I 18
have chosen; but that the Scripture may be
fulfilled, 'He who eats bread with me has lifted
up his heel against me.' I tell you now before it 19
comes to pass, that when it has come to pass you
may believe that I am he. Amen, amen, I say to 20
you, he who receives anyone I send, receives me;
and he who receives me, receives him who sent
me."

The Betrayer

When Jesus had said these things | MAY 20 | 21
he was troubled in spirit, and said | Nov. 19 |
solemnly, "Amen, amen, I say to you, one of you
will betray me." The disciples therefore looked 22
at one another, uncertain of whom he was speaking.

Now one of his disciples, he whom Jesus 23
loved, was reclining at Jesus' bosom. Simon 24
Peter therefore beckoned to him, and said to
him, "Who is it of whom he speaks?" He there- 25
fore, leaning back upon the bosom of Jesus, said
to him, "Lord, who is it?" Jesus answered, "It 26

is he for whom I shall dip the bread, and give it
to him." And when he had dipped the bread, he
27 gave it to Judas Iscariot, the son of Simon. And
after the morsel, Satan entered into him. And
Jesus said to him, "What thou dost, do quickly."
28 But none of those at the table understood why
29 he said this to him. For some thought that because Judas held the purse, Jesus had said to
him, "Buy the things we need for the feast"; or
30 that he should give something to the poor. When,
therefore, he had received the morsel, he went
out quickly. Now it was night.

The New Commandment

31　　When, therefore, he had gone out, Jesus said,
"Now is the Son of Man glorified, and God is
32 glorified in him. If God is glorified in him, God
will also glorify him in himself, and will glorify
him at once.

33　　"Little children, yet a little while I am with
you. You will seek me, and, as I said to the Jews,
'Where I go you cannot come,' so to you also I
34 say it now. A new commandment I give you,
that you love one another: that as I have loved
35 you, you also love one another. By this will all
men know that you are my disciples, if you have
love for one another."

Peter's Denials Predicted

36　　Simon Peter said to him, "Lord, where art
thou going?" Jesus answered, "Where I am
going thou canst not follow me now, but thou

13, 27: *Satan entered into him:* Judas now gave himself
entirely into the power of Satan (St. Thomas). It probably marks a definite decision on the part of Judas to
carry out the betrayal of his Master at once.

shalt follow later." Peter said to him, "Why can ₃₇
I not follow thee now? I will lay down my life for
thee." Jesus answered him, "Wilt thou lay down ₃₈
thy life for me? Amen, amen, I say to thee, the
cock will not crow before thou dost deny me
thrice.

A Word of Comfort

"Let not your heart be troubled. ┌─────────┐ **14** ₁
You believe in God, believe also in │ MAY 21 │
me. In my Father's house there are many │ Nov. 20 │
mansions. Were it not so, I should have └─────────┘
told you, be- ₂
cause I go to prepare a place for you. And if I go ₃
and prepare a place for you, I am coming again,
and I will take you to myself; that where I am,
there you also may be. And where I go you know, ₄
and the way you know."

Thomas said to him, "Lord, we do not know ₅
where thou art going, and how can we know the
way?" Jesus said to him, "I am the way, and the ₆
truth, and the life. No one comes to the Father
but through me. If you had known me, you would ₇
also have known my Father. And henceforth you
do know him, and you have seen him."

Philip said to him, "Lord, show us the Father ₈
and it is enough for us." Jesus said to him, "Have ₉
I been so long a time with you, and you have not
known me? Philip, he who sees me sees also the
Father. How canst thou say, 'Show us the
Father?' Dost thou not believe that I am in the ₁₀
Father and the Father in me? The words that I
speak to you I speak not on my own authority.
But the Father dwelling in me, it is he who does
the works. Do you believe that I am in the Father ₁₁
and the Father in me? Otherwise believe be- ₁₂
cause of the works themselves. Amen, amen, I
say to you, he who believes in me, the works that
I do he also shall do, and greater than these he

13 shall do, because I am going to the Father. And whatever you ask in my name, that I will do, in order that the Father may be glorified in
14 the Son. If you ask me anything in my name, I will do it.

15 "If you love me, keep my commandments. And
16 I will ask the Father and he will give you another
17 Advocate to dwell with you forever, the Spirit of truth whom the world cannot receive, because it neither sees him nor knows him. But you shall know him, because he will dwell with you, and be in you.

18 "I will not leave you orphans; I will come to
19 you. Yet a little while and the world no longer sees me. But you see me, for I live and you also
20 live. In that day you will know that I am in my
21 Father, and you in me, and I in you. He who has my commandments and keeps them, he it is who loves me. But he who loves me will be loved by my Father, and I will love him and manifest myself to him."

22 Judas, not the Iscariot, said to him, "Lord, how is it that thou art about to manifest thyself
23 to us, and not to the world?" Jesus answered and said to him, "If anyone love me, he will keep my word, and my Father will love him, and we will come to him and make our abode with him.
24 He who does not love me does not keep my words. And the word that you have heard is not mine, but the Father's who sent me.

14, 16: *Advocate:* or Paraclete. The latter is a Greek term which is better rendered into English by Advocate or Intercessor. Cf. 1 John 2, 1. The function of the One thus designated is protection, assistance, defense. The thought of Consoler is not wanting from the context (St. Thomas, St. Jerome, St. Augustine).

14, 19: *But you see me:* i.e., the world will not see me, but you will see me.

"These things I have spoken to you while yet 25
dwelling with you. But the Advocate, the Holy 26
Spirit, whom the Father will send in my name,
he will teach you all things, and bring to your
mind whatever I have said to you.

"Peace I leave with you, my peace I give to 27
you; not as the world gives do I give to you. Do
not let your heart be troubled, or be afraid. You 28
have heard me say to you, 'I go away and I am
coming to you.' If you loved me, you would indeed rejoice that I am going to the Father, for
the Father is greater than I. And now I have told 29
you before it comes to pass, that when it has
come to pass you may believe. I will no longer 30
speak much with you, for the prince of the world
is coming, and in me he has nothing. But he 31
comes that the world may know that I love the
Father, and that I do as the Father has commanded me. Arise; let us go from here.

Union with Christ

"I am the true vine, and my 15 1
Father is the vine-dresser. Every | MAY 22 |
branch in me that bears no fruit he will take | Nov. 21 | 2
away; and every branch that bears fruit he will
cleanse, that it may bear more fruit. You are 3
already clean because of the word that I have
spoken to you. Abide in me, and I in you. As the 4
branch cannot bear fruit of itself unless it remain
on the vine, so neither can you unless you abide
in me. ' I am the vine, you are the branches. He 5
who abides in me, and I in him, he bears much

14, 30f: *In me he has nothing:* i.e., he has no claim on me
or power over me. The success of the powers of darkness
in the death of Christ was only apparent. This was permitted to show Christ's perfect correspondence with the
will of the Father. On this rested His triumph over sin
and death.

6 fruit; for without me you can do nothing. If anyone does not abide in me, he shall be cast outside as the branch and wither; and they shall gather them up and cast them into the fire, and
7 they shall burn. If you abide in me, and if my words abide in you, ask whatever you will and
8 it shall be done to you. In this is my Father glorified, that you may bear very much fruit,
9 and become my disciples. As the Father has loved me, I also have loved you. Abide in my
10 love. If you keep my commandments you will abide in my love, as I also have kept my Father's
11 commandments, and abide in his love. These things I have spoken to you that my joy may be in you, and that your joy may be made full.

12 "This is my commandment, that you love one
13 another as I have loved you. Greater love than this no one has, that one lay down his life for
14 his friends. You are my friends if you do the
15 things I command you. No longer do I call you servants, because the servant does not know what his master does. But I have called you friends, because all things that I have heard from my Father I have made known to you.
16 You have not chosen me, but I have chosen you, and have appointed you that you should go and bear fruit, and that your fruit should remain; that whatever you ask the Father in my name he may
17 give you. These things I command you, that you may love one another.

The World's Hatred

18 "If the world hates you, know
19 that it has hated me before you. If you were of the world, the world would love what is its own. But because you are not of the world, but I have chosen you out of the world, therefore

MAY 23
Nov. 22

the world hates you. Remember the word that 20
I have spoken to you: No servant is greater than
his master. If they have persecuted me, they
will persecute you also; if they have kept my
word, they will keep yours also. But all these 21
things they will do to you for my name's sake,
because they do not know him who sent me.
If I had not come and spoken to them, they would 22
have no sin. But now they have no excuse for
their sin. He who hates me hates my Father also. 23
If I had not done among them works such as no 24
one else has done, they would have no sin. But
now they have seen, and have hated both me and
my Father; but that the word written in their Law 25
may be fulfilled, 'They have hated me without
cause.'

"But when the Advocate has come, whom I 26
will send you from the Father, the Spirit of truth
who proceeds from the Father, he will bear witness concerning me. And you also bear witness, 27
because from the beginning you are with me.

Persecution Predicted

"These things I have spoken to you that you **16** 1
may not be scandalized. They will expel you from 2
the synagogues. Yes, the hour is coming for
everyone who kills you to think that he is offering
worship to God. And these things they will do 3
because they have not known the Father nor me.
But these things I have spoken to you, that 'when 4
the time for them has come you may remember
that I told you. These things, however, I did not
tell you from the beginning, because I was with
you.

The Role of the Advocate

5   "And now I am going to him who MAY 24
Nov. 23 sent me, and no one of you asks me,

6   'Where art thou going?' But because I have spoken to you these things, sorrow has filled

7   your heart. But I speak the truth to you; it is expedient for you that I depart. For if I do not go, the Advocate will not come to you; but if I go,

8   I will send him to you. And when he has come he will convict the world of sin, and of justice, and

9   of judgment: of sin, because they do not believe

10   in me; of justice, because I go to the Father, and

11   you will see me no more; and of judgment, because the prince of this world has already been judged.

12   "Many things yet I have to say to you, but

13   you cannot bear them now. But when he, the Spirit of truth, has come, he will teach you all the truth. For he will not speak on his own authority, but whatever he will hear he will speak, and the things that are to come he will declare

14   to you. He will glorify me, because he will receive of what is mine and declare it to you.

15   All things that the Father has are mine. That is why I have said that he will receive of what

16   is mine, and will declare it to you. A little while and you shall see me no longer; and again a little while and you shall see me, because I go to the Father."

17   Some of his disciples therefore said to one another, "What is this he says to us, 'A little while and you shall not see me, and again a little while and you shall see me'; and, 'I go to

18   the Father'?"' They kept saying therefore, "What

16, 8: *Convict:* bring conviction relative to these truths. Elsewhere the term is rendered "expose."

is this 'little while' of which he speaks? We do not know what he is saying."

But Jesus knew that they wanted to ask him, 19 and he said to them, "You inquire about this among yourselves because I said, 'A little while and you shall not see me, and again a little while and you shall see me.' Amen, amen, I 20 say to you, that you shall weep and lament, but the world shall rejoice; and you shall be sorrowful, but your sorrow shall be turned into joy. A woman about to give birth has sorrow, 21 because her hour has come. But when she has brought forth the child, she no longer remembers the anguish for her joy that a man is born into the world. And you therefore have sorrow 22 now; but I will see you again, and your heart shall rejoice, and your joy no one shall take from you. And in that day you shall ask me 23 nothing. Amen, amen, I say to you, if you ask the Father anything in my name, he will give it to you. Hitherto you have not asked anything 24 in my name. Ask, and you shall receive, that your joy may be full.

"These things I have spoken to you in para- 25 bles. The hour is coming when I will no longer speak to you in parables, but will speak to you plainly of the Father. In that day you shall ask in 26 my name; and I do not say to you that I will ask the Father for you, for the Father himself loves 27 you because you have loved me, and have believed that I came forth from God. I came 28 forth from the Father and have come into the world. Again I leave the world and go to the Father."

His disciples said to him, "Behold, now thou 29 speakest plainly, and utterest no parable. Now 30 we know that thou knowest all things, and dost not need that anyone should question thee. For this reason we believe that thou camest forth from God."

31 Jesus answered them, "Do you now believe?
32 Behold, the hour is coming, and has already come, for you to be scattered, each one to his own house, and to leave me alone. But I am not alone, because the Father is with me.
33 These things I have spoken to you that in me you may have peace. In the world you will have affliction. But take courage, I have overcome the world."

Christ's Priestly Prayer for Unity

17 1 These things Jesus spoke; and raising his eyes to heaven, he said, MAY 25 / Nov. 24 "Father, the hour has come! Glorify thy Son,
2 that thy Son may glorify thee,' even as thou hast given him power over all flesh, in order that to all thou hast given him he may give
3 everlasting life. Now this is everlasting life, that they may know thee, the only true God, and
4 him whom thou hast sent, Jesus Christ. I have glorified thee on earth; I have accomplished
5 the work that thou hast given me to do. And now do thou, Father, glorify me with thyself, with the glory that I had with thee before the world existed.

6 "I have manifested thy name to the men whom thou hast given me out of the world. They were thine, and thou hast given them to
7 me, and they have kept thy word. Now they have learnt that whatever thou hast given me is

---

17, 2: Christ glorifies the Father by faithfully accomplishing His mission. But He also glorifies Him in another way: by raising man to a state in which he also can glorify God both here and in heaven. To this end the Father has given power over all men to the Son, to open for them a way to eternal life.

from thee; because the words that thou hast 8
given me I have given to them. And they have
received them, and have known of a truth that
I came forth from thee, and they have believed
that thou didst send me.

"I pray for them; not for the world do I pray, 9
but for those whom thou hast given me, because they are thine; and all things that are 10
mine are thine, and thine are mine; and I am
glorified in them. And I am no longer in the 11
world, but these are in the world, and I am
coming to thee. Holy Father, keep in thy name
those whom thou hast given me, that they may
be one even as we are. While I was with them, 12
I kept them in thy name. Those whom thou
hast given me I guarded; and not one of them
perished except the son of perdition, in order
that the Scripture might be fulfilled. But now I 13
am coming to thee; and these things I speak
in the world, in order that they may have my
joy made full in themselves. I have given them 14
thy word; and the world has hated them, because they are not of the world, even as I am
not of the world. I do not pray that thou take 15
them out of the world, but that thou keep them
from evil. They are not of the world, even as I 16
am not of the world. Sanctify them in the truth. 17
Thy word is truth. ' Even as thou hast sent me 18
into the world, so I also have sent them into
the world. And for them I sanctify myself, that 19
they also may be sanctified in truth.

17, 19: *Sanctify myself:* by offering Himself as a victim
to be immolated. *That they also may be sanctified:* that
they also may be set aside for God's work. *In truth:* i.e.,
"in contrast to all human purpose"; or for that truth which
is to be the object of their mission, as it is of Christ's.

20　"Yet not for these only do I pray, but for those also who through their word are to be-
21　lieve in me, ' that all may be one, even as thou, Father, in me and I in thee; that they also may be one in us, that the world may believe
22　that thou hast sent me. And the glory that thou hast given me, I have given to them, that they
23　may be one, even as we are one: I in them and thou in me; that they may be perfected in unity, and that the world may know that thou hast sent me, and that thou hast loved them even as thou hast loved me.

24　"Father, I will that where I am, they also whom thou hast given me may be with me; in order that they may behold my glory, which thou hast given me, because thou hast loved me
25　before the creation of the world. Just Father, the world has not known thee, but I have known thee, and these have known that thou
26　hast sent me. And I have made known to them thy name, and will make it known, in order that the love with which thou hast loved me may be in them, and I in them."

2. The Passion and Death of Jesus

Jesus Arrested

18 1　AFTER SAYING THESE THINGS, Jesus went forth with his disciples beyond the torrent of Cedron, where there was a garden into which he and his disciples en-
2　tered. Now Judas, who betrayed him, also knew the place, since Jesus had often met there
3　together with his disciples. Judas, then, taking

MAY 26
Nov. 25

17, 22: *Glory:* what Christ conferred upon His disciples was something of the divine nature, a further aspect of the principle of unity.

the cohort, and attendants from the chief priests and Pharisees, came there with lanterns, and torches, and weapons.

Jesus therefore knowing all that was to come upon him, went forth and said to them, "Whom do you seek?" ¹ They answered him, "Jesus of Nazareth." Jesus said to them, "I am he." Now Judas, who betrayed him, was also standing with them. When, therefore, he said to them, "I am he," they drew back and fell to the ground. So he asked them again, "Whom do you seek?" And they said, "Jesus of Nazareth." Jesus answered, "I have told you that I am he. If, therefore, you seek me, let these go their way." That the word which he said might be fulfilled, "Of those whom thou hast given me, I have not lost one."

Simon Peter therefore, having a sword, drew it and struck the servant of the high priest and cut off his right ear. Now the servant's name was Malchus. Jesus therefore said to Peter, "Put up thy sword into the scabbard. Shall I not drink the cup that the Father has given me?"

Peter's Denial

The cohort therefore and the tribune and the attendants of the Jews seized Jesus and bound him. And they brought him to Annas first, for he was the father-in-law of Caiphas, who was the high priest that year. Now it was Caiphas who had given the counsel to the Jews that it was expedient that one man should die for the people.

But Simon Peter was following Jesus, and so was another disciple. Now that disciple was known to the high priest, and he entered with Jesus into the courtyard of the high priest.

16 ¹ But Peter was standing outside at the gate. So the other disciple, who was known to the high priest, went out and spoke to the portress, and brought Peter in.

17 The maid, who was portress, said therefore to Peter, "Art thou also one of this man's dis-
18 ciples?" He said, "I am not." ¹ Now the servants and attendants were standing at a coal fire and warming themselves, for it was cold. And Peter also was with them, standing and warming himself.

19 The high priest therefore ques- | MAY 27
tioned Jesus concerning his dis- | Nov. 26
20 ciples, and concerning his teaching. Jesus answered him, "I have spoken openly to the world; I have always taught in the synagogue and in the temple, where all the Jews gather,
21 and in secret I have said nothing. Why dost thou question me? Question those who have heard what I spoke to them; behold, these know what I have said."

22 Now when he had said these things, one of the attendants who was standing by struck Jesus a blow, saying, "Is that the way thou dost answer
23 the high priest?" Jesus answered him, "If I have spoken ill, bear witness to the evil; but if well, why dost thou strike me?"

24 And Annas sent him bound to Caiphas, the high priest.

25 But Simon Peter was standing and warming himself. They therefore said to him, "Art thou also one of his disciples?" He denied it, and said,
26 "I am not." ¹ One of the servants of the high priest, a relative of him whose ear Peter had cut off, said, "Did I not see thee in the garden with
27 him?" Again, therefore, Peter denied it; and at that moment a cock crowed.

Jesus before Pilate

They therefore led Jesus from Caiphas to the 28
prætorium. Now it was early morning, and they
themselves did not enter the prætorium, that
they might not be defiled, but might eat the
passover.

Pilate therefore went outside to them, and 29
said, "What accusation do you bring against
this man?" They said to him in answer, "If he 30
were not a criminal we should not have handed
him over to thee." Pilate therefore said to them, 31
"Take him yourselves, and judge him according
to your law." The Jews, then, said to him, "It is
not lawful for us to put anyone to death." This 32
was in fulfillment of what Jesus had said, indicating the manner of his death.

Pilate therefore again entered into the præ- 33
torium, and he summoned Jesus, and said to
him, "Art thou the king of the Jews?" Jesus 34
answered, "Dost thou say this of thyself, or
have others told thee of me?" Pilate answered, 35
"Am I a Jew? Thy own people and the chief
priests have delivered thee to me. What hast thou
done?" Jesus answered, "My kingdom is not of 36
this world. If my kingdom were of this world,
my followers would have fought that I might
not be delivered to the Jews. But, as it is, my
kingdom is not from here." Pilate therefore said 37
to him, "Thou art then a king?" Jesus answered,
"Thou sayest it; I am a king. This is why I was
born, and why I have come into the world, to
bear witness to the truth. Everyone who is of
the truth hears my voice." Pilate said to him, 38
"What is truth?"

And when he had said this, he went outside
to the Jews again, and said to them, "I find no
guilt in him. But you have a custom that I should 39

release someone to you at the Passover. Do you wish, therefore, that I release to you the king of
40 the Jews?" They all therefore cried out again, "Not this man, but Barabbas!" Now Barabbas was a robber.

The Scourging and Crowning

19 1　Pilate, then, took Jesus and had | MAY 28
2　him scourged. And the soldiers, | Nov. 27
plaiting a crown of thorns, put it upon his head,
3　and arrayed him in a purple cloak. And they kept coming to him and saying, "Hail, King of the Jews!" and striking him.

4　Pilate therefore again went outside and said to them, "Behold, I bring him out to you, that
5　you may know that I find no guilt in him." Jesus therefore came forth, wearing the crown of thorns and the purple cloak. And he said to them,
6　"Behold, the man!" ' When, therefore, the chief priests and the attendants saw him, they cried out, saying, "Crucify him! Crucify him!" Pilate said to them, "Take him yourselves and crucify
7　him, for I find no guilt in him." The Jews answered him, "We have a Law, and according to that Law he must die, because he has made himself Son of God."

8　Now when Pilate heard this statement, he
9　feared the more. And he again went back into the prætorium, and said to Jesus, "Where art thou from?" But Jesus gave him no answer.
10　Pilate therefore said to him, "Dost thou not speak to me? Dost thou not know that I have power to crucify thee, and that I have power to
11　release thee?" Jesus answered, "Thou wouldst have no power at all over me were it not given thee from above. Therefore, he who betrayed me to thee has the greater sin."

And from then on Pilate was looking for a way 12
to release him. But the Jews cried out, saying,
"If thou release this man, thou art no friend of
Cæsar; for everyone who makes himself king
sets himself against Cæsar."

Pilate therefore, when he heard these words, 13
brought Jesus outside, and sat down on the
judgment-seat, at a place called Lithostrotos,
but in Hebrew, Gabbatha. Now it was the Prepa- 14
ration Day for the Passover, about the sixth
hour. And he said to the Jews, "Behold, your
king!" But they cried out, "Away with him! 15
Away with him! Crucify him!" Pilate said to
them, "Shall I crucify your king?" The chief
priests answered, "We have no king but Cæsar."
Then he handed him over to them to be cruci- 16
fied. And so they took Jesus and led him away.

The Crucifixion

And bearing the cross for himself, he went 17
forth to the place called the Skull, in Hebrew,
Golgotha, ' where they crucified him, and with 18
him two others, one on each side and Jesus in
the center.

And Pilate also wrote an inscription and had it 19
put on the cross. And there was written, "Jesus
of Nazareth, the King of the Jews." Many of the 20
Jews therefore read this inscription, because the
place where Jesus was crucified was near the
city; and it was written in Hebrew, in Greek and
in Latin. The chief priests of the Jews said 21
therefore to Pilate, "Do not write, 'The King of
the Jews,' but, 'He said, I am the King of the
Jews.' " Pilate answered, "What I have written, 22
I have written."

The soldiers therefore, when they had cruci- 23
fied him, took his garments and made of them
four parts, to each soldier a part, and also the

24 tunic. Now the tunic was without seam, woven in one piece from the top. They therefore said to one another, "Let us not tear it, but let us cast lots for it, to see whose it shall be." That the Scripture might be fulfilled which says, "They divided my garments among them; and for my vesture they cast lots." These things therefore the soldiers did.

The Death of Jesus

25 Now there were standing by the cross of Jesus his mother and his

MAY 29
Nov. 28

26 mother's sister, Mary of Cleophas, and Mary Magdalene. When Jesus, therefore, saw his mother and the disciple standing by, whom he loved, he said to his mother, "Woman, behold,
27 thy son." Then he said to the disciple, "Behold, thy mother." And from that hour the disciple took her into his home.

28 After this Jesus, knowing that all things were now accomplished, that the Scripture might be
29 fulfilled, said, "I thirst." Now there was standing there a vessel full of common wine; and having put a sponge soaked with the wine on a stalk of
30 hyssop, they put it to his mouth. Therefore, when Jesus had taken the wine, he said, "It is consummated!" And bowing his head, he gave up his spirit.

The Burial

31 The Jews therefore, since it was the Preparation Day, in order that the bodies might not remain upon the cross on the Sabbath (for that Sabbath was a solemn day), besought Pilate that their legs might be broken, and that they
32 might be taken away. The soldiers therefore came and broke the legs of the first, and of the
33 other, who had been crucified with him. But

when they came to Jesus, and saw that he was already dead, they did not break his legs; but one 34 of the soldiers opened his side with a lance, and immediately there came out blood and water.

And he who saw it has borne witness, and his 35 witness is true; and he knows that he tells the truth, that you also may believe. For these 36 things came to pass that the Scripture might be fulfilled, "Not a bone of him shall you break." And again another Scripture says, "They shall 37 look upon him whom they have pierced."

Now after these things Joseph of Arimathea, 38 because he was a disciple of Jesus (although for fear of the Jews a secret one), besought Pilate that he might take away the body of Jesus. And Pilate gave permission. He came, therefore, and took away the body of Jesus. And there also 39 came Nicodemus (who at first had come to Jesus by night), bringing a mixture of myrrh and aloes, in weight about a hundred pounds. They there- 40 fore took the body of Jesus and wrapped it in linen cloths with the spices, after the Jewish manner of preparing for burial. Now in the place 41 where he was crucified there was a garden, and in the garden a new tomb in which no one had yet been laid. There, accordingly, because of the 42 Preparation Day of the Jews, for the tomb was close at hand, they laid Jesus.

3. THE RESURRECTION OF JESUS

Mary Magdalene

NOW ON THE FIRST DAY of the week, Mary Magdalene came early to the tomb, while it was still dark, and she saw the stone taken away from the tomb. She ran 2 therefore and came to Simon Peter, and to the other disciple whom Jesus loved, and said to

| MAY 30 | **20** 1 |
| Nov. 29 | |

them, "They have taken the Lord from the tomb, and we do not know where they have laid him."

3 Peter therefore went out, and the other dis-
4 ciple, and they went to the tomb. The two were running together, and the other disciple ran on before, faster than Peter, and came first to the
5 tomb. And stooping down he saw the linen
6 cloths lying there, yet he did not enter. Simon Peter therefore came following him, and he went into the tomb, and saw the linen cloths
7 lying there, and the handkerchief which had been about his head, not lying with the linen
8 cloths, but folded in a place by itself. Then the other disciple also went in, who had come first to
9 the tomb. And he saw and believed; ' for as yet they did not understand the Scripture, that he
10 must rise from the dead. The disciples therefore went away again to their home.

11 But Mary was standing outside weeping at the tomb. So, as she wept, she stooped down and
12 looked into the tomb, and saw two angels in white sitting, one at the head and one at the feet, where the body of Jesus had been laid.
13 They said to her, "Woman, why art thou weeping?" She said to them, "Because they have taken away my Lord, and I do not know where they have laid him."
14 When she had said this she turned round and beheld Jesus standing there, and she did not
15 know that it was Jesus. Jesus said to her, "Woman, why art thou weeping? Whom dost thou seek?" She, thinking that he was the gardener, said to him, "Sir, if thou hast removed him, tell me where thou hast laid him and I will take him
16 away." ' Jesus said to her, "Mary!" Turning, she said to him, "Rabboni!" (that is to say,
17 Master). Jesus said to her, "Do not touch me, for I have not yet ascended to my Father, but go

to my brethren and say to them, 'I ascend to my Father and your Father, to my God and your God.' "

Mary Magdalene came, and announced to the disciples, "I have seen the Lord, and these things he said to me." 18

The Disciples

When it was late that same day, the first of the week, though the doors where the disciples gathered had been closed for fear of the Jews, Jesus came and stood in the midst and said to them, "Peace be to you!" And when he had said this, he showed them his hands and his side. The disciples therefore rejoiced at the sight of the Lord. He therefore said to them again, "Peace be to you! As the Father has sent me, I also send you." When he had said this, he breathed upon them, and said to them, "Receive the Holy Spirit; whose sins you shall forgive, they are forgiven them; and whose sins you shall retain, they are retained." 19 20 21 22 23

Thomas

Now Thomas, one of the Twelve, called the Twin, was not with them when Jesus came. The other disciples therefore said to him, "We have seen the Lord." But he said to them, "Unless I see in his hands the print of the nails, and put my finger into the place of the nails, and put my hand into his side, I will not believe." 24 25

And after eight days, his disciples were again inside, and Thomas with them. Jesus came, the doors being closed, and stood in their midst, and said, "Peace be to you!" Then he said to Thomas, "Bring here thy finger, and see my hands; and bring here thy hand, and put it into 26 27

my side; and be not unbelieving, but believing."
28 Thomas answered and said to him, "My Lord
29 and my God!" Jesus said to him, "Because thou
hast seen me, thou hast believed. Blessed are
they who have not seen, and yet have believed."

The Evangelist's Epilogue

30 Many other signs also Jesus worked in the
sight of his disciples, which are not written in
31 this book. But these are written that you may
believe that Jesus is the Christ, the Son of God,
and that believing you may have life in his name.

The Manifestation in Galilee

21 1 After these things, Jesus manifested himself again at the sea of
Tiberias. Now he manifested himself in this

MAY 31
Nov. 30

2 way. There were together Simon Peter and
Thomas, called the Twin, and Nathanael, from
Cana in Galilee, and the sons of Zebedee, and
3 two others of his disciples. Simon Peter said
to them, "I am going fishing." They said to
him, "We also are going with thee." And they
went out and got into the boat. And that night
4 they caught nothing. But when day was breaking, Jesus stood on the beach; yet the disciples
5 did not know that it was Jesus. Then Jesus
said to them, "Young men, have you any fish?"
6 They answered him, "No." ¹ He said to them,
"Cast the net to the right of the boat and you
will find them." They cast therefore, and now
they were unable to draw it up for the great
7 number of fishes. The disciple whom Jesus
loved said therefore to Peter, "It is the Lord."
Simon Peter therefore, hearing that it was the
Lord, girt his tunic about him, for he was stripped,
8 and threw himself into the sea. But the other
disciples came with the boat (for they were

not far from land, only about two hundred cubits off), dragging the net full of fishes.

When, therefore, they had landed, they saw 9 a fire ready, and a fish laid upon it, and bread. Jesus said to them, "Bring here some of the 10 fishes that you caught just now." Simon Peter 11 went aboard and hauled the net onto the land full of large fishes, one hundred and fifty-three in number. And though there were so many, the net was not torn. Jesus said to them, "Come 12 and breakfast." And none of those reclining dared ask him, "Who art thou?" knowing that it was the Lord. And Jesus came and took the 13 bread, and gave it to them, and likewise the fish. This is now the third time that Jesus appeared to the disciples after he had risen from the dead.

The Primacy of Peter

When, therefore, they had breakfasted, Jesus 15 said to Simon Peter, "Simon, son of John, dost thou love me more than these do?" He said to him, "Yes, Lord, thou knowest that I love thee." He said to him, "Feed my lambs." ' He said to 16 him a second time, "Simon, son of John, dost thou love me?" He said to him, "Yes, Lord, thou knowest that I love thee." He said to him, "Feed my lambs." A third time he said to him, 17 "Simon, son of John, dost thou love me?" Peter was grieved because he said to him for the third time, "Dost thou love me?" And he said to him, "Lord, thou knowest all things, thou knowest that I love thee." He said to him, "Feed my sheep."

"Amen, amen, I say to thee, when thou wast 18 young thou didst gird thyself and walk where thou wouldst. But when thou art old thou wilt stretch forth thy hands, and another will gird thee, and lead thee where thou wouldst not."

19 Now this he said to signify by what manner of death he should glorify God. And having spoken thus, he said to him, "Follow me."

20 Turning round, Peter saw following them the disciple whom Jesus loved, the one who, at the supper, had leaned back upon his breast and said, "Lord, who is it that will betray thee?"

21 Peter therefore, seeing him, said to Jesus, "Lord,
22 and what of this man?" Jesus said to him, "If I wish him to remain until I come, what is it to thee?

23 Do thou follow me." This saying therefore went abroad among the brethren, that that disciple was not to die. But Jesus had not said to him, "He is not to die"; but rather, "If I wish him to remain until I come, what is it to thee?"

Second Epilogue

24 This is the disciple who bears witness concerning these things, and who has written these things, and we know that his witness is true.

25 There are, however, many other things that Jesus did; but if every one of these should be written, not even the world itself, I think, could hold the books that would have to be written. Amen.

ACTS OF THE APOSTLES

Introduction

This book was written about 63 A. D. by St. Luke,
the author of the third Gospel. It ends with the statement that St. Paul preached in Rome for two years
while still under arrest. St. Luke had been with him
on the voyage from Palestine to Rome, since the
account of this voyage is given in the first person
plural, and he was still with him, as is clear from the
Epistle to Philemon, when the Apostle was confident
of soon being released. From this final statement it
appears that the book dates from the close of the two
years' imprisonment (63 A. D.), but before St. Paul's
acquittal.

Beginning with our Lord's farewell instructions to
the Apostles just before His Ascension, it first narrates the chief events in the history of the infant
Church up to about the year 42, when St. Peter definitely departed from Palestine. A feature of the latter
part of this period was the new policy of preaching
the Gospel to the Gentiles. From this point the Acts
traces the spread of the Church, principally through
the missionary journeys of St. Paul, and closes with a
short account of his labors in Rome. In this way it
covers a period of about thirty-five years from the
Ascension to the second year of St. Paul's imprisonment. Keeping to the main course of events as showing the growth of the Church, it is silent about the
internal development of the churches after their
establishment; many of these internal details are
recorded in the Epistles of St. Paul, but without in
any way contradicting the general facts given by St.
Luke.

The Acts is a necessary and beautiful supplement
to the history of the Gospels, describing with great
accuracy and literary charm the fulfillment of our
Lord's promise to send the Holy Spirit to sanctify
and guide His Church, and so it has aptly been called
the Gospel of the Holy Spirit.

ACTS OF THE APOSTLES

Prelude

The Ascension

1 1   IN THE FORMER BOOK, O Theo- JUNE 1
Dec. 1
philus, I spoke of all that Jesus did
2 and taught from the beginning ' until the day
on which he was taken up, after he had given
commandments through the Holy Spirit to the
3 apostles whom he had chosen. To them also
he showed himself alive after his passion by
many proofs, during forty days appearing to
them and speaking of the kingdom of God.
4 And while eating with them, he charged them
not to depart from Jerusalem, but to wait for
the promise of the Father, "of which you have
5 heard," said he, "by my mouth; for John indeed baptized with water, but you shall be
baptized with the Holy Spirit not many days
hence."

6   They therefore who had come together began
to ask him, saying, "Lord, wilt thou at this time
restore the kingdom to Israel?"

7   But he said to them, "It is not for you to know
the times or dates which the Father has fixed
8 by his own authority; but you shall receive
power when the Holy Spirit comes upon you,
and you shall be witnesses for me in Jerusalem
and in all Judea and Samaria and even to the
very ends of the earth."

9   And when he had said this, he was lifted up
before their eyes, and a cloud took him out of
10 their sight. And while they were gazing up to

1, 5: *You shall be baptized:* not the sacrament of
Baptism, which they had already undoubtedly received,
but the fuller outpouring of the Holy Spirit on Pentecost.

1, 10: *Two men:* angels in human form.

heaven as he went, behold, two men stood by them in white garments, and said to them, 11 "Men of Galilee, why do you stand looking up to heaven? This Jesus who has been taken up from you into heaven, shall come in the same way as you have seen him going up to heaven."

Then they returned to Jerusalem from the 12 mount called Olivet, which is near Jerusalem, a Sabbath day's journey. And when they had 13 entered the city, they mounted to the upper room where were staying Peter and John, James and Andrew, Philip and Thomas, Bartholomew and Matthew, James the son of Alpheus, and Simon the Zealot, and Jude the brother of James. All these with one mind continued steadfastly in prayer with the women 14 and Mary, the mother of Jesus, and with his brethren.

Matthias Chosen

In those days Peter stood up in the midst 15 of the brethren (now the number of persons met together was about a hundred and twenty), and he said, ' "Brethren, the Scripture must be 16 fulfilled which the Holy Spirit declared before by the mouth of David concerning Judas, who was the guide of those who arrested Jesus; inasmuch as he had been numbered among us 17 and was allotted his share in this ministry. And he indeed bought a field with the price of 18 his iniquity and, being hanged, burst asunder in the midst, and all his bowels gushed out. And it became known to all the residents of 19 Jerusalem, so that the field came to be called

---

1, 11: *In the same way:* on the clouds.
1, 12: *Sabbath day's journey:* about two-thirds of a mile.

in their language Haceldama, that is, the Field
20 of Blood. For it is written in the book of Psalms,
'Let their habitation become desolate and let
there be none to dwell in it.' And, 'His ministry
let another take.'

21 "Therefore, of these men who have been in
our company all the time that the Lord Jesus
22 moved among us, from John's baptism until
the day that he was taken up from us, of these
one must become a witness with us of his
resurrection."

23 And they put forward two: Joseph, called
Barsabbas, who was surnamed Justus, and
24 Matthias. And they prayed and said, "Thou,
Lord, who knowest the hearts of all, show which
25 of these two thou hast chosen ' to take the
place in this ministry and apostleship from
which Judas fell away to go to his own place."

26 And they drew lots between them, and the
lot fell upon Matthias; and he was numbered
with the eleven apostles.

I: THE CHURCH IN PALESTINE AND SYRIA

1. Growth of the Church in Jerusalem

Descent of the Holy Spirit

2 1 AND WHEN THE DAYS OF PEN- | JUNE 2
TECOST were drawing to a close, | Dec. 2
2 they were all together in one place. And suddenly there came a sound from heaven, as of a
violent wind blowing, and it filled the whole
3 house where they were sitting. And there appeared to them parted tongues as of fire, which
4 settled upon each of them. And they were
all filled with the Holy Spirit and began to speak
in foreign tongues, even as the Holy Spirit
prompted them to speak.

5 Now there were staying at Jerusalem devout

Jews from every nation under heaven. And 6
when this sound was heard, the multitude
gathered and were bewildered in mind, because each heard them speaking in his own
language. But they were all amazed and mar- 7
velled, saying, "Behold, are not all these that
are speaking Galileans? And how have we heard 8
each his own language in which he was born?
Parthians and Medes and Elamites, and in- 9
habitants of Mesopotamia, Judea, and Cappadocia, Pontus and Asia, ' Phrygia and Pam- 10
phylia, Egypt and the parts of Libya about
Cyrene, and visitors from Rome, ' Jews also 11
and proselytes, Cretans and Arabians, we have
heard them speaking in our own languages of
the wonderful works of God."

And all were amazed and perplexed, saying 12
to one another, "What does this mean?" But 13
others said in mockery, "They are full of new
wine."

Peter's Discourse

But Peter, standing up with the Eleven, 14
lifted up his voice and spoke out to them:
"Men of Judea and all you who dwell in Jerusalem, let this be known to you, and give ear
to my words. These men are not drunk, as you 15
suppose, for it is only the third hour of the day.
But this is what was spoken through the prophet 16
Joel: 'And it shall come to pass in the last days, 17
says the Lord, that I will pour forth of my Spirit
upon all flesh; and your sons and your daughters shall prophesy, and your young men shall
see visions, and your old men shall dream
dreams. And moreover upon my servants and 18
upon my handmaids in those days will I pour

2, 15: *Third hour:* nine in the morning, since the hours
were counted from sunrise at about six.

19 forth of my Spirit, and they shall prophesy. And I will show wonders in the heavens above and signs on the earth beneath, blood and fire and
20 vapor of smoke. The sun shall be turned into darkness, and the moon into blood, before the day of the Lord comes, the great and manifest
21 day. And it shall come to pass that whoever calls upon the name of the Lord shall be saved.'

22 "Men of Israel, hear these words. Jesus of Nazareth was a man approved by God among you by miracles and

> JUNE 3
> Dec. 3

wonders and signs, which God did through him in the midst of you, as you yourselves know.
23 Him, when delivered up by the settled purpose and foreknowledge of God, you have crucified
24 and slain by the hands of wicked men. But God has raised him up, having loosed the sorrows of hell, because it was not possible that
25 he should be held fast by it. For David says with reference to him, 'I saw the Lord before me always, because he is at my right hand,
26 lest I be moved. This is why my heart has made merry and my tongue has rejoiced; moreover my
27 flesh also will rest in hope, because thou wilt not abandon my soul to hell, neither wilt thou
28 let thy Holy One undergo decay. Thou hast made known to me the ways of life; thou wilt fill me with joy in thy presence.'

29 "Brethren, let me say to you freely of the patriarch David that he both died and was buried, and his tomb is with us to this very day.
30 Therefore, since he was a prophet and knew that God 'had sworn to him with an oath that

---

2, 24: *Hell:* limbo, where the souls of the just awaited the redemption; in Greek, "death." In both readings the thought is of all that makes death grievous, beginning with the state of separation of soul and body.

of the fruit of his loins one should sit upon his throne,' he, foreseeing it, spoke of the resurrection of the Christ. For neither was he abandoned to hell, nor did his flesh undergo decay. This Jesus God has raised up, and we are all witnesses of it. Therefore, exalted by the right hand of God, and receiving from the Father the promise of the Holy Spirit, he has poured forth this Spirit which you see and hear. For David did not ascend into heaven, but he says himself, 'The Lord said to my Lord: Sit thou at my right hand, ' until I make thy enemies thy footstool.'

"Therefore, let all the house of Israel know most assuredly that God has made both Lord and Christ, this Jesus whom you crucified."

The Result

Now on hearing this they were pierced to the heart and said to Peter and the rest of the apostles, "Brethren, what shall we do?"

But Peter said to them, "Repent and be baptized every one of you in the name of Jesus Christ for the forgiveness of your sins; and you will receive the gift of the Holy Spirit. For to you is the promise and to your children and to all who are far off, even to all whom the Lord our God calls to himself."

And with very many other words he bore witness, and exhorted them, saying, "Save yourselves from this perverse generation."

2, 36: *Made:* manifestly proved the divinity of our Lord and His office as Messias. By the Resurrection and Ascension Jesus enters on the perfect glory belonging to Him and is proved to be the Son of God and the Messias (Christ).

2, 39: *Far off:* the Gentiles; the Church is universal.

41   Now they who received his word were baptized, and there were added that day about three thousand souls.

Fervor of the Early Church

42   And they continued steadfastly in the teaching of the apostles and in the communion of the breaking of the bread and in the prayers.
43 And fear came upon every soul; many wonders also and signs were done by means of the apostles in Jerusalem, and great fear came
44 upon all. And all who believed were together
45 and held all things in common, ' and would sell their possessions and goods and distribute them among all according as anyone had need.
46 And continuing daily with one accord in the temple, and breaking bread in their houses, they took their food with gladness and sim-
47 plicity of heart, praising God and being in favor with all the people. And day by day the Lord added to their company such as were to be saved.

A Lame Beggar

3 1   Now Peter and John were going up into the temple at the ninth hour

JUNE 4
Dec. 4

2 of prayer. And a certain man, who had been lame from his mother's womb, was being car-

---

2, 44: *In common:* all were ready to help the needy and, as occasion demanded, they even sold their possessions to do so; this spirit of fraternal charity is widely different from modern Communism.

2, 46: *The temple:* there was to be no sudden break with the past, but the disciples had their own sacrifice, the Eucharist, *in their houses* where they also took their evening meal beforehand, as our Lord did at the institution of the Eucharist.

3, 1: *Ninth hour:* about three in the afternoon, the time of the evening sacrifice.

ried by, whom they laid daily at the gate of
the temple called the Beautiful, that he might
ask alms of those going into the temple. And 3
he, seeing Peter and John about to go into the
temple, asked for an alms. But Peter, gazing 4
upon him with John, said, "Look at us." And 5
he looked at them earnestly, hoping to receive
something from them. But Peter said, "Silver 6
and gold I have none; but what I have, that I
give thee. In the name of Jesus Christ of Nazareth, arise and walk."

And taking him by the right hand, he raised 7
him up, and immediately his feet and ankles
became strong. And leaping up, he stood and 8
began to walk, and went with them into the
temple, walking and leaping and praising God.
And all the people saw him walking and praising 9
God. And they recognized him as the man who 10
used to sit for alms at the Beautiful Gate of
the temple, and they were filled with wonder
and amazement at what had happened to him.

Now as he clung to Peter and John, all the 11
people ran to them in the portico called Solomon's, greatly wondering.

Peter's Discourse

But when Peter saw it, he said to the people: 12
"Men of Israel, why do you marvel at this, or
why do you stare at us, as though by any power
or holiness of our own we had made this man
walk? The God of Abraham and the God of 13
Isaac and the God of Jacob, the God of our
fathers, has glorified his Son Jesus, whom you
indeed delivered up and disowned before the
face of Pilate, when he had decided that he
should be released. But you disowned the Holy 14
and Just One, and asked that a murderer
should be granted to you; but the author of 15

life you killed, whom God has raised up from
16 the dead; whereof we are witnesses. And it is
his name, by means of faith in his name, that
has made strong this man whom you behold
and recognize; moreover it is the faith that
comes through Jesus that has given him the
perfect health you all see.

17 "And now, brethren, I know that you acted
18 in ignorance, as did also your rulers. But in
this way God fulfilled what he had announced
beforehand by the mouth of all the prophets,
19 namely, that his Christ should suffer. Repent
therefore and be converted, that your sins may
20 be blotted out ' in order that, when the times of
refreshment shall come from the presence of
the Lord, he may send him who has been
21 preached to you, Jesus Christ. For heaven indeed must receive him until the times of the
restoration of all things, of which God has
spoken by the mouth of his holy prophets who
22 have been from of old. For Moses said, 'The
Lord your God shall raise up to you a prophet
from among your brethren, as he raised up me;
to him you shall hearken in all things that he
23 shall speak to you. And it shall be that every
soul that will not hearken to that prophet, shall
24 be destroyed from among the people.' And all
the prophets who have spoken, from Samuel
onwards, have also announced these days.
25 You are the children of the prophets and of the
covenant that God made with your fathers,
saying to Abraham, 'And in thy offspring shall
all the families of the earth be blessed.' To you
26

3, 16: Faith in Christ (in the name of Christ) is the true
explanation of the miracle.

3, 22: *As he raised up me,* or "like me": both Christ
and Moses were mediators between God and man.

first God, raising up his Son, has sent him to bless you, that everyone may turn from his wickedness."

Arrest and Release of Peter and John

Now while they were speaking to the people, the priests and the officer of the temple and the Sadducees came upon them, being grieved because they were teaching the people and proclaiming in the case of Jesus the resurrection from the dead. And they set hands upon them and placed them in custody till the next day; for it was already evening. But many of those who had heard the word believed, and the number of the men came to be five thousand.

JUNE 5
Dec. 5

4 1

2

3

4

Now it came to pass on the morrow that their rulers and elders and Scribes were gathered together in Jerusalem ' with Annas, the high priest, and Caiphas and John and Alexander and as many as belonged to the high-priestly family. And setting them in the midst, they began to inquire, "By what authority or in what name have you done this?"

5

6

7

Then Peter, filled with the Holy Spirit, said to them, "Rulers of the people and elders, ' if we are on trial today about a good work done to a cripple, as to how this man has been cured, be it known to all of you and to all the people of Israel that in the name of Jesus Christ of Nazareth, whom you crucified, whom God has raised from the dead, even in this name does he stand here before you, sound. This is 'The stone that was rejected by you, the builders, which has become the corner stone.' Neither is there salvation in any other. For there is no other name under heaven given to men by which we must be saved."

8

9

10

11

12

13   Now seeing the boldness of Peter and John, and finding that they were uneducated and ordinary men, they began to marvel, and to
14 recognize them as having been with Jesus. And seeing the man who had been cured standing
15 with them, they could say nothing in reply. So they ordered them to withdraw from the council
16 chamber; and they conferred together, ' saying, "What shall we do with these men? For that indeed an evident miracle has been done by them is manifest to all the inhabitants of Jeru-
17 salem, and we cannot deny it. But lest it spread further among the people, let us warn them to speak no more about this name to any man."
18 And summoning them, they charged them not to speak or to teach at all in the name of Jesus.
19   But Peter and John answered and said to them, "Whether it is right in the sight of God to listen to you rather than to God, decide for
20 yourselves. For we cannot but speak of what
21 we have seen and heard." But they, after threatening them, let them go, not finding any way of punishing them, because of the people; for all were glorifying what had come to pass.
22 For the man upon whom this miraculous cure had been done was more than forty years old.

Thanksgiving

23   Now after their dismissal, they came to their companions and re-

                                          JUNE 6
                                          Dec. 6

ported all that the chief priests and the elders
24 had said to them. But they, when they heard it, lifted up their voice with one accord to God and said, "Lord, it is thou who didst make heaven and
25 earth and the sea and all that is in them, ' who didst say by the Holy Spirit through the mouth of our father David, thy servant, 'Why did the Gentiles rage and the peoples plan vain things?

[316]

The kings of the earth stood up, and the rulers 26
assembled together against the Lord and against
his Christ.' For of a truth there assembled to- 27
gether in this city against thy holy servant Jesus,
whom thou hast anointed, Herod and Pontius
Pilate with the Gentiles and the peoples of Israel,
to do what thy hand and thy counsel decreed to 28
be done. And now, Lord, take note of their 29
threats, and grant to thy servants to speak thy
word with all boldness, while thou stretchest 30
forth thy hand to cures and signs and wonders to
be wrought by the name of thy holy servant Jesus."

And when they had prayed, the place where 31
they had assembled was shaken, and they were
all filled with the Holy Spirit, and spoke the
word of God with boldness.

Manner of Life of Christians

Now the multitude of the believers were of 32
one heart and one soul, and not one of them said
that anything he possessed was his own, but they
had all things in common. And with great power 33
the apostles gave testimony to the resurrection
of Jesus Christ our Lord; and great grace was in
them all. Nor was there anyone among them in 34
want. For those who owned lands or houses
would sell them and bring the price of what they
sold ' and lay it at the feet of the apostles, and 35

4, 32: *In common:* as in 2, 44, while they still held private property, all were ready to use it for those in want,
and the more fervent went to the extent of selling their
possessions in whole or in part and turning over the proceeds to a fund for the poor. That this latter practice was
not obligatory or general, even in Jerusalem, is clear
from the special mention of Barnabas in v. 36, and from
5, 4, where Ananias is reminded that he need not have
sold his land, and that, if he did, he need not have given
the money to the Apostles.

distribution was made to each, according as any
36 one had need. Now Joseph, who by the apostles
was surnamed Barnabas (which is translated
Son of Consolation), a Levite and a native of
37 Cyprus, ' sold the field that he had, and brought
the price and laid it at the feet of the apostles.

Ananias and Sapphira

5 1   A man named Ananias, with Sapphira his wife,
2 sold a piece of land ' and by fraud kept back part
of the price of the land, with the connivance of
his wife, and bringing a part only, laid it at the
3 feet of the apostles. But Peter said, "Ananias,
why has Satan tempted thy heart, that thou
shouldst lie to the Holy Spirit and by fraud keep
4 back part of the price of the land? While it yet
remained, did it not remain thine; and after it
was sold, was not the money at thy disposal?
Why hast thou conceived this thing in thy heart?
5 Thou hast not lied to me, but to God." And
Ananias, hearing these words, fell down and expired. And great fear came upon all who heard of
6 it. And the young men got up and removed him
and, carrying him out, buried him.

7   About three hours later his wife, not knowing
8 what had happened, came in. And Peter said to
her, "Tell me, did you sell the land for so much?"
9 And she said, "Yes, for so much." ' And Peter
said to her, "Why have you agreed to tempt the
Spirit of the Lord? Behold the feet of those who
have buried thy husband are at the door, and
10 they will carry thee out." And she fell down
immediately at his feet and expired. And the
young men, coming in, found her dead, and
carrying her out they buried her beside her
11 husband. And great fear came upon the whole
church and upon all who heard of this.

Miracles

Now by the hands of the apostles

many signs and wonders were done 12
among the people. And with one accord they all
would meet in Solomon's portico; but of the rest, 13
no one dared to associate with them, yet the
people made much of them. And the multitude 14
of men and women who believed in the Lord
increased still more, so that they carried the sick 15
into the streets and laid them on beds and pallets
that, when Peter passed, his shadow at least
might fall on some of them. And there came also 16
multitudes from the towns near Jerusalem,
bringing the sick and those troubled with unclean spirits, and they were all cured.

Arrest of the Apostles

But the high priest rose up, and all those who 17
were with him (that is the party of the Sadducees),
and being filled with jealousy ' seized the apostles 18
and put them in the public prison. But during the 19
night an angel of the Lord opened the doors of
the prison and led them out, and said, "Go, stand 20
and speak in the temple to the people all the
words of this life." And when they heard this, 21
they went into the temple about daybreak and
began to teach.

But the chief priest and his party came and
they called together the Sanhedrin and all the
elders of the children of Israel, and sent to the
prison to have them brought. But when the 22
officers came and, opening the prison, did not
find them there, they returned and reported,
' saying, "The prison indeed we found securely 23
locked, and the guards standing before the doors,
but on opening it we found no one inside." Now 24
when the officer of the temple and the chief
priests heard these words, they were much per-

plexed concerning them as to what might come
25 of this. But someone came and told them, "Behold, the men whom you put in prison are stand-
26 ing in the temple and teaching the people." Then the captain went off with the officers and brought them without violence, for they feared the people lest they should be stoned.

27 And having brought them, they set them before the Sanhedrin. And the high priest ques-
28 tioned them, ' saying, "We strictly charged you not to teach in this name, and behold, you have filled Jerusalem with your teaching, and want to bring this man's blood upon us."

29 But Peter and the apostles answered and said, "We must obey God rather than men.
30 The God of our fathers raised Jesus, whom you
31 put to death, hanging him on a tree. Him God exalted with his right hand to be Prince and Savior, to grant repentance to Israel and for-
32 giveness of sins. And we are witnesses of these things, and so is the Holy Spirit, whom God has given to all who obey him."

33 But they, when they heard this, were cut to the heart and wanted to slay them.

34 But there stood up one in the Sanhedrin, a Pharisee named Gamaliel, a teacher of the Law respected by all the people, and he ordered that the men be put outside for a little while.
35 And he said to them, "Men of Israel, take care
36 what you are about to do to these men. For some time ago there rose up Theodas, claiming to be somebody, and a number of men, about four hundred, joined him; but he was slain, and all his followers were dispersed and he
37 was brought to nothing. After him rose up Judas the Galilean in the days of the census and drew some people after him; he too perished, and all his followers were scattered

abroad. So now I say to you, Keep away from 38
these men and let them alone. For if this plan
or work is of men, it will be overthrown; but if 39
it is of God, you will not be able to overthrow
it. Else perhaps you may find yourselves fighting even against God."

And they agreed with him ' and, calling in the 40
apostles and having them scourged, they charged
them not to speak in the name of Jesus, and
then let them go. So they departed from the 41
presence of the Sanhedrin, rejoicing that they
had been counted worthy to suffer disgrace for
the name of Jesus. And they did not for a single 42
day cease teaching and preaching in the temple
and from house to house the good news of Jesus
as the Christ.

The Deacons

Now in those days, as the num- | JUNE 8 | **6** 1
ber of the disciples was increasing, | Dec. 8 |
there arose a murmuring among the Hellenists
against the Hebrews that their widows were
being neglected in the daily ministration. So 2
the Twelve called together the multitude of the
disciples and said, "It is not desirable that we
should forsake the word of God and serve at
tables. Therefore, brethren, select from among 3
you seven men of good reputation, full of the
Spirit and of wisdom, that we may put them in
charge of this work. But we will devote our- 4
selves to prayer and to the ministry of the
word." And the plan met the approval of the 5
whole multitude, and they chose Stephen, a
man full of faith and of the Holy Spirit, and
Philip and Prochorus and Nicanor and Timon
and Parmenas and Nicholas, a proselyte from
Antioch. These they set before the apostles, 6
and after they had prayed they laid their hands

7 upon them. And the word of the Lord continued to spread, and the number of the disciples increased rapidly in Jerusalem; a large number also of the priests accepted the faith.

Stephen's Arrest

8 Now Stephen, full of grace and power, was working great wonders and signs among the 9 people. But there arose some from the synagogue which is called that of the Freedmen, and of the Cyrenians and of the Alexandrians and of those from Cilicia and the province of 10 Asia, disputing with Stephen. And they were not able to withstand the wisdom and the 11 Spirit who spoke. Then they bribed men to say they had heard him speaking blasphemous words against Moses and against God.

12 And they stirred up the people and the elders and the Scribes, and, running together, they seized him and brought him to the Sanhedrin. 13 And they brought forward false witnesses to say, "This man never ceases speaking words 14 against the Holy Place and the Law; for we have heard him say that this Jesus of Nazareth will destroy this place and will change the tradi- 15 tions which Moses handed down to us." Then all who sat in the Sanhedrin, gazing upon him, saw his face as though it were the face of an **7** 1 angel. And the high priest said, "Are these things so?"

Stephen's Discourse: the Patriarchs

2 Then he said, "Brethren and fathers, hear. The God of glory appeared to our father Abraham when he was in Mesopotamia, before he 3 settled in Haran, ¹ and said to him, 'Go forth from thy country and from thy kindred, and 4 come into the land that I will show thee.' Then

he went forth from the land of the Chaldeans and settled in Haran. From there, after the death of his father, God removed him into this land where you now dwell. And he gave him no 5 property in it, not even a foot of land, but he promised 'to give it for a possession to him and to his offspring after him,' when as yet he had no son. And God said, 'His offspring shall 6 sojourn in a strange country, and they shall enslave and oppress them four hundred years. And the nation to which they have been in 7 bondage, I will judge,' said God, 'and afterwards they shall go forth and shall worship me in this place.' And he gave him the covenant 8 of circumcision, and so he begot Isaac and circumcised him on the eighth day; and Isaac begot Jacob, and Jacob the twelve patriarchs.

Joseph

"Out of jealousy the patriarchs sold Joseph 9 into Egypt, but God was with him ' and rescued 10 him from all his tribulations, and gave him favor and wisdom 'in the sight of Pharaoh king of Egypt, and he made him governor over Egypt and over all his household.' Now there came a 11 famine over all Egypt and Canaan, and great tribulation, and our fathers found no food. But when Jacob heard that there was grain in 12 Egypt, he sent our fathers there a first time, and 13 on their second visit Joseph was recognized by his brothers, and his family became known to Pharaoh. And Joseph sent for his father Jacob 14 and all his kindred, seventy-five souls in all. And Jacob went down to Egypt, and he and our 15 fathers died ' and were taken to Sichem and laid 16 in the tomb which Abraham bought for a sum of silver from the sons of Hemor, the son of Sichem.

Moses

17 "Now when the time of the
promise drew near that God had
made to Abraham, the people increased and
18 multiplied in Egypt ¹ till 'another king arose in
19 Egypt who knew nothing of Joseph.' He dealt
craftily with our race and oppressed our fathers
by forcing them to expose their infants so that
20 they might not live. At this time Moses was
born, and he was acceptable to God; he was
nourished three months in his father's house,
21 and when he was exposed, Pharaoh's daughter
adopted him and brought him up as her own
22 son. And Moses was instructed in all the wisdom of the Egyptians, and he was mighty in
23 his words and in his deeds. And when he was
forty years old, it occurred to him to visit his
24 brethren, the children of Israel. And when he
had seen one of them being imposed upon,
he defended him and, striking down the Egyptian, he avenged him who was being illtreated.
25 Now, he thought that the brethren understood
that by his hand God was giving them de-
26 liverance; but they did not understand. The
next day he came across them fighting and he
tried to reconcile them in peace, saying, 'Men,
you are brethren; why do you injure each
27 other?' But the man who was wronging his
neighbor thrust him aside, saying, 'Who has
28 appointed thee ruler and judge over us? Dost
thou mean to kill me as thou didst the Egyptian
29 yesterday?' At those words Moses fled, and
lived for a time in the land of Madian, where
he begot two sons.
30 "When forty years had passed, there appeared to him in the desert of Mount Sinai an
31 angel in a flame of fire in a bush. But when
Moses saw it, he marvelled at the sight; but

as he drew near to look, there came the voice of the Lord, saying, 'I am the God of thy fathers, 32 the God of Abraham, the God of Isaac and the God of Jacob.' And Moses trembled and did not dare to look. Then the Lord said to him, 33 'Remove the sandals from thy feet, for the place where thou art standing is holy ground. I have 34 seen all the oppression of my people in Egypt, and I have heard their groaning, and I have come down to deliver them. And now come, I will send thee to Egypt.'

"This Moses whom they disowned, saying, 35 'Who has made thee ruler and judge?'—him God sent to be ruler and redeemer, with the help of the angel who appeared to him in the bush. This is he who led them out, working 36 wonders and signs in the land of Egypt and in the Red Sea and in the desert, forty years. This 37 is the Moses who said to the children of Israel, 'God will raise up to you a prophet from among your brethren, as he raised up me; to him shall you hearken.' This is he who was in the as- 38 sembly in the wilderness with the angel who spoke to him on Mount Sinai, and with our fathers, and he received the words of life to give to us. But our fathers would not obey him, 39 but thrust him aside and in their hearts turned back to Egypt, ' saying to Aaron, 'Make us 40 gods to go before us. As for this Moses who brought us out of the land of Egypt, we do not know what has become of him.' And they made 41 a calf in those days and offered sacrifice to the idol and rejoiced in the works of their own hands. But God turned and gave them up to 42 serve the host of heaven, even as it is written in the book of the Prophets: 'Did you offer victims and sacrifices to me for forty years in the desert, O house of Israel? Why, you took up with you 43

the tabernacle of Moloch and the star of your
god Rempham, images that you made to worship. And I will carry you away beyond Babylon.'

The Temple

44 　"Our fathers had in the desert | JUNE 10
the tent of the testimony, as God | Dec. 10
arranged when he told Moses to make it ac-
45 cording to the model that he had seen. This tent
also our fathers inherited, and they brought it
here with them when under Josue they took
possession of the territory of the Gentiles that
God drove out before our fathers; and it re-
46 mained down to the time of David. He found
favor before God and asked that he might find
47 a dwelling place for the God of Jacob. But
48 Solomon built him a house. Yet not in houses
made by hands does the Most High dwell, even
49 as the prophet says, 'The heaven is my throne,
and the earth a footstool for my feet. What
house will you build me, says the Lord, or what
50 shall be the place of my resting? Did not my
hand make all this?'

Conclusion

51 　"Stiff-necked and uncircumcised in heart and
ear, you always oppose the Holy Spirit; as your
52 fathers did, so you do also. Which of the prophets
have not your fathers persecuted? And they
killed those who foretold the coming of the
Just One, of whom you have now been the be-
53 trayers and murderers, you who received the
Law as an ordinance of angels and did not
keep it."

Stephen's Martyrdom

54 　Now as they heard these things, they were
cut to the heart and gnashed their teeth at him.

But he, being full of the Holy Spirit, looked up 55
to heaven and saw the glory of God, and Jesus
standing at the right hand of God; and he said, 56
"Behold, I see the heavens opened, and the Son
of Man standing at the right hand of God."
But they cried out with a loud voice and stopped 57
their ears and rushed upon him all together. And 58
they cast him out of the city and stoned him.
And the witnesses laid down their garments
at the feet of a young man named Saul. And 59
while they were stoning Stephen he prayed and
said, "Lord Jesus, receive my spirit." And falling 60
on his knees, he cried out with a loud voice,
saying, "Lord, do not lay this sin against them."
And with these words he fell asleep. And Saul
approved of his death.

Persecution

Now there broke out on that day a great 8 1
persecution against the Church in Jerusalem,
and all except the apostles were scattered
abroad throughout the land of Judea and Samaria. And devout men took care of Stephen's 2
burial and made great lamentation over him. But 3
Saul was harassing the Church; entering house
after house, and dragging out men and women,
he committed them to prison.

2. The Church in Judea and Samaria

Samaria

NOW THOSE WHO WERE scat- | JUNE 11 | 4
tered abroad went about preaching | Dec. 11 |
the word. And Philip went down to the city of 5
Samaria and preached the Christ to them. And 6
the crowds with one accord gave heed to what
was said by Philip, listening to him and seeing

7, 60: *He fell asleep:* he died.

7 the miracles that he worked. For unclean spirits,
crying with a loud voice, went out of many pos-
8 sessed persons, and many paralytics and cripples
9 were cured. So there was great joy in that city.

Now a man named Simon had previously
been practising sorcery in that city and astound-
ing the people of Samaria, claiming to be some-
10 one great; and all from least to greatest listened
to him, saying, "This man is the power of God,
11 which is called great." And they gave heed to
him because for a long time he had bewitched
12 them with his sorceries. But when they believed
Philip as he preached the kingdom of God and
the name of Jesus Christ, they were baptized,
13 both men and women. And Simon also himself
believed, and after his baptism attached himself to Philip; and at sight of the signs and exceedingly great miracles being wrought, he was
amazed.

14 Now when the apostles in Jerusalem heard
that Samaria had received the word of God,
15 they sent to them Peter and John. On their
arrival they prayed for them, that they might
16 receive the Holy Spirit; for as yet he had not
come upon any of them, but they had only been
17 baptized in the name of the Lord Jesus. Then
they laid their hands on them and they re-
18 ceived the Holy Spirit. But when Simon saw that
the Holy Spirit was given through the laying on
of the apostles' hands, he offered them money,
19 ' saying, "Give me also this power, so that anyone on whom I lay my hands may receive the
Holy Spirit."

20 But Peter said to him, ' "Thy money go to

8, 15: *Holy Spirit:* they had received the Holy Spirit in
Baptism, but not in the fullness with which He is imparted in Confirmation. Being only a deacon, Philip could
not administer Confirmation.

destruction with thee, because thou hast thought that the gift of God could be purchased with money. Thou hast no part or lot in this matter; for thy heart is not right before God. Repent therefore of this wickedness of thine and pray to God, that perhaps this thought of thy heart may be forgiven thee; for I see thou art in the gall of bitterness and in the bond of iniquity." But Simon answered, "Do you pray for me to the Lord, that nothing of what you have said may happen to me." 21 22 23 24

So they, after bearing witness and preaching the gospel of the Lord, returned to Jerusalem, and preached the gospel to many Samaritan villages. 25

An Ethiopian

But an angel of the Lord spoke to Philip, saying, "Arise and go south to the road that goes down from Jerusalem to Gaza." (This road is desert.) ' And he arose and went. And behold, an Ethiopian, a eunuch, a minister of Candace, queen of Ethiopia, who was in charge of all her treasures, had come to Jerusalem to worship ' and was returning, sitting in his carriage and reading the prophet Isaias. And the Spirit said to Philip, "Go near and keep close to this carriage." And Philip, running up, heard him reading the prophet Isaias, and he said, "Dost thou then understand what thou art reading?" But he said, "Why, how can I, unless someone shows me?" And he asked Philip to get up and sit with him. 26 27 28 29 30 31

> JUNE 12
> Dec. 12

Now the passage of Scripture which he was reading was this: "He was led like a sheep to slaughter; and just as a lamb dumb before its shearer, so did he not open his mouth. In humiliation his judgment was denied him; who 32 33

[329]

shall declare his generation? for his life is
34 taken from the earth." And the eunuch answered Philip and said, "I pray thee, of whom
is the prophet saying this? Of himself or of
someone else?"

35 Then Philip opened his mouth and, beginning
36 from this Scripture, preached Jesus to him. And
as they went along the road, they came to some
water; and the eunuch said, "See, here is water;
what is there to prevent my being baptized?"
37 [And Philip said, "If thou dost believe with all
thy heart, thou mayest." And he answered, and
said, "I believe Jesus Christ to be the Son of
38 God."] And he ordered the carriage to stop; and
both Philip and the eunuch went down into the
39 water, and he baptized him. But when they came
up out of the water, the Spirit of the Lord took
Philip away, and the eunuch saw him no more,
40 but he went on his way rejoicing. But Philip was
found in Azotus, and passing through he preached
the gospel to all the cities till he came to Cæsarea.

The Vision of Saul

9 1 But Saul, still breathing threats
of slaughter against the disciples of
2 the Lord, went to the high priest ' and asked him
for letters to the synagogues at Damascus,
that if he found any men or women belonging to
this Way, he might bring them in bonds to Jeru-
3 salem. And as he went on his journey, it came to
pass that he drew near to Damascus, when suddenly a light from heaven shone round about
4 him; and falling to the ground, he heard a voice
saying to him, "Saul, Saul, why dost thou per-
5 secute me?" And he said, "Who art thou, Lord?"
And he said, "I am Jesus, whom thou art perse-

JUNE 13
Dec. 13

9, 2: *This Way:* in Greek, "the Way," used for Christianity.

cuting. [It is hard for thee to kick against the goad." And he, trembling and amazed, said, "Lord, what wilt thou have me do?" ' And the Lord said to him,] "Arise and go into the city, and it will be told thee what thou must do." Now the men who journeyed with him stood speechless, hearing indeed the voice, but seeing no one. And Saul arose from the ground, but when his eyes were opened, he could see nothing. And leading him by the hand, they brought him into Damascus. And for three days he could not see, and he neither ate nor drank.

Saul's Baptism

Now there was in Damascus a certain disciple named Ananias, and the Lord said to him in a vision, "Ananias." And he said, "Here I am, Lord." And the Lord said to him, "Arise and go to the street called Straight and ask at the house of Judas for a man of Tarsus named Saul. For behold, he is praying." (And he saw a man named Ananias come in and lay his hands upon him that he might recover his sight.) But Ananias answered, "Lord, I have heard from many about this man, how much evil he has done to thy saints in Jerusalem. And here too he has authority from the high priests to arrest all who invoke thy name." But the Lord said to him, "Go, for this man is a chosen vessel to me, to carry my name among nations and kings and the children of Israel. For I will show him how much he must suffer for my name."

So Ananias departed and entered the house,

9, 12: This parenthesis describes a vision which St. Paul had while our Lord was speaking to Ananias.

9, 13: *Saints:* those separated from other men and united to Christ. They are sanctified by the presence in Him of the Holy Spirit.

and laying his hands upon him, he said, "Brother Saul, the Lord has sent me — Jesus, who appeared to thee on thy journey — that thou mayest recover thy sight and be filled with the Holy
18 Spirit." And straightway there fell from his eyes something like scales, and he recovered his
19 sight, and arose, and was baptized. And after taking some food, he regained his strength.

Saul's Zeal

Now for some days he joined the
20 disciples in Damascus, and straightway in the synagogues he began to preach that
21 Jesus is the Son of God. And all who heard him were amazed and said, "Is not this he who used to make havoc in Jerusalem of those who called upon this name, and who has come here for the purpose of taking them in bonds to the chief priests?"

JUNE 14
Dec. 14

22 But Saul grew all the stronger and confounded the Jews who were living in Damascus, proving that this is the Christ.

23 But as time passed on the Jews made a plot to
24 kill him. But their plot became known to Saul. They were even guarding the gates both day and
25 night in order to kill him; but his disciples took him by night and let him down over the wall, lowering him in a basket.

26 Now on his arrival at Jerusalem he tried to join the disciples, and they were all afraid of
27 him, not believing that he was a disciple. But Barnabas took him and brought him to the apostles, and he told them how on his journey he had seen the Lord, that the Lord had spoken to him, and how in Damascus he had acted
28 boldly in the name of Jesus. And he moved freely among them in Jerusalem, acting boldly
29 in the name of the Lord; he also spoke and dis-

puted with the Hellenists; but they sought to kill him. When the brethren got to know this, they took him down to Cæsarea and sent him away to Tarsus. 30

Peter Visits the Churches

Now throughout all Judea and Galilee and Samaria the Church was in peace and was being built up, walking in fear of the Lord, and it was filled with the consolation of the Holy Spirit. And it came to pass that Peter, while visiting all the saints, came to those living at Lydda. And he found there a certain man named Aeneas who had kept his bed eight years, being a paralytic. And Peter said to him, "Aeneas, Jesus Christ heals thee; get up and make thy bed." And straightway he got up. And all who lived at Lydda and in Sharon saw him, and they turned to the Lord. 31 32 33 34 35

Now at Joppa there was a certain disciple named Tabitha (which is translated Dorcas); this woman had devoted herself to good works and acts of charity. But it happened that at this time she fell ill and died; and they washed her, and laid her in an upper room. And as Lydda was near Joppa, the disciples, hearing that Peter was there, sent two men to him with the request, "Come on to us without delay." And Peter arose and went with them, and on his arrival they took him to the upper room. And all the widows stood about him weeping and showing him the tunics and cloaks which Dorcas used to make for them. But Peter, putting them all out, knelt down and prayed; and turning to the body, he said, "Tabitha, arise." And she opened her eyes and, seeing Peter, she sat up. Then Peter gave her his hand and raised her up; and calling the saints and the 36 37 38 39 40 41

42 widows, he gave her back to them alive. And it became known all over Joppa, and many
43 believed in the Lord. And it came to pass that he stayed some time in Joppa at the house of one Simon, a tanner.

3. Spread of the Church to the Gentiles

Cornelius: the Visions

10 1 NOW THERE WAS IN CÆSAREA a man named Cornelius, a centurion
2 of the cohort called Italian; he was devout and God-fearing, as was all his household, giving much alms to the people and praying to God
3 continually. About the ninth hour of the day he saw distinctly in a vision an angel of God come in to him and say to him, "Cornelius."
4 And he, gazing at him in terror, said, "What is it, Lord?" And he said to him, "Thy prayers and thy alms have gone up and been remem-
5 bered in the sight of God. And now send men to Joppa and fetch one Simon, surnamed Peter;
6 he is lodging with Simon, a tanner, who has a
7 house by the seaside." When the angel who was speaking to him had departed, he called two of his servants, and a God-fearing soldier
8 from among his personal attendants, and after telling them the whole story sent them to Joppa.

9 Now the next day, while they were still on their journey and were just drawing near to the city, Peter went up to the roof to pray,
10 about the sixth hour; but he got very hungry, and wanted something to eat. But while they were getting it ready, he fell into an ecstasy,
11 ' and saw heaven standing open and a certain vessel coming down like a great sheet, let down
12 by the four corners from heaven to earth; and in it were all the four-footed beasts and creep-

ing things of the earth, and birds of the air. And there came a voice to him, "Arise, Peter, 13 kill and eat." But Peter said, "Far be it from 14 me, Lord, for never did I eat anything common or unclean." And there came a voice a second 15 time to him, "What God has cleansed, do not thou call common." Now this happened three 16 times, and straightway the vessel was taken up into heaven.

Now while Peter was still wondering as to 17 what the vision he had had might mean, behold, the men sent by Cornelius stood at the door, inquiring for Simon's house; and they 18 called out to ask whether Simon, surnamed Peter, was staying there. But while Peter was 19 pondering over the vision, the Spirit said to him, "Behold, three men are looking for thee. Arise, therefore, go down and depart with them 20 without any hesitation, for I have sent them." So Peter went down to the men and said, 21 "Behold, I am the man you are asking for; what is the reason for your coming?" And they 22 said, "Cornelius, a centurion, a just and God-fearing man, to whom the whole nation of the Jews bear witness, has been directed by a holy angel to fetch thee to his house and to hear words from thee." So he invited them in and 23 entertained them.

Peter Meets Cornelius

And the next day he arose and started off with them, and certain | JUNE 16 / Dec. 16 | of the brethren from Joppa accompanied him. The following day he reached Cæsarea. Now 24 Cornelius was waiting for them, having invited in his relatives and his intimate friends. And as 25

10, 15: The distinction made by the Mosaic Law between clean and unclean food is no longer to hold good.

Peter entered, Cornelius met him and, falling
26 at his feet, made obeisance to him. But Peter
raised him up, saying, "Get up, I myself also
27 am a man." And as he talked with him, he went
28 in and found many assembled, and he said to
them, "You know it is not permissible for a Jew
to associate with a foreigner or to visit him;
but God has shown me that I should not call
any man common or unclean; therefore I came
29 without hesitation when I was sent for. I ask,
therefore, why you have sent for me."

30 And Cornelius said, "Three days ago, at this
very hour, I was praying in my house at the
ninth hour, and behold, a man stood before me
31 in shining garments, and said, 'Cornelius, thy
prayer has been heard and thy alms have been
32 remembered in the sight of God. Send therefore
to Joppa and call Simon, surnamed Peter; he is
lodging in the house of Simon, a tanner, by the
33 sea.' Immediately therefore I sent to thee, and
thou hast very kindly come. Now, therefore,
we are all present in thy sight to hear whatever
has been commanded thee by the Lord."

Peter's Discourse

34 But Peter began, and said, "Now I really
understand that God is not a respecter of per-
35 sons, but in every nation he who fears him and
36 does what is right is acceptable to him. He sent
his word to the children of Israel, preaching
peace through Jesus Christ (who is Lord of all).
37 You know what took place throughout Judea; for
he began in Galilee after the baptism preached
38 by John: how God anointed Jesus of Nazareth
with the Holy Spirit and with power, and he
went about doing good and healing all who were
in the power of the devil; for God was with him.
39 And we are witnesses of all that he did in the

country of the Jews and in Jerusalem; and yet
they killed him, hanging him on a tree. But God 40
raised him on the third day and caused him to
be plainly seen, [1] not by all the people, but by 41
witnesses designated beforehand by God, that
is, by us, who ate and drank with him after he
had risen from the dead. And he charged us to 42
preach to the people and to testify that he it is
who has been appointed by God to be judge
of the living and of the dead. To him all the 43
prophets bear witness, that through his name all
who believe in him may receive forgiveness
of sins."

The Baptism

While Peter was still speaking these words, 44
the Holy Spirit came upon all who were listening to his message. And the faithful of the cir- 45
cumcision, who had come with Peter, were
amazed, because on the Gentiles also the grace
of the Holy Spirit had been poured forth; for 46
they heard them speaking in tongues and mag-
nifying God. Then Peter answered, "Can any- 47
one refuse the water to baptize these, seeing
that they have received the Holy Spirit just as
we did?" And he ordered them to be baptized 48
in the name of Jesus Christ. Then they besought
him to stay on there a few days.

Explanation at Jerusalem

Now the apostles and the brethren all over Judea heard that the
Gentiles also had received the word of God. But 2
when Peter went up to Jerusalem, they of the
circumcision found fault with him, saying, 3

| JUNE 17 | **11** 1 |
| Dec. 17 | |

10, 46: *In tongues:* i. e., in foreign languages as on
Pentecost.

"Why didst thou visit men uncircumcised and eat with them?"

4 Then Peter began to explain the matter to
5 them in order, saying, "I was praying in the city of Joppa and while in ecstasy I had a vision, a certain vessel coming down something like a great sheet, let down from heaven by its four
6 corners, and it came right down to me. And gazing upon it, I began to observe, and I saw the four-footed creatures of the earth, and the wild beasts and the creeping things, and the birds of
7 the air. And I also heard a voice saying to me,
8 'Arise, Peter, kill and eat.' And I said, 'By no means, Lord, for nothing common or unclean has
9 ever entered my mouth.' But the voice answered a second time, 'What God has cleansed, do not
10 thou call common.' This happened three times, and then it was all drawn up back into heaven.
11 And behold, immediately three men came to the house where I was, having been sent from
12 Cæsarea to me; and the Spirit bade me not to hesitate to go with them. And these six brethren also went with me, and we entered the man's
13 house. And he told us how he had seen the angel in his house stand and say to him, 'Send to
14 Joppa and fetch Simon, surnamed Peter; he will speak to thee words by which thou shalt be
15 saved, thou and all thy household.' But when I began to speak, the Holy Spirit fell upon them, just as it did upon us at the beginning. And I re-
16 membered the word of the Lord, how he had said, 'John indeed baptized with water, but you shall be
17 baptized with the Holy Spirit.' Therefore, if God gave to them the same grace as he gave to us who believed in the Lord Jesus Christ, who was I
18 that I should be able to interfere with God?" On hearing this they held their peace, and glorified

God, saying, "Therefore to the Gentiles also God
has given repentance unto life."

The Converts at Antioch

Now those who had been dispersed by the 19
persecution that had broken out over Stephen,
went all the way to Phœnicia and Cyprus and
Antioch, speaking the word to none except to
Jews only. But some of them were Cyprians and 20
Cyreneans, who on reaching Antioch began to
speak to the Greeks also, preaching the Lord
Jesus. And the hand of the Lord was with them, 21
and a great number believed and turned to the
Lord. And news concerning them came to the 22
ears of the church in Jerusalem, and they sent
Barnabas as far as Antioch. Now when he came 23
and saw the grace of God, he rejoiced and exhorted them all to continue in the Lord with
steadfast heart; for he was a good man and full 24
of the Holy Spirit and of faith. And a great multitude was added to the Lord. And he went forth 25
to Tarsus to look for Saul, and on finding him he
brought him to Antioch. And for a whole year 26
they took part in the meetings of the church and
taught a great multitude. And it was in Antioch
that the disciples were first called "Christians."

Now in those days some prophets from Jeru- 27
salem came down to Antioch, and one of them 28
named Agabus got up and revealed through the
Spirit that there would be a great famine all over
the world. The famine occurred in the reign of
Claudius. So the disciples, each according to his 29
means, determined to send relief to the brethren
dwelling in Judea. And this they did, sending it 30
to the presbyters by the hands of Barnabas and
Saul.

11, 30: *Presbyters:* literally, "elders." This is the term

Conclusion: Persecution of the Church by Herod Agrippa

Peter in Prison

12 1   NOW AT THIS TIME Herod the king set hands on certain members 2 of the Church to persecute them. He killed James 3 the brother of John with the sword, and seeing that it pleased the Jews, he proceeded to arrest Peter also, during the days of the Unleavened 4 Bread. After arresting him he cast him into prison, committing the custody of him to four guards of soldiers, four in each guard, intending to bring him forth to the people after the Pass-5 over. So Peter was being kept in the prison; but prayer was being made to God for him by the Church without ceasing.

JUNE 18
Dec. 18

His Deliverance

6   Now when Herod was about to bring him forth, that same night Peter was sleeping between two soldiers, bound with two chains, and 7 outside the door sentries guarded the prison. And behold, an angel of the Lord stood beside him, and a light shone in the room; and he struck Peter on the side and woke him, saying, "Get up quickly." The chains dropped from his hands. 8 And the angel said to him, "Gird thyself and put on thy sandals." And he did so; and he said to him, "Wrap thy cloak about thee and follow me."

from which our "priest" is derived. But here and in the rest of Acts, and in many of the Epistles, it designates the priests who held office as rulers of the early Church. "Presbyter" also distinguishes these priests from the Jewish "elders."

12, 3: *Days of the Unleavened Bread:* the seven days following the paschal supper.

And he followed him out, without knowing 9
that what was being done by the angel was real,
for he thought he was having a vision. They 10
passed through the first and second guard and
came to the iron gate that leads into the city;
and this opened to them of its own accord. And
they went out, and passed on through one street,
and straightway the angel left him. Then Peter 11
came to himself, and he said, "Now I know for
certain that the Lord has sent his angel and
rescued me from the power of Herod and from
all that the Jewish people were expecting."

When he realized his situation, he went to the 12
house of Mary, the mother of John who was
surnamed Mark, where many had gathered together and were praying. When he knocked at 13
the door, a maid named Rhoda came to answer
it. And as soon as she recognized Peter's voice, 14
in her joy she did not open the gate, but ran in
and announced that Peter was standing before
the gate. But they said to her, "Thou art mad." 15
But she insisted that it was so. Then they said,
"It is his angel." But Peter continued knocking; 16
and when they opened, they saw him and were
amazed. But he motioned to them with his hand 17
to be quiet, and related how the Lord had brought
him out of the prison. And he said, "Tell this to
James and to the brethren." And he departed,
and went to another place.

Herod Punished

Now when morning came, there was no little 18
stir among the soldiers as to what had become of
Peter. When Herod had searched for him and 19
had not found him, he examined the guards and
ordered them to be put to death; then he went

12, 15: *Angel:* guardian angel.

down from Judea to Cæsarea and stayed there.
20 Now he was very angry with the Tyrians and Sidonians; but they came to him in a body and, having won over Blastus, the king's chamberlain, they asked for peace, because their country
21 depended on him for its food supply. So a day was fixed and on it Herod, arrayed in kingly
22 apparel, sat in the judgment-seat and began to address them. And the people shouted, "It is
23 the voice of a god, and not of a man." But immediately an angel of the Lord struck him down, because he had not given the honor to God; and he was eaten by worms, and died.

24 But the word of the Lord continued to grow
25 and spread. Now Barnabas and Saul, when they had fulfilled their mission, returned from Jerusalem, taking with them John, who was surnamed Mark.

II: THE CHURCH IN ASIA MINOR AND EUROPE
THE MISSIONARY JOURNEYS OF ST. PAUL

1. First Missionary Journey
Antioch

13 1 NOW IN THE CHURCH AT ANTIOCH [JUNE 19 / Dec. 19] there were prophets and teachers, among whom were Barnabas and Simon, called Niger, and Lucius of Cyrene, and Manahen the foster-brother of Herod the tetrarch, and Saul.
2 And as they were ministering to the Lord and fasting, the Holy Spirit said, "Set apart for me Saul and Barnabas unto the work to which I have
3 called them." Then, having fasted and prayed and laid their hands upon them, they let them go.

13, 2: *Ministering:* in some form of public worship, probably the Mass. From the Greek word used here comes our "liturgy."

13, 3: *Laid their hands upon them:* consecrating them

Cyprus

So they, sent forth by the Holy Spirit, went to 4
Seleucia and from there sailed to Cyprus. On 5
their arrival at Salamis they began to preach the
word of God in the synagogues of the Jews; and
they had also John as assistant. They went, pass- 6
ing through the whole island as far as Paphos,
and there they came across a Jewish magician
and false prophet named Bar-Jesus, who was 7
attached to the proconsul Sergius Paulus, a man
of discernment. He sent for Barnabas and Saul,
and sought to hear the word of God; but Elymas, 8
the sorcerer (for so his name is translated), opposed them, trying to turn away the proconsul
from the faith. But Saul (also called Paul), filled 9
with the Holy Spirit, gazed at him [1] and said, 10
"O full of all guile and of all deceit, son of the
devil, enemy of all justice, wilt thou not cease to
make crooked the straight ways of the Lord? And 11
now, behold, the hand of the Lord is upon thee,
and thou shalt be blind, not seeing the sun for
a time." And instantly there fell upon him a mist
of darkness, and he groped about for someone
to lead him by the hand. Then the proconsul, 12
seeing what had happened, believed and was
astonished at the Lord's teaching.

Antioch in Pisidia

Putting to sea from Paphos, Paul and his 13
companions came to Perge in Pamphylia; but

---

as bishops, or (more probably) giving them merely a
special blessing for the new work.

13, 6: *Bar-Jesus:* a patronymic, "Bar" meaning "son
of," as in Barnabas. "Jesus" is another form of "Josue."
His proper name was "Elymas," meaning "sorcerer" or
"magician." Cf. v. 8.

13, 9: *Saul:* A Jewish name. He may have adopted the
Roman name "Paul" either at this time or earlier, for
use among the Gentiles.

14 John left them and returned to Jerusalem. But they passed through Perge and reached the Pisidian Antioch; and entering the synagogue on
15 the Sabbath, they sat down. After the reading of the Law and the Prophets, the rulers of the synagogue sent to them, saying, "Brethren, if you have any word of exhortation for the people, speak."

Paul's Discourse

16 Then Paul arose, and motioning with his hand for silence, said, "Israelites and you who fear
17 God, hearken. The God of the people of Israel chose our fathers and exalted the people when they were sojourners in the land of Egypt, and
18 with uplifted arm led them forth out of it. And for a period of forty years he bore with their
19 ways in the desert, and after destroying seven nations in the land of Canaan, he divided their
20 land among them by lot ' after about four hundred and fifty years. After that he gave them judges, until the time of Samuel the prophet.
21 Then they demanded a king, and God gave them Saul, the son of Cis, a man of the tribe of Ben-
22 jamin, for forty years. And removing him, he raised up David to be their king, and to him he bore witness and said, 'I have found David, the son of Jesse, a man after my heart, who will do all that I desire.'

23 "From his offspring, God according- ⎡ JUNE 20
ing to promise brought to Israel a ⎢ Dec. 20
24 Savior, Jesus; John having first preached before his coming a baptism of repentance to all the
25 people of Israel. And when John was coming to the end of his career, he would say, 'I am not he whom you suppose me to be; but behold, there comes one after me, the sandals of whose feet I
26 am not worthy to loose.' Brethren, children of

the race of Abraham, and all among you who fear God, to you the word of this salvation has been sent. For the inhabitants of Jerusalem and its 27 rulers, not knowing him and the utterances of the prophets which are read every Sabbath, fulfilled them by sentencing him; and though they 28 found no ground for putting him to death, they asked of Pilate permission to kill him. And 29 when they had carried out all that had been written concerning him, they took him down from the tree and laid him in a tomb. But God raised 30 him from the dead on the third day; and he was 31 seen during many days by those who had come up with him from Galilee to Jerusalem; and they are now witnesses for him to the people.

"So we now bring you the good news that the 32 promise made to our fathers, God has fulfilled 33 to our children, in raising up Jesus, as also it is written in the second Psalm, 'Thou art my son, this day have I begotten thee.' And to show that 34 he has raised him up from the dead, never again to return to decay, he has said thus, 'I will give you the holy and sure promises of David.' Because he says also in another Psalm, 'Thou 35 wilt not let thy Holy One undergo decay.'

"For David, after he had in his own generation 36 served God's purposes, fell asleep and was laid among his fathers and did undergo decay; but 37 he whom God raised to life did not undergo it. Be it known therefore to you, brethren, that 38 through him forgiveness of sins is proclaimed to you, and in him everyone who believes is ac- 39 quitted of all the things of which you could not be acquitted by the Law of Moses. Beware, 40 therefore, that what is said in the Prophets may not prove true of you, ' 'Behold, you despisers, 41 then wonder and perish, because I work a work in your days, a work which you will not believe, if anyone relates it to you.' "

42 Now as they were going out, the people asked to have all this said to them on the following
43 Sabbath. And after the synagogue had broken up, many of the Jews and the worshipping converts went away with Paul and Barnabas, and they talked with them and urged them to hold
44 fast to the grace of God. And the next Sabbath almost the whole city gathered to hear the word
45 of the Lord. But on seeing the crowds, the Jews were filled with jealousy and contradicted what
46 was said by Paul, and blasphemed. Then Paul and Barnabas spoke out plainly: "It was necessary that the word of God should be spoken to you first, but since you reject it and judge yourselves unworthy of eternal life, behold, we now
47 turn to the Gentiles. For so the Lord has commanded us, 'I have set thee for a light to the Gentiles, to be a means of salvation to the very ends of the earth.' "

48 On hearing this the Gentiles were delighted, and glorified the word of the Lord, and all who
49 were destined for eternal life believed. And the word of the Lord spread throughout the whole
50 country. But the Jews incited the worshipping women of rank and the chief men of the city, and stirred up a persecution against Paul and Barnabas and drove them from their district.
51 But they shook off the dust of their feet in pro-
52 test against them and went to Iconium. And the disciples continued to be filled with joy and with the Holy Spirit.

Iconium

Now it came to pass at Iconium
that they went in the same way
into the synagogue of the Jews and so spoke
that a great multitude of Jews and of Greeks
believed. But the disbelieving Jews stirred up 2
and poisoned the minds of the Gentiles against
the brethren. They stayed a long time, there- 3
fore, acting fearlessly in the Lord, who gave
testimony to the word of his grace by permitting signs and wonders to be done by their
hands. But the people of the city were divided, 4
some siding with the Jews and some with the
apostles. But when there was a movement on 5
the part of the Gentiles and of the Jews with
their rulers to insult and stone them, hearing 6
of it, they escaped to the Lycaonian cities Lystra
and Derbe and the whole country round about,
and there they went on preaching the gospel.

14 1

JUNE 21
Dec. 21

Lystra

And in Lystra a certain man used to sit 7
whose feet were crippled. He had been lame
from his very birth, and had never been able
to walk. He listened to Paul as he spoke; when 8
Paul, gazing at him and seeing that he had
faith to be cured,' said with a loud voice, "Stand 9
upright on thy feet." And he sprang up and
began to walk.

Then the crowds, seeing what Paul had done, 10
lifted up their voice saying in the Lycaonian
language, "The gods have come down to us in
the likeness of men." And they called Barnabas 11
Jupiter, and Paul Mercury, because he was the
chief speaker. And the priest of the Jupiter 12
that stood at the entrance to the city brought
oxen and garlands to the gateways, and with

[347]

13 the people would have offered sacrifice. But
on hearing of this, the apostles Barnabas and
Paul rushed into the crowd, tearing their
14 clothes, ' and shouting, "Men, why are you
doing this? We also are mortals, human beings
like you, bringing to you the good news that
you should turn from these vain things to the
living God who made heaven and earth and the
15 sea and all things that are in them. In the
generations that are past he let all the nations
16 follow their own ways; and yet he did not leave
himself without testimony, bestowing blessings,
giving rains from heaven and fruitful seasons,
17 filling your hearts with food and gladness." And
even with these words they could hardly restrain
the crowds from offering sacrifice to them.

18   But some Jews arrived from Antioch and
Iconium; and after winning over the crowds,
they stoned Paul and dragged him outside the
19 city, thinking that he was dead. But the disciples gathered round him and he got up and
re-entered the city.

Derbe; the Return

    The next day he set out with Barnabas for
20 Derbe. After preaching the gospel to that city
and teaching many, they returned to Lystra and
21 Iconium and Antioch, reassuring the disciples
and exhorting them to continue in the faith,
and reminding them that through many tribula-
22 tions we must enter the kingdom of God. And
when they had appointed presbyters for them
in each church, with prayer and fasting, they
commended them to the Lord in whom they had
23 believed. Crossing Pisidia, they came to Pam-
24 phylia, and after speaking the word of the Lord
25 in Perge they went down to Attalia, and from

there they sailed back to Antioch, where they had first been entrusted to the grace of God for the work which they had now finished. On 26 their arrival they called the church together and reported all that God had done with them, and how he had opened to the Gentiles a door of faith. And they stayed no little time with 27 the disciples.

Dissension at Antioch

But some came down from Judea and began to teach the brethren, saying, "Unless you be circumcised after the manner of Moses, you cannot be saved." And when no little objection was made against 2 them by Paul and Barnabas, they decided that Paul and Barnabas and certain others of them should go up to the apostles and presbyters at Jerusalem about this question. So they, sent 3 on their way by the church, passed through Phœnicia and Samaria, relating the conversion of the Gentiles, and they caused great rejoicing among all the brethren. On arriving at Jerusalem they were welcomed by the church and 4 the apostles and the presbyters, and they proclaimed all that God had done with them. But 5 some of the Pharisees' sect, who had accepted the faith, got up and said, "They must be circumcised and also told to observe the Law of Moses."

| JUNE 22 | **15** 1 |
| Dec. 22 | |

Peter's Decision

So the apostles and the presbyters had a 6 meeting to look into this matter. And after 7 a long debate, Peter got up and said to them, "Brethren, you know that in early days God made choice among us, that through my mouth the Gentiles should hear the word of the gospel

8 and believe. And God, who knows the heart, bore witness by giving them the Holy Spirit
9 just as he did to us; and he made no distinction between us and them, but cleansed their hearts
10 by faith. Why then do you now try to test God by putting on the neck of the disciples a yoke which neither our fathers nor we have been
11 able to bear? But we believe that we are saved through the grace of the Lord Jesus, just as they are."

12 Then the whole meeting quieted down and listened while Barnabas and Paul told of the great signs and wonders that God had done among the Gentiles through them.

Advice from James

13 After these had finished speaking, James made this answer, saying, "Brethren, listen to
14 me. Simon has told how God first visited the Gentiles to take from among them a people to
15 bear his name. And with this the words of the
16 prophets agree, as it is written, 'After these things I will return and will rebuild the tabernacle of David which has fallen down, and the ruins thereof I will rebuild, and I will set it up;
17 that the rest of mankind may seek after the Lord, and all the nations upon whom my name is invoked, says the Lord, who does these things.'
18 'To the Lord was his own work known from the
19 beginning of the world.' Therefore my judgment is not to disquiet those who from among
20 the Gentiles are turning to the Lord; but to send them written instructions to abstain from anything that has been contaminated by idols and from immorality and from anything strangled
21 and from blood. For Moses for generations past has had his preachers in every city in the synagogues, where he is read aloud every Sabbath."

The Decision

Then the apostles and the presby- | JUNE 23 | 22
ters with the whole church decided | Dec. 23 |
to select representatives and to send them to
Antioch with Paul and Barnabas. These were
Judas, surnamed Barsabbas, and Silas, leading
men among the brethren. They were bearers 23
of the following letter:

"The brethren who are apostles and presbyters send greeting to the brethren of Gentile
origin in Antioch and Syria and Cilicia. As we 24
have heard that some of our number have disturbed you with their teaching, unsettling your
minds, persons to whom we had given no instruction, ' we have decided, being assembled 25
together, to select representatives and send them
to you with our beloved Barnabas and Paul:
men who have pledged their lives for the name 26
of our Lord Jesus Christ. We have therefore 27
sent Judas and Silas, who themselves also by
word of mouth will give you the same message.
For the Holy Spirit and we have decided to lay 28
no further burden upon you but this indis-
pensable one, that you abstain from things sac- 29
rificed to idols and from blood and from what
is strangled and from immorality; keep yourselves from these things, and you will get on
well. Farewell."

So the delegates went down to Antioch and, 30
gathering the community together, they delivered the letter. And they, having read it, were 31
delighted with the encouragement it gave them.
As Judas and Silas were themselves prophets, 32
they exhorted the brethren with many words
and strengthened them. After spending some 33
time there, they were let go by the brethren
with a greeting to those who had sent them.

34 [Silas however decided to stay there, and so
35 Judas departed alone for Jerusalem.] But Paul
and Barnabas stayed on in Antioch, teaching and
preaching the word of the Lord, with many
others.

2. Second Missionary Journey

Paul and Barnabas Separate

36   NOW SOME TIME AFTER Paul said to Barnabas,
"Let us return and visit the brethren in all the
cities where we have preached the word of the
37 Lord, to see how they are doing." But Barnabas
wanted to take with them John also, who was sur-
38 named Mark. But Paul asked that he, inasmuch
as he had deserted them in Pamphylia instead of
going on with them to their work, should not
39 again be taken along. And a sharp contention
sprang up so that they separated from each other,
and Barnabas took Mark and sailed for Cyprus.
40 But Paul chose Silas and set out, the brethren
41 commending him to the grace of the Lord; and
he travelled through Syria and Cilicia, and
strengthened the churches [and commanded
them to keep the precepts of the apostles and
presbyters].

Timothy

16 1   And he reached Derbe and Lystra.

JUNE 24
Dec. 24

And behold, a certain disciple was
there named Timothy, son of a believing Jewess,
2 but of a Gentile father. And he was highly
thought of by the brethren in Lystra and Icon-
3 ium. This man Paul wished to go forth with him,
and he took and circumcised him on account
of the Jews who were in those parts, for they
4 all knew that his father was a Gentile. And as
they passed through the cities, they delivered
to the brethren for their observance the de-

cisions arrived at by the apostles and presbyters in Jerusalem. So the churches grew stronger and 5 stronger in the faith and increased in numbers daily.

Departure for Macedonia

Passing through Phrygia and the Galatian 6 country, they were forbidden by the Holy Spirit to speak the word in the province of Asia. And when they came to Mysia, they tried 7 to get into Bithynia, but the Spirit of Jesus did not permit them; so passing by Mysia, they 8 went down to Troas. And Paul had a vision 9 one night; a Macedonian was standing, appealing to him and saying, "Come over into Macedonia and help us." As soon as he had 10 the vision, straightway we made efforts to set out for Macedonia, being sure that God had called us to preach the gospel to them.

Preaching at Philippi

So sailing from Troas, we ran a straight 11 course to Samothrace, and the next day to Neapolis, ' and thence to Philippi, the principal 12 city of a part of Macedonia, a Roman colony. We stayed some days in this city; ' and on the 13 Sabbath we went outside the gate to the bank of the river, where there seemed to be a place of prayer. And we sat down and spoke to the women who had gathered there. And a certain 14 woman named Lydia, a seller of purple from the city of Thyatira, who worshipped God, was listening; and the Lord touched her heart to give heed to what was being said by Paul. And when she and her household had been 15 baptized, she appealed to us and said, "If you have judged me to be a believer in the Lord,

---

16, 10: *We:* St. Luke is now accompanying the Apostle.

come into my house and stay there." And she insisted upon our coming.

A Possessed Girl

16   Now it came to pass as we were going to the place of prayer that a girl met us who possessed a divining spirit and brought her masters much
17 profit by soothsaying. She followed Paul and ourselves and kept crying out, saying, "These men are servants of the most high God and they
18 proclaim to you a way of salvation." This she did for many days; until Paul, being very much grieved, turned and said to the spirit, "I order thee in the name of Jesus Christ to go out of her." And it went out that very moment.

Arrest of Paul and Silas

19   But on seeing that their hope of profit was gone, her masters seized

JUNE 25
Dec. 25

Paul and Silas and dragged them into the
20 market place to the rulers; and bringing them to the magistrates, they said, "These men are making a great disturbance in our city; they
21 are Jews, and are advocating practices which it is against the law for us to adopt or observe,
22 since we are Romans." And the people joined in the attack against them; and the magistrates tore off their clothes and ordered them
23 to be beaten with rods; and after inflicting many lashes upon them they cast them into prison,
24 charging the jailer to keep them safely. On receiving such orders, he cast them into the inner prison and fastened their feet in the stocks.

25   But at midnight Paul and Silas were praying, singing the praises of God, and the prisoners
26 were listening to them; and suddenly there was such a great earthquake that the foundations of the prison were shaken. And at once all the

doors flew open, and everyone's chains were unfastened. And the jailer, roused out of sleep 27 and seeing that the doors of the prison were open, drew his sword and was about to kill himself, thinking that the prisoners had escaped. But Paul cried with a loud voice, saying, 28 "Do thyself no harm, for we are all here." Then 29 calling for a light, he ran in and trembling for fear fell down before Paul and Silas; and 30 bringing them out, he said, "Sirs, what must I do to be saved?" And they said, "Believe in the 31 Lord Jesus, and thou shalt be saved, and thy household." And they spoke the word of the 32 Lord to him and to all who were in his household. And he took them at that very hour of the 33 night and washed their wounds; and he and all his family were baptized immediately. And 34 taking them into his house, he set food before them, and rejoiced with all his household over his faith in God.

Freedom

But when day came, the magistrates sent the 35 lictors with the instructions, "Let these men go." And the jailer reported these words to Paul: 36 "The magistrates have sent word that you are to be released; now therefore come forth and go in peace." But Paul said to them, "They have 37 beaten us publicly and without trial, although we are Romans, and have cast us into prison; and now are they going to put us out secretly? By no means, but let them come themselves ' and take 38 us out." The lictors reported these words to the magistrates, and on hearing that they were Romans they were alarmed ' and came and appealed to them; and taking them out, besought 39 them to leave the city. And leaving the prison 40 they went to Lydia's house, and after seeing the brethren and encouraging them, they departed.

Thessalonica

17 1 Now after passing through Amphipolis and Apollonia, they came to Thessalonica, where there was a synagogue 2 of the Jews. And Paul, as was his custom, went in to them and for three Sabbaths reasoned with 3 them from the Scriptures; explaining and showing that the Christ had to suffer and rise from the dead, and that this is the Christ, even Jesus, 4 whom I preach to you. And some of them believed and joined Paul and Silas, along with a large number of the worshipping Greeks and of 5 the Gentiles, and not a few women of rank. But the Jews, moved with jealousy, took certain base loafers, and forming a mob, set the city in an uproar. They attacked Jason's house and 6 sought to bring them out to the people; but not finding them, they dragged Jason and certain brethren before the magistrates of the city, shouting, "These men who are setting the world 7 in an uproar have come here too, and Jason has taken them in; and they are all acting contrary to the decrees of Cæsar, saying that there is 8 another king, Jesus." And they stirred up the people and the magistrates of the city who heard 9 this; and they accepted bail from Jason and the rest and then let them go.

Beroea

10 But the brethren straightway sent Paul and Silas away by night to Berœa, and on their arrival there they went into the synagogue of 11 the Jews. Now these were of a nobler character than those of Thessalonica and they received the word with great eagerness, studying the Scriptures every day to see whether these things were 12 so. Many of them became believers, and so did no small number of prominent Gentiles, women

and men. But when the Jews of Thessalonica 13
found out that in Berœa too the word of God had
been preached by Paul, they came there also to
stir up and excite the multitude. Then straight- 14
way the brethren sent forth Paul to go as far as
the sea, while Silas and Timothy remained there.
But those who escorted Paul took him as far as 15
Athens, and receiving instructions from him to
Silas and Timothy to rejoin him as soon as possible, they set out.

Athens

Now while Paul was waiting for them at 16
Athens, he was exasperated to see how the city
was wholly given to idolatry. He had discussions 17
therefore in the synagogue with the Jews and
those who worshipped God, and in the market
place every day with those who were there. And 18
some of the Epicurean and Stoic philosophers
debated with him; and some said, "What is this
babbler trying to say?" But others, "He seems
to be a herald of strange gods," because he proclaimed to them Jesus and the resurrection. And 19
they took him and brought him to the Areopagus,
saying, "May we know just what is this new
doctrine which thou teachest? For thou bringest 20
some strange things to our ears; we wish therefore to know what these things mean." (Now all 21
the Athenians and the visitors there from abroad
used to spend all their leisure telling or listening
to something new.)

Paul's Discourse

Then Paul stood up in the midst of the Areo- 22
pagus, and said, "Men of Athens, I see that in

17, 21: *New:* not so much mere "news" as novel theories
and opinions.

17, 22: *Religious:* honoring a multitude of gods. There

23 every respect you are extremely religious. For as I was going about and observing objects of your worship, I found also an altar with this inscription: 'To the Unknown God.' What therefore you worship in ignorance, that I proclaim to you.

24 God, who made the world and all that is in it, since he is Lord of heaven and earth, does not

25 dwell in temples built by hands; neither is he served by human hands as though he were in need of anything, since it is he who gives to all

26 men life and breath and all things. And from one man he has created the whole human race and made them live all over the face of the earth, determining their appointed times and the bound-

27 aries of their lands; that they should seek God, and perhaps grope after him and find him, though

28 he is not far from any one of us. For in him we live and move and have our being, as indeed some of your own poets have said, 'For we are

29 also his offspring.' If therefore we are the off-spring of God, we ought not to imagine that the Divinity is like to gold or silver or stone, to an

30 image graven by human art and thought. The times of this ignorance God has it is true over-looked, but now he calls upon all men everywhere

31 to repent; inasmuch as he has fixed a day on which he will judge the world with justice by a Man whom he has appointed, and whom he has guaranteed to all by raising him from the dead."

32 Now when they heard of a resurrection of the dead, some began to sneer, but others said, "We

33 will hear thee again on this matter." So Paul

---

seems to be a touch of sarcasm in this.

17, 23: *Unknown God:* any god whom they might otherwise have neglected. St. Paul takes the expression and applies it to the true God whom in fact they did not know.

17, 24: *Does not dwell:* is not confined to.

went forth from among them. Certain persons 34
however joined him and became believers;
among them were Dionysius the Areopagite and
a woman named Damaris, and others with them.

Corinth

After this he departed from Athens and came to Corinth. And there he found a certain Jew named Aquila, a native of Pontus, who had recently come from Italy with his wife Priscilla, because Claudius had ordered all Jews to leave Rome. Paul visited them ' and, as he was of the same trade, he stayed with them and he set to work; for they were tent-makers by trade. And he would preach in the synagogue every Sabbath, [bringing in the name of the Lord Jesus] and try to convince Jews and Greeks. But when Silas and Timothy came from Macedonia, Paul was wholly occupied with the word, emphatically assuring the Jews that Jesus is the Christ. But as they contradicted him and blasphemed, he shook his garments in protest and said to them, "Your blood be upon your own heads; I am innocent of it. Henceforth I will go to the Gentiles." And he departed from there, and went into the house of a man named Titus Justus, a worshipper of God; his house adjoined the synagogue. But Crispus, the president of the synagogue, believed in the Lord and so did all his household, and many of the Corinthians heard Paul, and believed, and were baptized. And one night the Lord said to Paul in a vision, "Do not fear, but speak and do not keep silence; because I am with thee, and no one shall attack thee or injure thee, for I have many people in this city." So he

| JUNE 27 |
| Dec. 27 |

18 1
2
3
4
5
6
7
8
9
10
11

settled there a year and six months, teaching the
word of God among them.

Gallio

12 But when Gallio was proconsul of Achaia, the
Jews made a concerted attack upon Paul and
13 took him before the tribunal, saying, ' "This fel-
low is persuading men to worship God contrary
14 to the Law." But as Paul was about to open his
mouth, Gallio said to the Jews, "If there were
some question of misdemeanor or serious crime,
O Jews, I should with reason bear with you.
15 But if these are questions of doctrine and of
titles and of your Law, look to it yourselves; I
16 have no wish to decide such matters." And he
17 drove them from the tribunal. Then they all
seized Sosthenes, the president of the synagogue, and beat him in front of the tribunal; but
Gallio paid no attention to it.

Return to Antioch

18 But Paul, after staying there some time
longer, took leave of the brethren and sailed for
Syria with Priscilla and Aquila; at Cenchræ he
had his head shaved, because of a vow he had
19 made. He arrived at Ephesus and there he left
them; but he himself entered the synagogue and
20 had a discussion with the Jews. But when they
besought him to stay some time longer, he did
21 not consent, ' but bade them farewell, saying, "I
will come back to you, God willing." He put to
22 sea from Ephesus, ' and landing at Cæsarea, he
went up to Jerusalem to pay his respects to the
church and then went down to Antioch.

3. Third Missionary Journey

Return to Ephesus

AFTER SPENDING SOME TIME | JUNE 28 | 23
there he departed, and travelled | Dec. 28 |
through the Galatian country and Phrygia in
turn, strengthening all the disciples.

Now a certain Jew named Apollos, a native of 24
Alexandria, came to Ephesus. He was an elo-
quent man, and mighty in the Scriptures. He 25
had been instructed in the Way of the Lord, and
being fervent in spirit, used to speak and teach
carefully whatever had to do with Jesus, though
he knew of John's baptism only. This man there- 26
fore began to speak confidently in the synagogue, and on hearing him Priscilla and Aquila
took him more home and expounded the Way of God
to him more precisely. And as he wanted to go 27
to Achaia, the brethren encouraged him and
wrote to the disciples to welcome him. On his
arrival there he was of great service to those who
had believed, for he vigorously refuted the Jews 28
in public and showed from the Scriptures that
Jesus is the Christ.

Now it was while Apollos was in Corinth that **19** 1
Paul, after passing through the upper districts,
came to Ephesus and found certain disciples;
and he said to them, "Did you receive the Holy 2
Spirit when you became believers?" But they
said to him, "We have not even heard that there
is a Holy Spirit." And he said, "How then were 3
you baptized?" They said, "With John's baptism." Then Paul said, "John baptized the people 4
with a baptism of repentance, telling them to believe in him who was to come after him, that is,
in Jesus." On hearing this they were baptized in 5
the name of the Lord Jesus; and when Paul laid 6
his hands on them, the Holy Spirit came upon

them, and they began to speak in tongues and
7 to prophesy. There were about twelve men in all.
8   Now for three months he used to go to the synagogue and speak confidently, holding discussions
and trying to persuade them about the kingdom
9 of God. But when some were obstinate and refused to believe, speaking evil of the Way before
the community, he left them and withdrew his
disciples from them, and held daily discussions
10 in the school of one Tyrannus. Now this went on
for two years, so that all who lived in the province
11 of Asia, both Jews and Gentiles, heard the word
12 of the Lord. And God worked more than the usual
miracles by the hand of Paul; so that even hand-
kerchiefs and aprons were carried from his body
to the sick, and the diseases left them and the
evil spirits went out.

13   But certain of the itinerant Jews, exorcists,
also attempted to invoke the name of the Lord
Jesus over those who had evil spirits in them,
saying, "I adjure you by the Jesus whom Paul
14 preaches." And a certain Sceva, a Jewish high
15 priest, had seven sons who were doing this. But
the evil spirit answered and said to them, "Jesus
I acknowledge, and Paul I know, but who are
16 you?" And the man in whom the evil spirit was
sprang at them and overpowered them both with
such violence that they fled from that house
tattered and bruised.

17   And this became known to all the Jews and
Gentiles living in Ephesus, and fear fell on them
all, and the name of the Lord Jesus came to be
18 held in high honor. And many of those who believed kept coming, and openly confessed their

---

19, 16: *Them both:* perhaps only two of the seven were
actively engaged on this occasion. It is not unlikely,
however, that the word here translated "both" may have
meant "all" in the Greek of St. Luke's time.

practices. And many who had practised magical 19
arts collected their books and burnt them publicly; and they reckoned up the prices of them,
and found the sum to be fifty thousand pieces of
silver. Thus mightily did the word of the Lord 20
spread and prevail.

After all this, Paul resolved in the | JUNE 29 | 21
Spirit to pass through Macedonia | Dec. 29 |
and Achaia and to go to Jerusalem, saying, "After
I have been there, I must also see Rome." So he 22
sent two of his assistants, Timothy and Erastus,
to Macedonia, while he himself stayed on for a
while in the province of Asia.

Now at that time there arose no small commo- 23
tion about the Way. For a silversmith named 24
Demetrius, by making silver shrines of Diana,
brought no small gain to the craftsmen; and 25
these he got together, along with workmen of
like occupation, and said, "Men, you know that
our wealth comes from this trade; and you see 26
and hear that not only at Ephesus, but almost over
the whole province of Asia, this man Paul has
persuaded and turned away numbers of people,
saying, 'Gods made by human hands are not
gods at all.' And there is danger, not only that 27
this business of ours will be discredited, but also
that the temple of the great Diana will be regarded
as nothing, and even the magnificence of her
whom all Asia and the world worship will be on
the decline." On hearing this they were filled 28
with wrath and cried out, saying, "Great is
Diana of the Ephesians."

And the city was filled with confusion, and 29
they rushed by a common impulse into the

19, 19: *Their books:* containing magic formulæ.

19, 23: *Way:* the Christian manner of life.

19, 29: *Theatre:* the large open-air assembly place.

30 theatre, dragging along the Macedonians Gaius and Aristarchus, Paul's fellow-travellers. But when Paul wanted to go before the people, the

31 disciples would not let him; and some of the Asiarchs who were friends of his, sent to him and begged him not to venture into the theatre.

32 Meanwhile, some were shouting one thing and some another; for the assembly was in confusion, and most of them did not know why they

33 had gathered together. Then some of the crowd called upon Alexander, as the Jews were pushing him forward; and Alexander, motioning with his hand for silence, wanted to give an explan-

34 ation to the people. But as soon as they saw that he was a Jew, they all with one voice for about two hours shouted, "Great is Diana of the Ephesians."

35 But when the town clerk had quieted the crowd, he said, "Men of Ephesus, what man indeed is there who does not know that the city of the Ephesians is a worshipper of the great

36 Diana and of Jupiter's offspring? Since therefore this is undeniable, you ought to be calm

37 and do nothing rash. For you have brought these men here who are neither guilty of sacri-

38 lege nor blasphemers of your goddess. Therefore, if Demetrius and the craftsmen with him have a complaint against anyone, court days are kept and there are proconsuls; let them

39 take action against one another. And if you require anything further, it shall be settled in

40 the lawful assembly. For we are even in danger of being accused of riot over today's uproar, since there is no culprit whom we can hold liable for this disorderly gathering." And with these words he dismissed the assembly.

19, 31: *Asiarchs:* officers in charge of the religious feasts and of certain other matters in the province of Asia.

Macedonia and Greece

20 Now when the tumult had ceased, Paul sent for the disciples and encouraged them; then he took leave of them and started for Macedonia. After travelling through those parts and giving them much encouragement, he came to Greece. When he had spent three months there and was about to sail for Syria, a plot was laid against him by the Jews; so he resolved to return through Macedonia. And there accompanied him Sopater of Berœa, the son of Pyrrhus; and of the Thessalonians, Aristarchus and Secundus, and Gaius of Derbe, and Timothy; and of the province of Asia, Tychicus and Trophimus. These, having gone in advance, waited for us at Troas; but we ourselves sailed from Philippi after the days of the Unleavened Bread, and five days later joined them at Troas, and there we stayed seven days.

Troas

And on the first day of the week, when we had met for the breaking of bread, Paul addressed them, as he was to leave the next morning, and he prolonged his address until midnight. Now there were many lamps in the upper room where we had assembled. And a young man named Eutychus, who was sitting at the window, was overcome with drowsiness and, as Paul addressed them at great length, he went fast asleep and fell down from the third story to the ground and was picked up dead. Paul went down to him and laid himself upon him, and embracing him, said, "Do not be alarmed, life is still in him." Then he went up and broke

---

20, 7: *The first day of the week:* Sunday had replaced the Sabbath (Saturday) as the day of worship. *Breaking of bread:* the Holy Eucharist, celebrated in the evening.

bread and ate, and having spoken to them a
12 good while, even till daybreak, he departed. And
they took away the boy alive and were not a
little comforted.

13 But we went on board the ship and sailed
for Assos, intending to take Paul on board there.
That was the arrangement he had made, as he
14 intended to travel by land. So when he
met us at Assos, we took him on board and came
15 to Mitylene. Sailing from there, we arrived on
the following day off Chios; the next day we
made Samos, and the day after we reached
16 Miletus. For Paul had decided to sail past
Ephesus, lest he should be delayed in the
province of Asia; for he was hastening to be in
Jerusalem, if it were possible for him, by the
day of Pentecost.

Discourse at Miletus

17 From Miletus, however, he sent   JULY 1
to Ephesus for the presbyters of the   Dec. 31
18 church; and when they had come to him and
were assembled, he said to them:

"You know in what manner I have lived with
you all the time since the first day that I came
19 into the province of Asia, serving the Lord with
all humility and with tears and in trials that
20 befell me because of the plots of the Jews; how
I have kept back nothing that was for your good,
but have declared it to you and taught you in
21 public and from house to house, urging Jews
and Gentiles to turn to God in repentance and
22 to believe in our Lord Jesus Christ. And now,
behold, I am going to Jerusalem, compelled
by the Spirit, not knowing what will happen to
23 me there; except that in every city the Holy
Spirit warns me, saying that imprisonment and
24 persecution are awaiting me. But I fear none of
these, nor do I count my life more precious

than myself, if only I may accomplish my course and the ministry that I have received from the Lord Jesus, to bear witness to the gospel of the grace of God.

"And now, behold, I know that you all among 25 whom I went about preaching the kingdom of God, will see my face no longer. Therefore I call 26 you to witness this day that I am innocent of the blood of all; for I have not shrunk from de- 27 claring to you the whole counsel of God. Take 28 heed to yourselves and to the whole flock in which the Holy Spirit has placed you as bishops, to rule the Church of God, which he has pur- chased with his own blood. I know that after 29 my departure fierce wolves will get in among you, and will not spare the flock. And from 30 among your own selves men will rise speaking perverse things, to draw away the disciples after them. Watch, therefore, and remember 31 that for three years night and day I did not cease with tears to admonish every one of you.

"And now I commend you to God and to the 32 word of his grace, who is able to build up and to give the inheritance among all the sanctified. I have coveted no one's silver or gold or apparel. 33 You yourselves know that these hands of mine 34 have provided for my needs and those of my companions. In all things I have shown you that 35 by so toiling you ought to help the weak and remember the word of the Lord Jesus, that he himself said, 'It is more blessed to give than to receive.' "

Having said this, he knelt down and prayed 36 with them all. And there was much weeping 37 among them all and they fell on Paul's neck and kissed him, being grieved most of all at his 38 saying that they would no longer see his face. And they escorted him to the ship.

Tyre

21 1 And when we had parted from them and had set sail, we made a straight course and came to Cos, and the next
2 day to Rhodes, and from there to Patara. There we found a ship crossing over to Phœnicia, and
3 we went on board and set sail. After sighting Cyprus and leaving it to the left, we sailed for Syria and landed at Tyre, for there the ship
4 was to unload her cargo. Having looked up the disciples, we stayed there seven days. And they told Paul through the Spirit not to go to Jeru-
5 salem. But when our time was up we left there and went on, and all of them with their wives and children escorted us till we were out of the city; and we knelt down on the shore and
6 prayed. And having said farewell to one another, we went on board the ship and they returned home.

JULY 2
Jan. 1

Ptolemais and Caesarea

7 After completing the voyage from Tyre, we landed at Ptolemais where we greeted the
8 brethren and spent a day with them. The next day we departed and came to Cæsarea, where we went to the house of Philip the evangelist, who was one of the seven, and stayed with him.
9 He had four daughters, virgins, who had the
10 gift of prophecy. And while we were staying on there for some days, there came down from
11 Judea a certain prophet named Agabus. Coming to us, and taking Paul's girdle, he bound his own feet and hands, and said, "Thus says the Holy Spirit: The man whose girdle this is the

---

21, 4: *Told:* a warning about the danger ahead; having learnt this through the Holy Spirit, they naturally entreated St. Paul not to proceed.

Jews will bind like this at Jerusalem, and they will deliver him into the hands of the Gentiles." On hearing this, we ourselves and the people 12 there begged him not to go to Jerusalem. Then Paul answered and said, "What do you 13 mean by weeping and breaking my heart? For I am ready not only to be bound but even to die at Jerusalem for the name of the Lord Jesus." And when we could not persuade him we 14 acquiesced and said, "The Lord's will be done." After this we made our preparations and went 15 our way to Jerusalem. And some of the disciples 16 from Cæsarea went with us, taking with them Mnason, a Cypriot, an early disciple, whose guests we were to be.

4. Imprisonment in Palestine

Jerusalem

ON OUR ARRIVAL AT JERUSALEM | JULY 3 | 17
the brethren gave us a hearty wel- | Jan. 2 |
come. On the next day Paul went with us to 18
James, and all the presbyters came in. After 19
greeting them, he related in detail what God had done among the Gentiles through his ministry.

They praised God when they heard it and they 20
said to him, "Thou seest, brother, how many thousands of believers there are among the Jews, all of them zealous upholders of the Law. Now, 21
they have heard about thee that thou dost teach the Jews who live among the Gentiles to depart from Moses, telling them they should not cir-cumcise their children nor observe the customs.
' What then? The multitude is sure to assemble, 22
for they will hear that thou hast come. So do 23
what we tell thee. We have four men who are under a vow; take them and sanctify thyself 24
along with them, and pay for them that they may

shave their heads; and all will know that what
they have heard of thee is false, but that thou
25 thyself also observest the Law. But as for the
Gentile believers, we ourselves have written
our decision that they abstain from idol offerings
and from blood and from what is strangled and
from immorality."

26 Then Paul took the men, and the next day
after being purified along with them he entered
the temple and announced the completion of the
days of purification, when the sacrifice would be
offered for each of them.

Paul's Arrest

27 But when the seven days were almost over,
the Jews from the province of Asia, seeing him
in the temple, stirred up all the people and seized
28 him, shouting, "Men of Israel, help. This is the
man who teaches all men everywhere against the
people and the Law and this place, and moreover
he has brought Gentiles also into the temple and
29 has desecrated this holy place." For they had
seen Trophimus the Ephesian in the city with
him and they supposed that Paul had taken him
30 into the temple. And the whole city was thrown
into confusion, and the people ran together, and
seizing Paul, they proceeded to drag him out of
the temple; whereupon the doors were immediately shut.

31 They were trying to kill him, when news
reached the tribune of the cohort that all Jeru-
32 salem was in a tumult. And he, immediately taking soldiers and centurions, ran down to them;
and when they saw the tribune and the soldiers,
33 they stopped beating Paul. Then the tribune
came up and seized him and ordered him to be
bound with two chains, and inquired who he was
34 and what he had been doing. Some in the crowd

shouted one thing, and some another, and as he could not learn anything certain on account of the tumult, he ordered him to be taken into the barracks. And when he came to the steps, he was 35 actually being carried by the soldiers owing to the violence of the crowd; for the mass of the 36 people followed, shouting, "Away with him!"

And as Paul was about to be taken into the 37 barracks, he said to the tribune, "May I say something to thee?" He said, "Dost thou know Greek? Art not thou the Egyptian who recently 38 stirred up to sedition and led out into the desert the four thousand assassins?" But Paul said to 39 him, "I am a Jew from Tarsus in Cilicia, a citizen of no insignificant city. But I beg thee, give me leave to speak to the people."

Discourse to the People

He gave him leave, and Paul, | JULY 4 | 40
standing on the steps, motioned with | Jan. 3 |
his hand to the people and when they had become quiet he addressed them in Hebrew, saying:

"Brethren and fathers, listen to what I have **22** 1 to say to you in my defense."

And when they heard him speak to them in 2 Hebrew, they became even more quiet.

And he said: "I am a Jew, and I was born at 3 Tarsus in Cilicia, but was brought up here in this city, a pupil of Gamaliel, and instructed according to the strict acceptation of the Law of our fathers. I was zealous for the Law just as all of you are today. And I persecuted this Way even 4 to the death, binding and committing to prisons both men and women, as the high priest can bear 5 me witness, and all the elders. In fact I received letters from them to the brethren in Damascus, and I was on my way to arrest those who were there and bring them back to Jerusalem for punishment.

6   "And it came to pass that, as I was on my way and approaching Damascus, suddenly about noon there shone round about me a great light from

7 heaven; and I fell to the ground and heard a voice saying to me, 'Saul, Saul, why dost thou

8 persecute me?' And I answered, 'Who art thou, Lord?' And he said to me, 'I am Jesus of

9 Nazareth, whom thou art persecuting.' And my companions saw indeed the light, but they did not hear the voice of him who was speak-

10 ing to me. And I said, 'What shall I do, Lord?' And the Lord said to me, 'Get up and go into Damascus, and there thou shalt be told of all

11 that thou art destined to do.' And as I could not see because of the dazzling light, my companions had to lead me by the hand, and so I reached Damascus.

12   "Now one Ananias, an observer of the Law,

13 respected by all the Jews who lived there, ' came to me and, standing beside me, said to me, 'Brother Saul, regain thy sight.' And instantly I

14 looked at him. And he said, 'The God of our fathers has appointed thee beforehand to learn his will and to see the Just One and to hear a

15 voice from his mouth; for thou shalt be his witness before all men of what thou hast seen and

16 heard. ' And now why dost thou delay? Get up and be baptized and wash away thy sins, calling on his name.'

17   "And it came to pass that, when I had returned to Jerusalem and was praying in the temple, I

18 was in an ecstasy ' and saw him as he said to me, 'Make haste and go quickly out of Jerusalem, for they will not receive thy testimony concerning

19 me.' And I said, 'Lord, they themselves know that I used to imprison and beat in one syna-

gogue after another those who believed in thee; and when the blood of Stephen, thy witness, was shed, I was standing by and approved it, and took charge of the garments of those who killed him.' And he said to me, 'Go, for to the Gentiles far away I will send thee.' " 20 21

Paul's Citizenship

Now, till he said this they were listening to him, but then they lifted up their voice and shouted, "Away from the earth with such a one! for it is not right that he should live." And as they were shouting and throwing off their garments and casting dust into the air, the tribune ordered him to be taken into the barracks and to be scourged and tortured that he might find out why they shouted so against him. 22 23 24

JULY 5
Jan. 4

But when they had bound him with the straps, Paul said to the centurion who was standing by, "Is it legal for you to scourge a Roman, and that without a trial?" When the centurion heard this, he went to the tribune and reported, saying, "What art thou about to do? This man is a Roman citizen." Then the tribune came and said to him, "Tell me, art thou a Roman?" And he said, "Yes." And the tribune answered, "I obtained this citizenship at a great price." And Paul said, "But I am a citizen by birth." At once therefore those who had been going to torture him left him; and the tribune himself was alarmed to find that Paul was a Roman citizen, and that he had bound him. 25 26 27 28 29

The Sanhedrin

The next day, as he wished to find out the real reason why he was accused by the Jews, he loosed him and ordered the priests and all the Sanhe- 30 drin to assemble; and taking Paul forth, he placed him in front of them.

23 1   Then Paul, looking steadily at the Sanhedrin, said, "Brethren, I have conducted myself before God with a perfectly good conscience up to this 2 day." But the high priest Ananias ordered those who were standing by him to strike him on the 3 mouth. Then Paul said to him, "God will strike thee, thou whitewashed wall. Dost thou sit there to try me by the Law, and in violation of the Law 4 order me to be struck?" But the bystanders said, 5 "Dost thou insult God's high priest?" And Paul said, "I did not know, brethren, that he was the high priest; for it is written, 'Thou shalt not speak evil of a ruler of thy people.'"

6   Then Paul, knowing that part of them were Sadducees and part of them Pharisees, cried out in the Sanhedrin, "Brethren, I am a Pharisee, the son of Pharisees; it is about the hope and the resurrection of the dead that I am on trial." 7 And when he said that, there arose a dispute between the Pharisees and the Sadducees, and 8 the multitude was divided. For the Sadducees say that there is no resurrection, and that there are no angels or spirits, whereas the Pharisees 9 believe in both. So there was a great uproar, and some of the Pharisees got up and began to insist, saying, "We find no evil in this man; what if a spirit has really spoken to him, or an angel?" 10 And as the dispute was becoming violent, the tribune, fearing lest Paul should be torn to pieces by them, ordered the soldiers to come down and

---

23, 3: *Whitewashed wall:* with a thin coating of white hiding its ugliness; or perhaps in the sense of "the whited sepulchres" of Matt. 23, 27.

23, 6: *The hope:* for the coming of the Messias.

23, 8: *Both:* the Pharisees believed both in a resurrection and in the existence of spiritual beings.

take him by force from among them and bring him into the barracks. But on the following night 11 the Lord stood by him and said, "Be steadfast; for just as thou hast borne witness to me in Jerusalem, bear witness in Rome also."

A Conspiracy

Now when day broke, some Jews assembled and bound themselves

> JULY 6
> Jan. 5

12

under a curse, saying that they would neither eat nor drink till they had killed Paul. There were 13 more than forty that had made this conspiracy; and they went to the chief priests and the 14 elders and said, "We have bound ourselves under a great curse to taste nothing until we have killed Paul. Now therefore do you, with the Sanhedrin, suggest to the tribune that he bring him 15 to you as though you mean to look into his case more carefully; but we are ready to kill him before he gets here."

Now the son of Paul's sister heard of the 16 ambush, and he came and entered the barracks and told Paul. Paul called one of the centurions 17 to him and said, "Take this young man to the tribune, for he has something to report to thee." So he took him and brought him to the tribune 18 and said, "The prisoner Paul called me and asked me to bring this young man to thee, for he has something to say to thee." So the tribune 19 took him by the hand, and going aside with him, asked him, "What is it that thou hast to tell me?" And he said, "The Jews have agreed to ask thee 20 to bring Paul to the Sanhedrin tomorrow, on the plea that they intend to have a more thorough investigation made into his case. But do not 21 believe them; for more than forty of them are lying in wait for him, having bound themselves under a curse not to eat or drink until they have killed him; and they are now ready, only waiting for thy promise."

To Caesarea

22 The tribune therefore let the young man go, charging him not to divulge to anyone that he
23 had given him this information. Then he called two centurions and said to them, "Get ready by the third hour of the night two hundred soldiers to go as far as Cæsarea, and seventy cavalry and
24 two hundred spearmen; and provide beasts to mount Paul and take him in safety to Felix the
25 governor." [For he was afraid that the Jews might seize him by force and kill him, and he himself should afterwards be slandered, as though he intended to receive money.]

26 And he wrote a letter in these terms: ' "Claudius Lysias to His Excellency Felix the governor,
27 greeting. Whereas this man had been seized by the Jews and was on the point of being killed by them, I came on them with the troops and rescued
28 him, having learnt that he was a Roman. And wishing to know what charge they had preferred against him, I took him down into their San-
29 hedrin. I found him accused about questions of their Law, but not of any crime deserving of
30 death or imprisonment. And when I was told of an ambush which they had prepared for him, I sent him to thee, directing his accusers also to state the case before thee. Farewell."

31 So the soldiers, in accordance with their instructions, took Paul and conducted him by
32 night to Antipatris; and the next day they returned to the barracks, leaving the cavalry to
33 go on with him. When they reached Cæsarea, they delivered the letter to the governor and
34 also handed Paul over to him. On reading it he

asked from what province he was; and learning that he was from Cilicia, ¹ "I will hear thee," he ³⁵ said, "when thy accusers have come." And he ordered him to be kept in Herod's palace.

The Accusation

Now five days later the high priest Ananias came down with some of the elders and one Tertullus, an attorney; and they presented their case against Paul before the governor. When Paul had been summoned, ² Tertullus began to accuse him, saying:

"Whereas we live in much peace through thee, and whereas many reforms are in progress by thy foresight, we always and everywhere receive ³ them, most excellent Felix, with all thankfulness. But not to detain thee too long, I entreat thee to ⁴ be kind enough to grant us a brief hearing. We ⁵ have found this man a pest, and a promoter of seditions among all the Jews throughout the world, and a ringleader of the sedition of the Nazarene sect. He even tried to desecrate the ⁶ temple, but we caught him [and wished to judge him according to our Law. But Lysias, the trib- ⁷ une, came upon us and with great violence took him away out of our hands, ordering his accusers ⁸ to come to thee]. By examining him thyself, thou wilt be able to discover all these things we charge him with." And the Jews also supported the ⁹ charge, saying that this was so.

The Defense

Then when the governor nodded to him to ¹⁰ speak, Paul answered, "As I know that for many years thou hast been a judge for this nation, I shall answer for myself with good courage. For ¹¹ thou canst take as certain that it is not more than twelve days since I went up to worship in

12 Jerusalem; and neither in the temple did they
find me disputing with anyone or creating a disturbance among the people, nor in the syna-
13 gogues, nor about the city; ' neither can they
prove to thee the charges that they now make
14 against me. But this I admit to thee, that according to the Way, which they call a sect, so I
serve the God of my fathers; believing all
things that are written in the Law and the
15 Prophets, having a hope in God which these men
themselves also look for, that there is to be a
16 resurrection of the just and unjust; and in this
I too strive always to have a clear conscience
before God and before men.

17 "Now after several years I came to bring alms
to my nation and to offer sacrifice and fulfill
18 vows; in which they found me engaged in the
temple, after having been purified, with no
19 crowd or disturbance at all. But there were some
Jews from the province of Asia, who ought to
have been here before thee and to have presented their charges, if they had any, against me;
20 or else let these men themselves say what they
found wrong in me when I stood before the
21 Sanhedrin, unless it be for the one thing I
shouted out as I stood among them, 'It is about
the resurrection of the dead that I am being
judged by you this day.'"

The Prisoner

22 Felix, however, having precise information
about the Way, adjourned the trial, saying,
"When Lysias the tribune comes down, I will
23 decide your case." And he instructed the centurion to keep Paul in custody but to allow him

---

24, 16: *In this:* in this expectation and all that it implies
for the conduct of life.

some liberty, and not to prevent any of his friends from looking after him.

Now some days later, Felix came with his 24 wife Drusilla, who was a Jewess, and sent for Paul and heard what he had to say about the faith in Christ Jesus. But as he talked of justice 25 and chastity and the judgment to come, Felix became alarmed and answered, "For the present go thy way; but when I get an opportunity, I will send for thee." At the same time he was 26 hoping that money would be given him by Paul, and for this reason he would send for him often and talk with him. But after two years Felix was 27 succeeded by Porcius Festus; and as he wanted to ingratiate himself with the Jews, Felix left Paul in prison.

Festus

Festus accordingly entered his | JULY 8 | **25** 1
province, and three days afterwards | Jan. 7 |
he went up from Cæsarea to Jerusalem. And 2 the chief priests and Jewish leaders presented their charges against Paul, and begged him, ' asking it as a favor against Paul, that he would 3 have him fetched to Jerusalem. Meanwhile they were laying an ambush to kill him on the way. But Festus answered that Paul was being kept 4 in custody at Cæsarea and that he himself would be going there shortly. "Let, therefore, 5 your influential men go down with me," he said, "and if there is anything wrong with the man, let them present charges against him."

After staying among them not more than eight 6 or ten days, he went down to Cæsarea, and the next day he took his seat on the tribunal and ordered Paul brought in. And when he was fetched, 7 the Jews who had come down from Jerusalem surrounded him and brought many serious

charges against him, which they were unable to
8 prove. Paul said in his own defense, "Neither
against the Law of the Jews nor against the
temple nor against Cæsar have I committed any
9 offense." But Festus, wishing to do the Jews a
favor, answered Paul and said, "Art thou willing
to go up to Jerusalem and be tried there before
me on these charges?"

10 But Paul said, "I am standing at the tribunal
of Cæsar; there I ought to be tried. To Jews I
have done no wrong, as thou thyself very well
11 knowest. For if I have done any wrong or committed a crime deserving of death, I do not refuse to die. But if there is no ground to their
charges against me, no one can give me up to
12 them; I appeal to Cæsar." Then Festus, after
conferring with the council, answered, "Thou
hast appealed to Cæsar; to Cæsar thou shalt go."

Agrippa

13 And after an interval of some days, King
Agrippa and Bernice came to Cæsarea to pay
14 their respects to Festus. And as they were staying there several days, Festus laid Paul's case
before the king, saying, "There is a certain man
15 left a prisoner by Felix, and when I was at
Jerusalem the chief priests and elders of the
Jews presented their case against him, and asked
16 for his conviction. But I told them that Romans
are not accustomed to give any man up before
the accused has met his accusers face to face
and has been given a chance to defend himself
17 against the charges. Therefore, when they had
assembled here, I lost no time, but on the follow-

25, 11: *Appeal to Cæsar:* when a Roman citizen under
trial appealed to the emperor, the case passed out of the
jurisdiction of all other magistrates.

ing day took my seat on the tribunal and ordered the man to be brought in. But when his accusers 18 got up, they did not charge him with any of the crimes that I had expected. But they had against 19 him certain questions about their own religion and about a certain Jesus, who had died, but who Paul affirmed was alive. Being at a loss as to 20 how to investigate such matters, I asked him if he was willing to go to Jerusalem and be tried on these charges there. But when Paul entered an 21 appeal to have his case reserved for the decision of Augustus, I ordered him kept in custody till I could send him to Cæsar." And Agrippa said to 22 Festus, "I myself also could have wished to hear the man." "Tomorrow," said he, "thou shalt hear him."

So the next day Agrippa and Bernice came with 23 great pomp and entered the audience hall with the tribunes and principal men of the city, and by order of Festus Paul was brought in. And 24 Festus said, "King Agrippa and all men here present with us, you see this man about whom the whole multitude of the Jews pleaded with me at Jerusalem and here, insisting and crying out that he ought not to live any longer. But I, 25 for my part, found that he had done nothing deserving of death. But as he himself made the appeal, I decided to send him to Augustus. Still I have nothing definite to write to my lord 26 about him. So I have brought him forth before you, and especially before thee, King Agrippa, that after an examination of him has been made I may have something to put in writing. For it 27 seems to me unreasonable to send a prisoner without stating the charges against him."

Paul's Discourse

26 1   Then Agrippa said to Paul, "Thou art permitted to speak for thyself."

Then Paul stretched forth his hand, and began his defense.

2   "I think myself fortunate, King Agrippa, that I am to defend myself today before thee against
3 all the accusations of the Jews, especially as thou art well acquainted with all the Jewish customs and controversies; I beg thee therefore to listen to me with patience.

4   "My life, then, from my youth up, the early part of which was spent among my own nation
5 and at Jerusalem, all the Jews know; for they have long known me, if only they are willing to give evidence, that according to the strictest
6 sect of our religion I lived a Pharisee. And now for the hope in the promise made by God to our
7 fathers I am standing trial; to which promise our twelve tribes hope to attain as they worship night and day; and it is about this hope, O king,
8 that I am accused by the Jews. Why is it deemed incredible with you if God does raise the dead?

9   "And I then thought it my duty to do many things contrary to the name of Jesus of Nazareth.
10 And this I did in Jerusalem; and many of the saints I shut up in prison, having received authority from the chief priests to do so; and when they were put to death, I cast my vote against
11 them; and oftentimes in all the synagogues I punished them and tried to force them to blaspheme; and in my extreme rage against them I even pursued them to foreign cities.

12   "But while I was journeying on this business to Damascus with authority and permission from
13 the chief priests, ' at midday, O king, I saw on the way a light from heaven brighter than the sunshine round about me and my companions.

We all fell to the ground, and I heard a voice 14
saying to me in Hebrew, 'Saul, Saul, why dost
thou persecute me? It is hard for thee to kick
against the goad.' And I said, 'Who art thou, 15
Lord?' And the Lord said, 'I am Jesus, whom
thou art persecuting. But rise and stand upon 16
thy feet; for I have appeared to thee for this
purpose, to appoint thee to be a minister and a
witness to what thou hast seen, and to the visions
thou shalt have of me; delivering thee from the 17
people and from the nations, to whom I am now
sending thee, to open their eyes that they may 18
turn from darkness to light and from the dominion of Satan to God; that they may receive forgiveness of sins and an inheritance among those
sanctified by faith in me.'

"Therefore, King Agrippa, I was not disobedi- 19
ent to the heavenly vision; but first to the people 20
of Damascus and Jerusalem, and then all over
Judea and to the Gentiles, I set about declaring
that they should repent and turn to God, doing
works befitting their repentance. This is why 21
the Jews seized me in the temple and tried to
kill me. But aided to this day by the help of God, 22
I stand here to testify to both high and low, saying nothing beyond what the Prophets and
Moses said would come to pass: that the Christ 23
was to suffer, that he first by his resurrection
from the dead was to proclaim light to the people
and to the Gentiles."

The Result

While he was saying this in his defense, Fes- 24
tus said with a loud voice, "Paul, thou art mad;
thy great learning is driving thee to madness."

26, 14: *It is hard*, etc.: a proverb; oxen were driven by
goads, and kicking only made the goading more painful.
The grace of God was prodding St. Paul in a similar way.

25 "I am not mad, excellent Festus," said Paul,
26 "but I speak words of sober truth. For the king knows about these things and to him also I speak without hesitation. For I am sure that none of these things escaped him; for none of them hap-
27 pened in a corner. Dost thou believe the prophets, King Agrippa? I know that thou dost."
28 But Agrippa said to Paul, "In a short while thou wouldst persuade me to become a Christian."
29 And Paul answered, "I would to God that, whether it be long or short, not only thou but also all who hear me today might become such as I am,
30 except for these chains." Then the king arose and the governor and Bernice, and those who
31 had sat with them; and after withdrawing they kept talking the matter over together, saying, "This man has done nothing to deserve death or
32 imprisonment." And Agrippa said to Festus, "This man might have been set at liberty, if he had not appealed to Cæsar."

5. Imprisonment in Rome

Departure for Rome

27 1 NOW WHEN IT WAS DECIDED that he should sail for Italy, and that JULY 10 Jan. 9 Paul, with the other prisoners, should be turned over to a centurion named Julius, of the Augus-
2 tan cohort, we went on board a ship of Adrumythium which was bound for the ports of the province of Asia, and set sail; Aristarchus, a Macedonian from Thessalonica, being one of our party.

3 The next day we reached Sidon and Julius treated Paul kindly, allowing him to go to his
4 friends and receive attention. And putting to sea from there, we passed under the lee of Cyprus,
5 as the winds were against us, and sailing over

the sea that lies off Cilicia and Pamphylia, we reached Myra in Lycia. There the centurion 6 found a ship of Alexandria bound for Italy and put us on board her.

For many days we made slow progress and had 7 difficulty in arriving off Cnidus. Then as the wind kept us from going on, we sailed under the lee of Crete off Salmone, and coasting along it with 8 difficulty we came to a place called Fair Havens, near the town of Thalassa.

But as much time had been spent and naviga- 9 tion was now unsafe, for the Fast was already over, Paul began to admonish them, ' saying to 10 them, "Men, I see that this voyage is threatening to bring disaster and heavy loss, not only to the cargo and the ship, but to our lives also." But the 11 centurion gave more heed to the pilot and the captain than to what Paul had to say; and as the 12 harbor was unsuitable for wintering in, the majority favored sailing from there to try wheth- er they could get to Phœnis, a harbor in Crete facing southwest and northwest, to winter there. So when a light south wind sprang up, thinking 13 they had secured their object, they weighed an- chor and ran close along the coast of Crete.

A Storm

But not long afterwards a violent wind called 14 Euroaquilo burst against it; and when the ship 15 was caught in it and could not face the wind, we gave way and were driven along. We ran under 16 the lee of a small island called Cauda, where we managed with difficulty to secure the boat; ' after hoisting it on board, they used supports to 17 undergird the ship, and as they were afraid of

27, 9: *The Fast:* of the Day of Atonement, about September 15. Navigation was considered dangerous after
the middle of September.

being driven on the Syrtis quicksands, they lowered the mainsail and so were driven along.

18 As we were being tossed about by the violence of the storm, the next day they threw some of the

19 cargo overboard; and on the third day with their own hands they threw the ship's gear overboard.

20 As neither sun nor stars were visible for many days and no small storm was raging, all hope of our being saved was in consequence given up.

21 Then, when they had eaten noth- ┌─────────┐
ing for a long time, Paul got up in the │ JULY 11 │
midst of them and said, "Men, you should in- │ Jan. 10 │
deed have listened to me and not have sailed └─────────┘
from Crete, thus sparing yourselves this disaster

22 and loss. And now I beg you to be of good cheer, for there will be no loss of life among you, but

23 only of the ship. For last night an angel of the

24 God I belong to and serve, stood by me, ' saying, 'Do not be afraid, Paul; thou must stand before Cæsar; and behold, God has granted thee all who

25 are sailing with thee.' So, men, be of good cheer; for I have faith in God that it will be as it has

26 been told me. But we are to reach a certain island."

Shipwreck

27 It was the fourteenth night, and we were sail- ing in the Adria, when about midnight the sailors began to suspect that they were drawing near to

28 some land. On taking soundings, they found twenty fathoms, and a little further on they

29 found fifteen; then fearing that we might go on the rocks, they dropped four anchors from the

30 stern and longed for daylight. But as the sailors were trying to escape from the ship and had lowered the boat into the sea, pretending that they were going to cast anchors from the bow,

31 Paul said to the centurion and the soldiers,

"Unless these men remain in the ship, you cannot be saved." Then the soldiers cut away the 32 ropes of the boat and let her drift off.

And when it began to grow light, Paul begged 33 them all to take food, saying, "This is the fourteenth day that you have been constantly on the watch and fasting, without taking anything to eat. So I beg you to take some food for your safety; 34 for not a hair from the head of any one of you shall perish." With these words he took bread 35 and gave thanks to God before them all and broke it and began to eat. Then all became more 36 cheerful and took food themselves. Now, we 37 were in all two hundred and seventy-six souls on board. And after eating their fill, they pro- 38 ceeded to lighten the ship by throwing the wheat into the sea.

When day broke they could not make out the 39 land; but they noticed a bay with a beach, and they proposed to run the ship ashore there if they could. So they slipped the anchors and com- 40 mitted themselves to the sea, at the same time unlashing the fastenings of the rudders; and hoisting the foresail to the breeze, they made for the beach. But we struck a place open to two 41 seas, and they ran the ship aground. The prow stuck fast and remained immovable, but the stern began to break up under the violence of the sea. Now the soldiers planned to kill the pris- 42 oners lest any of them should swim ashore and escape, but the centurion, wishing to save Paul, 43 put a stop to their plan. He ordered those who could swim to jump overboard first and get to land, ' and they brought the rest in, some on 44 planks and others on various pieces from the ship. And so it came to pass that all got safely to land.

Malta

28 1   After our escape we learned that JULY 12
Jan. 11
the island was called Malta. And

2 the natives showed us no little kindness, for they
kindled a fire and refreshed us all because of the

3 rain that had set in, and the cold. Now Paul
gathered a bundle of sticks and laid them on
the fire, when a viper came out because of the heat

4 and fastened on his hand. When the natives saw
the creature hanging from his hand, they said
to one another, "Surely this man is a murderer,
for though he has escaped the sea, Justice does

5 not let him live." But he shook off the creature

6 into the fire and suffered no harm. Now they
were expecting that he would swell up and suddenly fall down and die; but after waiting a long
time and seeing no harm come to him, they
changed their minds and said that he was a god.

7   Now in the vicinity there were estates belonging to the head man of the island, whose name
was Publius, and he received us and entertained

8 us hospitably for three days. And it happened
that the father of Publius was laid up with fever
and dysentery; but Paul went in, and after praying and laying his hands on him, he healed him.

9 After this all the sick on the island came and

10 were cured; and they honored us with many
marks of honor, and when we sailed, they provided us with such things as we needed.

To Rome

11   We set sail after three months in an Alex-
andrian ship with the Twins on her figurehead,

12 which had wintered at the island. We put in at

28, 4: *Justice:* or Vengeance, as pursuing criminals,
was a familiar goddess among Greeks and Romans, and
the natives here speak of it as a goddess.

Syracuse, and stayed there three days. Then, following the coast, we reached Rhegium; and one day later a south wind sprang up, and on the second day we arrived at Puteoli, where we found brethren and were entreated to stay with them seven days; and so we came to Rome. And the brethren there, having had news of us, came as far as the Market of Appius and the Three Taverns; and when Paul saw them, he gave thanks to God and took courage. On our arrival at Rome, Paul was given permission to live by himself with a soldier to guard him.

At Rome

Three days later he called together the leading Jews, and when they had assembled he said to them, "Brethren, although I have done nothing against the people or against the customs of our fathers, yet I was handed over to the Romans as a prisoner from Jerusalem. After an examination they were ready to release me, since I was innocent of any crime that deserved death; but as the Jews objected, I was forced to appeal to Cæsar — not that I had any charge to bring against my nation. This, then, is why I asked to see you and speak with you. For it is because of the hope of Israel that I am wearing this chain." But they said to him, "We ourselves have received no letters about thee from Judea, and none of the brethren, upon arrival, has reported or spoken any evil of thee. But we want to hear from thee what thy views are; for as regards this sect, we know that everywhere it is spoken against."

So they fixed a day, and very many came to him at his lodging; and to them he explained the matter, bearing witness to the kingdom of

God and trying from morning till evening to convince them concerning Jesus from the Law

24 of Moses and from the Prophets. And some believed what was said; and some disbelieved;

25 ¹ and as they could not agree among themselves, they began to depart, when Paul added this one word: "Well did the Holy Spirit speak through

26 Isaias the prophet to our fathers, ¹ saying, 'Go to this people and say: With the ear you will hear and will not understand; and seeing you will see

27 and will not perceive. For the heart of this people has been hardened, and with their ears they have been hard of hearing, and their eyes they have closed; lest perhaps they see with their eyes, and hear with their ears, and understand with their heart, and be converted, and I heal them.'

28 Be it known to you therefore that this salvation of God has been sent to the Gentiles, and they

29 will listen to it." [When he had said this, the Jews departed, having much argument among themselves.]

30 And for two full years he remained in his own hired lodging; and he welcomed all who came

31 to him, preaching the kingdom of God and teaching about the Lord Jesus Christ with all boldness and unhindered. Amen.

THE LIFE AND EPISTLES OF ST. PAUL

St. Paul was born at Tarsus, Cilicia, of Jewish parents who were descended from the tribe of Benjamin (Acts 9, 11; 21, 39; 22, 3). He was a Roman citizen from birth (Acts 22, 27f). As he was "a young man" at the stoning of St. Stephen (Acts 7, 58) and calls himself "an old man" when writing to Philemon (v. 9), about the year 63, we may conclude that he was born around the beginning of the Christian era.

In his youth Paul acquired a threefold education. First, he learned the Greek language in his Tarsian environment, as is evident from his later skill in writing his Epistles. Secondly, his father probably initiated him into his own trade, which was that of tent-making, and thus Paul during his apostolic labors was able to defray the cost of his food and lodging by the work of his own hands (Acts 18, 3; 1 Cor. 4, 12; 1 Thess. 2, 9; 2 Thess. 3, 8). Thirdly, in his father's house at Tarsus his education was strongly Pharisaic (Acts 23, 6). To complete his schooling Paul was sent to Jerusalem, where he sat at the feet of the learned Gamaliel and was educated in the strict observance of the ancestral Law (Acts 22, 3). Here he also acquired a good knowledge of exegesis and was trained in the practice of disputation. As a convinced and zealous Pharisee he returned to Tarsus before the public life of Christ opened in Palestine, for he never refers to personal acquaintance with Christ during the Savior's mortal life.

Some time after the death of our Lord Paul returned to Palestine. His profound conviction and emotional character made his zeal develop into a religious fanaticism against the infant Church. He took part in the stoning of the first martyr, St. Stephen, and in the fierce persecution of the Christians that followed.

Entrusted with a formal mission from the high priest, he departed for Damascus to arrest the Christians there and bring them bound to Jerusalem. As he was nearing Damascus, about noon, a light descended from heaven suddenly blazed round him. Jesus with His glorified body appeared to him and addressed him, turning him away from his apparently successful career. An immediate transformation was wrought in the soul of Paul. He was suddenly converted to the Christian faith and arose an Apostle (Acts 9, 3-19; 22, 6-16; 26, 12-18).

He remained some days in Damascus after his Baptism (Acts 9, 10-19), and then went to Arabia (Gal. 1, 17), possibly for a year or two, to prepare himself for his future missionary activity. Having returned to Damascus, he stayed there for a time, preaching in the synagogues, that Jesus is the Christ, the Son of God. For this he incurred the hatred of the Jews, and had to flee from the city (Acts 9, 23-25; 2 Cor. 11, 32f). He then went to Jerusalem to see Peter (Gal. 1, 18), to pay his homage to the head of the Church. Later he went back to his native Tarsus (Acts 9, 30) and began to evangelize his own province (Gal. 1, 21) until called by Barnabas to Antioch (Acts 11, 25). After one year, on the occasion of a famine, both Barnabas and Paul were sent with alms to the poor Christian community at Jerusalem (Acts 11, 27-30). Having fulfilled their mission, they returned to Antioch (Acts 12, 25).

Soon after this Paul and Barnabas made the first missionary journey (44/45-49/50 A. D.), visiting the island of Cyprus, then Pamphylia, Pisidia and Lycaonia, all in Asia Minor, and establishing churches at Pisidian Antioch, Iconium, Lystra and Derbe (Acts 13—14).

After the Apostolic Council of Jerusalem Paul, accompanied by Silas and later also by Timothy and Luke, made his second missionary journey (50-52/53 A. D.), first revisiting the churches previously established by him in Asia Minor and then passing through Galatia (Acts 16, 6). At Troas a vision of a Macedonian was had by Paul, which impressed him as a call from God to evangelize Macedonia. He accordingly sailed for Europe, and preached the Gospel in Philippi, Thessalonica, Berœa, Athens and Corinth. Then he returned to Antioch by way of Ephesus and Jerusalem (Acts 15, 36—18, 22).

On his third missionary journey (53/54-58 A. D.) Paul visited nearly the same regions as on the second, but made Ephesus, where he remained nearly three years, the center of his missionary activity. He laid plans also for another missionary journey, intending to leave Jerusalem for Rome and Spain. But persecutions by the Jews hindered him from accomplishing his purpose. After two years of imprisonment at Cæsarea he finally reached Rome, where he was kept another two years in chains (Acts 18, 23—28, 31).

The Acts of the Apostles gives us no further information on the life of the Apostle. We gather, however, from the Pastoral Epistles and from tradition that at the end of the two years St. Paul was released from his Roman imprisonment, and then travelled to Spain (Rom. 15, 24. 28), later to the East again, and then back to Rome, where he was imprisoned a second time, and in 67 was beheaded.

St. Paul's untiring interest in and paternal affection for the various churches established by him have given us 14 canonical Epistles. It is, however, quite certain that he wrote other letters which are no longer extant.

These Epistles are not arranged in our Bible according to chronological order. In the first place are given the Epistles addressed to communities, according to the relative dignity of the church receiving the Epistle, and the length of the subject-matter; in the second place we have those addressed to individuals; and finally, the Epistle to the Hebrews.

All of the Epistles were written in Greek. Though St. Paul on occasion could speak that language with grace, he did not strive after literary elegance in his compositions. Because of the pressure of his work and cares, he usually dictated his Epistles and wrote the final salutation with his own hand (Rom. 16, 22; 1 Cor. 16, 21; Gal. 6, 11; 2 Thess. 3, 17). At times his thoughts are so overflowing and forceful that the rules of grammar and style are neglected. As a consequence, a mode of expression or an entire sentence is now and then difficult or obscure for us (2 Pet. 3, 16).

And yet, in spite of these grammatical faults and irregularities of style, no one can read the Epistles of St. Paul without being amazed at his natural eloquence. St. Jerome remarks that the words of the Apostle Paul seem to him like peals of thunder. His mental acumen and depth of feeling impart to his language loftiness, amazing power and beauty.

THE EPISTLE TO THE ROMANS

Introduction

St. Paul's Epistle to the Romans is given the position of honor at the head of all the New Testament Epistles. It was written at Corinth during the winter 57-58 A. D., at the close of St. Paul's third missionary journey, prior to his voyage to Jerusalem, where at the instigation of his bitter Jewish adversaries he was to be arrested and afterwards held prisoner for several years. This date for the composition of the Epistle is arrived at by comparing the circumstances and persons to which it alludes with those at Corinth during St. Paul's sojourn there at the close of his third missionary journey.

St. Paul during this period of his missionary activity had rather thoroughly covered the territory in the eastern world, and was looking for new fields to evangelize in the West. He purposed, accordingly, after visiting Jerusalem, to journey to Spain, stopping en route at Rome. In this letter he wished to inform the Romans of his intended visit and to set before them the fruits of his meditations on the great religious question of the day, justification by faith and the relation of this new system of salvation to the Mosaic religion. Although he had previously dealt briefly with the question in the Epistle to the Galatians, St. Paul had not thus far had the opportunity of fully developing in writing his doctrine on this point. But now wishing to introduce himself to the Romans, he seized the opportunity of setting forth a lengthy statement and defense of his doctrine, not only for the Romans but also for the various Christian communities throughout the world.

THE EPISTLE OF ST. PAUL THE APOSTLE TO THE ROMANS

Introduction

Greeting

PAUL, THE SERVANT of Jesus Christ, called to be an apostle, set apart for the gospel of God, which he had promised beforehand through his prophets in the holy Scriptures, concerning his Son who was born to him according to the flesh of the offspring of David; who was foreordained Son of God by an act of power in keeping with the holiness of his spirit, by resurrection from the dead, Jesus Christ our Lord, through whom we have received the grace of apostleship to bring about obedience to faith among all the nations for his name's sake; among whom are you also called to be Jesus Christ's—to all God's beloved who are in Rome, called to be saints: grace be to you and peace from God our Father and from the Lord Jesus Christ.

JULY 13
Jan. 12

Commendation and Desire to Visit Them

First I give thanks to my God through Jesus Christ for all of you, because your faith is proclaimed all over the world. For God is my witness, whom I serve in my spirit in the gospel of his Son, how unceasingly I make mention of you, always imploring in my prayers that somehow I may at last by God's will come to you after a safe journey. For I long to see you that I may impart some spiritual grace unto you to strengthen you, ' that is, that among you I may be comforted together with you by that faith which is common to us both, yours and mine.

Why He Wishes to Visit Them

13 Now I would not, brethren, have you ignorant, that I have often intended to come to see you (and have been hindered until now) that I may produce some results among you also, as well as

14 among the rest of the Gentiles. To Greeks and to foreigners, to learned and unlearned, I am

15 debtor; so, for my part, I am ready to preach the gospel to you also who are at Rome.

Theme of the Epistle

16 For I am not ashamed of the gospel, for it is the power of God unto salvation to everyone who

17 believes, to Jew first and then to Greek. For in it the justice of God is revealed, from faith unto faith, as it is written, "He who is just lives by faith."

I: DOCTRINAL

THE GOSPEL THE POWER OF GOD FOR THE SALVATION OF ALL WHO BELIEVE

1. Humanity without Christ

The Pagans Adore Idols

18 FOR THE WRATH OF GOD is revealed from heaven against all ungodliness and wickedness of those men who in wickedness hold back the

19 truth of God, seeing that what may be known about God is manifest to them. For God has

20 manifested it to them. For since the creation of the world his invisible attributes are clearly seen —his everlasting power also and divinity—being understood through the things that are made.

1, 17: *The justice of God:* the real, intrinsic holiness and justice that God imparts to man, transforming him from a sinner into a son of God by adoption, and an heir to heaven.

And so they are without excuse, ' seeing that, 21
although they knew God, they did not glorify
him as God or give thanks, but became vain in
their reasonings, and their senseless minds have
been darkened. For while professing to be wise, 22
they have become fools, ' and they have changed 23
the glory of the incorruptible God for an image
made like to corruptible man and to birds and
four-footed beasts and creeping things.

Punishment of Idolators

Therefore God has given them up in the lust- 24
ful desires of their heart to uncleanness, so that
they dishonor their own bodies among themselves—they who exchanged the truth of God for 25
a lie, and worshipped and served the creature
rather than the Creator who is blessed forever,
amen.

For this cause God has given them up to 26
shameful lusts; for their women have exchanged
the natural use for that which is against nature,
and in like manner the men also, having aban- 27
doned the natural use of the woman, have
burned in their lusts one towards another, men
with men doing shameless things and receiving
in themselves the fitting recompense of their
perversity. And as they have resolved against 28
possessing the knowledge of God, God has
given them up to a reprobate sense, so that they
do what is not fitting, being filled with all iniquity, 29
malice, immorality, avarice, wickedness; being
full of envy, murder, contention, deceit, malig-

1, 24: *God has given them up:* as St. Thomas Aquinas
says, not by impelling them to evil, but by deserting them.
He justly withdrew His grace from them in punishment
of their idolatry, and being thus abandoned by God, men
followed the bent of fallen nature, and fell into the deg-
radation of unnatural vice.

30 nity; being whisperers, ' detractors, hateful to God, irreverent, proud, haughty, plotters of
31 evil; disobedient to parents, ' foolish, dissolute, without affection, without fidelity, without mercy.
32 Although they have known the ordinance of God, they have not understood that those who practise such things are deserving of death. And not only do they do these things, but they applaud others doing them.

All Will Be Rewarded or Punished

2 1　Wherefore, thou art inexcusable, O man, whoever thou art who judgest. For wherein thou judgest another, thou dost condemn thyself. For thou who judgest
2 dost the same things thyself. And we know that the judgment of God is according to truth
3 against those who do such things. But dost thou think, O man who judgest those who do such things and dost the same thyself, that thou wilt
4 escape the judgment of God? Or dost thou despise the riches of his goodness and patience and long-suffering? Dost thou not know that the goodness of God is meant to lead thee to re-
5 pentance? But according to thy hardness and unrepentant heart, thou dost treasure up to thyself wrath on the day of wrath and of the revela-
6 tion of the just judgment of God, who will render
7 to every man according to his works. Life eternal indeed he will give to those who by patience in good works seek glory and honor and immortal-
8 ity; but wrath and indignation to those who are contentious, and who do not submit to the truth
9 but assent to iniquity. Tribulation and anguish shall be visited upon the soul of every man who
10 works evil; of Jew first and then of Greek. But glory and honor and peace shall be awarded to everyone who does good, to Jew first and then

JULY 14
Jan. 13

to Greek. Because with God there is no respect of 11
persons.

Gentiles to Be Judged by the Natural Law

For whoever have sinned without the Law, 12
will perish without the Law; and whoever have
sinned under the Law, will be judged by the Law.
For it is not they who hear the Law that are just 13
in the sight of God; but it is they who follow the
Law that will be justified. When the Gentiles 14
who have no law do by nature what the Law pre-
scribes, these having no law are a law unto themselves. They show the work of the Law written 15
in their hearts. Their conscience bears witness
to them, even when conflicting thoughts accuse
or defend them. This will take place on the day 16
when, according to my gospel, God will judge the
hidden secrets of men through Jesus Christ.

The Jews Transgress the Law

But if thou art called "Jew," and dost rely 17
upon the Law, and dost glory in God, ' and dost 18
know his will, and dost approve the better things,
being informed by the Law, ' thou art confident 19
that thou art a guide to the blind, a light to those
who are in darkness, an instructor of the unwise, 20
a teacher of children, having in the Law the pattern of knowledge and of truth. Thou therefore 21
who teachest another, dost thou not teach thyself? Thou who preachest that men should not
steal, dost thou steal? Thou who sayest that 22
men should not commit adultery, dost thou commit adultery? Thou who dost abominate idols,
dost thou commit sacrilege? Thou who dost glory 23
in the Law, dost thou dishonor God by trans-

2, 12: In this verse, as in the whole passage, the Mosaic
Law is probably meant.

24 gressing the Law? "For the name of God," as it is written, "is blasphemed through you among the Gentiles."

True Circumcision

25 Circumcision, indeed, profits if thou keep the Law; but if thou be a transgressor of the Law, thy circumcision has become uncircumcision.
26 Therefore if the uncircumcised keep the precepts of the Law, will not his uncircumcision be reck-
27 oned as circumcision? And he who is by nature uncircumcised, if he fulfill the Law, will judge thee who with the letter and circumcision art
28 a transgressor of the Law. For he is not a Jew who is so outwardly; nor is that circumcision
29 which is so outwardly in the flesh; but he is a Jew who is so inwardly, and circumcision is a matter of the heart in the spirit, not in the letter. His praise is not from men but from God.

Objections Answered

3 1 What advantage then remains to the Jew, or what is the use of cir-

JULY 15 Jan. 14

2 cumcision? Much in every respect. First, indeed, because the oracles of God were entrusted to
3 them. For what if some of them have not be-lieved? Will their unbelief make void the fidelity
4 of God? By no means! For God is true, and every man is a liar, as it is written, "That thou mayest be justified in thy words, and mayest be
5 victorious when thou art judged." But if our wickedness shows forth the justice of God, what shall we say? Is God unjust who inflicts punish-
6 ment? (I speak after a purely human manner.) By no means! Otherwise, how is God to judge
7 the world? But if through my lie the truth of God

2, 29: Circumcision of the heart means the uprooting of vices and evil tendencies from the heart.

has abounded unto his glory, why am I also still judged as a sinner? And why should we not, as 8 some calumniously accuse us of teaching, do evil that good may come from it? The condemnation of such is just.

The Scriptures Attest Universal Sin

What then? Are we better off than they? Not 9 at all. For we have argued that Jews and Greeks are all under sin, ' as it is written, "There is not 10 one just man; there is none who understands; 11 there is none who seeks after God. All have gone 12 astray together; they have become worthless. There is no one who does good, no, not even one. Their throat is an open sepulchre; with their 13 tongues they have dealt deceitfully. The venom of asps is beneath their lips; their mouth is full 14 of cursing and bitterness. Their feet are swift to 15 shed blood; destruction and misery are in their 16 ways. And the path of peace they have not 17 known. There is no fear of God before their 18 eyes."

This Concerns the Jews

Now we know that whatever the Law says, 19 it is speaking to those who are under the Law; in order that every mouth may be shut, and the whole world may be made subject to God. For 20 by the works of the Law no human being shall be justified before him, for through law comes the recognition of sin.

2. Salvation through Faith in Christ

Justice Comes through Faith in Christ

BUT NOW THE JUSTICE OF GOD has been 21 made manifest independently of the Law, being attested by the Law and the Prophets; the justice 22 of God through faith in Jesus Christ upon all who

23 believe. For there is no distinction,' as all have
24 sinned and have need of the glory of God. They
are justified freely by his grace through the re-
25 demption which is in Christ Jesus, whom God
has set forth as a propitiation by his blood
26 through faith, to manifest his justice, ' God in his
patience remitting former sins; to manifest his
justice at the present time, so that he himself is
just, and makes just him who has faith in Jesus.

Justification Excludes Boasting

27 Where then is thy boasting? It is excluded.
By what law? Of works? No, but by the law of
28 faith. For we reckon that a man is justified by
faith independently of the works of the Law.
29 Is God the God of the Jews only, and not of the
30 Gentiles also? Indeed of the Gentiles also. ' For
there is but one God who will justify the circumcised by faith, and the uncircumcised through
31 the same faith. Do we therefore through faith
destroy the Law? By no means! Rather we establish the Law.

Abraham Justified by Faith

4 1 What then shall we say that Abra-
ham, our father according to the | JULY 16 / Jan. 15
2 flesh, acquired? For if Abraham was justified by
works, he has reason to boast, but not before
3 God. ' For what does the Scripture say? "Abraham believed God and it was credited to him as
4 justice." Now to him who works, the reward is
not credited as a favor but as something due.
5 But to him who does not work, but believes in
him who justifies the impious, his faith is cred-
6 ited to him as justice. Thus David declares the
blessedness of the man to whom God credits
7 justice without works: "Blessed are they whose
iniquities are forgiven, and whose sins are cov-

ered; blessed is the man to whom the Lord will 8
not credit sin."

Justified before Circumcision

Does this blessedness hold good, then, only 9
for the circumcised, or also for the uncircumcised? For we say that unto Abraham faith was
credited as justice. How then was it credited? 10
When he was in the state of circumcision or in
that of uncircumcision? Not in circumcision but
in uncircumcision. And he received the sign of 11
circumcision as the seal of the justice of faith
which he had while uncircumcised, in order that
he may be the father of all who, while uncircumcised, believed, that to them also it may be
credited as justice; and the father of the circum- 12
cised, not of those merely who are circumcised,
but also of those who follow in the steps of the
faith that was our father Abraham's while yet
uncircumcised.

Not Justified by the Works of the Law

For not through the Law but through the jus- 13
tice of faith was the promise made to Abraham
and to his posterity that he should be heir of the
world. For if they who are of the Law are heirs, 14
faith is made empty, the promise is made void.
For the Law works wrath; for where there is no 15
law, neither is there transgression. Therefore 16
the promise was the outcome of faith, that it
might be a favor, in order that it might be secure
for all the offspring, not only for those who are of
the Law, but also for those who are of the faith
of Abraham, who is the father of us all; as it is 17
written, "I have appointed thee the father of
many nations." He is our father in the sight of
God, whom he believed, who gives life to the

dead and calls things that are not as though they were.

The Strength of His Faith

18 Abraham hoping against hope believed, so that he became the father of many nations, according to what was said, "So shall thy offspring
19 be." And without weakening in faith, he considered his own deadened body (for he was almost a hundred years old) and the deadened
20 womb of Sara; and yet in view of the promise of God, he did not waver through unbelief but was
21 strengthened in faith, giving glory to God, ' being fully aware that whatever God has promised he
22 is able also to perform. Therefore it was credited to him as justice.

The Model of Our Faith

23 Now not for his sake only was it written that
24 "It was credited to him," ' but for the sake of us also, to whom it will be credited if we believe in him who raised Jesus our Lord from the dead,
25 who was delivered up for our sins, and rose again for our justification.

3. The Superabundance of This Justification

Christ's Death Assures Us Hope and Peace

5 1 HAVING BEEN JUSTIFIED therefore by faith, let us have peace with God | JULY 17 Jan. 16
2 through our Lord Jesus Christ, ' through whom we also have access by faith unto that grace in which we stand, and exult in the hope of the glory of
3 the sons of God. And not only this, but we exult in tribulations also, knowing that tribulation
4 works out endurance, and endurance tried vir-
5 tue, and tried virtue hope. And hope does not disappoint, because the charity of God is poured forth in our hearts by the Holy Spirit who has

been given to us. For why did Christ, at the set 6
time, die for the wicked when as yet we were
weak? For scarcely in behalf of a just man does 7
one die; yet perhaps one might bring himself to
die for a good man. But God commends his 8
charity towards us, because when as yet we were
sinners, Christ died for us. 9

Christ's Death Assures Our Salvation

Much more now that we are justified by his
blood, shall we be saved through him from the
wrath. For if when we were enemies we were 10
reconciled to God by the death of his Son, much
more, having been reconciled, shall we be saved
by his life. And not this only, but we exult also in 11
God through our Lord Jesus Christ, through
whom we have now received reconciliation.

In Adam All Have Sinned

Therefore as through one man sin entered 12
into the world and through sin death, and thus
death has passed unto all men because all have
sinned—for until the Law sin was in the world, 13
but sin is not imputed when there is no law;
yet death reigned from Adam until Moses even 14
over those who did not sin after the likeness of
the transgression of Adam, who is a figure of him
who was to come.

Grace and Life Superabound through Christ

But not like the offense is the gift. For if by 15
the offense of the one the many died, much more
has the grace of God, and the gift in the grace
of the one man Jesus Christ, abounded unto the
many. Nor is the gift as it was in the case of one 16
man's sin, for the judgment was from one man
unto condemnation, but grace is from many
offenses unto justification. For if by reason of the 17

one man's offense death reigned through the one man, much more will they who receive the abundance of the grace and of the gift of justice reign
18 in life through the one Jesus Christ. Therefore as from the offense of the one man the result was unto condemnation to all men, so from the justice of the one the result is unto justification of
19 life to all men. For just as by the disobedience of the one man the many were constituted sinners, so also by the obedience of the one the many will be constituted just.

Purpose of the Law

20 Now the Law intervened that the offense might abound. But where the offense has
21 abounded, grace has abounded yet more; so that as sin has reigned unto death, so also grace may reign by justice unto life everlasting through Jesus Christ our Lord.

4. Justification and the Christian Life

Christians Dead to Sin

6 1 WHAT THEN SHALL WE SAY? Shall we continue in sin that grace ⎡JULY 18⎤
2 may abound? By no means! For how shall we ⎣Jan. 17⎦
3 who are dead to sin still live in it? Do you not know that all we who have been baptized into Christ Jesus have been baptized into his death?
4 For we were buried with him by means of Baptism into death, in order that, just as Christ has arisen from the dead through the glory of the

---

6, 3: St. Paul alludes to the manner in which Baptism was ordinarily conferred in the primitive Church, by immersion. The descent into the water is suggestive of the descent of the body into the grave, and the ascent is suggestive of the resurrection to a new life. St. Paul obviously sees more than a mere symbol in the rite of Baptism. As a result of it we are incorporated into Christ's mystical body and live a new life.

Father, so we also may walk in newness of life. For if we have been united with him in the likeness of his death, we shall be so in the likeness of his resurrection also. For we know that our old self has been crucified with him, in order that the body of sin may be destroyed, that we may no longer be slaves to sin; for he who is dead is acquitted of sin. But if we have died with Christ, we believe that we shall also live together with Christ; for we know that Christ, having risen from the dead, dies now no more, death shall no longer have dominion over him. For the death that he died, he died to sin once for all, but the life that he lives, he lives unto God. Thus do you consider yourselves also as dead to sin, but alive to God in Christ Jesus.

The Reign of Sin

Therefore do not let sin reign in your mortal body so that you obey its lusts. And do not yield your members to sin as weapons of iniquity, but present yourselves to God as those who have come to life from the dead and your members as weapons of justice for God; for sin shall not have dominion over you, since you are not under the Law but under grace.

Slavery to Sin

What then? Are we to sin because we are not under the Law but under grace? By no means! Do you not know that to whom you offer yourselves as slaves for obedience, to him whom you obey you are the slaves, whether to sin unto death or to obedience unto justice? But thanks

---

6, 6: We are no longer slaves to the evil inclinations of bodily concupiscence.

6, 17: *Into which you have been delivered:* i.e., "in which you have been instructed."

be to God that you who were the slaves of sin
have now obeyed from the heart that form of
18 doctrine into which you have been delivered, and
having been set free from sin, you have become
19 the slaves of justice. I speak in a human way
because of the weakness of your flesh; for as
you yielded your members as slaves of uncleanness and iniquity unto iniquity, so now yield your
members as slaves of justice unto sanctification.
20 For when you were the slaves of sin, you were
21 free as regards justice. But what fruit had you
then from those things of which you are now
ashamed? For the end of these things is death.
22 But now set free from sin and become slaves to
God, you have your fruit unto sanctification, and
23 as your end, life everlasting. For the wages of
sin is death, but the gift of God is life everlasting
in Christ Jesus our Lord.

Christians Freed from the Law

7 1   Do you not know, brethren (for I [JULY 19]
speak to those who know law), that [Jan. 18]
the Law has dominion over a man as long as he
2 lives? For the married woman is bound by the
Law while her husband is alive; but if her husband die, she is set free from the law of the
3 husband. Therefore while her husband is alive,
she will be called an adulteress if she is with
another man; but if her husband dies, she is set
free from the law of the husband, so that she is
not an adulteress if she has been with another
4 man. Therefore, my brethren, you also, through
the body of Christ, have been made to die to the
Law, so as to belong to another who has risen
from the dead, in order that we may bring forth

7, 4: St. Thomas Aquinas says, "It is evident that
through the death by which we die with Christ, the obli-
gation of the old Law ceases."

fruit unto God. For when we were in the flesh 5
the sinful passions, which were aroused by the
Law, were at work in our members so that they
brought forth fruit unto death. But now we have 6
been set free from the Law, having died to that
by which we were held down, so that we may
serve in a new spirit and not according to the
outworn letter.

The Law the Occasion of Sin

What shall we say then? Is the Law sin? By no 7
means! Yet I did not know sin save through the
Law. For I had not known lust unless the Law
had said, "Thou shalt not lust." But sin, having 8
thus found an occasion, worked in me by means
of the commandment all manner of lust, for
without the Law sin was dead. Once upon a time 9
I was living without law, but when the commandment came, sin revived, ' and I died, and the 10
commandment that was unto life was discovered
in my case to be unto death. For sin, having taken 11
occasion from the commandment, deceived me,
and through it killed me. So that the Law indeed 12
is holy and the commandment holy and just
and good.

Sin the Cause of Death

Did then that which is good become death to 13
me? By no means! But sin, that it might be
manifest as sin, worked death for me through
that which is good, in order that sin by reason

7, 5: *When we were in the flesh:* deprived of the grace
of God which comes from union with Christ through
Baptism. *The sinful passions:* i.e., evil inclinations which
incite to sin. These evil inclinations were *aroused by
the Law.* Prohibition whets desire.

7, 8: *Without the Law sin was dead:* i.e., sin was com-
paratively weak. The restraint which prohibitive laws put
on liberty stirred it up to rebellion, and thus in law sin
found a powerful ally.

of the commandment might become immeasur-
14 ably sinful. For we know that the Law is spiritual
15 but I am carnal, sold into the power of sin. For I
do not understand what I do, for it is not what I
16 wish that I do, but what I hate, that I do. But if
I do what I do not wish, I admit that the Law is
17 good. Now therefore it is no longer I who do it,
18 but the sin that dwells in me. For I know that in
me, that is, in my flesh, no good dwells, because
to wish is within my power, but I do not find the
19 strength to accomplish what is good. For I do
not the good that I wish, but the evil that I do
20 not wish, that I perform. Now if I do what I do
not wish, it is no longer I who do it, but the sin
21 that dwells in me. Therefore, when I wish to do
good I discover this law, namely, that evil is at
22 hand for me. For I am delighted with the law of
23 God according to the inner man, but I see another
law in my members, warring against the law of
my mind and making me prisoner to the law of
sin that is in my members.

Deliverance Due to the Grace of God

24 Unhappy man that I am! Who will deliver me
25 from the body of this death? The grace of God
through Jesus Christ our Lord. Therefore I myself with my mind serve the law of God, but with
my flesh the law of sin.

The Faithful Need Fear No Condemnation

8 1   There is therefore now no con-   JULY 20
demnation for those who are in   Jan. 19
Christ Jesus, who do not walk according to the

7, 15: Here St. Paul vividly depicts the inner struggle
which goes on in all human beings between the lower,
sensual nature, and the higher aspirations of the soul.
He concludes by saying that the higher aspirations gain
victory through the grace of God merited for mankind by
Jesus Christ.

flesh. For the law of the Spirit of the life in Christ 2
Jesus has delivered me from the law of sin and
of death. For what was impossible to the Law, 3
in that it was weak because of the flesh, God has
made good. By sending his Son in the likeness of
sinful flesh as a sin-offering, he has condemned
sin in the flesh, ' in order that the requirements 4
of the Law might be fulfilled in us, who walk not
according to the flesh but according to the spirit.

The Flesh and the Spirit

Now they who are according to the flesh mind 5
the things of the flesh, but they who are according to the spirit mind the things of the spirit. For 6
the inclination of the flesh is death, but the inclination of the spirit, life and peace. For the 7
wisdom of the flesh is hostile to God, for it is not
subject to the law of God, nor can it be. And they 8
who are carnal cannot please God.

You, however, are not carnal but spiritual, if 9
indeed the Spirit of God dwells in you. But if
anyone does not have the Spirit of Christ, he
does not belong to Christ. But if Christ is in you, 10
the body, it is true, is dead by reason of sin, but
the spirit is life by reason of justification.' But if 11
the Spirit of him who raised Jesus from the dead
dwells in you, then he who raised Jesus Christ
from the dead will also bring to life your mortal
bodies because of his Spirit who dwells in you.

A Solemn Warning

Therefore, brethren, we are debtors, not to the 12
flesh, that we should live according to the flesh,
' for if you live according to the flesh you will die; 13
but if by the spirit you put to death the deeds of
the flesh, you will live.

The Faithful Sons of God

14 For whoever are led by the Spirit of God, they
15 are the sons of God. Now you have not received
a spirit of bondage so as to be again in fear, but
you have received a spirit of adoption as sons, by
16 virtue of which we cry, "Abba! Father!" The
Spirit himself gives testimony to our spirit that
17 we are sons of God. But if we are sons, we are
heirs also: heirs indeed of God and joint heirs
with Christ, provided, however, we suffer with
him that we may also be glorified with him.

Yearning of All Creation

18 For I reckon that the sufferings of | JULY 21 |
the present time are not worthy to | Jan. 20 |
19 be compared with the glory to come that will be revealed in us. For the eager longing of creation
20 awaits the revelation of the sons of God. For
creation was made subject to vanity—not by
its own will but by reason of him who made it
21 subject—in hope, ' because creation itself also
will be delivered from its slavery to corruption
into the freedom of the glory of the sons of God.
22 For we know that all creation groans and travails
in pain until now.

Yearning of Human Beings

23 And not only it, but we ourselves also who
have the first-fruits of the Spirit—we ourselves
groan within ourselves, waiting for the adoption
24 as sons, the redemption of our body. For in hope
were we saved. But hope that is seen is not hope.
25 For how can a man hope for what he sees? ' But if
we hope for what we do not see, we wait for it
with patience.

The Holy Spirit Aids Us

But in like manner the Spirit also helps our 26 weakness. For we do not know what we should pray for as we ought, but the Spirit himself pleads for us with unutterable groanings. And 27 he who searches the hearts knows what the Spirit desires, that he pleads for the saints according to God.

God's Designs

Now we know that for those who love God all 28 things work together unto good, for those who, according to his purpose, are saints through his call. For those whom he has foreknown he has 29 also predestined to become conformed to the image of his Son, that he should be the firstborn among many brethren. And those whom he has 30 predestined, them he has also called; and those whom he has called, them he has also justified, and those whom he has justified, them he has also glorified.

Unshakable Hope in God

What then shall we say to these things? If 31 God is for us, who is against us? He who has not 32 spared even his own Son but has delivered him for us all, how can he fail to grant us also all things with him? Who shall make accusation 33 against the elect of God? It is God who justifies! Who shall condemn? It is Christ Jesus who 34 died; yes, and rose again, he who is at the right hand of God, who also intercedes for us!

Indomitable Love of Christ

Who shall separate us from the love of Christ? 35 Shall tribulation, or distress, or persecution, or hunger, or nakedness, or danger, or the sword?

36 Even as it is written, "For thy sake we are put to death all the day long. We are regarded as sheep
37 for the slaughter." But in all these things we
38 overcome because of him who has loved us. For I am sure that neither death, nor life, nor angels, nor principalities, nor things present, nor things
39 to come, nor powers, ' nor height, nor depth, nor any other creature will be able to separate us from the love of God, which is in Christ Jesus our Lord.

5. The Problem of the Rejection of Israel

Paul Grieves for the Jews

9 1 I SPEAK THE TRUTH IN CHRIST, I do not lie, my conscience bearing me
2 witness in the Holy Spirit, that I have great sad-
3 ness and continuous sorrow in my heart. For I could wish to be anathema myself from Christ for the sake of my brethren, who are my kins-
4 men according to the flesh; who are Israelites, who have the adoption as sons, and the glory and the covenants and the legislation and the wor-
5 ship and the promises; who have the fathers, and from whom is the Christ according to the flesh, who is, over all things, God blessed forever, amen.

JULY 22
Jan. 21

God's Election Depends on His Free Choice

6 It is not that the word of God has failed. For they are not all Israelites who are sprung from
7 Israel; nor because they are the descendants of Abraham, are they all his children; but "Through
8 Isaac shall thy posterity bear thy name." That

9, 3: That these words are merely an emphatic way of declaring his great devotion to his people and that they are not to be taken literally is evident from what St. Paul has said above, 8, 38.

is to say, they are not sons of God who are the children of the flesh, but it is the children of promise who are reckoned as posterity. For this is a word of promise: "About this time I will come and Sara shall have a son." And not she only; but also Rebecca, who conceived by one man, Isaac our father; for before the children had yet been born, or had done aught of good or evil, in order that the selective purpose of God might stand, ' depending not on deeds, but on him who calls, it was said to her, "The elder shall serve the younger"; ' as it is written, "Jacob I have loved, but Esau I have hated."

God Is Not Unjust

What then shall we say? Is there injustice with God? By no means! ' For he says to Moses, "I will have mercy on whom I have mercy, and I will show pity to whom I will show pity." So then there is question not of him who wills nor of him who runs, but of God showing mercy. For the Scripture says to Pharaoh, "For this very purpose I have raised thee up that I may show in thee my power, and that my name may be proclaimed in all the earth." Therefore he has mercy on whom he will, and whom he will he hardens.

9, 16: *Not of him who wills:* the primary and ultimate factor in man's destiny is the activity of God's grace, which of course does not exclude man's co-operation.

9, 17: *For this very purpose:* it is not to be understood that God's primary and express purpose in creating Pharaoh was to make a sinner out of him. But God raised him up to rule the Egyptian people, and, foreseeing that Pharaoh would abuse grace and fall into sin, God decreed to use Pharaoh according to his demerits for the further manifestation of His own divine attributes and for the realization of the designs of His all-wise providence.

9, 18: *He hardens:* i.e., by withdrawing divine grace in punishment of demerits.

His Power and Glory

19 Thou sayest to me: Why then does he still find fault? For who re-
20 sists his will? O man, who art thou to reply to God? Does the object moulded say to him who
21 moulded it: Why hast thou made me thus? Or is not the potter master of his clay, to make from the same mass one vessel for honorable, another
22 for ignoble use? But what if God, wishing to show his wrath and to make known his power, endured with much patience vessels of wrath, ready for
23 destruction, that he might show the riches of his glory upon vessels of mercy, which he has pre-
24 pared unto glory—even us whom he has called not only from among the Jews but also from among the Gentiles?

Witness of the Old Testament

25 As he says in Osee, "A people not mine I will call my people, and an unbeloved, beloved, and her who had not obtained mercy, one who has
26 obtained mercy. And it shall be in the place where it was said to them: you are not my people; there they shall be called sons of the liv-
27 ing God." And Isaias cries out concerning Israel, "Though the number of the children of Israel are as the sands of the sea, the remnant shall be
28 saved. For the Lord fulfills his word speedily in justice, because a speedy word will the Lord
29 accomplish on earth." And as Isaias foretold, "Unless the Lord of Hosts had left us a posterity, we should have become as Sodom and should have been like Gomorrah."

9, 21: St. John Chrysostom says, "St. Paul here so speaks not by way of denying free will but to show to what extent we are to submit to God. For we should be no more ready to demand reasons from God than the clay vessel" (Hom. 16 on Romans).

Jews' Refusal to Believe

What then shall we say? That the Gentiles 30
who were not pursuing justice have secured
justice, but a justice that is from faith; but Israel, 31
by pursuing a law of justice, has not attained to
the law of justice.' And why? Because they sought 32
it not from faith, but as it were from works. For
they stumbled at the stumbling-stone, as it is 33
written, "Behold I lay in Sion a stumbling-stone
and rock of scandal: and whoever believes in
him shall not be disappointed."

Ignorance of the Justice of God

Brethren, my heart's desire and ⟨JULY 24 / Jan. 23⟩ **10** 1
my prayer to God is in their behalf
unto their salvation. For I bear them witness 2
that they have zeal for God, but not according to
knowledge; for, ignorant of the justice of God 3
and seeking to establish their own, they have not
submitted to the justice of God. For Christ is the 4
consummation of the Law unto justice for everyone who believes.

This Justice Comes through Faith

For Moses wrote that the man who does that 5
justice which is of the Law shall live by it. But 6
the justice that is of faith says, "Do not say in
thy heart: Who shall ascend into heaven?" (that
is, to bring down Christ); "or, Who shall descend 7
into the abyss?" (that is, to bring up Christ from
the dead). But what does it say? "The word is 8
near thee, in thy mouth and in thy heart" (that

10, 5-13: St. Paul here seeks to establish the ease with
which this justice of the Christian dispensation may be
acquired, in contrast to the system which prevailed under
the Mosaic dispensation.

9 is, the word of faith, which we preach). For if
thou confess with thy mouth that Jesus is the
Lord, and believe in thy heart that God has raised
10 him from the dead, thou shalt be saved. For with
the heart a man believes unto justice, and with
the mouth profession of faith is made unto
11 salvation. For the Scripture says, "Whoever
12 believes in him shall not be disappointed." For
there is no distinction between Jew and Greek,
for there is the same Lord of all, rich towards all
13 who call upon him. "For whoever calls upon the
name of the Lord shall be saved."

Refusal to Believe the Gospel

14 How then are they to call upon him in whom
they have not believed? But how are they to
believe him whom they have not heard? And how
15 are they to hear, if no one preaches? And how
are men to preach unless they be sent? As it is
written, "How beautiful are the feet of those who
preach the gospel of peace; of those who bring
16 glad tidings of good things!" But all did not obey
the gospel. For Isaias says, "Lord, who has be-
17 lieved our report?" Faith then depends on hear-
18 ing, and hearing on the word of Christ. But I say:
Have they not heard? Yes, indeed, "Their voice
has gone forth into all the earth, and their words
19 unto the ends of the world." But I say: Has not
Israel known? First of all, Moses says, "I will
provoke you to jealousy of those who are not a
nation; I will stir you to anger against a senseless
20 nation." Then Isaias dares to say, "I was found
by those who did not seek me; I appeared openly
21 to those who made no inquiry of me." But to
Israel he says, "All the day long I stretched out
my hand to a people unbelieving and contradicting."

[418]

A Remnant of the Jews Will Be Saved

I say then: Has God cast off his people? By no means! For I also am

JULY 25   **11** 1
Jan. 24

an Israelite of the posterity of Abraham, of the tribe of Benjamin. God has not cast off his people 2 whom he foreknew. Or do you not know what the Scripture says in the account of Elias, how he lodges complaint with God against Israel? "Lord, they have slain thy prophets, they have 3 razed thy altars; and I only am left, and they are seeking my life." But what does the divine an- 4 swer say to him? "I have left for myself seven thousand men, who have not bowed their knees to Baal." Even so, then, at the present time there 5 is a remnant left, selected out of grace. And if out 6 of grace, then not in virtue of works; otherwise grace is no longer grace.

Witness of the Scriptures

What then? What Israel was seeking after, 7 that it has not obtained; but the chosen have obtained it, and the rest have been blinded, [1] as it 8 is written, "God has given them a spirit of stupor until this present day, eyes that they may not see, and ears that they may not hear." And David 9 says, "Let their table become a snare and a trap and a stumbling-block and a recompense unto them; let their eyes be darkened that they may 10 not see, and let them bow their backs always."

Israel's Fall the Gentiles' Salvation

I say then: have they so stumbled as to fall? 11 By no means! But by their offense salvation has come to the Gentiles, that they may be jealous

---

11, 8: *God has given them,* etc.: i.e., by permitting them, in punishment of their pride and hypocrisy, to be blinded to the truth of the Christian revelation.

11, 11: *Jealous:* must be understood here in a good sense.

12 of them. Now if their offense is the riches of the world, and their decline the riches of the Gentiles, how much more their full number!

The Gentiles Must Be Humble

13 For I say to you Gentiles: As long, indeed, as I am an apostle of the Gentiles, I will honor
14 my ministry, in the hope that I may provoke to jealousy those who are my flesh, and may save
15 some of them. For if the rejection of them is the reconciliation of the world, what will the recep-
16 tion of them be but life from the dead? Now if the first handful of the dough is holy, so also is the lump of the dough; and if the root is holy, so
17 also are the branches. But if some of the branches have been broken off, and if thou, being a wild olive, art grafted in their place, and hast become a partaker of the stem and fatness of the olive
18 tree, ' do not boast against the branches. But if thou dost boast, still it is not thou that support-
19 est the stem, but the stem thee. Thou wilt say, then, "Branches were broken off that I might be
20 grafted in." True, but they were broken off because of unbelief, whereas thou by faith stand-
21 est. Be not high-minded, but fear. ' For if God has not spared the natural branches, perhaps he
22 may not spare thee either. See, then, the goodness and the severity of God: his severity towards those who have fallen, but the goodness of God towards thee if thou abidest in his goodness; otherwise thou also wilt be cut off.

Israel Can Yet Be Saved

23 And they also, if they do not continue in unbelief, will be grafted in;
24 for God is able to graft them back. For if thou hast been cut off from the wild olive tree which is natural to thee, and contrary to nature, hast

JULY 26
Jan. 25

[420]

been grafted into the cultivated olive tree, how much more shall these, the natural branches, be grafted into their own olive tree!

Israel's Final Conversion

For I would not, brethren, have you ignorant 25 of this mystery, lest you should be wise in your own conceits, that a partial blindness only has befallen Israel, until the full number of the Gentiles should enter, and thus all Israel should 26 be saved, as it is written, "There will come out of Sion the deliverer and he will turn away impiety from Jacob; and this is my covenant with 27 them, when I shall take away their sins." In view of the gospel, they are enemies for your 28 sake; but in view of the divine choice, they are most dear for the sake of the fathers. For the 29 gifts and the call of God are without repentance.

Ultimate Triumph of God's Mercy

For as you also at one time did not believe 30 God, but now have obtained mercy by reason of their unbelief, so they too have not now believed 31 by reason of the mercy shown you, that they too may obtain mercy. For God has shut up all in un- 32 belief, that he may have mercy upon all.

God's Ways Unsearchable

Oh, the depth of the riches of the wisdom and 33 of the knowledge of God! How incomprehensible are his judgments and how unsearchable his ways! For "Who has known the mind of the 34

11, 29: *The gifts and the call of God are without repentance:* this statement must be understood, in the light of the context, of the gifts mentioned in 9, 4, especially of the gift of being the chosen people. The Jews remain the people of God's predilection, and will eventually be converted and saved.

35 Lord, or who has been his counsellor? Or who has first given to him, that recompense should
36 be made him?" For from him and through him and unto him are all things. To him be the glory forever, amen.

II: MORAL

The Duties of Christians

Conclusion of the Foregoin

12 1 I EXHORT YOU THEREFORE, brethren, by the mercy of God, to pre- JULY 27 Jan. 26 sent your bodies as a sacrifice, living, holy,
2 pleasing to God—your spiritual service. And be not conformed to this world, but be transformed in the newness of your mind, that you may discern what is the good and acceptable and perfect will of God.

Humility and Concord

3 By the grace that has been given to me, I say to each one among you: let no one rate himself more than he ought, but let him rate himself according to moderation, and according as God has apportioned to each one the measure of
4 faith. For just as in one body we have many members, yet all the members have not the same
5 function, so we, the many, are one body in Christ, but severally members one of another.
6 But we have gifts differing according to the grace that has been given us, such as prophecy to be
7 used according to the proportion of faith; or ministry, in ministering; or he who teaches, in
8 teaching; he who exhorts, in exhorting; he who gives, in simplicity; he who presides, with carefulness; he who shows mercy, with cheerfulness.

Fraternal Charity

Let love be without pretense. Hate what is 9
evil, hold to what is good. Love one another with 10
fraternal charity, anticipating one another with
honor. Be not slothful in zeal, be fervent in spirit, 11
serving the Lord, ' rejoicing in hope. Be patient 12
in tribulation, persevering in prayer. Share the 13
needs of the saints, practising hospitality. Bless 14
those who persecute you; bless and do not curse.
Rejoice with those who rejoice; weep with those 15
who weep. Be of one mind towards one another. 16
Do not set your mind on high things but con-
descend to the lowly. Be not wise in your own
conceits. To no man render evil for evil, but 17
provide good things not only in the sight of God,
but also in the sight of all men. If it be possible, 18
as far as in you lies, be at peace with all men.
Do not avenge yourselves, beloved, but give 19
place to the wrath, for it is written, "Vengeance
is mine; I will repay, says the Lord." But "If thy 20
enemy is hungry, give him food; if he is thirsty,
give him drink; for by so doing thou wilt heap
coals of fire upon his head." Be not overcome by 21
evil, but overcome evil with good.

Obedience

Let everyone be subject to the | JULY 28 | **13** 1
higher authorities, for there exists | Jan. 27 |
no authority except from God, and those who
exist have been appointed by God. Therefore he 2
who resists the authority resists the ordinance
of God; and they that resist bring on themselves
condemnation. For rulers are a terror not to the 3
good work but to the evil. Dost thou wish, then,
not to fear the authority? Do what is good and
thou wilt have praise from it. For it is God's 4
minister to thee for good. But if thou dost what is
evil, fear, for not without reason does it carry the

[423]

sword. For it is God's minister, an avenger to
5 execute wrath on him who does evil. Wherefore
you must needs be subject, not only because of
6 the wrath, but also for conscience' sake. For this
is also why you pay tribute, for they are the min-
7 isters of God, serving unto this very end. Render
to all men whatever is their due; tribute to whom
tribute is due; taxes to whom taxes are due; fear
to whom fear is due: honor to whom honor is due.

Charity a Social Duty

8 Owe no man anything except to love one
another; for he who loves his neighbor has ful-
9 filled the Law. For "Thou shalt not commit adultery; Thou shalt not kill; Thou shalt not steal;
Thou shalt not covet"; and if there is any other
commandment, it is summed up in this saying,
10 "Thou shalt love thy neighbor as thyself." ' Love
does no evil to a neighbor. Love therefore is the
fulfillment of the Law.

The Spirit of Christ

11 And this do, understanding the time, for it is
now the hour for us to rise from sleep, because
now our salvation is nearer than when we came
12 to believe. The night is far advanced; the day is
at hand. Let us therefore lay aside the works of
13 darkness, and put on the armor of light. Let us
walk becomingly as in the day, not in revelry and
drunkenness, not in debauchery and wanton-
14 ness, not in strife and jealousy. But put on the
Lord Jesus Christ, and as for the flesh, take no
thought for its lusts.

Mutual Forbearance

14 1 But him who is weak in faith, receive, without
2 disputes about opinions. For one believes that he
may eat all things; but he who is weak, let him

eat vegetables. Let not him who eats despise him ³
who does not eat, and let not him who does not
eat judge him who eats; for God has received
him. Who art thou to judge another's servant? ⁴
To his own lord he stands or falls; but he will
stand, for God is able to make him stand. For ⁵
one esteems one day above another; another
esteems every day alike. Let everyone be convinced in his own mind. He who regards the day, ⁶
regards it for the Lord; and he who eats, eats for
the Lord, for he gives thanks to God. And he who
does not eat, abstains for the Lord, and gives
thanks to God. For none of us lives to himself, ⁷
and none dies to himself; for if we live, we live to ⁸
the Lord, or if we die, we die to the Lord. Therefore, whether we live or die, we are the Lord's.
For to this end Christ died and rose again, that ⁹
he might be Lord both of the dead and of the
living. But thou, why dost thou judge thy ¹⁰
brother? Or thou, why dost thou despise thy
brother? For we shall all stand at the judgment-
seat of God; for it is written, "As I live, says the ¹¹
Lord, to me every knee shall bend, and every
tongue shall give praise to God."

Charity and Peace

Therefore every one of us will ¹²
render an account for himself to | JULY 29 |
God. Therefore let us no longer judge one an- ¹³
other, but rather judge this, that you should not
put a stumbling-block or a hindrance in your
brother's way. I know and am confident in the ¹⁴
Lord Jesus that nothing is of itself unclean; but
to him who regards anything as unclean, to him

14, 1: *Weak in faith:* those who had an erroneous conscience concerning the implications of the Christian teaching, especially concerning certain foods. The strong in
faith are those who are better instructed and understand
that no food is of itself unclean and forbidden.

15 it is unclean. If, then, thy brother is grieved because of thy food, no longer dost thou walk according to charity. Do not with thy food destroy
16 him for whom Christ died. Let not, then, our
17 good be reviled. For the kingdom of God does not consist in food and drink, but in justice and
18 peace and joy in the Holy Spirit; for he who in this way serves Christ pleases God and is ap-
19 proved by men. Let us, then, follow after the things that make for peace, and let us safeguard
20 the things that make for mutual edification. Do not for the sake of food destroy the work of God! All things indeed are clean; but a thing is evil
21 for the man who eats through scandal. It is good not to eat meat and not to drink wine, nor to do anything by which thy brother is offended or
22 scandalized or weakened. ' Thou hast faith. Keep it to thyself before God. Blessed is he who does
23 not condemn himself by what he approves. But he who hesitates, if he eats, is condemned, because it is not from faith; for all that is not from faith is sin.

Self-Denial and Patience

15 1 Now we, the strong, ought to bear the infirmities of the weak, and not to please ourselves.
2 Let every one of you please his neighbor by do-
3 ing good, for his edification; for Christ did not please himself, but as it is written, "The reproaches of those who reproach thee have fallen
4 upon me." For whatever things have been written have been written for our instruction, that through the patience and the consolation afforded by the Scriptures we may have hope. May
5 then the God of patience and of comfort grant

14, 22f: *Faith:* here means conscience enlightened by faith.

you to be of one mind towards one another according to Jesus Christ; that, one in spirit, you 6 may with one mouth glorify the God and Father of our Lord Jesus Christ.

Mercy

Wherefore receive one another, even as Christ 7 has received you to the honor of God. For I say 8 that Christ Jesus has been a minister of the circumcision in order to show God's fidelity in confirming the promises made to our fathers, but 9 that the Gentiles glorify God because of his mercy, as it is written, "Therefore will I praise thee among the Gentiles, and will sing to thy name." And again he says, "Rejoice, you Gen- 10 tiles, with his people." And again, "Praise the 11 Lord, all you Gentiles; and sing his praises, all you peoples." And again Isaias says, "There 12 shall be the root of Jesse, and he who shall arise to rule the Gentiles . . . in him the Gentiles shall hope." Now may the God of hope fill you with all 13 joy and peace in believing, that you may abound in hope and in the power of the Holy Spirit.

Conclusion

Personal Explanations and Greetings

Apostle of the Gentiles

NOW I FOR MY PART, my breth- | JULY 30 | 14
ren, am convinced with regard to | Jan. 29 |
you that you yourselves are full of love, filled with all knowledge, so that you are able to admonish one another. But I have written to you 15 rather boldly here and there, brethren — as it were to refresh your memory — because of the grace that has been given me by God, that I 16 should be a minister of Christ Jesus to the

Gentiles; sanctifying the gospel of God, that the offering up of the Gentiles may become accept-
17 able, being sanctified by the Holy Spirit. I have therefore this boast in Christ Jesus as regards
18 the work of God. For I do not make bold to mention anything but what Christ has wrought through me to bring about the obedience of the
19 Gentiles, by word and deed, ' with mighty signs and wonders, by the power of the Holy Spirit, so that from Jerusalem round about as far as Illyricum I have completed the evangelization of
20 Christ. But I have not preached this gospel where Christ has already been named, lest I might
21 build on another man's foundation; but even as it is written, "They who have not been told of him shall see, and they who have not heard shall understand."

St. Paul's Plans

22 This is why I was hindered these many times
23 from coming to you. But now, having no more work in these parts, and having had for many
24 years a great desire to come to you, when I set out for Spain I hope to see you as I pass through (and by you to be sped on my way there), having
25 first enjoyed being with you for a while. Now, however, I will set out for Jerusalem to minister
26 to the saints. For Macedonia and Achaia have thought it well to make a contribution for the
27 poor among the saints at Jerusalem. So it has pleased them, and their debtors they are. For if the Gentiles have shared in their spiritual blessings, they should also minister to them in ma-
28 terial things. Therefore, when I have completed this, and have delivered to them the proceeds, I
29 will set out by way of you for Spain. And I know

that when I come to you, I shall come with the fullness of Christ's blessing.

Request for Prayers

Now I exhort you, brethren, through our Lord 30
Jesus Christ, and through the charity of the
Spirit, that you help me by your prayers to God
for me, that I may be delivered from the unbe- 31
lievers in Judea, and that the offering of my
service may be acceptable to the saints in Jerusalem; that I may come to you in joy, by the will of 32
God, and may be refreshed with you. Now the 33
God of peace be with you all. Amen.

Commendation of Phoebe

But I commend to you Phœbe, | JULY 31 | 16 1
our sister, who is in the ministry of | Jan. 30 |
the church at Cenchræ, that you may receive her 2
in the Lord as becomes saints, and that you may
assist her in whatever business she may have
need of you. For she too has assisted many,
including myself.

Greetings to Individuals

Greet Prisca and Aquila, my helpers in Christ 3
Jesus, who for my life have risked their own 4
necks. To them not only I give thanks but also
all the churches of the Gentiles. Greet also the 5
church that is in their house. Greet my beloved
Epænetus, who is the first-fruits of Asia to Christ.
Greet Mary who has labored much among you. 6
Greet Andronicus and Junias, my kinsmen and 7
my fellow-prisoners, who are distinguished among
the apostles, who also were in Christ before me.
Greet Ampliatus, beloved to me in the Lord. 8
Greet Urbanus, our helper in Christ, and my 9
beloved Stachys. Greet Apelles, approved in 10

11 Christ. Greet the members of Aristobulus' household. Greet Herodion, my kinsman. Greet the
12 members of Narcissus' household who are in the Lord. Greet Tryphæna and Tryphosa who labor in the Lord. Greet the beloved Persis who
13 has labored much in the Lord. Greet Rufus, the elect in the Lord, and her who is his mother and
14 mine. Greet Asyncritus, Phlegon, Hermas, Patrobas, Hermes, and the brethren who are with
15 them. Greet Philologus and Julia, Nereus and his sister, and Olympias, and all the saints who
16 are with them. Greet one another with a holy kiss. All the churches of Christ greet you.

Warning to Trouble-makers

17 Now I exhort you, brethren, that you watch those who cause dissensions and scandals contrary to the doctrine that you have learned, and
18 avoid them. For such do not serve Christ our Lord but their own belly, and by smooth words
19 and flattery deceive the hearts of the simple. For your submission to the faith has been published everywhere. I rejoice therefore over you. Yet I would have you wise as to what is good, and
20 guileless as to what is evil. But the God of peace will speedily crush Satan under your feet. The grace of our Lord Jesus Christ be with you.

Greetings from Corinth

21 Timothy, my fellow-laborer, greets you, and Lucius, and Jason, and Sosipater, my kinsmen.
22 I, Tertius, who have written this epistle, greet
23 you in the Lord. Gaius, my host, and the host of the whole church, greets you. Erastus, the city treasurer, and Quartus, our brother, greet you.
24 [May the grace of our Lord Jesus Christ be with you all, amen.]

Doxology

Now to him who is able to strengthen you in 25
accordance with my gospel, and the preaching of
Jesus Christ, according to the revelation of the
mystery which has been kept in silence from
eternal ages, which is manifested now through 26
the writings of the prophets according to the
precept of the eternal God, and made known to
all the Gentiles to bring about obedience to faith
— ' to the only wise God, through Jesus Christ, 27
be honor forever and ever. Amen.

THE FIRST EPISTLE
TO THE CORINTHIANS
Introduction

Corinth was a Roman colony built upon the remains of an old Greek city. At the time of the Apostles it was materially prosperous and morally corrupt.

On his second missionary journey, Paul preached about two years in Corinth, first to the Jews in the synagogue and then to the Gentiles in the house of Titus Justus (Acts 18, 1-18). After his disappointment in the use of a philosophical approach to Christianity at Athens (Acts 17, 15ff), Paul used at Corinth a simpler presentation of his doctrine. According to the divine promise (Acts 18, 9f), he made many converts, but suffered much from the hostility of the Jews. He left for Ephesus some time after Gallio became proconsul of Achaia, i. e., about 52 A. D.

It is quite probable that St. Paul wrote an Epistle to the Corinthians prior to the two that we now possess (1 Cor. 5, 9). The Epistle called St. Paul's First to the Corinthians was occasioned by the visit to Ephesus of members of the Corinthian church (1 Cor. 1, 11; 16, 12. 17). St. Paul, who had meanwhile returned to Antioch and undertaken his third missionary journey, learned from these messengers of certain disorders in the church at Corinth. Questions were also proposed by the neophytes to their spiritual father for solution. To correct those disorders and to answer these questions, St. Paul wrote this masterly Epistle.

From 1 Cor. 16, 5-8 it is clear that the letter was written at Ephesus some time before Pentecost, probably in the beginning of the year 57 A. D.

THE FIRST EPISTLE OF ST. PAUL THE APOSTLE TO THE CORINTHIANS

Introduction

Greeting

PAUL, CALLED BY THE WILL OF GOD to be an apostle of Jesus Christ, and Sosthenes our brother, to the church of God at Corinth, to you who have been sanctified in Christ Jesus and called to be saints with all who call upon the name of our Lord Jesus Christ in every place—their Lord as well as ours. Grace be to you and peace from God our Father and the Lord Jesus Christ. ₁ ₂ ₃

| AUG. 1 |
| Jan. 31 |

The Gifts of God

I give thanks to my God always concerning you for the grace of God which was given you in Christ Jesus, because in everything you have been enriched in him, in all utterance and in all knowledge; even as the witness to the Christ has been made so firm in you ' that you lack no grace, while awaiting the appearance of our Lord Jesus Christ, who will also keep you secure unto the end, unimpeachable in the day of the coming of our Lord Jesus Christ. God is trustworthy, by him you have been called into fellowship with his Son, Jesus Christ our Lord.

I: PARTY SPIRIT

Nature of the Division

NOW I BESEECH YOU, brethren, by the name of our Lord Jesus Christ, that you all say the same thing; and that there be no dissensions among you, but that you be perfectly united in one mind and in one judgment. For I have been

informed about you, my brethren, by those of the house of Chloe, that there are strifes among
12 you. Now this is what I mean: each of you says, I am of Paul, or I am of Apollos, or I am of Cephas,
13 or I am of Christ. Has Christ been divided up? Was Paul crucified for you? Or were you bap-
14 tized in the name of Paul? I thank God that I baptized none of you but Crispus and Gaius,
15 ' lest anyone should say that you were baptized
16 in my name. I baptized also the household of Stephanas. I am not aware of having baptized anyone else.

Salvation Not by Wisdom of Words

17 For Christ did not send me to baptize, but to preach the gospel, not with wisdom of words, lest
18 the cross of Christ be made void. For the doctrine of the cross is foolishness to those who perish, but to those who are saved, that is, to us,
19 it is the power of God. For it is written, "I will destroy the wisdom of the wise, and the prudence
20 of the prudent I will reject." Where is the "wise man"? Where is the scribe? Where is the disputant of this world? Has not God turned to fool-
21 ishness the "wisdom" of this world? For since, in God's wisdom, the world did not come to know God by "wisdom," it pleased God, by the foolishness of our preaching, to save those who
22 believe. For the Jews ask for signs, and the
23 Greeks look for "wisdom"; but we, for our part, preach a crucified Christ—to the Jews indeed a stumbling-block and to the Gentiles foolishness,
24 ' but to those who are called, both Jews and Greeks, Christ, the power of God and the wis-

---

1, 17: *Not . . . to baptize:* as his principal office. Like Christ (John 4, 2) and Peter (Acts 10, 48), Paul usually left the baptismal rite to others. *Wisdom of words:* eloquence.

dom of God. For the foolishness of God is wiser 25
than men, and the weakness of God is stronger
than men.

Their Case an Example

For consider your own call, breth- 26
ren; that there were not many wise
according to the flesh, not many mighty, not
many noble. But the foolish things of the world 27
has God chosen to put to shame the "wise,"
and the weak things of the world has God chosen
to put to shame the strong, and the base things 28
of the world and the despised has God chosen,
and the things that are not, to bring to naught
the things that are; lest any flesh should pride 29
itself before him. From him you are in Christ 30
Jesus, who has become for us God-given wisdom, and justice, and sanctification, and redemption; so that, just as it is written, "Let him who 31
takes pride, take pride in the Lord."

AUG. 2
Feb. 1

Paul's Method of Preaching

And I, brethren, when I came to you, did not **2** 1
come with pretentious speech or wisdom, announcing unto you the witness to Christ. For I 2
determined not to know anything among you,
except Jesus Christ and him crucified. And I was 3
with you in weakness and in fear and in much
trembling. And my speech and my preaching 4
were not in the persuasive words of wisdom, but
in the demonstration of the Spirit and of power,
' that your faith might rest, not on the wisdom 5
of men, but on the power of God.

True Wisdom

Wisdom, however, we speak among those 6
who are mature, yet not a wisdom of this world
nor of the rulers of this world, who are passing

7 away. But we speak the wisdom of God, mysterious, hidden, which God foreordained before the
8 world unto our glory, a wisdom which none of the rulers of this world has known; for had they known it, they would never have crucified the
9 Lord of glory. But, as it is written, "Eye has not seen nor ear heard, nor has it entered into the heart of man, what things God has prepared for
10 those who love him." But to us God has revealed them through his Spirit. For the Spirit searches
11 all things, even the deep things of God. For who among men knows the things of a man save the spirit of the man which is in him? Even so, the things of God no one knows but the Spirit of
12 God. Now we have received not the spirit of the world, but the spirit that is from God, that we may know the things that have been given us by
13 God. These things we also speak, not in words taught by human wisdom, but in the learning of
14 the Spirit, combining spiritual with spiritual. But the sensual man does not perceive the things that are of the Spirit of God, for it is foolishness to him and he cannot understand, because it is
15 examined spiritually. But the spiritual man judges all things, and he himself is judged by no
16 man. For "who has known the mind of the Lord, that he might instruct him?" But we have the mind of Christ.

They Cannot Receive Full Doctrine

3 1   And I, brethren, could not speak to you as to spiritual men but only
2 as carnal, as to little ones in Christ. I fed you

AUG. 3
Feb. 2

2, 13: *Combining spiritual with spiritual:* may mean explaining spiritual subjects to spiritual men, or using spiritual instruction for spiritual subjects, or judging spiritual things according to spiritual standards.

3, 2: *Milk:* elementary doctrine. *Solid food:* more advanced teaching.

with milk, not with solid food, for you were not yet ready for it. Nor are you now ready for it, for you are still carnal. For since there are jeal- 3 ousy and strife among you, are you not carnal, and walking as mere men? For whenever one 4 says, "I am of Paul," but another, "I am of Apollos," are you not mere men?

The Office of God's Ministers

What then is Apollos? What indeed is Paul? They are the servants of him whom you have 5 believed — servants according as God has given to each to serve. I have planted, Apollos wa- 6 tered, but God has given the growth. So then 7 neither he who plants is anything, nor he who waters, but God who gives the growth. Now he 8 who plants and he who waters are one, yet each will receive his own reward according to his labor. For we are God's helpers, you are God's 9 tillage, God's building.

Their Responsibility and Reward

According to the grace of God which has been 10 given to me, as a wise builder, I laid the founda- tion, and another builds thereon. But let every- one take care how he builds thereon. For other 11 foundation no one can lay, but that which has been laid, which is Christ Jesus. But if anyone 12 builds upon this foundation, gold, silver, precious stones, wood, hay, straw — ' the work of each 13 will be made manifest, for the day of the Lord will declare it, since the day is to be revealed in fire. The fire will assay the quality of everyone's work: if his work abides which he has built 14 thereon, he will receive reward; if his work burns 15 he will lose his reward, but himself will be saved, yet so as through fire.

3, 8: *Are one: equal fellow-workers in the service of God.*

16 Do you not know that you are the temple of God and that the Spirit of God dwells in you?
17 If anyone destroys the temple of God, him will God destroy; for holy is the temple of God, and this temple you are.

Pride Not to Be Taken in Man

18 Let no one deceive himself. If any one of you thinks himself wise in this world, let him become
19 a fool, that he may come to be wise. For the wisdom of this world is foolishness with God.
20 For it is written, "I will catch the wise in their craftiness." And again, "The Lord knows the thoughts of the wise, that they are empty."
21,22 Therefore let no one take pride in men. For all things are yours, whether Paul, or Apollos, or Cephas; or the world, or life, or death; or things present, or things to come — all are yours,
23 and you are Christ's, and Christ is God's.

Ministers of Gospel Judged by Christ

4 1 Let a man so account us, as servants of Christ and stewards of the

AUG. 4
Feb. 3

2 mysteries of God. Now here it is required in
3 stewards that a man be found trustworthy. But with me it is a very small matter to be judged by you or by man's tribunal. Nay I do not even
4 judge my own self. For I have nothing on my conscience, yet I am not thereby justified; but he
5 who judges me is the Lord. Therefore, pass no

3, 15: *Lose his reward:* he will lose the special reward of preaching but will be saved if his conscience is otherwise clear. The teaching of this verse implies the teaching of Christian tradition on purgatory. If the venial offenses of preachers are punished on the last day, similarly other venial sins will be punished after the particular judgment.

4, 1: *Mysteries:* includes doctrines and rites the excellence of which is God's secret, surpassing human understanding.

judgment before the time, until the Lord comes, who will both bring to light the things hidden in darkness and make manifest the counsels of hearts; and then everyone will have his praise from God.

Corinthians Contrasted with Apostles

Now, brethren, I have applied these things to 6 myself and Apollos by way of illustration for your sakes, that in our case you may learn not to be puffed up one against the other over a third party, transgressing what is written. For who 7 singles thee out? Or what hast thou that thou hast not received? And if thou hast received it, why dost thou boast as if thou hadst not received it?' You are already filled! You are already made 8 rich! Without us you reign! And would that you did reign, that we too might reign with you! For 9 I think God has set forth us the apostles last of all, as men doomed to death, seeing that we have been made a spectacle to the world, and to angels, and to men. We are fools for Christ, but 10 you are wise in Christ! We are weak, but you are strong! You are honored, but we are without honor! To this very hour we hunger and thirst, 11 and we are naked and buffeted, and have no fixed abode. And we toil, working with our own 12 hands. We are reviled and we bless, we are persecuted and we bear with it, we are maligned 13 and we entreat, we have become as the refuse of this world, the offscouring of all, even until now!

I write these things not to put you to shame, 14 but to admonish you as my dearest children. For 15 although you have ten thousand tutors in Christ, yet you have not many fathers. For in Christ

---

4, 15: The tutor, i.e., "pedagogue," the slave, often not much loved, who accompanied the youth to and from his real teacher.

Jesus, through the gospel, did I beget you.
16 Therefore, I beg you, be imitators of me, as I am
17 of Christ. For this very reason I have sent to you Timothy, who is my dearest son and faithful in the Lord. He will remind you of my ways, which are in Christ Jesus, even as I teach everywhere in every church.

18 Now some are puffed up, as if I were not com-
19 ing to you. But I shall come to you shortly, if the Lord is willing, and I shall learn the power of
20 those who are puffed up, not the promises. For the kingdom of God is not in word, but in power.
21 What is your wish? Shall I come to you with a rod, or in love and in the spirit of meekness?

II: MORAL DISORDERS

1. The Incestuous Man

Action to Be Taken

5 1 IT IS ACTUALLY REPORTED that there is immorality among you, and such immorality as is not found even among the Gentiles, that a man should have his father's
2 wife. And you are puffed up, and have not rather mourned so that he who has done this deed
3 might be put away from your midst. I indeed, absent in body but present in spirit, have already,
4 as though present, passed judgment ' in the name of our Lord Jesus Christ on the one who has so acted — you and my spirit gathered to-
5 gether with the power of our Lord Jesus — ' to deliver such a one over to Satan for the destruction of the flesh, that his spirit may be saved in

AUG. 5
Feb. 4

5, 3ff: St. Paul indicates to the Corinthian church the action they should already have taken. *To deliver such a one over to Satan:* implies a) excommunication, b) trials, even physical, without the normal aids of the Church against Satan. *The destruction of the flesh:* the destruction of sinful tendencies.

the day of our Lord Jesus Christ. Your boasting 6
is unseemly. Do you not know that a little leaven
ferments the whole lump? Purge out the old 7
leaven, that you may be a new dough, as you
really are without leaven. For Christ, our passover, has been sacrificed. Therefore let us keep 8
festival, not with the old leaven, nor with the
leaven of malice and wickedness, but with the
unleavened bread of sincerity and truth.

Punishment by Excommunication

I wrote to you in the letter not to associate 9
with the immoral — ' not meaning, of course, 10
the immoral of this world, or the covetous, or
the greedy, or idolators; otherwise you would
have to leave the world. But now I write to you 11
not to associate with one who is called a brother,
if he is immoral, or covetous, or an idolator, or
evil-tongued, or a drunkard, or greedy; with
such a one not even to take food. For what have 12
I to do with judging those outside? Is it not those
inside whom you judge? For those outside God 13
will judge. "Expel the wicked man from your
midst."

2. Lawsuits before Pagans
Public Litigation

DARE ANY OF YOU, having a matter against **6** 1
another, bring your case to be judged before
the unjust and not before the saints? Do you 2
not know that the saints will judge the world?
And if the world will be judged by you, are you
unworthy to judge the smallest matters? Do you 3
not know that we shall judge angels? How much
more worldly things! If, therefore, you have 4

5, 6-8: Fermentation was considered as a kind of corruption. Therefore leaven was removed from Jewish houses
for the observance of the Passover to symbolize removal
of sin, the corruption of the soul.

cases about worldly matters to be judged, appoint
those who are rated as nothing in the Church to
5 judge.' To shame you I say it. Can it be that there
is not one wise man among you competent to
6 settle a case in his brother's matter? But brother
goes to law with brother and that before unbelievers.

7 Nay, to begin with, it is altogether a defect in
you that you have lawsuits one with another.
Why not rather suffer wrong? Why not rather
8 be defrauded? But you yourselves do wrong and
9 defraud, and that to your brethren. Or do you
not know that the unjust will not possess the
kingdom of God? Do not err; neither fornicators,
10 nor idolators, nor adulterers,' nor the effeminate,
nor sodomites, nor thieves, nor the covetous,
nor drunkards, nor the evil-tongued, nor the
11 greedy will possess the kingdom of God. And
such were some of you, but you have been
washed, you have been sanctified, you have
been justified in the name of our Lord Jesus
Christ, and in the Spirit of our God.

3. The Evil of Immorality

Sacredness of the Body

12 ALL THINGS ARE LAWFUL FOR ME,
but not all things are expedient. All

AUG. 6
Feb. 5

things are lawful for me, but I will not be brought
13 under the power of anyone. Food for the belly
and the belly for food, but God will destroy both
the one and the other. Now the body is not for
immorality, but for the Lord, and the Lord for
14 the body. Now God has raised up the Lord and
15 will also raise us up by his power. Do you not
know that your bodies are members of Christ?
Shall I then take the members of Christ and
make them members of a harlot? By no means!

Or do you not know that he who cleaves to a 16 harlot, becomes one body with her? "For the two," it says, "shall be one flesh." But he who 17 cleaves to the Lord is one spirit with him. Flee immorality. Every sin that a man commits 18 is outside the body, but the immoral man sins against his own body. Or do you not know that 19 your members are the temple of the Holy Spirit, who is in you, whom you have from God, and that you are not your own? For you have been 20 bought at a great price. Glorify God and bear him in your body.

III: ANSWERS TO QUESTIONS

1. Marriage and Celibacy

Advice to the Married

NOW CONCERNING THE THINGS whereof you **7** 1 wrote to me: It is good for man not to touch woman. Yet, for fear of fornication, let each 2 man have his own wife, and let each woman have her own husband. Let the husband render 3 to the wife her due, and likewise the wife to the husband. The wife has not authority over her 4 body, but the husband; the husband likewise has not authority over his body, but the wife. Do 5 not deprive each other, except perhaps by consent, for a time, that you may give yourselves to prayer; and return together again lest Satan tempt you because you lack self-control. But 6 this I say by way of concession, not by way of commandment. For I would that you all were 7 as I am myself; but each one has his own gift from God, one in this way, and another in that.

Advice to the Unmarried

8 But I say to the unmarried and to widows, it is good for them if they so | AUG. 7 / Feb. 6 |
9 remain, even as I. But if they do not have self-control, let them marry, for it is better to marry
10 than to burn. But to those who are married, not I, but the Lord commands that a wife is not to
11 depart from her husband, and if she departs, that she is to remain unmarried or be reconciled to her husband. And let not a husband put away his wife.

Obligation of the Believing Spouse

12 To the others I say, not the Lord: If any brother has an unbelieving wife and she consents to live with him, let him not put her away.
13 And if any woman has an unbelieving husband and he consents to live with her, let her not put
14 away her husband. For the unbelieving husband is sanctified by the believing wife, and the unbelieving wife is sanctified by the believing husband; otherwise your children would be un-
15 clean, but, as it is, they are holy. But if the unbeliever departs, let him depart. For a brother or sister is not under bondage in such cases, but
16 God has called us to peace. For how dost thou know, O wife, whether thou wilt save thy husband? Or how dost thou know, O husband, whether thou wilt save thy wife?

No Change to Be Sought

17 Only, as the Lord has allotted to each, as when God has called each, so let him walk —
18 and so I teach in all the churches. Was one

7, 12: *Not the Lord:* not the express teaching of Christ during His earthly life, but a law made by the Apostles on the authority of Christ. It is known as the "Pauline privilege."

called having been circumcised? Let him not become uncircumcised. Was one called being uncircumcised? Let him not be circumcised. Circumcision does not matter, and uncircumcision does not matter; but the keeping of the commandments of God is what matters. Let every man remain in the calling in which he was called. ' Wast thou a slave when called? Let it not trouble thee. But if thou canst become free, make use of it rather. For a slave who has been called in the Lord, is a freedman of the Lord; just as a freeman who has been called is a slave of Christ. You have been bought with a price; do not become the slaves of men. Brethren, in the state in which he was when called, let every man remain with God.

The State of Virginity

Now concerning virgins I have no commandment of the Lord, yet I give an opinion, as one having obtained mercy from the Lord to be trustworthy. I think, then, that this is good on account of the present distress — that it is good for a man to remain as he is. ' Art thou bound to a wife? Do not seek to be freed. Art thou freed from a wife? Do not seek a wife. But if thou takest a wife, thou hast not sinned. And if a virgin marries, she has not sinned. Yet such will have tribulation of the flesh. But I spare you that.

But this I say, brethren, the time is short; it remains that those who have wives be as if they had none; and those who weep, as though not weeping; and those who rejoice, as though not

| AUG. 8 |
| Feb. 7 |

19
20
21
22
23
24
25
26
27
28
29
30

7, 29: *The time is short:* i.e., for meriting in this life before the coming of Christ, whether in the particular or in the general judgment.

rejoicing; and those who buy, as though not
31 possessing; and those who use this world, as
though not using it, for this world as we see it is
32 passing away. I would have you free from care.
He who is unmarried is concerned about the
things of the Lord, how he may please God.
33 Whereas he who is married is concerned about
the things of the world, how he may please his
34 wife; and he is divided. And the unmarried
woman, and the virgin, thinks about the things
of the Lord, that she may be holy in body and
in spirit. Whereas she who is married thinks
about the things of the world, how she may please
35 her husband. Now this I say for your benefit,
not to hold you in check, but to promote what is
proper, and to make it possible for you to pray to
the Lord without distraction.

Duty of Father to Virgin Daughter

36 But if any man thinks that he incurs disgrace
with regard to his virgin, since she is over age,
and that it ought so to be done, let him do what
37 he will; he does not sin if she should marry. But
he who stands firm in his heart, being under no
constraint, but is free to carry out his own will,
and has decided to keep his virgin — he does
38 well. Therefore both he who gives his virgin in
marriage does well, and he who does not give
her does better.

Widows

39 A woman is bound as long as her husband is
alive, but if her husband dies, she is free. Let her
marry whom she pleases, only let it be in the
40 Lord. But she will be more blessed, in my judgment, if she remains as she is. And I think that
I also have the spirit of God.

2. Idol Offerings
General Principles

NOW CONCERNING THINGS sacrificed to idols, **8** 1 we know that we all have knowledge. Knowledge puffs up, but charity edifies. If anyone thinks that 2 he knows anything, he has not yet known as he ought to know. But if anyone loves God, the 3 same is known by him. Now as for food sacrificed 4 to idols, we know that there is no such thing as an idol in the world, and that there is no God but one. For even if there are what are called gods, 5 whether in heaven or on earth (for indeed there are many gods, and many lords), ' yet for us 6 there is only one God, the Father from whom are all things, and we unto him; and one Lord, Jesus Christ, through whom are all things, and we through him.

Practical Rules

But such knowledge is not in everyone. Some, 7 still idol-conscious, eat idol offerings as such, and their conscience, being weak, is defiled. Now 8 food does not commend us to God. For neither shall we suffer any loss if we do not eat, nor if we do eat shall we have any advantage. Still, 9 take care lest perhaps this right of yours become a stumbling-block to the weak. For if a man sees 10 one who "has knowledge" reclining at table in an idol place, will not his conscience, weak as it is, be emboldened to eat idol offerings? And 11 through thy "knowledge" the weak one will perish, the brother for whom Christ died. Now when 12 you sin thus against the brethren, and wound their weak conscience, you sin against Christ. Therefore, if food scandalizes my brother, I will 13 eat flesh no more forever, lest I scandalize my brother.

3. Paul's Rights as an Apostle
His Claim of Rights

9 1   AM I NOT FREE? Am I not an apostle? Have I not seen Jesus our

AUG. 9
Feb. 8

2 Lord? Are not you my work in the Lord? ' And if to others I am not an apostle, yet to you I am.
3 For you are the seal set upon my apostleship in the Lord. My defense against those who question
4 me is this: Have we not a right to eat and to
5 drink? Have we not a right to take about with us a woman, a sister, as do the other apostles, and
6 the brethren of the Lord, and Cephas? Or is it only Barnabas and I who have not the right to do
7 this? What soldier ever serves at his own expense? Who plants a vineyard and does not eat of its fruit? Who feeds the flock, and does not
8 eat of the milk of the flock? Do I speak these things on human authority? Or does not the Law
9 also say these things? For it is written in the Law of Moses, "Thou shalt not muzzle the ox that treads cut the grain." Is it for the oxen that
10 God has care? Or does he say this simply for our sakes? These things were written for us. For he who plows should plow in hope, and he who
11 threshes, in hope of partaking of the fruits. If we have sown for you spiritual things, is it a great
12 matter if we reap from you carnal things? If others share in this right over you, why not we rather? But we have not used this right, but we bear all things, lest we offer hindrance to the
13 gospel of Christ. Do you not know that they who minister in the temple eat what comes from the

---

9, 5: *Woman:* the Greek text has "a sister woman." There is no question of a right to marry. The Apostles had that right, but there is no evidence that many of them used it. Paul here is defending his right to support from the Church, not only for himself, but also for a "sister" who would attend to his needs.

temple, and that they who serve the altar, have their share with the altar? So also the Lord 14 directed that those who preach the gospel should have their living from the gospel.

Reason for Not Using Rights

But I for my part have used none of these 15 rights. Neither do I write these things that so it should be done in my case. For it were better for me to die than that anyone should make void my boast. For even if I preach the gospel, I have 16 therein no ground for boasting, since I am under constraint. For woe to me if I do not preach the gospel! If I do this willingly, I have a reward. 17 But if unwillingly, it is a stewardship that has been entrusted to me. ' What then is my reward? 18 That preaching the gospel, I deliver the gospel without charge, so as not to abuse my right in the gospel.

Paul Is All to All

For, free though I was as to all, unto all I 19 have made myself a slave that I might gain the more converts. And I have become to the Jews a 20 Jew that I might gain the Jews; to those under 21 the Law, as one under the Law (though not myself under the Law), that I might gain those under the Law; to those without the Law, as one without the Law (though I am not without the law of God, but am under the law of Christ), that I might gain those without the Law. To the weak 22 I became weak, that I might gain the weak. I became all things to all men, that I might save all. I do all things for the sake of the gospel, that 23 I may be made partaker thereof.

He Makes Sure His Reward

Do you not know that those who run in a race, 24 all indeed run, but one receives the prize? So

25 run as to obtain it. And everyone in a contest abstains from all things — and they indeed to receive a perishable crown, but we an imperish-
26 able. I, therefore, so run as not without a purpose;
27 I so fight as not beating the air; but I chastise my body and bring it into subjection, lest perhaps after preaching to others I myself should be rejected.

4. Against Overconfidence

Warning from Old Testament

10 1   FOR I WOULD NOT have you ignorant, brethren, that our fathers

AUG. 10
Feb. 9

were all under the cloud, and all passed through
2 the sea, and all were baptized in Moses, in the
3 cloud and in the sea. And all ate the same spiritu-
4 al food, and all drank the same spiritual drink (for they drank from the spiritual rock which
5 followed them, and the rock was Christ). Yet with most of them God was not well pleased, for "they were laid low in the desert."

6   Now these things came to pass as examples to us, that we should not lust after evil things
7 even as they lusted. And do not become idolaters, even as some of them were, as it is written, "The people sat down to eat and drink, and rose
8 up to play." Neither let us commit fornication, even as some of them committed fornication, and there fell in one day twenty-three thousand.
9 Neither let us tempt Christ, as some of them
10 tempted, and perished by the serpents. Neither murmur, as some of them murmured, and per-

---

10, 3f: *Spiritual food, spiritual drink:* so called because of the miraculous nature of the manna and the water from the rock. *Spiritual rock . . .* Christ, pre-existing as God, protected the Jews, and produced this food and drink, which were types of sacraments that He would later institute.

ished at the hands of the destroyer. Now all 11
these things happened to them as a type, and
they were written for our correction, upon whom
the final age of the world has come.

Application

Therefore let him who thinks he stands take 12
heed lest he fall. May no temptation take hold 13
of you but such as man is equal to. God is
faithful and will not permit you to be tempted
beyond your strength, but with the temptation
will also give you a way out that you may be
able to bear it.

5. Discussion of Idol Offerings Resumed

The Table of the Lord

THEREFORE, BELOVED, flee from the worship 14
of idols. I am speaking as to men of sense; judge 15
for yourselves what I say. The cup of blessing 16
that we bless, is it not the sharing of the blood of
Christ? And the bread that we break, is it not
the partaking of the body of the Lord? Because 17
the bread is one, we though many, are one body,
all of us who partake of the one bread. Behold 18
Israel according to the flesh, are not they who
eat of the sacrifices partakers of the altar? What 19
then do I say? That what is sacrificed to idols is
anything, or that an idol is anything? No; but I 20
say that what the Gentiles sacrifice, "they sacrifice to devils and not to God"; and I would not
have you become associates of devils. You can- 21
not drink the cup of the Lord and the cup of
devils; you cannot be partakers of the table of
the Lord and of the table of devils. Or are we 22
provoking the Lord to jealousy? Are we stronger
than he?

Practical Directions

All things are lawful, but not all things are
23 expedient. All things are lawful, but not all
24 things edify. Let no one seek his own interests,
25 but those of his neighbor. Anything that is sold
in the market, eat, asking no question for con-
26 science' sake. "The earth is the Lord's, and the
27 fullness thereof." If one of the unbelievers in-
vites you, and you wish to go, eat whatever is
set before you, and ask no question for con-
28 science' sake. But if someone says, "This has
been sacrificed to idols," do not eat of it, for
the sake of him who told you and for conscience'
29 sake — ' I mean the other's conscience, not
thine. For why should my liberty be called to
30 judgment by another's conscience? If I partake
with thanksgiving, why am I ill spoken of for
that for which I give thanks?

Give No Offense

31 Therefore, whether you eat or drink, or do
32 anything else, do all for the glory of God. Do
not be a stumbling-block to Jews and Greeks
33 and to the church of God, even as I myself in
all things please all men, not seeking what is
profitable to myself but to the many, that they
11 1 may be saved. Be imitators of me as I am of
Christ.

IV. RELIGIOUS GATHERINGS

1. The Headdress of Women

Rules for Men and Women

2 NOW I PRAISE YOU, brethren, because in all things you are mindful
of me and hold fast my precepts as I gave them
3 to you. But I would have you know that the head

AUG. 11
Feb. 10

of every man is Christ, and the head of the woman is the man, and the head of Christ is God. Every man praying or prophesying with his head 4 covered, disgraces his head. But every woman 5 praying or prophesying with her head uncovered disgraces her head, for it is the same as if she were shaven. For if a woman is not covered, let 6 her be shaven. But if it is a disgrace for a woman to have her hair cut off or her head shaved, let her cover her head. A man indeed 7 ought not to cover his head, because he is the image and glory of God. But woman is the glory of man. For man is not from woman, but woman 8 from man. For man was not created for woman, 9 but woman for man. This is why the woman 10 ought to have a sign of authority over her head, because of the angels.

Yet neither is man independent of woman, 11 nor woman independent of man in the Lord. For as the woman is from the man, so also is 12 the man through the woman, but all things are from God. Judge for yourselves: does it become 13 a woman to pray to God uncovered? Does not 14 nature itself teach you that for a man to wear his hair long is degrading; but for a woman to 15 wear her hair long is a glory to her? Because her hair has been given her as a covering. But if 16 anyone is disposed to be contentious — we have no such custom, neither have the churches of God.

11, 3-10: Christian teaching raised the position of women. There was naturally a tendency to push equality with men beyond due limits. Paul is opposing this in a practical way.

11, 10: *Because of the angels:* who assist at the divine service and are interested in having all done properly.

2. The Eucharist

An Abuse

17   BUT IN GIVING THIS CHARGE, I do not commend you in that you
18 meet not for the better but for the worse. For first of all I hear that when you meet in church there are divisions among you, and in part I
19 believe it. For there must be factions, so that those who are approved may be made manifest
20 among you. So then when you meet together, it is no longer possible to eat the Lord's Supper.
21 For at the meal, each one takes first his own supper, and one is hungry, and another drinks
22 overmuch. Have you not houses for your eating and drinking? Or do you despise the church of God and put to shame the needy? What am I to say to you? Am I to commend you? In this I do not commend you.

Institution of the Eucharist

23   For I myself have received from the Lord (what I also delivered to you), that the Lord Jesus, on the night in which he was betrayed,
24 took bread, ' and giving thanks broke, and said, "This is my body which shall be given up for
25 you; do this in remembrance of me." In like manner also the cup, after he had supped, saying, "This cup is the new covenant in my blood; do this as often as you drink it, in remembrance

---

11, 19: *Must be factions:* considering man's pride and obstinacy there must be factions, but from this evil arises good in that the true and genuine Christians are made manifest.

11, 20-22: Among the early Christians, in imitation of the Last Supper, a slight meal, the Agape or love-feast, preceded the Eucharistic service. Paul reprobates the abuses of this supper. Possibly, abuses of this kind motivated the Church in prescribing the Eucharist fast.

11, 25: *The new covenant:* Sacrificial blood sealed the old covenant; cf. Ex. 24, 8. This is the sacrificial blood that makes effective the new order established by God.

of me. For as often as you shall eat this bread 26 and drink the cup, you proclaim the death of the Lord, until he comes." Therefore whoever 27 eats this bread or drinks the cup of the Lord unworthily, will be guilty of the body and the blood of the Lord. But let a man prove himself, 28 and so let him eat of that bread and drink of the cup; for he who eats and drinks unworthily, 29 without distinguishing the body, eats and drinks judgment to himself. This is why many among 30 you are infirm and weak, and many sleep. But 31 if we judged ourselves, we should not thus be judged. But when we are judged, we are being 32 chastised by the Lord that we may not be condemned with this world. Wherefore, my brethren, when you come together to eat, wait for 33 one another. If anyone is hungry, let him eat at 34 home, lest you come together unto judgment. The rest I shall set in order when I come.

V: THE SPIRITUAL GIFTS

1. Their Distribution

A Principle of Discrimination

NOW CONCERNING SPIRITUAL GIFTS, brethren, I would not have you ignorant. I would that when you were 2 Gentiles, you went to dumb idols according as you were led. Wherefore I give you to understand that no one speaking in the Spirit of God 3 says "Anathema" to Jesus. And no one can say "Jesus is Lord," except in the Holy Spirit.

12 1

AUG. 13
Feb. 12

Now there are varieties of gifts, but the same 4 Spirit; and there are varieties of ministries, but 5 the same Lord; and there are varieties of workings, but the same God, who works all things in 6 all. Now the manifestation of the Spirit is given 7 to everyone for profit. To one through the Spirit 8

is given the utterance of wisdom; and to another the utterance of knowledge, according to the
9 same Spirit; to another faith, in the same Spirit; to another the gift of healing, in the one Spirit;
10 ' to another the working of miracles; to another prophecy; to another the distinguishing of spirits; to another various kinds of tongues; to another
11 interpretation of tongues. But all these things are the work of one and the same Spirit, who allots to everyone according as he will.

12 For as the body is one and has many members, and all the members of the body, many as they are, form one body, so also is it with Christ.

13 For in one Spirit we were all baptized into one body, whether Jews or Gentiles, whether slaves or free; and we were all given to drink of one
14 Spirit. For the body is not one member, but
15 many. If the foot says, "Because I am not a hand, I am not of the body," is it therefore not of the
16 body? And if the ear says, "Because I am not an eye, I am not of the body," is it therefore not of the body?

17 If the whole body were an eye, where would be the hearing? If the whole body were hearing,
18 where would be the smelling? But as it is, God has set the members, each of them, in the body
19 as he willed. Now if they were all one member,
20 where would the body be? But as it is, there are indeed many members, yet but one body.
21 And the eye cannot say to the hand, "I do not need thy help"; nor again the head to the feet,
22 "I have no need of you." Nay, much rather, those that seem the more feeble members of
23 the body are more necessary; and those that we think the less honorable members of the body, we surround with more abundant honor, and our uncomely parts receive a more abundant
24 comeliness, whereas our comely parts have no

need of it. But God has so tempered the body together in due portion as to give more abundant honor where it was lacking; that there may be 25 no disunion in the body, but that the members may have care for one another. And if one 26 member suffers anything, all the members suffer with it, or if one member glories, all the members rejoice with it.

Christ's Mystical Body

Now you are the body of Christ, member for 27 member. And God indeed has placed some in 28 the Church, first apostles, secondly prophets, thirdly teachers; after that miracles, then gifts of healing, services of help, power of administration, and the speaking of various tongues. ' Are all apostles? Are all prophets? Are all 29 teachers? ' Are all workers of miracles? Do all 30 have the gift of healing? Do all speak with tongues? Do all interpret? ' Yet strive after the 31 greater gifts.

2. A Digression on Charity

Its Excellence

AND I POINT OUT TO YOU a yet more excellent way. If I should | AUG. 14 | **13** 1 | Feb. 13 | speak with the tongues of men and of angels, but do not have charity, I have become as sounding brass or a tinkling cymbal. And if I 2 have prophecy and know all mysteries and all knowledge, and if I have all faith so as to remove mountains, yet do not have charity, I am nothing. And if I distribute all my goods to 3

12, 31: *Greater gifts:* greater than those just described is charity, which follows.

13, 1: *Charity:* here is meant the supernatural virtue comprising love of God above all things and love of neighbor for God.

feed the poor, and if I deliver my body to be burned, yet do not have charity, it profits me nothing.

4 Charity is patient, is kind; charity does not
5 envy, is not pretentious, is not puffed up, ' is not ambitious, is not self-seeking, is not provoked;
6 thinks no evil,' does not rejoice over wickedness,
7 but rejoices with the truth; bears with all things, believes all things, hopes all things, endures all things.

Contrast with Other Gifts

8 Charity never fails, whereas prophecies will disappear, and tongues will cease, and knowl-
9 edge will be destroyed. For we know in part
10 and we prophesy in part; but when that which is perfect has come, that which is imperfect will
11 be done away with. When I was a child, I spoke as a child, I felt as a child, I thought as a child. Now that I have become a man, I have put away
12 the things of a child. We see now through a mirror in an obscure manner, but then face to face. Now I know in part, but then I shall know
13 even as I have been known. So there abide faith, hope and charity, these three; but the greatest of these is charity.

3. The Gifts of Tongues and Prophecy

Superiority of Prophecy

14 1 AIM AT CHARITY, yet strive after the spiritual gifts, but especially that
2 you may prophesy. For he who speaks in a tongue does not speak to men but to God; for no one

AUG. 15
Feb. 14

14, 1: In the early church "Prophecy" was the gift of speaking extemporaneously under special inspiration of God.

14, 2: The gift of tongues in the early church was the gift of speaking new languages without previous instruction.

understands, as he is speaking mysteries in his spirit. But he who prophesies speaks to men for edification, and encouragement, and consolation. He who speaks in a tongue edifies himself, but he who prophesies edifies the church. Now I should like you all to speak in tongues, but still more to prophesy; for he who prophesies is greater than he who speaks in tongues, unless he can interpret so that the church may receive edification.

Tongues Require Interpretation

But now, brethren, if I come to you speaking in tongues what shall I profit you, unless I speak to you either in revelation, or in knowledge, or in prophecy, or in teaching? Even inanimate instruments, like the flute or the harp, may produce sound, but if there is no difference in the notes, how shall it be known what is piped or harped? If the trumpet give forth an uncertain sound, who will prepare for battle? So likewise you — unless with the tongue you utter intelligible speech — how shall it be known what is said? For you will be speaking to the empty air. There are, for example, so many kinds of languages in this world and none without a meaning. If, then, I do not know the meaning of the language, I shall be to the one to whom I speak, a foreigner; and he who speaks, a foreigner to me. So also you, since you strive after spiritual gifts, seek to have them abundantly for the edification of the church.

Therefore let him who speaks in a tongue pray that he may interpret. For if I pray in a tongue, my spirit prays, but my understanding is unfruitful.' What, then, is to be done? I will pray with the spirit, but I will pray with the understanding also; I will sing with the spirit, but I

16 will sing with the understanding also. Else if
thou givest praise with the spirit alone, how shall
he who fills the place of the uninstructed say
"Amen" to thy thanksgiving? For he does not
17 know what thou sayest. For thou, indeed, givest
18 thanks well, but the other is not edified. I thank
19 God that I speak with all your tongues; yet in
the church, I had rather speak five words with
my understanding, that I may also instruct
others, than ten thousand words in a tongue.

Functions of These Gifts

20 Brethren, do not become children | AUG. 16
in mind, but in malice be children | Feb. 15
21 and in mind mature. In the Law it is written
that "In other tongues and with other lips I will
speak to this people, and not even so will they
22 listen to me, says the Lord." Wherefore tongues
are intended as a sign, not to believers, but to
unbelievers; whereas prophecies, not to unbe-
23 lievers, but to believers. Therefore, if the whole
church be assembled together and, while all are
speaking with tongues, there should come in
uninstructed persons or unbelievers, will they
24 not say that you are mad? Whereas if, while all
are prophesying, there should come in an unbeliever or uninstructed person, he is convicted
25 by all, he is put on trial by all; the secrets of his
heart are made manifest, and so, falling on his
face, he will worship God, declaring that God is
truly among you.

Practical Directions

26 What then is to be done, brethren? When you
come together each of you has a hymn, has an
instruction, has a revelation, has a tongue, has
an interpretation. Let all things be done unto
27 edification. If anyone speaks in a tongue, let it

be by twos or at most by threes, and let them
speak in turn, and let one interpret. But if there   28
is no interpreter let him keep silence in the
church, and speak to himself and to God. Of the   29
prophets, let two or three speak at a meeting,
and let the rest act as judges. But if anything is   30
revealed to another sitting by, let the first keep
silence. For you all can prophesy one by one, so   31
that all may learn and all may be encouraged.
For the spirits of the prophets are under the   32
control of the prophets. For God is a God of   33
peace, not of disorder.

Order Necessary

Thus I likewise teach in all the churches of
the saints. Let women keep silence in the   34
churches, for it is not permitted them to speak,
but let them be submissive, as the Law also
says. But if they wish to learn anything let them   35
ask their husbands at home, for it is unseemly
for a woman to speak in church.

What, was it from you that the word of God   36
went forth? Or was it unto you only that it
reached? If anyone thinks that he is a prophet   37
or spiritual, let him recognize that the things I
am writing to you are the Lord's commandments. If anyone ignores this, he shall be   38
ignored. So then, brethren, desire earnestly the   39
gift of prophesying and do not hinder the gift of
speaking in tongues. Only let all things be done   40
properly and in order.

VI: THE RESURRECTION

Christ's Resurrection

NOW I RECALL TO YOUR MINDS,
brethren, the gospel that I preached
to you, which also you received, wherein also

| AUG. 17 | **15** 1 |
| Feb. 16 | |

2 you stand, through which also you are being saved, if you hold it fast, as I preached it to you
3 — unless you have believed to no purpose. For I delivered to you first of all, what I also received, that Christ died for our sins according
4 to the Scriptures,¹ and that he was buried, and that he rose again the third day, according to
5 the Scriptures, and that he appeared to Cephas,
6 and after that to the Eleven. Then he was seen by more than five hundred brethren at one time, many of whom are with us still, but some have
7 fallen asleep. After that he was seen by James,
8 then by all the apostles. And last of all, as by one born out of due time, he was seen also by
9 me. For I am the least of the apostles, and am not worthy to be called an apostle, because I
10 persecuted the Church of God. But by the grace of God I am what I am, and his grace in me has not been fruitless — in fact I have labored more than any of them, yet not I, but the grace of
11 God with me. Whether it is I or they, so we preach, and so you have believed.

The False Doctrine

12   Now if Christ is preached as risen from the dead, how do some among you say that there is
13 no resurrection of the dead? But if there is no resurrection of the dead, neither has Christ
14 risen; and if Christ has not risen, vain then is
15 our preaching, vain too is your faith. Yes, and we are found false witnesses as to God, in that we have borne witness against God that he raised Christ — whom he did not raise, if the dead do
16 not rise. For if the dead do not rise, neither has
17 Christ risen; and if Christ has not risen, vain is
18 your faith, for you are still in your sins. Hence they also who have fallen asleep in Christ, have
19 perished. If with this life only in view we have

had hope in Christ, we are of all men the most
to be pitied.

Christ the First-fruits

But as it is, Christ has risen from | AUG. 18 | 20
the dead, the first-fruits of those | Feb. 17 |
who have fallen asleep. For since by a man came 21
death, by a man also comes resurrection of the
dead.

For as in Adam all die, so in Christ all will 22
be made to live. But each in his own turn, Christ 23
as first-fruits, then they who are Christ's, who
have believed, at his coming. Then comes the 24
end, when he delivers the kingdom to God the
Father, when he does away with all sovereignty,
authority and power. For he must reign, until 25
"he has put all his enemies under his feet." And 26
the last enemy to be destroyed will be death, for
"he has put all things under his feet." But when
he says ' all things are subject to him, undoubt- 27
edly he is excepted who has subjected all things
to him. And when all things are made subject 28
to him, then the Son himself will also be made
subject to him who subjected all things to him,
that God may be all in all.

Practical Faith

Else what shall they do who receive Baptism 29
for the dead? If the dead do not rise at all, why
then do people receive Baptism for them? And 30
we, why do we stand in jeopardy every hour?
I die daily, I affirm it, by the very pride that I 31

15, 29: From this it seems that the Christians were accustomed to receive Baptism externally as substitutes for
the catechumens who had received it only in desire. It
did not have sacramental effect, but was tolerated as
being the performance of an act the catechumens desired
but could not themselves receive. It showed a belief in
the Resurrection.

take in you, brethren, in Christ Jesus our Lord.
32 If, as men do, I fought with beasts at Ephesus, what does it profit me? If the dead do not rise, "let us eat and drink for tomorrow we shall die."
33 Do not be led astray, "evil companionships corrupt
34 good morals." Awake as you should, and do not sin; for some have no knowledge of God. To your shame I say so.

The Mode of the Resurrection

35 But someone will say, "How do the dead rise? Or with what kind of
36 body do they come?" Senseless man, what thou thyself sowest is not brought to life, unless it
37 dies. And when thou sowest, thou dost not sow the body that shall be, but a bare grain, perhaps
38 of wheat or something else. But God gives it a body even as he has willed, and to each of the
39 seeds a body of its own. All flesh is not the same flesh, but there is one flesh of men, another of
40 beasts, another of birds, another of fishes. There are also heavenly bodies and earthly bodies, but of one kind is the glory of the heavenly, of
41 another kind the glory of the earthly. There is one glory of the sun, and another glory of the moon, and another of the stars; for star differs
42 from star in glory. So also it is with the resurrection of the dead. What is sown in corruption rises in
43 incorruption; what is sown in dishonor rises in glory; what is sown in weakness rises in power;
44 what is sown a natural body rises a spiritual body.

> AUG. 19
> Feb. 18

The Natural and the Spiritual Body

If there is a natural body, there is also a
45 spiritual body. So also it is written, [1] "The first man, Adam, became a living soul"; the last

Adam became a life-giving spirit. But it is not 46
the spiritual that comes first, but the physical,
and then the spiritual. The first man was of the 47
earth, earthy; the second man is from heaven,
heavenly. As was the earthy man, such also are 48
the earthy; and as is the heavenly man, such
also are the heavenly. Therefore, even as we 49
have borne the likeness of the earthy, let us
bear also the likeness of the heavenly.

Final Glory of the Body

Now this I say, brethren, that flesh and blood 50
can obtain no part in the kingdom of God, neither
shall corruption have any part in incorruption.
Behold, I tell you a mystery: we shall all indeed 51
rise, but we shall not all be changed — ' in a 52
moment, in the twinkling of an eye, at the last
trumpet. For the trumpet shall sound, and the
dead shall rise incorruptible and we shall be
changed. For this corruptible body must put on 53
incorruption, and this mortal body must put on
immortality. But when this mortal body puts on 54
immortality, then shall come to pass the word
that is written, "Death is swallowed up in victory!' O death, where is thy victory? O death, 55
where is thy sting?"

Now the sting of death is sin, and the power 56
of sin is the Law. But thanks be to God who has 57
given us the victory through our Lord Jesus Christ.

Therefore, my beloved brethren, be steadfast 58
and immovable, always abounding in the work
of the Lord, knowing that your labor is not in
vain in the Lord.

15, 51: The reading of most of the Greek MSS is to be
preferred: "We shall not all sleep (die), but we shall all
be changed." The meaning would then be that while
those who are living at the last day will not die, they must
undergo the change spoken of in the previous verses,
from the natural body to the spiritual body.

Conclusion

The Collection

16 1   NOW CONCERNING THE COLLEC- | AUG. 20 |
TION being made for the saints, as | Feb. 19 |
I have ordered the churches of Galatia, do you
2 also. On the first day of the week, let each one
of you put aside at home and lay up whatever
he has a mind to, so that the collections may
3 not have to be made after I have come. But
when I am with you, whomever you may author-
ize by giving credentials, them I will send to
4 carry your gift to Jerusalem. And if it is important
enough for me also to go, they shall go with me.

St. Paul's Plans

5   But I shall come to you after passing through
Macedonia (for I mean to pass through Mace-
6 donia); but with you I shall perhaps remain or
7 even winter, so that you may speed me wherever
I may be going. For I do not wish to see you just
8 now in passing by, for I hope to stay some time
with you, if the Lord permits. But I shall stay
9 on at Ephesus until Pentecost. For a door has
been opened to me, great and evident, and there
are many adversaries.

10   Now if Timothy comes, see that he be with
you without fear, for he works the work of the
11 Lord just as I do. Therefore, let no one despise
him, but speed him on his way in peace that he
may come to me, for I am awaiting him with
the brethren.

12   With regard to our brother Apollos, I earnestly
besought him to come to you with the brethren,
and he was quite unwilling to come at present;
but he will come when he has leisure.

Final Directions and Greetings

Watch, stand fast in the faith, act like men, 13
be strong. Let all that you do be done in charity. 14
Now I beseech you, brethren — you know that 15
the household of Stephanas and of Fortunatus
are the first-fruits of Achaia, and have devoted
themselves to the service of the saints — to such 16
as these do you also be subject, and to every
helper and worker. I rejoice at the presence of 17
Stephanas and Fortunatus and Achaicus, because what was lacking on your part they have
supplied; for they have refreshed both my spirit 18
and yours. To such as these, therefore, give
recognition.

The churches of Asia greet you. Aquila and 19
Priscilla with the church at their house greet
you heartily in the Lord. All the brethren greet 20
you. Greet one another with a holy kiss.

I Paul greet you, with my own hand. If any 21, 22
man does not love the Lord Jesus Christ, let him
be anathema. Maranatha. The grace of our 23
Lord Jesus be with you. My love is with you 24
all in Christ Jesus. Amen.

THE SECOND EPISTLE
TO THE CORINTHIANS

Introduction

St. Paul wrote this second canonical Epistle to the Christians of Corinth from Macedonia towards the close of his third missionary journey, and therefore very probably around the year 57 of our era. The Apostle had lately come from Ephesus, where he had spent over two years, and was on his way to Corinth. He had previously sent Titus to Corinth to visit the new community and to ascertain the effect on the faithful there of a severe letter which he had been obliged to write them some time before.

Paul and Titus had first arranged to meet at Troas, a Mysian seaport on the eastern shore of the Aegean Sea; but St. Paul arrived there ahead of schedule, and being anxious for news from Corinth, went across the sea to Philippi in Macedonia, and it was probably there that he met his envoy.

The report given by Titus of the effect on the Corinthians of St. Paul's letter from Ephesus occasioned this Epistle, in which the Apostle defends his life and ministry, urges that the collection—already requested and begun—be made for the poor Christians in Jerusalem, and replies to his bitter opponents. The Epistle ranks with those to Timothy and the Galatians as the most intensely personal of St. Paul's writings. But unlike the letters to Timothy, which are calmly pastoral and directive, this Epistle is vehement and hotly polemical, especially in the four closing chapters. The writer will have his critics and adversaries understand that he is a true apostle of Jesus Christ, and that his sincerity and authority have been amply attested by extraordinary visitations from heaven and by unparalleled labors and sufferings in behalf of the Gospel.

THE SECOND EPISTLE OF ST. PAUL THE APOSTLE TO THE CORINTHIANS

Introduction

Greeting

PAUL, AN APOSTLE OF JESUS | AUG. 21 | **1** 1
CHRIST by the will of God, and | Feb. 20 |
Timothy our brother, to the church of God that
is at Corinth, with all the saints that are in the
whole of Achaia: grace be to you and peace from   2
God our Father and from the Lord Jesus Christ.

Comfort in Trouble

Blessed be the God and Father of our Lord   3
Jesus Christ, the Father of mercies and the God
of all comfort, who comforts us in all our afflic-   4
tions, that we also may be able to comfort those
who are in any distress by the comfort wherewith we ourselves are comforted by God. For   5
as the sufferings of Christ abound in us, so also
through Christ does our comfort abound. For   6
whether we are afflicted, it is for your instruction
and salvation; or whether we are comforted, it
is for your comfort; which shows its efficacy in
the endurance of the selfsame sufferings that
we also suffer. And our hope for you is steadfast,   7
knowing that as you are partakers of the sufferings, so will you also be of the comfort.

Persecution and Deliverance

For we would not, brethren, have you ignorant   8
of the affliction which came upon us in Asia.
We were crushed beyond measure — beyond
our strength, so that we were weary even of
life. Yes, we have been carrying, within our   9

1, 9: *Death sentence:* the Apostle had passed through a
serious illness.

very selves, our death sentence; in order that
we may not trust in ourselves, but in God who
10 raises the dead. He it is who delivered us, and
will deliver us, from such great perils; and in
him we have hope to be delivered yet again,
11 through the help of your prayers for us. Thus,
for the gift bestowed on us at the instance of
many persons, thanks will be given by many on
our behalf.

His Sincerity

12 For our boast is this, the testimony of our
conscience that in simplicity and godly sincerity
— not in carnal wisdom, but in the grace of
God — we conducted ourselves in the
world, and especially in our relations with you.
13 For we write nothing to you that you do not read
and understand. Indeed, I hope you will always
14 understand, even as you have understood us in
part, that we are your boast, as you will also be
ours, in the day of our Lord Jesus Christ.

I: PERSONAL DEFENSE

1. The Apostle Explains His Delay

He Is Not Fickle

15 WITH THIS ASSURANCE I meant, in order that
you might enjoy a double grace, to visit you
16 first, and to pass through you into Macedonia,
and from Macedonia to come again to you, and
by you to be sent forward on my way to Judea.
17 Now in this my intention, did I show fickleness?
Or are my plans made according to the flesh,
so that with me it is now "Yes" and now "No?"
18 God is my witness that our message to you is
19 not both "Yes" and "No." For the Son of God,
Jesus Christ, who was preached among you by
us — by me and Silvanus and Timothy — was

[470]

not now "Yes" and now "No," but only "Yes"
was in him. For all the promises of God find 20
their "Yes" in him; and therefore through him
also rises the "Amen" to God unto our glory.
Now it is God who is warrant for us and for you 21
in Christ, who has anointed us, ' who has also 22
stamped us with his seal and has given us the
Spirit as a pledge in our hearts.

His Wish to Spare Them

Now I call God to witness against | AUG. 22 | 23
my soul that it was to spare you that | Feb. 21 |
I did not again come to Corinth. Not that we lord
it over your faith, but rather we are fellow-
workers in your joy; for in faith you stand.

But I made up my mind not to come to you **2** 1
again in sorrow. For if I make you sad, who can 2
gladden me, save the very one that is grieved
by me? And I wrote to you as I did, that when I 3
come I may not have sorrow upon sorrow from
those who ought to give me joy; for I trust in you
all that my joy is the joy of you all. For I wrote 4
to you in much affliction and anguish of heart,
with many tears, not that you might be grieved,
but that you might know the great love I have
for you.

He Pardons the Offender

Now if anyone has caused grief, he has not 5
grieved me, but in a measure (not to be too
severe) all of you. For such a one this punish- 6
ment meted out by the many is sufficient. On 7
the contrary, then, you should rather forgive
and comfort him, lest perchance he be over-
whelmed by too much sorrow. Therefore I exhort 8
you to assure him of your love for him. For to 9
this very end also did I write, that I might test
you and know whether you are obedient in all

10 things. Whom you pardon anything, I also pardon. Indeed, what I have forgiven — if I have forgiven anything — I have done for your sakes,
11 in the person of Christ, that we may not be defeated by Satan; for we are not unaware of his devices.

Thanksgiving for Good News

12 Now when I came to Troas to preach the gospel of Christ, though I had there a great
13 opportunity in the Lord, I had no peace of mind, because I did not find Titus my brother. And so, bidding them farewell, I went on to Macedonia.
14 But thanks be to God who always leads us in triumph in Christ Jesus, manifesting through us
15 the odor of his knowledge in every place. For we are the fragrance of Christ for God, alike as regards those who are saved and those who are
16 lost; to these an odor that leads to death, but to those an odor that leads to life. And for such
17 offices, who is sufficient? We, at least, are not, as many others, adulterating the word of God; but with sincerity, as coming from God, we preach in Christ in God's presence.

2. The Apostle Defends His Assurance

They Are His Commendation

3 1 ARE WE BEGINNING AGAIN to commend ourselves? Or do we | AUG. 23 Feb. 22 |
need, as some do, letters of commendation to
2 you or from you? You are our letter, written on our hearts, which is known and read by all men;
3 clearly you are a letter of Christ, composed by us, written not with ink but with the Spirit of the living God, not on tablets of stone but on fleshly tablets of the heart.

Excellence of the New Law

Such is the assurance I have through Christ 4
towards God. Not that we are sufficient of our- 5
selves to think anything, as from ourselves, but
our sufficiency is from God. He also it is who 6
has made us fit ministers of the new covenant,
not of the letter but of the spirit; for the letter
kills, but the spirit gives life.

Now if the ministration of death, which was 7
engraved in letters upon stones, was inaugurated
in such glory that the children of Israel could not
look steadfastly upon the face of Moses on account of the transient glory that shone upon it,
shall not the ministration of the spirit be still 8
more glorious? For if there is glory in the mini- 9
stration that condemned, much more does the
ministration that justifies abound in glory. For 10
though the former ministration was glorified, yet
in this regard it is without glory, because of the
surpassing glory of the latter. For if that which 11
was transient was glorious, much more is that
glorious which abides.

The Veil Is Taken Away

Having therefore such hope, we show great 12
boldness. We do not act as Moses did, who used 13
to put a veil over his face that the Israelites
might not observe the glory of his countenance,
which was to pass away. But their minds were 14
darkened; for to this day, when the Old Testament is read to them, the selfsame veil remains,
not being lifted to disclose the Christ in whom

3, 7: *Ministration of death:* the Mosaic Law, which
had no power, apart from faith and grace, to save from
spiritual death.

3, 8: *Ministration of the spirit:* the New Law, the gospel.

3, 12: *Such hope:* of one day enjoying the fullness of the
glory spoken of in v. 8.

15 it is made void. Yes, down to this very day, when Moses is read, the veil covers their hearts;
16 but when they turn in repentance to God, the
17 veil shall be taken away. Now the Lord is the spirit; and where the Spirit of the Lord is, there
18 is freedom. But we all, with faces unveiled, reflecting as in a mirror the glory of the Lord, are being transformed into his very image from glory to glory, as through the Spirit of the Lord.

4 1   Discharging therefore this ministry in accordance with the mercy

AUG. 24
Feb. 23

2 shown us, we do not lose heart. On the contrary, we renounce those practices which shame conceals, we avoid unscrupulous conduct, we do not corrupt the word of God; but making known the truth, we commend ourselves to every man's
3 conscience in the sight of God. And if our gospel also is veiled, it is veiled only to those who are
4 perishing. In their case, the god of this world has blinded their unbelieving minds, that they should not see the light of the gospel of the glory
5 of Christ, who is the image of God. For we preach not ourselves, but Jesus Christ as Lord, and ourselves merely as your servants in Jesus.
6 For God, who commanded light to shine out of darkness, has shone in our hearts, to give enlightenment concerning the knowledge of the glory of God, shining on the face of Christ Jesus.

Frailty and Support

7   But we carry this treasure in vessels of clay, to show that the abundance of the power is
8 God's and not ours. In all things we suffer tribulation, but we are not distressed; we are

4, 4: *The image of God:* Christ is the image of God, (a) as having the same nature as the Father; (b) as being the Son of the Father; (c) as being equal to the Father (St. Thomas).

sore pressed, but we are not destitute; we en- 9
dure persecution, but we are not forsaken; we
are cast down, but we do not perish; always 10
bearing about in our body the dying of Jesus,
so that the life also of Jesus may be made manifest in our bodily frame. For we the living are 11
constantly being handed over to death for Jesus'
sake, that the life also of Jesus may be made
manifest in our mortal flesh. Thus death is at 12
work in us, but life in you. But since we have the 13
same spirit of faith, as shown in that which is
written — "I believed, and so I spoke" — we
also believed, wherefore we also speak. For we 14
know that he who raised up Jesus will raise
up us also with Jesus, and will place us with you.
For all things are for your sakes, so that the 15
grace which abounds through the many may
cause thanksgiving to abound, to the glory of God.

Wherefore we do not lose heart. On the con- 16
trary, even though our outer man is decaying,
yet our inner man is being renewed day by day.
For our present light affliction, which is for the 17
moment, prepares for us an eternal weight of
glory that is beyond all measure; while we look 18
not at the things that are seen, but at the things
that are not seen. For the things that are seen
are temporal, but the things that are not seen
are eternal.

Reward after Death

For we know that if the earthly | AUG. 25   **5** 1
house in which we dwell be destroyed, | Feb. 24
we have a building from God, a house not made
by human hands, eternal in the heavens. And 2
indeed, in this present state we groan, yearning

4, 14: *And will place us with you:* in heaven.
4, 17: This verse proves that the good works of the just
on earth are meritorious of eternal life, as the Council of
Trent teaches.

to be clothed over with that dwelling of ours
3 which is from heaven, if indeed we shall be
4 found clothed, and not naked. For we who are
in this tent sigh under our burden, because we
do not wish to be unclothed, but rather clothed
over, that what is mortal may be swallowed up
5 by life. Now he who made us for this very thing
is God, who has given us the Spirit as its pledge.

6   Always full of courage, then, and knowing that
while we are in the body we are exiled from the
7 Lord — for we walk by faith and not by sight —
8 we even have the courage to prefer to be exiled
from the body and to be at home with the Lord.
9 And therefore we strive, whether in the body or
10 out of it, to be pleasing to him. For all of us must
be made manifest before the tribunal of Christ,
so that each one may receive what he has won
through the body, according to his works,
whether good or evil.

3. The Apostle Defends His Sincerity

His Labor for God and Souls

11   KNOWING THEREFORE the fear of the Lord,
we try to persuade men; but to God we are
manifest. And I hope also that in your con-
sciences we are manifest.

12   We are not again commending ourselves to
you; but we are giving you occasion to boast
about us, that you may have an answer for them

5, 5: *The Spirit as its pledge:* The Holy Spirit received
in Baptism is the earnest, the warrant, a foretaste of
eternal life.

5, 6: The Apostle means to say, if death is necessary
before we can be with Christ, then welcome death.

5, 13: When the Apostle spoke of the graces and priv-
ileges he had received from God, his adversaries accused
him of madness; but he spoke thus for the glory of God
and the welfare of the faithful.

who glory in appearances and not in heart. For 13
if we were out of our mind, it was for God; if
we are sane, it is for you. For the love of Christ 14
impels us, because we have come to the conclusion that, since one died for all, therefore all
died, ' and that Christ died for all, in order that 15
they who are alive may live no longer for themselves, but for him who died for them and rose
again.

So that henceforth we know no one according 16
to the flesh. And even though we have known
Christ according to the flesh, yet now we know
him so no longer. If then any man is in Christ, 17
he is a new creature: the former things have
passed away; behold, they are made new! But 18
all things are from God, who has reconciled us
to himself through Christ and has given to us
the ministry of reconciliation.

For God was truly in Christ, reconciling the 19
world to himself by not reckoning against men
their sins and by entrusting to us the message
of reconciliation.

Ambassadors of Christ

On behalf of Christ, therefore, we | AUG. 26 | 20
are acting as ambassadors, God, as | Feb. 25 |
it were, appealing through us. We exhort you,
for Christ's sake, be reconciled to God. For our 21
sakes he made him to be sin who knew nothing
of sin, so that in him we might become the
justice of God.

Yes, working together with him we entreat **6** 1
you not to receive the grace of God in vain. For 2
he says, "In an acceptable time I have heard
thee, and in the day of salvation I have helped
thee." Behold, now is the acceptable time; behold, now is the day of salvation! We give no 3
offense to anyone, that our ministry may not be

4 blamed. On the contrary, let us conduct ourselves in all circumstances as God's ministers, in much patience; in tribulations, in hardships,
5 in distresses; ' in stripes, in imprisonments, in tumults; in labors, in sleepless nights, in fast-
6 ings; in innocence, in knowledge, in long-sufferings; in kindness, in the Holy Spirit, in unaffected
7 love; in the word of truth, in the power of God; with the armor of justice on the right hand and
8 on the left; in honor and dishonor, in evil report and good report; as deceivers and yet truthful,
9 as unknown and yet well known, ' as dying and
10 behold, we live, as chastised but not killed, ' as sorrowful yet always rejoicing, as poor yet enriching many, as having nothing yet possessing all things.

11 We are frank with you, O Corinthians; our
12 heart is wide open to you. In us there is no lack of room for you, but in your heart there is no
13 room for us. Now as having a recompense in like kind — I speak as to my children — be you also open wide to us.

Avoid Marriage with Unbelievers

14 Do not bear the yoke with unbelievers. For what has justice in common with iniquity? Or
15 what fellowship has light with darkness? What harmony is there between Christ and Belial? Or what part has the believer with the unbe-
16 liever? And what agreement has the temple of God with idols? For you are the temple of the living God, as God says, "I will dwell and move among them, I will be their God and they shall

---

6, 14: *Bear the yoke:* the reference is to marriage, though the principle has application to all relations of Christians and pagans.

6, 15: *Belial,* or *Beliar:* a Hebrew word meaning "nothingness," "uselessness."

be my people." Wherefore, "Come out from 17
among them, be separated, says the Lord, and
touch not an unclean thing; and I will welcome 18
you in, and will be a Father to you, and you shall
be my sons and daughters, says the Lord
almighty."

Having therefore these promises, beloved, let **7** 1
us cleanse ourselves from all defilement of the
flesh and of the spirit, perfecting holiness in the
fear of God.

4. The Apostle Defends His Previous Letter

Love for the Corinthians

MAKE ROOM FOR US. We have | AUG. 27 | 2
wronged no one, we have corrupted | Feb. 26 |
no one, we have taken advantage of no one.
I am not saying this to condemn you; for I have 3
already said that you are in our hearts, to die
together and to live together. Great is my con- 4
fidence in you, great my boasting about you.
I am filled with comfort, I overflow with joy in
all our troubles.

For indeed when we came to Macedonia, our 5
flesh had no rest; we had troubles on every side,
conflicts without and anxieties within. But God, 6
who comforts the humble, comforted us by the
arrival of Titus. And not by his arrival only, but 7
also by the comfort which he himself experienced
in you. He told us of your longing, of your sorrow,
of your zeal for me, so that I rejoiced yet more.

Their Repentance

Wherefore, although I made you sorry by my 8
letter, I do not regret it. And even if I did regret
it, seeing that the same letter did for a while
make you sorry, ' now I am glad; not because 9
you were made sorry, but because your sorrow

led you to repentance. For you were made sorry according to God, that you might suffer no loss

10 at our hands. For the sorrow that is according to God produces repentance that surely tends to salvation, whereas the sorrow that is according

11 to the world produces death. For behold this very fact that you were made sorry according to God, what earnestness it has wrought in you, nay, what explanations, what indignation, what fear, what yearning, what zeal, what readiness to avenge! In everything you have showed yourselves to be innocent in the matter.

12 If then I did write to you, it was not for the sake of him who did the wrong, nor for the sake of him who suffered the wrong; but to make

13 clear the zeal we have for you, ' before God. This is why we have been comforted. But besides our own comfort, we more especially rejoiced at the joy of Titus, because his mind had been set at

14 rest by you all. And if I did boast to him all about you, I have not been put to shame; but just as we have spoken all things in truth to you, so also has the boasting we made to Titus

15 been found to be true. And his affection for you is all the more abundant, as he recalls how obedient you all were and how you received him

16 with fear and trembling. I rejoice that in all things I can have confidence in you.

II: THE COLLECTION FOR THE POOR CHRISTIANS IN JERUSALEM

Example of the Macedonians

8 1   NOW WE MAKE KNOWN TO YOU, | AUG. 28
brethren, the grace of God that has | Feb. 27
been bestowed upon the churches of Macedonia;

2 where, amid much testing of tribulation, their overflowing joy and their very deep poverty have

resulted in rich generosity. For according to their 3
means — I bear them witness — yes, beyond
their means, they gave, 'earnestly begging of 4
us the favor of sharing in the ministry that is in
behalf of the saints. And beyond our expecta- 5
tions they gave themselves, first to the Lord,
and then by the will of God to us. This led us 6
to exhort Titus to complete among you also this
same gracious work, of which he had made a
beginning before.

Exhortation

Now, as you abound in everything — in faith, 7
in utterance, in knowledge, in all zeal, and in
your love for us — may you excel in this gracious
work also. I do not speak as commanding, but 8
as testing the sincerity of your own charity by
means of the zeal of others. For you know the 9
graciousness of our Lord Jesus Christ — how,
being rich, he became poor for your sakes, that
by his poverty you might become rich.

In this matter I am giving advice. It is to your 10
interest, since a year ago you not only began to
do, but also to have the will. Now therefore 11
complete the doing also; so that your readiness
to begin it may be equalled by your desire to
carry it through, according to your ability. For 12
if there is willingness, it is welcome according
to what one has, not according to what one does
not have.

For I do not mean that the relief of others 13
should become your burden, but that there
should be equality; that at the present time your 14
abundance may supply their want, and that their
abundance may, in its turn, make up what you
lack, thus establishing an equality, 'as it is 15
written, "He who had much had nothing over,
and he who had little had not less."

The Mission of Titus

16 Now thanks be to God, who has inspired Titus
17 with this same zeal for you. For not only has he
accepted our exhortation, but being very zealous
himself, he has gone to you of his own choice.
18 And we have sent along with him the brother
whose services to the gospel are praised in all
19 the churches; and what is more, who was also
appointed by the churches to travel with us in
this work of grace which is being done by us, to
the glory of the Lord and to show our own readi-
20 ness. We are on our guard, lest anyone should
slander us in the matter of our administration of
21 this generous amount. For we take forethought
for what is honorable, not only before God, but
22 also in the sight of men. And we have sent with
them also our brother, whom we have proved to
be zealous often and in many things, but who
now is more in earnest than ever, because of his
23 great confidence in you, whether as regards
Titus, who is my companion and fellow-worker
among you, or as regards our brethren, the mes-
24 sengers of the churches, the glory of Christ. Give
them therefore, in the sight of the churches, a
proof of your charity and of our boasting on your
behalf.

The Collection to Be Made Promptly

9 1   For it is indeed superfluous for me
to write to you with reference to this

AUG. 29
Feb. 28

2 charitable service to the saints. For I know your
eagerness, whereof I boast about you to the
Macedonians—that Achaia has been ready since
last year—and your zeal has stimulated very
3 many. Still, I have sent the brethren, lest our
boasting concerning you should be found empty
in this instance; that, as I was saying, you may

be ready, ' lest, if any Macedonians come with 4
me and find you unprepared, we — not to say
yourselves — should be put to shame for having
been so sure. I have therefore thought it neces- 5
sary to exhort the brethren to go to you in advance and to get ready this promised contribution, so that it may be as a matter of bounty, and
not of extortion.

Exhortation to Generosity

Mark this: he who sows sparingly will also reap 6
sparingly, and he who sows bountifully will also
reap bountifully. Let each one give according as 7
he has determined in his heart, not grudgingly or
from compulsion, for "God loves a cheerful
giver." And God is able to make all grace abound 8
in you, so that always having ample means, you
may abound in every good work, ' as it is written, 9
"He has scattered abroad and has given to the
poor, his justice remains forever."

Now he who provides the sower with seed will 10
both give you bread to eat and will multiply your
seed, and will increase the growth of the fruits of
your justice; that, being enriched in all things, 11
you may contribute with simplicity of purpose,
and thus through us evoke thanksgiving to God;
for the administration of this service not only 12
supplies the want of the saints, but overflows also
in much gratitude to the Lord. The evidence 13
furnished by this service makes them glorify God
for your obedient profession of Christ's gospel
and for the sincere generosity of your contribu-
tions to them and to all; while they themselves, 14
in their prayers for you, yearn for you, because
of the excellent grace God has given you. Thanks 15
be to God for his unspeakable gift!

III: THE APOSTLE DEFENDS HIS APOSTOLATE

His Authority

10 1 NOW I MYSELF, PAUL, appeal to you by the meekness and gentleness of Christ—I who to your face indeed am diffident when among you, but when absent am fearless 2 towards you! Yes, I beseech you that I may not when I come have to be bold, with that assurance wherewith I am thought to be bold, against those who regard us as walking according to the flesh. 3 For though we walk in the flesh, we do not make 4 war according to the flesh; for the weapons of our warfare are not carnal, but powerful before God to the demolishing of strongholds, the destroying 5 of reasoning—' yes, of every lofty thing that exalts itself against the knowledge of God, bringing every mind into captivity to the obedience of 6 Christ, and being prepared to take vengeance on all disobedience when once your own submission is complete.

7 Look at what is before you. If anyone is confident that he is Christ's, let him reflect within himself that even as he is Christ's, so too are we. 8 For even if I boast somewhat more about our authority (which the Lord has given for your upbuilding, and not for your destruction), I shall 9 not be put to shame. But that I may not seem to 10 terrify you, as it were, by letters ' ("for his letters," they say, "are weighty and telling, but his bodily appearance is weak and his speech of 11 no account"), let such people understand that what we are in word by letters when absent, such are we also in deed when bodily present.

12 Of course we have not the boldness to class ourselves or to compare ourselves with certain ones who commend themselves. We, on the contrary, measure ourselves by ourselves and com-

AUG. 30
Feb. 29

pare ourselves with ourselves; and so we do not 13
boast beyond our limits, but within the limits of
the commission which God has given us — limits
which include you also. For we are not going 14
beyond our commission, as if it did not embrace
you, since we reached even as far as you with the
gospel of Christ.

We do not boast beyond our limits, in the 15
labors of other men; but we hope, as your faith
increases, greatly to enlarge through you the
province allotted to us, so as even to preach the 16
gospel in places that lie beyond you, instead of
boasting in another man's sphere about work
already done. "But he who boasts, let him boast 17
in the Lord." For he is not approved who com- 18
mends himself, but he whom the Lord commends.

He Preached Gratuitously

Would to God that you could bear
with a little of my foolishness! Nay,

11 1

do bear with me! For I am jealous for you with a 2
divine jealousy. For I betrothed you to one
spouse, that I might present you a chaste virgin
to Christ. But I fear lest, as the serpent seduced 3
Eve by his guile, so your minds may be corrupted
and fall from a single devotion to Christ. For if he 4
who comes preaches another Christ whom we
did not preach, or if you receive another Spirit
whom you have not received, or another gospel
which you did not accept, you might well bear
with him. For I regard myself as nowise inferior 5
to the great apostles. Even though I be rude in 6
speech, yet I am not so in knowledge; but in
every way we have made ourselves clear to you.

11, 1: *Foolishness:* the folly of self-praise which the Corinthians have forced the Apostle to indulge in for the moment.

11, 4: The supposition here is impossible since there is only one Christ, one Holy Spirit, one heavenly Gospel.

7 Or did I do wrong when I humbled myself that you might be exalted, preaching to you the gospel
8 of God free of charge? I stripped other churches, taking pay from them so as to minister to you.
9 And when I was with you and in want, I was a burden to no one; for the brethren from Macedonia supplied my needs. Thus in all things I have kept myself from being a burden to you, and
10 so I intend to keep myself. By the truth of Christ which is in me, this boast shall not be taken from
11 me in the districts of Achaia. ' Why so? Because I
12 do not love you? God knows I do. ' But what I do I will go on doing, that I may deprive them of the occasion who are seeking an occasion to boast
13 that they are doing the same as we do. For they are false apostles, deceitful workers, disguising
14 themselves as apostles of Christ. And no wonder, for Satan himself disguises himself as an angel
15 of light. It is no great thing, then, if his ministers disguise themselves as ministers of justice. But their end will be according to their works.

His Ministry of Labor and Suffering

16 I repeat, let no one think me ┌──────────┐
foolish. But if so, then regard me │ SEPT. 1 │
│ Mar. 2 │
17 as such, that I also may boast a little. What I └──────────┘
am saying in this confidence of boasting, I am not speaking according to the Lord, but as it
18 were in foolishness. Since many boast according
19 to the flesh, I too will boast. For you gladly put up with fools, because you are wise yourselves!
20 For you suffer it if a man enslaves you, if a man devours you, if a man takes from you, if a man
21 is arrogant, if a man slaps your face! I speak to my own shame, as though we had been weak. But wherein any man is bold—I am speaking
22 foolishly — I also am bold. Are they Hebrews? So am I! Are they Israelites? So am I! Are they

offspring of Abraham? So am I! Are they ministers of Christ? I — to speak as a fool — am more: in many more labors, in prisons more frequently, in lashes above measure, often exposed to death. From the Jews five times I received forty lashes less one. Thrice I was scourged, once I was stoned, thrice I suffered shipwreck, a night and a day I was adrift on the sea; in journeyings often, in perils from floods, in perils from robbers, in perils from my own nation, in perils from the Gentiles, in perils in the city, in perils in the wilderness, in perils in the sea, in perils from false brethren; in labor and hardships, in many sleepless nights, in hunger and thirst, in fastings often, in cold and nakedness. Besides those outer things, there is my daily pressing anxiety, the care of all the churches! Who is weak, and I am not weak? Who is made to stumble, and I am not inflamed? If I must boast, I will boast of the things that concern my weakness.

The God and Father of the Lord Jesus, who is blessed forevermore, knows that I do not lie. In Damascus the governor under King Aretas was guarding the city of the Damascenes in order to arrest me, but I was lowered in a basket through a window in the wall, and escaped his hands.

His Revelations

If I must boast — it is not indeed expedient **12** to do so — but I will come to visions and revelations of the Lord. I know a man in Christ who fourteen years ago — whether in the body I do

---

12, 2: *A man in Christ:* St. Paul humbly speaks of himself in the third person. *Whether in the body,* etc.: the Apostle at the time was totally abstracted from the senses, as in ecstasy. *The third heaven:* i.e., paradise, the abode of the blessed.

not know, or out of the body I do not know, God
knows — such a one was caught up to the third
3 heaven. And I know such a man — whether in
the body or out of the body I do not know, God
4 knows — that he was caught up into paradise
and heard secret words that man may not repeat.
5 Of such a man I will boast; but of myself I will
6 glory in nothing save in my infirmities. For if I
do wish to boast, I shall not be foolish; for I
shall be speaking the truth. But I forbear, lest
any man should reckon me beyond what he sees
in me or hears from me.

His Infirmities

7 And lest the greatness of the revelations
should puff me up, there was given me a thorn
for the flesh, a messenger of Satan, to buffet
8 me. Concerning this I thrice besought the Lord
9 that it might leave me. And he has said to me,
"My grace is sufficient for thee, for strength is
made perfect in weakness." Gladly therefore I
will glory in my infirmities, that the strength of
10 Christ may dwell in me. Wherefore I am satisfied, for Christ's sake, with infirmities, with
insults, with hardships, with persecutions, with
distresses. For when I am weak, then I am strong.

He Has Been Forced to Boast

11 I have become foolish! You have forced me.
For I ought to have been commended by you,
since in no way have I fallen short of the most
eminent apostles, even though I am nothing.
12 Indeed, the signs of the apostle were wrought
among you in all patience, in miracles and won-
13 ders and deeds of power. For in what have you
been less favored than the other churches —
unless in this, that I was no burden to you?
Pardon me this wrong!

[488]

His Third Visit

Behold, this is the third time that
I am ready to come to you. And I will
not be a burden to you; for I do not seek yours,
but you. For the children should not save up for
the parents, but the parents for the children. But
I will most gladly spend and be spent myself for
your souls, even though, loving you more, I be
loved less.

But be it so: I was no burden to you, but, being
crafty, I caught you by guile. Did I take advantage of you through any of these whom I sent to
you? I urged Titus to go, and I sent our brother
with him. Did Titus take advantage of you?
Have we not walked in the same spirit, have we
not walked in the same steps?

Are you thinking all this time that we are defending ourselves before you? We speak before
God in Christ; but in all things, beloved, for
your own edification. For I fear lest perhaps
when I come I may not find you as I should
wish, and lest I may be found by you not as you
would wish—lest perhaps there be found among
you contentions, envyings, animosities, dissensions, detractions, gossiping, arrogance, disorders — lest when I come again God should
humiliate me before you, and I should mourn
over many who sinned before and have not repented of the uncleanness and immorality and
licentiousness that they practised.

Warnings

Behold, this is the third time that I am coming
to you: "On the word of two or three witnesses
every word shall be confirmed." I have already
warned, when present, and now in my absence
I warn again those who sinned before, and all

[489]

the rest, that, if I come again, I will not spare.
3 Do you seek a proof of the Christ who speaks in me, who is not weak in your regard, nay, is
4 powerful in you? For though he was crucified through weakness, yet he lives through the power of God. Yes, we also are weak in him, yet we shall live with him through the power of God in your regard.

5 Put your own selves to test, whether you are in the faith; prove yourselves. Do you not know yourselves that Christ Jesus is in you? unless
6 perhaps you are reprobate! But I hope that you
7 will come to know that we are not reprobate. But we pray God that you may do no evil at all, not wishing ourselves to appear approved, but that you may do what is good, and we ourselves pass
8 as reprobate. For we can do nothing against the
9 truth, but only for the truth. And so we rejoice when we are weak but you are strong. This we also pray for, your perfecting.

10 Wherefore I write these things while absent, that when present I may not act more severely, according to the power that the Lord has given me for upbuilding, and not for destruction.

Conclusion

Farewell

11 IN CONCLUSION, brethren, rejoice, be perfected, be comforted, be of the same mind, be at peace; and the God of peace and love will be
12 with you. Greet one another with a holy kiss. All the saints send you greetings.

13 The grace of our Lord Jesus Christ, and the charity of God, and the fellowship of the Holy Spirit be with you all. Amen.

13, 5: Christ dwells in the intellect by faith, in the heart and affections by charity, in the soul by grace.

THE EPISTLE TO THE GALATIANS

Introduction

The Galatians to whom this Epistle was written lived between Cappadocia and Phrygia, in Asia Minor. They were Gentile Christians, and were converted by St. Paul about the year 52 A. D. His ministry among them had borne great fruit; they had been baptized, and had received the Holy Spirit; miracles worked among them had given evidence of the presence of the Spirit in their hearts. The Apostle visited them a second time, and by his exhortations confirmed them in the faith. But after his second visit St. Paul learned, by letter or by special messenger sent to him, that some Jewish teachers who had lately arrived among his new converts were teaching, contrary to his doctrines, that for salvation it was necessary to be circumcised and to observe the Mosaic rites. Furthermore, these Judaizers sought to undermine the authority of the Apostle by questioning his divine commission. They claimed that his teaching seemed to be only human and differed widely in many respects from that of Christ and of the other Apostles. They asserted that he disregarded the sacredness of the Mosaic Law and circumcision, which were an external sign of God's covenant with man, and thereby doubted the truth of the divine promises. Such were the difficulties that reached the ears of St. Paul in Ephesus; and since he was unable to be with his converts, he met the serious situation by this Epistle.

The Epistle contains a defense of his person and of his doctrine. In indignation he asserts the divine origin of his teaching and of his authority; he shows that justification is not through the Mosaic Law, but through faith in Jesus Christ, who was crucified and who rose from the dead; he concludes that consequently the Mosaic Law was something transient and not permanent, that it is not an essential part of Christianity. Nor does he fail to insist on the necessity of the evangelical virtues, especially charity, the offspring of faith.

The subject-matter of the Epistle resembles closely

THE EPISTLE OF ST. PAUL THE APOSTLE TO THE GALATIANS

Introduction

Greeting

1 1 PAUL, AN APOSTLE, sent not from men nor by man, but by Jesus Christ and God the Father who raised him from the
2 dead, ' and all the brethren who are with me, to
3 the churches of Galatia. Grace and peace be to you from God the Father, and from our Lord
4 Jesus Christ, ' who gave himself for our sins, that he might deliver us from the wickedness of this present world according to the will of our God and
5 Father; to whom is glory forever and ever. Amen.

| SEPT. 3 |
| Mar. 4 |

Surprise and Rebuke

6 I marvel that you are so quickly deserting him who called you to the grace of Christ, changing to
7 another gospel; which is not another gospel, except in this respect that there are some who trouble you, and wish to pervert the gospel of
8 Christ. But even if we or an angel from heaven should preach a gospel to you other than that which we have preached to you, let him be
9 anathema! As we have said before, so now I say again: If anyone preach a gospel to you other than that which you have received, let him he

that of the Epistle to the Romans, and also of the Second Epistle to the Corinthians. The reason for this similarity is that these Epistles were written when the Apostle was more or less in the same frame of mind, indignant that his converts were being perverted by Pharisaic emissaries.

The Epistle was probably written at Ephesus about the year 54 A. D. It may, however, have been written somewhat later, from either Macedonia or Corinth. Its authenticity was admitted by all antiquity.

anathema! For am I now seeking the favor of 10
men, or of God? Or am I seeking to please men?
If I were still trying to please men, I should not
be a servant of Christ.

I: PERSONAL DEFENSE

1. A Defense of His Apostolate

Not of Human Origin

FOR I GIVE YOU TO UNDERSTAND, brethren, 11
that the gospel which was preached by me is not
of man. For I did not receive it from man, nor 12
was I taught it; but I received it by a revelation
of Jesus Christ. For you have heard of my former 13
manner of life in Judaism; how beyond all measure I persecuted the Church of God, and ravaged
it. And I advanced in Judaism above many of my 14
contemporaries in my nation, showing much more
zeal for the traditions of my fathers. But when it 15
pleased him who from my mother's womb set me
apart and called me by his grace, ¹ to reveal his 16
Son in me, that I might preach him among the
Gentiles, immediately, without taking counsel
with flesh and blood, and without going up to 17
Jerusalem to those who were appointed apostles
before me, I retired into Arabia, and again returned to Damascus.

Then after three years I went to Jerusalem to 18
see Peter, and I remained with him fifteen days.
But I saw none of the other apostles, except 19
James, the brother of the Lord. Now in what I 20
am writing to you, behold, before God, I do not
lie. Then I went into the regions of Syria and 21
Cilicia. And I was unknown by sight to the 22
churches of Judea which were in Christ. But 23
they had heard only that he who formerly persecuted us, now preaches the faith which once he
ravaged. And they glorified God in me. 24

2. A Defense of His Gospel

Approved by the Apostles

2 1   THEN AFTER FOURTEEN YEARS I | SEPT. 4 |
went up again to Jerusalem with | Mar. 5 |
2 Barnabas, taking also Titus along with me. And
I went up in consequence of a revelation, and I
conferred with them on the gospel which I preach
among the Gentiles, but separately with the men
of authority; lest perhaps I should be running, or
3 had run in vain. But not even Titus, who was
with me, Gentile though he was, was compelled
4 to be circumcised, ¹ although it was urged on
account of false brethren who were brought in
secretly, who slipped in to spy upon our liberty
which we have in Christ Jesus, that they might
5 bring us into slavery. Now to these we did not
yield in submission, no, not for an hour, that the
6 truth of the gospel might continue with you. But
from the men of authority (what they once were
matters not to me; God accepts not the person
of man) — the men of authority laid no further
7 burden on me. On the contrary, when they saw
that to me was committed the gospel for the
uncircumcised, as to Peter that for the circum-
8 cised (for he who worked in Peter for the apostleship of the circumcised worked also in me among
9 the Gentiles) — and when they recognized the
grace that was given to me, James and Cephas
and John, who were considered the pillars, gave
to me and to Barnabas the right hand of fellowship, that we should go to the Gentiles, and they
10 to the circumcised; provided only that we should
be mindful of the poor, the very thing I was eager
to do.

Paul Reproves Peter

But when Cephas came to Antioch, I with- 11 stood him to his face, because he was deserving of blame. For before certain persons came from 12 James, he used to eat with the Gentiles; but when they came, he began to withdraw and to separate himself, fearing the circumcised. And 13 the rest of the Jews dissembled along with him, so that Barnabas also was led away by them into that dissimulation. But when I saw that they were 14 not walking uprightly according to the truth of the gospel, I said to Cephas before them all: If thou, though a Jew, livest like the Gentiles, and not like the Jews, how is it that thou dost compel the Gentiles to live like the Jews?

We are Jews by birth, and not sinners from 15 among the Gentiles. But we know that man is not 16 justified by the works of the Law, but by the faith of Jesus Christ. Hence we also believe in Christ Jesus, that we may be justified by the faith of Christ, and not by the works of the Law; because by the works of the Law no man will be justified. But if, while we are seeking to be justi- 17 fied in Christ, we ourselves also are found sinners, is Christ therefore the minister of sin? By no means. ' For if I reconstruct the things 18 that I destroyed, I make myself a sinner. For I 19 through the Law have died to the Law that I may live to God. With Christ I am nailed to the cross. It is now no longer I that live, but Christ lives in 20 me. And the life that I now live in the flesh, I live in the faith of the Son of God, who loved me and gave himself up for me. ' I do not cast away 21 the grace of God. For if justice is by the Law, then Christ died in vain.

II: DOCTRINAL

1. Justification from Faith Not from the Law

Proved from the Galatians' Experience

3 1 O FOOLISH GALATIANS! who has bewitched you, before whose eyes SEPT. 5
Mar. 6
2 Jesus Christ has been depicted crucified? This only I would learn from you: Did you receive the Spirit in virtue of the works of the Law, or
3 in virtue of hearing and believing? Are you so foolish that after beginning in the Spirit, you
4 now make a finish in the flesh? Have you suffered so much in vain? if indeed it be in vain.
5 He therefore who gives the Spirit to you, and works miracles among you, does he do it by the works of the Law, or by the message of faith?
6 Even thus "Abraham believed God, and it was credited to him as justice."

The Example of Abraham

7 Know therefore that the men of faith are the
8 real sons of Abraham. And the Scripture, foreseeing that God would justify the Gentiles by faith, announced to Abraham beforehand, "In
9 thee shall all the nations be blessed." Therefore the men of faith shall be blessed with faithful Abraham.

The Nature of the Law

10 For those who rely on the works of the Law are under a curse. For it is written, "Cursed is everyone who does not hold to all things that are written in the book of the Law, to perform
11 them." But that by the Law no man is justified before God is evident, because "who is just
12 lives by faith." But the Law does not rest on faith; but, "he who does these things, shall live
13 by them." Christ redeemed us from the curse

of the Law, becoming a curse for us; for it is written, "Cursed is everyone who hangs on a gibbet"; that the blessing of Abraham might 14 come to the Gentiles through Christ Jesus, that through faith we might receive the promise of the Spirit.

The Promise of God

Brethren (I speak after the manner of men); 15 yet even a man's will, once it has been ratified, no one annuls or alters. The promises were made 16 to Abraham and to his offspring. He does not say, "And to his offsprings," as of many; but as of one, "And to thy offspring," who is Christ. Now I mean this: The Law which was made four 17 hundred and thirty years later does not annul the covenant which was ratified by God, so as to make the promise void. For if the right to 18 inherit be from the Law, it is no longer from a promise. But God gave it to Abraham by promise.

The Purpose of the Law

What then was the Law? It was enacted on 19 account of transgressions, being delivered by angels through a mediator, until the offspring should come to whom the promise was made. Now there is no intermediary where there is 20 only one; but God is one. Is the Law then con- 21 trary to the promises of God? By no means. For if a law had been given that could give life, jus- tice would truly be from the Law. But the Scrip- 22 ture shut up all things under sin, that by the faith of Jesus Christ the promise might be given to those who believe.

But before the faith came we were kept im- 23 prisoned under the Law, shut up for the faith that was to be revealed. Therefore the Law has 24 been our tutor unto Christ, that we might be

25 justified by faith. But now that faith has come,
26 we are no longer under a tutor. For you are all
the children of God through faith in Christ Jesus.
27 For all you who have been baptized into Christ,
28 have put on Christ. There is neither Jew nor
Greek; there is neither slave nor freeman; there
is neither male nor female. For you are all one
29 in Christ Jesus. And if you are Christ's, then you
are the offspring of Abraham, heirs according to
promise.

2. Christians Live in a State of Freedom

Slavery and Freedom

4 1 NOW I SAY, as long as the heir is ⎡ SEPT. 6 ⎤
a child, he differs in no way from a ⎣ Mar. 7 ⎦
2 slave, though he is the master of all; but he is
under guardians and stewards until the time set
3 by his father. So we too, when we were children,
were enslaved under the elements of the world.
4 But when the fullness of time came, God sent
his Son, born of a woman, born under the Law,
5 that he might redeem those who were under
the Law, that we might receive the adoption of
6 sons. And because you are sons, God has sent
the Spirit of his Son into our hearts, crying,
7 "Abba, Father." ' So that he is no longer a slave,
but a son; and if a son, an heir also through
God.

No Return to Slavery

8 But then indeed, not knowing God, you served
9 those who really are not gods. But now that you
have come to know God, or rather to be known
by God, how is it that you turn again to the
weak and beggarly elements, which you desire to
10 serve again? You are observing days and months
11 and seasons and years. I fear for you, lest perhaps I have labored among you in vain.

Become like me, because I also have become 12
like you, brethren, I beseech you! You have done
me no wrong. And you know that on account of 13
a physical infirmity I preached the gospel to you
formerly; and though I was a trial to you in my
flesh, ' you did not reject or despise me; but you 14
received me as an angel of God, even as Christ
Jesus. Where then is your self-congratulation? 15
For I bear you witness that, if possible, you would
have plucked out your very eyes and given them
to me. Have I then become your enemy, because 16
I tell you the truth? They court you from no good 17
motive; but they would estrange you, that you
may court them. But court the good from a good 18
motive always, and not only when I am present
with you, ' my dear children, with whom I am 19
in labor again, until Christ is formed in you! But 20
I wish I could be with you now, and change my
tone, because I do not know what to make of you.

Ismael and Isaac

Tell me, you who desire to be under the Law, 21
have you not read the Law? For it is written that 22
Abraham had two sons, the one by a slave-girl
and the other by a free woman. And the son of 23
the slave-girl was born according to the flesh,
but the son of the free woman in virtue of the
promise. ' This is said by way of allegory. For 24
these are the two covenants: one indeed from
Mount Sinai, bringing forth children unto bondage, which is Agar. For Sinai is a mountain in 25
Arabia, which corresponds to the present Jerusalem, and is in slavery with her children. But 26
that Jerusalem which is above is free, which is
our mother. For it is written, "Rejoice thou 27
barren, that dost not bear; break forth and cry,
thou that dost not travail; for many are the
children of the desolate, more than of her that

28 has a husband." Now we, brethren, are the
29 children of promise, as Isaac was. But as then
he who was born according to the flesh persecuted him who was born according to the spirit,
30 so also it is now. But what does the Scripture
say? "Cast out the slave-girl and her son, for
the son of the slave-girl shall not be heir with
31 the son of the free woman." Therefore, brethren,
we are not children of a slave-girl, but of the
free woman — in virtue of the freedom wherewith Christ has made us free.

III: MORAL

1. General Counsels

Circumcision Now Voidance of Christ

5 1 STAND FAST, AND DO NOT be
caught again under the yoke of
2 slavery. Behold, I, Paul, tell you that if you be
circumcised, Christ will be of no advantage to
3 you. And I testify again to every man who has
himself circumcised, that he is bound to observe
4 the whole Law. You who would be justified in the
Law are estranged from Christ; you have fallen
5 away from grace. For we in the Spirit wait for
6 the hope of justice in virtue of faith. For in Christ
Jesus neither circumcision is of any avail, nor
uncircumcision, but faith which works through
charity.

> SEPT. 7
> Mar. 8

Judgment on Seducers

7 You were running well; who hindered you
8 from obeying the truth? This persuasion is not
9 from him who calls you. A little leaven ferments
10 the whole mass. I have confidence in you in the
Lord, that you will not think otherwise; but he
who disturbs you will bear the penalty, whoever

he may be. But I, brethren, if I still preach circumcision, why am I still persecuted? Then is the stumbling-block of the cross removed! Would that those who are unsettling you would mutilate themselves! 11 12

How Christians Should Live

For you have been called to liberty, brethren; only do not use liberty as an occasion for sensuality, but by charity serve one another. For the whole Law is fulfilled in one word: Thou shalt love thy neighbor as thyself. But if you bite and devour one another, take heed or you will be consumed by one another. 13 14 15

But I say: Walk in the Spirit, and you will not fulfill the lusts of the flesh. For the flesh lusts against the spirit, and the spirit against the flesh; for these are opposed to each other, so that you do not do what you would. But if you are led by the Spirit, you are not under the Law. Now the works of the flesh are manifest, which are immorality, uncleanness, licentiousness, ' idolatry, witchcrafts, enmities, contentions, jealousies, anger, quarrels, factions, parties, ' envies, murders, drunkenness, carousings, and suchlike. And concerning these I warn you, as I have warned you, that they who do such things will not attain the kingdom of God. But the fruit of the Spirit is: charity, joy, peace, patience, kindness, goodness, ' faith, modesty, continency. Against such things there is no law. And they who belong to Christ have crucified their flesh with its passions and desires. If we live by the Spirit, by the Spirit let us also walk. Let us not become desirous of vainglory, provoking one another, envying one another. 16 17 18 19 20 21 22 23 24 25 26

2. Specific Counsels

6 1   BRETHREN, EVEN IF a person is caught doing something wrong, you

SEPT. 8
Mar. 9

who are spiritual instruct such a one in a spirit of meekness, considering thyself, lest thou also 2 be tempted. Bear one another's burdens, and so 3 you will fulfill the law of Christ. For if anyone thinks himself to be something, whereas he is 4 nothing, he deceives himself. But let everyone test his own work, and so he will have glory in himself only, and not in comparison with another. 5 For each one will bear his own burden.

Good Works

6   And let him who is instructed in the word share 7 all good things with his teacher. Be not deceived, 8 God is not mocked. For what a man sows, that he will also reap. For he who sows in the flesh, from the flesh also will reap corruption. But he who sows in the spirit, from the spirit will reap 9 life everlasting. And in doing good let us not grow tired; for in due time we shall reap if we 10 do not relax. Therefore, while we have time, let us do good to all men, but especially to those who are of the household of faith.

Conclusion

Summary

11   SEE WITH WHAT large letters I am writing to 12 you with my own hand! As many as wish to please in the flesh compel you to be circumcised simply that they may not suffer persecution for 13 the cross of Christ. For not even they who are

---

6, 1: *Caught:* i.e., led away by passion or surprise into a fault.

circumcised keep the Law; but they desire you to be circumcised, that they may make a boast of your flesh. But as for me, God forbid that I 14 should glory save in the cross of our Lord Jesus Christ, through whom the world is crucified to me, and I to the world. For in Christ Jesus 15 neither circumcision nor uncircumcision but a new creation is of any account.

And whoever follow this rule, peace and mercy 16 upon them, even upon the Israel of God.

Henceforth let no man give me trouble, for I 17 bear the marks of the Lord Jesus in my body. The 18 grace of our Lord Jesus Christ be with your spirit, brethren. Amen.

6, 16: *This rule:* i.e., the teaching concerning the new creation. *Israel of God:* i.e., the Church. Those who have the faith of true Israelites.

6, 17: The scars on St. Paul's body were those inflicted in persecutions; they attested his faithfulness to Christ.

THE EPISTLE TO THE EPHESIANS

Introduction

This Epistle was written by St. Paul towards the close of his first imprisonment in Rome, in the year 63 A. D. It was brought to its destination in Asia Minor by Tychicus, who also carried with him the Epistle to the Colossians. He was accompanied by Onesimus bearing the Epistle to Philemon.

In spite of this traditional title it is uncertain to whom St. Paul originally addressed this Epistle. Either it was indeed written to the Ephesians, as was commonly believed from the end of the second century A. D. and indicated by the presence of the words "at Ephesus" (1, 1) in most MSS; or it is to be identified with the Epistle mentioned in Col. 4, 16, which St. Paul wrote to the Christians of Laodicea, a town not far from Colossæ and Ephesus; or, finally, it may have been written, not to any one community in particular, but as a sort of circular letter to the various Christian communities in that part of Asia Minor in which Ephesus and Colossæ are situated.

Ephesus, then the chief city of western Asia Minor, had been evangelized by St. Paul about 53-56 A. D. Soon afterwards the important town of Laodicea, about a hundred miles to the east, had received Christianity from some Ephesian Christians. The great majority of converts in all this territory were from among the pagan Gentiles, Jews forming only a small minority.

Very similar in theme and language to the Epistle to the Colossians, but much more abstract, profound and systematic, this Epistle's central thought is the Church regarded as the mystical body of Christ, through which God pours out the divine life of grace in most generous fashion to its members, the Christians, in and through its head, Jesus Christ. The spiritual, organic unity of its members with Christ and with one another is emphasized as the basic principle of the life of the mystical body. Then comes exhortation to lead the new life that befits those incorporated into the sublime unity of the mystical body.

THE EPISTLE OF ST. PAUL THE APOSTLE TO THE EPHESIANS

Introduction

Greeting

PAUL, AN APOSTLE OF JESUS | SEPT. 9 | **1** 1
CHRIST by the will of God, to all the | Mar. 10 |
saints who are at Ephesus, the faithful in Christ
Jesus: grace be to you and peace from God our   2
Father and the Lord Jesus Christ.

The Eternal Plan of the Father

Blessed be the God and Father of our Lord   3
Jesus Christ, who has blessed us with
every spiritual blessing on high in Christ. Even as he   4
chose us in him before the foundation of the
world, that we should be holy and without blemish in his sight in love. He predestined us to be   5
adopted through Jesus Christ as his sons, according to the purpose of his will, ' unto the praise of   6
the glory of his grace, with which he has favored
us in his beloved Son.

Realized in the Son

In him we have redemption through his blood,   7
the remission of sins, according to the riches of
his grace. This grace has abounded beyond mea-   8
sure in us in all wisdom and prudence, so that he   9
may make known to us the mystery of his will
according to his good pleasure. And this his good
pleasure he purposed in him ' to be dispensed in   10
the fullness of the times: to re-establish all things
in Christ, both those in the heavens and those
on the earth.

1, 5: *The purpose:* the original Greek reads "the good
pleasure." This Epistle insists repeatedly on the gratuitous
character of the divine gift of redemption.

Fulfilled through the Holy Spirit

11 In him, I say, in whom we also have been called by a special choice, having been predestined in the purpose of him who works all things
12 according to the counsel of his will, to contribute to the praise of his glory — we who before hoped
13 in Christ. And in him you too, when you had heard the word of truth, the good news of your salvation, and believed in it, were sealed with
14 the Holy Spirit of the promise, ' who is the pledge of our inheritance, for a redemption of possession, for the praise of his glory.

I: DOCTRINAL

1. The Church Is One with Christ

Thanksgiving and Prayer

15 WHEREFORE I ON MY PART, hearing of your faith in the Lord Jesus, and of your love for all
16 the saints, do not cease to give thanks for you,
17 making mention of you in my prayers, that the God of our Lord Jesus Christ, the Father of glory, may grant you the spirit of wisdom and
18 revelation in deep knowledge of him: the eyes of your mind being enlightened, so that you may know what is the hope of his calling, what the riches of the glory of his inheritance in the saints,
19 and what the exceeding greatness of his power towards us who believe.

Its measure is the working of his mighty
20 power, ' which he has wrought in Christ in raising him from the dead, and setting him at his
21 right hand in heaven ' above every Principality and Power and Virtue and Domination — in short, above every name that is named, not

---

1, 12f: *We . . . you too:* the Jewish Christians . . . the Gentile Christians.

only in this world, but also in that which is to
come. And all things he made subject under his 22
feet, and him he gave as head over all the
Church, ' which indeed is his body, the comple- 23
tion of him who fills all with all.

All Brought into Christ's Life

You also, when you were dead by | SEPT. 10 | **2** 1
reason of your offenses and sins, | Mar. 11 |
wherein once you walked according to the fash- 2
ion of this world, according to the prince of the
power of the air about us, the prince of the spirit
which now works on the unbelievers — indeed, 3
in the company of these even we, all of us, once
led our lives in the desires of our flesh, doing the
promptings of our flesh and of our thoughts, and
were by nature children of wrath even as the
rest. But God, who is rich in mercy, by reason of 4
his very great love wherewith he has loved us
even when we were dead by reason of our sins, 5
brought us to life together with Christ (by grace
you have been saved), ' and raised us up to- 6
gether, and seated us together in heaven in
Christ Jesus, that he might show in the ages to 7
come the overflowing riches of his grace in kindness towards us in Christ Jesus. For by grace you 8
have been saved through faith; and that not
from yourselves, for it is the gift of God; not as 9
the outcome of works, lest anyone may boast. For 10
his workmanship we are, created in Christ Jesus
in good works, which God has made ready beforehand that we may walk in them.

2, 2: *The prince,* etc: Satan, the prince of demoniacal
power.

2, 3: *Children of wrath:* deserving of God's anger.

2, 6: *In heaven:* literally, as in 1, 3, "on high." The
divine life of the Christian on earth is an initial stage of
the heavenly state, since it unites him to God in the
glorified Christ.

Gentile and Jew United

11   Wherefore, bear in mind that once you, the
Gentiles in flesh, who are called "uncircumcision" by the so-called "circumcision" in flesh
12   made by human hand — bear in mind that you
were at that time without Christ, excluded as
aliens from the community of Israel, and strangers to the covenants of the promise, having no
13   hope, and without God in the world. But now in
Christ Jesus you, who were once afar off, have
been brought near through the blood of Christ.
14   For he himself is our peace, he it is who has
made both one, and has broken down the intervening wall of the enclosure, the enmity, in his
15   flesh. The Law of the commandments expressed
in decrees he has made void, that of the two he
might create in himself one new man, and make
16   peace ' and reconcile both in one body to God by
the cross, having slain the enmity in himself.
17   And coming, he announced the good tidings of
peace to you who were afar off, and of peace to
18   those who were near; because through him we
both have access in one Spirit to the Father.
19   Therefore, you are now no longer strangers and
foreigners, but you are citizens with the saints
20   and members of God's household: you are built
upon the foundation of the apostles and prophets
with Christ Jesus himself as the chief corner
21   stone. In him the whole structure is closely fitted
together and grows into a temple holy in the
22   Lord, in him you too are being built together into
a dwelling place for God in the Spirit.

2. Paul's Commission to Preach the Mystery

Paul Instructed

FOR THIS REASON, I, PAUL, the prisoner of Christ Jesus for the sake of you, the Gentiles — for I suppose you have heard of the dispensation of the grace of God that was given to me in your regard; how that by revelation was made known to me the mystery, as I have written above in brief; and so by reading you can perceive how well versed I am in the mystery of Christ, ' that mystery which in other ages was not known to the sons of men, as now it has been revealed to his holy apostles and prophets in the Spirit: namely, that the Gentiles are joint heirs, and fellow-members of the same body, and joint partakers of the promise in Christ Jesus through the gospel.

SEPT. 11
Mar. 12

3 1

2

3

4

5

6

Assigned to Preach to the Gentiles

Of that gospel I was made a minister by the gift of God's grace, which was given to me in accordance with the working of his power. Yes, to me, the very least of all saints, there was given this grace, to announce among the Gentiles the good tidings of the unfathomable riches of Christ, and to enlighten all men as to what is the dispensation of the mystery which has been hidden from eternity in God, who created all things; in order that through the Church there be made known to the Principalities and the Powers in the heavens the manifold wisdom of God ' according to the eternal purpose which he accomplished in Christ Jesus our Lord. In him we have assurance and confident access through faith in him. Therefore I pray you not to be disheartened at my tribulations for you, for they are your glory.

7

8

9

10

11

12

13

3. A Prayer for His Readers

14 FOR THIS REASON I bend my knees to the
15 Father of our Lord Jesus Christ, from whom all
fatherhood in heaven and on earth receives its
16 name, that he may grant you from his glorious
riches to be strengthened with power through his
17 Spirit unto the progress of the inner man; and to
have Christ dwelling through faith in your hearts:
18 so that, being rooted and grounded in love, you
may be able to comprehend with all the saints
19 what is the breadth and length and height and
depth, and to know Christ's love which surpasses
knowledge, in order that you may be filled unto
all the fullness of God.

20 Now, to him who is able to accomplish all
things in a measure far beyond what we ask or
conceive, in keeping with the power that is at
21 work in us — to him be glory in the Church and
in Christ Jesus down through all the ages of
time without end. Amen.

II: MORAL

1. For Christians in General

Unity in the Mystical Body

4 1 I THEREFORE, the prisoner in the ┌─────────┐
Lord, exhort you to walk in a manner │ SEPT. 12 │
│ Mar. 13 │
worthy of the calling with which you were called, └─────────┘
2 with all humility and meekness, with patience,
3 bearing with one another in love, careful to preserve the unity of the Spirit in the bond of peace:
4 one body and one Spirit, even as you were called
5 in one hope of your calling; one Lord, one faith,
6 one Baptism; one God and Father of all, who is
above all, and throughout all, and in us all.

4, 12: *The body of Christ:* the mystical body, of which
Christ is the head and the source of supernatural life.

Diversity of Graces

But to each one of us grace was given accord- 7
ing to the measure of Christ's bestowal. Thus it 8
says, "Ascending on high, he led away captives;
he gave gifts to men." Now this, "he ascended," 9
what does it mean but that he also first descended
into the lower parts of the earth? He who de- 10
scended, he it is who ascended also above all the
heavens, that he might fill all things. And he 11
himself gave some men as apostles, and some as
prophets, others again as evangelists, and others
as pastors and teachers, in order to perfect the 12
saints for a work of ministry, for building up the
body of Christ, until we all attain to the unity of 13
the faith and of the deep knowledge of the Son of
God, to perfect manhood, to the mature measure
of the fullness of Christ. And this he has done 14
that we may be now no longer children, tossed to
and fro and carried about by every wind of
doctrine devised in the wickedness of men, in
craftiness, according to the wiles of error. Rather 15
are we to practise the truth in love, and so grow
up in all things in him who is the head, Christ.
For from him the whole body (being closely joined 16
and knit together through every joint of the
system according to the functioning in due measure of each single part) derives its increase to
the building up of itself in love.

Change of Self

This, therefore, I say and testify in the Lord, 17
that henceforward you are not to walk as the
Gentiles walk in the futility of their mind, having 18
their understanding clouded in darkness, estranged from the life of God through the ignorance that is in them, because of the blindness of
their heart. For they have given themselves up 19

in despair to sensuality, greedily practising every
20 kind of uncleanness. But you have not so learned
21 Christ — for surely you have heard of him and
have been taught in him (as truth is in Jesus)
22 that as regards your former manner of life you
are to put off the old man, which is being cor-
23 rupted through its deceptive lusts. But be renewed
24 in the spirit of your mind, ' and put on the new
man, which has been created according to God
in justice and holiness of truth.

Vices to Be Avoided

25   Wherefore, put away lying and speak truth
each one with his neighbor, because we are
26 members of one another. "Be angry and do not
sin": do not let the sun go down upon your anger:
27,28 do not give place to the devil. He who was wont
to steal, let him steal no longer, but rather let him
labor, working with his hands at what is good,
that he may have something to share with him
29 who suffers need. Let no ill speech proceed from
your mouth, but whatever is good for supplying
what fits the current necessity, that it may give
30 grace to the hearers. And do not grieve the Holy
Spirit of God, in whom you were sealed for the
31 day of redemption. Let all bitterness, and wrath,
and indignation, and clamor, and reviling, be re-
32 moved from you, along with all malice. On the

4, 22: *The old man:* human nature under the domination of sin.
4, 23: *The spirit of your mind:* spirit here seems to
mean that interior and higher aspect of the mind by which
it is open to the influence of grace, in contrast to the
futility of the Gentiles' mind spoken of in v. 17.
4, 24: *The new man:* human nature restored by grace
and obedient to the Holy Spirit.
4, 26: The quotation is from Ps. 4, 5. Even in just anger
one must be careful not to sin by excess.
4, 30: *The day of redemption:* the last day, when redemption will be completed.

contrary, be kind to one another, and merciful, generously forgiving one another, as also God in Christ has generously forgiven you.

Be you, therefore, imitators of God, as very dear children ¹ and walk in love, as Christ also loved us and delivered himself up for us an offering and a sacrifice to God to ascend in fragrant odor.

SEPT. 13
Mar. 14

5 1

2

But immorality and every uncleanness or covetousness, let it not even be named among you, as becomes saints; ¹ or obscenity or foolish talk or scurrility, which are out of place, but rather thanksgiving. For know this and understand, that no fornicator, or unclean person, or covetous one (for that is idolatry) has any inheritance in the kingdom of Christ and God. Let no one lead you astray with empty words; for because of these things the wrath of God comes upon the children of disobedience. Do not, then, become partakers with them. For you were once darkness, but now you are light in the Lord. Walk, then, as children of light (for the fruit of the light is in all goodness and justice and truth), testing what is well pleasing to God; and have no fellowship with the unfruitful works of darkness, but rather expose them. For of the things that are done by them in secret it is shameful even to speak; ¹ but all the things that are exposed are made manifest by the light: for all that is made manifest is light. Thus it says, "Awake, sleeper, and arise from among the dead, and Christ will enlighten thee." See to it therefore, brethren, that you walk with care: not as unwise ¹ but as wise, making the most of your time, because the days are evil. Therefore do not become foolish, but understand what the will of the Lord is. And do not be drunk with wine, for in that is debauchery; but be filled with the Spirit, speaking to one another in psalms

3

4

5

6

7

8

9

10

11

12

13

14

15

16

17

18

19

20 and hymns and spiritual songs, singing and making melody in your hearts to the Lord, giving thanks always for all things in the name of our Lord Jesus Christ to God the Father.

2. The Christian Home

The Wife and the Husband

21 BE SUBJECT TO ONE ANOTHER in the fear of
22 Christ. Let wives be subject to their husbands as
23 to the Lord; because a husband is head of the wife, just as Christ is head of the Church, being
24 himself savior of the body. But just as the Church is subject to Christ, so also let wives be to their husbands in all things.

25 Husbands, love your wives, just as Christ also loved the Church, and delivered himself up for
26 her, ' that he might sanctify her, cleansing her in
27 the bath of water by means of the word; in order that he might present to himself the Church in all her glory, not having spot or wrinkle or any such thing, but that she might be holy and with-
28 out blemish. Even thus ought husbands also to love their wives as their own bodies. He who
29 loves his own wife, loves himself. For no one ever hated his own flesh; on the contrary he nourishes and cherishes it, as Christ also does the Church
30 (because we are members of his body, made from
31 his flesh and from his bones). "For this cause a man shall leave his father and mother, and cleave

---

5, 24: *In all things:* i. e., in all things that pertain to the right relationship of husband and wife. Note well that the subjection inculcated in these verses is not a brutal or slavish subjection as to a tyrant, but that of the loved one to her lover, who is according to right order head of the family, as Christ is head of the Church.

5, 26: *The bath of water:* the Sacrament of Baptism.

to his wife; and the two shall become one flesh."
This is a great mystery — I mean in reference to ₃₂
Christ and to the Church. However, let each one ₃₃
of you also love his wife just as he loves himself;
and let the wife respect her husband.

Children and Parents

Children, obey your parents in the | SEPT. 14 | **6** ₁
Lord, for that is right. "Honor thy | Mar. 15 | ₂
father and thy mother" — such is the first commandment with a promise — "that it may be well ₃
with thee, and that thou mayest be long-lived
upon the earth."

And you, fathers, do not provoke your children ₄
to anger, but rear them in the discipline and
admonition of the Lord.

Slaves and Masters

Slaves, obey your masters according to the ₅
flesh, with fear and trembling in the sincerity of
your heart, as you would Christ: ' not serving to ₆
the eye as pleasers of men, but as slaves of
Christ, doing the will of God from your heart, ' giv- ₇
ing your service with good will as to the Lord and
not to men, in the knowledge that whatever good ₈
each does, the same he will receive back from
the Lord, whether he is slave or freeman.

And you, masters, do the same towards them, ₉
and give up threatening, knowing that their Lord
who is also your Lord is in heaven, and that with
him there is no respect of persons.

6, 5-8: St. Paul does not laud slavery as an institution
but in the circumstances he exhorts those already slaves
to humble acceptance of it in corporal activity for a supernatural motive.

3. The Christian Warfare

The Armor of God

10 FOR THE REST, brethren, be strengthened in
11 the Lord and in the might of his power. Put on
the armor of God, that you may be able to stand
12 against the wiles of the devil. For our wrestling
is not against flesh and blood, but against the
Principalities and the Powers, against the world-
rulers of this darkness, against the spiritual
13 forces of wickedness on high. Therefore take up
the armor of God, that you may be able to resist
in the evil day, and stand in all things perfect.
14 Stand, therefore, having girded your loins with
truth, and having put on the breastplate of justice,
15 and having your feet shod with the readiness of
16 the gospel of peace, in all things taking up the
shield of faith, with which you may be able to
quench all the fiery darts of the most wicked one.
17 And take unto you the helmet of salvation and the
sword of the spirit, that is, the word of God.

Assiduous Prayer

18 With all prayer and supplication pray at all
times in the Spirit, and therein be vigilant in all
perseverance and supplication for all the saints
19 —' and for me, that when I open my mouth,
utterance may be granted to me fearlessly to
20 make known the mystery of the gospel, ' for
which I am an ambassador in chains; so that
therein I may dare to speak as I ought.

6, 15: *Readiness:* that prompt vigilance which is provided by the gospel to win a victorious peace.

Conclusion

BUT THAT YOU TOO MAY KNOW my circum- 21
stances and what I am doing, Tychicus, our
dearest brother and faithful minister in the Lord,
will tell you everything. Him I have sent to you 22
for this very purpose, that you may learn our circumstances, and that he may comfort your hearts:

Peace be to the brethren, and love with faith, 23
from God the Father and the Lord Jesus Christ.
Grace be with all those who have a love unfailing 24
for our Lord Jesus Christ. Amen.

THE EPISTLE TO THE PHILIPPIANS

Introduction

The church at Philippi was St. Paul's first founda-tion on European soil. The vision of a man of Mace-donia calling for aid brought the Apostle, St. Timothy and their comrades from Asia into Europe. In Acts (16, 11-40) St. Luke narrates the conversions at Philippi, the cure of a girl possessed by a demon, the Apostle's imprisonment, his release and depar-ture from that city.

On at least two other occasions Philippi had the joy of welcoming its beloved Apostle. The people were deeply attached to St. Paul, helping him by alms in his missionary work; and Paul's special affection for them manifests itself in this Epistle. He hopes to be able to visit them soon.

The occasion of its composition can be gathered from the Epistle. Learning that St. Paul had been cast into prison, the church at Philippi, in order to assist him, sent Epaphroditus with a sum of money and with instructions to remain beside the Apostle as his companion and servant. While thus employed, Epaphroditus fell sick and nearly died. Upon his recovery, St. Paul decided to send him back to Philippi. The Epistle expresses gratitude to the church for its gift and commends the service rendered by Epaphroditus.

At the same time Paul takes the opportunity of exhorting the faithful to compose their dissensions, and he warns them against Jewish converts who wished to make Old Testament practices obligatory for Christians.

No one but St. Paul could have composed such a letter. It was written from Rome in the year 63 A. D.

THE EPISTLE OF ST. PAUL THE APOSTLE TO THE PHILIPPIANS

Introduction

Greeting

PAUL AND TIMOTHY, servants of **1** 1
Jesus Christ, to all the saints in
Christ Jesus that are at Philippi, with the bishops
and deacons: grace be to you, and peace from 2
God our Father, and from the Lord Jesus Christ.

Thanksgiving and Prayer

I give thanks to my God in all my remem- 3
brance of you, always in all my prayers making 4
supplications for you all with joy, because of 5
your association with me in spreading the gospel
of Christ from the first day until now. I am con- 6
vinced of this, that he who has begun a good work
in you will bring it to perfection until the day of
Christ Jesus. And I have the right to feel so 7
about you all, because I have you in my heart, all
of you, alike in my chains and in the defense and
confirmation of the gospel, as sharers in my joy.
For God is my witness how I long for you all in 8
the heart of Christ Jesus. And this I pray, that 9
your charity may more and more abound in
knowledge and all discernment, so that you may 10
approve the better things, that you may be upright and without offense unto the day of Christ,
filled with the fruit of justice, through Jesus 11
Christ, to the glory and praise of God.

I: PERSONAL NEWS

Propagation of the Gospel

NOW I WISH YOU TO KNOW, brethren, that 12
my experiences have turned out rather for the
advancement of the gospel, so that the chains I 13

bear for the sake of Christ have become manifest as such throughout the prætorium and in all
14 other places. And the greater number of the brethren in the Lord, gaining courage from my chains, have dared to speak the word of God
15 more freely and without fear. Some indeed preach Christ even out of envy and contentious-
16 ness, but some also out of good will. Some proclaim Christ out of love since they know I am
17 appointed for the defense of the gospel; but some out of contentiousness, not sincerely, thinking to
18 stir up affliction for me in my chains. But what of it? Provided only that in every way, whether in pretense or in truth, Christ is being proclaimed;
19 in this I rejoice, yes and I shall rejoice. For I know that this will turn out for my salvation, thanks to your prayer and the assistance of the
20 Spirit of Jesus Christ, in accord with my eager longing and hope that in nothing I shall be put to shame, but that with complete assurance now as at all times Christ will be glorified in my body, whether through life or through death.

Sentiments of St. Paul

21   For to me to live is Christ and to die is gain.
22 But if to live in the flesh is my lot, this means for me fruitful labor, and I do not know which to
23 choose. Indeed I am hard pressed from both sides — desiring to depart and to be with Christ,
24 a lot by far the better; yet to stay on in the flesh
25 is necessary for your sake. And with this conviction I know that I shall stay on and continue with you all for your progress and joy in the faith,
26 that your rejoicing in my regard may abound in Christ Jesus through my coming to you again.

1, 18: *In pretense:* some used the gospel as an excuse for furthering their own ambitions. *In truth:* they preach Christ without any selfish motives.

II: EXHORTATION

Firmness

ONLY LET YOUR LIVES be worthy of the gospel 27
of Christ; so that, whether I come and see you,
or remain absent, I may hear about you, that you
are steadfast in one spirit, with one mind striving
together for the faith of the gospel. Do not be 28
terrified in any way by the adversaries; for this
is to them a reason for destruction, but to you for
salvation, and that from God. For you have been 29
given the favor on Christ's behalf — not only to
believe in him but also to suffer for him, while 30
engaged in the same struggle in which you have
seen me and now have heard of me.

Unity and Humility

If, therefore, there is any comfort **2** 1
in Christ, any encouragement from
charity, any fellowship in the Spirit, any feelings
of mercy, ' fill up my joy by thinking alike, having 2
the same charity, with one soul and one mind. Do 3
nothing out of contentiousness or out of vainglory, but in humility let each one regard the
others as his superiors, each one looking not to 4
his own interests but to those of others.

SEPT. 16
Mar. 17

Have this mind in you which was also in Christ 5
Jesus, ' who though he was by nature God, did 6
not consider being equal to God a thing to be
clung to, ' but emptied himself, taking the nature 7
of a slave and being made like unto men. And
appearing in the form of man, he humbled him- 8
self, becoming obedient to death, even to death
on a cross. Therefore God also has exalted him 9
and has bestowed upon him the name that is

2, 7: *Emptied himself:* not by surrendering the divine
nature, which is impossible, but by foregoing the glory
attached to it.

10　above every name, so that at the name of Jesus
every knee should bend of those in heaven, on
11　earth and under the earth, and every tongue
should confess that the Lord Jesus Christ is in
the glory of God the Father.

Fear and Joy in Serving

12　Wherefore, my beloved, obedient as you have
always been, not as in my presence only, but
now much more in my absence, work out your
13　salvation with fear and trembling. For it is God
who of his good pleasure works in you both the
14　will and the performance. Do all things without
15　murmuring and without questioning, so as to be
blameless and guileless, children of God without
blemish in the midst of a depraved and perverse
generation. For among these you shine like stars
16　in the world, holding fast the word of life to my
glory against the day of Christ; because not in
vain have I run, neither in vain have I labored.
17　But even if I am made the libation for the sacrifice and service of your faith, I joy and rejoice
18　with you. And in the same way do you also joy
and rejoice with me.

III: TIMOTHY AND EPAPHRODITUS
Timothy

19　NOW I HOPE IN THE LORD JESUS shortly to
20　send Timothy to you, that I also may be of good
cheer when I know your circumstances. For I
have no one so like-minded who is so genuinely
21　solicitous for you. For they all seek their own
22　interests, not those of Jesus Christ. But know his
worth: as child serves father, so he has served

2, 17: *Made the libation:* the Philippians are the priests,
their faith is the sacrificial animal on the altar, Paul's life
blood is poured out as a libation. *Service:* the Greek
means divine worship.

with me in spreading the gospel. I hope then to 23
send him to you as soon as I see how things stand
with me. But I trust in the Lord that I myself also 24
shall come to you shortly.

Epaphroditus

But I have thought it necessary to send to you 25
Epaphroditus, my brother and fellow-worker and
fellow-soldier, but for you a messenger and the
minister to my need. For he was longing for all of 26
you and was grieved because you had heard that
he was sick. Yes, he was sick, almost unto death. 27
But God had mercy on him, and not on him only
but on me also, that I might not have sorrow upon
sorrow. Therefore I send him the more speedily, 28
in order that seeing him again you may rejoice
and that I may be free from sorrow. Welcome 29
him, then, with all joy in the Lord and show
honor to men like him, because for the work of 30
Christ he drew near to death, risking his life to
supply what was lacking for your service to me.

IV: WARNINGS AGAINST FALSE TEACHERS

The Christian Spirit

FOR THE REST, MY BRETHREN, | SEPT. 17 | **3** 1
rejoice in the Lord. To write you the | Mar. 18 |
same things indeed is not irksome to me, but it is
necessary for you. Beware of the dogs, beware of 2
the evil workers, beware of the mutilation. For we 3
are the circumcision, we who serve God in spirit,
who glory in Christ Jesus and have no confidence
in the flesh—though I too might have confidence 4
even in the flesh. If anyone else thinks he may
have confidence in the flesh, yet more may I: cir- 5
cumcised the eighth day, of the race of Israel, of
the tribe of Benjamin, a Hebrew of Hebrews; as
regards the Law, a Pharisee; as regards zeal, a 6

persecutor of the Church of God; as regards the justice of the Law, leading a blameless life.

Renunciation for the Sake of Christ

7 But the things that were gain to me, these, for
8 the sake of Christ, I have counted loss. Nay more, I count everything loss because of the excelling knowledge of Jesus Christ, my Lord. For his sake I have suffered the loss of all things, and I count
9 them as dung that I may gain Christ ' and be found in him, not having a justice of my own, which is from the Law, but that which is from faith in Christ, the justice from God based
10 upon faith; so that I may know him and the power of his resurrection and the fellowship of his
11 sufferings: become like to him in death, ' in the hope that somehow I may attain to the resurrec-
12 tion from the dead. Not that I have already obtained this, or already have been made perfect, but I press on hoping that I may lay hold of that for which Christ Jesus has laid hold of me.
13 Brethren, I do not consider that I have laid hold of it already. But one thing I do: forgetting what is behind, I strain forward to what is before,
14 I press on towards the goal, to the prize of God's heavenly call in Christ Jesus.

15 Let us then, as many as are perfect, be of this mind; and if in any point you are minded other-
16 wise, this also God will reveal to you. Still in what we have attained let us be of the same mind, and let us also continue in this same rule.

Followers and Opponents of the Cross

17 Brethren, be imitators of me, and mark those
18 who walk after the pattern you have in us. For many walk, of whom I have told you often and now tell you even weeping, that they are enemies
19 of the cross of Christ. Their end is ruin, their god

is the belly, their glory is in their shame, they mind the things of earth. But our citizenship is in heaven from which also we eagerly await a Savior, our Lord Jesus Christ,' who will re-fashion the body of our lowliness, conforming it to the body of his glory by exerting the power by which he is able also to subject all things to himself. So then, my brethren, beloved and longed for, my joy and my crown, stand fast thus in the Lord, beloved.

Conclusion
Concord

I ENTREAT EVODIA and I exhort Syntyche to be of one mind in the Lord. And I beseech thee also, my loyal comrade, help them, for they have toiled with me in the gospel, as have Clement and the rest of my fellow-workers whose names are in the book of life.

SEPT. 18
Mar. 19

Peace and Joy in the Lord

Rejoice in the Lord always; again I say, rejoice. Let your moderation be known to all men. The Lord is near. Have no anxiety, but in every prayer and supplication with thanksgiving let your petitions be made known to God. And may the peace of God which surpasses all understand-ing guard your hearts and your minds in Christ Jesus.

For the rest, brethren, whatever things are true, whatever honorable, whatever just, what-ever holy, whatever lovable, whatever of good repute, if there be any virtue, if anything worthy of praise, think upon these things. And what you have learned and received and heard and seen

---

3, 19: *Their god is the belly:* they are slaves of their grosser appetites.

in me, these things practise. And the God of peace will be with you.

Their Gift

10 I have rejoiced in the Lord greatly that now at last your concern for me has revived. Indeed you were always concerned, but lacked opportunity.
11 Not that I speak because I was in want. For I have learned to be self-sufficing in whatever cir-
12 cumstances I am. I know how to live humbly and I know how to live in abundance (I have been schooled to every place and every condition), to be filled and to be hungry, to have abundance
13 and to suffer want. I can do all things in him who
14 strengthens me. Still, you have done well by
15 sharing in my affliction. But, Philippians, you yourselves also know that in the first days of the gospel, when I left Macedonia, no church went into partnership with me in the matter of giving and receiving but you only.
16 For even in Thessalonica, you sent once and
17 twice something for my need. Not that I am eager for the gift, but I am eager for the profit
18 accumulating to your account. I have all and more than enough. I am fully supplied now that I have received from Epaphroditus what you have sent, a sweet odor, an acceptable sacrifice, well pleas-
19 ing to God. But may my God supply your every need according to his riches in glory in Christ
20 Jesus. Now to our God and Father be glory for endless ages. Amen.

Farewell

21, 22 ' Greet every saint in Christ Jesus. ' The breth-ren with me here greet you. All the saints greet
23 you, especially those of Cæsar's household. The grace of our Lord Jesus Christ be with your spirit. Amen.

THE EPISTLE TO THE COLOSSIANS
Introduction

During Paul's stay at Ephesus from about 53 to 56 A. D. (Acts 19, 1—20, 2), the message of the Gospel was carried inland by his zealous converts. Among these was Epaphras, who evangelized the towns of Colossæ, Laodicea and Hierapolis (4, 12f), situated in the valley of the Lycus River little more than a hundred miles east of Ephesus. The Apostle took a personal interest in the work of his disciple (2, 1). A few years later, while he was being detained at Rome for trial before Cæsar, he had news of the Colossians through Epaphras. Though the report of the evangelist was, on the whole, favorable (1, 4-8; 2, 5f), he saw dangerous tendencies in the young Christian community. Self-appointed teachers claimed for angels a very high place of honor (2, 18f), and boasted of a deeper knowledge of Christianity, insisting on Judaic observances (2, 16) and a false asceticism (2, 20-23). Concerned lest his work be destroyed, Epaphras had come to Rome to seek help from Paul.

Paul met the danger by sending (63 A. D.) a letter to Colossæ, borne by Tychicus (4, 7-9). To counter the errors he set forth in clear terms the true doctrine concerning Christ, our Redeemer, head of the mystical body, the Church (1, 15—2, 3), and drew up rules for an ideal Christian life (3, 5—4, 6). Between these positive sections, the Apostle inserted a vigorous condemnation of the false teachings (2, 4—3, 4). Because of the emphatic statement of Christ's divinity that they contain, the first two chapters of the letter are of great doctrinal importance.

The Epistle to the Colossians bears a remarkable resemblance to the Epistle to the Ephesians. Most of the words and phrases of this shorter letter are met with in the other also. Written at the same time, both were addressed to communities of Jewish and pagan converts, struggling in like circumstances to maintain the purity of their faith. The two Epistles should be read and studied together.

THE EPISTLE OF ST. PAUL THE APOSTLE TO THE COLOSSIANS

Introduction

Greeting

1 1 PAUL, AN APOSTLE OF JESUS CHRIST by the will of God, and our 2 brother Timothy, ' to the brethren in Colossæ, 3 holy and faithful in Christ Jesus: grace be to you and peace from God our Father.

SEPT. 19
Mar. 20

Thanksgiving

We give thanks to the God and Father of our 4 Lord Jesus Christ, praying always for you, ' for we have heard of your faith in Christ Jesus and of 5 the love that you bear towards all the saints ' because of the hope that is laid up for you in heaven. Of that hope you have heard in the word 6 of the gospel truth ' which has reached you, even as it is in the whole world, both bearing fruit and growing; just as it does among you since the day that you heard and recognized the grace of God 7 in truth. Thus you learned from our most dear fellow-servant Epaphras. He is a faithful minister 8 of Christ Jesus in your behalf; and it was he who made known to us your love in the Spirit.

Prayer for Their Progress

9 This is why we too have been praying for you unceasingly, since the day we heard this, and asking that you may be filled with knowledge of his will, in all spiritual wisdom and understand-10 ing. May you walk worthily of God and please him in all things, bearing fruit in every good 11 work and growing in the knowledge of God. May you be completely strengthened through his glorious power unto perfect patience and long-

suffering; joyfully ' rendering thanks to the 12
Father, who has made us worthy to share the lot
of the saints in light. He has rescued us from 13
the power of darkness and transferred us into
the kingdom of his beloved Son, in whom we 14
have our redemption, the remission of our sins.

I: THE PRE-EMINENCE OF CHRIST

God, Creator, Head

HE IS THE IMAGE of the invisible God, the 15
firstborn of every creature. For in him were 16
created all things in the heavens and on the
earth, things visible and things invisible, whether
Thrones, or Dominations, or Principalities, or
Powers. All things have been created through
and unto him, ' and he is before all creatures, 17
and in him all things hold together. Again, he is 18
the head of his body, the Church; he, who is the
beginning, the firstborn from the dead, that in
all things he may have the first place. For it has 19
pleased God the Father that in him all his fullness should dwell, and that through him he 20
should reconcile to himself all things, whether on
the earth or in the heavens, making peace
through the blood of his cross.

Conciliator

You yourselves were at one time estranged 21
and enemies in mind through your evil works.
But now he has reconciled you in his body of 22
flesh through his death, to present you holy and
undefiled and irreproachable before him. Only 23
you must remain firmly founded in the faith and
steadfast and not withdrawing from the hope of
the gospel which you have heard. It has been
preached to every creature under heaven; and
of it I, Paul, have become a minister.

Center of Preaching

24 I rejoice now in the sufferings I bear for your
sake; and what is lacking of the sufferings of
Christ I fill up in my flesh for his body, which is
25 the Church; whose minister I have become in
virtue of the office that God has given me in your
regard. For I am to preach the word of God
26 fully — the mystery which has been hidden for
ages and generations, but now is clearly shown
27 to his saints. To them God willed to make known
how rich in glory is this mystery among the
Gentiles — Christ in you, your hope of glory!
28 Him we preach, admonishing every man and
teaching every man in all wisdom, that we may
29 present every man perfect in Christ Jesus. At
this, too, I work and strive, according to the
2 1 power which he mightily exerts in me. For I wish
you to know what great concern I have for you
and for the Laodiceans and for all who have not
2 seen me in the flesh; that their hearts may be
comforted, and they themselves well equipped in
charity and in all the riches of complete understanding, so as to know the mystery of God the
3 Father of Christ Jesus, in whom are hidden all
the treasures of wisdom and knowledge.

II: WARNINGS AGAINST FALSE TEACHERS

A General Admonition

4 NOW I SAY THIS so that no one
may deceive you by persuasive | SEPT. 20
Mar. 21
5 words. For though I am absent in body, yet in
spirit I am with you, rejoicing at the sight of your
orderly array and the steadfastness of your faith
6 in Christ. Therefore, as you have received Jesus
7 Christ our Lord, so walk in him; be rooted in him
and built up on him, and strengthened in the

faith, as you also have learnt, rendering thanks abundantly.

Speculative Errors

See to it that no one deceives you by philosophy and vain deceit, according to human traditions, according to the elements of the world and not according to Christ. For in him dwells all the fullness of the Godhead bodily, and in him who is the head of every Principality and Power you have received of that fullness. In him, too, you have been circumcised with a circumcision not wrought by hand, but through putting off the body of the flesh, a circumcision which is of Christ. For you were buried together with him in Baptism, and in him also rose again through faith in the working of God who raised him from the dead. And you, when you were dead by reason of your sins and the uncircumcision of your flesh, he brought to life along with him, forgiving you all your sins, cancelling the decree against us, which was hostile to us. Indeed, he has taken it completely away, nailing it to the cross. Disarming the Principalities and Powers, he displayed them openly, leading them away in triumph by force of it.

Erroneous Practices

Let no one, then, call you to account for what you eat or drink or in regard to a festival or a new moon or a Sabbath. These are a shadow of things to come, but the substance is of Christ. Let no one cheat you who takes pleasure in self-abasement and worship of the angels, and enters vainly

---

2, 8: *The elements of the world:* a term used in the syncretistic worship practised in Asia Minor, signifying the demons whom the heathens in their superstition held to be in control of the four elements and the heavenly bodies.

into what he has not seen, puffed up by his mere
19 human mind. Such a one is not united to the head,
from whom the whole body, supplied and built
up by joints and ligaments, attains a growth that
is of God.

20 If you have died with Christ to the elements of
the world, why, as if still living in the world, do
21 you lay down the rules: "Do not touch; nor taste;
22 nor handle!" — things that must all perish in
their very use? In this you follow "the precepts
23 and doctrines of men," ' which, to be sure, have
a show of wisdom in superstition and self-abasement and hard treatment of the body, but are not
to be held in esteem, and lead to the full gratifica-
tion of the flesh.

Mystical Death and Resurrection

3 1 Therefore, if you have risen with
Christ, seek the things that are | SEPT. 21 / Mar. 22 |
above, where Christ is seated at the right hand
2 of God. Mind the things that are above, not the
3 things that are on earth. For you have died and
4 your life is hidden with Christ in God. When
Christ, your life, shall appear, then you too will
appear with him in glory.

III: THE IDEAL CHRISTIAN LIFE IN THE WORLD

Renounce Vices

5 THEREFORE MORTIFY YOUR MEMBERS, which
are on earth: immorality, uncleanness, lust, evil
desire and covetousness (which is a form of idol-
6 worship). Because of these things the wrath of
7 God comes upon the unbelievers, and you yourselves once walked in them when they were your
8 life. But now do you also put them all away:

anger, wrath, malice, abusive language and foul-mouthed utterances. Do not lie to one another. 9 Strip off the old man with his deeds ' and put on 10 the new, one that is being renewed unto perfect knowledge "according to the image of his Creator." Here there is not "Gentile and Jew," 11 "circumcised and uncircumcised," "Barbarian and Scythian," "slave and freeman"; but Christ is all things and in all.

Practise Virtues

Put on therefore, as God's chosen ones, holy 12 and beloved, a heart of mercy, kindness, humility, meekness, patience. Bear with one another 13 and forgive one another, if anyone has a grievance against any other; even as the Lord has forgiven you, so also do you forgive. But above all these 14 things have charity, which is the bond of perfection. And may the peace of Christ reign in your 15 hearts; unto that peace, indeed, you were called in one body. Show yourselves thankful. ' Let the 16 word of Christ dwell in you abundantly: in all wisdom teach and admonish one another by psalms, hymns and spiritual songs, singing in your hearts to God by his grace. Whatever you 17 do in word or in work, do all in the name of the Lord Jesus, giving thanks to God the Father through him.

The Christian Family

Wives, be subject to your husbands, as is becoming in the Lord. Husbands, love your wives 19 and do not be bitter towards them. Children, 20 obey your parents in all things, for that is pleasing in the Lord. Fathers, do not provoke your 21 children to anger, that they may not be discouraged.

[533]

Slaves and Masters

22 Slaves, obey in all things your masters according to the flesh; not with eye-service seeking to please men, but in singleness of heart from fear
23 of the Lord. Whatever you do, work at it from the
24 heart as for the Lord and not for men, knowing that from the Lord you will receive the inheri-
25 tance as your reward. Serve the Lord Christ. ' For he who does a wrong will reap the wrong he did,
4 1 and there is no respect of persons. Masters, give your slaves what is just and fair, knowing that you too have a Master in heaven.

Prayer and Prudence

2 Be assiduous in prayer, being wakeful therein with thanksgiving.

SEPT. 22
Mar. 23

3 At the same time pray for us also, that God may give us an opportunity for the word, to announce the mystery of Christ (for which also I am in
4 chains), that I may openly announce it as I ought
5 to speak. Walk in wisdom as regards outsiders,
6 making the most of your time. Let your speech, while always attractive, be seasoned with salt, that you may know how you ought to answer each one.

Conclusion
Tychicus and Onesimus

7 ALL MY CIRCUMSTANCES TYCHICUS, our dear-
8 est brother and faithful minister and fellow-servant in the Lord, will tell you. Him I have sent to you for this very purpose, that he may learn
9 your circumstances and comfort your hearts. With him is Onesimus, our most dear and faithful

---

4, 5: Look for favorable openings to win outsiders to the faith.

brother, who is one of you. They will tell you all that is going on here.

From Paul's Co-workers

Aristarchus, my fellow-prisoner, sends you 10 greetings; so does Mark, Barnabas' cousin (concerning whom you have received instructions — if he comes to you, welcome him), ' and Jesus 11 who is called Justus. Of men circumcised, these only are my fellow-workers in the kingdom of God; they have been a comfort to me. Epaphras, 12 who is one of you, sends you greetings — a servant of Christ Jesus, who is ever solicitous for you in his prayers, that you may remain perfect and completely in accord with all the will of God. Yes, I bear him witness that he labors much for 13 you and for those who are at Laodicea and at Hierapolis. Luke, our most dear physician, and 14 Demas send you greetings.

A Message for the Laodiceans

Greetings to the brethren who are at Laodicea 15 and to Nymphas and the church that is in his house. And when this letter has been read among 16 you, see that it be read in the church of the Laodiceans also; and that you yourselves read the letter from Laodicea. And say to Archippus: 17 "Look to the ministry which thou hast received in the Lord, that thou fulfill it."

I, Paul, greet you by my own hand. Remember 18 my chains. Grace be with you. Amen.

THE FIRST EPISTLE
TO THE THESSALONIANS

Introduction

St. Paul founded the church at Thessalonica during the early part of his second great missionary journey, i.e., about 51 A.D. Thessalonica, the capital of Macedonia, was a large and important city. Its population was predominantly Gentile, but Jews dwelt there in sufficient numbers to have a synagogue. Paul succeeded in converting some of the Jews and a large number of Gentiles. But his success stirred up the envy of the unbelieving Jews, who by calumny and riot compelled him to flee to Berœa. From there he went to Athens and Corinth, and it was in the latter city that this letter was written.

While at Athens Paul, fearing lest the persecution which continued against the church at Thessalonica should cause his new converts to abandon the faith, sent Timothy to ascertain conditions in the church and to comfort and strengthen its members. Timothy reported to Paul at Corinth, bringing the cheering news of their constancy in the face of persecution. He likewise informed Paul that the Thessalonians required further instruction on the Second Coming of Christ, and this topic forms the main doctrinal subject of the Epistle, which was written shortly after Timothy's return from Thessalonica. The Second Epistle to the Thessalonians was written soon after the First, and these two Epistles are generally regarded as the earliest of Paul's writings.

THE FIRST EPISTLE OF ST. PAUL THE APOSTLE TO THE THESSALONIANS

Introduction

Greeting

PAUL AND SILVANUS AND TIMO- | SEPT. 23 | **1** 1
THY, to the church of the Thessa- | Mar. 24 |
lonians in God the Father and in the Lord Jesus
Christ: grace be to you and peace.   2

Thanksgiving for Their Faith

We give thanks to God always for you all,
continually making a remembrance of you in our
prayers; being mindful before God our Father   3
of your work of faith, and labor, and charity, and
your enduring hope in our Lord Jesus Christ.
We know, brethren, beloved of God, how you   4
were chosen. For our gospel was not delivered to   5
you in word only, but in power also, and in the
Holy Spirit, and in much fullness, as indeed you
know what manner of men we have been among
you for your sakes. And you became imitators   6
of us and of the Lord, receiving the word in
great tribulation, with joy of the Holy Spirit, ' so   7
that you became a pattern to all the believers in
Macedonia and in Achaia. For from you the word   8
of the Lord has been spread abroad, not only in
Macedonia and Achaia, but in every place your
faith in God has gone forth, so that we need say
nothing further. For they themselves report con-   9
cerning us how we entered among you, and how
you turned to God from idols, to serve the living
and true God, ' and to await from heaven Jesus,   10
his Son, whom he raised from the dead, who has
delivered us from the wrath to come.

1, 10: *Wrath to come:* eternal punishment.

I: PAUL'S PAST RELATIONS AND PRESENT INTEREST

His Mission Among Them

2 1 FOR YOU YOURSELVES, brethren, know that 2 our coming among you was not in vain. But although we had previously experienced suffering and shameful treatment at Philippi, as you know, we had confidence in our God to preach to you 3 the gospel of God amid much anxiety. For our exhortation was not from error, nor from impure 4 motives, nor from guile. But as approved by God to be entrusted with the gospel, so we speak not as pleasing men, but God, who proves our hearts. 5 For at no time have we used words of flattery, as you know, nor any pretext for avarice, God is 6 witness, nor have we sought glory from men, 7 neither from you nor from others. Although as the apostles of Christ we could have claimed a position of honor among you, still while in your midst we were as children: as if a nurse were 8 cherishing her own children, so we in our love for you would gladly have imparted to you not only the gospel of God, but also our own souls; because you had become most dear to us.

9 For you remember, brethren, our labor and toil. We worked night and day so as not to be a burden to any of you while we preached to you 10 the gospel of God. You are witnesses and God also, how holy and just and blameless was our 11 conduct towards you who have believed; inasmuch as you are aware of how we entreated and comforted each one of you, acting towards you as 12 a father towards his children, declaring to you that you should walk worthily of God, who called you unto his kingdom and glory.

2, 18: *Satan hindered us:* i. e., through evil men, whether Jews or Gentiles, who served as his agents to interfere with Paul's ministry.

Thanksgiving for Their Constancy

Therefore we too give thanks to God without 13
ceasing, because when you heard and received
from us the word of God, you welcomed it not as
the word of men, but, as it truly is, the word of
God, who works in you who have believed. For 14
you, brethren, have become imitators of the
churches of God which are in Judea in Christ
Jesus, in that you also have suffered the same
things from your own countrymen as they have
from the Jews, who both killed the Lord Jesus 15
and the prophets, and have persecuted us. They
are displeasing to God, and are hostile to all men,
because they hinder us from speaking to the 16
Gentiles, that they may be saved. Thus they are
always filling up the measure of their sins, for
the wrath of God has come upon them to the
utmost.

But we, brethren, being bereaved of you for a 17
short time, in sight, not in heart, have made more
than ordinary efforts to hasten to see you, so
great has been our desire. For we wanted to 18
come to you — I, Paul, more than once — but
Satan hindered us. For what is our hope, or joy, 19
or crown of glory, if not you before our Lord
Jesus Christ at his coming? Yes, you are our 20
glory and joy.

The Mission of Timothy

And so when we could bear it no   SEPT. 24   **3** 1
longer we decided to remain at   Mar. 25
Athens alone, ' and we sent Timothy, our brother 2
and a servant of God in the gospel of Christ, to
strengthen and comfort you in your faith, lest 3
any should be shaken by these tribulations. For
you yourselves know that we are appointed thereto. Indeed even when we were with you we used 4
to tell you that we should suffer tribulations, as

5 also it has come to pass, and you know. Consequently when I could bear it no longer I sent in order to know your faith, lest perhaps the tempter might have tempted you, and our labor might come to naught.

6 But now that Timothy has come to us from you, and has made known to us your faith and charity, and your kindly remembrance of us at all times, and that you long to see us just as we long to see

7 you, we have accordingly found comfort in you, brethren, amid all our trials and tribulations, on

8 account of your faith; because now we live, if you

9 stand fast in the Lord. For what thanks can we return to God for you for all the joy wherewith

10 we rejoice for your sakes before our God? Night and day we pray more and more that we may see you again, and may supply those things that are lacking to your faith.

11 May God our Father and our Lord Jesus direct

12 our way unto you. And may the Lord make you to increase and abound in charity towards one another, and towards all men just as we do

13 towards you, that he may strengthen your hearts, blameless in holiness before God our Father, at the coming of our Lord Jesus Christ, with all his saints. Amen.

Exhortation to Chastity and Charity

4 1 Moreover, brethren, even as you have learned from us how you ought to walk to please God — as indeed you are walking — we beseech and exhort you in the Lord Jesus to make even

2 greater progress. For you know what precepts I

3 have given to you by the Lord Jesus. For this is the will of God, your sanctification; that you ab-

4 stain from immorality; that every one of you learn how to possess his vessel in holiness and

5 honor, not in the passion of lust like the Gentiles

who do not know God; that no one transgress 6
and overreach his brother in the matter, because
the Lord is the avenger of all these things, as we
have told you before and have testified. For God 7
has not called us unto uncleanness, but unto
holiness. Therefore, he who rejects these things 8
rejects not man but God, who has also given his
Holy Spirit to us.

But concerning brotherly charity there is no 9
need for us to write to you, for you yourselves
have learned from God to love one another. For 10
indeed you practise it towards all the brethren
all over Macedonia. But we exhort you, brethren,
to make even greater progress. Strive to live 11
peacefully, minding your own affairs, working
with your own hands, as we charged you, so 12
that you may walk becomingly towards outsiders,
and may need nothing.

II: THE SECOND COMING OF OUR LORD

Witnessed by the Dead

BUT WE WOULD NOT, brethren, | SEPT. 25 | 13
have you ignorant concerning those | Mar. 26 |
who are asleep, lest you should grieve, even as
others who have no hope. For if we believe that 14
Jesus died and rose again, so with him God will
bring those also who have fallen asleep through
Jesus. For this we say to you in the word of the 15
Lord, that we who live, who survive until the
coming of the Lord, shall not precede those who
have fallen asleep. For the Lord himself with cry 16
of command, with voice of archangel, and with
trumpet of God will descend from heaven; and

4, 4: *Vessel:* may refer to a man's body or to his wife. The
first meaning seems preferable. In this sense of "body,"
Paul is forbidding the use of it for immorality. In the
sense of "wife," two translations are given: a) acquire a
wife, b) possess a wife; a) avoid sexual indulgence before
marriage, b) make a proper use of marriage.

17 the dead in Christ will rise up first. Then we who live, who survive, shall be caught up together with them in clouds to meet the Lord in the air, and so we shall ever be with the Lord.
18 Wherefore, comfort one another with these words.

Time Unknown

5 1 But of the times and seasons, brethren, you
2 have no need that we write to you, for you yourselves know well that the day of the Lord is
3 to come as a thief in the night. For when they shall say, "Peace and security," even then sudden destruction will come upon them, as birth pangs upon her who is with child, and they will not escape.

Be Always Prepared

4 But you, brethren, are not in darkness, that
5 that day should overtake you as a thief; for you are all children of the light and children of the day. We are not of night, nor of darkness.
6 Therefore, let us not sleep as do the rest, but let
7 us be wakeful and sober. For they who sleep, sleep at night, and they who are drunk, are
8 drunk at night. But let us, who are of the day, be sober. Let us put on the breastplate of faith and charity, and for a helmet the hope of salvation.
9 For God has not destined us unto wrath, but to gain salvation through our Lord Jesus Christ,
10 who died for us in order that, whether we wake or sleep, we should live together with him.
11 Wherefore, comfort one another and edify one another, even as indeed you do.

4, 15: *We:* applies to the faithful, whoever they may be, who are alive at the end of the world. Those living at the Second Coming of Christ shall have no advantage over those who have died, because the living shall not go before them to glory or receive glory without them. The Thessalonians, therefore, need not grieve over the lot of the dead.

Conclusion

Obedience, Patience and Charity

NOW WE BESEECH YOU, brethren, to appre-   12
ciate those who labor among you, and who are
over you in the Lord and admonish you. Esteem   13
them with a more abundant love on account of
their work. Be at peace with them.'And we exhort   14
you, brethren, reprove the irregular, comfort the
fainthearted, support the weak, be patient
towards all men. See that no one renders evil   15
for evil to any man; but always strive after good
towards one another and towards all men.

Rejoice always. Pray without ceasing. In all 16-18
things give thanks; for this is the will of God in
Christ Jesus regarding you all. Do not extinguish   19
the Spirit. Do not despise prophecies. But test all 20, 21
things; hold fast that which is good. Keep your-   22
selves from every kind of evil.

Final Blessing and Greeting

And may the God of peace himself sanctify   23
you completely, and may your spirit and soul and
body be preserved sound, blameless at the coming of our Lord Jesus Christ. He who called you   24
is faithful and will do this.

Brethren, pray for us. Greet all the brethren 25, 26
with a holy kiss. I charge you by the Lord that   27
this epistle be read to all the holy brethren. The   28
grace of our Lord Jesus Christ be with you. Amen.

5, 19: *Do not extinguish the Spirit:* make use of the
charismatic gifts such as tongues and prophecy.

5, 21: *Test all things:* they are to make certain that the
gifts are genuine.

5, 23: *Spirit:* the human soul as the principle of intelli-
gence and will. *Soul:* the human soul as the principle of
animal and sensitive life, hence as the seat of the affections
and feelings. *Spirit, soul* and *body,* are the terms in which
Paul sums up man and his activities. Consequently he
prays that under the grace of God they may be wholly
sanctified.

Preface

The First Epistle failed to quiet the doubts and fears of the Thessalonians, and so Paul hastened to supply them with fuller information on the subject of the *parousia*, or Second Coming of Christ. He informed them that the *parousia* was not at hand. It could not take place until a great apostasy occurred and Antichrist appeared. Some of the Thessalonians who were convinced that the Second Coming of Christ was at hand thought it useless to work, and consequently lived irregularly. Paul condemned this practice, and ordered the offenders to be corrected. He urged all to adhere to his teachings, whether these were given orally or in writing.

THE SECOND EPISTLE OF ST. PAUL THE APOSTLE TO THE THESSALONIANS

Introduction

Greeting

1 1 PAUL AND SILVANUS AND TIMOTHY, to the church of the Thessalonians in God our Father and the Lord Jesus 2 Christ: grace be to you and peace from God our Father and the Lord Jesus Christ.

SEPT. 26
Mar. 27

Their Faith and Constancy

3 We are bound to give thanks to God always for you, brethren. It is fitting that we should, because your faith grows exceedingly and your 4 charity each one for the other increases. And because of this we ourselves boast of you in the churches of God for your patience and faith in all your persecutions and the tribulations that 5 you are enduring. In this there is a proof of the just judgment of God counting you worthy of the

kingdom of God, for which also you suffer. Indeed it is just on the part of God to repay with affliction those who afflict you, and to give you who are afflicted rest with us at the revelation of the Lord Jesus, who will come from heaven with the angels of his power, ' in flaming fire, to inflict punishment on those who do not know God, and who do not obey the gospel of our Lord Jesus Christ. These will be punished with eternal ruin, away from the face of the Lord and the glory of his power, when on that day he shall come to be glorified in his saints, and to be marvelled at in all those who have believed. For our testimony before you has been believed.

Prayer for Their Glorification

To this end also we pray always for you, that our God may make you worthy of his calling, and may fulfill with power every good purpose and work of faith, that the name of our Lord Jesus Christ may be glorified in you, and you in him, according to the grace of our God and the Lord Jesus Christ.

I: THE SECOND COMING OF OUR LORD

Preludes to the Second Coming

WE BESEECH YOU, BRETHREN, by the coming **2** of our Lord Jesus Christ and our being gathered together unto him, not to be hastily shaken from your right mind, nor terrified, whether by spirit, or by utterance, or by letter attributed to us, as though the day of the Lord were near at hand. Let no one deceive you in any way, for the day of the Lord will not come unless the apostasy comes

---

2, 3: The *parousia* must be preceded by a great apostasy, i. e., a great religious revolt, and the advent of the man of sin, i. e., Antichrist. *Son of perdition:* one entirely deserving of eternal punishment.

first, and the man of sin is revealed, the son of
4 perdition, who opposes and is exalted above all
that is called God, or that is worshipped, so that
he sits in the temple of God and gives himself
5 out as if he were God. Do you not remember
that when I was still with you, I used to tell you
6 these things? And now you know what restrains
him, that he may be revealed in his proper time.
7 For the mystery of iniquity is already at work;
provided only that he who is at present restraining it, does still restrain, until he is gotten out of
the way.

8   And then the wicked one will be revealed,
whom the Lord Jesus will slay with the breath
of his mouth and will destroy with the brightness
of his coming.

9   And his coming is according to the working of
Satan with all power and signs and lying wonders,
10 and with all wicked deception to those who are
perishing. For they have not received the love of
11 truth that they might be saved. Therefore God
sends them a misleading influence that they may

2, 4: Antichrist will be characterized by great impiety and
pride. *He sits in the temple of God,* etc.: he will aspire to
be treated as God and proclaim that he is really God.

2, 7: *Mystery of iniquity:* the evil power of which Antichrist is to be the public exponent and champion. *He who
is at present restraining it:* the obstacle is now spoken
of as a person.

2, 8: When Christ appears in glory, He will inflict defeat
and death on Antichrist by a mere word of command.

2, 9f: By the aid of Satan Antichrist will perform prodigies
which men will falsely regard as miracles, and by means
of which they will be led to adopt sinful practices and
erroneous doctrines.

2, 11: *God sends:* God will allow their willful rejection of
truth to have its natural results of spiritual blindness,
impenitence and damnation.

believe falsehood, that all may be judged who   12
have not believed the truth, but have preferred
wickedness.

Thanksgiving for Their Election

But we, brethren beloved of God, | SEPT. 27 | 13
are bound to give thanks to God | Mar. 28 |
always for you, because God has chosen you as
first-fruits unto salvation through the sanctification of the Spirit and belief of the truth. For this   14
purpose he also called you by our preaching to
gain the glory of our Lord Jesus Christ. So then,   15
brethren, stand firm, and hold the teachings that
you have learned, whether by word or by letter
of ours. And may our Lord Jesus Christ himself   16
and God our Father, who has loved us and has
given us through grace everlasting consolation
and good hope, comfort and strengthen your   17
hearts in every good work and word.

II: EXHORTATION

Request for Mutual Prayer

IN CONCLUSION, BRETHREN, pray for us, that **3** 1
the word of the Lord may run and be glorified
even as among you, and that we may be delivered   2
from troublesome and evil men; for not all men
have the faith.

But the Lord is faithful, who will strengthen   3
you and guard you from evil. And we have con-   4
fidence in the Lord as regards you, that you
both do and will do the things that we enjoin.
And may the Lord direct your hearts into the love   5
of God and the patience of Christ.

Against Idleness

And we charge you, brethren, in the name of   6
our Lord Jesus Christ, to withdraw yourselves

[547]

from every brother who lives irregularly, and not
7 according to the teaching received from us. For
you yourselves know how you ought to imitate
us; for we were not unruly while with you,
8 neither did we eat any man's bread at his cost,
but we worked night and day in labor and toil,
9 so that we might not burden any of you. Not that
we did not have the right to do so, but that we
might make ourselves an example for you to
10 imitate us. For indeed when we were with you, we
used to charge you: if any man will not work,
11 neither let him eat. For we have heard that some
among you are living irregularly, doing no work
12 but busy at meddling. Now such persons we
charge and exhort in the Lord Jesus Christ that
they work quietly and eat their own bread.

13　　But you, brethren, do not grow tired of well-
14 doing. And if anyone does not obey our word by
this letter, note that man and do not associate
15 with him, that he may be put to shame. Yet do
not regard him as an enemy, but admonish him
as a brother.

Conclusion

Final Blessing and Greeting

16　　AND MAY THE LORD of peace himself give you
everlasting peace in every place. The Lord be
17 with you all. I, Paul, greet you with my own hand.
This is the mark in every letter. Thus I write.
18 The grace of our Lord Jesus Christ be with you
all. Amen.

3, 6: *Irregularly:* here, as in v. 11, the term refers to
deliberate avoidance of work, or malingering.

3, 8f: He did not insist on his right to their support, but
provided for himself by the labor of his own hands.

THE FIRST EPISTLE TO TIMOTHY

Introduction

The two Epistles to St. Timothy and the one to St. Titus are called Pastoral Epistles because they are addressed directly, not to any church as a group, but rather to its head or pastor for his guidance in the rule of the church. All three Epistles are closely connected in form and content. From earliest times these letters have been recognized as inspired and canonical by the eastern and western Fathers.

St. Timothy was of Lystra in Lycaonia, born of a Greek father and a Jewish mother (Acts 16, 1). He was educated in the assiduous reading of the Scriptures (2 Tim. 3, 15). His mother Eunice and his grandmother Lois (2 Tim. 1, 5), as well as Timothy himself, probably embraced the faith during St. Paul's first stay at Lystra, since they were already Christians at his return on the second missionary journey (Acts 16, 1). It was at that time that Timothy was highly recommended by the Christians and the Apostle chose him as a missionary companion. Since Timothy was uncircumcised, the Apostle performed this rite upon him to facilitate his preaching among the Jewish colonists in the regions of Phrygia (Acts 16, 3) and elsewhere. Thereafter Timothy was seldom parted from St. Paul, who employed him in some difficult and confidential missions (2 Thess. 3, 1-8; 1 Cor. 4, 17; 16, 10; Phil. 2, 19-23; Heb. 13, 23). During the first imprisonment of the Apostle at Rome Timothy was with his master (Col. 1, 1; Philem. 1; Phil. 1, 1). After this imprisonment he accompanied the Apostle on his last missionary journey and was left at Ephesus to take charge of the church there (1 Tim. 1, 3). The Apostle shortly before his death wrote Timothy to come to him before the winter (2 Tim. 1, 4; 4, 9. 21). According to tradition Timothy spent the rest of his life at Ephesus as its bishop and was martyred during the winter of 97 A.D. His feast is celebrated in the Latin Church on January 24.

This first Epistle was written between Paul's liberation from the first imprisonment (63 A.D.) and his

THE FIRST EPISTLE OF ST. PAUL
THE APOSTLE TO TIMOTHY

Introduction
Greeting

1 1 PAUL, AN APOSTLE OF JESUS SEPT. 28
CHRIST, by the order of God our Mar. 29
2 Savior, and of Christ Jesus our hope, ' to Timothy, his beloved son in the faith: grace, mercy and peace from God the Father and from Christ Jesus our Lord.

I: AGAINST FALSE TEACHERS
Timothy's Mission at Ephesus

3 WHEN I WENT TO MACEDONIA, I asked thee
4 to stay on at Ephesus that thou mightest charge some not to teach novel doctrines, and not to study fables and endless genealogies which be-
5 get controversies rather than godly edification which is in the faith. Now the purpose of this
6 charge is charity, from a pure heart and a good conscience and faith unfeigned. Some going

---

death (67 A.D.), on one of his journeys not mentioned in the Acts of the Apostles (1 Tim. 1, 3; cf. also 2 Tim. 4, 13. 20; Titus 3, 12), since it presupposes an ecclesiastical hierarchy as well as false teachers at Ephesus, who were not there during the Apostle's third missionary journey (Acts 20, 29f). For these reasons Catholic authors commonly hold that the Epistle was written in 65 or 66 A.D. from Macedonia (1 Tim. 1, 3).

A twofold thought is dominant in this Epistle. Timothy must energetically combat false teachers and actively engage in the work of organizing the community. The thought of the Apostle moves restlessly back and forth on these two points, since he was fully aware from his own experience of the dangers that threatened.

astray from these things have turned aside to vain babbling, desiring to be teachers of the 7 Law, when they understand neither what they say nor the things about which they make assertion.

Role of the Law

But we know that the Law is good, if a man 8 uses it rightly, knowing that the Law is not made 9 for the just, but for the unjust and rebellious, for the ungodly and sinners, for criminals and the defiled, for parricides and matricides, for murderers, for immoral people, for sodomites, for 10 kidnappers, for liars, for perjurers, and whatever else is contrary to the sound doctrine, according 11 to the gospel of the glory of the blessed God, which has been committed to my trust.

The Apostle's Own Life

I give thanks to Christ Jesus our Lord, who has 12 strengthened me, because he counted me trustworthy in making me his minister. For I formerly 13 was a blasphemer, a persecutor and a bitter adversary; but I obtained the mercy of God because I acted ignorantly, in unbelief. Indeed, the grace 14 of our Lord has abounded beyond measure in the faith and love that is in Christ Jesus. This saying 15 is true and worthy of entire acceptance, that Jesus Christ came into the world to save sinners, of whom I am the chief. But for this reason I 16 obtained mercy, that in me first Christ Jesus might show forth all patience, as an example to those who shall believe in him for the attainment of life everlasting. To the King of the ages, 17 who is immortal, invisible, the one only God, be honor and glory forever and ever. Amen.

Fidelity to Vocation

18 I commit to thee this charge, my son Timothy, that according to the prophecies once made concerning thee, thou mayest fight the good fight
19 by means of them, having faith and a good conscience. Some rejecting this have made ship-
20 wreck of the faith, among whom are Hymeneus and Alexander, whom I have delivered up to Satan that they may learn not to blaspheme.

II: PASTORAL CHARGE

Directions on Prayer

2 1 I URGE THEREFORE, first of all, that supplications, prayers, interces-

SEPT. 29
Mar. 30

2 sions and thanksgivings be made for all men; for kings, and for all in high positions, that we may lead a quiet and peaceful life in all piety and
3 worthy behavior. This is good and agreeable in
4 the sight of God our Savior, who wishes all men to be saved and to come to the knowledge of the
5 truth. For there is one God, and one Mediator between God and men, himself man, Christ
6 Jesus, ' who gave himself a ransom for all, bear-
7 ing witness in his own time. To this I have been appointed a preacher and an apostle (I tell the truth, I do not lie), a teacher of the Gentiles in faith and truth.

Women in Public Assemblies

8 I wish, then, that the men pray everywhere, lifting up pure hands, without wrath and conten-
9 tion. In like manner I wish women to be decently dressed, adorning themselves with modesty and dignity, not with braided hair or gold or pearls or
10 expensive clothing, ' but with good works such as
11 become women professing godliness. Let a
12 woman learn in silence with all submission. For I do not allow a woman to teach, or to exercise

[552]

authority over men; but she is to keep quiet. For 13 Adam was formed first, then Eve. And Adam was 14 not deceived, but the woman was deceived and was in sin. Yet women will be saved by child- 15 bearing, if they continue in faith and love and holiness with modesty.

Qualities of a Bishop

This saying is true: If anyone is eager for the **3** 1 office of bishop, he desires a good work. A bishop 2 then, must be blameless, married but once, reserved, prudent, of good conduct, hospitable, a teacher, not a drinker or a brawler, but moder- 3 ate, not quarrelsome, not avaricious. He should 4 rule well his own household, keeping his children under control and perfectly respectful. For if a 5 man cannot rule his own household, how is he to take care of the church of God? He must not be a 6 new convert, lest he be puffed up with pride and incur the condemnation passed on the devil. Besides this he must have a good reputation with 7 those who are outside, that he may not fall into disgrace and into a snare of the devil.

Qualities of a Deacon

Deacons also must be honorable, not double- 8 tongued, not given to much wine, not greedy for base gain, but holding the mystery of faith in a 9 pure conscience. And let them first be tried, and 10 if found without reproach let them be allowed to serve. In like manner let the women be honor- 11 able, not slanderers, but reserved, faithful in all things. Deacons should be men who have 12 been married but once, ruling well their children and their own households. And those who have 13 fulfilled well this office will acquire a good position and great confidence in the faith that is in Christ Jesus.

[553]

III: AGAINST FALSE DOCTRINE

Pillar and Mainstay of the Truth

14 I WRITE THESE THINGS to thee

15 hoping to come to thee shortly, but | SEPT. 30 / Mar. 31 | in order that thou mayest know, if I am delayed, how to conduct thyself in the house of God, which is the Church of the living God, the pillar

16 and mainstay of the truth. And obviously great is the mystery of godliness: Which was manifested in the flesh, was justified in the spirit, appeared to angels, was preached to Gentiles, believed in the world, taken up in glory.

Lying Teachers

4 1 Now the Spirit expressly says that in after times some will depart from the faith, giving heed

2 to deceitful spirits and doctrines of devils, speaking lies hypocritically, and having their conscience

3 branded. They will forbid marriage, and will enjoin abstinence from foods, which God has created to be partaken of with thanksgiving by

4 the faithful and by those who know the truth. For every creature of God is good, and nothing is to be

5 rejected that is accepted with thanksgiving. For it is sanctified by the word of God and prayer.

Piety and False Asceticism

6 By recommending these things to the brethren, thou wilt be a good minister of Christ Jesus, nourished with the words of faith and of the

---

4, 2: Fugitive slaves and criminals were often branded on the forehead.

4, 3-5: St. Paul condemns abstinence when it is the result of the false principle that matter is bad because produced by the evil spirit. From right motives of self-denial and mortification, commanded by the Church, the practice of fast and abstinence is good.

good doctrine to which thou hast attained. But 7 avoid foolish fables and old wives' tales and train thyself in godliness. For bodily training is of little 8 profit, while godliness is profitable in all respects, since it has the promise of the present life as well as of that which is to come. This saying is true 9 and worthy of entire acceptance; for we work 10 and are reviled for this reason, that we hope in the living God, who is the Savior of all men, especially of believers.

Zeal in His Office

Command and teach these things. Let no man 11,12 despise thy youth, but be thou an example to the faithful in speech, in conduct, in charity, in faith, in chastity. Until I come, be diligent in 13 reading, in exhortation and in teaching. Do not 14 neglect the grace that is in thee, granted to thee by reason of prophecy with the laying on of hands of the presbyterate. Meditate on these things, 15 give thyself entirely to them, that thy progress may be manifest to all. Take heed to thyself and 16 to thy teaching, be earnest in them. For in so doing thou wilt save both thyself and those who hear thee.

IV: DUTIES TOWARDS THE FLOCK

Different Classes

DO NOT REBUKE an elderly man, but exhort him as you would a father, | OCT. 1 / Apr. 1 | **5** 1 and young men as brothers, elderly women as 2 mothers, younger women as sisters in all chastity.

Widows

Honor widows who are truly widowed. But if a 3, 4 widow has children or grandchildren, let these

---

4, 14: *Presbyterate:* i. e., the priesthood.

first learn to provide for their own household and make some return to their parents, for this is

5 pleasing to God. But she who is truly a widow, and left solitary, has set her hope on God and continues in supplications and prayers night and

6 day. For she who gives herself up to pleasures is

7 dead while she is still alive. And command them

8 to be blameless. But if anyone does not take care of his own, and especially of his household, he has denied the faith and is worse than an unbeliever.

9 Let a widow who is selected be not less than sixty years old, having been married but once,

10 with a reputation for her good works in bringing up children, in practising hospitality, in washing the saints' feet, in helping those in trouble, in

11 carefully pursuing every good work. But refuse younger widows, for when they have wantonly turned away from Christ, they wish to marry,

12 and are to be condemned because they have

13 broken their first troth. And further, being idle, they learn to go about from house to house, and are not only idle but gossipers as well and busy-

14 bodies, mentioning things they ought not. I desire therefore that the younger widows marry, bear children, rule their households, and give the

15 adversary no occasion for abusing us. For already

16 some have turned aside after Satan. If any believing woman has widowed relatives, let her provide for them and do not let the Church be burdened, in order that there may be enough for those who are truly widows.

5, 3: *Truly widowed:* i. e., one who is alone, solitary, with no relatives to provide for her. *Honor:* implies support, like our word "honorarium."

5, 11: *Refuse:* reject, do not admit to an official position.

Presbyters

Let the presbyters who rule well be held 17
worthy of double honor, especially those who
labor in the word and in teaching. For the Scrip- 18
ture says, "Thou shalt not muzzle the ox that
treads out the grain," and, "The laborer is
worthy of his wages." Do not listen to an accusa- 19
tion against a presbyter unless it is supported by
two or three witnesses. When they sin, rebuke 20
them in the presence of all, that the rest also may
have fear. I charge thee before God and Christ 21
Jesus and the elect angels that thou observe
these things impartially, in no way favoring either
side. Do not lay hands hastily upon anyone, and 22
do not be a partner in other men's sins. Keep
thyself chaste. Stop drinking water only, but 23
use a little wine for thy stomach's sake and thy
frequent infirmities. Some men's sins are mani- 24
fest even before investigation, other men's sins
only afterwards. In like manner also the good 25
works are manifest, and those that are otherwise
cannot be hidden.

Slaves

Let slaves who are under the yoke | OCT. 2 | **6** 1
account their masters deserving of | Apr. 2 |
all honor, that the name of the Lord and his
teaching be not blasphemed. And when they have 2
masters who are believers, let them not despise
them because they are brethren, but let them
serve them all the more because they who receive
their services are believers and beloved. Teach
and exhort these things.

Lying Teachers

If anyone teaches otherwise and does not agree 3
with the sound instruction of our Lord Jesus
Christ, and that doctrine which is according to

4 godliness, ' he is proud, knowing nothing, but doting about controversies and disputes of words. From these arise envies, quarrels, blasphemies,
5 base suspicions, ' the wranglings of men corrupt in mind and bereft of truth, supposing godliness
6 to be gain. And godliness with contentment is
7 indeed great gain. For we brought nothing into the world, and certainly we can take nothing out;
8 but having food and sufficient clothing, with these
9 let us be content. But those who seek to become rich fall into temptation and a snare and into many useless and harmful desires, which plunge men
10 into destruction and damnation. For covetousness is the root of all evils, and some in their eagerness to get rich have strayed from the faith and have involved themselves in many troubles.

Final Plea

11 But thou, O man of God, flee these things; but pursue justice, godliness, faith, charity, patience,
12 mildness. Fight the good fight of the faith, lay hold on the life eternal, to which thou hast been called, and hast made the good confession before
13 many witnesses. I charge thee in the sight of God, who gives life to all things, and in the sight of Christ Jesus, who bore witness before Pontius
14 Pilate to the good confession, that thou keep the commandment without stain, blameless until the
15 coming of our Lord Jesus Christ. This coming he in his own time will make manifest, who is the Blessed and only Sovereign, the King of kings
16 and Lord of lords; who alone has immortality and dwells in light inaccessible, whom no man has seen or can see, to whom be honor and everlasting dominion. Amen.

The Rich

Charge the rich of this world not to be proud, 17
or to trust in the uncertainty of riches, but in
God, who provides all things in abundance for
our enjoyment. Let them do good and be rich in 18
good works, giving readily, sharing with others,
and thus providing for themselves a good founda- 19
tion against the time to come, in order that they
may lay hold on the true life.

Conclusion

Exhortation and Greeting

O TIMOTHY, guard the trust and keep free from 20
profane novelties in speech and the contradic-
tions of so-called knowledge, which some have 21
professed and have fallen away from the faith.
Grace be with thee. Amen.

Preface

The Second Epistle to Timothy was written in 66 or 67 A.D., while St. Paul was a prisoner in Rome for the second and last time.

The Apostle describes himself as still in prison and abandoned by nearly all his companions, who for various reasons have left Rome (4, 9f). Only Luke the physician, of whom he seems to have special need, is with him (4, 11). He feels his isolation keenly, particularly since his relations with the Roman church are much restricted. He feels the need of seeing Mark and Timothy, for whom Tychicus was to substitute at Ephesus (4, 11f). He sees his death near (4, 6-8). The Epistle is an urgent invitation to Timothy to join him, yet the Apostle is concerned to strengthen the spirit of his beloved disciple and to urge him again to act energetically against the separatist teachers.

THE SECOND EPISTLE OF ST. PAUL THE APOSTLE TO TIMOTHY

Introduction

Greeting

1 1   PAUL, AN APOSTLE OF JESUS CHRIST, by the will of God, in accordance with the promise of life in Christ Jesus,   OCT. 3
Apr. 3
2 to Timothy, my beloved son: grace, mercy and peace from God the Father and from Christ Jesus our Lord.

Thanksgiving and Prayer

3   I give thanks to God, whom I serve as did my forefathers, with a clear conscience, that I remember thee without ceasing in my prayers night 4 and day. Recalling thy tears, I long to see thee, 5 that I may be filled with joy. I remember that unfeigned faith of thine, which dwelt first in thy

grandmother Lois and in thy mother Eunice, and dwells, I am certain, in thee also.

I: PASTORAL CHARGE

Paul's Example

FOR THIS REASON I admonish thee to stir up 6 the grace of God which is in thee by the laying on of my hands. For God has not given us the spirit 7 of fear, but of power and of love and of prudence. Do not, therefore, be ashamed of testimony for 8 our Lord, nor of me, his prisoner, but enter into my sufferings for the gospel through the power of God. He has redeemed us and called us with a 9 holy calling, not according to our works, but according to his own purpose and the grace which was granted to us in Christ Jesus before this world existed, but is now made known by the 10 manifestation of our Savior Jesus Christ. He has destroyed death and brought to light life and incorruption by the gospel, of which I have been 11 appointed a preacher and an apostle and a teacher of the Gentiles. That is why also I am 12 suffering these things; yet I am not ashamed. For I know whom I have believed, and I am certain that he is able to guard the trust committed to me against that day. Hold to the form of sound 13 teaching which thou hast heard from me, in the faith and love which are in Christ Jesus. Guard 14 the good trust through the Holy Spirit, who dwells in us.

Loyalty and Defections

This thou knowest that all in the province of 15 Asia have turned away from me, among them, Phigelus and Hermogenes. May the Lord grant 16

1, 10: *Incorruption:* immortality, eternal happiness.

mercy to the house of Onesiphorus, because he
often comforted me and was not ashamed of my
17 chains; but when he came to Rome, he sought
18 me out diligently and found me. May the Lord
grant him to find mercy from the Lord on that
day. And thou knowest very well the many services he rendered me at Ephesus.

Devotion to His Office

2 1   Therefore, my child, be strengthened in the grace which is in Christ

OCT. 4
Apr. 4

2 Jesus; and the things that thou hast heard from
me through many witnesses, commend to trustworthy men who shall be competent in turn to
3 teach others. Conduct thyself in work as a good
4 soldier of Christ Jesus. No one serving as God's
soldier entangles himself in worldly affairs, that
he may please him whose approval he has se-
5 cured. And again, one who enters a contest is not
6 crowned unless he has competed according to the
rules. The farmer who toils must be the first to
7 partake of the fruits. Take in what I tell thee, for
the Lord will give thee understanding in all
things.

The Thought of Christ

8   Remember that Jesus Christ rose from the
dead and was descended from David; this is my
9 gospel, ' in which I suffer even to bonds, as a
10 criminal. But the word of God is not bound. ' This
is why I bear all things for the sake of the elect,
that they also may obtain the salvation that is in
11 Christ Jesus, with heavenly glory. This saying is
true: If we have died with him, we shall also live
12 with him; if we endure, we shall also reign with
him; if we disown him, he also will disown us;
13 if we are faithless, he remains faithful, for he
cannot disown himself.

[562]

II: FIDELITY TO HIS OFFICE
False Teachers

RECALL THESE THINGS to their minds, charging them in the sight of the Lord not to dispute with words, for that is useless, leading to the ruin of the listeners. Use all care to present thyself to God as a man approved, a worker that cannot be ashamed, rightly handling the word of truth. But avoid profane and empty babblings, for they contribute much to ungodliness, and their speech spreads like a cancer. Of this sort are Hymeneus and Philetus, who have erred from the truth in saying that the resurrection has taken place already; and they are destroying the faith of some.

The Faithful Servant

But the sure foundation of God stands firm, bearing this seal: "The Lord knows who are his"; and, "Let everyone depart from iniquity who names the name of the Lord."

But in a great house there are vessels not only of gold and silver, but also of wood and clay; and some are for honorable uses, but some for ignoble. If anyone, therefore, has cleansed himself from these, he will be a vessel for honorable use, sanctified and useful to the Lord, ready for every good work. But flee the cravings of youth and pursue justice, faith, charity and peace with those who call on the Lord from a pure heart. Avoid also foolish and ignorant controversies, knowing that they breed quarrels. But the ser-

14 15 16 17 18 19 20 21 22 23 24

2, 18: They taught the immortality of the soul but seem to have denied the resurrection of the body.

2, 19: These are the two fundamental truths of the relations of God to man: on God's part, predestination; on man's part, the free rejection of sin.

vant of the Lord must not quarrel, but be gentle

25 towards all, ready to teach, patient, ' gently admonishing those who resist, in case God should

26 give them repentance to know the truth, and they recover themselves from the snare of the devil, to whose will they are held captive.

Against New Teachers

3 1 But know this, that in the last days
2 dangerous times will come. Men will OCT. 5 Apr. 5 be lovers of self, covetous, haughty, proud, blasphemers, disobedient to parents, ungrateful,
3 criminal, ' heartless, faithless, slanderers, incon-
4 tinent, merciless, unkind, ' treacherous, stubborn, puffed up with pride, loving pleasure more than
5 God, ' having a semblance indeed of piety, but
6 disowning its power. Avoid these. ' For of such are they who make their way into houses and captivate silly women who are sin-laden and led
7 away by various lusts: ever learning yet never
8 attaining knowledge of the truth. Just as Jamnes and Mambres resisted Moses, so these men also resist the truth, for they are corrupt in mind,
9 reprobate as regards the faith. But they will make no further progress, for their folly will be obvious to all, as was that of those others.

Paul's Example and Doctrine

10 But thou hast closely followed my doctrine, my conduct, my purpose, my faith, my long-suffer-
11 ing, my love, my patience, ' my persecutions, my afflictions; such as befell me at Antioch, Iconium and Lystra — such persecutions as I suffered,
12 and out of them all the Lord delivered me. And all who want to live piously in Christ Jesus will
13 suffer persecution. But the wicked and impostors will go from bad to worse, erring and leading
14 into error. But do thou continue in the things that

[564]

thou hast learned and that have been entrusted to thee, knowing of whom thou hast learned them. For from thy infancy thou hast known the 15 Sacred Writings, which are able to instruct thee unto salvation by the faith which is in Christ Jesus. All Scripture is inspired by God and useful 16 for teaching, for reproving, for correcting, for instructing in justice; that the man of God may 17 be perfect, equipped for every good work.

Preach Sound Doctrine

I charge thee, in the sight of God and Christ Jesus, who will judge the living and the dead by his coming and by his kingdom, preach the word, be urgent in season, 2 out of season; reprove, entreat, rebuke with all patience and teaching. For there will come a time 3 when they will not endure the sound doctrine; but having itching ears, will heap up to themselves teachers according to their own lusts, and they 4 will turn away their hearing from the truth and turn aside rather to fables. But do thou be watch- 5 ful in all things, bear with tribulation patiently, work as a preacher of the gospel, fulfill thy ministry.

OCT. 6
Apr. 6

4 1

Reward

As for me, I am already being poured out in 6 sacrifice, and the time of my deliverance is at hand. I have fought the good fight, I have 7 finished the course, I have kept the faith. For the 8 rest, there is laid up for me a crown of justice, which the Lord, the just Judge, will give to me in that day; yet not to me only, but also to those who love his coming.

3, 14: *Of whom:* refers to Timothy's mother and grand-mother, as well as to St. Paul.

3, 16: This is the classic text for the divine inspiration of the Scriptures.

Conclusion

Paul's Loneliness

9 MAKE HASTE TO COME to me shortly; for Demas has deserted me, loving this world, and 10 has gone to Thessalonica, Crescens to Galatia, 11 Titus to Dalmatia. Luke only is with me. Take Mark and bring him with thee, for he is useful 12 to me for the ministry. But Tychicus I have sent 13 to Ephesus. When thou comest, bring with thee the cloak that I left at Troas with Carpus, and the 14 books, especially the parchments. Alexander, the coppersmith, has done me much harm; the Lord 15 will render to him according to his deeds. Do thou also avoid him for he has vehemently opposed our words.

His Trial

16 At my first defense no one came to my support, but all forsook me, may it not be laid to their 17 charge. But the Lord stood by me and strengthened me, that through me the preaching of the gospel might be completed, and that all the Gentiles might hear, and I was delivered from 18 the lion's mouth. The Lord will deliver me from every work of evil, and will preserve me for his heavenly kingdom; to whom be the glory forever and ever. Amen.

Greetings

19 Greet Prisca and Aquila and the household of 20 Onesiphorus. Erastus stayed at Corinth, but Tro- 21 phimus I left sick at Miletus. Hasten to come before winter. Eubulus, Pudens, Linus and 22 Claudia and all the brethren greet thee. The Lord Jesus Christ be with thy spirit. Grace be with you. Amen.

4, 6: *Poured out:* i. e., as a libation.

THE EPISTLE TO TITUS

Introduction

St. Titus was born of Greek parents. He accompanied Sts. Paul and Barnabas to the Council of Jerusalem (Gal. 2, 1. 3). He was uncircumcised, and although at the Council Judaizers insisted that he submit to this rite, St. Paul refused to permit it. Titus is addressed in this Epistle as "beloved son" (1, 4), probably because he was converted to the faith by the Apostle. He was sent by the latter on several important missions during the third missionary journey (2 Cor. 2, 13; 7, 6; 8, 6. 16; 12, 18). We lose sight of him after this, as he is not mentioned in the Epistles of the Captivity. From this Epistle we learn that St. Paul entrusted him with the organization of the church in Crete (1, 5). Afterwards he was summoned by the Apostle to Nicopolis in Epirus (3, 12), and during Paul's final Roman imprisonment he was sent on a mission to Dalmatia (2 Tim. 4, 10). According to tradition he returned to Crete to exercise his episcopal office, and died there.

The journey of St. Paul to the island of Crete (1, 5) cannot be inserted anywhere in the life of the Apostle before the first Roman imprisonment. Hence the visit, as well as the composition of this Epistle, took place between St. Paul's liberation from this first imprisonment and his death. Catholic authors commonly hold that the Epistle was written shortly after the writing of 1 Timothy, in either 65 or 66 A.D.

The religious situation in Crete and the mission of Titus correspond to what confronted Timothy at Ephesus (compare 3, 9 with 1 Tim. 1, 4). Because of the character of the inhabitants and the spread of erroneous doctrines (1, 10f. 14; 3, 9-11), Titus' task was a difficult one. Before leaving Titus at Crete St. Paul had instructed him how to organize and rule the churches. In this Epistle the Apostle gives him counsels and instructions to guide him in his episcopal office.

THE EPISTLE OF ST. PAUL THE APOSTLE TO TITUS

Introduction

Greeting

1 1 PAUL, A SERVANT OF GOD and apostle of Jesus Christ, in accordance with the faith of God's elect and the full knowledge of the truth which is according to
2 piety, ' in the hope of life everlasting which God, who does not lie, promised before the ages be-
3 gan — he has in due times manifested his word through the preaching committed to my trust by
4 the command of God our Savior — to Titus, my beloved son in the common faith: grace and peace from God the Father, and from Christ Jesus our Savior.

| OCT. 7 |
| Apr. 7 |

I: PASTORAL CHARGE

Titus' Mission

5 FOR THIS REASON I left thee in Crete, that thou shouldst set right anything that is defective and shouldst appoint presbyters in every city, as
6 I myself directed thee to do. They must be blameless, married but once, having believing children who are not accused of impurity or dis-
7 obedience. For a bishop must be blameless as being the steward of God, not proud, or ill-tempered, or a drinker, or a brawler, or greedy
8 for base gain; but hospitable, gentle, reserved,
9 just, holy, continent; holding fast the faithful word which is in accordance with the teaching, that he may be able both to exhort in sound doctrine and to confute opponents.

Special Needs in Crete

For there are also many disobedient, vain 10
babblers and deceivers, especially those of the
circumcision. These must be rebuked, for they 11
upset whole households, teaching things that they
ought not, for the sake of base gain. One of 12
themselves, a prophet of their own, said, "Cretans,
always liars, evil beasts, lazy gluttons." This 13
statement is true. Hence rebuke them sharply that
they may be sound in faith, and may not listen to 14
Jewish fables and the commandments of men
who turn away from the truth. For the clean all 15
things are clean, but for the defiled and unbelieving nothing is clean; for both their mind and their
conscience are defiled. They profess to know 16
God, but by their works they disown him, being
abominable and unbelieving and worthless for
any good work.

II: CHARGE TO TEACH THE CHRISTIAN LIFE

Different Classes

BUT DO THOU SPEAK what befits | OCT. 8 | **2** 1
the sound doctrine: that elderly men | Apr. 8 | 2
be reserved, honorable, prudent, sound in faith,
in love, in patience; that elderly women, in like 3
manner, be marked by holiness of behavior, not
slanderers, nor enslaved to much wine; teaching
what is right, that they may train the younger 4
women to be wise, to love their husbands and
their children, ' to be discreet, chaste, domestic, 5
gentle, obedient to their husbands, so that the
word of God be not reviled. Exhort the younger 6
men, in like manner, to be self-controlled. Show 7
thyself in all things an example of good works, in

1, 15: The reference is to the distinction between clean
and unclean meats in the Mosaic Law, abrogated by
the gospel.

8 teaching, in integrity and dignity; let thy speech be sound and blameless, so that anyone opposing may be put to shame, having nothing bad to say
9 of us. Exhort slaves to obey their masters, pleasing them in all things and not opposing them;
10 ' not pilfering, but showing faithfulness in all things, so as to adorn in all things the teaching of God our Savior.

Changed Life

11 For the grace of God our Savior has appeared
12 to all men, ' instructing us, in order that, rejecting ungodliness and worldly lusts, we may live temperately and justly and piously in this world;
13 looking for the blessed hope and glorious coming
14 of our great God and Savior, Jesus Christ, ' who gave himself for us that he might redeem us from all iniquity and cleanse for himself an acceptable
15 people, pursuing good works. Thus speak, and exhort, and rebuke, with all authority. Let no one despise thee.

3 1 Admonish them to be subject to princes and authorities, obeying commands, ready for every
2 good work, ' speaking evil of none, not quarrelsome but moderate, showing all mildness to all
3 men. For we ourselves also were once unwise, unbelieving, going astray, slaves to various lusts and pleasures, living in malice and envy, hateful
4 and hating one another. But when the goodness
5 and kindness of God our Savior appeared, then not by reason of good works that we did ourselves, but according to his mercy, he saved us through the bath of regeneration and renewal
6 by the Holy Spirit; whom he has abundantly poured out upon us through Jesus Christ our
7 Savior, ' in order that, justified by his grace, we may be heirs in the hope of life everlasting.

[570]

Good Works and Truth

This saying is true, and concerning these 8 things I desire thee to insist, that they who believe in God may be careful to excel in good works. These things are good and useful to men. But avoid foolish controversies and genealogies 9 and quarrels and disputes about the Law; for they are useless and futile. A factious man avoid 10 after a first and a second admonition, knowing 11 that such a one is perverted and sins, being self-condemned.

Conclusion

Closing Messages

WHEN I SEND ARTEMAS or Tychicus to thee, 12 make every effort to come to me at Nicopolis; for there I have decided to spend the winter. Help 13 Zenas the lawyer and Apollos on their way, taking care that nothing be wanting to them. And 14 let our people also learn to excel in good works, in order to meet cases of necessity, that they may not be unfruitful.

Greeting

All my companions greet thee. Greet those 15 who love us in the faith. The grace of God be with you all. Amen.

Introduction

During his first Roman imprisonment (A. D. 61-63), St. Paul came to know a slave named Onesimus, who had deserted his master Philemon, a wealthy Christian of Colossæ in Phrygia. After the Apostle had won the fugitive over to Christianity, he looked for a favorable opportunity to send him back to his master. This opportunity offered itself when he was dispatching a letter to the Colossians in the year 63 A. D. Onesimus accompanied St. Paul's messenger Tychicus (Col. 4, 7-9). To Philemon the Apostle addressed this touching appeal, entreating his friend to deal kindly with the runaway.

THE EPISTLE OF ST. PAUL THE APOSTLE TO PHILEMON

Address and Greeting

1 PAUL, A PRISONER OF CHRIST JESUS, and our brother Timothy, to

OCT. 9
Apr. 9

2 Philemon, our beloved and fellow-worker,' and to Appia, the sister, and to Archippus, our fellow-soldier, and to the church that is in our house: 3 grace be to you and peace from God our Father and from the Lord Jesus Christ.

Philemon's Faith and Charity

4 I give thanks to my God, always making re-
5 membrance of thee in my prayers, as I hear of thy charity and of the faith that thou hast in our
6 Lord Jesus and towards all the saints. May the sharing of thy faith be made evident in full knowledge of all the good that is in you, in Christ
7 Jesus. For I had great joy and consolation in thy charity, because through thee, brother, the hearts of the saints have found rest.

Plea for Onesimus

8 For this reason, though I am very confident that I might charge thee in Christ Jesus to do

what is fitting, yet for the sake of charity I prefer 9
to plead, since thou art such as thou art; as
Paul, an old man — and now also a prisoner of
Jesus Christ — I plead with thee for my own 10
son, whom I have begotten in prison, for Onesimus. He once was useless to thee, but now is 11
useful both to me and to thee. I am sending him 12
back to thee, and do thou welcome him as though
he were my very heart. I had wanted to keep him 13
here with me that in thy stead he might wait on
me in my imprisonment for the gospel; but I did 14
not want to do anything without thy counsel, in
order that thy kindness might not be as it were
of necessity, but voluntary.

Perhaps, indeed, he departed from thee for a 15
short while so that thou mightest receive him
forever, 'no longer as a slave, but instead of a 16
slave as a brother most dear, especially to me,
and how much more to thee, both in the flesh and
in the Lord! If, therefore, thou dost count me as 17
a partner, welcome him as thou wouldst me. And 18
if he did thee any injury or owes thee anything,
charge it to me. I, Paul, write it with my own 19
hand: I will repay it — not to say to thee that
thou owest me thy very self. Yes, indeed, 20
brother! May I, too, make use of thee in the
Lord! Console my heart in the Lord!

Hopes, Greetings, Blessings

Trusting in thy compliance I am writing to 21
thee, knowing that thou wilt do even beyond
what I say. At the same time make ready a 22
lodging for me too, for I hope that through your
prayers I shall be restored to you. Epaphras, my 23
fellow-prisoner in Christ Jesus, ' Mark, Aristar- 24
chus, Demas and Luke, my fellow-workers, send
thee greetings. The grace of our Lord Jesus 25
Christ be with your spirit. Amen.

THE EPISTLE TO THE HEBREWS

Introduction

Apart from some doubts expressed unofficially in the West before the fourth century, the traditional Catholic view has always maintained the Pauline authorship of the Epistle to the Hebrews, at least in the sense that it was conceived by St. Paul and written under his direction. Its thought is thoroughly Pauline, and much of its phraseology is also distinctly Pauline. The excellent literary style, however, is generally superior to that found in the other Epistles of St. Paul, and ranks with the best in the New Testament.

The time, place of composition and destination of the Epistle are not stated explicitly, and there is but little evidence elsewhere bearing upon these matters. Opinions, based on the few vague indications available, differ widely. As plausible as any is the common view that the Epistle was written at Rome about 63 A. D., shortly after St. Paul's release from his first Roman imprisonment, and that it was destined for the Jewish Christians of Palestine, who under the stress of trials were in danger of relapsing into Judaism.

The Epistle describes most eloquently the eminent superiority of the new dispensation over the old. Inaugurated by the Son of God Himself, this new dispensation was God's final revelation to man. It completed the message of the prophets, and brought to perfection all that was of permanent value in the Mosaic covenant. The Incarnate Son of God was its High Priest, and His glorious sacrifice was truly efficacious before God in the forgiveness of sin. As suffering and humiliation had an important place in His victory, His followers are exhorted to forego worldly advantage, to bear their trials patiently, and to persevere heroically in the faith.

THE EPISTLE OF ST. PAUL THE APOSTLE TO THE HEBREWS

I: SUPERIORITY OF THE NEW DISPENSATION OVER THE OLD

1. A Superior Mediator

Christ Superior to the Angels

GOD, WHO AT SUNDRY TIMES and in divers manners spoke in times past to the fathers by the prophets, last of all in these days has spoken to us by his Son, whom he appointed heir of all things, by whom also he made the world; who, being the brightness of his glory and the image of his substance, and upholding all things by the word of his power, has effected man's purgation from sin and taken his seat at the right hand of the Majesty on high, having become so much superior to the angels as he has inherited a more excellent name than they. For to which of the angels has he ever said, "Thou art my son, I this day have begotten thee"? and again, "I will be to him a father, and he shall be to me a son"? And again, when he brings the firstborn into the world, he says, "And let all the angels of God adore him." And of the angels indeed he says, "He makes his angels spirits, and his ministers a flame of fire." But of the Son, "Thy throne, O God, is forever and ever, and a sceptre of equity is the sceptre of thy kingdom. Thou hast loved justice and hated iniquity; therefore God, thy God, has anointed thee with the oil of gladness above thy fellows." And, "Thou in the beginning, O Lord,

OCT. 10
Apr. 10

1 1

2

3

4

5

6

7

8

9

10

1, 4: *Having become*: or, "showing himself to be." "The humanity of Christ was exalted in glory far above the angels, because He alone was truly the Son."

didst found the earth, and the heavens are works
11 of thy hands. They shall perish, but thou shalt
continue; and they shall all grow old as does a
12 garment, and as a vesture shalt thou change
them, and they shall be changed. But thou art
13 the same, and thy years shall not fail." Now to
which of the angels has he ever said, "Sit at my
right hand, until I make thy enemies the foot-
14 stool of thy feet"? Are they not all ministering
spirits, sent for service, for the sake of those who
shall inherit salvation?

Warning and Exhortation

2 1　　Therefore ought we the more earnestly to
observe the things that we have heard, lest per-
2 haps we drift away. For if the word spoken by
angels proved to be valid, and every transgression and disobedience received a just punish-
3 ment, how shall we escape if we neglect so great
a salvation? For it was first announced by the
Lord and was confirmed unto us by those who
4 heard him; God also, according to his own will,
bearing them witness by signs and wonders, and
by manifold powers, and by impartings of the
Holy Spirit.

Christ Suffered for His Brethren

5　　For he has not subjected to angels ┌──────────┐
the world to come, whereof we │ OCT. 11 │
│ Apr. 11 │
6 speak. Rather someone has testified └──────────┘ somewhere,
saying, "What is man that thou art mindful of
him, or the son of man that thou visitest him?
7 Thou hast made him a little lower than the
angels, thou hast crowned him with glory and

2, 2: *Word spoken by angels:* the Mosaic Law.

2, 5: *World to come:* here means the Christian dispensation, not the future life.

honor, and hast set him over the works of thy hands; thou hast put all things under his feet." 8 For in subjecting all things to man, he left nothing that is not subject to him. But now we do not see as yet all things subject to him. But we do see 9 him who was made "a little lower than the angels," namely, Jesus, crowned with glory and honor because of his having suffered death, that by the grace of God he might taste death for all. For it became him for whom are all things and 10 through whom are all things, who had brought many sons into glory, to perfect through sufferings the author of their salvation. For both he 11 who sanctifies and they who are sanctified are all from one. For which cause he is not ashamed to call them brethren, saying, "I will declare thy 12 name to my brethren; in the midst of the church I will praise thee." And again, "I will put my 13 trust in him." And again, "Behold, I and my children whom God has given me." Therefore 14 because children have blood and flesh in common, so he in like manner has shared in these; that through death he might destroy him who had the empire of death, that is, the devil; and might 15 deliver them, who throughout their life were kept in servitude by the fear of death. For, of course, 16 it is not angels that he is succoring, but he is succoring the offspring of Abraham. Wherefore it 17 was right that he should in all things be made like unto his brethren, that he might become a merciful and faithful high priest before God to expiate the sins of the people. For in that he 18 himself has suffered and has been tempted, he is able to help those who are tempted.

2, 11: *All from one:* probably, from one family, with God as the Father of all.

2, 14: *Blood and flesh:* i. e., having the same human nature.

Christ Superior to Moses

3 1 Therefore, holy brethren, partakers of a heavenly calling, consider the apostle and high priest
2 of our confession, Jesus, ' who is faithful to him who made him, as was Moses also "in all his
3 house." For he was deemed worthy of greater glory than Moses, just as the builder of a house has greater honor than the house that he has
4 built. For every house is built by someone; but
5 he who created all things is God. And Moses indeed was faithful "in all his house" as a servant, to testify concerning those things that were
6 to be spoken; but Christ is faithful as the Son over his own house. We are that house, if we hold fast our confidence and the hope in which we glory unto the end.

Exhortation

7 Therefore, as the Holy Spirit says, "Today if you shall hear his voice,

OCT. 12
Apr. 12

8 do not harden your hearts as in the provocation,
9 during the day of temptation in the desert, ' where your fathers tried me, proved and saw my works
10 ' forty years. Wherefore I was offended with this generation, and said, 'They always err in heart,
11 and they have not known my ways.' As I have sworn in my wrath, they shall not enter into my
12 Rest." Take heed, brethren, lest perhaps there be in any of you an evil, unbelieving heart that
13 would turn away from the living God. But exhort one another every day, while it is still Today, that none of you be hardened by the deceitful-
14 ness of sin. For we have been made partakers of Christ, provided only that we hold fast our first
15 confidence in him unto the end. While it is said, "Today if you shall hear his voice, do not harden
16 your hearts as in that provocation" — for some

who heard gave provocation, but not all those who came out of Egypt under Moses — with 17 whom then was he offended forty years? Was it not with those who sinned, whose corpses fell in the desert? And to whom did he swear that they 18 should not enter into his Rest, but to those who were unbelieving? And we see that they could 19 not enter in because of unbelief.

Our Promised Land

Let us therefore fear lest perhaps, while the **4** 1 promise of entering into his Rest remains, any of you should be thought wanting. For to us also it 2 has been declared, just as to them. But the word that was heard did not profit them, since they had no faith in what they heard. We then who have 3 believed shall enter into his Rest, even as he said, "As I have sworn in my wrath, they shall not enter into my Rest." And indeed his works were completed at the foundation of the world. For somewhere he spoke of the seventh day thus, 4 "And God rested the seventh day from all his works"; and in this place again, "They shall not 5 enter into my Rest." Since then it follows that 6 some are to enter into it, and they to whom it was first declared did not enter in because of unbelief, he again fixes another day to be Today, saying by 7 David after so long a time, as quoted above, "Today if you shall hear his voice, do not harden your hearts." For if Josue had given them rest, 8 God would never afterwards be speaking of another day. There remains therefore a Sabbath 9 Rest for the people of God. For he who has 10 entered into his Rest, has himself also rested from his own works, even as God did from his. Let us therefore hasten to enter into that Rest, 11 lest anyone fall by following the same example of unbelief. For the word of God is living and 12 efficient and keener than any two-edged sword, and extending even to the division of soul and spirit, of joints also and of marrow, and a discerner of the thoughts and intentions of the 13 heart. And there is no creature hidden from his sight, but all things are naked and open to the eyes of him to whom we have to give account.

2. A Superior High Priest

Confidence in Christ

14   HAVING THEREFORE a great high priest who has passed into the heavens, Jesus the Son of God, let us hold fast our 15 confession. For we have not a high priest who cannot have compassion on our infirmities, 16 one tried as we are in all things except sin. Let us therefore draw near with confidence to the throne of grace, that we may obtain mercy and find grace to help in time of need.

OCT. 13
Apr. 13

Christ the High Priest

5 1   For every high priest taken from among men is appointed for men in the things pertaining to God, that he may offer gifts and sacrifices for 2 sins. He is able to have compassion on the ignorant and erring, because he himself also is 3 beset with weakness, and by reason thereof is obliged to offer for sins, as on behalf of the people, 4 so also for himself. And no man takes the honor to himself; he takes it who is called by God, as 5 Aaron was. So also Christ did not glorify himself with the high priesthood, but he who spoke to him, "Thou art my son, I this day have begotten 6 thee." As he says also in another place, "Thou art a priest forever, according to the order of 7 Melchisedech." For Jesus, in the days of his earthly life, with a loud cry and tears, offered up prayers and supplications to him who was able to save him from death, and was heard because of his reverent submission. And he, Son though 8 he was, learned obedience from the things that he suffered; and when perfected, he became to 9 all who obey him the cause of eternal salvation, called by God a high priest according ɪo the order 10 of Melchisedech.

Importance of the Doctrine

On this point we have much to say, and it is 11 difficult to explain it, because you have grown dull of hearing. For whereas by this time you 12 ought to be masters, you need to be taught again the rudiments of the words of God; and you have become such as have need of milk and not of solid food. For everyone who is fed on milk is 13 unskilled in the word of justice; he is but a child. But solid food is for the mature, for those 14 who by practice have their faculties trained to discern good and evil.

An Appeal for Progress

Therefore, leaving the elemen- | OCT. 14 | **6** 1
tary teaching concerning Christ, let | Apr. 14 |
us pass on to things more perfect, not laying again a foundation of repentance from dead works and of faith towards God, of the doctrine 2 of baptisms and the laying on of hands, of the resurrection of the dead and of eternal judgment. And this we will do, if God permits. 3

Danger of Apostasy

For it is impossible for those who were once 4 enlightened, who have both tasted the heavenly gift and become partakers of the Holy Spirit,

---

6, 4: *Impossible:* i. e., extremely difficult.

5 who have moreover tasted the good word of God
6 and the powers of the world to come, and then
have fallen away, to be renewed again to repentance; since they crucify again for themselves the
7 Son of God and make him a mockery. For the
earth that drinks in the rain that often falls upon
it, and produces vegetation that is of use to those
by whom it is tilled, receives a blessing from
8 God; but that which brings forth thorns and
thistles is worthless, and is nigh unto a curse,
and its end is to be burnt.

Expectation of Better Things

9 But in your case, beloved, we are confident of
better things, things that promise salvation, even
10 though we speak thus. For God is not unjust,
that he should forget your work and the love that
you have shown in his name, you who have
11 ministered and do minister to the saints. But we
want every one of you to show to the very end
the same earnestness for the fulfillment of your
12 hopes; so that you may become not sluggish but
imitators of those who by faith and patience will
inherit the promises.

Certainty of God's Promise

13 For when God made his promise to Abraham,
since he had no one greater to swear by, he swore
14 by himself, ' saying, "I will surely bless thee,
15 and I will surely multiply thee." And thus after
patient waiting, Abraham obtained the promise.
16 For men swear by one greater than themselves,
and an oath given as a guarantee is the final
17 settlement of all their disagreement. Hence God,
meaning to show more abundantly to the heirs of
the promise the unchangeableness of his will,

6, 6: *Make him a mockery:* by apostasy.

interposed an oath, ' that by two unchangeable 18
things, in which it is impossible for God to deceive, we may have the strongest comfort—we
who have sought refuge in holding fast the hope
set before us. This hope we have, as a sure and 19
firm anchor of the soul, reaching even behind the
veil ' where our forerunner Jesus has entered 20
for us, having become a high priest forever according to the order of Melchisedech.

Melchisedech More Than Abraham

For this Melchisedech was king 7 1
of Salem, priest of the most high

OCT. 15
Apr. 15

God, who met Abraham returning from the
slaughter of the kings and blessed him; to whom 2
Abraham divided the tithes of all. First, as his
name shows, he is King of Justice, and then
also he is King of Salem, that is, King of Peace.
Without father, without mother, without geneal- 3
ogy, having neither beginning of days nor end of
life, but likened to the Son of God, he continues
a priest forever.

Melchisedech More Than Levi

Now consider how great this man is, to whom 4
even Abraham the patriarch gave tithes out of
the best portions of the spoils. And indeed they 5
who are of the priestly sons of Levi, have a commandment to take tithes from the people according to the Law, that is, from their brethren,
though these also have come from the loins of
Abraham. But he whose genealogy is not re- 6
corded among them received tithes of Abraham
and blessed him who had the promises. Now 7
beyond all contradiction, that which is less is
blessed by the superior. And in the one case 8
indeed, mortal men receive tithes, while in
the other, it is one of whom it is testified that he

9 lives on. And even Levi, the receiver of tithes, was also, so to speak, through Abraham made
10 subject to tithes, for he was still in the loins of his father when Melchisedech met him.

Levitical Priesthood Imperfect

11 If then perfection was by the Levitical priesthood (for under it the people received the Law), what further need was there that another priest should rise, according to the order of Melchisedech, and said not to be according to the
12 order of Aaron? For when the priesthood is changed, it is necessary that a change of law be
13 made also. For he of whom these things are said is from another tribe, from which no one has ever
14 done service at the altar. For it is evident that our Lord has sprung out of Juda, and Moses spoke nothing at all about priests when referring
15 to this tribe. And it is yet far more evident if there arise another priest, according to the like-
16 ness of Melchisedech, who has become so not according to the Law of carnal commandment,
17 but according to a life that cannot end. For it is testified of him, "Thou art a priest forever, according to the order of Melchisedech."

Superseded by Priesthood of Christ

18 On the one hand there is the rejection of the former commandment, because of its weakness
19 and unprofitableness (for the Law brought nothing to perfection), and on the other hand a bringing in of a better hope, through which we draw near to God.

A Priest by Divine Oath

20 And inasmuch as it is not without an oath (for the others indeed were made priests without an
21 oath, but he with an oath through him who said

[584]

to him, "The Lord has sworn and will not repent,
thou art a priest forever"), ¹ all the more has   22
Jesus become surety of a superior covenant.
And the other priests indeed were numerous,   23
because they were prevented by death from continuing in office; but he, because he continues   24
forever, has an everlasting priesthood. Therefore   25
he is able at all times to save those who come to
God through him, since he lives always to make
intercession for them.

Sinless and Perfect

For it was fitting that we should have such a   26
high priest, holy, innocent, undefiled, set apart
from sinners, and become higher than the heavens. He does not need to offer sacrifices daily (as   27
the other priests did), first for his own sins, and
then for the sins of the people; for this latter he
did once for all in offering up himself. For the   28
Law appoints as priests men who are weak; but
the word of the oath, which came after the Law,
appoints a Son who is forever perfect.

3. A Superior Covenant

Christ in the Heavenly Sanctuary

NOW THE MAIN POINT in what   OCT. 16   **8** 1
we are saying is this. We have such   Apr. 16
a high priest, who has taken his seat at the right
hand of the throne of Majesty in the heavens,
¹ a minister of the Holies, and of the true taber-   2
nacle, which the Lord has erected and not man.
For every high priest is appointed to offer gifts   3
and sacrifices; therefore it is necessary that this
one also should have something to offer. If then   4
he were on earth, he would not even be a priest,
since there are already others to offer gifts according to the Law. The worship they offer is a   5

mere copy and shadow of things heavenly, even as Moses was warned when he was completing the tabernacle: "See," God said, "that thou make all things according to the pattern that was shown thee on the mount."

Mediator of a Superior Covenant

6 But now he has obtained a superior ministry, in proportion as he is mediator of a superior covenant, enacted on the basis of superior prom-
7 ises. For had the first been faultless, place would
8 not of course be sought for a second. For finding fault with them he says, "Behold, days are coming, says the Lord, when I will make a new covenant with the house of Israel and with the
9 house of Juda, not according to the covenant that I made with their fathers on the day when I took them by the hand to lead them forth out of the land of Egypt; for they did not abide by my covenant, and I did not regard them, says the
10 Lord. For this is the covenant that I will make with the house of Israel after those days, says the Lord: I will put my laws into their mind, and upon their hearts I will write them, and I will be
11 their God, and they shall be my people. And they shall not teach, each his neighbor, and each his brother, saying, 'Know the Lord'; for all shall know me, from least to greatest among them.
12 Because I will be merciful to their iniquities, and
13 their sins I will remember no more." Now in saying "a new covenant," he has made obsolete the former one; and that which is obsolete and has grown old is near its end.

4. A Superior Sacrifice
The Earthly Sanctuary

THE FIRST COVENANT also had ritual ordinances and a sanctuary, though an earthly one. For there was set up a tabernacle in the outer part of which were the lamp-stand and the table and the showbread, and this is called the Holy Place; but beyond the second veil was the tabernacle which is called the Holy of Holies, having a golden censer and the ark of the covenant, overlaid on every side with gold. In the ark was a golden pot containing the manna and the rod of Aaron which had budded, and the tablets of the covenant; and above it were the cherubim of glory overshadowing the mercy-seat. But of all these we cannot now speak in detail.

OCT. 17
Apr. 17

9 1
2
3
4
5

A Type of the Heavenly Sanctuary

Such then being the arrangements, the priests always used to enter into the first tabernacle to perform the sacred rites; but into the second tabernacle the high priest alone entered once a year, not without blood, which he offered for his own and the people's sins of ignorance. The Holy Spirit signified by this that the way into the Holies was not yet thrown open while the first tabernacle was still standing. This first tabernacle is a figure of the present time, inasmuch as gifts and sacrifices are offered that cannot perfect the worshipper in conscience, since they refer only to food and drink ' and various ablutions and bodily regulations imposed until a time of reformation.

6
7
8
9
10

9, 11: *Greater and more perfect tabernacle:* the tabernacle of the heavens.

Christ the High Priest and Victim

11 But when Christ appeared as high priest of the good things to come, he entered once for all through the greater and more perfect tabernacle, not made by hands (that is, not of this 12 creation), nor again by virtue of blood of goats and calves, but by virtue of his own blood, into the Holies, having obtained eternal redemption. 13 For if the blood of goats and bulls and the sprinkled ashes of a heifer sanctify the unclean 14 unto the cleansing of the flesh, how much more will the blood of Christ, who through the Holy Spirit offered himself unblemished unto God, cleanse your conscience from dead works to serve the living God?

Redemption through Christ

15 And this is why he is mediator of a new covenant, that whereas a death has taken place for redemption from the transgressions committed under the former covenant, they who have been called may receive eternal inheritance 16 according to the promise. For where there is a testament, the death of the testator must inter- 17 vene; for a testament is valid only when men are dead, otherwise it has as yet no force as long as the testator is alive.

The Blood of Victims

18 Hence not even the first has been inaugurated 19 without blood; for when every commandment of the Law had been read by Moses to all the people, he took the blood of the calves and of the goats, with water and scarlet wool and hyssop, and sprinkled both the book itself and all the 20 people, ' saying, "This is the blood of the covenant 21 which God has commanded you for you." The taber-

nacle also and all the vessels of the ministry he
sprinkled likewise with blood; and with blood　22
almost everything is cleansed according to the
Law, and without the shedding of blood there is
no forgiveness.

The Blood of Christ

It was necessary, therefore, that | OCT. 18 |　23
the copies of the heavenly realities | Apr. 18 |
should be cleansed by these things; but the
heavenly realities themselves require better
sacrifices than these. For Jesus has not entered　24
into a Holies made by hands, a mere copy of the
true, but into heaven itself, to appear now before
the face of God on our behalf; nor yet has he　25
entered to offer himself often, as the high priest
enters into the Holies year after year with blood
not his own; for in that case he must have　26
suffered often since the beginning of the world.
But as it is, once for all at the end of the ages,
he has appeared for the destruction of sin by the
sacrifice of himself. And just as it is appointed　27
unto men to die once and after this comes the
judgment, so also was Christ offered once to　28
take away the sins of many; the second time with
no part in sin he will appear unto the salvation of
those who await him.

One Sacrifice Supplants Many

For the Law, having but a shadow of the good **10** 1
things to come, and not the exact image of the
objects, is never able by the sacrifices which
they offer continually, year after year the same,
to perfect those who draw near; for in that case　2
would they not have ceased to be offered, because the worshippers, once cleansed, would no
longer have any consciousness of sin? Yet in　3
these sacrifices sins are brought to remembrance

4 year by year. For it is impossible that sins should be taken away with blood of bulls and of goats.
5 Therefore in coming into the world, he says, "Sacrifice and oblation thou wouldst not, but a
6 body thou hast fitted to me: in holocausts and
7 sin-offerings thou hast had no pleasure. Then said I, 'Behold, I come — (in the head of the book it is written of me) — to do thy will, O
8 God.'" In saying in the first place, "Sacrifices and oblations and holocausts and sin-offerings thou wouldst not, neither hast thou had pleasure in them" (which are offered according to the
9 Law), and then saying, "Behold, I come to do thy will, O God," he annuls the first covenant in
10 order to establish the second. It is in this "will" that we have been sanctified through the offering of the body of Jesus Christ once for all.

Its Eternal Efficacy

11 And every priest indeed stands daily ministering, and often offering the same sacrifices, which
12 can never take away sins; but Jesus, having offered one sacrifice for sins, has taken his seat
13 forever at the right hand of God, waiting thenceforth until his enemies be made the footstool
14 under his feet. For by one offering he has per-
15 fected forever those who are sanctified. Thus also the Holy Spirit testifies unto us. For after having
16 said, "This is the covenant that I will make with them after those days, says the Lord: I will put my laws upon their hearts, and upon their minds I
17 will write them," he then adds, "And their sins and their iniquities I will remember no more."
18 Now where there is forgiveness of these, there is no longer offering for sin.

10, 26: *Sin willfully*: by apostasy.

II: EXHORTATIONS

1. To Perseverance in Faith

First Motive: the Judgment

SINCE THEN, BRETHREN, we are 19 free to enter the Holies in virtue of | OCT. 19 / Apr. 19 | the blood of Christ, a new and living way which 20 he inaugurated for us through the veil (that is, his flesh), and since we have a high priest over 21 the house of God, let us draw near with a true 22 heart in fullness of faith, having our hearts cleansed from an evil conscience by sprinkling, and the body washed with clean water. Let us 23 hold fast the confession of our hope without wavering, for he who has given the promise is faithful. And let us consider how to arouse one 24 another to charity and good works; not forsaking 25 our assembly as is the custom of some, but exhorting one another, and this all the more as you see the Day drawing near.

Guilt of Apostasy

For if we sin willfully after receiving the 26 knowledge of the truth, there remains no longer a sacrifice for sins, but a certain dreadful expecta- 27 tion of judgment, and "the fury of a fire which will consume the adversaries." A man making 28 void the Law of Moses dies without any mercy on the word of two or three witnesses; how 29 much worse punishments do you think he de- serves who has trodden under foot the Son of God, and has regarded as unclean the blood of the covenant through which he was sanctified, and has insulted the Spirit of grace? For we 30 know him who has said, "Vengeance is mine, I will repay." And again, "The Lord will judge his people." It is a fearful thing to fall into the hands 31 of the living God.

Second Motive: Trials Well Borne

32　But call to mind the days gone by, in which, after you had been enlightened, you endured
33　a great conflict of sufferings; partly by being made a public spectacle through reproaches and tribulations, and partly by making common cause
34　with those who fared thus. For you both have had compassion on those in prison and have joyfully accepted the plundering of your own goods, knowing that you have a better possession and a
35　lasting one. Do not, therefore, lose your con-
36　fidence, which has a great reward. For you have need of patience that, doing the will of God, you
37　may receive the promise: "For yet a very little while, and he who is to come, will come, and
38　will not delay. Now my just one lives by faith. But if he draws back, he will not please my soul."
39　We, however, are not of those who draw back unto destruction, but of those who have faith to the saving of the soul.

Third Motive: Old Testament Examples

11　1　Now faith is the substance of things to be hoped for, the evidence OCT. 20 Apr. 20
2　of things that are not seen; for by it the men of
3　old had testimony borne to them. By faith we understand that the world was fashioned by the word of God; and thus things visible were made out of things invisible.

Abel

4　By faith Abel offered to God a sacrifice more excellent than did Cain, through which he

---

11, 1: The sense is: faith is assurance in the case of things that are hoped for, it is conviction about things that are not seen.

11, 2: *Had testimony borne to them:* i. e., they gained God's approval.

obtained a testimony that he was just, God giving testimony to his gifts; and through his faith, though he is dead, he yet speaks.

Henoch

By faith Henoch was taken up lest he should 5 see death; and he was not found, because God took him up. For before he was taken up he had testimony that he pleased God, and without 6 faith it is impossible to please God. For he who comes to God must believe that God exists and is a rewarder to those who seek him.

Noe

By faith Noe, having been warned concerning 7 things not seen as yet, prepared with pious fear an ark in which to save his household. Having thus condemned the world, he was made heir of the justice which is through faith.

Abraham

By faith he who is called Abraham obeyed by 8 going out into a place which he was to receive for an inheritance; and he went out, not knowing where he was going. By faith he abode in the 9 Land of Promise as in a foreign land, dwelling in tents with Isaac and Jacob, the co-heirs of the same promise; for he was looking for the city 10 with fixed foundations, of which city the architect and the builder is God.

Sara

By faith even Sara herself, who was barren, 11 received power for the conception of a child when she was past the time of life, because she believed that he who had given the promise was faithful. And so there sprang from one man, 12 though he was as good as dead, issue like the stars of heaven in number and innumerable as the sand that is by the seashore.

The Heavenly Country

13 In the way of faith all these died without receiving the promises, but beholding them afar off, and saluting them and acknowledging that

14 they were pilgrims and strangers on earth. For they who say these things show plainly that they

15 seek a country of their own. And indeed if they were thinking of the country from which they went out, they certainly would have had oppor-

16 tunity to return; but as it is they seek after a better, that is, a heavenly country. Therefore God is not ashamed to be called their God, for he has prepared for them a city.

Abraham's Trial

17 By faith Abraham, when he was put to the test, offered Isaac; and he who had received the

18 promises¹ (to whom it had been said, "In Isaac thy seed shall be called") was about to offer up

19 his only-begotten son, reasoning that God has power to raise up even from the dead; whence also he received him back as a type.

Isaac, Jacob, Joseph

20 By faith Isaac blessed Jacob and Esau even

21 regarding things to come. By faith Jacob, when dying, blessed each of the sons of Joseph and bowed in worship towards the top of his staff.

22 By faith Joseph, when dying, made mention of the departure of the sons of Israel and gave orders concerning his bones.

11, 19: *As a type:* i. e., of the Resurrection.

Amram and Jochabed

By faith Moses was hidden by his parents for three months after his birth, because they saw he was a beautiful babe and they did not fear the king's edict. 23

OCT. 21
Apr. 21

Moses

By faith Moses, when he was grown up, denied 24 that he was a son of Pharaoh's daughter; choos- 25 ing rather to be afflicted with the people of God than to have the enjoyment of sin for a time, esteeming the reproach of Christ greater riches 26 than the treasures of the Egyptians; for he was looking to the reward. By faith he left Egypt, not 27 fearing the wrath of the king; for he persevered as if seeing him who cannot be seen. By faith he 28 celebrated the Passover and the sprinkling of blood, that he who destroyed the firstborn might not touch them.

The Israelites

By faith they passed through the Red Sea, as 29 through dry land; whereas the Egyptians, attempting it, were swallowed up. By faith the walls 30 of Jericho fell after they had gone around them for seven days.

Rahab

By faith Rahab the harlot, who had received 31 the spies in peace, did not perish with the unbelievers.

More Heroes of Faith

And what more shall I say? For time will fail 32 me if I tell of Gideon, of Barac, of Samson, of Jephthe, of David and of Samuel and the prophets, who by faith conquered kingdoms, 33 wrought justice, obtained promises, stopped the mouths of lions, ' quenched the violence of fire, 34

escaped the edge of the sword, recovered strength
from weakness, became valiant in battle, put to
35 flight armies of aliens. Women had their dead
restored to them by resurrection. Others were
tortured, refusing to accept release, that they
36 might find a better resurrection. Others had
experience of mockery and stripes, yes even of
37 chains and prisons. They were stoned, they were
sawed asunder, they were tempted, they were
put to death by the sword. They went about in
sheepskins and goatskins, destitute, distressed,
38 afflicted — ' of whom the world was not worthy
— wandering in deserts, mountains, caves and
holes in the earth.

Imperfection of Their State

39 And all these, though they had been approved
by the testimony of faith, did not receive what
40 was promised, for God had something better in
view for us; so that they should not be perfected
without us.

2. Other Virtues

Constancy

12 1 THEREFORE LET US ALSO, having
such a cloud of witnesses over us,
put away every encumbrance and the sin entan-
gling us, and run with patience to the fight set
2 before us; looking towards the author and
finisher of faith, Jesus, who for the joy set before
him, endured a cross, despising shame, and sits
3 at the right hand of the throne of God. Consider,
then, him who endured such opposition from sinners against himself, so that you may not grow
weary and lose heart.

4 For you have not yet resisted unto blood in the
5 struggle with sin. And you have forgotten the
exhortation that is addressed to you as sons,

OCT. 22
Apr. 22

saying, "My son, neglect not the discipline of the Lord, neither be thou weary when thou art rebuked by him. For whom the Lord loves, he 6 chastises; and he scourges every son whom he receives."

Continue under discipline. God deals with you 7 as with sons; for what son is there whom his father does not correct? But if you are without 8 discipline, in which all have had a share, then you are illegitimate children and not sons. Furthermore, we had fathers of our flesh to correct 9 us, and we reverenced them. Shall we not much more obey the Father of spirits and live? For 10 they indeed corrected us for a few days, as they saw fit; but he for our benefit, that we may share his holiness. Now all discipline seems for the 11 present to be a matter not for joy but for grief; but afterwards it yields the most peaceful fruit of justice to those who have been exercised by it. Therefore brace up the hands that hang 12 down, and the tottering knees, and make 13 straight paths for your feet; that no one who is lame may go out of the way, but rather be healed.

Peace and Holiness

Strive for peace with all men, and for that 14 holiness without which no man will see God. Take heed lest anyone be wanting in the grace 15 of God; lest any root of bitterness springing up cause trouble and by it the many be defiled; lest 16 there be any immoral or profane person, such as Esau, who for one meal sold his birthright. For 17 know that even afterwards, when he desired to inherit the blessing, he was rejected; for he found no opportunity for repentance, although he had sought after it with tears.

Sinai and the New Sion

18 For you have not approached a mountain that may be touched, and a burning fire, and whirl-
19 wind and darkness and storm, and sound of trumpet, and sound of words; which sound was such that those who heard entreated that the
20 word should not be spoken to them; for they could not bear what was being said: "And if even a beast touches the mount, it shall be
21 stoned." And so terrible was the spectacle that Moses said, "I am greatly terrified and trem-
22 bling." But you have come to Mount Sion, and to the city of the living God, the heavenly Jerusalem, and to the company of many thousands
23 of angels, and to the Church of the firstborn who are enrolled in the heavens, and to God, the judge of all, and to the spirits of the just made
24 perfect, and to Jesus, mediator of a new covenant, and to a sprinkling of blood which speaks
25 better than Abel. See that you do not refuse him who speaks. For if they did not escape who rejected him who spoke upon earth, much more shall we not escape who turn away from him who
26 speaks to us from heaven. His voice then shook the earth, but now he promises thus, "Yet once, and I will shake not the earth only but heaven
27 also." Now by this expression, "yet once," he announces the removal of things which can be shaken — created things — in order that the things which cannot be shaken may remain.
28 Therefore, since we receive a kingdom that cannot be shaken, we have grace, through which we may offer pleasing service to God with fear and
29 reverence. For our God is a consuming fire.

Brotherly Love and Purity

Let brotherly love abide in you,
and do not forget to entertain strangers; for thereby some have entertained angels
unawares. Remember those who are in bonds as
if you were bound with them, and those who are
illtreated, as tarrying yourselves also in the body.
Let marriage be held in honor with all, and let
the marriage bed be undefiled. For God will
judge the immoral and adulterers.

13 1
2
3

4

God Will Never Fail You

Let your manner of life be without avarice; be
content with what you have, for he himself has
said, "I will not leave thee, neither will I forsake
thee." So that we may confidently say, "The
Lord is my helper: I will not fear what man shall
do to me."

5

6

Loyalty to Christ and Superiors

Remember your superiors, who spoke to you
the word of God. Consider how they ended their
lives, and imitate their faith. Jesus Christ is the
same, yesterday and today, yes, and forever.

7

8

Do not be led away by various and strange
doctrines. For it is good to make steadfast the
heart by grace, not by foods, in which those who
walked found no profit. We have an altar, from
which they have no right to eat who serve the
tabernacle. For the bodies of those animals
whose blood is brought into the Holies by the
high priest for sin, are burned outside the camp;
and so Jesus also, that he might sanctify the
people by his blood, suffered outside the gate.
Let us therefore go forth to him outside the camp,

9

10

11

12

13

14 bearing his reproach; for here we have no permanent city, but we seek for the city that is to
15 come. Through him, therefore, let us offer up a sacrifice of praise always to God, that is, fruit of
16 lips praising his name. And do not forget kindness and charity, for by such sacrifices God's
17 favor is obtained. Obey your superiors and be subject to them, for they keep watch as having to render an account of your souls; so that they may do this with joy, and not with grief, for that would not be expedient for you.

Conclusion

Request for Prayer

18 PRAY FOR US. For we are confident that we have a good conscience, desiring to live uprightly
19 in all things. But I more especially exhort you to do this, that I may be restored to you the sooner.

Blessing

20 Now may the God of peace, who brought forth from the dead the great pastor of the sheep, our Lord Jesus, in virtue of the blood of an everlast-
21 ing covenant, fit you with every good thing to do his will; working in you that which is well pleasing in his sight, through Jesus Christ, to whom is glory forever and ever. Amen.

Greetings

22 And I beseech you, brethren, to bear with this word of exhortation; for I have written to you in
23 few words. Know that our brother Timothy has been set free; with whom (if he comes soon) I
24 will see you. Greet all your superiors and all the saints. The brethren from Italy send you greet-
25 ings. ' Grace be with you all. Amen.

THE EPISTLE OF ST. JAMES

Introduction

Besides the fourteen Epistles of St. Paul, there are seven Catholic Epistles: one of St. James, two of St. Peter, three of St. John, and one of St. Jude. From the earliest days of the Church these have been called "Catholic" on account of their universal appeal. With the exception of the Second and Third Epistles of St. John, they were circular or encyclical letters sent by these Apostles to various Christian communities of the Church.

St. James the Less, the author of the first Catholic Epistle, was the son of Alpheus or Cleophas (Matt. 10, 3). His mother Mary was a sister, or a close relative, of the Blessed Virgin, and for that reason, according to Jewish custom, he was sometimes called the brother of the Lord (Gal. 1, 19; cf. also Matt. 13, 55; Mark 6, 3). The Apostle held a distinguished position in the early Christian community at Jerusalem. St. Paul tells us he was a witness of the Resurrection of Christ (1 Cor. 15, 7); he is also called a "pillar" of the Church, whom St. Paul consulted about the gospel (Gal. 2, 2. 9). According to tradition, he was the first Bishop of Jerusalem, and was at the Council of Jerusalem about the year 50 (Acts 1, 13; 15, 4ff; 21, 18; Gal. 1, 19). The historians Eusebius and Hegesippus relate that St. James was martyred for the faith by the Jews in the spring of the year 62, although they greatly esteemed his person and had given him the surname of "James the Just."

Catholic tradition has always recognized St. James as the author of this Epistle. Internal evidence based on the language, style and teaching of the Epistle reveals its author as a Jew familiar with the Old Testament, and a Christian thoroughly grounded in the teachings of the gospel. External evidence from the early Fathers and councils of the Church confirms its authenticity and canonicity.

The date of its writing cannot be determined exactly. According to some scholars it was written

THE EPISTLE OF ST. JAMES
THE APOSTLE

Introduction

Greeting

1 1 JAMES, THE SERVANT OF GOD | OCT. 24
and of our Lord Jesus Christ, to the | Adr. 24
twelve tribes that are in the Dispersion: greeting.

I: EXHORTATION TO PATIENCE IN TRIALS

Wisdom in Trials

2 ESTEEM IT ALL JOY, my brethren, when you
3 fall into various trials, knowing that the trying
4 of your faith begets patience. And let patience
have its perfect work, that you may be perfect
and entire, lacking nothing.

5 But if any of you is wanting in wisdom, let
him ask it of God, who gives abundantly to all
men, and does not reproach; and it will be
6 given to him. But let him ask with faith, without hesitation. For he who hesitates is like a
wave of the sea, driven and carried about by
7 the wind. Therefore, let not such a one think
that he will receive anything from the Lord,

---

about the year 49. Others, however, claim it was
written after St. Paul's Epistle to the Romans (composed during the winter of 57-58). It was probably
written between the years 60 and 62.

St. James addresses himself to the "twelve tribes
that are in the Dispersion" (1, 1), that is, to Christians
outside Palestine; but nothing in the Epistle indicates that he is thinking only of Jewish Christians.
St. James realizes full well the temptations and
difficulties they encounter in the midst of paganism,
and as a spiritual father, he endeavors to guide and
direct them in the faith. Therefore the burden of
his discourse is an exhortation to practical Christian
living.

'being a double-minded man, unstable in all 8 his ways.

But let the brother of lowly condition glory 9 in his high estate, and the rich man in his low 10 condition; for he will pass away like the flower of the grass. For the sun rises with a burning 11 heat and parches the grass, and its flower falls and the beauty of its appearance perishes. So too will the rich man wither in his ways.

Blessed is the man who endures temptation; 12 for when he has been tried, he will receive the crown of life which God has promised to those who love him.

Sources of Evil and Good

Let no man say when he is tempted, that he is 13 tempted by God; for God is no tempter to evil, and he himself tempts no one. But everyone is 14 tempted by being drawn away and enticed by his own passion. Then when passion has con- 15 ceived, it brings forth sin; but when sin has matured, it begets death. Therefore, my be- 16 loved brethren do not err.

Every good gift and every perfect gift is from 17 above, coming down from the Father of Lights, with whom there is no change, nor shadow of alteration. Of his own will he has begotten us 18 by the word of truth, that we might be, as it were, the first-fruits of his creatures.

II: LIVING AND ACTIVE FAITH

Hearers and Doers of the Word of God

YOU KNOW THIS, my beloved brethren. But 19 let every man be swift to hear, slow to speak,

---

1, 8: *Double-minded:* an irresolute person who enter-
tains conflicting sentiments.

1, 13: *God is no tempter to evil:* the meaning probably is
that God is not subject to temptation, neither does he
tempt any man.

20 and slow to wrath. For the wrath of man does
21 not work the justice of God. Therefore, casting
aside all uncleanness and abundance of malice,
with meekness receive the ingrafted word,
22 which is able to save your souls. But be doers
of the word, and not hearers only, deceiving
23 yourselves. For if anyone is a hearer of the
word, and not a doer, he is like a man looking
24 at his natural face in a mirror: for he looks at
himself and goes away, and presently he for-
25 gets what kind of man he is. But he who has
looked carefully into the perfect law of liberty
and has remained in it, not becoming a forget-
ful hearer but a doer of the work, shall be
26 blessed in his deed. And if anyone thinks himself to be religious, not restraining his tongue
but deceiving his own heart, that man's religion
27 is vain. Religion pure and undefiled before God
the Father is this: to give aid to orphans and
widows in their tribulation, and to keep oneself
unspotted from this world.

Impartiality

2 1   My brethren, do not join faith in | OCT. 28
our glorious Lord Jesus Christ with | Apr. 25
2 partiality towards persons. For if a man in fine
apparel, having a gold ring, enters your assembly, and a poor man in mean attire enters
3 also, and you pay attention to him who is
clothed in fine apparel and say, "Sit thou here
in this good place"; but you say to the poor
man, "Stand thou there," or, "Sit by my foot-
4 stool"; are you not making distinctions among
yourselves, and do you not become judges with
5 evil thoughts? Listen, my beloved brethren!

1, 22: The word of God has already been received by the
Christians to whom St. James is writing; but they must
understand it better and obey it.

Has not God chosen the poor of this world to
be rich in faith and heirs of the kingdom which
God has promised to those who love him? But 6
you have dishonored the poor man. Do not the
rich use their power to oppress you, and do
they not drag you before judgment-seats? Do 7
they not blaspheme the good name by which
you are called?

If, however, you fulfill the royal law, ac- 8
cording to the Scriptures, "Thou shalt love thy
neighbor as thyself," you do well. But if you 9
show partiality towards persons, you commit sin,
being convicted by the law as transgressors. For 10
whoever keeps the whole law, but offends in
one point, has become guilty in all. For he who 11
said, "Thou shalt not commit adultery," said
also, "Thou shalt not kill." Now if thou wilt not
commit adultery, yet wilt commit murder, thou
hast become a transgressor of the law. So speak 12
and so act as men about to be judged by the
law of liberty. For judgment is without mercy 13
to him who has not shown mercy; but mercy
triumphs over judgment.

Practical Faith

What will it profit, my brethren, if a man 14
says he has faith, but does not have works?
Can the faith save him? And if a brother or a 15
sister be naked and in want of daily food, and 16
one of you say to them, "Go in peace, be warmed
and filled," yet you do not give them what is
necessary for the body, what does it profit? So 17
faith too, unless it has works, is dead in itself.
But someone will say, "Thou hast faith, and I 18
have works." Show me thy faith without works,

2, 10f: The whole Law and each article of it must be
observed. He who transgresses a single Law despises the
supreme Lawgiver.

and I from my works will show thee my faith.
19 Thou believest that there is one God. Thou
dost well. The devils also believe, and tremble.
20 But dost thou want to know, O senseless
21 man, that faith without works is useless? Was
not Abraham our father justified by works,
when he offered up Isaac his son upon the
22 altar? Dost thou see that faith worked along
with his works, and by the works the faith was
23 made perfect? And the Scripture was fulfilled
which says, "Abraham believed God, and it
was reckoned to him as justice, and he was
24 called the friend of God." You see that by
works a man is justified, and not by faith only.
25 In like manner, was not Rahab the harlot also
justified by works, when she welcomed the
messengers and sent them out another way?
26 For just as the body without the spirit is dead,
so faith also without works is dead.

III: THE HAZARD OF TEACHING

Abuses of the Tongue

3 1 LET NOT MANY OF YOU become
teachers, my brethren, knowing that
OCT. 26
Apr. 26
2 you will receive a greater judgment. For in
many things we all offend. If anyone does not
offend in word, he is a perfect man, able also to
3 lead round by a bridle the whole body. For if
we put bits into horses' mouths that they may
4 obey us, we control their whole body also. Behold, even the ships, great as they are, and
driven by boisterous winds, are steered by a
5 small rudder wherever the touch of the steers-
man pleases. So the tongue also is a little member, but it boasts mightily. Behold, how small
6 a fire — how great a forest it kindles! And the
tongue is a fire, the very world of iniquity. The

tongue is placed among our members, defiling the whole body, and setting on fire the course of our life, being itself set on fire by hell. For 7 every kind of beast and bird, and of serpents and the rest, is tamed and has been tamed by mankind; but the tongue no man can tame—a 8 restless evil, full of deadly poison. With it we 9 bless God the Father; and with it we curse men, who have been made after the likeness of God. Out of the same mouth proceed blessing 10 and cursing. These things, my brethren, ought not to be so. Does the fountain send forth sweet 11 and bitter water from the same opening? Can 12 a fig tree, my brethren, bear olives, or a vine figs? So neither can salt water yield fresh water.

True Wisdom

Who is wise and instructed among you? Let 13 him by his good behavior show his work in the meekness of wisdom. But if you have bitter 14 jealousy and contentions in your hearts, do not glory and be liars against the truth. This is not 15 the wisdom that descends from above. It is earthly, sensual, devilish. For where there is 16 envy and contentiousness, there is instability and every wicked deed. But the wisdom that 17 is from above is first of all chaste, then peaceable, moderate, docile, in harmony with good things, full of mercy and good fruits, without judging, without dissimulation. The fruit of jus- 18 tice is sown in peace by those who make peace.

IV: SPECIAL ADMONITIONS
Sources of Discord

WHENCE DO WARS and quarrels OCT. 27 Apr. 27 **4** 1 come among you? Is it not from this, from your passions, which wage war in your members? You covet and do not have; 2

you kill and envy, and cannot obtain. You quarrel and wrangle, and you do not have be-
3 cause you do not ask. You ask and do not receive, because you ask amiss, that you may
4 spend it upon your passions. Adulterers, do you not know that the friendship of this world is enmity with God? Therefore, whoever wishes to be a friend of this world becomes an enemy
5 of God. Or do you think that the Scripture says in vain, "The Spirit which dwells in you
6 covets unto jealousy"? But he gives a greater grace. For this reason it says, "God resists
7 the proud, but gives grace to the humble." Be subject therefore to God, but resist the devil,
8 and he will flee from you. Draw near to God, and he will draw near to you. Cleanse your hands, you sinners, and purify your hearts, you
9 double-minded. Be sorrowful, and mourn, and weep; let your laughter be turned into mourn-
10 ing, and your joy into sadness. Humble yourselves in the sight of the Lord, and he will exalt you.

Presumption

11 Brethren, do not speak against one another. He who speaks against a brother, or judges his brother, speaks against the law and judges the law. But if thou judgest the law, thou art
12 not a doer of the law, but a judge. There is one Lawgiver and Judge, he who is able to destroy
13 and to save. But thou who judgest thy neighbor, who art thou?

Behold now, you who say, "Today or tomorrow we will go into such a city, and spend a
14 year there, and trade and make money"; you

4, 4: A worldly soul is guilty of spiritual infidelity or adultery.

4, 6: *But he gives a greater grace:* i. e., He gives us more valuable gifts than the world or its votaries can offer.

who do not know what will happen tomorrow.
For what is your life? It is a mist that appears 15
for a little while, and then vanishes. You ought
rather to say, "If the Lord will," and, "If we
live, we will do this or that." But now you 16
boast in your arrogance. All such boasting is
evil. Therefore he who knows how to do good, 17
and does not do it, commits a sin.

The Unjust Rich

Come now, you rich, weep and | OCT. 28 | **5** 1
howl over your miseries which will | Apr. 28 |
come upon you. Your riches have rotted, and 2
your garments have become moth-eaten. Your 3
gold and silver are rusted; and their rust will be
a witness against you, and will devour your flesh
as fire does. You have laid up treasure in the
last days. Behold, the wages of the laborers 4
who reaped your fields, which have been kept
back by you unjustly, cry out; and their cry
has entered into the ears of the Lord of Hosts.
You have feasted upon earth, and you have 5
nourished your hearts on dissipation in the day
of slaughter. You have condemned and put to 6
death the just, and he did not resist you.

Conclusion

Patience in Affliction

BE PATIENT, THEREFORE, brethren, until the 7
coming of the Lord. Behold, the farmer waits
for the precious fruit of the earth, being patient
until it receives the early and the late rain. Do 8
you also be patient; strengthen your hearts; for
the coming of the Lord is at hand. Do not com- 9
plain against one another, brethren, that you
may not be judged. Behold, the judge is standing at the door. Take, brethren, as an example 10
of labor and patience, the prophets who spoke

11 in the name of the Lord. Behold, we call them blessed who have endured. You have heard of the patience of Job, and you have seen the purpose of the Lord, how the Lord is merciful and
12 compassionate. But above all things, my brethren, do not swear, either by heaven or by the earth, or any other oath; but let your yes be yes, your no, no; that you may not fall under judgment

Last Anointing, Confession and Prayer

13 Is any one of you sad? Let him pray. Is any
14 one in good spirits? Let him sing a hymn. Is any one among you sick? Let him bring in the presbyters of the Church, and let them pray over him, anointing him with oil in the name of
15 the Lord. And the prayer of faith will save the sick man, and the Lord will raise him up, and if he be in sins, they shall be forgiven him.
16 Confess, therefore, your sins to one another, and pray for one another, that you may be saved. For the unceasing prayer of a just man
17 is of great avail. Elias was a man like ourselves, subject to the same infirmities; and he prayed earnestly that it might not rain upon the earth, and it did not rain for three years and six
18 months. He prayed again, and the heavens gave rain and the earth brought forth its fruit.

Conversion of a Sinner

19 My brethren, if any one of you strays from
20 the truth and someone brings him back, he ought to know that he who causes a sinner to be brought back from his misguided way, will save his soul from death, and will cover a multitude of sins.

5, 14: According to the teaching of the Council of Trent (Sess. 14, c. 3) St. James promulgated here the Sacrament of Extreme Unction. *Presbyters:* certainly here in the sense of "priests."

THE FIRST EPISTLE OF ST. PETER

Introduction

St. Peter, also called Simon (Acts 15, 14; 2 Pet. 1, 1), was the son of a certain John from the town of Bethsaida in Galilee (John 1, 42-44). He was led by his brother Andrew to the Lord, who conferred upon him the name Cephas, i. e., "rock" or Peter (John 1, 42; Matt. 16, 17-19; Mark 3, 16; Luke 6, 14). Thereupon he followed the Lord and became the "Prince of the Apostles." After the Resurrection the primacy was conferred upon him and immediately after the Ascension he began to exercise it. After preaching in Jerusalem and Palestine he went to Rome, probably after his liberation from prison (Acts 12, 17). Some years later he was in Jerusalem for the first Church Council (Acts 15, 6ff), and shortly afterwards at Antioch (Gal. 2, 11-14). In the year 67 he was martyred in Rome.

The Epistle names St. Peter, Apostle of Jesus Christ, as its author (1, 1; cf. also 5, 12-14), and the testimony of the early centuries of Christianity re-affirms this evidence. So constant was this testimony that Eusebius, the Church historian, placed the Epistle among the books of the Bible accepted by all. Its authorship is also confirmed by the contents of the Epistle, in which the author appears as an immediate witness of the sufferings of Christ (5, 1), and by its similarity to St. Peter's discourses in Acts.

The Epistle is addressed to the Christian communities of Asia Minor that were being distressed by the enmity of their pagan neighbors. By their acceptance of Christianity they had become separated from their own countrymen, who abused and persecuted them. The Apostle therefore instructs his readers that Christianity is the true religion in spite of their trials and sufferings, and exhorts them to lead good Christian lives.

The place of composition is given as "Babylon" (5, 13). From the Apocalypse (14, 8; 16, 19, etc.), the Jewish writings and the Sibylline books of the first century, we know that this name was a cryptic

THE FIRST EPISTLE OF ST. PETER THE APOSTLE

Introduction

Greeting

1 1   PETER, AN APOSTLE of Jesus
Christ, to the sojourners of the Dis- | OCT. 29 Apr. 29 |
persion in Pontus, Galatia, Cappadocia, Asia
2 and Bithynia, chosen ' unto the sanctification of
the Spirit according to the foreknowledge of
God the Father, unto obedience to Jesus Christ
and the sprinkling of his blood: grace and peace
be given you in abundance.

Thanksgiving

3   Blessed be the God and Father of our Lord
Jesus Christ, who according to his great mercy
has begotten us again, through the resurrection
of Jesus Christ from the dead, unto a living
4 hope, ' unto an incorruptible inheritance—undefiled and unfading, reserved for you in heaven.
5 By the power of God you are guarded through
faith for salvation, which is ready to be revealed
6 in the last time. Over this you rejoice; though
now for a little while, if need be, you are made
7 sorrowful by various trials, that the temper of
your faith—more precious by far than gold
which is tried by fire—may be found unto
praise and glory and honor at the revelation of
8 Jesus Christ. Him, though you have not seen,

designation of the City of Rome. Since the author
seems to be familiar with the Epistle to the Ephesians, which was written in 63 A.D., and since he
makes no reference to the persecution of Nero,
which began about the end of 64 A.D., it appears
very likely that the letter was written in the latter
part of 63 or the beginning of 64.

you love. In him, though you do not see him, yet believing, you exult with a joy unspeakable and triumphant; receiving, as the final issue 9 of your faith, the salvation of your souls. The 10 prophets who foretold the grace that was to come for you made earnest inquiry and search concerning this salvation. They searched what 11 time or circumstances the Spirit of Christ in them was signifying, when he foretold the sufferings of Christ, and the glories that would follow. To them it was revealed that not to 12 themselves but to you they were ministering those things which now have been declared to you by those who preached the gospel to you by the Holy Spirit sent from heaven. Into these things angels desire to look.

I: GENERAL COUNSELS OF CHRISTIAN HOLINESS
Filial Obedience and Fear

THEREFORE, HAVING GIRDED UP the loins 13 of your understanding, be sober and set your hope completely upon that grace which is brought to you in the revelation of Jesus Christ. As obedient children, do not conform to the 14 lusts of former days when you were ignorant; but as the One who called you is holy, be you 15 also holy in all your behavior; for it is written, 16 "You shall be holy, because I am holy."

And if you invoke as Father him who without 17 respect of persons judges according to each one's work, conduct yourselves with fear in the time of your sojourning. You know that you were re- 18 deemed from the vain manner of life handed down from your fathers, not with perishable things, with silver or gold, ' but with the precious 19

1, 17: *With fear:* the reverential fear of children towards a just father. *Sojourning:* life on earth is but a pilgrimage.

blood of Christ, as of a lamb without blemish and
20 without spot. Foreknown, indeed, before the
foundation of the world, he has been manifested
21 in the last times for your sakes. Through him you
are believers in God who raised him up from the
dead and gave him glory, so that your faith and
hope might be in God.

Brotherly Love

22 Now that your obedience to charity has purified your souls for a
brotherly love that is sincere, love one another
23 heartily and intensely. For you have been reborn,
not from corruptible seed but from incorruptible,
through the word of God who lives and abides
24 forever. For, "All flesh is as grass, and all its
glory as the flower of grass; the grass withered,
25 and the flower has fallen— ' but the word of the
Lord endures forever." Now this is the word of
the gospel that was preached to you.

OCT. 30
Apr. 30

Growth in Holiness

2 1 Lay aside therefore all malice, and all deceit,
2 and pretense, and envy, and all slander. Crave,
as newborn babes, pure spiritual milk, that by
3 it you may grow to salvation; if, indeed, you
4 have tasted that the Lord is sweet. Draw near to
him, a living stone, rejected indeed by men but
5 chosen and honored by God. Be you yourselves
as living stones, built thereon into a spiritual
house, a holy priesthood, to offer spiritual sacrifices acceptable to God through Jesus Christ.
6 Hence Scripture says, "Behold, I lay in Sion a
chief corner stone, chosen, precious; and he who
7 believes in it shall not be put to shame." For you,
therefore, who believe is this honor; but to those

2, 2: Neophytes will attain to maturity more readily when
strengthened by the *spiritual milk,* the pure and un-
adulterated word of God.

who do not believe, "A stone which the builders
rejected, the same has become the head of the
corner,"¹ and, "A stumbling-stone, and a rock of   8
scandal," to those who stumble at the word, and
who do not believe. For this also they are destined. You, however, are a chosen race, a royal   9
priesthood, a holy nation, a purchased people;
that you may proclaim the perfections of him who
has called you out of darkness into his marvellous
light. You who in times past were not a people,   10
but are now the people of God; who had not
obtained mercy, but now have obtained mercy.

II: PARTICULAR COUNSELS
OF CHRISTIAN CONDUCT

Good Example

BELOVED, I EXHORT YOU as strangers and   11
pilgrims to abstain from carnal desires which war
against the soul. Behave yourselves honorably   12
among the pagans; that, whereas they slander
you as evildoers, they may, through observing
you, by reason of your good works glorify God in
the day of visitation.

For the Citizen

Be subject to every human creature for God's   13
sake, whether to the king as supreme,¹ or to   14
governors as sent through him for vengeance on
evildoers and for the praise of the good. For such   15
is the will of God, that by doing good you should
put to silence the ignorance of foolish men. Live   16
as freemen, yet not using your freedom as a
cloak for malice but as servants of God. Honor   17
all men; love the brotherhood; fear God; honor
the king.

2, 12: *The day of visitation:* this may refer to the last
judgment, or, more probably, to the time when the call of
grace shall be given to the pagan. Hence the exhortation
to good example.

For the Slave

18   Servants, be subject to your masters in all fear, not only to the good ┌─────────┐ OCT. 31 / May 1 └─────────┘

19 and moderate, but also to the severe. This is indeed a grace, if for consciousness of God any-

20 one endures sorrows, suffering unjustly. For what is the glory if, when you sin and are buffeted, you endure it? But if, when you do right and suffer, you take it patiently, this is accept-

21 able with God. Unto this, indeed, you have been called, because Christ also has suffered for you, leaving you an example that you may follow

22 in his steps: "Who did no sin, neither was deceit

23 found in his mouth." Who, when he was reviled, did not revile, when he suffered, did not threaten, but yielded himself to him who judged him un-

24 justly; who himself bore our sins in his body upon the tree, that we, having died to sin, might live to justice; and by his stripes you were healed.

25 For you were as sheep going astray, but now you have returned to the shepherd and guardian of your souls.

For the Wife and the Husband

3 1   In like manner also let wives be subject to their husbands; so that even if any do not believe the word, they may without word be won through

2 the behavior of their wives, observing rever-

3 ently your chaste behavior. Let not theirs be the outward adornment of braiding the hair, or of

4 wearing gold, or of putting on robes; but let it be the inner life of the heart, in the imperishableness of a quiet and gentle spirit, which is of

5 great price in the sight of God. For after this manner in old times the holy women also who hoped in God adorned themselves, while being

---

2, 19: *For consciousness of God:* for religious motives.

subject to their husbands. So Sara obeyed Abra- 6
ham, calling him lord. You are daughters of hers
when you do what is right and fear no disturbance.

Husbands, in like manner dwell with your 7
wives considerately, paying honor to the woman
as to the weaker vessel, and as co-heir of the
grace of life, that your prayers be not hindered.

In Christian Charity

Finally, be all like-minded, compassionate, 8
lovers of the brethren, merciful, humble; not 9
rendering evil for evil, or abuse for abuse, but
contrariwise, blessing; for unto this were you
called that you might inherit a blessing. For, "He 10
who would love life, and see good days, let him
refrain his tongue from evil, and his lips that
they speak no deceit. Let him turn away from 11
evil and do good, let him seek after peace and
pursue it. For the eyes of the Lord are upon the 12
just, and his ears unto their prayers; but the
face of the Lord is against those who do evil."

In Christian Suffering

And who is there to harm you, if 13
you are zealous for what is good?

| NOV. 1 |
| May 2 |

But even if you suffer anything for justice' sake, 14
blessed are you. So have no fear of their fear and
do not be troubled. But hallow the Lord Christ in 15
your hearts. Be ready always with an answer to
everyone who asks a reason for the hope that is
in you. Yet do so with gentleness and fear, having 16
a good conscience, so that wherein they speak in
disparagement of you they who revile your good
behavior in Christ may be put to shame. For it is 17
better, if the will of God should so will, that you

3, 6: *Fear no disturbance:* in marriage Christian wives
are obliged to obey God's law regardless of intimidation
from non-Christian husbands.

18 suffer for doing good than for doing evil. Because
Christ also died once for sins, the Just for the
unjust, that he might bring us to God. Put to
death indeed in the flesh, he was brought to life
19 in the spirit, ' in which also he went and preached
20 to those spirits that were in prison. These in
times past had been disobedient when the
patience of God waited in the days of Noe while
the ark was building. In that ark a few, that is,
21 eight souls were saved through water. Its counter-
part, Baptism, now saves you also (not the putting
off of the filth of the flesh, but the inquiry of a
good conscience after God), through the resur-
22 rection of Jesus Christ; who is at the right hand
of God, swallowing up death that we might be
made heirs of eternal life; for he went into
heaven, Angels, Powers and Virtues being made
subject to him.

In Christian Faithfulness

4 1   Since Christ therefore has suffered in the
flesh, do you also arm yourselves with the same
intent; because he who has suffered in the flesh
2 has ceased from sins; that during the rest of his
time in the flesh he may live no longer according
to the lusts of men, but according to the will of
3 God. For sufficient is the time past for those to
have accomplished the desire of the pagans,
walking, as they did, in dissipation, lusts, drunkenness, revellings, carousings and unlawful wor-
4 ship of idols. They are amazed that you do not
run with them into the same flood of dissipation,
5 and they abuse you. But they will render an account to him who is ready to judge the living and
6 the dead. For to this end was the gospel preached
even to the dead, that they may be judged indeed as men in flesh but may live as God lives
in spirit.

III: CHRISTIAN SERVICE AND THE COMING JUDGMENT

Mutual Charity

BUT THE END of all things is at hand. Be prudent therefore and watchful in prayers. But above all things have a constant mutual charity among yourselves; for charity covers a multitude of sins. Be hospitable to one another without murmuring. According to the gift that each has received, administer it to one another as good stewards of the manifold grace of God. If anyone speaks, let it be as with words of God. If anyone ministers, let it be as from the strength that God furnishes; that in all things God may be honored through Jesus Christ, to whom are the glory and the dominion forever. Amen.

Blessings of Persecution

Beloved, do not be startled at the trial by fire that is taking place among you to prove you, as if something strange were happening to you; but rejoice, in so far as you are partakers of the sufferings of Christ, that you may also rejoice with exultation in the revelation of his glory. If you are upbraided for the name of Christ, blessed will you be, because the honor, the glory and the power of God and his Spirit rest upon you. Let none of you suffer as a murderer, or a thief, or a slanderer, or as one coveting what belongs to others. But if he suffer as a Christian, let him not be ashamed, but let him glorify God under this name. For the time has come for the judgment to begin with the

NOV. 2
May 3

3, 18: *Brought to life in the spirit:* a reference to the new activity of Christ's soul in limbo.

4, 6: *The gospel preached even to the dead:* a reference to the good tidings Christ brought to the souls in limbo.

household of God; but if it begin first with us, what will be the end of those who do not believe
18 the gospel of God? And if the just man scarcely will be saved, where will the impious and the
19 sinner appear? Therefore let them also who suffer according to the will of God commend their souls in well-doing to a faithful Creator.

For the Ministry

5 1   Now I exhort the presbyters among you — I, your fellow-presbyter and witness of the sufferings of Christ, the partaker also of the glory that
2 is to be revealed in time to come — tend the flock of God which is among you, governing not under constraint, but willingly, according to God; nor yet for the sake of base gain, but
3 eagerly; nor yet as lording it over your charges, but becoming from the heart a pattern to the
4 flock. And when the Prince of the shepherds appears, you will receive the unfading crown of glory.

Counsels to the Laity

5   Likewise, you who are younger, be subject to the presbyters. And all of you practise humility towards one another, for, "God resists the proud,
6 but gives grace to the humble." Humble yourselves, therefore, under the mighty hand of God, that he may exalt you in the time of visitation,
7 cast all your anxiety upon him, because he cares
8 for you. Be sober, be watchful! For your adversary the devil, as a roaring lion, goes about seek-
9 ing someone to devour. Resist him, steadfast in the faith, knowing that the same suffering befalls
10 your brethren all over the world. But the God of all grace, who has called us unto his eternal

---

5, 1: *Fellow-presbyter*: i. e., fellow-priest or bishop.

glory in Christ Jesus, will himself, after we have suffered a little while, perfect, strengthen and establish us. To him is the dominion forever and 11 ever. Amen.

Conclusion

Farewell

BY SILVANUS, the faithful brother as I account 12 him, I have written to you thus briefly, exhorting and testifying that this is the true grace of God. Stand firmly in it. ' The church which is at Baby- 13 lon, chosen together with you, greets you, and so does my son Mark. Greet one another with a 14 holy kiss. Grace be to you all who are in Christ. Amen.

Preface

In this Second Epistle St. Peter refers to his previous letter and to the doctrine contained in it (3, 1f). It was most likely addressed to the same Christian communities of Asia Minor as the former Epistle, and was occasioned by the appearance among the Christians of false teachers (2, 1), heretics and deceivers (3, 3), who promised them freedom (2, 19), corrupting their good morals (2, 18) and denying the Second Coming of Christ and the end of the world (3, 4ff). Its purpose, therefore, was to encourage the Christians to persevere in the faith, and to protect them against the dangers of the false teachers.

The contents of this Epistle, especially chapter 2, bear such a striking resemblance to the Epistle of St. Jude that it seems probable St. Peter was familiar with the Epistle of his fellow-Apostle and made use of some of his thoughts.

The author calls himself "Simon Peter, a servant and Apostle of Jesus Christ" (1, 1). This statement of authorship is confirmed by the Epistle itself, the author of which describes himself as an eyewitness of our Lord's Transfiguration (1, 16-18), and calls Paul his dear brother (3, 15).

The time and place of its composition are deduced from 1, 13-15. The Apostle knows that his death is close at hand. As St. Peter died a martyr in Rome, we may conclude that the Epistle was written from Rome during his imprisonment, 66-67 A.D.

THE SECOND EPISTLE OF ST. PETER THE APOSTLE

Introduction
Greeting

1 1 SIMON PETER, A SERVANT and apostle of Jesus Christ, to those who have obtained an equal privilege of faith with ourselves through the justice of our God and 2 Savior Jesus Christ. May grace and peace be

NOV. 3
May 4

given you in abundance in the knowledge of our Lord.

I: CHRISTIAN VIRTUE— ITS NECESSITY AND MOTIVES

Life of a Christian

FOR INDEED HIS DIVINE POWER has granted 3 us all things pertaining to life and piety through the knowledge of him who has called us by his own glory and power — through which he has 4 granted us the very great and precious promises, so that through them you may become partakers of the divine nature, having escaped from the corruption of that lust which is in the world. Do 5 you accordingly on your part strive diligently to supply your faith with virtue, your virtue with knowledge, your knowledge with self-control, 6 your self-control with patience, your patience with piety, your piety with fraternal love, your 7 fraternal love with charity.

Necessity of Virtue

For if you possess these virtues and they 8 abound in you, they will render you neither inactive nor unfruitful in the knowledge of our Lord Jesus Christ. For he who lacks them is blind, 9 groping his way, and has forgotten that he was cleansed from his former sins. Therefore, breth- 10 ren, strive even more by good works to make your calling and election sure. For if you do this, you will not fall into sin at any time. Indeed, in 11 this way will be amply provided for you the en-

---

1, 4: *Through which:* Christ's glory and power are the foundation of our hope.

1, 4: *Partakers of the divine nature:* the adopted sons of God share in a supernatural way in the nature of God. Grace makes them like Him; and in heaven they will see Him as He is.

trance into the everlasting kingdom of our Lord and Savior Jesus Christ.

12 Therefore I shall begin to remind you always of these things; although indeed you know them and are well established in the present truth.

13 As long as I am in this tabernacle, I think it right

14 to arouse you by a reminder, knowing as I do that the putting off of my tabernacle is at hand, just as our Lord Jesus Christ signified to me.

15 Moreover I will endeavor that even after my death you may often have occasion to call these things to mind.

Sovereignty of Christ

16 For we were not following fictitious tales when we made known to you the power and coming of our Lord Jesus Christ, but we had been eye-

17 witnesses of his grandeur. For he received from God the Father honor and glory, when from out the majestic glory a voice came down to him, speaking thus: "This is my beloved Son in whom

18 I am well pleased." And this voice we ourselves heard borne from heaven when we were with him on the holy mount.

19 And we have the word of prophecy, surer still, to which you do well to attend, as to a lamp shining in a dark place, until the day dawns and

20 the morning star rises in your hearts. This, then, you must understand first of all, that no prophecy of Scripture is made by private interpretation.

21 For not by will of man was prophecy brought at any time; but holy men of God spoke as they were moved by the Holy Spirit.

1, 13: *This tabernacle:* the human body.

1, 18: *The holy mount:* the Mount of Transfiguration.

1, 19: *Until the day dawns:* the day of the Lord, a reference to the Second Coming of Christ. It will resemble the morning star in splendor.

II: FALSE TEACHERS

Punishment of Lying Teachers

BUT THERE WERE FALSE PROPH- | NOV. 4 | **2** 1
ETS also among the people, just as | May 8 |
among you there will be lying teachers who will
bring in destructive sects. They even disown the
Lord who bought them, thus bringing upon
themselves swift destruction. And many will 2
follow their wanton conduct, and because of
them the way of truth will be maligned. And out 3
of greed they will with deceitful words use you
for their gain. Their condemnation, passed of
old, is not made void, and their destruction does
not slumber.

Warning from the Past

For God did not spare the angels when they 4
sinned, but dragged them down by infernal ropes
to Tartarus, and delivered them to be tortured
and kept in custody for judgment. Nor did he 5
spare the ancient world, but preserved (with
seven others) Noe a herald of justice, when he
brought a flood upon the world of the impious.
And he condemned the cities of Sodom and Go- 6
morrah to destruction, reducing them to ashes,
thus making them an example to those who in the
future should live impiously; whereas he de- 7
livered just Lot, who was distressed by the law-
less behavior of the wicked. For by what that just 8
man saw and heard while dwelling among them,
they tormented his just soul day after day with
their wicked deeds. The Lord knows how to 9
deliver the God-fearing from temptation and to
reserve the wicked for torment on the day of
judgment, but especially those who follow the 10
flesh in unclean lust and despise authority.

The Vices of Heresy

Rash and self-willed, such men in their derid-
11 ing do not regard majesty; whereas angels,
though greater in strength and power, do not
12 bring against themselves an abusive charge. But
these men, like irrational animals created by
nature for capture and destruction, deride what
they do not understand, and will perish in their
13 own corruption, receiving thereby the recompense of their wrongdoing. They regard as
pleasure their daylight revelry; they are spots
and blemishes, they abound in wantonness while
14 banqueting with you. They have eyes full of
adultery and turned unceasingly towards sin.
They entice unstable souls; they have their hearts
exercised in covetousness; they are children of
15 a curse. They have forsaken the right way and
have gone astray; they have followed the way of
Balaam, the son of Bosor, who loved the wages
16 of wrongdoing. But he was rebuked for his madness; a dumb beast of burden spoke with the
voice of a man and checked the folly of the
prophet.
17 These men are springs without water and
mists driven by storms; the blackness of dark-
18 ness is reserved for them. For by high-sounding,
empty words they entice with sensual allure-
ments of carnal passion those who are just
19 escaping from such as live in error. They
promise them freedom, whereas they themselves are the
slaves of corruption; for by whatever a man is
20 overcome, of this also he is the slave. For if
after escaping the defilements of the world
through the knowledge of our Lord and Savior

2, 18: These lying teachers had interpreted Christian
liberty as freedom from the moral law. *Escaping from
such as live in error:* Christian converts who were hardly
free from former pagan habits.

Jesus Christ, they are again entangled therein and overcome, their latter state has become worse for them than the former. For it were 21 better for them not to have known the way of justice, than having known it, to turn back from the holy commandment delivered to them. For 22 what that true proverb says has happened to them, "A dog returns to his vomit," and "A sow even after washing wallows in the mire."

The Second Coming

This, beloved, is now the second epistle that I am writing to you **3** 1

NOV. 5 / May 6

wherein I stir up your pure mind to remembrance, that you may be mindful of what I formerly 2 preached of the words of the holy prophets and of your apostles, which are the precepts of the Lord and Savior. This first you must know, that 3 in the last days there will come deceitful scoffers, men walking according to their own lusts, ¹ say- 4 ing, "Where is the promise or his coming? For since the fathers fell asleep, all things continue as they were from the beginning of creation." For of this they are willfully ignorant, that there 5 were heavens long ago, and an earth formed out of water and by water through the word of God. By these means the world that then was, deluged 6 with water, perished. But the heavens that now 7 are, and the earth, by that same word have been stored up, being reserved for fire against the day of judgment and destruction of ungodly men.

But, beloved, do not be ignorant of this one 8 thing, that one day with the Lord is as a thousand years, and a thousand years as one day. The 9

3, 4: *Fathers:* the first converts to Christianity, many of whom were at this time dead.
3, 7: The word that created the world and destroyed it by water, now preserves the world for the general conflagration at the end of time.

Lord does not delay in his promises, but for your sake is long-suffering, not wishing that any should perish but that all should turn to repen-
10 tance. But the day of the Lord will come as a thief; at that time the heavens will pass away with great violence, and the elements will be dissolved with heat, and the earth, and the works that are
11 in it, will be burned up. Seeing therefore that all these things are to be dissolved, what manner of men ought you to be in holy and pious behavior,
12 you who await and hasten towards the coming of the day of God, by which the heavens, being on fire, will be dissolved and the elements will melt
13 away by reason of the heat of the fire. But we look for new heavens and a new earth, according to his promises, wherein dwells justice.

Conclusion

Exhortation, Doxology

14   THEREFORE, BELOVED, while you look for these things, endeavor to be found by him with-
15 out spot and blameless, in peace. And regard the long-suffering of our Lord as salvation. Just as our most dear brother Paul also, according to the
16 wisdom given him, has written to you,' as indeed he did in all his epistles, speaking in them of these things. In these epistles there are certain things difficult to understand, which the un-learned and the unstable distort, just as they do the rest of the Scriptures also, to their own destruction.
17   You therefore, brethren, since you know this beforehand, be on your guard lest, carried away by the error of the foolish, you fall away from
18 your own steadfastness. But grow in grace and knowledge of our Lord and Savior, Jesus Christ. To him be the glory, both now and to the day of eternity. Amen.

THE FIRST EPISTLE OF ST. JOHN

Introduction

That St. John the Apostle, the author of the Fourth Gospel, is also the author of this Epistle is the verdict of historical evidence, both implicit and explicit, reaching as far back as St. Polycarp. The internal evidence of the book itself is sufficiently strong; for the writer speaks with authority, as an Apostle would. Moreover, when the Epistle is compared with the Gospel of St. John, the resemblance both in thought and in expression is so striking that identity of authorship is admitted by most commentators.

From this close relation to the Fourth Gospel many commentators are of the opinion that the Epistle was written shortly before or shortly after the Gospel to serve as an introduction, or as a postscript, to it, or at least with the intention that both should be read together. Beyond this, there is nothing to indicate the time and place of its composition; but from this close connection we may say that it was written at Ephesus towards the close of the first century.

The Apostle wrote this letter probably as a circular letter to the faithful of Asia Minor, to remind them of what he had written and preached concerning the divinity of Christ, and thus to strengthen them against the heresies of the day. For it seems certain that, in the churches to which the letter is directed, there had risen false teachers and prophets—antichrists who denied that Jesus was the Messias, and Incarnate Son of God.

The fundamental thought of the Epistle is this: God is made known to us in Jesus Christ; hence, fellowship with the Father is through the Son. There are three main currents of thought: (1) God is light (1, 5—2, 27); (2) God is justice (2, 28—4, 6); (3) God is love (4, 7—5, 12).

Hence, if we are to have fellowship with the Father through the Son, we must walk in light, in justice or holiness, and in love. Thus the Apostle calls those who deny that Jesus is the Christ and the

THE FIRST EPISTLE OF ST. JOHN
THE APOSTLE

Introduction

The Witness to the Word of Life

1 1 I WRITE OF WHAT was from the beginning, what we have heard, | NOV. 6 / May 7 | what we have seen with our eyes, what we have looked upon and our hands have handled: of the 2 Word of Life. And the Life was made known and we have seen, and now testify and announce to you, the Life Eternal which was with the 3 Father, and has appeared to us. What we have seen and have heard we announce to you, in order that you also may have fellowship with us, and that our fellowship may be with the Father, 4 and with his Son Jesus Christ. And these things we write to you that you may rejoice, and our joy may be full.

I: GOD IS LIGHT

Walk in Light

5 AND THE MESSAGE which we have heard from 6 him and announce to you, is this: that God is light, and in him is no darkness. If we say that we have fellowship with him, and walk in darkness, we lie, and are not practising the truth. 7 But if we walk in the light as he also is in the light, we have fellowship with one another, and

---

Incarnate Son of God, liars and antichrists. He especially emphasizes the sublimity and excellence of love, the love of God finding expression in brotherly love. The Apostle further shows how to distinguish the children of God from the children of the devil; he describes the baseness and gravity of sin; and finally, he shows how the sinner may hope for pardon.

the blood of Jesus Christ, his Son, cleanses us from all sin.

If we say that we have no sin, we deceive 8 ourselves, and the truth is not in us. If we ac- 9 knowledge our sins, he is faithful and just to forgive us our sins and to cleanse us from all iniquity. If we say that we have not sinned, we 10 make him a liar, and his word is not in us.

My dear children, these things I write to you 2 1 in order that you may not sin. But if anyone sins, we have an advocate with the Father, Jesus Christ the just; and he is a propitiation for our 2 sins, not for ours only but also for those of the whole world.

Observe the Commandments Especially Charity

And by this we can be sure that we know 3 him, if we keep his commandments. He who 4 says that he knows him, and does not keep his commandments, is a liar and the truth is not in him. But he who keeps his word, in him the love 5 of God is truly perfected; and by this we know that we are in him. He who says that he abides 6 in him, ought himself also to walk just as he walked.

Beloved, no new commandment am I writing 7 to you, but an old commandment which you had from the beginning. The old commandment is the word which you have heard. Again, a new 8 commandment I am writing to you, and this is true both in him and in you. Because the darkness has passed away and the true light is now shining. He who says that he is in the light, and 9

2, 7f: The *old* and the *new* commandments are really one and the same commandment of love, promulgated in the Old Testament, but renewed by Christ, especially in the new motives and other helps supplied by Him.

10 hates his brother, is in the darkness still. He who loves his brother abides in the light, and
11 for him there is no stumbling. But he who hates his brother is in the darkness, and walks in the darkness, and he does not know whither he goes; because the darkness has blinded his eyes.

Reasons for Writing

12 I am writing to you, dear children, | NOV. 7 because your sins are forgiven you | May 8
13 for his name's sake. I am writing to you, fathers, because you know him who is from the beginning.
14 I am writing to you, young men, because you have conquered the evil one. I am writing to you, little ones, because you know the Father. I am writing to you, fathers, because you know him who is from the beginning. I am writing to you, young men, because you are strong and the word of God abides in you, and you have con-
15 quered the evil one. Do not love the world, or the things that are in the world. If anyone loves the world, the love of the Father is not in him;
16 because all that is in the world is the lust of the flesh, and the lust of the eyes, and the pride of life; which is not from the Father, but from the
17 world. And the world with its lust is passing away, but he who does the will of God abides forever.

Against False Teachers

18 Dear children, it is the last hour; and as you have heard that Antichrist is coming, so now many antichrists have arisen; whence we know

---

2, 18: *It is the last hour:* the meaning probably is that it is the last age of the world, the age of the Church. How long it will last no one knows. *Antichrist:* St. John supposes that the doctrine concerning the coming of Antichrist is already known to his readers. "Antichrist" is commonly understood as a personal opponent of Christ at the end of time. Cf. 2 John 7.

that it is the last hour. They have gone forth 19 from us, but they were not of us. For if they had been of us, they would surely have continued with us; but they were to be made manifest, that not one of them is of us. But you have an anoint- 20 ing from the Holy One and you know all things. I have not written to you as to those who do not 21 know the truth, but as to those who know it, and because no lie is of the truth. Who is the 22 liar but he who denies that Jesus is the Christ? He is the Antichrist who denies the Father and the Son. [1] No one who disowns the Son has the 23 Father. He who confesses the Son has the Father also. As for you, let that which you have 24 heard from the beginning abide in you. If that abides in you which you have heard from the beginning, you also will abide in the Son and in the Father. And this is the promise that he 25 has given us, the life everlasting.

These things I have written to you concerning 26 those who lead you astray. And as for you, let 27 the anointing which you have received from him, dwell in you, and you have no need that anyone teach you. But as his anointing teaches you concerning all things, and is true and is no lie, even as it has taught you, abide in him.

II: GOD IS JUSTICE
Children of God

AND NOW, DEAR CHILDREN, abide in him, so that when he ap-

| NOV. 8 | 28 |
| May 9 | |

pears we may have confidence, and may not shrink ashamed from him at his coming. If you 29 know that he is just, know that everyone also

2, 19: The antichrists who teach erroneous and subversive doctrines formerly belonged to the Church. Before they left the Christian community they were no longer ours: they were not in the state of grace and not real Christians.

who does what is just has been born of him.

3 1 Behold what manner of love the Father has bestowed upon us, that we should be called children of God; and such we are. This is why the world does not know us, because it did not know

2 him. Beloved, now we are the children of God, and it has not yet appeared what we shall be. We know that, when he appears, we shall be like to him, for we shall see him just as he is.

3 And everyone who has this hope in him makes himself holy, just as he also is holy.

4 Everyone who commits sin commits iniquity

5 also; and sin is iniquity. And you know that he appeared to take our sins away, and sin is not

6 in him. No one who abides in him commits sin; and no one who sins has seen him, or has known him.

Children of the Devil

7 Dear children, let no one lead you astray. He who does what is just is just, even as he is just.

8 He who commits sin is of the devil, because the devil sins from the beginning. To this end the Son of God appeared, that he might destroy

9 the works of the devil. Whoever is born of God does not commit sin, because his seed abides in him and he cannot sin, because he is born of God.

10 In this the children of God and the children of the devil are made known.

Whoever is not just is not of God, nor is he

11 just who does not love his brother. For this is the message that you have heard from the begin-

---

2, 20: *Anointing from the Holy One:* the expression is usually understood to refer to the conferring of the Holy Spirit.

3, 9: *Does not commit sin:* this does not mean that it is impossible for him who has been spiritually reborn in Baptism to commit sin, but simply that he will not sin as long as he keeps the seed of grace in himself. This grace, however, can be lost through sin.

ning, that we should love one another; not like 12
Cain, who was of the evil one, and killed his
brother. And wherefore did he kill him? Because his own works were wicked, but his
brother's just. Do not be surprised, brethren, if 13
the world hates you. We know that we have 14
passed from death to life, because we love the
brethren. He who does not love abides in death. 15
Everyone who hates his brother is a murderer.
And you know that no murderer has eternal
life abiding in him.

True Charity

In this we have come to know his love, that 16
he laid down his life for us; and we likewise
ought to lay down our life for the brethren. He 17
who has the goods of this world and sees his
brother in need and closes his heart to him,
how does the love of God abide in him? My dear 18
children, let us not love in word, neither with the
tongue, but in deed and in truth.

A Good Conscience

In this we know that we are of the truth, and 19
in his sight we set our hearts at rest. Because 20
if our heart blames us, God is greater than our
heart and knows all things. Beloved, if our heart 21
does not condemn us, we have confidence towards God, and whatever we ask, we shall re- 22
ceive from him, because we keep his commandments and do those things that are pleasing in
his sight.

And this is his commandment, that we should 23
believe in the name of his Son Jesus Christ,
and love one another, even as he gave us commandment. And he who keeps his command- 24
ments abides in God, and God in him. And in
this we know that he abides in us, by the Spirit
whom he has given us.

[635]

True and False Spirits

4 1   Beloved, do not believe every spirit, but test the spirits to see whether they are of God; because many false 2 prophets have gone forth into the world. By this is the spirit of God known: every spirit that confesses that Jesus Christ has come in the flesh, 3 is of God. And every spirit that severs Jesus, is not of God, but is of Antichrist, of whom you have heard that he is coming, and now is already in the world.

NOV. 9
May 10

4   You are of God, dear children, and have over-5 come him, because greater is he who is in you than he who is in the world. They are of the world; therefore of the world they speak and 6 the world listens to them. ' We are of God. He who knows God listens to us; he who is not of God does not listen to us. By this we know the spirit of truth and the spirit of error.

III: GOD IS LOVE

Love Unites Us with God

7   BELOVED, LET US LOVE ONE ANOTHER, for 8 love is from God. And everyone who loves is born of God, and knows God. He who does not 9 love does not know God; for God is love. In this has the love of God been shown in our case, that God has sent his only-begotten Son into the world that we may live through him. 10 In this is the love, not that we have loved God,

---

4, 1: *Test the spirits:* the expression probably refers to those Christians who claimed extraordinary gifts of the Holy Spirit (cf. 1 Cor. 14, 32). These spirits should be examined to see whether their teaching is in agreement with Catholic faith and the doctrine of Christ and His Church.

4, 3: *And every spirit that severs Jesus:* i. e., everyone who teaches that there are two distinct persons in Jesus.

but that he has first loved us, and sent his Son a propitiation for our sins. Beloved, if God has so 11 loved us, we also ought to love one another.

No one has ever seen God. If we love one 12 another, God abides in us and his love is perfected in us. In this we know that we abide in 13 him and he in us, because he has given us of his Spirit. And we have seen, and do testify, that 14 the Father has sent his Son to be Savior of the world. Whoever confesses that Jesus is the Son 15 of God, God abides in him and he in God. And 16 we have come to know, and have believed, the love that God has in our behalf. God is love, and he who abides in love abides in God, and God in him.

In this is love perfected with us, that we may 17 have confidence in the day of judgment; because as he is, even so are we also in this world. There is no fear in love; but perfect love casts 18 out fear, because fear brings punishment. And he who fears is not perfected in love. Let us 19 therefore love, because God first loved us. If 20 anyone says, "I love God," and hates his brother, he is a liar. For how can he who does not love his brother, whom he sees, love God, whom he does not see? And this commandment 21 we have from him, that he who loves God should love his brother also.

The Basis of Love

Everyone who believes that Jesus is the Christ is born of God. And everyone who loves him who begot, loves also

| NOV. 10 | **5** 1 |
| May 11 | |

4, 18: *There is no fear in love:* perfect love banishes human, doubtful and servile fear. It does not, however, exclude the wholesome fear of God's judgments, nor the *fear and trembling* with which man must work out his salvation (Phil. 2, 12).

2 the one begotten of him. In this we know that
we love the children of God, when we love God
3 and do his commandments. For this is the love
of God, that we keep his commandments; and
4 his commandments are not burdensome. Because all that is born of God overcomes the
world; and this is the victory that overcomes the
5 world, our faith. Who is there that overcomes
the world if not he who believes that Jesus is
the Son of God?

Witnesses to Christ

6 This is he who came in water and in blood,
Jesus Christ; not in the water only, but in the
water and in the blood. And it is the Spirit that
7 bears witness that Christ is the truth. For there
are three that bear witness [in heaven: the
Father, the Word, and the Holy Spirit; and these
8 three are one. And there are three that bear
witness on earth]: the Spirit, and the water, and
9 the blood; and these three are one. If we receive
the testimony of men, the testimony of God is
greater; for this is the testimony of God which is
greater, that he has borne witness concerning
10 his Son. He who believes in the Son of God has
the testimony of God in himself. He who does
not believe the Son, makes him a liar; because
he does not believe the witness that God has
borne concerning his Son.

11 And this is the testimony, that God has given
12 us eternal life; and this life is in his Son. He

5, 6: *The water . . . the blood:* probably refers to the
baptism and death of Christ.

5, 7f: According to the evidence of many manuscripts, and
the majority of commentators, these verses should read:
"For there are three that bear witness: the Spirit, and
the water, and the blood; and these three are one." The
Holy See reserves to itself the right to pass finally on the
origin of the present reading.

who has the Son has the life. He who has not the Son has not the life.

These things I am writing to you that you may **13** know that you have eternal life—you who believe in the name of the Son of God.

Confidence in Prayer

And the confidence that we have towards him **14** is this, that if we ask anything according to his will, he hears us. And we know that he hears **15** us whatever we ask; we know that the requests we make of him are granted.

He who knows his brother is committing a sin **16** that is not unto death, shall ask, and shall give life to him who does not commit a sin unto death. There is sin unto death; I do not mean that anyone should ask as to that. All lawlessness is sin, **17** and there is a sin unto death.

Conclusion

WE KNOW THAT NO ONE who is born of God **18** commits sin; but the Begotten of God preserves him and the evil one does not touch him. We **19** know that we are of God, and the whole world is in the power of the evil one. And we know **20** that the Son of God has come and has given us understanding, that we may know the true God and may be in his true Son. He is the true God and eternal life.

Dear children, guard yourselves from the idols. **21** Amen.

5, 16f: It is difficult to determine just what St. John means by *sin . . . not unto death* and *sin unto death*. The former is probably a grievous or mortal sin, because *life shall be given;* the latter is probably a willful apostasy and the sin of final unrepentance. St. John does not forbid us to pray for such sinners, because God alone can determine whether one is finally impenitent or not. Our faith teaches us that God desires not the death of the sinner, but that he be converted and live (Ezech. 33, 11).

Preface

The direct external evidence that this as well as the following Epistle was written by St. John the Apostle, is not extensive. Yet sufficient references to both Epistles are found in early patristic literature to prove their authorship and authenticity. Besides, we have a number of indirect testimonies in the citation of passages obviously derived from either the Second or the Third Epistle. Again, the vocabulary throughout is precisely that which is found in the Gospel and in the First Epistle.

The ideas and expressions of the Second Epistle are the same as those of the First; hence its composition must have been prompted by the same or similar occasions. It was probably written towards the end of the first century.

The recipient of the Second Epistle is addressed as "Elect Lady." The meaning of the title is obscure. Many have thought that an individual is meant, one whose name was Kuria or Elect, or simply "an elect lady." Others have seen in the title a mere symbol, either of the universal Church, or of some particular church in Asia Minor.

The Apostle commends the recipients of the letter for their steadfastness in the true faith, and exhorts them to persevere, lest they lose the reward of their labors. He exhorts them to love one another, but warns them to have no fellowship with heretics, and not even to greet them.

THE SECOND EPISTLE OF ST. JOHN THE APOSTLE

Introduction

Greeting

1　THE PRESBYTER to the Elect Lady | NOV. 11
and to her children whom I love in | May 12
truth — and not I alone, but also all who have
2 known the truth — for the sake of the truth
which abides in us, and will be with us forever:
3 grace, mercy and peace be with you from God the

Father and from Christ Jesus, the Son of the
Father, in truth and love.

TEACHING OF THE APOSTLE

Brotherly Love

I REJOICED GREATLY that I found some of 4
thy children walking in truth, according to the
commandment that we have received from the
Father. And now I beseech thee, lady, not as 5
writing to thee a new commandment, but that
which we have had from the beginning, that we
love one another. And this is love, that we walk 6
according to his commandments. This is the
commandment, that, just as you have heard
from the beginning, you should walk in it.

Against False Teachers

For many deceivers have gone forth into the 7
world who do not confess Jesus as the Christ
coming in the flesh. This is the deceiver and the
Antichrist.

Look to yourselves, that you do not lose what 8
you have worked for, but that you may receive a
full reward. Anyone who advances and does not 9
abide in the doctrine of Christ, has not God; he
who abides in the doctrine, he has both the
Father and the Son. If anyone comes to you 10
and does not bring this doctrine, do not receive
him into the house, or say to him, Welcome.
For he who says to him, Welcome, is sharer in 11
his evil works.

Conclusion

THOUGH I HAVE MUCH to write to you, I do 12
not wish to do so with paper and ink; for I hope
to be with you and to speak face to face, that your
joy may be full.

The children of thy sister Elect greet thee. 13

Preface

The Third Epistle of St. John is addressed to a certain Gaius. Whether he is to be identified with a Christian of the same name mentioned in Acts 19, 29 and 20, 4 is uncertain.

The time and place of composition of this Epistle are likewise uncertain. The similarity of content and form, however, suggests that it was written about the same time as the Second Epistle.

The Epistle, though brief, vividly portrays certain features in the life of the early Church. Gaius is praised for his hospitality and for walking in the truth. Diotrephes on the contrary is censured for his ambition and lack of hospitality. A certain Demetrius is also commended for his virtue.

THE THIRD EPISTLE OF ST. JOHN THE APOSTLE

Introduction

Salutation

1 THE PRESBYTER to the beloved Gaius, whom I love in truth.

PRAISE OF GAIUS

2 BELOVED, I PRAY that in all things thou mayest prosper and be in health, even as thy soul prospers.
3 I rejoiced greatly when some brethren came and bore witness to thy truth, even as thou
4 walkest in the truth. I have no greater joy than to hear that my children are walking in the truth.
5 Beloved, thou dost in accordance with faith whatever thou workest for the brethren, and that

even when they are strangers. They have borne 6
witness to thy love before the church. Thou wilt
do well to see them off on their journey in a
manner worthy of God. For on behalf of the 7
Name they have gone forth, taking nothing from
the pagans. We therefore ought to support such 8
as these, that we may be fellow-workers for
the truth.

DIOTREPHES AND DEMETRIUS

I WOULD HAVE WRITTEN perhaps to the 9
church; but Diotrephes, who loves to have the
first place among them, does not receive us.
Therefore if I come, I will recall to mind his 10
works, prating against us with evil words; and
as if this were not enough for him, he himself
does not receive the brethren, and those who do
so he hinders, and casts them out of the church.

Beloved, do not imitate evil, but that which 11
is good. He who does what is good is of God; he
who does what is evil has not seen God. Witness 12
is borne to Demetrius by all, and by the truth
itself, yes, we also bear witness; and thou knowest that our witness is true.

Conclusion

I HAD MUCH to write to thee; but I do not 13
want to write to thee with pen and ink. But I 14
hope to see thee shortly, and we will speak face
to face.

Peace be to thee. The friends greet thee. 15
Greet the friends by name.

THE EPISTLE OF ST. JUDE

Introduction

By designating himself "the brother of James" (v. 1), the writer of this Epistle evidently wished to reveal himself to his readers. At the time the Epistle was written, there was no one of prominence in the Church having the name of James except the Apostle James the Less, Bishop of Jerusalem and author of the Epistle that bears his name. St. James the Less was one of the "brethren of the Lord" (Gal. 1, 19), and had a brother named Jude (Matt. 13, 55; Mark 6, 3). In the two lists of the Apostles given by St. Luke (Luke 6, 16; Acts 1, 15), one is named "Jude of James." He is called Thaddeus by the other evangelists (Matt. 10, 3; Mark 3, 18). It is clear that Luke refers to Jude the brother of James. Little more is known of the life of this Apostle. According to a tradition he preached the gospel in Syria and suffered martyrdom at Beirut. The Church celebrates the feast of Sts. Simon and Jude on October 28.

The author of this Epistle presupposes that his readers are familiar with the Old Testament and with Jewish traditions. It is likely, therefore, that it was addressed to converts from Judaism who also knew the Apostle James.

The Epistle is both brief and practical. It was occasioned by the teachings and practices of certain heretics within the Church. By their evil lives they were denying that Jesus is the only Lord and Master. They were opposed to all law and authority, and changed Christian liberty into unrestrained license. The Epistle is a warning to them.

The Epistle was written between the years 62 and 67 A. D., as may be concluded from the following indications. The warnings from the past (vv. 5-7) contain no mention of the fall of Jerusalem. It was written before the death of St. Peter. It was written after the death of St. James, Bishop of Jerusalem, for on the authority of Hegesippus we know that the church in Palestine was free from heresies during his administration.

THE EPISTLE OF ST. JUDE THE APOSTLE

Introduction

Purpose of Address

JUDE, THE SERVANT of Jesus | NOV. 12 | 1
Christ and the brother of James, to | May 13 |
the called who have been loved in God the Father
and preserved for Christ Jesus: mercy and peace 2
and charity be given you in abundance.

Beloved, while I was making every endeavor 3
to write to you about our common salvation, I
found it necessary to write to you, exhorting you
to contend earnestly for the faith once for all
delivered to the saints. For certain men have 4
stealthily entered in, who long ago were marked
out for this condemnation, ungodly men who
turn the grace of God into wantonness and disown our only Master and Lord, Jesus Christ.

I: WARNING AGAINST FALSE TEACHERS

Divine Judgments

BUT I DESIRE TO REMIND YOU, though once 5
for all you have come to know all things, that
Jesus, who saved the people from the land of
Egypt, the next time destroyed those who did not
believe. And the angels also who did not preserve 6
their original state, but forsook their abode, he
has kept in everlasting chains under darkness for
the judgment of the great day. Just as Sodom and 7
Gomorrah, and the neighboring cities which like

The Fathers, and Catholic tradition in general,
ascribe this Epistle to the Apostle St. Jude. St.
Peter made use of it in his Second Epistle. The
Muratorian canon enumerates it among the sacred
books.

them committed sins of immorality and practised unnatural vice, have been made an example, undergoing the punishment of eternal fire.

Evil Life of Heretics

8 In like manner do these men also defile the
9 flesh, disregard authority, deride majesty. Yet when Michael the archangel was fiercely disputing with the devil about the body of Moses, he did not venture to bring against him an accusation of blasphemy, but said, "May the Lord
10 rebuke thee." But these men deride whatever they do not know; and the things they know by instinct like the dumb beasts, become for them a
11 source of destruction. Woe to them! for they have gone in the way of Cain, and have rushed on thoughtlessly into the error of Balaam for the sake of gain, and have perished in the rebellion of
12 Core. These men are stains on their feasts, banqueting together without fear, looking after themselves; clouds without water, carried about by the winds; trees in the fall, unfruitful, twice
13 dead, uprooted; wild waves of the sea, foaming up their shame; wandering stars, for whom the storm of darkness has been reserved forever.

1, 6: The rebellious angels lost the dignity conferred on them through grace and were cast into hell. On the last day final sentence will be passed upon them, and the fullness of punishment will be meted out to them.

1, 9: This dispute between Michael and the devil is nowhere else recorded in the Scriptures. The cause of the dispute is not assigned, but it is certain the devil wished to make some evil use of the body of Moses.

1, 11: *Way of Cain:* who slew his brother. *Error of Balaam:* who for the sake of a reward would have led the people astray. *Rebellion of Core:* who opposed Moses, a divinely appointed authority. The heretics resemble these men, and will be punished as they were.

Judgment of Heretics

Now of these also Henoch, the seventh from 14 Adam, prophesied, saying, "Behold, the Lord has come with thousands of his holy ones ' to execute 15 judgment upon all, and to convict all the impious of all their impious works, and of all the hard things that impious sinners have spoken against him." These are grumbling murmurers walking 16 according to their lusts. And haughty in speech, they cultivate people for the sake of gain. But as 17 for you, beloved, be mindful of the words that have been spoken beforehand by the apostles of our Lord Jesus Christ, who kept saying to you 18 that at the end of time there will come scoffers, walking impiously according to their lusts. These 19 are they who set themselves apart, sensual men, not having the Spirit.

II: ADMONITIONS FOR CHRISTIANS

Perseverance and Charity

BUT AS FOR YOU, BELOVED, build up your- 20 selves upon your most holy faith, praying in the Holy Spirit. Keep yourselves in the love of God, 21 looking for the mercy of our Lord Jesus Christ unto life everlasting. And some, who are judged, 22 reprove; but others, save, snatching them from 23 the fire. And to others be merciful with fear, hating even the garment which is soiled by the flesh.

Conclusion

NOW TO HIM who is able to preserve you with- 24 out sin and to set you before the presence of his glory, without blemish, in gladness, ' to the only 25 God our Savior, through Jesus Christ our Lord, belong glory and majesty, dominion and authority, before all time, and now, and forever. Amen.

THE APOCALYPSE

Introduction

The Apocalypse is a revelation of the things that were, are and will be. We are actually witnessing some of the events foretold in this book, but many still lie in the future. It is Christ who commands John to write to the seven churches, opens the seven seals, reveals the sufferings of the saints, opens the little book, overcomes the beast, reigns during the period of the first resurrection, judges the dead, both great and small, according to their works at His Second Coming, rules over all things from the beginning, presides over all the changing scenes of earth's history, and is the King of kings and Lord of lords.

The book presents Christ as the Coming One; it reveals the dealings of Him who came, and who is to come. It opens with the solemn hope that the Coming One will come soon, and closes with the impressive prediction that the Coming One will come quickly.

The book is one of hope, but also one of warning; its aim is to assure the Church of the advent of her Lord in victory. The precise time of this victory lies hidden with God, but it is certain, although the crown will not be won without a struggle. Heaven will be stormed and carried away through suffering and conflict. And all who keep the words of this book will take part in the conflict and share in the victory.

The conflict is presented under the form of symbols. It is not easy to give a full interpretation of all the types, but the general symbols are not difficult to understand. Jerusalem stands as the type of the good cause, and this is the Church of Christ. Babylon appears as the type of the evil cause, and this is the world power. The heavenly Jerusalem has the assistance of divine power. The earthly Babylon has the help of evil powers, the dragon, the beast and the false prophet. The scenes in the great conflict arrange themselves around these types of good and

[648]

APOCALYPSE OF ST. JOHN
THE APOSTLE

Prologue

The Book — Its Source and Contents

THE REVELATION OF JESUS CHRIST which God gave him, to make known to his servants the things that must shortly come to pass; and he sent and signified them through his angel to his servant John; who bore witness to the word of God and to the testimony of Jesus Christ, to whatever he saw. Blessed is he who reads and those who hear the words of this prophecy, and keep the things that are written therein; for the time is at hand.

NOV. 13 / May 14 **1** 1

2

3

Greetings

John to the seven churches that are in Asia: grace be to you and peace from him who is and who was and who is coming, and from the seven spirits who are before his throne, and from Jesus Christ, who is the faithful witness, the firstborn of the dead, and the ruler of the kings of the earth. To him who has loved us, and washed us from our sins in his own blood, and made us to be a kingdom, and priests to God his Father — to him belong glory and dominion forever and ever. Amen.

4

5

6

---

of evil. The numbers, the seals, the trumpets and the bowls are phases in the development and consummation of the conflict.

John has arranged the scenes in a sevenfold structure; even in the subordinate visions he keeps to this arrangement. Commentators, however, are not agreed in marking off the limits of each structure.

The book was written in Greek by St. John the Evangelist, on the island of Patmos, about the year 96 A. D.

Christ's Coming

7   Behold, he comes with the clouds, and every eye shall see him, and they also who pierced him. And all the tribes of the earth shall wail 8 over him. Even so. Amen. ' "I am the Alpha and the Omega, the beginning and the end," says the Lord God, "who is and who was and who is coming, the Almighty."

I: THE SEVEN LETTERS

1. Preparatory Vision

John Told to Write His Visions

9   I, JOHN, YOUR BROTHER and partner in the tribulation and kingdom and patience that are in Jesus, was on the island which is called Patmos, because of the word of God and the testimony of 10 Jesus. I was in the spirit on the Lord's day, and I heard behind me a great voice, as of a trumpet, 11 ' saying, "What thou seest write in a book, and send to the seven churches, to Ephesus, and to Smyrna, and to Pergamum, and to Thyatira, and to Sardis, and to Philadelphia, and to Laodicea."

Vision of the Son of Man

12   And I turned to see the voice that was speaking to me. And having turned, I saw seven golden 13 lamp-stands; and in the midst of the seven lamp-stands One like to a son of man, clothed with a garment reaching to the ankles, and girt about 14 the breasts with a golden girdle. But his head and his hair were white as white wool, and as 15 snow, and his eyes were as a flame of fire; his feet were like fine brass, as in a glowing furnace,

---

1, 4: *Asia:* the Roman Province of Asia, the western part of what is now known as Asia Minor. *The seven spirits:* the Holy Spirit, whose seven gifts are diffused among all the churches; or the phrase may refer to seven angels.

and his voice like the voice of many waters. And 16 he had in his right hand seven stars. And out of his mouth came forth a sharp two-edged sword; and his countenance was like the sun shining in its power.

And when I saw him, I fell at his feet as one 17 dead. And he laid his right hand upon me, saying, "Do not be afraid; I am the First and the Last, 'and he who lives; I was dead, and behold, I am 18 living forevermore; and I have the keys of death and of hell. Write therefore the things that thou 19 hast seen, and the things that are, and the things that are to come hereafter. As for the mystery of 20 the seven stars that thou sawest in my right hand, and the seven golden lamp-stands — the seven stars are the angels of the seven churches, and the seven lamp-stands are the seven churches."

2. The Letters

To the Church at Ephesus

"TO THE ANGEL of the church at Ephesus write: Thus says he who holds the seven stars in his right hand, who walks in the midst of the seven golden lamp-stands: I know thy works and thy labor and thy patience, 2 and that thou canst not bear evil men; but hast tried them who say they are apostles and are not, and hast found them false. And thou hast pa- 3 tience and hast endured for my name, and hast not grown weary.

NOV. 14
May 15

2 1

"But I have this against thee, that thou hast 4 left thy first love. Remember therefore whence 5 thou hast fallen, and repent and do the former works; or else I will come to thee, and will move thy lamp-stand out of its place, unless thou repentest. But this thou hast: thou hatest the 6 works of the Nicolaites, which I also hate.

[651]

7   "He who has an ear, let him hear what the Spirit says to the churches: Him who overcomes I will permit to eat of the tree of life, which is in the paradise of my God.

To the Church at Smyrna

8   "And to the angel of the church at Smyrna
9 write: Thus says the First and the Last, who was dead and is alive: I know thy tribulation and thy poverty, but thou art rich; and that thou art slandered by those who say they are Jews and
10 are not, but are a synagogue of Satan. Fear none of those things that thou art about to suffer. Behold, the devil is about to cast some of you into prison that you may be tested, and you will have tribulation for ten days. Be thou faithful unto death, and I will give thee the crown of life.
11   "He who has an ear, let him hear what the Spirit says to the churches: He who overcomes shall not be hurt by the second death.

To the Church at Pergamum

12   "And to the angel of the church at Pergamum
13 write: Thus says he who has the sharp two-edged sword: I know where thou dwellest, where the throne of Satan is; and thou holdest fast my name and didst not disown my faith, even in the days of Antipas, my faithful witness, who was slain among you where Satan dwells.
14   "But I have a few things against thee, because thou hast there some who hold the teaching of Balaam, who taught Balak to cast a stumbling-block before the children of Israel, that they
15 might eat and commit fornication. So thou hast

2, 10: *Ten days:* the period of trial would be limited and would be short.

2, 11: *Second death:* a death which is other than the death of the body, i. e., the final condemnation of sinners.

also some who hold the teaching of the Nicolaites. In like manner repent, or else I will come to thee quickly, and will fight against them with the sword of my mouth. 16

"He who has an ear, let him hear what the Spirit says to the churches: To him who overcomes, I will give the hidden manna, and I will give him a white pebble, and upon the pebble a new name written, which no one knows except him who receives it. 17

To the Church at Thyatira

"And to the angel of the church at Thyatira write: Thus says the Son of God, who has eyes like to a flame of fire, and whose feet are like fine brass: I know thy works, thy faith, thy love, thy ministry, thy patience and thy last works, which are more numerous than the former. 18

19

"But I have against thee that thou sufferest the woman Jezebel, who calls herself a prophetess, to teach, and to seduce my servants, to commit fornication, and to eat of things sacrificed to idols. And I gave her time that she might repent, and she does not want to repent of her immorality. Behold, I will cast her upon a bed, and those who commit adultery with her into great tribulation, unless they repent of their deeds. And her children I will strike with death, and all the churches shall know that I am he who searches desires and hearts, and I will give to each of you according to your works. 20

21

22

23

"But to you I say, ' to the rest in Thyatira, as many as do not hold this teaching and do not know the depths of Satan, as they call them, I will not put upon you any other burden. But that which you have, hold fast till I come. And to him who overcomes, and who keeps my works unto the end, I will give authority over the 24

25

26

27 nations. And he shall rule them with a rod of
28 iron, and like the potter's vessel they shall be
dashed to pieces, as I also have received from
my Father; and I will give him the morning star.
29 "He who has an ear, let him hear what the
Spirit says to the churches.

To the Church at Sardis

3 1 "And to the angel of the church | NOV. 15 |
at Sardis write: Thus says he who | May 16 |
has the seven spirits of God and the seven stars:
I know thy works; thou hast the name of being
2 alive, and thou art dead. Be watchful and
strengthen the things that remain, but which
were ready to die. For I do not find thy works
3 complete before my God. Remember therefore
what thou hast received and heard, and observe
it and repent. Therefore, if thou wilt not watch,
I will come upon thee as a thief, and thou shalt
not know at what hour I shall come upon thee.
4 But thou hast a few persons at Sardis who have
not defiled their garments, and they shall walk
5 with me in white; for they are worthy. He who
overcomes shall be arrayed thus in white garments, and I will not blot his name out of the
book of life, but I will confess his name before
my Father, and before his angels.
6 "He who has an ear, let him hear what the
Spirit says to the churches.

To the Church at Philadelphia

7 "And to the angel of the church at Philadelphia write: Thus says the holy one, the true one,
he who has the key of David, he who opens and
no one shuts, and who shuts and no one opens:

3, 7: *Who opens and no one shuts:* an affirmation of the
divinity of Christ. Cf. Job 12, 14 where this power is attributed to God alone.

¹ I know thy works. Behold, I have caused a door 8
to be opened before thee which no one can shut,
for thou hast scanty strength, and thou hast kept
my word and hast not disowned my name. Be- 9
hold, I will bring some of the synagogue of
Satan who say they are Jews, and are not, but
are lying — behold, I will make them come and
worship before thy feet. And they shall know that
I have loved thee. Because thou hast kept the 10
word of my patience, I too will keep thee from
the hour of trial, which is about to come upon
the whole world to try those who dwell upon the
earth. I come quickly; hold fast what thou hast, 11
that no one receive thy crown. He who over- 12
comes, I will make him a pillar in the temple of
my God, and never more shall he go outside.
And I will write upon him the name of my God,
and the name of the city of my God — the new
Jerusalem, which comes down out of heaven
from my God — and my new name.

"He who has an ear, let him hear what the 13
Spirit says to the churches.

To the Church at Laodicea

"And to the angel of the church at Laodicea 14
write: Thus says the Amen, the faithful and true
witness, who is the beginning of the creation of
God: I know thy works; thou art neither cold nor 15
hot. I would that thou wert cold or hot. But be- 16
cause thou art lukewarm, and neither cold nor
hot, I am about to vomit thee out of my mouth;
because thou sayest, 'I am rich and have grown 17
wealthy and have need of nothing,' and dost not
know that thou art the wretched and miserable
and poor and blind and naked one.

"I counsel thee to buy of me gold refined by 18

3, 14: *Amen:* a Hebrew word, used here as a personal
name.

fire, that thou mayest become rich, and mayest be clothed in white garments, and that the shame of thy nakedness may not appear, and to anoint thy eyes with eye salve that thou may-
19 est see. As for me, those whom I love I rebuke and chastise. Be earnest therefore and repent.
20 Behold, I stand at the door and knock. If any man listens to my voice and opens the door to me, I will come in to him and will sup with him,
21 and he with me. He who overcomes, I will permit him to sit with me upon my throne; as I also have overcome and have sat with my Father on his throne.
22 "He who has an ear, let him hear what the Spirit says to the churches."

II: THE SEVEN SEALS

1. Preparatory Vision

The Court of Heaven

4 1 AFTER THIS I LOOKED, and be- | NOV. 16
hold, a door standing open in heav- | May 17
en, and the former voice, which I had heard as of a trumpet speaking with me, said, "Come up hither, and I will show thee the things that must
2 come to pass hereafter." Immediately I was in the spirit; and behold, there was a throne set in heaven, and upon the throne One was sitting.
3 And he who sat was in appearance like to a jasper-stone and a sardius, and there was a rainbow round about the throne, in appearance like to an emerald.
4 And round about the throne are twenty-four seats; and upon the seats twenty-four elders sitting, clothed in white garments, and on their
5 heads crowns of gold. And from the throne pro- ceed flashes of lightning, rumblings, and peals of thunder; and there are seven lamps burning

before the throne, which are the seven spirits of God. And before the throne there is, as it were, 6 a sea of glass like to crystal, and in the midst of the throne, and round the throne, are four living creatures, full of eyes before and behind. And the 7 first living creature is like a lion and the second like a calf, and the third has the face, as it were, of a man, and the fourth is like an eagle flying. And the four living creatures have each 8 of them six wings; round about and within they are full of eyes. And they do not rest day and night, saying, "Holy, holy, holy, the Lord God almighty, who was, and who is, and who is coming."

And when those living creatures give glory 9 and honor and benediction to him who sits on the throne, who lives forever and ever, ' the twenty- 10 four elders will fall down before him who sits upon the throne, and will worship him who lives forever and ever, and will cast their crowns before the throne, saying, ' "Worthy art thou, O 11 Lord our God, to receive glory and honor and power; for thou hast created all things, and because of thy will they existed, and were created."

The Scroll and the Lamb

And I saw upon the right hand of him who sits **5** 1 upon the throne a scroll written within and without, sealed with seven seals. And I saw a strong 2 angel proclaiming with a loud voice, "Who is worthy to open the scroll, and to break the seals thereof?" And no one in heaven, or on earth, 3 or under the earth, was able to open the scroll or to look thereon. And I wept much, because 4 no one was found worthy to open the scroll or to look thereon.

And one of the elders said to me, "Do not 5 weep; behold, the lion of the tribe of Juda, the

root of David, has overcome to open the scroll
6 and its seven seals." And I saw, and behold, in
the midst of the throne and of the four living
creatures, and in the midst of the elders, a Lamb
standing, as if slain, having seven horns and
seven eyes, which are the seven spirits of God
7 sent forth into all the earth. And he came and
took the scroll out of the right hand of him who
8 sat upon the throne. And when he had opened
the scroll, the four living creatures and the
twenty-four elders fell down before the Lamb,
having each a harp and golden bowls full of
incense, which are the prayers of the saints.

The Three Songs of Praise

9 And they sing a new canticle, saying, "Worthy
art thou to take the scroll and to open its seals;
for thou wast slain, and hast redeemed us for
God with thy blood, out of every tribe and tongue
10 and people and nation, and hast made them for
our God a kingdom and priests, and they shall
reign over the earth."

11 And I beheld, and I heard a voice of many
angels round about the throne, and the living
creatures and the elders, and the number of
12 them was thousands of thousands, saying
with a loud voice, "Worthy is the Lamb who was
slain to receive power and divinity and wisdom
and strength and honor and glory and blessing."
13 And every creature that is in heaven and on the
earth and under the earth, and such as are on the
sea, and all that are in them, I heard them all
saying, "To him who sits upon the throne, and to
the Lamb, blessing and honor and glory and
14 dominion, forever and ever." And the four living

5, 5: *Root of David:* the lion is also the symbol of the
royal house of David. Christ comes of the seed of David
and the prophets described Him as the branch that would
spring from the ancient stock.

creatures said, "Amen," and the elders fell
down and worshipped him who lives forever
and ever.

2. The Breaking of the First Six Seals

War

AND I SAW that the Lamb had | NOV. 17 | **6** 1
opened the first of the seven seals, | May 18 |
and I heard one of the four living creatures saying, as with a voice of thunder, "Come!" And I
saw,' and behold, a white horse, and he who was 2
sitting on it had a bow, and there was given
him a crown, and he went forth as a conqueror
to conquer.

Strife

And when he opened the second seal, I heard 3
the second living creature saying, "Come!" ' And 4
there went forth another horse, a red one; and
to him who was sitting on it, it was given to take
peace from the earth, and that men should kill
one another, and there was given him a great
sword.

Famine

And when he opened the third seal, I heard 5
the third living creature saying, "Come!" And
I saw, and behold, a black horse, and he who
was sitting on it had a balance in his hand.
And I heard as it were a voice in the midst of the 6
four living creatures, saying, "A measure of
wheat for a denarius, and three measures of
barley for a denarius, and do not harm the wine
and the oil."

Pestilence

And when he opened the fourth seal, I heard 7
the voice of the fourth living creature saying,
"Come!" And I saw, ' and behold, a pale-green 8

horse, and he who was sitting on it — his name is Death, and hell was following him. And there was given him power over the four parts of the earth, to kill with sword, with famine, and with death, and with the beasts of the earth.

The Martyrs

9 And when he opened the fifth seal, I saw under the altar the souls of those who had been slain for the word of God, and for the witness that 10 they bore. And they cried with a loud voice, saying, "How long, O Lord (holy and true), dost thou refrain from judging and from avenging our 11 blood on those who dwell on the earth?" And there was given to each of them a white robe; and they were told to rest a little while longer, until the number of their fellow-servants and their brethren who are to be slain, even as they had been, should be complete.

Signs on Earth and in Heaven.

12 And I saw, when he opened the sixth seal, and there was a great earthquake, and the sun became black as sackcloth of hair; and the whole 13 moon became as blood. And the stars of heaven fell upon the earth, as the fig tree sheds its unripe 14 figs when it is shaken by a great wind. And heaven passed away as a scroll that is rolled up; and every mountain and the islands were moved 15 out of their places. And the kings of the earth, and the princes, and the tribunes, and the rich, and the strong, and everyone, bond and free, hid themselves in the caves and in the rocks of 16 the mountains. And they said to the mountains and to the rocks, "Fall upon us, and hide us from the face of him who sits upon the throne, 17 and from the wrath of the Lamb; for the great day of their wrath has come, and who is able to stand?"

3. An Intermediate Vision, and the Opening of the Seventh Seal

Sealing of the Spiritual Israel

AFTER THIS I SAW four angels standing at the four corners of the NOV. 18 | May 19 **7** 1 earth, holding fast the four winds of the earth, that no wind should blow over the earth, or over the sea, or upon any tree. And I saw an- 2 other angel ascending from the rising of the sun, having the seal of the living God; and he cried with a loud voice to the four angels, who had it in their power to harm the earth and the sea, saying, "Do not harm the earth or the sea or the 3 trees, till we have sealed the servants of our God on their foreheads." And I heard the number 4 of those who were sealed, a hundred and forty-four thousand sealed, out of every tribe of the children of Israel; of the tribe of Juda, twelve 5 thousand sealed; of the tribe of Ruben, twelve thousand; of the tribe of Gad, twelve thousand; of the tribe of Aser, twelve thousand; of the 6 tribe of Nephthali, twelve thousand; of the tribe of Manasses, twelve thousand; of the tribe of 7 Simeon, twelve thousand; of the tribe of Levi, twelve thousand; of the tribe of Issachar, twelve thousand; of the tribe of Zabulon, twelve thou- 8 sand; of the tribe of Joseph, twelve thousand; of the tribe of Benjamin, twelve thousand sealed.

Blessedness of the Sealed

After this I saw a great multitude which no 9 man could number, out of all nations and tribes and peoples and tongues, standing before the throne and before the Lamb, clothed in white robes, and with palms in their hands. And they 10 cried with a loud voice, saying, "Salvation belongs to our God who sits upon the throne, and to the Lamb." And all the angels were 11

standing round about the throne, and the elders
and the four living creatures; and they fell on
their faces before the throne and worshipped
12 God,' saying, "Amen. Blessing and glory and
wisdom and thanksgiving and honor and power
and strength to our God forever and ever. Amen."

The Seventh Seal

13 And one of the elders spoke and said to me,
"These who are clothed in white robes, who are
14 they? and whence have they come?" And I said
to him, "My lord, thou knowest." And he said to
me, "These are they who have come out of the
great tribulation, and have washed their robes
and made them white in the blood of the Lamb.
15 Therefore they are before the throne of God, and
serve him day and night in his temple, and
he who sits upon the throne will dwell with
16 them. They shall neither hunger nor thirst any
more, neither shall the sun strike them nor any
17 heat. For the Lamb who is in the midst of the
throne will shepherd them, and will guide them
to the fountains of the waters of life, and God
will wipe away every tear from their eyes."
8 1 And when he opened the seventh seal, there
was silence in heaven, as it were for half an hour.

iii: THE SEVEN TRUMPETS

1. Preparatory Vision

Seven Angels with Trumpets

2 AND I SAW the seven angels who
stand before God, and there were   NOV. 19 / Mav 20
3 given to them seven trumpets. And another angel
came and stood before the altar, having a golden
censer; and there was given to him much incense,
that he might offer it with the prayers of all the
saints upon the golden altar which is before the

throne. And with the prayers of the saints there ₄
went up before God from the angel's hand the
smoke of the incense. And the angel took the ₅
censer and filled it with the fire of the altar and
threw it down upon the earth, and there were
peals of thunder, rumblings, and flashes of lightning and an earthquake. And the seven angels ₆
who had the seven trumpets prepared themselves
to sound the trumpet.

2. The First Six Trumpets

The First Four Trumpets

AND THE FIRST ANGEL sounded the trumpet, ₇
and there followed hail and fire mingled with
blood, and it was cast upon the earth; and the
third part of the earth was burnt up, and the
third part of the trees was burnt up, and all
green grass was burnt up.

And the second angel sounded the trumpet, ₈
and as it were a great mountain burning with
fire was cast into the sea; and the third part of
the sea became blood, ' and there died the third ₉
part of those creatures that have life in the sea,
and the third part of the ships was destroyed.

And the third angel sounded the trumpet, and ₁₀
there fell from heaven a great star, burning like
a torch, and it fell upon the third part of the
rivers and upon the fountains of waters. The ₁₁
name of the star is called Wormwood. And the
third part of the waters became wormwood; and
many people died of the waters because they
were made bitter.

And the fourth angel sounded the trumpet, ₁₂
and the third part of the sun was smitten, and
the third part of the moon, and the third part of
the stars, that the third part of them might be
darkened, and the day for the third part of it
might not shine, and the night likewise.

The Three Woes

13 And I beheld, and I heard the voice of an
eagle flying in midheaven, saying with a loud
voice, "Woe, woe, woe to the inhabitants of the
earth!" because of the rest of the trumpet-voices
of the three angels who were about to sound the
trumpet.

The Fifth Trumpet

9 1 And the fifth angel sounded the trumpet, and
I saw that a star had fallen from heaven upon the
earth, and there was given to him the key of the
2 bottomless pit. And he opened the bottomless
pit, and there came up smoke out of the pit like
the smoke of a great furnace; and the sun and
the air were darkened by the smoke of the pit.
3 And out of the smoke there came forth locusts
upon the earth. And there was given to them
power, as the scorpions of the earth have power.
4 And they were told not to hurt the grass of the
earth or any green thing or any tree; but only
the men who do not have God's seal upon their
5 foreheads. And they were not permitted to kill
anyone, but to torture them for five months; and
their torment was as the torment of a scorpion
when it strikes a man.

6 And in those days men will seek death and
will not find it; and they will long to die and
7 death will flee from them. And in appearance
the locusts were like horses made ready for
battle; and there were on their heads crowns
as it were like gold; and their faces were like
8 the faces of men. And they had hair like the
hair of women; and their teeth were like the
9 teeth of lions. And they had breastplates like
breastplates of iron; and the sound of their wings
was like the sound of many horse-chariots run-
10 ning to battle. And they had tails like those of
scorpions and there were stings in their tails;

and they had power to harm mankind for five months. And they had over them a king, the 11 angel of the abyss; his name in Hebrew is Abaddon, and in the Greek Apollyon; in Latin he has the name Exterminans.

The first woe is past; behold, two woes are 12 yet to come hereafter!

The Sixth Trumpet

And the sixth angel sounded the trumpet, and 13 I heard a voice from the four horns of the golden altar which is before God, ' saying to the sixth 14 angel who had the trumpet, "Loose the four angels who are bound at the great river Euphrates." And the four angels were loosed who 15 had been kept ready for the hour and day and month and year, that they might kill the third part of mankind. And the number of the army of 16 horsemen was twenty thousand times ten thousand. I heard the number of them.

And this is how I saw the horses in the vision: 17 they who sat upon them had breastplates like to fire and to hyacinth and to sulphur, and the heads of the horses were like the heads of lions; and from their mouths issued fire and smoke and sulphur. By these three plagues the third part of 18 mankind was killed, by the fire and the smoke and the sulphur which issued from their mouth. For the power of the horses is in their mouths 19 and in their tails. For their tails are like serpents, and have heads, and with them they do harm.

And the rest of mankind, they who were not 20 killed by these plagues, did not repent of the works of their hands so as not to worship the demons and the idols of gold and of silver and of brass and of stone and of wood, which can neither see nor hear nor walk. And they did not 21 repent of their murders or of their sorceries or of their immorality or of their thefts.

3. An Intermediate Vision and the Seventh Trumpet

The Angel with the Little Scroll

10 1   AND I SAW another angel, a strong one, coming down from heaven, clothed in a cloud, and the rainbow was over his

NOV. 20
May 21

head, and his face was like the sun, and his feet
2 like pillars of fire. And he had in his hand a little open scroll; and he set his right foot upon the
3 sea but his left upon the earth. And he cried with a loud voice as when a lion roars. And when he had cried, the seven thunders spoke out their
4 voices. And when the seven thunders had spoken, I was about to write; and I heard a voice from heaven saying, "Seal up the things that the seven thunders spoke, and do not write them."
5   And the angel whom I saw standing on the sea and on the earth, lifted up his hand to heaven,
6 and swore by him who lives forever and ever, who created heaven and the things that are therein, and the earth and the things that are therein, and the sea and the things that are
7 therein, that there shall be delay no longer; but that in the days of the voice of the seventh angel, when he begins to sound the trumpet, the mystery of God will be accomplished, as he declared by his servants the prophets.
8   And the voice that I heard from heaven was speaking with me again, and saying, "Go, take the open scroll from the hand of the angel who
9 stands upon the sea and upon the earth." And I went away to the angel, telling him to give me the scroll. And he said to me, "Take the scroll and eat it up, and it will make thy stomach bitter, but in thy mouth it will be sweet as honey."
10   And I took the scroll from the angel's hand, and ate it up, and it was in my mouth sweet as honey, and when I had eaten it my stomach was made

bitter. And they said to me, "Thou must proph- 11
esy again to many nations and peoples and
tongues and kings."

The Measuring of the Temple

And there was given me a reed like to a rod, **11** 1
and I was told: "Rise and measure the temple
of God, and the altar and those who worship
therein. But the court outside the temple, reject 2
it, and do not measure it; for it has been given
to the nations, and the holy city they will trample
under foot for forty-two months. And I will grant 3
unto my two witnesses to prophesy for a thousand two hundred and sixty days, clothed in
sackcloth."

The Two Witnesses

These are the two olive trees and the two 4
lamp-stands that stand before the Lord of the
earth. And if anyone desires to harm them, fire 5
will come out of their mouths, and will devour
their enemies. And if anyone desires to injure
them, he must in this manner be killed. These 6
have power to shut heaven, so that it will not
rain during the days of their prophesying; and
they have power over the waters to turn them
into blood, and to smite the earth with every
plague as often as they desire.

And when they have finished their testimony, 7
the beast that comes up out of the abyss will
wage war against them, and will conquer them
and will kill them. And their dead bodies will 8
lie in the streets of the great city, which is called
mystically Sodom and Egypt, where their Lord
also was crucified. And men from the tribes and 9
peoples and tongues and nations will look upon
their bodies three days and a half; and they will
not allow their dead bodies to be laid in tombs.
And the inhabitants of the earth will rejoice over 10

them and make merry; and they will send gifts to one another because these two prophets tormented the inhabitants of the earth.

11 And after the three days and a half, the breath of life from God entered into them. And they stood up on their feet, and a great fear fell upon

12 those who saw them. And they heard a great voice from heaven saying to them, "Come up hither." And they went up to heaven in a cloud,

13 and their enemies saw them. And at that hour there was a great earthquake and the tenth part of the city fell; and there were killed in the earthquake seven thousand persons; and the rest were affrighted and gave glory to the God of heaven.

14 The second woe is past; and behold, the third woe will come quickly.

The Seventh Trumpet

15 And the seventh angel sounded the trumpet; and there were loud voices in heaven saying, "The kingdom of this world has become the kingdom of our Lord and of his Christ, and he

16 shall reign forever and ever." And the twenty-four elders who sit upon their thrones before God fell on their faces and worshipped God, say-

17 ing, "We give thee thanks, O Lord God almighty, who art, and who wast, because thou hast taken

18 thy great power and hast begun thy reign. And the nations were angered, but thy wrath came and the time for the dead to be judged, and for giving the reward to thy servants — the prophets, and the saints, and those who fear thy name, the small and the great — and for destroying those

19 who corrupted the earth." And the temple of God in heaven was opened, and there was seen the ark of his covenant in his temple, and there came flashes of lightning, and peals of thunder, and an earthquake, and great hail.

[668]

IV: THE SEVEN SIGNS

The Woman and the Dragon

AND A GREAT SIGN appeared in heaven: a woman clothed with the sun, and the moon was under her feet, and upon her head a crown of twelve stars. And being **2** with child, she cried out in her travail and was in the anguish of delivery. And another sign was **3** seen in heaven, and behold, a great red dragon having seven heads and ten horns, and upon his heads seven diadems. And his tail was drag- **4** ging along the third part of the stars of heaven, and it dashed them to the earth; and the dragon stood before the woman who was about to bring forth, that when she had brought forth he might devour her son. And she brought forth a male **5** child, who is to rule all nations with a rod of iron; and her child was caught up to God and to his throne. And the woman fled into the wilder- **6** ness, where she has a place prepared by God, that there they may nourish her a thousand two hundred and sixty days.

> NOV. 21
> May 22

12 1

Michael Overcomes the Dragon

And there was a battle in heaven; Michael **7** and his angels battled with the dragon, and the dragon fought and his angels. And they did not **8** prevail, neither was their place found any more in heaven. And that great dragon was cast down, **9** the ancient serpent, he who is called the devil and Satan, who leads astray the whole world; and he

---

12, 1: *A woman:* this woman is not the Blessed Virgin, for the details of the prophecy do not fit her. The prophecy pictures the Church of the Old and New Covenants. The beams of the divine glory clothe her; the moon is beneath her feet; she is crowned with a crown of twelve stars, and she must bring forth Christ to the world. By accommodation the Church applies this verse to the Blessed Virgin.

was cast down to the earth and with him his angels were cast down.

The Song of Triumph

10 And I heard a loud voice in heaven saying, "Now has come the salvation, and the power and the kingdom of our God, and the authority of his Christ; for the accuser of our brethren has been cast down, he who accused them before

11 our God day and night. And they overcame him through the blood of the Lamb and through the word of their witness, for they did not love their

12 lives even in face of death. Therefore rejoice, O heavens, and you who dwell therein. Woe to the earth and to the sea, because the devil has gone down to you in great wrath, knowing that he has but a short time."

The Dragon and the Woman

13 And when the dragon saw that he was cast down to the earth, he pursued the woman who

14 had brought forth the male child. And there were given to the woman the two wings of the great eagle, that she might fly into the wilderness unto her place, where she is nourished for a time and times and a half time, away from the serpent.

15 And the serpent cast out of his mouth after the woman water like a river, that he might cause

16 her to be carried away by the river. And the earth helped the woman, and the earth opened her mouth and swallowed up the river that the

17 dragon had cast out of his mouth. And the dragon was angered at the woman, and went away to wage war with the rest of her offspring, who keep the commandments of God, and hold fast

18 the testimony of Jesus. And he stood upon the sand of the sea.

The Beast of the Sea

And I saw a beast coming up out of the sea, having seven heads and ten horns, and upon its horns ten diadems, and upon its heads blasphemous names. And the beast that I saw was like a leopard, and its feet were like the feet of a bear, and its mouth like the mouth of a lion. And the dragon gave it his own might and great authority. And one of its heads was smitten, as it were, unto death; but its deadly wound was healed. And all the earth followed the beast in wonder. And they worshipped the dragon because he gave authority to the beast, and they worshipped the beast, saying, "Who is like to the beast, and who will be able to fight with it?"

And there was given to it a mouth speaking great things and blasphemies; and there was given to it authority to work for forty-two months. And it opened its mouth for blasphemies against God, to blaspheme his name and his tabernacle, and those who dwell in heaven. And it was allowed to wage war with the saints and to overcome them. And there was given to it authority over every tribe, and people, and tongue, and nation. And all the inhabitants of the earth will worship it whose names have not been written in the book of life of the Lamb who has been slain from the foundation of the world.

If any man has an ear, let him hear. He who is for captivity, into captivity he goes; he who kills by the sword, by the sword must he be killed. Here is the patience and the faith of the saints.

The Beast of the Earth

And I saw another beast coming up out of the earth, and it had two horns like to those of a lamb, but it spoke as does a dragon. And it exercised all the authority of the former beast in its sight; and it made the earth and the inhabitants therein to worship the first beast, whose

13 deadly wound was healed. And it did great signs, so as even to make fire come down from heaven

14 upon earth in the sight of mankind. And it leads astray the inhabitants of the earth, by reason of the signs which it was permitted to do in the sight of the beast, telling the inhabitants of the earth to make an image to the beast which has

15 the wound of the sword, and yet lived. And it was permitted to give life to the image of the beast, that the image of the beast should both speak and cause that whoever should not wor-

16 ship the image of the beast should be killed. And it will cause all, the small and the great, and the rich and the poor, and the free and the bond, to have a mark on their right hand or on their

17 foreheads, and it will bring it about that no one may be able to buy or sell, except him who has the mark, either the name of the beast or the number of its name.

18 Here is wisdom. He who has understanding, let him calculate the number of the beast, for it is the number of a man; and its number is six hundred and sixty-six.

The Lamb and the Virgins

14 1 And I saw, and behold, the Lamb was standing upon Mount Sion, and | NOV. 23 May 24 |
with him a hundred and forty-four thousand having his name and the name of his Father writ-

---

13, 16: *Mark:* as slaves received a brand or a mark in their flesh, indicating to whom they belonged, so in the spiritual conflict there is on the side of good and of evil a brand or mark. St. Paul spoke of such marks in his own body that proved him a slave of Jesus Christ. So the false prophet seeks to impress a mark on all. Just what this mark is we do not know.

ten on their foreheads. And I heard a voice from 2
heaven like a voice of many waters, and like a
voice of loud thunder; and the voice that I heard
was as of harpers playing on their harps. And 3
they were singing as it were a new song before
the throne, and before the four living creatures
and the elders; and no one could learn the song
except those hundred and forty-four thousand,
who have been purchased from the earth. These 4
are they who were not defiled with women; for
they are virgins. These follow the Lamb wherever he goes. These were purchased from among
men, first-fruits unto God and unto the Lamb,
' and in their mouth there was found no lie; 5
they are without blemish.

The Three Angels

And I saw another angel flying in midheaven, 6
having an everlasting gospel to preach to those
who dwell upon the earth and to every nation
and tribe and tongue and people, ' saying with a 7
loud voice, "Fear God, and give him honor, for
the hour of his judgment has come; and worship him who made the heaven and the earth, the
sea and fountains of waters." And another angel 8
followed, saying, "She has fallen, Babylon the
great, who of the wine of the wrath of her immorality has given all the nations to drink."

And another, a third angel followed them, say- 9
ing with a loud voice, "If anyone worships the
beast and its image and receives a mark upon his
forehead or upon his hand, ' he also shall drink 10
of the wine of the wrath of God, which is poured
unmixed into the cup of his wrath; and he shall
be tormented with fire and brimstone in the sight
of the holy angels and in the sight of the Lamb.

14, 8: *Babylon:* in Jewish and Christian circles, Babylon
was a synonym for Rome.

11 And the smoke of their torments goes up forever and ever; and they rest neither day nor night, they who have worshipped the beast and its image, and anyone who receives the mark of its name."

Blessedness of the Saints

12 Here is the patience of the saints, who keep the commandments of God, and the faith of
13 Jesus. And I heard a voice from heaven saying, "Write: Blessed are the dead who die in the Lord henceforth. Yes, says the Spirit, let them rest from their labors, for their works follow them."

Vision of the Judgment

14 And I saw, and behold, a white cloud, and upon the cloud one sitting like to a son of man, having upon his head a crown of gold and in his hand a
15 sharp sickle. And another angel came forth out of the temple crying with a loud voice to him who sat upon the cloud, "Put forth thy sickle and reap, for the hour to reap has come, because
16 the harvest of the earth is ripe." And he who sat on the cloud cast his sickle upon the earth, and the earth was reaped.

17 And another angel came forth out of the temple that is in heaven, he also having a sharp sickle.
18 And another angel came forth from the altar, he who has authority over the fire, and he called with a loud voice to him who had the sharp sickle, saying, "Put forth thy sharp sickle and gather the clusters of the vine of the earth; for
19 its grapes are fully ripe." And the angel cast his sickle to the earth, and gathered the vintage of the earth, and cast it into the great wine press of
20 the wrath of God. And the wine press was trodden outside the city, and there came forth blood out of the wine press, up to the horses' bridles, for a thousand and six hundred stadia.

The Angels and the Plagues

And I saw another sign in heaven, great and marvellous, seven angels having the seven last plagues. For in them has been completed the wrath of God.

| NOV. 24 | **15** 1 |
| May 25 | |

The Sea of Glass

And I saw as it were a sea of glass mingled with fire, and those who had overcome the beast and its image and the number of its name, standing on the sea of glass, having the harps of God and singing the song of Moses, the servant of God, and the song of the Lamb, saying, "Great and marvellous are thy works, O Lord God almighty; just and true are thy ways, O King of the ages. Who will not fear thee, O Lord, and magnify thy name? for thou alone art holy. For all nations will come and worship before thee; because thy judgments are manifest."

V: THE SEVEN BOWLS

1. Preparatory Vision

The Angels and the Bowls

AND AFTER THIS I looked, and behold, the temple of the tabernacle of the testimony was opened in heaven, and there came forth out of the temple the seven angels who had the seven plagues, clothed with clean white linen, and girt about their breasts with golden girdles. And one of the four living creatures gave to the seven angels seven golden bowls, full of the wrath of God who lives forever and ever. And the temple was filled with smoke from the majesty of God, and from his power; and no one could enter into the temple till the seven plagues of the seven angels were finished.

2. The First Six Bowls

The First Three Bowls

16 1 AND I HEARD a loud voice from the temple saying to the seven angels, "Go and pour out the seven bowls of the wrath of God upon the earth."

2 And the first went and poured out his bowl upon the earth, and a sore and grievous wound was made upon the men who have the mark of the beast, and upon those who worshipped its

3 image. And the second poured out his bowl into the sea, and it became blood as of a dead man;

4 and every live thing in the sea died. And the third poured out his bowl upon the rivers and fountains of waters, and they became blood.

5 And I heard the angel of the waters saying, "Thou art just, O Lord, who art and who wast, O Holy One, because thou hast judged these

6 things; because they poured out the blood of saints and prophets, blood also thou hast given

7 them to drink; they deserve it!" And I heard the altar saying, "Yes, O Lord God almighty, true and just are thy judgments."

The Second Three Bowls

8 And the fourth poured out his bowl upon the sun, and he was allowed to scorch mankind with

9 fire. And mankind were scorched with great heat, and they blasphemed the name of God who has authority over these plagues, and they did not

10 repent and give him glory. And the fifth poured out his bowl upon the throne of the beast; and its kingdom became dark, and they gnawed their

11 tongues for pain. And they blasphemed the God of heaven because of their pains and their wounds, and they did not repent of their works.

12 And the sixth poured out his bowl upon the great river Euphrates, and dried up its waters, that a way might be made ready for the kings from the rising sun.

3. An Intermediate Vision and the Seventh Bowl

The Unclean Spirits

AND I SAW issuing from the mouth of the dragon, and from the mouth of the beast, and from the mouth of the false prophet, three unclean spirits like frogs. For they are spirits of demons working signs, and they go forth unto the kings of the whole earth to gather them together for the battle on the great day of God almighty. "Behold, I come as a thief! Blessed is he who watches and keeps his garments, lest he walk naked and they see his shame." And he gathered them together in a place that is called in Hebrew Armagedon.

The Seventh Bowl

And the seventh poured out his bowl upon the air, and there came forth a loud voice out of the temple from the throne, saying, "It has come to pass!" And there were flashes of lightning, rumblings and peals of thunder, and there was a great earthquake such as never has been since men were first upon the earth, so great an earthquake was it. And the great city came into three parts; and the cities of the nations fell. And Babylon the great was remembered before God, to give her the cup of the wine of his fierce wrath. And every island fled away, and the mountains could not be found. And great hail, heavy as a talent, came down from heaven upon men; and men blasphemed God because of the plague of the hail; for it was very great.

VI: BABYLON THE GREAT

The Woman on the Scarlet Beast

17 1   AND THERE CAME one of the seven angels who had the seven bowls, and he spoke with me, saying, "Come, I will show thee the condemnation of the great harlot 2 who sits upon many waters, with whom the kings of the earth have committed fornication, and the inhabitants of the earth were made drunk with the wine of her immorality."

3   And he took me away in spirit into a desert. And I saw a woman sitting upon a scarlet-colored beast, full of names of blasphemy, having seven 4 heads and ten horns. And the woman was clothed in purple and scarlet, and covered with gold and precious stones and pearls, having in her hand a golden cup full of abominations and the unclean- 5 ness of her immorality. And upon her forehead a name written — a mystery — Babylon the great, the mother of the harlotries and of the abomina- 6 tions of the earth. And I saw the woman drunk with the blood of the saints and with the blood of the martyrs of Jesus. And when I saw her, I wondered with a great wonder.

The Angel's Explanation

7   And the angel said to me, "Wherefore dost thou wonder? I will tell thee the mystery of the woman, and of the beast that carries her which 8 has the seven heads and the ten horns. The beast that thou sawest was, and is not, and is about to come up from the abyss, and will go to destruction. And the inhabitants of the earth — whose names have not been written in the book of life from the foundation of the world — will wonder when they see the beast which was, and is not. 9 And here is the meaning for him who has wisdom. The seven heads are seven mountains upon

which the woman sits; and they are seven kings; five of them have fallen, one is, and the other 10 has not yet come; and when he comes, he must remain a short time. And the beast that was, and 11 is not, is moreover himself eighth, and is of the seven, and is on his way to destruction.

"And the ten horns that thou sawest are ten 12 kings, who have not received a kingdom as yet, but they will receive authority as kings for one hour with the beast. These have one purpose, 13 and their power and authority they give to the beast. These will fight with the Lamb, and the 14 Lamb will overcome them, for he is the Lord of lords, and the King of kings, and they who are with him, called, and chosen, and faithful."

And he said to me, "The waters that thou 15 sawest where the harlot sits, are peoples and nations and tongues. And the ten horns that thou 16 sawest, and the beast, these will hate the harlot, and will make her desolate and naked, and will eat her flesh, and will burn her up in fire. For 17 God has put it into their hearts to carry out his purpose, to give their kingdom to the beast, until the words of God are accomplished. And the 18 woman whom thou sawest is the great city which has kingship over the kings of the earth."

The Fall of Babylon

And after this I saw another angel   NOV. 26   **18** 1
coming down from heaven, having   May 27
great authority, and the earth was lighted up by his glory. And he cried out with a mighty voice, 2 saying, "She has fallen, she has fallen, Babylon the great; and has become a habitation of demons, a stronghold of every unclean spirit, a stronghold of every unclean and hateful bird; because all the nations have drunk of the wrath of 3 her immorality, and the kings of the earth have

committed fornication with her, and by the power of her wantonness the merchants of the earth have grown rich."

Her Sins and Punishment

4 And I heard another voice from heaven saying, "Go out from her, my people, that you may not share in her sins, and that you may not receive

5 of her plagues. For her sins have reached even to heaven, and the Lord has remembered her

6 iniquities. Render to her as she also has rendered, and give her the double according to her works; in the cup that she has mixed, mix for her double.

7 As much as she glorified herself and gave herself to wantonness, so much torment and mourning give to her. Because in her heart she says, 'I sit a queen, I am no widow, and I shall not see

8 mourning.' Therefore in one day her plagues shall come, death and mourning and famine; and she shall be burnt up in fire; for strong is God who will judge her."

Dirge of the Kings

9 And the kings of the earth who with her committed fornication and lived wantonly will weep and mourn over her when they see the smoke

10 of her burning, standing afar off for fear of her torments, saying, "Woe, woe, the great city, Babylon, the strong city, for in one hour has thy judgment come!"

Dirge of the Merchants

11 And the merchants of the earth will weep and mourn over her; for no one will buy their mer-

18, 9-19: This passage does not appear to be an account of a vision but rather a direct prophecy, after the manner of the prophecies of Isaias and Ezechiel concerning Tyre. Tyre furnishes a type of the vengeance of God upon pride and luxury.

chandise any more: merchandise of gold and 12
silver, and precious stones and pearls, and fine
linen and purple, and silk and scarlet, and all
thyine wood, and all vessels of ivory, and all
vessels of precious stone, and of brass, and of
iron, and of marble, ' and cinnamon and amo- 13
mum and spices, and ointment and frankincense,
and wine and oil, and fine flour and wheat, and
beasts of burden and sheep and horses, and
chariots and slaves, and souls of men. And the 14
fruit which was the desire of thy soul departed
from thee; and all the fat and splendid things
perished from thee, and men will find them
nevermore. The merchants of these things, who 15
grew rich by her, will stand afar off for fear of
her torments, weeping and mourning, ' and say- 16
ing, "Woe, woe, the great city, which was clothed
in fine linen and purple and scarlet, and gilded
in gold, and precious stone, and pearls; for in 17
one hour riches so great were laid waste!"

Dirge of the Mariners

And every shipmaster, and everyone who sails
to a place, and mariners, and all who work upon
the sea, stood afar off, ' and cried out as they 18
saw the place of her burning, saying, "What city
is like to this great city?" And they cast dust on 19
their heads, and cried out weeping and mourning,
saying, "Woe, woe, the great city, wherein all
who had their ships at sea were made rich out
of her wealth; for in one hour she has been laid
waste!" Make merry over her, O heaven, and 20
you the saints and the apostles and the prophets,
for God has judged your cause upon her.

The Angel's Promise

And a strong angel took up a stone, as it were 21
a great millstone, and cast it into the sea, saying,

"With this violence will Babylon, the great city,
be overthrown, and will not be found any more.
22 And the sound of harpers and musicians and
flute-players and trumpet will not be heard in
thee any more; and no craftsman of any craft
will be found in thee any more; and sound of
23 millstone will not be heard in thee any more. And
light of lamp will not shine in thee any more; and
voice of bridegroom and of bride will not be
heard in thee any more; because thy merchants
were the great men of the earth, for by thy sorcery
24 all the nations have been led astray. And in her
was found blood of prophets and of saints, and
of all who have been slain upon the earth."

The Angelic Song

19 1 After these things I heard as it were a loud voice of a great crowd

NOV. 27
May 28

in heaven, saying, "Alleluia! salvation and glory
2 and power belong to our God. For true and just
are his judgments, who has judged the great
harlot who corrupted the earth with her fornication, and has avenged the blood of his servants
3 at her hands." And again they have said, "Alleluia! And the smoke of her goes up forever and
4 ever!" And the twenty-four elders and the four
living creatures fell down and worshipped God
who sits on the throne, and they said, "Amen!
5 Alleluia!" And a voice came forth from the
throne, saying, "Praise our God, all you his
servants, and you who fear him, the small and
the great!"

The Song of Triumph

6 And I heard as it were a voice of a great crowd,
and as the voice of many waters, and as the voice
of mighty thunders, saying, "Alleluia! for the
7 Lord, our God almighty, now reigns! Let us be

glad and rejoice, and give glory to him; for the marriage of the Lamb has come, and his spouse has prepared herself. And she has been permitted 8 to clothe herself in fine linen, shining, bright. For the fine linen is the just deeds of the saints."

And he said to me, "Write: Blessed are they 9 who are called to the marriage supper of the Lamb." And he said to me, "These are true words of God." And I fell down before his feet 10 to worship him. And he said to me, "Thou must not do that. I am a fellow-servant of thine and of thy brethren who give the testimony of Jesus. Worship God! for the testimony of Jesus is the spirit of prophecy."

VII: THE CONSUMMATION

The Divine Warrior

AND I SAW heaven standing open; and be- 11 hold, a white horse, and he who sat upon it is called Faithful and True, and with justice he judges and wages war. And his eyes are as a 12 flame of fire, and on his head are many diadems; he has a name written which no man knows except himself. And he is clothed in a garment 13 sprinkled with blood, and his name is called The Word of God. And the armies of heaven, clothed 14 in fine linen, white and pure, were following him on white horses.

King of Kings and Lord of Lords

And from his mouth goes forth a sharp sword 15 with which to smite the nations. And he will rule them with a rod of iron, and he treads the wine press of the fierce wrath of God almighty. And he has on his garment and on his thigh a 16 name written, "King of kings and Lord of lords."

Defeat of the Beast and the False Prophet

17 And I saw an angel standing in the sun, and he cried with a loud voice, saying to all the birds that fly in midheaven, "Come, gather yourselves
18 together to the great supper of God, that you may eat flesh of kings, and flesh of tribunes, and flesh of mighty men, and flesh of horses, and of those who sit upon them, and flesh of all men, free and bond, small and great."
19 And I saw the beast, and the kings of the earth and their armies gathered together to wage war against him who was sitting upon the horse, and
20 against his army. And the beast was seized, and with it the false prophet who did signs before it wherewith he deceived those who accepted the mark of the beast and who worshipped its image. These two were cast alive into the pool of fire that
21 burns with brimstone. And the rest were killed with the sword of him who sits upon the horse, the sword that goes forth out of his mouth; and all the birds were filled with their flesh.

Satan Chained

20 1 And I saw an angel coming down from heaven, having the key of the
2 abyss and a great chain in his hand. And he laid hold on the dragon, the ancient serpent, who is the devil and Satan, and bound him for a thou-
3 sand years. And he cast him into the abyss, and closed and sealed it over him, that he should deceive the nations no more, until the thousand years should be finished. And after that he must be let loose for a little while.

NOV. 28
May 29

Reign of the Saints

4 And I saw thrones, and men sat upon them and judgment was given to them. And I saw the souls of those who had been beheaded because

of the witness to Jesus and because of the word of God, and who did not worship the beast or his image, and did not accept his mark upon their foreheads or upon their hands. And they came to life and reigned with Christ a thousand years. The rest of the dead did not come to life till the 5 thousand years were finished. This is the first resurrection. Blessed and holy is he who has 6 part in the first resurrection! Over these the second death has no power; but they will be priests of God and Christ, and will reign with him a thousand years.

Satan Loosed

And when the thousand years are finished, 7 Satan will be released from his prison, and will go forth and deceive the nations which are in the four corners of the earth, Gog and Magog, and will gather them together for the battle; the number of whom is as the sand of the sea. And 8 they went up over the breadth of the earth and encompassed the camp of the saints, and the beloved city. And fire from God came down out of 9 heaven and devoured them. And the devil who deceived them was cast into the pool of fire and brimstone, where are also the beast ' and the 10 false prophet; and they will be tormented day and night forever and ever.

The Last Judgment

And I saw a great white throne and the one 11 who sat upon it; from his face the earth and heaven fled away, and there was found no place for them. And I saw the dead, the great and the 12 small, standing before the throne, and scrolls were opened. And another scroll was opened, which is the book of life; and the dead were judged out of those things that were written in

13 the scrolls, according to their works. And the sea gave up the dead that were in it, and death and hell gave up the dead that were in them; and they were judged each one, according to their works.

14 And hell and death were cast into the pool of fire. This is the second death, the pool of fire.

15 And if anyone was not found written in the book of life, he was cast into the pool of fire.

New Heaven and New Earth

21 1 And I saw a new heaven and a new earth. For the first heaven and the first earth passed away, and the sea is no

NOV. 29
May 30

2 more. And I saw the holy city, New Jerusalem, coming down out of heaven from God, made ready as a bride adorned for her husband. And

3 I heard a loud voice from the throne saying, "Behold the dwelling of God with men, and he will dwell with them. And they will be his people, and God himself will be with them as their God.

4 And God will wipe away every tear from their eyes. And death shall be no more; neither shall there be mourning, nor crying, nor pain any more, for the former things have passed away."

The Promise

5 And he who was sitting on the throne said, "Behold, I make all things new!" And he said, "Write, for these words are trustworthy and

6 true." And he said to me, "It is done! I am the Alpha and the Omega, the beginning and the end. To him who thirsts I will give of the fountain

7 of the water of life freely. He who overcomes shall possess these things, and I will be his God,

---

21, 1: *New:* there are two words that are translated "new" in our English versions. One refers to time: the other to quality. The quality of the earth will be changed but not the substance; there will be some resemblance between the old and the new.

and he shall be my son. But as for the cowardly 8
and unbelieving, and abominable and murderers,
and fornicators and sorcerers, and idolators and
all liars, their portion shall be in the pool that
burns with fire and brimstone, which is the
second death."

The Heavenly Jerusalem

And there came one of the seven angels who 9
had the bowls full of the seven last plagues;
and he spoke with me, saying, "Come, I will
show thee the bride, the spouse of the Lamb."
And he took me up in spirit to a mountain, great 10
and high, and showed me the holy city Jerusalem,
coming down out of heaven from God, ¹ having 11
the glory of God. Its light was like to a precious
stone, as it were a jasper-stone, clear as crystal.
And it had a wall great and high with twelve 12
gates, and at the gates twelve angels, and names
written on them, which are the names of the
twelve tribes of the children of Israel. On the 13
east are three gates, and on the north three
gates, and on the south three gates, and on the
west three gates. And the wall of the city has 14
twelve foundation stones, and on them twelve
names of the twelve apostles of the Lamb.

And he who spoke with me had a measure, a 15
golden reed, to measure the city and the gates
thereof and the wall. And the city stands four-
square, and its length is as great as its breadth, 16
and he measured the city with the reed, to twelve
thousand stadia: the length and the breadth and
the height of it are equal. And he measured its 17
wall, of a hundred and forty-four cubits, man's
measure, that is, angel's measure. And the mate- 18
rial of its wall was jasper; but the city itself was
pure gold, like pure glass. And the foundations 19
of the wall of the city were adorned with every

precious stone. The first foundation, jasper; the
second, sapphire; the third, agate; the fourth,
20 emerald;' the fifth, sardonyx; the sixth, sardius;
the seventh, chrysolite; the eighth, beryl; the
ninth, topaz; the tenth, chrysoprase; the eleventh,
21 jacinth; the twelfth, amethyst. And the twelve
gates were twelve pearls; that is, each gate was
of a single pearl. And the street of the city was
pure gold, as it were transparent glass.

God and the Lamb Give It Light

22 And I saw no temple therein. For the Lord
God almighty and the Lamb are the temple there-
23 of. And the city has no need of the sun or the
moon to shine upon it. For the glory of God lights
24 it up, and the Lamb is the lamp thereof. And the
nations shall walk by the light thereof; and the
kings of the earth shall bring their glory and
25 honor into it. And its gates shall not be shut by
26 day; for there shall be no night there. And they
shall bring the glory and the honor of nations
27 into it. And there shall not enter into it anything
defiled, nor he who practises abomination and
falsehood, but those only who are written in the
book of life of the Lamb.

The River and Tree of Life

22 1   And he showed me a river of the | NOV. 30
water of life, clear as crystal, coming | May 31
forth from the throne of God and of the Lamb.
2 In the midst of the city street, on both sides of
the river, was the tree of life, bearing twelve
fruits, yielding its fruit according to each month,
and the leaves for the healing of the nations.

The Throne of God and of the Lamb

And there shall be no more any accursed thing; 3
but the throne of God and of the Lamb shall be
in it, and his servants shall serve him. And they 4
shall see his face and his name shall be on their
foreheads. And night shall be no more, and they 5
shall have no need of light of lamp, or light of
sun, for the Lord God will shed light upon them;
and they shall reign forever and ever.

Epilogue

Confirmation

AND HE SAID to me, "These words are trust- 6
worthy and true; and the Lord, the God of the
spirits of the prophets, sent his angel to show
to his servants what must shortly come to pass.
And behold, I come quickly! Blessed is he who 7
keeps the words of the prophecy of this book."
And I, John, am he who heard and saw these 8
things. And when I heard and saw, I fell down to
worship at the feet of the angel who showed me
these things. And he said to me, "Thou must not 9
do that. I am a fellow-servant of thine and of thy
brethren the prophets, and of those who keep
the words of this book. Worship God!"

Words of Christ

And he said to me, "Do not seal up the words 10
of the prophecy of this book; for the time is at
hand. He who does wrong, let him do wrong 11
still; and he who is filthy, let him be filthy still;

22, 7: *I come quickly:* these are the words of Christ and
confirm the declaration of the last verse. He will come
quickly but the precise time is not determined. "One day
with the Lord is as a thousand years, and a thousand
years as one day!"

and he who is just, let him be just still; and he
12 who is holy, let him be hallowed still. ' Behold, I
come quickly! And my reward is with me, to
13 render to each one according to his works. I am
the Alpha and the Omega, the first and the last,
14 the beginning and the end!" Blessed are they
who wash their robes that they may have the
right to the tree of life, and that by the gates
15 they may enter into the city. Outside are the
dogs, and the sorcerers, and the fornicators, and
the murderers, and the idolators, and everyone
who loves and practises falsehood.

Final Attestation

16   "I, Jesus, have sent my angel to testify to you
these things concerning the churches. I am the
root and the offspring of David, the bright morn-
17 ing star." And the Spirit and the bride say,
"Come!" And let him who hears say, "Come!"
And let him who thirsts come; and he who
18 wishes, let him receive the water of life freely. I
testify to everyone who hears the words of the
prophecy of this book. If anyone shall add to
them, God will add unto him the plagues that
19 are written in this book. And if anyone shall
take away from the words of the book of this
prophecy, God will take away his portion from the
tree of life, and from the holy city, and from the
20 things that are written in this book. He who
testifies to these things says, "It is true, I come
21 quickly!" Amen! Come, Lord Jesus! ' The grace
of our Lord Jesus Christ be with all. Amen.

22, 17: *The Spirit:* the Holy Spirit. *The bride:* the Church
of Christ.

PALESTINE IN THE TIME OF CHRIST